Quality Assurance for Information Systems: Methods, Tools, and Techniques

Computer Books from QED

Quality Assurance for Information Systems: Methods, Tools, and Techniques

William E. Perry

QED Technical Publishing Group
Boston • Toronto • London

© 1991 by QED Information Sciences, Inc.
P.O. Box 82-181
Wellesley, MA 02181

Library of Congress Catalog Number: 91-14398
International Standard Book Number: 0-89435-347-0

Printed in the United States of America.
    93 10 9 8 7 6 5 4 3

Library of Congress Cataloging-in-Publication Data

Perry, William E.
    Quality assurance for information systems: methods, tools, and techniques/William E. Perry
        p.   cm.
    Includes index.
    ISBN 0-89435-347-0 :
    1. Computer software — Quality control.   I. Title.
QA76.76.Q35P47   1991
005 — dc20

Contents

List of Figures and Tables xix
Foreword xxv
Preface xxvii

PART 1:   THE QUALITY ASSURANCE FUNCTION 1

*CHAPTER 1: QUALITY ASSURANCE: AN ESSENTIAL
ELEMENT OF ELECTRONIC DATA PROCESSING* 3

What Is Quality? 4
What Is Quality Assurance? 5
Examples of Avoidable Problems 7
Quality Assurance Objectives 9
Why Is a Quality Assurance Group Needed? 11
   Challenges Facing the MIS Manager 11
When Is a Quality Assurance Function Needed? 16
Who Should Staff the Function? 17
Operation of the Quality Assurance Function 17
The Critical Difference Between Quality
Control and Quality Assurance 19
Summary 20

CHAPTER 2: ROLE OF A QUALITY ASSURANCE GROUP 21

Quality Assurance Functions 21
   Analyze MIS Errors 22

Develop Standards and Guidelines 24
Review and Build a Quality Environment 24
Provide Technical Advice 25
Review Applications 26
Project Application Evaluation Objectives 27
Criteria for Evaluating Goals 28
Criteria for Evaluating Compliance 28
Criteria for Evaluating Performance 29
Quality Assurance Group Tasks 29
Establishing the Quality Assurance Charter 33
Quality Assurance Group Role Worksheet 34
Quality Assurance Costs 36
Summary 44

APPENDIX: QUALITY ASSURANCE WORK PLAN **49**

**CHAPTER 3: DEVELOPING THE QUALITY
ASSURANCE FUNCTION** **63**

How to Get Started 64
Organizational Structure 64
Staffing Alternatives 66
Task Force Method 66
Full-Time Staff Method 68
Permanent Committee Method 68
Full-Time and Part-Time Combination 69
Characteristics of Quality Assurance Candidates 69
Developing the Quality Assurance Function 71
Organizational Structure 71
Staffing the Quality Assurance Function 72
Quality Assurance Support Staff 76
Support Needed for a Successful QA Function 78
Steps in Performing the Function 79
Objectivity 80
Summary 82

**CHAPTER 4: SYSTEMS REVIEW PRIORITIES:
ALLOCATING QA TIME** **85**

Methods of Selecting Applications for Review 85
Five Common Methods for Selecting Applications for Review 86
Rating Criteria 87

Type of Application 88
    Financial Applications 88
    Statutory Requirements...89
    Exposure to Loss 89
Complexity of Application 89
    Application History...89
    Effort to Develop Application 90
    Time Span to Complete Project..90
    Expected Number of Application Programs...............................90
    Number of Databases Updated 90
    Technology 90
People 91
    User Involvement...91
    Internal Audit Involvement 92
    Skill of the Project Team 92
Other Selection Criteria 92
Rating Individual Applications 93
    Assumptions and Caveats..93
    MIS Planning/Prioritization Process 94
    Nondiscretionary Reviews 94
    Risk Evaluation Levels and Dimensions 96
Level I 98
    Mission Impact/Strategic Value/Organization (Business)
    Criticality and Sensitivity Factors 98
Level II 99
    System Size/Scale/Complexity 99
    System Environment/Stability 100
    Reliability/Integrity 101
    Technology Integration 101
Risk Scoring: Application of the Work Priority Scheme 102
    Implementation of the Scheme 102
    Suggested Scoring Approach for Each Risk Dimension 102
    First Order System Risk Score 104
    Risk Level II Review Considerations 104
    The Second Order System Risk Score 105
    An Example..105
Systems Enhancements in the Review Process...............................106
Responding To Special Requests 107
Summary..107

PART 2: CONDUCTING REVIEWS OF APPLICATION SYSTEMS 113

CHAPTER 5: QUALITY ASSURANCE REVIEW OF AN APPLICATION SYSTEM 115

Reviewing Computer Systems Applications 115
Systems Failures..118
    Reasons for Failure to Achieve Goals 119
    Systems Failures — Methods 121
    Systems Failures — Performance 123
    Top-Down Review 126
Review of Goals 128
    Level 1 129
Review of Methods 134
Review of Performance 137
Summary..142

CHAPTER 6: INITIATING SYSTEMS REVIEW 145

Preparation for a Quality Assurance Group 146
Quality Assurance Review Points 149
    Feasibility Study 151
    Design Phase 152
    Program Phase...154
    System Test Phase 154
    Conversion Phase 155
Staffing the Quality Assurance Review........................155
Planning the Quality Assurance Review 156
    Administrative Planning 156
    Use of Gantt Chart 159
    Project Control 160
    Automating Scheduling 160
    General Planning.......................................161
    Application-Oriented Planning 161
Entrance Conference 162
    Entrance Conference Objectives 162
    Conducting the Entrance Conference 163
    Quality Assurance Documentation 164
Summary 167

CHAPTER 7: CONDUCTING A QUALITY
ASSURANCE REVIEW **171**

Quality Assurance Review Points 172
Conducting the Review 173
System Justification Phase 174
   Review Point 1: Mid-Justification Phase 176
   Review Point 2: End of Justification Phase 178
Systems Design Phase 179
   Review Point 3: Review of the Business Systems Solutions 181
   Review Point 4: Review of Computer Equipment Selection 183
   Review Point 5: Review of Computer Systems Design 183
Programming Phase 188
   Review Point 6: Program Design 188
   Review Point 7: Testing and Conversion Planning 191
   Review Point 8: Program Coding and Testing 191
Testing Phase 193
   Review Point 9: Detailed Test Plan 194
   Review Point 10: Test Results 196
Conversion Phase 197
   Review Point 11: Detail Conversion Planning and Programs 198
   Review Point 12: Review of Conversion Results 200
   Conversion Checklist 201
Determining if Concerns Have Been Adequately
Addressed by the Project Team 205
Summary 206

CHAPTER 8: REVIEWING THE ADEQUACY
OF APPLICATION CONTROLS **207**

Internal Control Defined 207
   Environment Control Objectives 208
   Application Control Objectives 209
Acceptable Level of Risk 210
Methods for Reducing Losses 212
Reduce the Frequency of Occurrence 214
Reduce Opportunity for Loss 214
Reduce Amount Subject to Loss 215
Reduce Impact of Loss 215
Types of Controls 215

Reviewing Controls 217
Common System Vulnerabilities 218
    Erroneous or Falsified Data Input 218
    Misuse by Authorized End Users 219
    Uncontrolled System Access 220
    Ineffective Security Practices for the Application 220
    Procedural Errors at the MIS Facility 221
    Program Errors 223
    Operating System Flaws 225
    Communications System Failure 226
Reviewing Environmental Controls 227
Reviewing Application Controls 236
    Data Is Accurate 237
    Data Is Complete 238
    Data Is Authorized 239
    Data Is Timely 240
    Data Is Supportable 241
    Application Control Review 242
Summary 259

**CHAPTER 9: QUALITY ASSURANCE
REVIEW TECHNIQUES 261**

Quality Assurance Review Techniques 261
Application of Techniques 264
Skills Needed for QA Review Techniques 264
Quality Assurance Techniques 269
    Project Documentation Review Technique 269
    Systems Documentation Quality Assurance Technique 270
    Interviewing QA Techniques 271
    Observation (Examination) QA Technique 272
    Checklist QA Review Technique 274
    Testing (Verification) QA Technique 277
    Test Data QA Technique 277
    Base Case QA Technique 279
    Judgment QA Technique 282
    Simulation/Modeling QA Technique 282
    Consultants (Advice) QA Technique 284
    Quantitative Analysis QA Techniques 285

Automating the Quality Assurance Function 290
Summary 291

**CHAPTER 10: REPORTING QUALITY
ASSURANCE RESULTS** **293**

Results Expected From QA Reviews 293
Writing Quality Assurance Reports 294
Planning for Writing a Report 296
Postreview Conference..304
Who Gets Quality Assurance Results? 306
Summary 307

**PART 3:   QUALITY ASSURANCE
RESPONSIBILITIES AND METHODS** **309**

**CHAPTER 11: VERIFICATION, VALIDATION,
AND TESTING**..**311**

Quality Assurance Through Verification 311
  Attributes of Quality Software 312
  Verification Throughout Life Cycle..............................315
An Overview of Testing..320
  Concepts 320
  Dynamic Testing 321
  Structural Versus Functional Testing 322
  Static Testing..323
  Manual Versus Automated Testing..............................324
Verification Techniques 325
  General Verification Techniques 326
  Test Data Generation 332
  Functional Testing Techniques 333
  Structural Testing Techniques 337
  Test Data Analysis 341
  Static Analysis Techniques..343
  Dynamic Analysis Techniques 348
  Combined Methods 350
  Test Support Tools..351
Summary 354

CHAPTER 12: IMPROVING SOFTWARE MAINTENANCE 361

Definition of Software Maintenance 364
  Functional Definition 364
The Software Maintenance Process 368
Software Maintenance Problems 370
  Software Quality 370
  Documentation 373
  Users 374
  Personnel 375
The Ideal Maintainer...375
System Maintenance Versus System Redesign 377
  Frequent System Failures 378
  Code Over Seven Years Old...378
  Overly Complex Program Structure and Logic Flow...379
  Code Written for Previous-generation Hardware...379
  Running in Emulation Mode...380
  Very Large Modules or Unit Subroutines...380
  Excessive Resource Requirements 380
  Hard-coded Parameters That Are Subject to Change...381
  Difficulty in Keeping Maintainers 381
  Seriously Deficient Documentation 381
  Missing or Incomplete Design Specifications 382
Controlling Software Changes...382
  Controlling Perfective Maintenance...382
  Controlling Adaptive Maintenance 385
  Controlling Corrective Maintenance 386
Improving Software Maintenance 387
  Source Code Guidelines 388
  Documentation Guidelines...392
  Coding and Review Techniques 393
  Change Control 396
  Testing Standards and Procedures 399
Software Maintenance Tools 399
  Cross-referencer 400
  Comparators 401
  Diagnostic Routines 401
  Application Utility Libraries 402
  On-line Documentation Libraries...402

On-line/Interactive Change and Debug Facilities 403
Generation and Retention of Test Data 403
Managing Software Maintenance 404
Goals of Software Maintenance Management 406
Establish a Software Maintenance Policy 407
Staffing and Management of Maintenance Personnel 410

CHAPTER 13: REUSE OF SOFTWARE **413**

The Software Crisis 414
The Nature of Software Reusability 415
The Software Reuse Process 417
Levels of Reusable Software Information 417
Reusable Software Classification 420
Software Commonality 421
Advantages of Software Reuse 422
Productivity 423
Quality 423
Difficulties in Software Reuse 424
A Software Professional Viewpoint 425
A Software Managerial Viewpoint 426
A Cognition/Cultural Viewpoint 426
Feasibility of Software Reuse 427
The Role of Prototyping in Software Reuse 432
Reusability and Software Acquisition..433
Software Portability 434
Summary..435

*CHAPTER 14: SPECIAL QUALITY ASSURANCE
GROUP TASKS* **439**

Typical Quality Assurance Special Tasks 442
Developing Control Standards..442
Hardware Selection Analysis..443
Software Selection Analysis 443
Develop Systems and Programming Practices 444
Training MIS Personnel in Control, System,
and Programming Practices 444
Providing Systems Consultant Services..445
Resolving the Technical Problems of Application Systems...................446
Bridging the Gap Between Systems and Operations Personnel 446

Developing More Effective MIS Methods 447
Reviewing Data Center Operations 447
Evaluation of Operational Application Systems 448
Advantages and Disadvantages of Special Assignments 448
Evaluating the Merits of Special Tasks 452
Summary 453

**CHAPTER 15: QUALITY ASSURANCE AND
THE PERSONAL COMPUTER** **455**

Introduction 455
Basic Security Concerns 455
Information Security Objectives 456
Threats 456
The Nature of the PC Security Problem 456
Physical Accessibility 457
Built-in Security Mechanisms 457
Nature of Data Being Handled 458
Users' Responsibilities 458
Is There Really a Security Problem? 459
Protecting the Equipment 459
Theft and Damage Protection 460
Environmental Controls 461
Magnetic Media Protection 462
Maintaining Perspective 464
System and Data Access Control 464
Authorization Rules 465
Identification 465
Logical Access Controls 468
Cryptography 470
Residue Control 473
Placement of Controls 474
Summary 474
Software and Data Integrity 475
Formal Software Development 475
Data Integrity Controls 476
Operational Controls 476
Documentation 477
Additional Guidance 477
Backup and Contingency Planning 477

Elements of Contingency Planning 477
Emergency Procedures 478
File Backup 478
Other Backup Considerations 480
Summary 482
Miscellaneous Considerations 482
Auditability 482
Multi-user Personal Computers 483
Communications Environments 484
Electromagnetic Emanations 485
The Micro as an Accomplice 485
Additional Issues 486
Managing the Security Problem 486
Information Security Management — An Overview 486
A Plan of Action 491
Opportunities 494
Personal Computer Self-Assessment Questionnaire 495
Personal Computer Security Products 495
Physical Access Control and Theft Protection 502
Electrical Power Quality Control 502
Environmental Protection 502
Magnetic Media Protection 502
System and File Access Control 503
Cryptographic Systems 503
Miscellaneous 504
Summary 504

PART 4: MEASUREMENTS/METRICS **507**

CHAPTER 16: QUANTITATIVE ANALYSIS
OF SYSTEM REVIEWS **509**

Value of Ratings 509
Rating Considerations 511
Review Point Evaluation Forms...514
Scoring the QA Review 514
Evaluating the Score 533
Adjusted Score/Explanation of Adjusted Score 534
Example of Review Point Evaluation 535
Other Methods for Evaluating Quality 539
Summary 539

CHAPTER 17: METRICS — A TOOL FOR DEFINING AND MEASURING QUALITY **541**

Quality Measurement in Perspective 542
Identifying Quality Requirements 543
    Procedures for Identifying Important Quality Factors 545
    An Example of Factors Specification 548
    Procedures for Identifying Critical Software Attributes 550
    Example of Identifying Software Criteria 550
    Procedures for Establishing Quantifiable Goals 552
    Example of Metrics 554
Summary 562

CHAPTER 18: MEASURING COMPUTER SYSTEM RELIABILITY **565**

Purpose and Scope 565
Fundamental Concepts 566
    Terminology 566
    Reliability Distinctions 567
    Reliability Requirements 567
Evaluating Reliability 569
    Sources of Reliability Data 569
    Reliability Metrics 578
    Assessing the Quality of the Computer System 583
Basic Techniques 588
    Design Features 589
    Implementation Techniques 592
Recovery Strategy 593
    Recovery Procedures 593
    Recovery Levels 594
The Reliability Program 595
    Implementing a Reliability Program 595
    Financial Considerations 596
    Activities for Establishing and Maintaining Reliability 597

PART 5: RELATIONSHIPS TO INTERNAL AUDIT **601**

CHAPTER 19: RELATIONSHIP TO INTERNAL AUDITING **603**

Internal Audit Responsibilities 604

Control in an MIS Environment 606
The Auditor and Control 608
Control and MIS Organization...609
Need for Quality Assurance 612
Working Relationships with Internal Auditors............................614
    Working with Auditors to Perform the Audit Function 615
    Using Auditors on the Quality Assurance Review Team 616
    Reliance by Auditors on QA Reviews 616
    Cross-Training 617
    Exchange of Reports...617
    Internal Audit Support of Quality Assurance 618
Summary..618

APPENDIX A: SAMPLE QUALITY
ASSURANCE MANUAL **621**
    Organization's Computer Philosophy 622
    Abbreviations Used 622
    Quality Assurance Philosophy...622
    How the Manual Is Used 623

APPENDIX B: TESTING TOOLS AND TECHNIQUES **677**
1.1.   Introduction 677
2.1.   Name. Algorithm Analysis 678
3.1.   Name. Analytic Modeling of Systems Designs 685
4.1.   Name. Assertion Generation...692
5.1.   Name. Assertion Processing 697
6.1.   Name. Cause-Effect Graphing...701
7.1.   Name. Code Auditor 706
8.1.   Name. Comparators...710
9.1.   Name. Control Structure Analyzer......................................712
10.1.   Name. Cross-Reference Generators.....................................715
11.1   Name. Data Flow Analyzers 719
12.1.   Name. Execution Time Estimators/Analyzers 722
13.1.   Name. Formal Reviews 725
14.1.   Name. Formal Verification..731
15.1.   Name. Global Roundoff Analysis
        of Algebraic Processes...735
16.1.   Name. Inspection..739
17.1.   Name. Interactive Test Aids...744

18.1.   Name. Interface Checker 747
19.1.   Name. Mutation Analysis 750
20.1.   Name. Peer Review 755
21.1.   Name. Physical Units Checking.. 766
22.1.   Name. Regression Testing 769
23.1.   Name. Requirements Analyzer 772
24.1.   Name. Requirements Tracing 775
25.1.   Name. Software Monitors.. 779
26.1.   Name. Specification-Based Functional Testing 782
27.1.   Name. Symbolic Execution 786
28.1.   Name. Test Coverage Analyzers... 791
29.1.   Name. Test Data Generator 794
30.1.   Name. Test Support Facilities 798
31.1.   Name. Walkthroughs.. 801

List of Figures
and Tables

Figure   *Page*

1.1. Evaluation objectives 6
1.2. Elements of QA objectives 10
1.3. Cost of project versus QA's
       ability to influence 12
1.4. Challenges of the MIS department 13
1.5. Operation of Quality Assurance function 18
2.1. Role of a Quality Assurance group 23
2.2. Evaluation objectives 27
2.3. Tasks of a Quality Assurance function 31
2.4. Quality Assurance group role worksheet 37
2.5. Task score worksheet 43
2.6. A typical QA charter 45
2.7. Quality Assurance costs and effort 46
2.8. The Quality Assurance function 47
3.1. Suggested MIS department organization 65
3.2. Quality Assurance staffing alternatives 67
3.3. Suggested Quality Assurance group structure 73
3.4. Job description: Quality Assurance manager 74
3.5. Job description: senior Quality Assurance analyst .. 75
3.6. Job description: Quality Assurance consultant 76

Figure   *Page*

3.7.   Job description: Quality Assurance analyst 77
3.8.   Constraints of the Quality Assurance review process 81
4.1.   Methods of selecting applications for review 87
4.2.   MIS planning/prioritization process 95
4.3.   Allocating review time by application worksheet 111
4.4.   Allocating review time by application worksheet 112
5.1.   Quality Assurance areas 117
5.2.   Systems failures — goals 120
5.3.   Systems failures — methods 122
5.4.   Systems failures — performance 124
5.5.   Top-down review 127
5.6.   Review of goals 129
5.7.   Goals evaluation matrix 133
5.8.   Review of methods 135
5.9.   Methods evaluation matrix 138
5.10.   Review of performance 141
5.11.   Performance evaluation matrix 143
6.1.   Sources of information for review planning 147
6.2.   Project review control sheet 150
6.3.   Project tickler card 158
6.4.   Gantt assignment chart 159
6.5.   Weekly status report 160
6.6.   Workpaper table of contents 168
7.1.   System justification phase 175
7.2.   Review point 1: mid-justification phase review 177
7.3.   Review point 2: end of justification phase review 180
7.4.   System design phase 182
7.5.   Review point 3: review of the business
        systems solution 184
7.6.   Review point 4: review of computer
        equipment selection 185
7.7.   Review point 5: review of computer
        system design 186

Figure		*Page*
7.8.	Testing phase	189
7.9.	Review point 6: review of program design	190
7.10.	Review point 7: review of testing and conversion planning	192
7.11.	Review point 8: review of program coding and testing	193
7.12.	Testing phase	195
7.13.	Review point 9: review of detailed test plan	196
7.14.	Review point 10: review of test results	197
7.15.	Conversion phase	199
7.16.	Review point 11: review of detail conversion planning and programs	200
7.17.	Review point 12: review of conversion results	201
8.1.	Cost-effectiveness curve of control	211
8.2.	Reducing risks	213
8.3.	Effectiveness and efficiency of controls	217
8.4.	Environmental control review questionnaire	229
8.5.	MIS department controls profile worksheet	235
8.6.	Application review questionnaire	244
8.7.	Computer application controls profile worksheet	258
9.1.	Quality Assurance review techniques	262
9.2.	Quality Assurance review points/review techniques matrix	265
9.3.	Skills needed to use Quality Assurance technique: project documentation	270
9.4.	Skills needed to use Quality Assurance technique: system documentation	272
9.5.	Skills needed to use Quality Assurance technique: fact finding (interviews)	273
9.6.	Skills needed to use Quality Assurance technique: observation (examination)	274
9.7.	Skills needed to use Quality Assurance technique: checklist	276

Figure   *Page*

9.8.   Skills needed to use Quality Assurance
       technique: testing (verification) 278

9.9.   Skills needed to use Quality Assurance
       technique: test data...279

9.10. Skills needed to use Quality Assurance
       technique: base case 280

9.11. Skills needed to use Quality Assurance
       technique: confirmation..281

9.12. Skills needed to use Quality Assurance
       technique: judgment 283

9.13. Skills needed to use Quality Assurance
       technique: simulation/modeling 284

9.14. Skills needed to use Quality Assurance
       technique: consultants (advice)..285

9.15. Skills needed to use Quality Assurance
       technique: quantitative analysis 286

9.16. Skills/techniques matrix 288

11.1. A hierarchy of software quality attributes 313

11.2. The software development life cycle 315

11.3. Life cycle verification activities 317

13.1   Three levels of reusable software information 418

13.2. Software package commonality index 422

13.3. Feasibility of software reuse...429

14.1. Special assignment/advantages-disadvantages
       matrix 450

15.1. Personal computer self-assessment questionnaire.................496

16.1. Quality Assurance review point #1:
       mid-justification phase review..515

16.2. Quality Assurance review point #2:
       end of justification phase review 516

16.3. Quality Assurance review point #3:
       review of business systems solution phase...........................518

16.4. Quality Assurance review point #4:
       review of equipment selection..519

Figure   *Page*

16.5.   Quality Assurance review point #5:
        review of computer system design 520

16.6.   Quality Assurance review point #6:
        review of program design 523

16.7.   Quality Assurance review point #7:
        review of testing and conversion planning 525

16.8.   Quality Assurance review point #8:
        review of program coding and testing 526

16.9.   Quality Assurance review point #9:
        review of detailed test plan 527

16.10. Quality Assurance review point #10:
        review of test results 528

16.11. Quality Assurance review point #11:
        review of detail conversion planning and programs 529

16.12. Quality Assurance review point #12:
        review of conversion results 530

16.13. Review score sheet 531

16.14. Adjusted score for comparative purposes 537

16.15. Review score sheet 538

17.1.   How software metrics complement Quality Assurance 543

17.2.   Framework for measuring quality 544

17.3.   Software quality requirements survey form 547

17.4.   System characteristics and related quality factors 548

17.5.   The impact of not specifying or measuring
        software quality factors 551

17.6.   Cost versus benefit trade-off 552

17.7.   Relationships between software quality factors 553

17.8.   Typical factor trade-offs 556

17.9.   Software criteria and related quality factors 557

17.10. Criteria definitions for software quality 558

17.11. Quality factor ratings 560

18.1.   System performance reports — examples of
        one type of accounting information analysis 571

Figure   *Page*

18.2.   System incident report 573
18.3.   Sample operator log 574
18.4.   Weekly log report 574
18.5.   Efficiency report..576
18.6.   Utilization statistics 577
18.7.   Failure categorization 577
18.8.   Measures of MTTF, MTBF, MTTR, and availability 581
18.9.   Assessment examples and classes of measurements............584
18.10. Classification of reliability techniques 590
18.11. Triple modular redundancy (TMR) system with voting 591
18.12. Bathtub curve — failure rate as a function of time 599

Tables
4.1.   Practice template for risk scoring of an AIS 108
4.2.   Dimension risk scores and system risk scores for AIS 1 109
4.3.   Dimension risk scores and system risk scores for AIS 2 110
11.1.   Summary of testing techniques 324
11.2.   Testing techniques and tools 357
12.1.   Software maintenance problems 363
12.2.   Functional definition of software maintenance.....................365
12.3.   Software maintenance process 369
12.4.   Characteristics of systems that are candidates
        for redesign 377
12.5.   Suggested policies for controlling software changes 383
12.6.   Factors that affect source code maintainability 387
12.7.   Documentation guidance 392
12.8.   Coding and review techniques..394
12.9.   Controlling changes 397
12.10. Software maintenance tools 400
12.11. Goals of software maintenance 406
12.12. Establishing a software maintenance policy 408
12.13. Managing the software maintenance function 412

Foreword

Is there any significant product that is not subject to a quality assurance operation? Automobiles, airplanes, buildings, refrigerators and television sets must pass tests assuring quality. Computer programs are equally significant works; however, each is different and considered more a work of art than an engineered product.

Programmers did not graduate from the same schools that produce the makers of products. Engineering students learn how to document their work. They learn production methods, testing, and project management. Programmers, I having been among the earliest, majored in mathematics, music, history, and accounting. We didn't know about engineering matters and, therefore, became cottage craftsmen and artists in the absence of the disciplines that transformed other crafts and arts into engineering.

Finally, only in recent years have programming and programmers been forced into the discipline necessary to economically produce the most complex structures known to man — computer programs. Software engineering, structured programming, and quality assurance are emerging in spite of the fact that our universities and colleges still have not advanced to producing software engineers.

The more advanced software-producing organizations are finally realizing the need for formalized life cycle standards and practices. Quality assurance, one important step in the life cycle, is recognized by these organizations as necessary for quality software. An independent testing of programs designed and documented so that they may be formally tested before entering productive use has been found essential — something engineers knew about at least a hundred years ago.

Effective quality assurance requires competent programmers to work in this specialty. We need test programmers or quality assurance programmers just as we have these specialties in engineering. They must be given an identity, stature, and a career path of continued growth of the specialty. A body of knowledge, formal methods, tools, and techniques are needed.

May this book be a significant contribution to the advancement of software engineering practices and quality assurance in particular.

Donn B. Parker
Menlo Park, CA

Preface

The rapid growth of computer technology during the past twenty years has had a substantial impact on organizations. During that time, data processing departments have placed their effort on expanding the use of the computer and discovering new applications. Progress has been substantial during these twenty years, but so have the problems. Data processing, once held in awe by most people, has now become the scapegoat for many organizational problems.

Management's attempt to control the computer has been directed at the symptoms rather than the problems. Management has established elaborate approval procedures for new applications. Users of the computer are charged for that use so that they are aware of, and are charged for, the cost of their applications. Management has frequently slowed the use of new technology by vetoing plans to install new equipment until it has been proven by several years of use.

Many of the problems associated with data processing applications can be attributed to the lack of an orderly installation process, properly supervised from inception through installation.

The emergence of quality assurance groups in data processing is an attempt by data processing management to reduce these problems. In manufacturing operations, the quality control function began decades ago. Data processing, being a production department for office operations, can use quality practices to perform the same function in MIS that quality control does in a manufacturing operation.

This book provides data processing organizations a methodology for implementing a quality control (QC) and quality assurance (QA) function. Guidance is provided for establishing, staffing, and promoting quality assurance. QC is presented as a function that continually reviews systems throughout the systems development life cycle. The book explains the techniques and methods for performing those reviews. A quality control/quality assurance manual prepared by a major organization is included in Appendix A. The review methods and techniques given in the book, together with a how-to-do-it manual, provide organizations with all the materials they need to build and develop an effective quality function in data processing.

One responsible for implementing and/or operating a quality assurance function must understand the critical difference between quality assurance and quality control. Many QA groups actually practice QC, and parts of this book reflect that practice. However, even though it may be necessary to practice QC initially, it is a poor practice. See The Critical Difference Between Quality Control and Quality Assurance, in Chapter 1, for a discussion of the difference between QA and QC.

William E. Perry
Executive Director
Quality Assurance Institute
Orlando, Florida

Part 1

The Quality Assurance Function

1

Quality Assurance: An Essential Element of Electronic Data Processing

Data processing technology continues to outpace systems analysts' ability to build well-controlled and easily maintainable applications. Data processing personnel continue to search for techniques to improve the quality of computerized applications. One such technique is the quality assurance (QA) function. For the last 20 years, data processing departments have been forming quality assurance groups within their domain at a steady rate.

The general function of these groups is threefold: 1) to ascertain compliance to the approved methods of building applications; 2) to assure a reasonable level of performance; and 3) to assure that the goals of the organization, and especially those of the system user, are satisfied. These goals can best be accomplished by establishing a quality-oriented MIS environment.

Organizations continually quest for quality products. Similarities abound between the problems of manufacturing a product and producing a computerized application. The early success of American industry hinged on its ability to consistently produce products of high quality. Those organizations that were able to maintain high quality were able to dominate their industries. The formation of a QA function provides data processing management with an additional degree of confidence that the computerized applications will be well controlled and easily maintainable.

Organizations that achieve high quality in their products first establish an acceptable level of quality and then build a mechanism that assures this level is maintained. In manufacturing that mechanism is known as quality control. The quality control group works with the manufacturing departments to assure that the desired level of quality is maintained. Quality control includes more than an evaluation of the end product. It begins with the examination of the raw materials and continues throughout the manufacturing cycle.

Data processing organizations must equate their function to manufacturing a product in order to see the need for a quality control function. Data processing must assume the responsibility of determining an acceptable level of quality, and then establish the mechanism — quality assurance function — to determine that level is maintained. If you, the data processing professional, say, "My product is hand crafted and it's a one-of-a-kind type product, so it cannot be measured and compared against a standard," QA has little chance of success in your organization. On the other hand, if you say, "My skill is finding better ways to perform work, but the end product can be measured and evaluated against a standard," then the QA function can perform a very viable service for you.

Many companies are now using or considering the use of structured design and structured programming techniques to improve the quality of their systems. These techniques go hand in hand with the quality assurance function. The two disciplines are compatible and mutually supportive. The use of structured techniques provides the standardization and documentation by which QA can measure. Conversely, it appears in practice that successful implementation of structured methods requires some form of QA function to ensure the proper use of the new techniques.

Quality assurance is a step along the path of evolution of data processing from an art to a science. A successful quality assurance function requires that standards be established against which quality can be measured. The function should be advisory to data processing personnel with its clout coming from management support.

WHAT IS QUALITY?

The dictionary defines *quality* as an attribute or characteristic that is associated with something. Thus quality cannot be universally defined but, rather, must be defined for the item in question. Quality becomes a stated list of attributes and characteristics. In a data processing environment quality must be defined by the organization. Definitions may vary significantly from one organization to another. For one organization a well-built Model T Ford is quality, while to another organization it is a fully loaded Cadillac. Quality cannot be built into a product, or measured, until it is defined. Most data processing organizations have only begun to address what high-quality computerized applications are. Thus, the first task of MIS quality assurance may be to define what is meant by quality in the organization.

WHAT IS QUALITY ASSURANCE?

Data processing professionals are no different from other employees of their organization. They want to do a good job and be amply commended and rewarded for that job. The problem faced by data processing personnel is that their technology is not well understood, so if the application they build "works," few people, if any, know whether they did an outstanding job or just a satisfactory job. A means to evaluate the caliber of their work is needed.

The QA function has the primary responsibility of determining if the users' needs have been adequately satisfied. But the needs of the user must be viewed in proper perspective with the needs of other users and the overall goals of the organization. It is important that the data processing systems support the objectives and goals of the organization. Figure 1.1 illustrates the evaluation objectives of a QA function.

QA evaluates systems prior to their implementation. This includes both the building of new systems and enhancing existing systems. As a means of determining if the users' needs are being satisfied, QA evaluates three areas.

1. *Goals.* Does the system achieve the objectives of both the user and the total organization? The goals of the organization come first, and the goals or requirements of the user second. Should the requirements of the user conflict with the goals of the organization, it is important for QA to point out this conflict. The goals of any one user should be in harmony with the goals of other users.

2. *Methods.* Are standardized methods utilized in performance of the data processing function? These methods are manifested as policies, procedures, standards, and guidelines. The QA function will evaluate compliance to these methods of performing work.

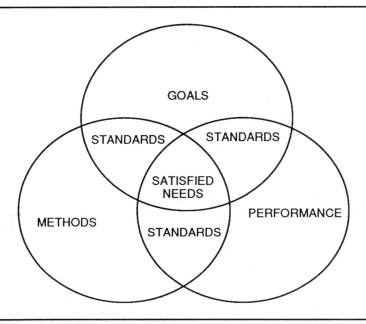

Figure 1.1. Evaluation objectives.

3. *Performance.* Have the systems analysts optimized the use of com-
    puter hardware and software when implementing applications?
    Optimization involves skilled systems design, the use of proper
    programming and systems techniques, as well as the best use of the
    available hardware and software.

Individuals appointed to a QA function work with systems analysts
and programmers to achieve these objectives. This does not give QA the
responsibility for systems design. The group should take on the role of
a counselor as opposed to the role of a policeman. Differences of opinion
are settled by management decisions.

Figure 1.1 illustrates that standards are extremely important in satisfying users' needs. Methods should not interfere with goals, nor should
methods reduce performance. Goals should not override performance, and
so on. However, it is only through standards that the proper balance
among goals, methods, and performance can be achieved. If the department fails to set standards, systems programmers will set them. Far too
often, data processing management relinquishes the setting of standards
to programmers — and later reprimands them for poor performance.

EXAMPLES OF AVOIDABLE PROBLEMS

The following are examples of unsatisfactory applications that have cost organizations large amounts of money. The systems were designed by experienced data processing personnel. They are cases where the existence of a QA function could have saved the data processing department embarrassment and the organization money.

Example 1. A large manufacturing company was designing an on-line order entry system to replace a batch-oriented system. Under the existing system, all orders for a day were processed in a batch overnight. The sales organizations were notified the next morning of stockouts, delays in delivery, and other information pertinent to the execution of the order.

The new on-line order entry system would give the sales office the necessary information immediately. Thus, sales representatives could confirm with customers (while taking the order) shipment dates, method of shipment, stockouts, and so on. The systems designers ran preliminary tests on the equipment, and built an extensive application costing several hundred thousand dollars. When the application was coupled with the vendor's software, however, the resulting performance degraded to the point that the response time was unacceptable at the sales location test site. This caused the data processing department to divert systems programmers to the function of building a specialized message switching system. After expending many thousands of dollars on additional programming effort, the decision was finally reached that the desired performance was unachievable.

A QA function challenging performance by questioning the ability of technology to produce the desired response times would have alerted data processing management to the problem many months and several hundred thousand dollars sooner than when the inability was actually discovered.

Example 2. A sales organization established an operating standard limiting program modules to 64K in order to create the proper job mix in a multitask environment. A systems designer building a new system realized that the 64K limitation would degrade performance significantly. By increasing the program's module size to 180K, the designer was able to eliminate several passes of a large file. As this was a frequently run system, the designer argued that the exception was warranted, and proceeded to build the application using the 180K module limit. The application was complete and tested before the operations personnel realized the desired standard had been exceeded. They let the system run nonetheless. But whenever the new application ran, the normal mix of work could not be run. This meant that while the designer's application achieved a higher level of performance, the net result was less throughput at the computer center during the day.

Example 3. A large job order manufacturing organization designed a production control system to handle the entire process. The system was designed so that the engineering department would enter the bill of materials necessary for a job. From that, the system would explode the subcomponents listed into their bill of material. The computer system would then determine schedules, order raw material, and issue the paperwork on the appropriate date. The net result was each work station would be given a daily list of jobs that were to be completed that day, together with the location of the parts. As status was reported using data terminals, the computer would adjust schedules to be reflected in the next day's work. The success of the system was dependent upon the correct entry of information from the shop floor. The system was designed by engineers. When the machine operators were asked to prepare computer input, the job was beyond their capabilities. To remedy this situation, the organization put data entry clerks on the shop floor. Since the machine operators' pay was used for calculating incentive payroll, they could no longer control the work they did to assure maximum incentive pay. Thus, rather than reporting actual production, the operators reported production that guaranteed them maximum pay. Within six months, the organization scrapped the new system and reverted to the manual paperwork system.

This is an example where the systems designer clearly over-engineered the system for the people it was designed to assist. Again, a QA group challenging the usability of an application would have alerted management of this potential problem during the systems design phase. The type of changes that could have been incorporated in the initial system would have been done, thus saving the organization the several hundred thousand dollars required to build another system that the machine operators could utilize.

Example 4. A user department in a life insurance company wanted a change made to an application. The change was extremely complex but would have simplified some operating procedures in the user department. The systems designer performed an evaluation and determined it was uneconomical to make that particular change. At the same time the systems programmers were converting from one version of an operating system to another. The change cost about $14,000, for which no economic justification was made.

In this situation it is difficult to evaluate which of the two decisions was correct. Were the goals of the organization relegated to second place and the desires of the data processing operation put first? If that $14,000 had been spent to satisfy the requirement of the user, would the overall functioning of the organization have been better? A difficult pair of questions, but a QA group could have provided a much needed independent viewpoint.

QUALITY ASSURANCE OBJECTIVES

The QA group works with the systems designer in designing new systems and enhancements to existing systems. In this process, QA evaluates goals, methods, and performance. The quality assurance group performs those functions that the data processing manager might do personally if time permitted. Figure 1.2 outlines the elements that make up the objectives of QA.

Under *goals,* the QA reviews each system to determine that

1. The system meets the needs of the user department(s) and other users.

2. The system is consistent with the needs of other users. One system does not infringe on the rights of other systems users.

3. The goals are consistent with the objectives of the organization. In all cases, the organization's objectives should have a higher priority than the goals of one user.

4. The goals of the system meet the MIS department objectives. If there is a conflict, resolve it before implementing the system.

5. The goals of the system are consistent with industry and government requirements. Where either the industry or government has set requirements for data processing systems or this specific application, those requirements need to be incorporated into the system.

GOALS	METHODS	PERFORMANCE
Meets user needs Consistent with needs of other users Consistent with organization objectives Meets MIS department objectives Consistent with industry and government requirements Controlled and auditable	The system was implemented using organization and MIS department: Policies Procedures Standards Guidelines	The system design is: Economical Effective Efficient

Figure 1.2. Elements of QA objectives.

6.   The system complies to the intent of management (i.e., controls are adequate) and the system is auditable.

Under *methods*, QA reviews systems to determine that the system being implemented is using the organization and MIS department's:

1.   *Policies.* The broad-based course of action selected by the organization.

2.   *Procedures.* The particular methods outlined by the organization to accomplish objectives.

3.   *Standards.* Rules set up by the organization for the measure of quantity or quality of work.

4.   *Guidelines.* Recommended methods for performing work.

Under *performance*, QA reviews systems to determine that the design is

1.   *Economical.* The system is to be performed in the way that requires the least cost.

2.   *Effective.* The system will accomplish the results desired with minimum effort.

3.   *Efficient.* The system as designed maximizes the use of people and machines.

While these terms sound somewhat synonymous, each requires a different evaluation of the system. *Economical* means dollar considerations. *Effectiveness* brings in the criteria of time and ease of performing the task. *Efficiency* considers such things as whether or not all or parts of the system should have been computerized, or whether it could have been done more efficiently manually.

WHY IS A QUALITY ASSURANCE GROUP NEEDED?

Experience has shown that the best time to influence the design of systems is in the earlier stages of development. Once the design of a system has been determined, it is costly to make significant changes. Adjustments during and after the programming stage tend to be more fine tuning than modifications of any magnitude. Figure 1.3 illustrates that while the majority of the cost of developing a system occurs after programming has commenced, the ability to influence the design is inversely proportional to the cost.

Management tends to become involved in the system when the cost becomes significant and the dates of implementation approach. Thus, we have the paradox of management's influence and concern coming at the point in the systems development life cycle where they are least able to influence the systems design.

The establishment of a QA function provides management with a degree of confidence that an independent, technically trained group is monitoring the goals, methods, and performance of applications from the beginning of the project. This relieves data processing management of personally performing this function.

Challenges Facing the MIS Manager

The MIS manager is faced with some unique problems in the performance of the data processing mandate. Figure 1.4 illustrates those challenges facing the MIS department which the establishment of a QA

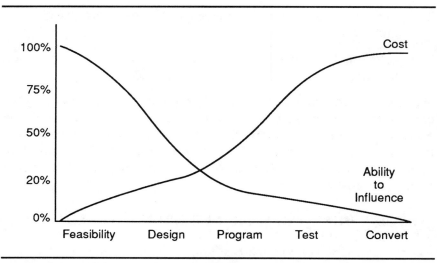

Figure 1.3. Cost of project versus QA's ability to influence.

group would help solve. The solutions are discussed in the later chapters of this book.

The data processing manager is responsible for a highly technical function that interfaces with most operating groups within the organization. In most highly technical departments, the manager is able to contain the technical aspects of the function within the department. This is not true in the data processing organization, since other departments and groups within the organization use and rely upon the result of MIS systems. This puts the MIS manager in an influential and responsible role in most departments within the organization.

Some of the unique challenges facing an MIS department relate specifically to the technical aspect of data processing. An independent evaluation group such as QA can assist the MIS manager in dealing with these challenges.

Changing Technology. Vendors continually offer new data processing hardware and software. This continual modification by vendors may obsolete existing systems and cause a significant percentage of data

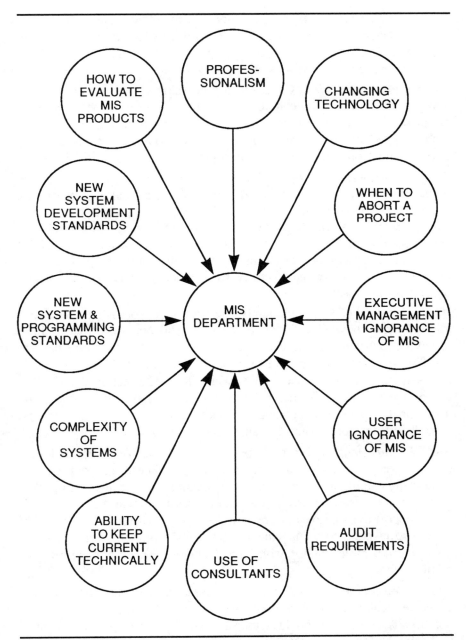

Figure 1.4. Challenges of the MIS department.

processing resources to be expended just to stay current with technological changes. The value of making many of these changes is rarely examined. Technology tends to trap organizations into continuing with one vendor's line of hardware and software.

When to Abort a Project. Once a data processing system is under development, it is rarely stopped unless a major disaster is pending. Few organizations have the proper criteria and information to make an early judgment as to when system development should be stopped on an uneconomical project or one that is running into technical difficulties.

Executive Management Ignorance of MIS. Few members of executive management have a detailed knowledge of the technical aspects of data processing. However, these same individuals are required to make decisions regarding the future of data processing. Too frequently, decisions are made on intuition as opposed to facts. Many of these decisions inhibit DP effectiveness because there appears to be distrust on the part of many members of executive management over economic evaluations of data processing proposals.

User Ignorance of MIS. Frequently, users of data processing have minimal technical knowledge of data processing. This puts them in a position of having to accept recommendations by data processing systems designers. The systems designers, in turn, have little knowledge of the needs and requirements of the user. Thus, while it may be technically feasible to provide the user with desired features in an application, neither the user nor the systems designer can properly match needs with technical capacity of data processing to satisfy those needs.

Audit Requirement. Auditors are becoming more active in evaluation of computer applications. Unfortunately, many of these auditors are not technically qualified to perform the evaluations they are making. This places an additional burden on the data processing department to technically support the auditor. Failure to support the audit effort may result in having to respond to management about audit comments for which the goals are desirable but for which the technology does not permit economical achievement.

Use of Consultants. No one individual in data processing can be knowledgeable on all aspects of designing and implementing a computer application. Ideally, consultants should be used as needed to assist in solving technical problems. Unfortunately, few organizations provide the systems designers access to a consultant.

Ability to Keep Current Technically. All members of the data processing department, especially management, have difficulty in keeping technically current in their field. As data processing systems become more segmented, this problem accelerates. Although it was possible 10 years ago for one person to implement an entire system, it now takes a group of individuals to perform the same function. Data processing management, because of its technical lag, has difficulty in assessing the adequacy of new ideas in system design and the adequacy of new hardware and software systems under consideration.

Complexity of Systems. As systems become more integrated, they become more complex. Chains of systems now flow through entire organizations. One transaction, such as an order, can trigger numerous transactions to be automatically generated by the computer system. Thus, the development of one system can affect the operation of many other systems. It now becomes necessary for a systems designer to comprehend fully the impact of a new system, or enhancement to an existing system, on all the systems affected by that development.

Few Systems and Programming Standards. Systems and programming work remains basically an art. Without standards, systems designers and programmers can innovate in ways which facilitate errors and incur high maintenance costs on computerized applications.

Few Systems Development Standards. The development process itself in most organizations remains a highly skilled craft. Individuals personalize applications so that each one is developed in a unique manner. The development process too frequently is one that meets the personal requirements of the lead systems designer. This uniqueness of the development process has led to executive management's reluctance to rely on MIS-proposed costs and schedules. There have been too many cost overruns and schedule extensions in implementing data processing applications.

How to Evaluate MIS Products. When hardware is purchased, software obtained, or applications built, it is difficult for management to evaluate the product. The lack of standards tends to make each product unique. Because of the time required to get data processing products operational, requirements and environments change during that process. Thus, economic evaluations and objectives stated in the proposal often change sufficiently by the implementation date to make evaluations difficult.

Professionalism. Many individuals within the data processing department are more loyal to the data processing profession than to the organization that employs them. Their divided loyalty can cause them to be more concerned about the technical aspects of data processing than meeting the needs of their own organization. This misplaced professionalism causes reluctance on the part of data processing professionals to use "canned" systems. They would rather specify and develop "personalized" systems, which may not be in the best interest of the organization but are technically valuable for the personal improvement of the data processing professional.

WHEN IS A QUALITY ASSURANCE FUNCTION NEEDED?

A recent study by the American Petroleum Institute showed that member companies having an MIS quality assurance function staffed that function at the ratio of 1 QA person per 40 systems designers and programmers. The survey indicated that the staffing rate was expected to increase to 1 QA person for each 15 systems designers and programmers in the near future. This is not an ideal to strive for but a needed staffing level for the function to be fully effective. The staffing ratios suggested by the API study appear to be in line with the ratios in other industries that have adopted the QA concept.

The staffing ratios indicate that when a data processing department has 10 or more systems designers and programmers, they need one full-time-equivalent to perform the quality assurance function. At fewer than 10 systems designers and programmers, the function should still be performed but would probably be done on a part-time basis. For example, a department of six would require half a full-time-equivalent position to perform the QA function. Six systems designers and programmers should be considered the entry point to add the QA function.

If your organization has its major financial systems computerized, QA takes on even greater importance. If any of the following questions can be answered affirmatively, the MIS department should seriously consider adding the function:

- Does the department have six or more systems designers or programmers?
- Are any of the organization's major financial systems computerized?
- Is the total data processing budget over $250,000 per year?

WHO SHOULD STAFF THE FUNCTION?

The QA function staff should be as knowledgeable in data processing as the senior systems analysts and designers in the department. If the function is not staffed by the best people in the data processing department, it will be ineffective. Designers who are having their systems reviewed must have respect for the individuals performing the review. Likewise, DP management must have respect for those performing the reviews if they are to support the reviewers' recommendations.

Assignment to the QA group can be done in one of three ways: full-time, part-time (in addition to the individual's regular assignments), or as a training mechanism for personnel in the data processing department. Those assigned to the group for training need not be in lead positions in the group.

Individuals assigned to the group should be expected to spend a considerable amount of time (8–12 weeks per year) maintaining their technical proficiency. This proficiency can be maintained through courses, conferences, and on-the-job training.

OPERATION OF THE QUALITY ASSURANCE FUNCTION

The QA function should be charged with the task of looking at all new data processing applications as well as major enhancements to existing applications. With limited resources available, it is important that the personnel in the group optimize its resources. The method that has proved effective is to have the group establish checkpoints at various key points in the MIS systems development life cycle. These checkpoints, which are illustrated in Figure 1.5, are the feasibility study, design, programming, testing, and conversion.

Checkpoints are of two kinds: 1) the point at which advice and counsel from the QA function will be most beneficial for the systems designers, and 2) points when the group can evaluate the status of the system being implemented. Status checkpoints serve as an independent evaluation when DP management or user management need to decide whether to commit more resources to continue the project.

During each of the five key phases in the systems development life cycle, QA interacts one or more times with the project development

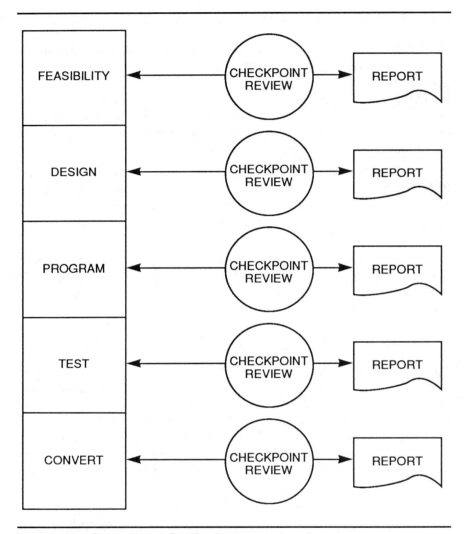

Figure 1.5. Operation of Quality Assurance function.

team. At the end of most of these checkpoint reviews (discussed in detail in later chapters), the QA person or group will make a report to management. The report may be either oral or written, and may be given to an appropriate level of management. Management will then take any action it feels is warranted.

THE CRITICAL DIFFERENCE BETWEEN QUALITY CONTROL AND QUALITY ASSURANCE

Quality is an attribute of a product that is either present or absent. For example, a quality attribute of a program is the job number. It is either present or absent. If present, the program is a quality program as far as job number is concerned; if it is absent then we say the program has a defect.

The role of quality control is to measure products against a standard or attribute like a job number to determine if it is there. The purpose of quality control is to identify defects and have them corrected so that defect-free products will be produced. Quality control is limited to looking at products. It is a function that should be performed by the workers. Tasks such as systems reviews and software testing are quality control tasks.

Quality assurance is a function that manages quality. It sets up quality control, but normally does not perform the actual quality control work of inspecting products. Quality assurance uses the results of quality control to evaluate and improve the "processes" that produce the products. Thus we see that quality assurance works with the processes, and quality control works with the products.

The quality dilemma that quality assurance people face is that they cannot properly do their job of working with the processes until

1. The processes are established (standards and procedures).

2. Quality control has been installed in the processes to provide quality assurance groups information on product defects.

Until formal processes are established and utilized, and quality control exists in those processes, many quality assurance groups will spend their time establishing process (standards and procedures) and performing quality control activities such as system development reviews. The purpose of reviews should be twofold for quality assurance groups: first, to help the projects by performing quality control for them, but second and more important, to learn how to do quality control so the QC process can be formalized and turned over to the projects.

In this book a lot of material is devoted to quality control activities, but they are labeled *quality assurance tasks*. The intent is to assist quality assurance groups in setting up quality control. However, the QA group should turn over all QC tasks to the projects or involved workers as quickly as those QC tasks can be perfected, documented, and the workers trained in how to perform those activities.

SUMMARY

QA groups are being established within data processing departments to provide management with an independent evaluation of the goals, methods, and performance of new systems under development and enhancements to existing systems. The function should be staffed with individuals as knowledgeable in data processing as the MIS department's senior personnel. When a data processing department exceeds six systems analysts/programmers, it should consider establishing this function. It can be staffed by full-time individuals, or by means of additional assignments for personnel in the data processing department. QA operates by conducting reviews at predetermined checkpoints. The basis of these checkpoint reviews is to assist the project team in systems design and to provide management with an independent evaluation of the system at that point in time. This independent evaluation will help data processing management make a decision whether or not to provide additional resources to complete the project.

Role of a Quality Assurance Group

From the time a project commences until it becomes operational, there is a wide range of possible solutions. Data processing department management wants assurance that DP systems are traversing the best solution path. The design of systems must satisfy both the users' needs and the proper utilization of technology. The role of quality assurance is to steer project development in the right direction. Its role is fourfold. The first is to assist the organization in developing the standards and guidelines necessary to build competent systems. Second, QA should review the adequacy of and adherence to general controls, such as the operating procedures and program change procedures. Adequate general controls will assure a proper environment in which to develop and operate systems. Third, QA should provide technical advice to the project team. Fourth, it must review the development of all applications to assure compliance with the organization's goals, methods, and performance criteria.

QUALITY ASSURANCE FUNCTIONS

In the American Petroleum Institute study on the quality assurance function mentioned in Chapter 1, one of the questions asked was "What duties are being performed by the quality assurance group in your organization?" The duties and percentages of responses are listed below.

Duties Performed	Percent of Responses
Review system controls	92
Develop control standards	92

Duties Performed	*Percent of Responses*
Review systems design for completeness	85
Assure documentation is complete	85
Provide technical advice	85
Recommend specific controls	77
Develop systems and programming practices	77
Review for conformance with systems test plan	77
Assure that systems and programming practices are being followed	69
Review for conformance to systems design	69

Among the other duties listed by respondents to the questionnaire were review economic justification, review operating and development cost, validate resource availability, and education. This information will be of value when the charter for QA is developed.

Because QA is organizationally a part of the data processing department, its primary role and function should be supportive of the data processing function. The group is an extension of the responsibilities of the data processing manager. It assumes part of the role currently performed by data processing line management. The role of QA is fivefold. Figure 2.1 illustrates this role. The role is illustrated as a pyramid because each segment of the role builds upon the previous segment.

Analyze MIS Errors

Most of the problems and concerns in a computerized environment are readily available in the form of documented or identified errors or problems. Analyzing these problems can provide the basis for improving the quality of the MIS environment. For example, if the major cause of program "hang-ups" is inadequate space allocation, providing a solution to this problem will improve programmers' performance, and thus improve quality.

Some quality assurance groups spend as much as half their effort tracking errors and analyzing them. This involves examining errors as they occur, pinpointing correction responsibilities, making sure that correction actually occurs, as well as looking for long-range solutions to the problems.

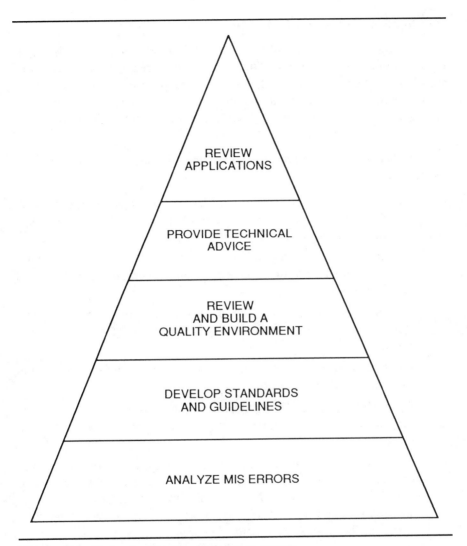

Figure 2.1. Role of a Quality Assurance group.

Some quality assurance groups issue an "error alert" report for common errors. An error alert serves two purposes. First, it helps programmers avoid repeating the same error, and second, it publicizes the fact that the quality assurance group is providing a positive service to all systems analysts and programmers.

Develop Standards and Guidelines

Developing standards and guidelines for the organization's data processing is a fundamental QA role. Obviously, if the organization already has satisfactory standards and guidelines, the group need not develop them. However, few data processing departments have adequate standards and guidelines for the development, implementation, and operation of data processing systems.

The types of standards and guidelines that are needed include the following.

- *System development process standards.* The steps and methods by which an organization approves, implements, and enhances computerized applications.

- *Documentation standards.* The types and contents of documentation that will be produced as a result of developing computerized applications.

- *Programming standards.* The methods and procedures that programmers will follow in designing, coding, documenting, and testing programs.

- *Control standards.* The methods by which computer system and programs will be controlled.

- *Operating standards.* The procedures that must be followed to place programs into production and operate programs in a production mode.

- *Hardware and software standards.* The types of hardware and software packages that will be used by the organizations and those features within software that will be utilized during operation. The standards should include the methods by which hardware and software can be modified or changed.

- *Performance standard.* The level or criteria to be achieved in doing work.

Review and Build a Quality Environment

QA should review the general controls in an operating environment and determine whether they are adequate and whether they comply with general controls. The organizations' standards and guidelines form the basis for developing general controls. Without detailed standards, it becomes difficult to enforce general controls. A review of the general controls can be done either as a special review or when a specific application is being reviewed. This review becomes a mechanism to provide data processing management on compliance to general controls.

Examples of General Controls:

• Segregation of duties between various functions as outlined in department charters, job descriptions, and an organization's policies and procedures.

• Policies and procedures for budgeting projects, reporting status, and scheduling work.

• Policies and procedures for following an organization's standards and guidelines.

Provide Technical Advice

There are three main areas in which project teams need advice: 1) understanding the intent and meaning of an organization's policies, procedures, standards, and guidelines; 2) determining the best method for using the organization's hardware and software; and 3) assessing the impact of the application being developed on other applications currently in operation or under development. Project teams have a full-time task getting their projects operational. The intent of project personnel is to do the best possible job, but their time is limited. In the three areas just listed, the project team will utilize the knowledge of the team members. However, the project team does not have time to do much exploration of the unknown. It is in this area that QA members can provide assistance to the project team.

The technical assistance QA provides takes two forms. The first is answering specific requests by the project team: this can be an interpretation of a standard, advice requested on how best to accomplish some part of the project requirements, or merely a general discussion on various approaches. The second is advice volunteered by QA members where they feel it is needed. This advice can be the result of personal experiences utilizing good techniques and understanding where the project team is violating standards or policies of the organization. It often takes the form of suggestions on how to avoid problems or reduce efforts.

Whether or not a project team accepts the QA group's technical advice is dependent upon good personal relationships between QA and the project team. If a trusting relationship can be fostered so the project team knows QA is working toward the betterment of the project, the advice will be well received.

It is important that QA not try to capitalize on providing this advice. If the project team accepts recommendations and QA claims credit for these recommendations, the future effectiveness of the QA group will be diminished.

REVIEW APPLICATIONS

The primary purpose of QA is to review applications. The earlier functions provide the base for the application review. For example, the review includes compliance to organization standards, guidelines, general controls, and good data processing practices. If QA has played an active role in the development and review of criteria, they will be more adept in assessing compliance.

The QA review comprises six parts:

1. Review the system under development for

    a.   technical competence of design

    b.   adequacy of internal controls

    c.   cost/benefit analysis of the system

    d.   satisfying needs of users

2. Determine that the systems development project is consistent with the plans and goals of the data processing department, other applications, and the organization.

3. Determine that the system under development is in compliance with the organization's policies, procedures, standards, and guidelines.

4. Determine that the system under development makes effective and economic use of the organization's hardware, software, and other resources.

5. Determine that the plan for testing the system is adequate.

6.   Determine that the plan for converting from one system to another or placing the new system into production is adequate.

PROJECT APPLICATION EVALUATION OBJECTIVES

This chapter began by discussing how QA helps steer the systems development project to the best solution. Next we reviewed the types and importance of controls. Last, we talked about the primary role being to review the systems application underdevelopment. Now, let's look at what specific objective should be achieved in each QA area (i.e., goals, methods, and performance) during each of the systems development life cycle phases prior to implementation (i.e., feasibility study, design, program, testing, and conversion). Figure 2.2, Evaluation Objectives, lists the objectives by system development life cycle phase.

SDLC PHASE / QUALITY ASSURANCE AREA	FEASIBILITY	DESIGN	PROGRAM	TESTING	CONVERSION
Goals	Goals are realistic, achievable, and compatible with organization goals	System design achieves goals	Program design achieves goals	Goals are met	Controlled conversion
Methods	Justification standards	Systems standards	Programming standards	Testings standards	Conversion standards
Performance	System is cost-effective	Optimizes people and machines	Optimizes hardware and software	Meets systems criteria	Economical conversion

Figure 2.2. Evaluation objectives.

Criteria for Evaluating Goals

When QA reviews an application system under development, they should verify that the goals of the MIS department, organization, and user are being achieved. For systems development life cycle phases, QA must make judgments on the following criteria.

1. *Feasibility phase.* The user goals are realistic. The project goals are achievable. The project goals are compatible with the goals of the organization and goals of the MIS department.

2. *Design phase.* The design specifications will achieve the project goals.

3. *Program phase.* The program specifications will accomplish what was specified during the system design phase.

4. *Testing phase.* The implemented system achieves the goals specified during the design phase.

5. *Conversion phase.* The conversion to the new system can be achieved without any loss of control over data and processing.

Criteria for Evaluating Compliance

One of the major functions performed by QA is verifying compliance to the organization's policies, procedures, standards, and guidelines. During each phase of the systems development life cycle, QA should assure the following:

1. *Feasibility phase.* The feasibility study has evaluated all the project criteria and the justification for implementing the project is in accordance with the organization's standards and procedures.

2. *Design phase.* The project is designed in accordance with the organization's standards and guidelines in such a manner that it can be programmed, operated, and maintained by the normal procedures of the organization.

3. *Programming phase.* The coding of programs will be in accordance with the standard methods of programming.

4. *Testing phase.* The testing of the programs and systems is adequate and done in accordance with the standards and guidelines of the organization.

5.   *Conversion phase.* The conversion is adequate and performed in accordance with the standards and guidelines of the organization.

Criteria for Evaluating Performance

The QA group should evaluate the efficiency, effectiveness, and economy of the systems design. Even if performance is not a specific objective, the group would be negligent if they did not make a professional judgment about performance. The QA group's evaluation of performance of a computerized application should include ascertaining the following:

1.   *Feasibility phase.* The proposed system is cost-effective. This includes both the proposed design as well as whether or not the application should be computerized.

2.   *Design phase.* The proposed design optimizes the use of people and machines. People perform those functions for which they are best suited, and machines perform those functions for which they are best suited.

3.   *Program phase.* The implementation of the design specifications through programming optimizes the use of hardware and software. (Are there any preprogrammed packages that could be used more economically to achieve the specification requirements?)

4.   *Testing phase.* The implemented systems meet those criteria of performance objectives outlined in the feasibility and design phase.

5.   *Conversion phase.* The conversion should be performed in the most economical manner. Because conversion is a one-time function, it may be more economical to do a manual conversion than to develop the computer programs necessary to make the required changes. Obviously, each conversion has to be analyzed as if it were a new computerized application being studied, designed, programmed, and tested.

QUALITY ASSURANCE GROUP TASKS

Within the role of QA are various tasks that may or may not be performed by QA. It is important that the role and tasks be established and known before the group becomes active. If the charter is well understood by all interested parties, the probability of success increases greatly. When the tasks they are given become a source of debate or argument because they are not understood by project teams or users, the group can spend more time justifying and explaining its role than actually performing its task.

Chapter 1 discussed many of the challenges facing the MIS department and the fact that QA can help the data processing department to meet those challenges. Figure 2.3 reviews the challenges and the role QA can perform in helping the MIS department with them. The challenges are categorized according to the four parts of the role of QA. Understanding these tasks and how they relate to the challenges of the MIS department will prove helpful in establishing the charter.

Listed below is a brief explanation of how QA can help the MIS department meet some of their challenges:

1. *Changing technology.* The quality assurance group works with new systems and new technology and must keep current in that technology to perform their function. Becoming knowledgeable, they can help other members in the MIS department, including management, keep current by discussing new technology in staff meetings, through writing papers, and personal counseling.

2. *When to abort a project.* By making evaluations at the end of each phase of the system development life cycle, the quality assurance group can advise data processing management when projects are in trouble. This early warning mechanism enables management to make informed decisions about aborting projects.

3. *Executive management ignorance of MIS.* An independent technical assessment of data processing applications and controls will give executive management additional assurance as to whether or not they are making proper decisions.

4. *User ignorance of MIS.* The quality assurance group can challenge both the user and the project team regarding whether or not the system meets the user's needs and requirements. These requirements are both those specified in the system and those that should be specified in the system.

ROLE	MIS DEPARTMENT CHALLENGE	QUALITY ASSURANCE TASKS
Review Application	When to abort a project	Evaluates system in all phases
	Executive management ignorance of MIS	Provides executive management with a technical assessment
	User ignorance of MIS	Ascertains user requirements are met
	Audit requirements	Ascertains audit requirements are met
Provide Technical Advice	Changing technology	Knows current technology
	Use of consultants	Acts as internal consultant
	Ability to keep current technically	Acts as a technical consultant to systems analysts
	Complexity of systems	Knows many system
Review and Build a Quality Environment	How to evaluate MIS products	Evaluates MIS products
	Build a quality environment	Counsel MIS management
Develop Standards and Guidelines	Few systems and programming standards	Helps set standards
	Few system development standards	Helps set standards
	Professionalism	Evaluates quality of work
Analyze MIS Errors	Know type of problems	Quantify problems
	Know cost of problems	Identify problems
	Know magnitude of problems	Determine cost of problem

Figure 2.3. Tasks of a Quality Assurance function.

5. *Audit requirements.* The auditors have requirements for computer data and a need to assess the adequacy of internal controls. Many auditors are unable to perform these tasks due to lack of data processing knowledge. The quality assurance group, once they understand audit requirements, can ascertain that those requirements are met in new applications.

6. *Use of consultants.* Because the QA group will be current technically and will work on a wide variety of projects, its members will be able to act as internal consultants to members in the data processing department on technical problems.

7. *Ability to keep current technically.* The use of the quality assurance concept will give the data processing manager some assurance that the implementation of new systems will utilize the most current technology. This is because QA can act as a technical consultant to the systems analyst, thus relieving the analyst of some of the pressure of having to maintain technical proficiency in all aspects of data processing.

8. *Complexity of systems.* The interrelationships of systems make it difficult for any one systems analyst to comprehend some of the problems they can cause. The QA group working with many systems will be able to ascertain that the totality of systems mesh into an integrated network of systems. The use and enforcement of structured techniques will further help the QA group in identifying and qualifying these interrelationships.

9. *Few systems and programming standards.* Where standards are missing, the quality assurance group can help set them. Their experience in working with many systems puts them in an ideal position to help set standards. The use of structured programming helps overcome the programming "art" syndrome and provides standard programming practices against which work can be measured.

10. *Few systems development standards.* Where standards are missing, the quality assurance group can help set them. Their experience in working with many systems puts them in an ideal position to help set standards. The implementation and enforcement of structured design techniques provides an excellent vehicle for the development of workable standards.

11. *How to evaluate MIS products.* The quality assurance group understands the needs of many systems and has an appreciation for the current technology. This background puts them in an ideal position to evaluate MIS products, both hardware and software.

12. *Professionalism.* After evaluating many computer applications over a period of time, the quality assurance group will be in a position to evaluate the technical aspects of the systems designer's and programmer's work. This will help the data processing manager assure upper management that the organization is getting good value for its data processing dollars.

The tasks listed are representative of the many tasks that can be performed by a quality assurance group. Projections state that systems will assume an even greater portion of an organization's business procedures. This increasing reliance on data processing mandates the need for a group to assure quality in data processing systems applications.

ESTABLISHING THE QUALITY ASSURANCE CHARTER

When QA is formed, a charter for the group should be established. The charter should be circulated to those organizations that will come in contact or use the services. This will eliminate all misunderstandings of what the group is authorized to do.

The following process is recommended to establish a charter:

1. Organize a task force to establish a draft charter. The task force should comprise
   a. the probable manager of the quality assurance function
   b. the manager or assistant manager of the data processing department
   c. one or more project leaders
   d. one or more key users of data processing applications
   e. the manager or assistant manager of computer operations
   f. the general auditor or MIS audit manager of the organization
   g. a member of executive management (suggest this individual be chairman of the task force)

2. Have each task force member fill out a worksheet rating the potential tasks (from very important to very unimportant) that could be performed by a quality assurance group. Figure 2.4 is such a worksheet. (This will be explained in a later section.)

3. Score the tasks in accordance with the rating given by those completing the worksheet (the scoring method will be explained in the section discussing the worksheet).

4. List the tasks in priority sequence based on their score. Then, using the material contained in the remainder of this book, estimate the amount of resources required to accomplish each task.

5. Determine with management consent the amount of manpower that will be allotted to staff the quality assurance function.

6. Incorporate into a charter those tasks that can logically be accomplished with available resources. Add as an appendix to the charter those tasks (in sequence) that should be accomplished when time becomes available or additional resources are added.

Following this process will result in drafting a realistic charter for the group. The charter will have those tasks considered to be most important by the task force. This does not exclude the use of judgment on the part of the task force to move items around once the priority listing has been established. It does have the advantage of approaching the problem from a scientific viewpoint.

Once the charter has been drafted, it can then be reviewed by various members of management to obtain their concurrence or recommendations. This gives the process another critique which assures that management's concerns will be addressed by the quality assurance group.

Quality Assurance Group Role Worksheet

The worksheet shown in Figure 2.4 provides a listing of QA tasks. The tasks are categorized by the four major roles of QA. The individuals on the quality assurance task force should rate each of these tasks according to their own personal beliefs.

Where individuals have some specific reaction to a task that they feel needs clarification, they should complete the Comments section.

These worksheets, when complete, show how the individual members of the task force see the role the QA group is to perform. Space is available to add tasks the individual feels should be performed by the group.

Because the individual members of the charter-drafting task force come from different disciplines, they will probably assign different rankings to the tasks. This is healthy because it allows the different groups associated with data processing to provide input about this important function.

Scoring the Quality Assurance Tasks. Once each member of the task force has completed the Quality Assurance Group Role Worksheet, a consensus of viewpoints must be reached. A Task Score Worksheet (Figure 2.5) is provided for this purpose. One Task Score Worksheet should be prepared for each task in Figure 2.4 (a total of 54 worksheets). For that task, the total number of times "very important" was checked should be inserted in the "Number of Times Checked"/"very important" checked block. Likewise, the same is done for "important," "neither important nor unimportant," "unimportant," and "very unimportant." For each of these ratings, multiply the number of times checked times the constant listed on the worksheet. For example, for the "very important" rating, the number of times checked is multiplied by 5 to arrive at a score. When the score for each of the five ratings has been determined, they should be added together to arrive at a total score. The score will be an algebraic number which can be either plus or minus.

The Task Score Worksheet should then be resequenced so that the highest score is on top and the lowest score on the bottom. The rank should then be filled in from 1 through 54, with rank number 1 being the highest score, and rank 54 being the lowest score. Once they have been ranked, an estimated man-days per year needs to be determined as a requirement for accomplishing this task. When the number of days per year equals the available resources for the quality assurance function, the accomplishable tasks have been determined. The tasks should then be drafted into a charter.

The charter is the authority provided the group to accomplish its function. The charter provides the authority to act. It should have three sections:

1.   *Scope of work.* The general area in which the group will operate, together with the responsibilities and authority allowed the group, listed in general terms.

2. *Role.* A discussion of each one of the four potential parts of the QA role: a) review applications, b) provide technical advice, c) review general controls, and d) develop standards and guidelines. If the task selection process does not include any tasks for one part of the role, eliminate that part. In that case, the charter only describes those parts of the role that will be performed by the group.

3. *Tasks.* Under each part of the role, the tasks to be performed should be briefly listed.

The group charter will be a job description for the quality assurance group. It will be more detailed than some organization department charters, but this is necessary because it will be a new function to most organizations. The charter serves three purposes. It outlines the responsibility of the group. It specifies the authority given the group in each aspect of its role. It educates the quality assurance group and other interested parties about the QA mandate. And, finally, it asserts that management expects high quality in data processing applications.

Figure 2.6 exemplifies a typical charter and can be used as a model for building a charter for a quality assurance group. The Appendix at the end of this chapter is a work plan developed by a quality assurance group to support its charter.

QUALITY ASSURANCE COSTS

The primary function of the quality assurance group is to review new applications. Time expended for other elements of the role supports this systems review function. The charter of the group, if established according to the criteria provided in this chapter, will give a breakdown of effort between application review and the other potential elements of the role. In an ideal situation, this would be 70 percent for system reviews and 30 percent for all other tasks.

Next, what is needed is a method of dividing up the amount of effort that will be expended on each application being reviewed. Figure 2.7 suggests such an allocation of effort. The figure divides the time among the five phases of the system development life cycle where the QA should be involved (feasibility, design, programming, testing, and conversion).

ROLE ELEMENT	QUALITY ASSURANCE TASK	RATING					COMMENTS
		Very Important	Important	Neither Important nor Unimportant	Unimportant	Very Unimportant	
REVIEW APPLICATION	**GOALS** 1. Determine if project goals are realistic 2. Determine if project goals are achievable 3. Determine if project goals are compatible with MIS Dept. Goals 4. Determine if project goals are compatible with Organization goals 5. Determine if project goals are compatible with other systems 6. Determine if system design will achieve project goals 7. Controls ensure compliance with the intent of management **METHODS** 8. Determine if program design will meet system specifications 9. Determine if testing plan is adequate 10. Determine if conversion plan is adequate						

Figure 2.4. Quality Assurance group role worksheet.

ROLE ELEMENT	QUALITY ASSURANCE TASK	RATING					COMMENTS
		Very Important	Important	Neither Important nor Unimportant	Unimportant	Very Unimportant	
	11. Determine if compliance with project justification standards						
	12. Determine if compliance with system standards						
	13. Determine compliance with programming standards						
	14. Determine compliance with control standards						
	15. Certifying systems prior to their attainment of production status						
	16. Reviewing the adequacy of security						
	17. Verify system is on time and within budget						
	18. Recommend specific controls						
	19. Determine compliance with documentation standards						
	20. Determine compliance with testing standards						
	21. Determine compliance with conversion standards						

Figure 2.4. Quality Assurance group role worksheet. (cont'd)

ROLE ELEMENT	QUALITY ASSURANCE TASK	RATING					COMMENTS
		Very Important	Important	Neither Important nor Unimportant	Unimportant	Very Unimportant	
PROVIDE TECHNICAL ADVICE	**PERFORMANCE**						
	22. Determine that the system is cost-effective						
	23. Determine that the system optimizes people and machines						
	24. Determine that the system optimizes hardware and software						
	25. Determine that the testing procedures are efficient						
	26. Determine that the conversion procedures are efficient						
	27. Measure hardware performance						
	28. Measure software performance						
	1. Advise on use of hardware						
	2. Advise on use of software						
	3. Advise on system design						
	4. Advise on program design						
	5. Advise on use of controls						
	6. Advise on test procedures						
	7. Advise on conversion procedures						

Figure 2.4. Quality Assurance group role worksheet. (cont'd)

ROLE ELEMENT	QUALITY ASSURANCE TASK	RATING					COMMENTS
		Very Important	Important	Neither Important nor Unimportant	Unimportant	Very Unimportant	
	8. Advise on MIS department standards and guidelines						
	9. Advise on user department standards and guidelines						
	10. Advise on organization standards and guidelines						
	11. Advise users on data processing capabilities						
	12. Advise executive management on data processing capabilities						
	13. Advise data processing management on data processing capabilities						
	14. Advise on intersystem interfaces						
REVIEW AND BUILD A QUALITY ENVIRONMENT	1. Review organization structure						
	2. Review job descriptions						
	3. Review system standards						
	4. Review programming standards						
	5. Review documentation standards						

Figure 2.4. Quality Assurance group role worksheet. (cont'd)

ROLE ELEMENT	QUALITY ASSURANCE TASK	RATING					COMMENTS
		Very Important	Important	Neither Important nor Unimportant	Unimportant	Very Unimportant	
	6. Review testing standards						
	7. Review conversion standards						
	8. Review budget and cost procedures						
	9. Review system change procedures						
	10. Review supervisory procedures						
	11. Review operating procedures						
	12. Review quality of technical work						
	13. Meet regularly with DP management to review problems						
	14. Train MIS personnel						
	15. Monitor project status						
DEVELOP STANDARDS AND GUIDELINES	1. Develop and/or improve justification standards						
	2. Develop and/or improve system standards						
	3. Develop and/or improve documentation standards						
	4. Develop and/or improve programming standards						

Figure 2.4. Quality Assurance group role worksheet. (cont'd)

ROLE ELEMENT	QUALITY ASSURANCE TASK	RATING					COMMENTS
		Very Important	Important	Neither Important nor Unimportant	Unimportant	Very Unimportant	
	5. Develop and/or improve testing standards						
	6. Develop and/or improve conversion standards						
	7. Develop and/or improve hardware standards						
	8. Develop and/or improve software standards						
	9. Develop and/or improve purchased application standards						
	10. Develop and/or improve operating standards						
	11. Develop and/or improve system development process standards						
	12. Develop and/or improve performance standards						
ANALYZE MIS ERRORS	1. On call to study all errors						
	2. Issue error alerts for common problems						
	3. Quantify errors and issue regular error reports						
	4. Develop recommendations/solutions for identified errors						

Figure 2.4. Quality Assurance group role worksheet. (cont'd)

TASK

SCORE CALCULATION:

RATING	NUMBER OF TIMES CHECKED	SCORE
VERY IMPORTANT		× 5 =
IMPORTANT		× 3 =
NEITHER IMPORTANT NOR UNIMPORTANT		× 0 = 0
UNIMPORTANT		× − 3 =
VERY IMPORTANT		× − 5 =

TOTAL SCORE

RANK

ESTIMATED DAYS/YEARS TO ACCOMPLISH

Figure 2.5. Task score worksheet.

The cost of quality assurance ideally should be included in the estimated project costs. If it is included as a line item in a project's budget, it should range somewhere between 2.5 and 5 percent of the total project cost. For example, if a project costs $100,000 to implement, then between $2,500 to $5,000 should be allocated for the quality assurance aspect of that project. The minimum level to be effective is 2.5 percent of the project costs, and ideally 5 percent of the project costs should be allocated.

The early part of the design process is where the application can be most readily influenced. If the QA group spends the largest percentage of its time during the design phase of the system, it can make the greatest impact on that system. The time expended in the programming, testing, and conversion area is one of checking compliance to design specifications and organizations' policies, procedures, standards, and guidelines.

SUMMARY

MIS quality assurance is accomplished by a fourfold role: first, to develop standards and guidelines; second, to review general controls; third, to be a technical advisor on MIS matters; and fourth, to review applications. The first three segments of the role support the fourth.

The application review is spread out over five phases of the systems development life cycle. These phases are feasibility, design, programming, testing, and conversion. The review in each phase has three objectives. These are to determine that organization, user and MIS department goals are (or will be) achieved; to determine compliance with standards, policies, procedures and guidelines; and to assure reasonable performance. These objectives are achieved through a review process. This process starts with planning, and includes tasks agreed upon by management. In the execution of these tasks, the quality assurance group uses various techniques and resources. Much of the success of the group is dependent upon establishing good working relationships with data processing personnel. At the end of each phase, the quality assurance function will make a judgment on whether or not the project should continue through the next phase. Figure 2.8 illustrates the function.

QUALITY ASSURANCE CHARTER

It is the policy of the data processing department to provide a quality assurance group as a means of improving the quality of computerized applications. The manager of data processing is assigned the responsibility for the quality assurance function and will see that:

1. Applications are reviewed at the appropriate times to determine if they meet the needs of the user; are developed according to policies, procedures, standards and guidelines; and are implemented in a technically competent manner.

2. The results of these reviews are made available to user and data processing management.

3. The project team makes satisfactory disposition, within 30 days, of any recommendations resulting from a quality assurance review.

The manager and staff of the quality assurance function shall have full, free, and unrestricted access to all the information, records, and personnel of the project under review.

Specifically the manager of quality assurance shall be responsible for execution of the following tasks:

1. During application reviews the QA manager shall determine if:
   - Project goals are achievable
   - System design will achieve project goals
   - Program design will meet system specifications
   - Testing plan is adequate
   - Conversion plan is adequate
   - There is compliance with all development standards

2. Developing and/or improving standards and guidelines for:
   - System standards
   - Programming standards
   - Conversion standards
   - Documentation standards
   - Testing standards

3. Reviewing general controls:
   - Quality of technical work

4. Providing technical advice on:
   - System design
   - Test procedures
   - Conversion procedures
   - Program design
   - MIS department standards and guidelines

Figure 2.6. A Typical QA charter.

DEVELOPMENT PHASE	% OF QA TIME EXPENDED	% OF TOTAL PROJECT COST	
		Minimum	Ideal
Feasibility	10%	.25%	.5%
Design	40	1.00	2.0
Programming	30	.75	1.5
Testing	10	.25	.5
Conversion	10	.25	.5
	100%	2.5%	5.0%

Figure 2.7. Quality assurance costs and effort.

Strong management support is essential if the function is to succeed. One method of obtaining this support is to get management agreement and support of a function charter that spells out the group's authority and responsibilities.

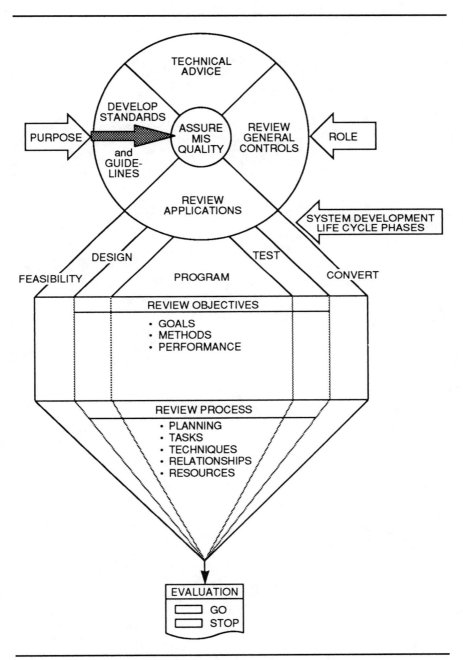

Figure 2.8. The Quality Assurance function.

Appendix: Quality Assurance Work Plan

I. SCOPE

It is the policy of the Information Systems organization to provide a Quality Assurance function as an internal means of maintaining the quality and effectiveness of applications, facilities, and services provided by Information Systems (I/S) to assure National Steel Corporation will be a world class producer of quality products recognized for excellence.

A primary purpose of the Quality Assurance function is to assure that adequate Information Systems policies, standards, and guidelines exist in accordance with the Company's strategic direction. The major emphasis is on the measuring and monitoring of the internal development and operational process at appropriate times ensuring quality systems and reduced business risk.

In defining the scope of quality assurance, the following should be highlighted:

1. The Quality Assurance function will establish reviews procedures from an internal Information Systems perspective for evaluating all Information Systems areas to assure through reviews that systems are being designed, implemented, and operated according to Information Systems policy, standards, and/or guidelines.

2. Reviews of operational systems will determine the effectiveness of, and adherence to, policy standards and design criteria related to overall controls and security features.

3.   Quality Assurance reviews will frequently be conducted on Information Systems (I/S) policies, procedures, standards, and/or operating guidelines without respect to a specific system. The internal coordination of these procedures and standards from one (1) internal Information Systems group to another will be reviewed for effectiveness.

Through the utilization of reviews Quality Assurance will be able to identify the processes that require changes to assure the production of quality products. However, the quality of products produced by Information Systems is the responsibility of the individual or team of individuals who are assigned to perform the task necessary to produce these products. The formalization of the Quality Assurance Program and the implementation of a Quality Assurance Review Program does not alter this responsibility. For this reason, the Quality Assurance Program will continue to be functionally decentralized. The areas of New Development, Data Administration, Systems Support, Process Control, Computer Sciences, Information Centers, and Telecommunications will continue to have primary responsibility for executing and, if necessary, developing Quality Assurance activities.

A.   Responsibility

Quality Assurance is responsible for the following functions:

1.   *Establish Quality Assurance Systems Review Guidelines*

Quality Assurance will develop guidelines to determine which systems require Quality Assurance review. Selection of which systems require reviews will be primarily based upon the significance of the application to business objectives, operations, strategic plans, and business risk.

Quality Assurance reviews examining the adherence to established Information Systems' (I/S) policies, procedures, standards, operating guidelines, and Quality Assurance guidelines relative to specific projects will be conducted on a scheduled basis.

2.   *Assist in Development of Annual Quality Assurance Review Plan*

Quality Assurance will assist Information Systems departments in developing an annual Quality Assurance Review (QAR) plan. This Plan should address all areas of Information Systems: Development, Maintenance,

Operations, Process Control, Data Base, Information Center, and Management Services.

Selecting from the annual planned objectives of each area (Development, Maintenance, Operation, Process Control, Information Center, Database, and Management Services) within Information Systems, Quality Assurance will coordinate its review objectives with the appropriate Information Systems management to confirm the Department's Annual Quality Assurance Schedule. On a quarterly basis, the schedule is reviewed with Information Systems management and updated.

In conducting systems development reviews, a phased approach will be followed. A review will be conducted at the completion of each of the following phases:

- System Requirements:
  - user requirements
  - system definition
  - advisability study
- System Design:
  - preliminary design
  - detail design
- System Programming:
  - program design
  - programming/program testing
- Implementation Phase:
  - implementation planning
  - system test/start-up preparation
  - operation turnover

Quality Assurance will have reasonable access to all the information, records, and personnel of the project or activities under review. Certain sensitive information may require user approval for access during the review process. Information Systems will determine the need for user approval prior to the start of the review.

Formal reports regarding accuracy of the findings and the achievability of recommendations will be agreed to by both Quality Assurance and the Information Systems area involved.

Quality Assurance will follow-up to ensure that all recommendations have planned implementation dates and are completed.

3.   *Standards Reviews*

Quality Assurance develops and maintains programs/plans for conducting Quality Assurance reviews to assure the adequacy of Information Systems policies, procedures, standards, operating guidelines and Quality Assurance guidelines.

All Information Systems quality assurance guidelines, policies, procedures, standards, and operating guidelines in effect will be utilized by Quality Assurance as the base from which to conduct their reviews.

As well as using this information as a base, there is an inherent responsibility of Quality Assurance to recognize and report the need for change. Recommendations will be provided to the appropriate Information Systems group's management for approval and implementation.

Policies, procedures, standards, and operating guidelines maintained and utilized by these groups are subject to review and recommendations provided by Quality Assurance.

4.   *Coordination-Audit*

Upon notification by internal audit of MIS-related audit reports and findings relative to Information Systems, the Quality Assurance function will review the recommendations as they relate to Information Systems (I/S) policies, standards, and guidelines.

When applicable, Quality Assurance will review proposed changes/ improvements to policies and standards with Information Systems management. A final report will be issued and the changes/improvements will be implemented by the responsible Information Systems area.

5.   *High Risk Review*

Annually, key operational systems will be selected either Commercial or Process Control by Quality Assurance for review to determine adherence to standards, procedures, operating guidelines and quality guidelines.

One measure of selection would be based on the volume and frequency of incidents requiring corrective action. Also, Data Center, Information Systems, and User Management can request a review based on their perspective of the system's condition.

Acting in a consultative capacity, Quality Assurance will perform these reviews to evaluate that Information Systems procedures, standards, and guidelines are being followed.

Included in these operational reviews will be the examination of contingency planning and file/data retention to guarantee adequate backup provisions.

6. *Security Standards*

Quality Assurance will interface with the data security officer through periodic meetings to share in the establishment of uniform Information Systems safety and security standards and guidelines.

In response to Information Systems management requests, review of computer centers and/or systems development departments will be performed. The review will cover existing safety and security operational and maintenance elements within the facility. Recommendations will be made to enhance protection and control through new or revised procedures or additional physical protection devices.

7. *Strategic Plan Reviews*

Strategic planning responsibilities within Information Systems will necessitate inventory-type operational reviews to gain an insight into the current systems environment. Identification of the need to upgrade hardware and/or software to be in line with future planning due to technology or standardization will be recommended.

8. *Quality Improvement Programs*

This function will coordinate the development implementation of Information Systems Quality Councils and Quality Circles. These functions will create the avenue to implement Quality Process improvements which guarantees Quality products.

9. *Establishing Quality Measuring Programs*

The function of these programs should be to ascertain whether quality is being achieved, and if not, why not. Once the "why not" has been identified, the processes can be changed to prevent those types of problems from recurring. This measurement cycle (i.e., identify a problem, identify the cause of the problem, change the process to correct the problem, and then remeasure) will bootstrap quality. Over time, quality will increase significantly if this remeasurement cycle is pursued.

10. *Managerial Review*

Quality Assurance will review the general management processes to confirm the compliance to corporate and departmental policies, procedures, and quality guidelines.

II. REVIEW POINTS

The following list of milestones indicates the subphases that require a Quality Review at their completion, the general identification of the Evaluators, and the typical composition of the review group. Because of the substantial diversity in types of systems that are built, it is impossible to specify the job titles of individuals who will play these roles. It is assumed that the reader will be able to directly translate the generalized descriptions shown in this list with the job titles and names of individuals who will best perform the required functions on his or her particular project.

The General Manager I/S, and the appropriate System General Manager are understood to always be ex officio members of any review group.

User Requirements

Purpose:

To determine the adequacy of the team's understanding of the current system and to evaluate the user requirements as defined.

Evaluated by:

Key User Supervisors
Key Systems Development Person-Analysis Project Control Administrator
Quality Assurance

Reviewed by:

Manager Information Systems
Systems General Manager

Systems Definitions

Purpose:

To evaluate the system as proposed by the team; to agree to the procedures and assumptions to be used if an advisability study is deemed necessary.

Evaluated by: Key User Supervisors
Project Control Administrator
Quality Assurance

Reviewed by: Manager Information Systems
Systems General Manager
Advisability Study

Purpose: To review the results of the advisability study; evaluate the scope, costs, and associated benefits of each alternative.

Evaluated by: Key User Supervisors
Database Administration
Key Systems Development Person-Analysis
Project Control Administrator
Quality Assurance

Reviewed by: Key User Managers
Manager, Information Systems
Systems General Manager
Sponsor

Preliminary Design

Purpose: To ensure that the preliminary design satisfies the user requirements; evaluate the feasibility of the design and the potential technical issues (i.e., Database design, teleprocessing requirements, etc.).

Evaluated by: Key User Supervisors
Key Systems Development Person-Design
Database Administration
Operations Representative
Project Control Administrator
Quality Assurance

Reviewed by: Systems General Manager
Manager, Information
Systems Sponsor

Program Design

Purpose:	To perform a technical review of the subsystems and programs to identify potential inefficiencies, cumbersome program designs; conformance to design standards.
Evaluated by:	Key Systems Development Person-Programming Operations Representative Project Control Administrator Quality Assurance
Reviewed by:	Manager, Information Systems Systems General Manager

Programming/Program Testing

Purpose:	To ensure that programs have been adequately tested and the test results provide an adequate level of confidence; review run procedures and conformance to programming standards.
Evaluated by:	Key Systems Development Person-Programming Operations Representative Project Control Administrator Quality Assurance
Reviewed by:	Systems General Manager Manager, Information Systems

Implementation Planning

Purpose:	To ensure that areas of potential impact within the system and external to the system such as job descriptions, work flow, conversion plans, etc. are adequately covered in the implementation plans; review the system test plan.
Evaluated by:	Key Users Key Systems Development Person Operations Representative Systems Support Representative Project Control Administrator Quality Assurance
Reviewed by:	Systems General Manager Manager, Information Systems

Systems Test/Start-Up Preparation

Purpose:	To evaluate the system to be turned over to operations to ensure adequate operating instructions and documentation.
Evaluated by:	Operations Manager Systems Support Manager Project Control Administrator Quality Assurance
Reviewed by:	Systems General Manager Manager, Information Systems

III.   PROJECT SELECTION PROCEDURES

Division Management of Information Systems identifies which project or areas are to be reviewed by the Quality Assurance Review Function. Some of the factors which may be used in making these determinations are

- Financial application

- Statutory requirements

- Exposure to loss

- Application history

- Effort to develop application

- Time span to complete project

- Expected number of application programs

- New hardware technology

- New software technology

- User involvement

- Internal audit involvement

- Skill level of project team

- Availability of quality assurance review resources

- Risk factor

IV. QUALITY ASSURANCE REVIEW AND ASSESSMENT PROCEDURES

A. Purpose

The purpose of this section is to outline the established guidelines and procedures which govern the conduct of Quality Assurance Review function, Management function, and the project team during the review process.

B. Responsibilities

1. Quality Assurance
    - Develops detailed Quality Assurance review plan for the project.
    - Gathers, conforms, and validates information needs to prepare Quality Assurance assessment reports.
    - Prepares and publishes Quality Assurance assessment reports.

2. Management
    - Reviews Quality Assurance assessment reports.
    - Responds to recommendation and requests prepared by Quality Assurance review function.

3. Project Team
    - Assists in developing detailed Quality Assurance Review plan for project.
    - Assists in gathering and providing Quality Assurance review function with information needs for Quality Assurance Assessment Reports.

C. Concept

The Quality Assurance Review Program is founded upon the principle that a review of Quality Assurance activities based upon agreed checklist and review procedures will lead to improved quality and a better product. It is not to be construed as a restrictive procedure or an effort to direct department efforts. Quality Assurance Reviews should be approached with a spirit of assistance relying ultimately upon close cooperation and mutual professional confidence.

D.   Procedures

1.   *Preliminary Review Procedure*

The purpose of this procedure is to initiate the Quality Assurance Review Processes for projects which are selected for review. This procedure occurs prior to the first Quality Assurance Review for the project.

Responsibility		*Action*
Quality Assurance	a)	Notifies Information Systems Project Leader of a schedule for Quality Assurance Kickoff Meeting
I/S Project Leader	b)	Acknowledges schedule for Kickoff Meeting, may suggest different date.
	c)	Coordinates with his/her project manager on Q.A. Kickoff Meeting.
	d)	Provides Quality Assurance with a copy of project request and any other information that would help Quality Assurance understand the project.
Quality Assurance	e)	Conducts Kickoff Meeting.
	f)	Provides copies of Quality Assurance Review Checklist to Project Team Member(s).
	g)	Reviews Overview of project as provided by Project Team Member(s).

Responsibility	*Action*
	h) Develops schedule* for first Quality Assurance Checkpoint Review.

2. Recurring Review Procedure

The purpose of this procedure is to outline the processes which will be followed in developing Quality Assurance Assessment Reports. This procedure occurs at each Quality Assurance Review point within the project.

I/S Project Leader	a) As soon as available, provides Quality Assurance with tangible item(s) to support each item on the checklist prior to Quality Assurance Checkpoint Review.
Quality Assurance	b) Conducts a schedule Quality Assurance Checkpoint Review.
	c) Reviews items on Quality Assurance Review Checklist and tangible items.
	d) If applicable, develops schedule* for subsequent Quality Assurance Reviews.
	e) Prepares preliminary Quality Assurance Assessment report for this review point.
	f) Discusses preliminary review point assessment report with Information Systems Project Leader.

---

* Quality Assurance Reviews are to be scheduled at a number of key checkpoints in the project life cycle.

Responsibility   *Action*

g) Discusses preliminary
   review point assessment
   report with Project
   Leader's Manager.

h) Discusses preliminary
   review point assessment
   report with Project
   Leader's Director.

i) Prepares finalized
   Quality Assurance Re-
   view/Checkpoint Assessment Report.

j) Sends finalized Quality
   Assurance Review Checkpoint Assessment Report
   to Project Leader and
   Project Leader's Man-
   ager and Director.

I/S Project Leader of   k) Suggests modification to
Quality Assurance   improve Quality Assur-
                                ance Quality Assurance
                                checklists for subsequent
                                review checkpoint(s) for
                                this project.

Quality Assurance   l) Reviews and obtains
                                approval of proposed
                                modification to Quality
                                Assurance Checklists
                                Leader, Project Leader's
                                Manager and Project
                                Leader's Director.

                             m) Makes approved modi-
                                fication to subsequent
                                Quality Assurance
                                Checklist(s) for this
                                project.

Responsibility	*Action*
	n) Provides modified Quality Assurance Checklist to Project Leader and appropriate Information Systems Management Staff.

3. Final Review Procedures

The purpose of this procedure is to identify opportunities to improve quality which may have been overlooked in the review point Assessment Reports. This procedure occurs after the last scheduled review point in the project.

Quality Assurance	a) Upon completion of the project an overall Quality Assurance Assessment Report will be prepared for Information Systems Division Management.

Developing the Quality Assurance Function

The quality assurance function can be initiated by executive data processing or internal auditing management. Once established, the QA group should report directly to the data processing manager. This high-level reporting assures the QA group of the authority and independence needed for success. There are four methods of staffing the function: 1) a full-time staff; 2) a combination of full-time and part-time personnel; 3) a permanent committee of data processing personnel; 4) a special task force to be established each time a review is undertaken.

The individuals staffing the function should be as skilled as the senior data processing personnel. The function will be more successful with a small number of highly skilled people than a large number of people with minimal data processing skills. The individuals in the group should be objective, naturally inquisitive, "take charge" type persons, and able to devote the necessary time to the successful fulfillment of the function. Last, it is important that the individuals in the group believe QA is necessary.

The key to success is strong management support. This support should be threefold: first, the function should be adequately staffed with highly skilled people; second, the function should be given the authority necessary to fulfill their responsibilities; and third, management must be supportive of recommendations. While this does not mean that all recommendations must be accepted, it does mean that they must be seriously considered and adopted if valid.

HOW TO GET STARTED

Normally QA groups are initiated by data processing departments. However, internal audit groups are beginning to become the prime instigator in the establishment of the function.

If a data processing department has six or more systems analysts, a major computerized financial system, or a budget over $250,000 per year, a QA function should be seriously considered.

To establish QA in an organization, the initiating group should:

1. *Prepare a preliminary report.* The report should state the advantages and disadvantages as well as costs and expected benefits.

2. *Establish a task force.* The objective of the task force would be to perform one or two quality assurance reviews. The task force should comprise senior MIS personnel. The preliminary report should recommend the establishment of this task force.

3. *Make final recommendations to management (after a test review).* This report should summarize the results of the task force quality assurance review. It should contain a recommendation regarding how the group should be staffed, its authority and responsibilities, its organization structure, to whom the group will report, and the methods of reporting findings.

Each organization needs to do some experimentation as to how such a group can be most effective for them. Creating a task force to perform one or two quality assurance reviews enables this experimentation to occur. It is also low in cost, and does not commit the organization to the formal establishment of a group until some firsthand review experience can be gotten.

The report recommending the establishment of QA should be sent to the individual to whom the data processing manager reports. If the request is initiated by the data processing department, they should solicit internal audit support and vice versa. It would be unwise for internal auditing to propose such a function without having data processing management support.

ORGANIZATIONAL STRUCTURE

The higher in the data processing structure the quality assurance function reports, the better the probability of success. The level of reporting is also indicative of management support. High-level reporting provides a degree of independence for the group because they can deal with other functions on an equal basis.

Within organizations the function is typically situated in one of three spots. First, in some companies it reports to the manager of systems. Second, it may be organizationally a coequal of the four major segments of data processing (operation, control, systems, and programming). Third, it may be a staff function reporting directly to the MIS manager. The recommended organizational structure is reporting as a staff function to the MIS manager. (See Figure 3.1.)

Such a structure offers several advantages. It will receive the attention of the MIS manager. The QA manager need not be involved in the day-to-day functioning of the department as do other first-line managers. It is organizationally independent of all other aspects of the data processing department. And, finally the manager of quality assurance does not have to be in the same pay bracket as other first-line managers in the data processing department.

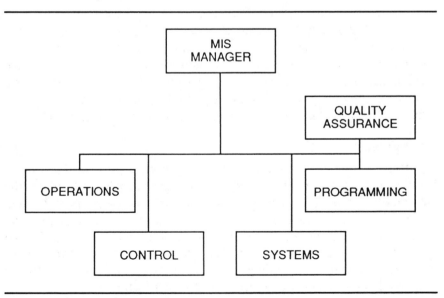

Figure 3.1. Suggested MIS department organization.

The group will be in contact with other departments within the organization. The two most frequently contacted departments will be the user department and the internal audit department. In addition, QA personnel will be in meetings with and sending reports to executive management from time to time. Very early in discussions on a proposed system, executive management may desire an independent viewpoint on the feasibility and probability of success of the system. The QA is ideally suited to provide this type of advice.

QA should be heavily involved in major data processing decisions. However, keep in mind that the decisions will be made by data processing management, not by QA. The role played by QA is that of advisor to the MIS manager. This advisory role adds another reason for having QA as a staff function reporting to the data processing manager. The advisory role is more suited to a staff function than a line function.

STAFFING ALTERNATIVES

Most organizations initiate QA with a task force that is organized for the purpose of reviewing one or more data processing systems. The task force should comprise leading MIS systems analysts and programmers. It should include the leading candidate for manager of the quality assurance function.

Three additional staffing alternatives are being used by various organizations. Ideally, a full-time staff should be available to perform quality assurance reviews. However, if an organization does not desire to make this commitment to the function, two other alternatives are available. These are a combination of full- and part-time personnel, and the establishment of a permanent committee of reviewers to perform quality assurance reviews. Figure 3.2 outlines the advantages and disadvantages of each alternative.

Task Force Method

The task force staffing method is most appropriate prior to the formalization of the QA function. This approach can also be utilized by the data processing manager whenever a review of a new system is desired. However, using the task force staffing method may mean there is no continuity between reviews. Each task force will tend to develop its own methods and procedures for the review. In addition, the task force members may have trouble finding sufficient time to perform the review properly if other tasks are competitors for their time.

STAFFING METHOD	ADVANTAGES	DISADVANTAGES
FULL-TIME STAFF	1. Continuity of reviewers 2. Commitment by management to function	1. Cannot add specialized knowledge 2. Losing touch with practice
COMBINATION FULL TIME AND PART TIME	1. Continuity of function 2. Specialized knowledge can be added	1. Competition for time of part-timers 2. Full-time members lose touch with practice
PERMANENT COMMITMENT	1. Continuity of function 2. Continuity of reviewers	1. Competition for reviewer's time 2. Committee not as authoritative as full-time group.
SPECIAL TASK FORCE FOR EACH REVIEW	1. Can build a group special- ized for each 2. Can be used as a training assignment	1. No continuity between reviews 2. Competition for reviewers' time

Figure 3.2. Quality Assurance staffing alternatives.

There are advantages to the task force concept. Such a group can be uniquely developed for each review. The data processing manager can analyze problem areas in a new system and assign task force members with an appropriate background for these areas. In addition, it is a good training assignment for systems designers because it puts them in a position of analyzing the competency of systems design. The experiences learned from participating on a task force can be immediately implemented in the day-to-day work of the systems analyst.

Full-Time Staff Method

The utilization of full-time staff has major advantages. First, it provides a continuity of reviewers. This is important to the data processing manager because the manager will know that all reviews are performed by the same methods. Another major advantage is the visible management support of the function by the assignment of full-time personnel. The task force concept could give the appearance of a lack of management confidence in the project team on a specific project. When task forces are assembled for only a limited number of projects, data processing personnel may question the motives of management for forming these task forces.

When full-time staffing is used, the competency of the review group is limited to the knowledge of the full-time staff. A task force can add specialized knowledge for specialized projects, but a full-time staff normally operates using the personnel available. In addition, it becomes difficult for full-time reviewers to maintain technical proficiency with current practice. It requires a special effort on the part of individuals to remain current with technology.

Permanent Committee Method

A step up from the task force approach is the formation of a permanent committee to perform reviews. The main difference between a permanent committee and a task force is the continuity of individual reviewers. A task force will be convened for the purpose of reviewing one system. A permanent committee will be convened for the purpose of reviewing many projects.

The permanent committee has the advantage of continuity of reviewers and continuity of the function. The permanent aspect of the committee says to project managers that their projects will be reviewed. It's not a hit or miss proposition dependent upon the whims of the MIS department manager. The fact that the function will be permanently established is indicative of a higher degree of management support than a specially convened task force.

The disadvantages of a permanent committee parallel those of the task force. These committees traditionally are part-time assignments for committee members. This means they have current work assignments competing for their time. As the intensity of the work assignment increases due to approaching target dates, individuals have less time and less desire to work as members of a review team. Also, it is still a committee. A committee can never be as authoritative as a function staffed with full-time personnel.

Full-Time and Part-Time Combination

Another staffing approach is to staff with one or more full-time personnel augmented by part-time personnel. The part-time personnel would fill out the review team to achieve the desired staffing level and expertise needed. The organization should begin by selecting one person as a full-time quality assurance manager.

Having one full-time member, the function gains continuity of purpose. A strong manager of the function will help assure that the part-time people perform their function. When the part-time staffers for the function feel torn between assignments, the full-time manager of quality assurance can work with other first-line managers to assure that the part-time members fulfill their obligations.

By utilizing part-time members, the group is able to add specialized knowledge where necessary. This has proven to be an excellent mechanism for improving the work. The full-time manager must insist on having only the best people assigned during the formative stages. It is extremely important the first series of reviews demonstrate unequivocally the value of the QA function. This does not mean that the function has to find major flaws in the system under review but, rather, that the assessment must prove accurate during the next phase of development of that application.

CHARACTERISTICS OF QUALITY ASSURANCE CANDIDATES

Obtaining the right individuals for the group is essential if it is to be successful. The characteristics that make a good systems analyst/programmer are not sufficient to assure that that same individual will be successful in the quality assurance group. The ability to review the work of others and to convince them there are better methods to perform their work takes some unique skills in dealing with people. QA reviewers must be respected for their technical ability and have a good talent for communicative and persuasive abilities.

The key member in the group is the manager. It is within this individual that we must look for all the traits necessary in a quality assurance reviewer. Others who are members of the group can succeed with only a subset of the desired characteristics if the manager is a very strong individual. Thus, we first must describe the manager of quality assurance.

The successful QA staff member must have

- A thorough understanding of data processing systems design and programming. The individual should be as knowledgeable in these skills as those being evaluated.

- An objective view so that the individual can distinguish between different methods of accomplishing a task that will produce acceptable results, and differences in quality of the methods where the results will not be the same.

- Leadership and take-charge personalities as reviewers will be working independently on special assignments. They cannot expect a lot of advice and guidance in performing their work. Therefore, the reviewers should be self-starters who will pursue assignments with interest and enthusiasm.

- An inquisitive nature because many of the problems and concerns to be uncovered in the review are not intuitively obvious. Thus, the individual who is a good reviewer needs to have the instinct to pursue leads and to put together bits of information that individually are meaningless but in total document the problem.

- An understanding of controls because any review of an application must include an internal control review.

- An ability to communicate both orally and in writing because much of the success of an individual in quality assurance can be ascribed to the ability to communicate needs and problems to project personnel. The more effective he or she is in communicating with data processing personnel, the more successful he or she will be in getting their ideas accepted.

- An ability to write reports. As the quality assurance reviewer must be able to transfer concerns and recommendations into written

reports. Much of his or her success in having formal recommendations implemented will be dependent on the reviewer's ability
to communicate the information to management through written
reports.

In addition, the individual should be personally convinced of the importance of quality assurance and must be willing and able to devote the
necessary time.

You should be able to perceive from this description that the quality assurance function is heavily people-dependent. The importance of
getting the right individuals cannot be overemphasized.

DEVELOPING THE QUALITY ASSURANCE FUNCTION

The development of a QA function entails establishing an organizational
structure for the group, obtaining the support of interested parties, building a staff, and establishing the steps or procedures under which the
function will operate. The staffing of the structure encompasses development of job descriptions. Support for the function is needed from project
leaders, project personnel, executive management, and internal auditing.
The steps and procedures are the methods by which a group will conduct
reviews.

Organizational Structure

The QA function should report directly to the data processing manager
as a staff function. The individual in charge of the function should be the
manager of quality assurance. Most organizations begin the function with
one individual. Four other positions could logically be established within
the function when it grows in size — three QA analysts and a secretary.

The individuals filling the technical positions must be highly skilled
data processing personnel. The approximate salary ranges necessary to
obtain individuals with necessary skills would be

- Quality assurance manager, $27,000 – $40,000

- Senior QA application review analyst or consultant, $25,000 – $32,000

- Quality assurance staff analyst, $22,000 – $30,000

Staffing the Quality Assurance Function

Regardless of whether the staff for the group is full-time or part-time, the qualifications needed for success are the same. To obtain better understanding of the job requirements, see the job descriptions in Figures 3.4, 3.5, 3.6 and 3.7. Each has five items of information:

1.   Job title — the name of the position.

2.   Report to — the individual in the organization's structure to whom this job reports.

3.   Function — general description of what the position should accomplish.

4.   Responsibilities and duties — those specific tasks that the individual is responsible to accomplish.

5.   Qualifications — the education, experience, and traits the individual should possess.

Job descriptions are designed to assist organizations in setting up positions for their own QA function. They can be used "as is" or modified to meet the special needs of your organization. Note that if only one position is established (i.e., quality assurance manager) that job description should include the responsibilities and duties of a senior quality assurance analyst. This is because the analyst job description contains the elements of the quality assurance review, while the manager job description is more supervisory oriented.

Figure 3.3 illustrates the structure of a mature QA group. The function would be headed by a manager. Reporting to the manager would be the quality assurance staff and the senior quality assurance application review analyst(s). As the workload and responsibility of the group grows, quality assurance analyst(s) and a secretary could be added. If the quality assurance manager was the only individual in the group, he would perform the functions of both the manager and the senior quality assurance analyst job.

If the function of the group entails highly technical aspects of data processing, one or more quality assurance consultants could be added to the group to provide this expertise. For example, if the QA function has responsibility for selecting and advising on operating systems features, this consultant could work with project and operating personnel on all aspects of operating systems as well as assisting in project reviews and the setting of standards. Such a consultant would be on the same level as a senior quality assurance analyst.

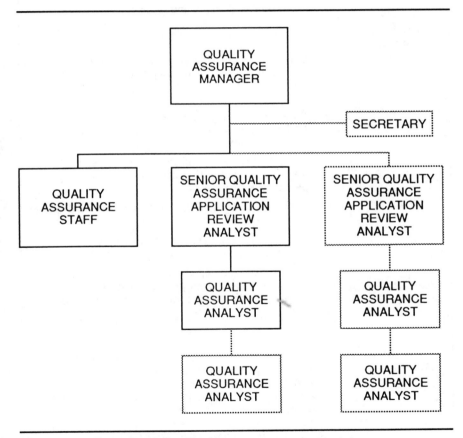

Figure 3.3. Suggested Quality Assurance group structure.

REPORTS TO: Data Processing Manager

FUNCTION: Assists the data processing manager in implementing the quality assurance policy. Determines quality assurance objectives, establishes long-range goals and develops an operating budget for the group. Plans and assigns units of work, sets performance objectives, motivates, counsels and develops staff to achieve performance and work objectives. Interviews and evaluates qualifications of job applicants.

DUTIES AND RESPONSI- BILITIES: The quality assurance manager is responsible for:

1. Establishing quality assurance policy for all computer systems and computer operations of the company and directing the group in carrying out the policy.

2. Establishing the general criteria for reviews for MIS systems to determine what should be evaluated and when.

3. Promoting quality assurance concepts throughout the MIS department by issuing guidelines and providing instruction.

4. Providing consultation to MIS personnel and users as necessary.

5. Conducts quality assurance reviews acting as a senior quality assurance analyst.

6. Deciding on and reporting to the data processing manager failure by project teams to respond in a reasonable time to systems recommendations.

7. Providing continuing research on how to review and improve the quality of MIS systems.

QUALIFICA- TIONS: Candidate must have a bachelor's degree in either business or computer science with specialized knowledge in all facets of computer systems development and operations. Should have 10 years in computer systems or programming. The individual in this position should possess a reasonable ability in writing, speaking, and dealing with people.

Figure 3.4. Job description: Quality Assurance manager.

REPORTS TO: Quality Assurance Manager

FUNCTION: Reviews MIS systems to determine that goals will be achieved, methods followed and performance is satisfactory. In this respect, develops control standards and guidelines for MIS systems, and functions as a central source of knowledge on technology and standards for all MIS personnel. Supervises Quality Assurance assignments of the group to ensure system maintains a satisfactory level of quality, that systems will function efficiently, and that the systems will operate in accordance with established procedures.

DUTIES AND RESPONSI-BILITIES: The senior quality assurance analyst is responsible for:

1.   Directing system reviews.

2.   Evaluating and approving work and reports of quality assurance analysts.

3.   Reviewing system during the feasibility, design, programming, testing and conversion phases. Advises data processing management of problems uncovered by this review.

4.   Reviewing general controls. Advises data processing management of weaknesses.

5.   Advising project team on MIS design and programming technology.

6.   Developing MIS standards and guidelines.

7.   Negotiating differences regarding systems implementation between assigned quality assurance analysts, systems designers, and user departments.

QUALIFICA-TIONS: Requires intensive knowledge of the systems of the organization, the policies, standards, and procedures of the organization as well as the long-range goals and its philosophy with respect to advances in computer technology in order to insure that policy and established procedures are adhered to. Requires intensive knowledge of review techniques as well as a broad knowledge of computer systems and programming. Individual should have five years' systems and programming experience.

Figure 3.5.   Job description: senior Quality Assurance analyst.

REPORTS TO:	Quality Assurance Manager
FUNCTION:	Within the entire electronic data processing environment, the incumbent provides any highly technical assistance necessary to assist project personnel in the performance of their function.
DUTIES AND: RESPONSI- BILITIES	The quality assurance consultant is responsible for:

1. Advising and assisting project personnel with *details* in the use of new solutions for systems and program development.

2. Assisting the group in evaluating highly technical aspects of systems and program design.

3. Participating in the review of applications being developed to provide assistance in advancing system design approach.

4. Maintaining liaison with equipment manufacturers and software firms to keep abreast of trends in data.

QUALIFICA- TIONS:	A bachelor's degree in computer science and considerable data processing experience is necessary. Incumbent should have at least five years of systems development and programming experience and excellent knowledge of computer programming and operating systems.

Figure 3.6. Job description: Quality Assurance consultant.

QUALITY ASSURANCE SUPPORT STAFF

As quality assurance groups mature many put more emphasis on establishing an environment in which quality can flourish and less effort needs to be spent on reviewing individual applications. Experience has shown that by reviewing a single application the most quality assurance can do is improve that application; however, by creating an environment encouraging quality, all applications can be improved. This also places quality assurance in a position where its contribution to the data processing function is more recognizable.

REPORTS TO:	Senior Quality Assurance Analyst
FUNCTION:	The incumbent assists in the performance of reviews of data processing systems.
DUTIES AND RESPONSI-BILITIES:	Under direct supervision, incumbent assists in the performance of reviews of the feasibility, design, programming, testing, and conversion efforts for new or modified computer systems. Incumbent may assist in the development of guidelines and standards. The incumbent assists in the preparation of formal reports of reviews. Any discrepancies and problems discovered during the review are referred to a higher level quality assurance analyst.
QUALIFICA-TIONS:	In many cases, the individuals in this classification work independently and must have demonstrated the ability to exercise considerable initiative when conducting reviews as well as a minor degree of analysis and good judgment in making recommendations to improve systems. Requires the capability for assuming limited responsibility for the work performed as well as for the preparation and presentation of the audit report. Requires the ability to work on several assignments simultaneously. Individual should have three years of systems and programming experience.

Figure 3.7. Job description: Quality Assurance analyst.

To establish a quality environment the QA function draws together those functions in the data processing department that support and improve quality systems. The purpose of putting all these support functions under the QA manager is to direct and coordinate their efforts in order to maximize quality. The support functions that are placed under the QA manager direct and coordinate their efforts in order to maximize quality. The support functions that are being placed under QA include the following (note that no one organization has included all of the following with their QA function).

- Error tracking
- Development of MIS application standards

- Development of software standards
- Authorization of deviations from standards
- Development of control standards
- Design of system controls
- Training of data processing personnel
- Tracking of production projects
- Performance analysis
- Hardware selection
- Software selection

Support Needed for a Successful QA Function

Part of the function of QA is to develop good working relationships with project personnel, internal auditing, and management. The support is necessary because QA operates as an advisory group. This advisory capacity of the group should be developed in a friendly environment as opposed to a hostile environment.

The day-to-day functioning of the group is with data processing personnel. This relationship is one of inquiry and discussion of future plans and alternatives under consideration. It is important for the QA reviewer to obtain honest and frank discussions with the project personnel. If a good working relationship has been achieved, these discussions will occur. On the other hand, if the project team is uncertain of the reviewer's motive, the working relationship will become very formal and the reviewer will have difficulty in obtaining the type of information needed. No information is volunteered and questions are answered in the briefest possible manner. Chapter 6 will discuss ways of building a good relationship.

Quality assurance and internal audit have some overlapping responsibilities. Properly established, the functions of the two groups should be complementary. The QA group is more qualified to evaluate the technical aspects of systems. On the other hand, internal audit is more qualified to comment on the adequacy of internal controls. Working together they can make a very strong team.

The function performed by QA could be performed by a highly technical competent internal audit group. However in practice, internal audit does not have the time or talent necessary to do a thorough quality assurance review. Without the available time and technically trained personnel, internal audit is either shortcutting these reviews or eliminating them altogether. Studies have shown that very few internal audit groups are involved in the systems design phase of new applications. QA should reach agreements with internal audit as to which aspects of data processing application reviews each will perform. There is more needed than the two groups can do combined, so reaching a logical division of work should not prove difficult. Chapter 12 will discuss this relationship with internal audit in detail.

The goals to which QA is dedicated will be supported by management. It is the method by which they are accomplished for which quality assurance needs the support. Quality assurance should primarily look to data processing management for support. However, support is also needed from user department management. Data processing management can help obtain user management support by explaining the role and responsibilities of QA.

Quality assurance should solicit support from data processing management to:

1. Provide the function with a sufficient number of competent personnel.

2. Provide the function with the authority necessary to carry out their responsibilities. This will assure the group of access to project information and personnel.

3. Have their recommendations considered and adopted. This can primarily be achieved through management interest and review of quality assurance reports, and a review by the project teams of the plan of action based on those recommendations.

Steps in Performing the Function

The QA group executes seven steps in the process of performing a review of an application under development. These steps include:

1. *Planning the review.* Developing plans and schedules to perform the review.

2. *Preliminary review.* Gathering information necessary as background before commencing the formal review process.

3.   *Feasibility review.* Studying the feasibility results.

4.   *Design review.* Analyzing of the system design and assessing whether that design satisfies the goals of the application.

5.   *Program review.* Checking compliance to standards and design criteria.

6.   *Testing review.* Determining whether the system meets design criteria.

7.   *Conversion review.* Determining that the conversion process is well controlled.

The constraints of the review steps are illustrated in Figure 3.8. Note that the steps result in a "go" or "no go" recommendation. This necessitates that QA has gathered enough information at the end of each of the reviews to recommend to management whether or not to proceed to the next phases of the project.

One constraint is the role or authority of the QA function. The function can do no more than authorized. The second constraint regards the QA methods and procedures which limit how and what the QA function does. QA is guided by two sets of procedures. The first is the standards, guidelines, policies, and procedures of the organization, which is supplemented by the technical advice they can offer the project team. The second is the policies and procedures of the QA group itself. These are the methods by which the function operates. These quality assurance group procedures will be discussed in detail in Chapters 4–10.

OBJECTIVITY

QA is asked to evaluate the competence and performance of their peers. This is especially difficult in QA groups that use part-time personnel.

Imagine for the moment yourself a member of QA group. You are assigned to the group on either a part-time basis or short-term assignment. You are assigned to review project X, headed by a person for whom you have worked in the past, and may again in the future. During the quality review process you note several items that may be potential

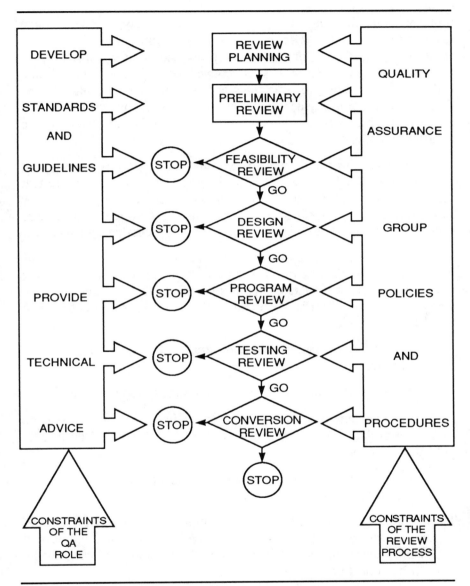

Figure 3.8. Constraints of the Quality Assurance review process.

problems in the future. However, you are not completely sure. The project leader assures you they will be handled at some time in the future. You must now prepare a report for the project leader's supervisor. Judging the facts you have gathered, you believe the project will have some difficulty in achieving its objectives and meeting the schedule. On the other hand, the project leader had told you the problems will be handled in the future. You realize you may well be working for this leader in the next few months. What would you put in your report?

There is no easy answer to this question. Certainly a long-term assignment to QA improves one's objectivity. This does not assure that the long-term person will be independent, nor the short-term person overly influenced by the prospect of future assignments. However, it does raise a question that needs to be addressed by data processing management.

One of the steps that can help improve independence is having QA personnel report individually and confidentially to the data processing manager on areas of concern. This has benefit to the QA members, but also has the effect of shifting some of their work responsibilities back to the data processing manager.

Other steps that can be taken to improve the independence of the QA group are:

1. Making long-term assignments to the quality assurance group.

2. Guaranteeing that a quality assurance reviewer will not be assigned to a project leader whom that individual has reviewed during the last X months.

3. Using the most senior personnel in the data processing department to perform the quality assurance function.

Those organizations using structured techniques will find that if the QA review is based on objective evaluation against the structured format imposed by the techniques, fewer personal implications of peer review have to be considered.

SUMMARY

Data processing management should assume primary responsibility for establishing the QA function. Once established, data processing management should support that group with a sufficient number of competent personnel, provide the group with the authority it needs to perform their function, and then determine that the group's recommendations are being given serious consideration by the project team. Recommendations from the group should be adopted unless there are very valid reasons for not implementing them.

When QA is being developed, there are four areas that require consideration: 1) the organizational structure of the group; 2) the caliber, method, and quantity of staff for the group; 3) soliciting support from management, users, and internal auditing; and 4) developing the procedures and methods by which the group will operate. Management should closely monitor these areas and provide what guidance they can to ascertain the developing group gets off to the best start possible.

Independence of QA personnel should remain a continual concern of data processing management. It is in its best interest that the group maintain as much independence as possible. Data processing management should take those steps necessary to affirm its support for an independent function.

Systems Review Priorities: Allocating QA Time

Ideally, QA is charged with reviewing all systems. As a practical matter it is rarely staffed sufficiently to review all systems in the appropriate depth. Therefore, some method is needed to assign priorities so as to allot the available review time among systems needing review.

This chapter will discuss the methods that can be used for selecting applications for review. A scientific approach based on four criteria is recommended. The criteria are the type of application, the complexity of the application, the technology being utilized to implement the application, and the people involved in specifying and implementing the system.

This approach assists in developing a plan for which applications to review and how much time should be expended on that review. The planning methodology calls for allocating 80% of the available review time, and leaving the remaining 20% as a contingency for special assignments and explaining the implications and solutions to problems associated with previous reviews.

METHODS OF SELECTING APPLICATIONS FOR REVIEW

After the QA is established, the next step is determining work priorities. One of the major criteria of success is in finding a good answer to the time allocation question. Without a plan for allocating resources, the work of the group can be dissipated in low-priority tasks.

One quality assurance manager practices saying "no" in front of the mirror so that he can turn down these requests. It is very easy to spend an hour or two trying to be a good guy. Unfortunately, hours have the tendency to mount into days and weeks over the course of a year.

Five Common Methods for Selecting Applications for Review

QA groups tend to make choices in one of five ways:

1. *Intuition.* The manager selects those applications which he or she believes to be in need of review. Under this method, the manager will have a "feel" as to which application is most likely to cause problems for the organization. Both the application and the amount of time allocated to its review are at the prerogative of the manager.

2. *Directed.* Management of the data processing department directs what applications to review. This direction can either be application by application, or a set of criteria (all telecommunication applications, for example) that instructs QA as to which application should be reviewed.

3. *Reactive.* In this approach, the group becomes involved with applications as they begin to develop problems. Again, it can be each application individually or by some criteria (i.e., 10 percent over budget or 90 days late) that causes involvement.

4. *Planned judgment.* Using judgment, QA will select which applications they will review and for how long. The primary difference between judgment and intuition is the planning effort involved. Judgment implies an evaluation of alternatives. Intuition considers each application individually.

5. *Planned scientific.* A mathematically oriented approach to selecting applications based on a predetermined set of criteria. Mathematical values will be assigned as a result of analysis of each criterion. The mathematical summing of the individual criterion will result in a numerical value that can be used in assigning priority.

Of the five approaches, the planned scientific is the most objective. The other four tend to be subjective evaluations. This scientific approach has proven very successful in those organizations whose management is scientifically oriented. On the other hand, in organizations where management runs the organization by "the seat of their pants," such an approach may run into opposition. Utilizing the planned scientific approach, the manager can provide documented explanations as to why resources have been assigned to reviews of specific applications.

The five methods for selecting applications are generally in conflict with one another (see Figure 4.1). It is difficult to work by more than one of these methods at a time.

The remainder of this chapter is oriented toward the planned scientific approach to selecting applications for review. However, if your quality assurance group uses one of the other approaches, the criteria and methodology can still prove helpful in your application selection process.

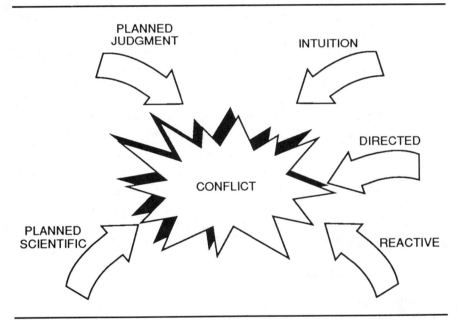

Figure 4.1. Methods of selecting applications for review.

RATING CRITERIA

Experience has shown four general categories of concern for computerized applications. These can be restated as categories for rating (or evaluating) applications for review.

1. *Type of application.* The function or area that is being computerized. Examples would be payroll, accounts receivable, inventory, budgeting, demand deposits, and unearned premium reserves. One can consider

software systems such as database managers, telecommunications systems, or bill or material processors, as types of applications.

2. *Complexity of applications.* The difficulty in computerizing and the amount of resources involved in building the application. Evaluation of complexity varies from person to person and installation to installation. What may be complex for a small computer installation may be a simple application to a large organization. Thus, complexity will be related to the size of the organization and skill of the personnel.

3. *Technology.* Problems with technology may be either hardware- or software-related. Most problems come from technology not previously utilized by the organization. When new hardware and software are involved in an application, it becomes more difficult to implement. This is due to the learning experience of individuals with those new products. There is also a correlation between the time the product has been on the market and difficulty in using it. When a product has been time-tested, its implementation is not as difficult as with a product newly introduced to the marketplace.

4. *People.* The skill, temperament, control orientation, dedication, and time available for the project all influence the type of job that can be performed by a specific individual. The complexity of current technology necessitates the team approach to developing a new application. These criteria are magnified by the number and backgrounds of individuals participating on the project team.

TYPE OF APPLICATION

The major criteria for determining if a system should be reviewed lies in the nature of the role of that application in the organization. Obviously, applications that control the assets of an organization are those of greatest concern. The higher the percentage of assets controlled, the greater the concern. The three aspects of types of applications that need to be evaluated are financial applications, statutory requirements, and exposure to loss.

Financial Applications

In merchandising organizations, the invoicing systems probably control the greatest percentage of resources. Next is the purchasing application, followed by the payroll application. It is thus the financial systems that merit the highest priority for review.

Statutory Requirements

Many data processing applications provide data to governmental agencies. This is especially true of regulated industries. In all industries, systems such as payroll interface with several governmental agencies. Invoicing systems that collect sales tax can interface with agencies of one or more states. Because of the necessity for correct reporting to governmental agencies, together with potential penalties for wrong information, extra time and effort are warranted on these systems. The larger the number of agencies involved, the greater the exposure of the organization.

Exposure to Loss

Computer applications are subject to exposure to loss. This exposure can be due to errors and omissions on the part of careless or dishonest employees or acts of sabotage on the part of disgruntled employees, and losses due to penetration by outsiders. Better than 95 percent of all losses will be those associated with employees of the organization. Therefore, undue effort should not be put on losses associated with outside individuals. The more liquid the assets of the organization (cash, readily salable inventory, etc.) the higher the exposure to loss. This factor needs to be considered in the evaluation criteria for reviewing applications.

COMPLEXITY OF APPLICATION

The complexity of an application will vary depending on the type of installation and the skill of data processing personnel. Complexity can be measured by many different criteria. The ones to consider are

1. Application history
2. Effort to develop application
3. Time span to complete project
4. Expected number of application programs
5. Number of databases updated

Application History

The nature of certain applications seems to make them complex to operate. A study of the history of an application provides some insight as to the complexity of operation. Another means of measuring complexity is the number of errors and problems that have occurred. This can be determined by a study of the history of an application. Analysis of past events will provide us with some indication of future trends.

Effort to Develop Application

The effort to develop an application needs to be measured in man-months of effort. This is the best common denominator for systems development effort. Again, the skill of people within an organization will affect the effort needed to develop a typical application.

Time Span to Complete Project

If a project team has sufficient time to complete a project, it can be done as an orderly process. When the project team is pressured to do its work on a crash basis, the individual pieces must be compressed, subjecting the project to error. While it can be argued that too much time results in a poor use of resources because the project team will use the available time inefficiently, too little time usually has more problems associated with it.

Expected Number of Application Programs

The larger the number of programs included in an application — whether utilities or applications — the greater the complexity of the system. The longer the chain of programs, the more times data is passed, the greater the number of interfaces, and the more spread out the logic. These all add to the complexity of the system.

Number of Databases Updated

Application programs interact with files that will be retained and updated the next time a transaction is processed or the application run. The greater the number of files updated, the greater the complexity of the system.

Technology

The type of technology utilized by the project team affects the difficulty in developing the application. When an organization is using time-tested hardware and software, the implementation is facilitated. When the newer technologies are utilized, the systems analysts and programmers have the dual problem of understanding the application and the supporting hardware and software technology. When systems problems occur, it may be difficult to pinpoint whether the problem is application or technical in nature. Unfamiliarity with the technology greatly increases the probability of problems. Technology can be divided into hardware technology and software technology.

Hardware technology has progressed from card batch systems through on-line disk systems with telecommunication. As systems move through that progression, the complexity increases geometrically.

Today, software appears to be causing more difficulty technically than hardware. Special-purpose packages designed exclusively for an organization (an advance release from a vendor of a new software package, or a routine that was specially developed by a vendor for a particular application) may be the most difficult to utilize. Once systems analysts and programmers have mastered a particular piece of software, additional applications using that software are much easier to implement.

PEOPLE

The skill level of the project team is a major ingredient in success for data processing applications. Three parties are involved in the development of most applications: users, internal auditors, and the project team.

The rating criteria described in this chapter can rate each of these groups independently. However, if the groups work together amicably, the probability of success increases greatly. Unfortunately, this is a difficult factor to rate. Therefore, the rater is cautioned that if known personality or departmental conflicts exist, the effectiveness of that party could be lessened because of this conflict.

User Involvement

Organizations that have a history of successful data processing applications attribute much of their success to user involvement. The amount of user involvement can be considered one of the keys to success. An important criterion is the time user personnel have available to contribute to development of an application. It is helpful, but not necessary, for user personnel to have a strong technical understanding of data processing. If they fully understand the application and have a strong desire to understand data processing, that should suffice.

Internal Audit Involvement

Internal auditors can play a major role in systems development if they are technically competent regarding data processing. Many of the functions that might normally be performed by a quality assurance group can be performed by internal audit if they are involved in the application development cycle. This relationship between quality assurance and internal auditing will be discussed in detail in Chapter 19.

Skill of the Project Team

The technical competence of the project team is a major element in the success of an application. When systems analysts and programmers are experienced and competent, the probability of success increases tremendously. Quality assurance personnel must seriously assess the effectiveness of the project team and adjust their involvement with the project accordingly. The skills needed by the project team are the same skills that are considered important for a good quality assurance analyst.

OTHER SELECTION CRITERIA

The proposed criteria are provided as an example of this method of selecting applications. These criteria are oriented toward a financial organization, such as a bank or insurance company. Nonfinancial organizations may have to revise these criteria.

The success of using a mathematical process to select applications for review depends upon how closely those criteria correlate to risk. If the criteria are good predictors of problems, the selection process will be successful. It may be necessary to experiment with different criteria prior to identifying those criteria that have a high correlation to risk.

Additional criteria for selecting applications for a quality assurance review include

- Age of the application
- Skill of user personnel in working with computerized applications
- Visibility of application system

- Type of logic (difficult, average, easy)
- Need for security
- Need for privacy
- Number of people on the project

RATING INDIVIDUAL APPLICATIONS

Each new application or major enhancement to an existing application should be rated by the quality assurance group. The rating should be done in conjunction with the group's normal planning cycle. This planning cycle may be either monthly, quarterly, or yearly. The objective of rating individual applications is to determine the group's workload over the next planning period — that is, to establish a work priority scheme.

Assumptions and Caveats

The use of the proposed work prioritizing scheme is based on certain ideal assumptions and caveats. These include:

- An inventory of all computer systems (AISs) — operational, under development, or undergoing major change — is maintained.
- The inventory may not be complete due to user development or system changes made outside the system development process.
- To use the priority scheme, certain minimal information is required or the assessment of the system may not be valid.
- The full priority scheme would most easily be performed by MIS groups in order to enlist multiple perspectives, especially where resources are known to be a concern.
- Management in the organization must agree that risk can be evaluated by a standardized scheme.
- Users should always be consulted in the risk evaluation to ensure appropriate assumptions, and to assure maximum effectiveness.
- Judgment is still needed!

Within this framework of assumptions and caveats the entire MIS work plan can then be developed. To the degree these assumptions differ from the reality of the organization's SDLC environment, the work planning methodology should be adjusted.

MIS Planning/Prioritization Process

The risk evaluation performed as part of the work priority scheme must be done within the context of the entire MIS planning process. There are elements of the process that need to be considered prior to the risk evaluation (such as nondiscretionary requirements) and other elements that require consideration afterward (such as resource constraints). Figure 4.2 and the following paragraphs present a suggested model for the entire prioritization process.

Nondiscretionary Reviews

As can be seen from the model in Figure 4.2, the review planning and prioritization process starts with front end qualifiers that must be considered by the auditor prior to making decisions with respect to which system(s) should be reviewed. These front end qualifiers consist of nondiscretionary factors which are beyond the reviewer's control. These nondiscretionary factors include, but are not limited to the following:

- External directives (laws, regulations, OMB circulars, and MIS standards).

- Internal directives and priorities (contractual requirements; requirements, standards, and policies of audit and data processing organizations; upper management directives).

- Business/organizational environment unique to the organization (effect of economy on organization, budget of organization, and technology available to or used by organization).

- Factors unique to the organization (presence and strength of quality assurance and security functions, management and control philosophy, structure, and policies).

- Geopolitical environment (public concern and politics).

- Resource constraints and economic health (dollars, time, expertise, training, tools, and techniques).

- Known problems with the system, from current logs or previous evaluations and audits (nature and magnitude of problems).

- Evaluations and audits planned by management.
- Reviewer's institutional knowledge of the organization's universe of systems.

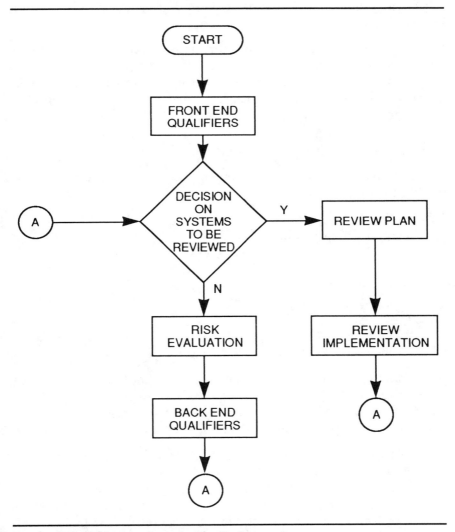

Figure 4.2. MIS planning/prioritization process.

After all of the front end qualifiers have been considered, it may be that the entire review plan is dictated by the nondiscretionary work. That is, external directives, internal directives, and/or resource constraints may require that certain audits be performed and these required reviews may use up the limited audit resources available. In this case, the priority scheme may still be useful for determining audit approaches and where to focus efforts.

If, on the other hand, additional review resources are available for discretionary reviews, the risk evaluation of the work priority scheme can be used to identify and rank the systems in greatest need of audit coverage. Ultimately, back end qualifiers may need to be considered for the discretionary reviews.

Risk Evaluation Levels and Dimensions

The work priority scheme expresses the risk concerns in terms of two levels and five dimensions.

Level I

1.   Criticality and mission impact

Level II

2.   Size/scale/complexity

3.   Environment/stability

4.   Reliability/integrity

5.   Technology integration

Each dimension is defined as a related set of characteristics which can measure or estimate the amount of risk posed by that dimension of a failure of the system. The chief concern of each dimension can be stated in the form of a question as follows:

1.   What is the impact or criticality of the system to the organization? A poorly developed or controlled system that is mission critical could jeopardize the basic operational or programmatic effectiveness; therefore, an impact/critical system commands audit attention. The larger the impact, the more important it is to audit.

2.   How complex is the system? (This includes size considerations.) The more complete the system, the more difficult is communication and control, and consequently, the higher the risk of failure. The greater the chance for failure, the more important it is to review the system.

3.   How stable is the system internally (structure) and externally (environment)? The less stable the system, the more difficult it is to develop procedures for communication and control, the greater the chance for failure, and the greater the need to review.

4.   How reliable is the system and the information it processes and generates? That is, what is the chance of the system failing or the data being wrong? The answer to this question is obtained by looking at the controls in the system (integrity controls) and prior review experience. The less reliable system and data, the more chance for failure and the need to review.

5.   How well is the technology integrated into the organization? The more poorly the system technology is integrated with the skills of the staff and the standards and procedures of the organization, the more chance for failure and the greater the need to review.

The overriding risk is criticality and mission impact. Systems with significant impact easily take precedence over all other dimensions in allocating MIS review resources. Because criticality and mission impact is so crucial, the work priority scheme assigns it to its own level. The two-level work priority scheme permits a high amount of flexibility depending on organizational need since it can be applied in any degree of detail required. For example, the results of Level I ranking may be adequate to prioritize all audit work, based on available time and resources. If additional ranking characteristics are necessary, the more detailed Level II can be used to further prioritize review work. A two-level review, additionally, enables the auditor to purge from consideration those systems which will definitely not be reviewed, for any number of reasons. Environment and resource issues enter here. The two-level work priority scheme follows in outline form, identifying the five dimensions and their related characteristics. (Note that the same characteristic may be used in more than one dimension because the question asked will be different.)

LEVEL I

Mission Impact/Strategic Value/Organization (Business) Criticality and Sensitivity Factors

- Criticality of the system to the organization's mission.
- Criticality/sensitivity of the system to the well-being, safety, or interest of the general public/clients/consumers.
- Criticality/sensitivity of data and information:
  competitive advantage
  confidence of the public in program/department
  privacy/confidentiality/security issues
- Materiality of resources controlled by system.
- Fraud potential.
- Life cycle costs of system (people and dollars).
  development cost budget
      people
      dollars
          hardware
          software
          facilities
  operating cost budget
      people
          data processing/systems (including training)
          users (including training)
      dollars
          hardware (CPU, peripherals, terminals, telecommunications)
              acquisition
              operation
      software
              acquisition
              maintenance
          supplies
          facilities
          configuration change control
- Degree of dependence on AIS.
- Criticality of interfaces with other systems and external organizations.

A Level I review, outlined above, provides a "first cut" at the total audit universe. This initial review will identify critical systems that require audit coverage. The additional dimensions to be reviewed in Level II should be used to rank these critical systems to find those most deserving of discretionary review coverage.

LEVEL II

System* Size/Scale/Complexity

- Size of user area impacted.
- Number/complexity of interfaces/relationships with other projects or systems.
- Complexity of AIS technology (network size, communication needs, system configuration, degree of centralization, nature of transaction coupling mechanisms, nature of security).
- Size/complexity of system
  size of system budget
  development costs
        maintenance/operation costs
  number/complexity of different inputs
  number/complexity of unique files
  number/complexity of unique outputs
  number/complexity of logical files (views) system will access
  number/complexity of major types of on-line inquiry
  number of source documents maintained/retained
  number/complexity of computer programs
  complexity of programming language
  complexity of system configuration
  number of human elements interfacing
  number of decision levels
  number of functions by devices
  number, types, and complexity of transactions
  number of external organizations impacted
- Nature of interactions with external organizations.

---

* The term "system" is used in place of "project" to signify the entire AIS life cycle and the possibility of review at any point in the development process or operations.

System Environment/Stability

- Organizational breadth (interfaces, dependencies, system configuration).
- Management involvement/commitment.
- Project management approach and structure.
- Configuration management program.
- Management efficiency and effectiveness.
- Specificity of, agreement on, and support for user requirements.
- Confidence in estimates — both cost and time — premising make-or-buy decisions, vendor selection, system testing/validation, etc.
- Number of vendors/contractors involved.
- Newness of function/process to user.
- Problems associated with current system performance and/or system development effort.
- Existence/scope of data processing standards, policies, and procedures, especially systems development life cycle methodology and documentation requirements.
- Availability of evidence — document and report preparation and maintenance for entire system life cycle (test/validation/certification results, operations manual, system specifications, audit trails, exception reporting).
- Quality and completeness of documentation.
- General controls:
  physical access controls
  environmental controls
  communication controls
  management controls environment
  document controls
  system change and test/validation/certification controls
- Ongoing concern issues/organization effect (will mission objectives be met in a timely manner?):
  interruption tolerance
  ability to maintain performance
  unsatisfactory system performance (adverse consequences from degradation or failure)
  unsatisfactory system development completion
  unsatisfactory conversion

- Labor relations (salary parity, hours, fringe benefits, etc.).
- Project team (management and staff effectiveness and training).
- Organizational and personnel changes (frequency, magnitude, and number).
- Functional requirements changes (frequency, number, and magnitude).
- Technical changes (frequency, magnitude, and number).
- Factors affecting cost/economic/budget climate.
- Availability and adequacy of back-up and recovery procedures.

Reliability/Integrity

- Hazards/risks to information system (data, hardware, communications, facilities)
- General controls:
    environmental (e.g., physical access controls, natural hazards controls)
    management
- Applications controls.
- Availability and adequacy of audit trails.
- Quality and quantity of automated error detection/correction procedures.
- Availability and adequacy of back-up and recovery procedures.
- Completeness, currency, and accuracy of documentation for audit.
- Prior reviews.
- Auditor judgment (intuitively obvious).

Technology Integration

- Makeup of project team in relation to technology used (number, training, and experience).
- Applicability of the data processing design methodologies and standards to the technology in use.
- Pioneering aspects (newness of technology and/or technological approaches used in this information system for application and organization).
- Technical complexity of information system (interrelationships of tasks).
- User knowledge of DP technology.

- Margin for error (i.e., Is there reasonable time to make adjustments, corrections, or perform analyses before the transaction is completed?).
- Utilization of equipment (tolerance for expansion).
- Availability of automated error detection/correction procedures.
- Completeness, currency, and accuracy of documentation for implementation/maintenance/operation (e.g., operations/maintenance manuals).
- Amount of hard-copy evidence.

RISK SCORING: APPLICATION OF THE WORK PRIORITY SCHEME

Implementation of the Scheme

For the scheme to be of use to the MIS auditor, an analysis approach for risk scoring must be employed using the dimensions and characteristics. The rest of this section describes *one possible approach* that could be used. User experience will undoubtedly lead to modifications and improvements in the application of the scheme. If the MIS reviewer for some reason does not wish to use the scoring methodology, he or she could still keep the dimensions and their characteristics in mind when performing a less formal review.

Suggested Scoring Approach for Each Risk Dimension

The method of ranking and rating suggested here in a simple approach commensurate with the softness of the data available. Each dimension of the scheme should be treated and ranked separately, with scores then combined. Criticality/Mission Impact, the Level I dimension of the proposed scheme, would be analyzed first. The procedure is as follows.

First, the n characteristics *within a dimension* are ranked according to their importance to that dimension. The rank number of characteristic i is $I(i)$ and ranges from 1 to n, with n correlated with the most important characteristic. For operational systems one can use discriminant analysis applied to equal sets of known system failures and successes to obtain this ranking. For developmental systems a consensus view of audit management can be used, ideally obtaining sponsor or user input.

Second, the rank, $I(i)$, is then converted to an importance weighting factor, $W(i)$, that is normalized to 20. (The reason for selecting 20 is explained later.) This means that the sum of the weighting factors for the characteristics within a dimension is set to 20 (or normalized to 20). Since each of the five dimensions has a different number of characteristics and we wish to treat the dimensions as equals, normalization will guarantee that the risk score range for each dimension will be the same.

The normalization factor, F, is the number which converts the rank $I(i)$ to the weighting factor $W(i)$. The relationships are

(1) $$W(i) = F \times I(i)$$

(2) $$\sum_{i=1 \text{ to } n} W(i) = \sum_{i=1 \text{ to } n} F \times I(t) = 20$$

Solving equation (2) for F, we find

(3) $$F = \frac{20}{\sum_{i=1 \text{ to } n} I(i)}$$

and substituting for F in equation (1) yields the importance weighting factor $W(i)$ for characteristic i:

(4) $$W(i) = \frac{20}{\sum_{i=1 \text{ to } n} I(i)}$$

Third, each characteristic is rated with respect to the risk of occurrence. One of the following risk ratings, $R(i)$, is assigned to characteristic i.

$$R(i) = 3 \text{ (for High Risk)}$$
$$R(i) = 2 \text{ (for Medium Risk)}$$
$$R(i) = 1 \text{ (for Low Risk)}$$

These ratings can be assigned by the auditor, again with user assistance if appropriate.

Finally, a dimension risk score (DRS) for the dimension of risk is obtained by multiplying the importance weighting by the risk rating of the characteristic and summing over the characteristics for that dimension. The equation for this is the following:

$$DRS(j) = \sum_{i=1 \text{ to } n} W(i) \times R(i)$$

where i = characteristics 1 to n

$W(i) =$ importance weighting for characteristic i

$R(i) =$ risk rating for characteristic i

$DRS(j) =$ dimension j's risk score, $j = 1$ to 5

The risk score for each of the five dimensions will range from 20 to 60 using these importance weighting and risk rating number assignments.

First Order System Risk Score

After completing a Level I review for an organization's universe of AISs, using the analysis scheme, the QA analyst can use the Criticality/Mission Impact dimension risk score as a first order approximation to a system risk score. Since these risk scores have all been normalized to the same number (20), it is possible to compare these risk scores across AISs and eliminate from further consideration AISs having a low risk with respect to Criticality/ Mission Impact.

Risk Level II Review Considerations

If it is decided that the more detailed Level II review is appropriate and affordable, one must decide upon a sequence for reviewing the remaining dimensions of the high risk, critical AISs. While there is no single "correct" way to do this, it might be appropriate to consider the following.

Since the Environment/Stability risk dimension includes the organization's general controls, including the strength and security functions throughout the SDLC (of both systems and major enhancements to existing systems), it may be most useful to review this dimension first in a Level II review. These general controls would heavily affect the need for review coverage as well as the scope and expertise necessary in that coverage. The MIS auditors could confidently reduce their scope and related testing of applications if they could rely on the organization's general controls and the safeguards these various review functions provide in the SDLC process. Any ranking or prioritizing of the elements in the work priority scheme, beyond the overriding factors described above (i.e., external influence and mission criticality), could not be reasonably accomplished without a survey of the organization's general and applications controls and without an institutional knowledge of the organization, its SDLC process, and any facts and circumstances affecting system development activities. The characteristics in all four Level II dimensions should be weighted and rated in the light of such background information, and the dimension risk score, DRS, obtained for each of the four Level II dimensions.

The Second Order System Risk Score

As a second order approximation one can treat the dimensions as equal contributors to the risk score for the AIS as a whole. Under this assumption the system risk score, (SRS) is then a simple sum of the five dimension risk scores, (DRS).

$$(5) \qquad SRS = \sum_{j=1 \text{ to } 5} DRS(j)$$

Since DRS(j) can range from 20 to 60, SRS will range from 100 to 300. The choice of 20 for the sum of the weights of the characteristics within a dimension is arbitrary and was made in order to place SRS in a reasonable range for comparing one system's risk score to another's.

An Example

It may be a useful exercise to go through an example of the arithmetic involved. Assume we wish to calculate dimension risk scores and system risk scores for two AISs. To simplify matters we shall assume small numbers of characteristics for each dimension. Dimension 1 has four characteristics, dimension 2 has three characteristics, dimension 3 has five characteristics, dimension 4 has three characteristics and dimension five has 2 characteristics. The importance ranking $I(i)$ and the risk ratings $R(i)$ are obtained from audit management and the auditor respectively. The rest of the numbers in Tables 4.2 and 4.3 are calculated using equations (1) – (5). (Table 4.1 is a practice template of the table to assist the reader in learning the methodology.)

Using dimension 1 as a first order system risk score, we find AIS 1, with DRS = 42, is more at risk than AIS 2, with DRS = 38. We obtain the second order risk score by adding the five dimension risk scores for each AIS. Using these numbers, AIS 1 with SRS = 191.4, is again more at risk than AIS 2, with its SRS = 180.0. Only experience with the method will enable the reviewer to obtain more refined interpretations of the calculations.

SYSTEMS ENHANCEMENTS IN THE REVIEW PROCESS

Systems are enhanced (or modified) under different circumstances. These enhancements can be categorized as follows:

- *Emergency changes.* Changes to systems that must occur before the application can run, usually within 24 hours or less.

- *Software system changes.* Changes to systems that must be modified because of changes in vendor-supplied software, such as operating systems, compilers, sorts, etc. These changes normally do not affect the application's processing rules and can be made independent of the application programs.

- *Short duration changes.* Changes for known errors or problems. Do not cause the system to "hang up" or produce unusable results, but must be corrected quickly. The change is normally installed within two weeks.

- *Scheduled changes.* Changes to the systems that are known in advance and can be implemented on an orderly basis. The usual duration is 10 to 90 days.

- *Major enhancements.* Changes of a substantial nature that can follow the procedures utilized in the building of new applications.

All major enhancements should be considered for review. These can be handled like any other new application because of their size. This type of change encompasses the largest single block of systems development and programming resources in many organizations.

Emergency changes and software system changes should probably not be reviewed by the quality assurance group. What should be reviewed in these cases are the procedures that control these types of changes. Without strong controls over changes of these types, unauthorized changes could be made, or major systems problems occur because of lack of control.

The questionable type of enhancements for review are those of short duration and scheduled changes. To determine QA involvement in these types of changes, the group should first determine the amount of data processing resources being utilized, and second, the exposure to the organization by making one of these types of changes to an application. Obviously, if it is an extremely sensitive application, QA should be involved. Application rating sheets will prove helpful in making this determination. For example, QA may ask each systems analyst to complete one of the application rating sheets (see Figures 4.3 and 4.4) for each short duration or scheduled change. The group can then pick a cutoff point. For example, if the score equals 75 or higher, the quality assurance group will become involved.

RESPONDING TO SPECIAL REQUESTS

Successful QA groups will receive a substantial number of requests for special assignments. There is value in responding to these requests if time is available. It is suggested that 20 percent of available review days be allocated to these types of requests. However, the manager of quality assurance should make a special effort to determine that no more than the allotted time is utilized for these types of requests.

When the requests exceed the amount of time allocated for them, the manager of quality assurance should discuss this situation with the manager of data processing. It is important to emphasize the primary objective for establishing the quality assurance group. If these objectives are subverted by satisfying special requests, the manager of quality assurance should not honor the requests.

SUMMARY

QA groups can have their efforts directed in a variety of ways. The method of direction can affect the effectiveness of the function. Those groups that are most successful are those that achieve the objectives for which they are established. In order to do this, the groups must plan the use of their resources.

The resources can be allocated by determining which applications are in most need of review, and then allocating the available resources to satisfy those needs. This chapter has provided a methodology to make this allocation. Once the allocation has been made, the manager of quality assurance may still need to exert judgment because certain systems will need extra effort due to unique problems.

One cannot overemphasize the importance of setting objectives for the group and then developing a plan to meet those objectives. Data processing is a very orderly, methodical process. To operate successfully in that environment, the quality assurance group must develop very orderly, methodical plans.

AIS _____

DIMENSION	$I(i)$	F	$W(i)$	$R(i)$	$W \times R$	$DRS(j)$
DIM 1 C (1) C (2) C (3) C (4)						
DIM 2 C (1) C (2) C (3)						
DIM 3 C (1) C (2) C (3) C (4) C (5)						
DIM 4 C (1) C (2) C (3)						
DIM 5 C (1) C (2)						

SRS _____

Table 4.1. Practice template for risk scoring of an AIS.

AIS ___1___

DIMENSION	$I(i)$	F	$W(i)$	$R(i)$	$W \times R$	$DRS(j)$
DIM 1						
C (1)	2	2	4	1	4	
C (2)	1	2	2	2	4	
C (3)	4	2	8	2	16	
C (4)	$\frac{3}{10}$	2 ___	$\frac{6}{20}$	3 ___	$\frac{18}{42}$	42.0
DIM 2						
C (1)	3	10/3	10	1	10	
C (2)	2	10/3	20/3	2	40/3	
C (3)	$\frac{1}{6}$	10/3 ___	$\frac{10/3}{20}$	3 ___	$\frac{10}{33.3}$	33.3
DIM 3						
C (1)	4	4/3	16/3	3	16	
C (2)	2	4/3	8/3	2	16/3	
C (3)	5	4/3	20/3	1	20/3	
C (4)	1	4/3	4/3	2	8/3	
C (5)	$\frac{3}{15}$	4/3 ___	$\frac{4}{20}$	3 ___	$\frac{12}{42.7}$	42.7
DIM 4						
C (1)	1	10/3	10/3	3	10	
C (2)	3	10/3	10	3	30	
C (3)	$\frac{2}{6}$	10/3 ___	$\frac{20/3}{20}$	1 ___	$\frac{46.7}{46.7}$	46.7
DIM 5						
C (1)	1	20/3	20/3	2	40/3	
C (2)	$\frac{2}{3}$	20/3 ___	$\frac{40/3}{20}$	1 ___	$\frac{40/3}{26.7}$	26.7

SRS ___191.4___

Note:
1st Order SRS (Range = 20 to 60) = DRS(1) = 42.0.
2nd Order SRS (Range = 100 to 300) = SRS = 191.4.

Table 4.2. Dimension risk scores and system risk scores for AIS 1.

AIS   2

DIMENSION	$I(i)$	F	$W(i)$	$R(i)$	$W \times R$	$DRS(j)$
DIM 1						
C (1)	4	2	8	3	24	
C (2)	2	2	4	1	4	
C (3)	1	2	2	2	4	
C (4)	3	2	6	1	6	
	10	—	20	—	38	38.0
DIM 2						
C (1)	2	10/3	20/3	3	20	
C (2)	1	10/3	10/3	1	10/3	
C (3)	3	10/3	10	2	20	
	6	—	20	—	43.3	43.3
DIM 3						
C (1)	5	4/3	20/3	3	20	
C (2)	3	4/3	4	1	4	
C (3)	1	4/3	4/3	2	8/3	
C (4)	2	4/3	8/3	1	8/3	
C (5)	4	4/3	16/3	3	16	
	15	—	20	—	45.4	45.4
DIM 4						
C (1)	1	10/3	10/3	2	40/3	
C (2)	3	10/3	10	1	10	
C (3)	2	10/3	20/3	3	10	
	6	—	20	—	33.3	33.3
DIM 5						
C (1)	2	20/3	40/3	1	40/3	
C (2)	1	20/3	20/3	1	40/3	
	3	—	20	—	20	20.0

SRS   180.0

Note:
1st Order SRS (Range = 20 to 60) = DRS(1) = 38.0
2nd Order SRS (Range = 100 to 300) = SRS = 180.0

Table 4.3. Dimension risk scores and system risk scores for AIS 2.

Application Name	Rating	% Review This Period	Adjusted Rating	% Total of all Ratings	Review Days

Figure 4.3. Allocating review time by application worksheet.

Application Name	Rating	% Review This Period	Adjusted Rating	% Total of all Ratings	Review Days
FIRST	90	60%	54	27%	40.5
SECOND	80	40%	32	16%	24
THIRD	70	20%	14	7%	10.5
FOURTH	60	100%	60	30%	45
FIFTH	50	80%	40	20%	30

Figure 4.4. Allocating review time by application worksheet.

Part 2

Conducting Reviews
of Application
Systems

Quality Assurance Review of an Application System

This chapter will examine what QA should do when reviewing an application. The "what" will be subdivided into goals, methods, and performance. In order to appreciate system problems, we will examine the reasons why some data processing applications are not successful.

The QA group is an aid to the data processing manager in solving the business problems of the organization. This objective must remain paramount as it performs its tasks. The QA group should undertake its review by a top-down approach, starting with management considerations: First, will the goals of the system solve the business problem? Second, are the methods in accordance with the organization's method of doing work? And third, will the data processing tasks be performed at a reasonable cost? The review approach is supportive of evaluating these three management considerations.

It is because quality assurance groups in different organizations perform different tasks, that this chapter discusses goals, methods, and performance independently. Most groups begin evaluating methods. It is only after they have achieved this successfully that they expand to review of goals and performance.

REVIEWING COMPUTER SYSTEMS APPLICATIONS

The QA review is a peer group activity. This means the project manager is reviewed by other project managers. The reviewers may be organizationally in a QA group, but they are part of the data processing department. Frequently the reviewers are good friends of the individuals being reviewed. The context and framework of the review must be taken from this perspective. The questions and procedures undertaken in the review must be fair, approved by supervisors, and in the best interest of the project being reviewed.

The QA group should have established a charter prior to undertaking reviews. The object of the charter is to define the scope of work undertaken during the review. The scope can involve goals, methods, and performance.

The easiest way to begin the QA function is to review methods. However, keep in mind that the objective of a computerized application is to solve a business problem. Even the best designed computer system in the world, developed exactly in accordance with the organization's methods of doing work, is a failure if it doesn't solve the business problem.

The business problem must be analyzed from the viewpoint of the user. Listed below are examples of typical business problems in four industries.

Banks. Should the bank make a loan to a specific individual and for what purposes?

Insurance. Is an individual insurable for the coverage being requested?

Retail. Should a customer be extended the amount of credit being requested?

Government. Is a recipient eligible for the service being requested?

It is apparent that these are not computer problems; they are business problems. The computer may or may not be utilized in solving a business problem. Too frequently, computer systems personnel come to believe that all business problems can be solved with the computer. This leads us back to the three areas of quality assurance illustrated in Figure 5.1.

The goals of a system should be aimed at solving a specific business problem. If QA is involved in goal review, then it needs to seriously consider whether or not the computer is the best mechanism to solve the business problem. The QA group normally becomes involved when the computer is being considered as an aid or solution to the business

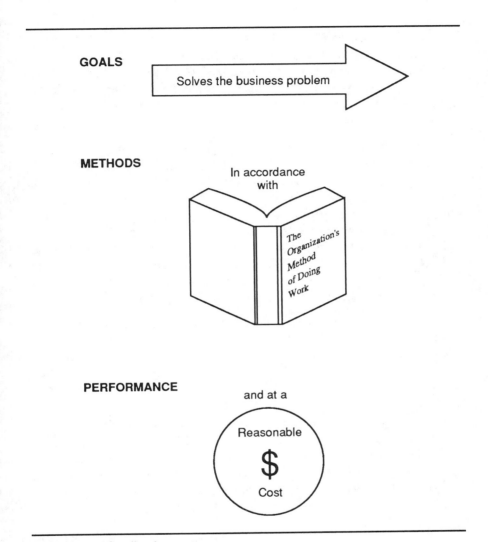

GOALS

Solves the business problem

METHODS

In accordance with

The Organization's Method of Doing Work

PERFORMANCE

and at a

Reasonable

$

Cost

Figure 5.1. Quality Assurance areas.

problem. In these cases, its function is to determine if the computer can assist in solving the business problem.

The main thrust of the review will be to determine that the methods utilized in the computer system are in compliance with the organization's methods. This includes all the policies and procedures (standards) of the organization that affect the application under review.

They need to consider the policies and procedures of the area being computerized as well as methods of the data processing department. For example, if the system being computerized is a bank's demand deposit system, the rules within the application should be consistent with the demand deposit department's policies and procedures, and consistent with banking regulations.

Some groups become involved in performance. Quality assurance personnel are employees of the organization and should be concerned with the overall well-being of the organization. Even where performance is not an integral part of their function, they should be alert to gross negligence, sloppy work, and poor performance. Obviously, a cursory review does not entail a performance review but, rather, a broad judgment between good and bad performance. The quality assurance reviewer has an obligation to make data processing management aware of poor performance. This may be done formally or informally, but it should be done. A detailed performance review is a complete and time-consuming task.

Companies that have adopted the team approach to design and programming have found that poor performance by an individual is usually detected early by the team.

SYSTEMS FAILURES

Many data processing departments prominently display the motto "If you must make a mistake, make a new one." This indicates that most people can accept mistakes the first time, but lose their tolerance if the same error is repeated. People who progress in organizations tend to learn from their own and others' failures. Failing to meet an objective or a goal can be a very frustrating but good educational experience.

Prior to commencing the discussion on how to review computer applications, let us first learn from the mistakes of others. An analysis of the literature on data processing over the past 20 years provides us some insight as to why systems have failed. It would be nicer to reverse this and discuss the traits that make systems succeed, but it is more difficult to isolate a specific success characteristic.

We will examine systems failures by categorizing them three ways: first, the reasons why systems failed to meet their goals; second, the reasons why project teams failed because of inadequate or unused methods; and third, reasons why systems failed to meet a desired level of performance. These should be studied and referred to continually as the QA group becomes involved in the review of a new application system.

Reasons for Failure to Achieve Goals

The system goal is to solve the business problem. Listed in Figure 5.2 and briefly explained below, are actual reasons why organizations failed to achieve their goals:

Lack of Knowledge by Users about Computer Capabilities and Limitations. Users know what is needed to solve their business problems, but frequently do not know whether those problems can be solved on the computer. In instances where they make unrealistic demands for computer systems, or fail to use the power of the computer, the installed application never realizes the potential possible when the user has a good comprehension of computer capabilities.

Computer Personnel Specify the System. Computer personnel have neither the responsibility for the accuracy and completeness of the processing by the system, nor an understanding as to what is needed to make the system successful. Unfortunately, many users abdicate their systems specification responsibility. Computer personnel tend to specify systems that work well on the computer, but may not be easy to set in practice. Frequently, these systems are overengineered for the caliber of people using the system in the performance of their daily work.

User's Fear of Loss of Control of the System to MIS Department. The user and the MIS department may develop adversary positions, particularly when the computer application encompasses the work of two or more departments. When users feel that the implementation of the system may result in a loss of responsibility or power to the data processing department, their objectivity and desire for success may be lost.

Lack of Interest by User Management. Without interest by user management, user personnel may not devote the necessary time and effort to making the system successful. If those responsible for the system detect a lackluster attitude by their management toward the system, it may lessen their desire to make the system successful.

Lack of Interest by Company Management. Top management lack of interest makes the implementation priority questionable. Either or both the user and data processing department may decide to let this system slide in lieu of other projects for which there is more management interest. The lack of motivation that results from lack of interest by user management occurs on the part of all involved when top management lacks interest.

Unwillingness to Accept Responsibility for the System Because It Belongs to the Other Guy. The "It's not my system" syndrome is a major cause of system failure. This was especially true in the early days of data processing when users assumed data processing to be responsible, and data processing assumed the user to be responsible. In many of these cases, the wrong person (the programmer) made systems decisions. This is one of the primary reasons current literature emphasizes the need for user involvement and responsibility.

SYSTEM GOAL: Solve the business problem.

Causes of Goal Failures:

- Lack of knowledge by users about computer capabilities and limitation
- Computer personnel specify the system
- User's fear of loss of control of the system to MIS department
- Lack of interest by user management
- Lack of interest by company management
- Unwillingness to accept responsibility for the system because it belongs to the "other guy"
- Organizational disputes over responsibilities
- Wrong application being developed
- No long-range systems plan

Figure 5.2. Systems failures — goals.

Organizational Disputes over Responsibilities. Many systems encompass the work and responsibilities of two or more departments. When these functions become consolidated into one system, it may be difficult to pinpoint organizational responsibility. Either both departments may feel responsible for a particular function, or neither department may assume responsibility. Top management should step in and resolve these organizational responsibility disputes as early as possible in the systems development process.

Wrong Application Being Developed. Many times the application being developed does not solve the business problem. It provides interesting information, information that may be helpful, and even information that is useful, but not at the proper time or in the proper format. For example, if the business problem is to determine whether or not an individual is insurable, but the data processing system does not contain the necessary attributes to make that decision, it has not been successful at solving the business problem.

No Long-Range Systems Plan. The objective of a systems plan is to make sure all the individual applications will fit together when complete. Without such a plan, there is no assurance that when the applications become operational, they will properly interconnect. For example, if a personnel system and a payroll system are developed independently at different times, they may collect data in different formats. When a decision is made to have the personnel system feed the payroll system, the data may be unexchangeable due to different formats, lengths, etc.

Systems Failures — Methods

The objective of reviewing system methods is to determine that the implementation conforms to the organization's policies and procedures. These policies and procedures ideally would be interpreted into standards. The causes of systems failures due to improper methods are listed in Figure 5.3 and briefly explained below.

Lack of Involvement by Users. Most organizations define responsibility by function. When users having responsibility for a function relinquish that responsibility to the data processing department, they are failing to follow the policies of their management. Top management has designated them responsible, and while they can delegate work they cannot delegate responsibility to the data processing department. This means users must be involved in the development of systems affecting their responsibility. Many organizations require by directive that users participate in the development of systems affecting their responsibility. Lack of involvement by users in systems development has frequently been called the number one cause of system failures.

Inadequate Planning. Speakers at many conferences on data processing joke that when you want to know what a system will cost you multiply the system development estimates by a factor. The only real discussion centers on whether the factor should be 3, 4, 5, etc. While many data processing managers try to substantiate their poor estimates by explaining that the product is custom made, the technology unknown, and the specifications changing, their arguments are unacceptable. The real cause is the lack of adequate planning. Planning may not produce exact costs in advance but will provide the criteria to advise management as soon as problems occur that can affect cost.

SYSTEM METHOD: Implementation conforms to the organization's policies and procedures (standards)

Causes of Methods Failures:

- Lack of involvement by users
- Inadequate planning
- Inadequate design
- Inadequate programming
- Inadequate testing
- Management unwillingness to enforce standards
- Lack of security
- Chaotic conversion

Figure 5.3. Systems failures — methods.

Inadequate Design. Systems analysts tend to overestimate their own abilities to solve problems at the later stages of systems development. This leads them to start programming prior to finalizing program specifications. The argument is that implementation can be facilitated, but practice has shown just the opposite. The structured top-down design approach places more attention on the design process and helps solve the problem of programming first and designing later.

Inadequate Programming. Programmers have argued that their work is an art and that to restrict them to standard programming methods lessens their creativity and performance. These arguments lead to situations in which the program logic and maintainability is dependent upon the continual employment of the programmer. Many organizations have found it easier to rewrite such programs than to understand and modify them. The use and enforcement of structured programming techniques will greatly enhance the maintainability of programs.

Inadequate Testing. Since it is impossible to test every possible condition that may be encountered in operation, testing is at best a risk situation. Also, testing is not one of the more rewarding aspects of a programmer's work. It is tedious, time-consuming, and unenjoyable. Therefore, unless adequate criteria are developed to determine when a system is acceptable, this phase tends to be cut short.

Management's Unwillingness to Enforce Standards. Data processing is extremely detailed. Effective standards likewise must be detailed, and enforcement requires some detection mechanism to know when standards are not being followed. If the mechanism is ineffective, or too late in the implementation process, management may be put in a difficult position of paying to redo work to conform to standards. Coupling these factors, many data processing managers are unwilling to "bite the bullet" and enforce standards regardless of the time and effort required.

Lack of Security. Far more than keeping unauthorized personnel from the computer room, security also involves the protection of input and output data. This protection is equally necessary against honest mistakes, incompetence, negligence, lack of interest, and other similar problems on the part of employees. Failure to protect information and programs has resulted in serious problems for many organizations.

Chaotic Conversion. Detailed planning is necessary if conversions are to be properly executed. Most analysts have little experience in this systems phase. Without adequate planning and control, a series of unexpected and time-consuming problems may develop resulting in the need for special programming, extra computer time, overtime operations, and all the other things one hopes will not happen just prior to a new system going operational.

Systems Failures — Performance

The objective of systems performance review is to determine that the system is implemented and operated at a reasonable cost. Causes of systems performance failures are listed in Figure 5.4 and explained briefly below.

SYSTEM PERFORMANCE: System is implemented and operated at a reasonable cost.

Causes of Performance Failures:

- Ambitions of systems and user personnel
- Human resistance to change
- Inadequate performance measurements
- Operating managers do not use the information generated by the computer
- High turnover of systems personnel
- Inadequate quality of systems design and project management
- Computer system overdesigned
- Manual support systems are underdesigned
- System provides too much information
- Late implementation
- Cost overruns
- Frequent changes of computer hardware and software
- Inflexible systems design
- Too many changes during the design process

Figure 5.4. Systems failures — performance.

Ambitions of Systems and User Personnel. Systems and user personnel may design applications more for their own personal whim and desires than for the organization's needs. For example, systems personnel may utilize a new hardware concept, such as on-line terminals, even though the application does not warrant the hardware. By manipulation of costs and schedules, however, the data processing professionals are able to justify the system.

Human Resistance to Change. There is a natural resistance to change by all people. This fact needs to be recognized and people reassured by explaining the reasons for the change and how they will be affected personally. The more that can be done to prepare people for the change, the higher the probability of success of the system.

Inadequate Performance Measurements. Unless management has developed adequate criteria, it is difficult to measure performance. Without being able to measure performance, management has little idea if and when the system is achieving even a minimal level of performance.

Operating Managers Do Not Use the Information Generated by the Computer. In the majority of computer system problems, the data to detect the problem were produced by the computer application but not acted upon by user personnel. Although this can be attributable to many causes, the fact remains that either the instructions and training were insufficient or users devoted too little time or interest. Ascertaining that error notification is causing some reaction should be made an integral part of first-line supervision's responsibility.

High Turnover of Systems Personnel. Because of the technical nature of data processing, and the extensive company background needed to develop an application, high turnover of systems personnel places any development project in jeopardy. Selection of systems personnel should take into account the stability of employment within an organization.

Computer System Overdesigned. Systems must be used by people. If the system is too complex for the mental capacity of the people who are using it, the system has problems. All systems design should take into account the caliber of personnel who will be putting data into the system and using data from the system.

Manual Support Systems Are Underdesigned. Too frequently, computer systems personnel put insufficient time and effort into the manual support systems. These include training, control, data reporting, authorization, and use of warning information produced by the system.

System Provides Too Much Information. We have all seen huge stacks of paper produced by high-speed printers. If people must have certain information to perform their function correctly, it should not be difficult for them to obtain that information from computer reports. It is essential that information be presented in a format where it is easy to locate, and in a visible format.

Late Implementation. Processing rules should be frozen during the latter parts of systems implementation; changes during the testing phase make evaluation of the system difficult. When a system implementation falls far behind scheduled implementation date, people lose interest and faith in the system. Also, continually changing conditions make it difficult to keep a system frozen for very long. Late implementation adds to the failure rate of systems.

Cost Overruns. Substantial cost overruns lessen management's faith in the project team. This loss of faith can magnify what otherwise might be minor problems in the system. However, "substantial cost overruns" may suggest existence of more than minor problems.

Frequent Changes of Computer Hardware and Software. Each change to system hardware and software has an effect on an application under development. Even where there is not a direct effect on the system (i.e., change in operating system version), there can be a ripple effect. Problems encountered with hardware and software changes can delay system implementation.

Inflexible Systems Design. Application systems in most organizations operate under a changing environment throughout the system life. The less flexible the system, the less it is able to incorporate changes necessitated by business conditions. When the series of items that cannot be incorporated into the system exceeds a certain level, the application must be replaced by a new system.

Too Many Changes During a Design Process. The system design is normally structured around and optimized for certain business characteristics (volume of business, for example). When business characteristics or the systems designers fail to recognize which business characteristics are pertinent, the design specifications must be changed. Should the number of changes become great enough, the system structure may no longer be effective. Also, when changes get too frequent, both the cost of the system and the implementation date may exceed expectations. This, in turn, causes other problems that can lead to the downfall of the system.

Top-Down Review

A systems review must begin at the highest level and work down to the lowest level. This is called a *top-down review* and its initial objective is to determine if the application system will solve the business problems according to the methods of the organization and at a reasonable cost. Without a top-down approach, the review may lose sight of that objective.

A top-down review by QA asks: What are the goals of the system? What methods need to be followed during implementation? And what level of performance is expected? Only after answers to these questions have been established should the review get into the details of systems design and programming. The review begins with a very broad scope, and then works its way down to lower and lower levels of detail.

The top-down review methodology outlined in Figure 5.5 shows each level splitting into the components it comprises. Level 1 items include reviewing, meeting goals, using methods, and achieving a reasonable level of performance. Each level 1 subdivides into a series of level 2 areas of review. In Figure 5.5 only level 1 of methods shows this

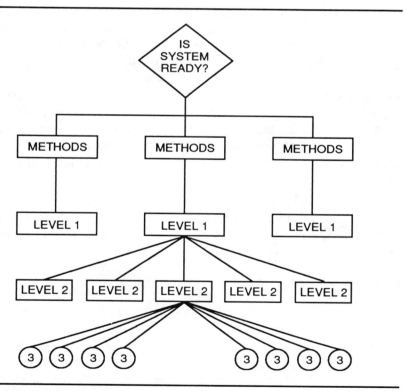

Figure 5.5. Top-down review.

breakdown, but in reality each level 1 is further divided into a group of level 2s. Each level 2, then, is further subdivided into a series of level 3 items. Thus, if we were to see Figure 5.5 broken out for each level 2 and level 3, it would be an extremely complex chart.

Level 1 of the top-down review is a very broad review of an evaluation area. This, in turn, is supported by a lower (level 2) review, which focuses on the implementation approach. The level 2 gets more specific in further subdefining what is meant by the area under review. For example, if we are reviewing methods (level 1), level 2 will involve a specific approach, such as standards for the system design phase. The third level goes into still more detail. In a review of methods, the third level review would determine if the systems designers understood the systems design standards.

Let us see how a top-down approach could be used in a court to interrogate a witness. A prosecutor is trying to establish a witness's presence at the scene of a crime. She begins by a general (level 1) question asking if anything unusual occurred on a specific date. If the witness says yes, the prosecutor proceeds to (level 2) questioning, which should lead to the location at which something occurred. The questioning would then proceed to level 3, which would get very specific about what the witness saw and heard at the location where the crime occurred. This is not to liken a computer system review to a criminal case but, rather, to illustrate that the most effective review techniques begin at the general and work down to the specific.

The remaining parts of this chapter will explain these three areas in detail. Keep in mind that this chapter is talking about "what" should be accomplished in the review. "How" the review is accomplished will be covered in Chapter 7.

REVIEW OF GOALS

A review of systems application goals is the most valuable contribution that a QA group can make, but it may also be the most difficult work the group has to do. QA cannot establish goals. If goals are not clearly stated, QA cannot determine if they are or can be met. Thus, QA is not an all-powerful group evaluating the performance of the project team. What they are doing is reviewing whether or not preestablished goals have been met. The review items for goals are listed in Figure 5.6.

Level 1

- Solves the business problem.

Level 2

- System goals are realistic.
- System goals are achievable.
- System goals are compatible with the goals of the organization.
- System goals are compatible with the goals of the user.

Level 3

- Business problem solution is compatible with system goals.
- Users can comprehend and use the system.
- User personnel want the system.
- Adequate resources are available to implement the system.
- System will be ready when needed.
- System will have a reasonable lifespan.
- Implemented system can run with existing technology for a reasonable period.
- System technology is understood by the organization.
- A plan exists to meet goals.
- Goals are achieved.

Figure 5.6. Review of goals.

Level 1

Level 1 items for review are the broad system problems to be solved. An example previously used was ascertaining whether or not an individual is insurable. This is, perhaps, only one of the many business problems that would be solved in a systems application by an insurance company.

Each level 1 goal needs to be further reviewed by four level 2 items. Again, goal review is not meant to usurp the authority of the data processing project manager. It is intended to review what the project team is doing to ascertain that its plans are in accordance with the goals given to that project team. The four level 2 items are:

System Goals Are Realistic. This item determines that the goal is a realistic (i.e., achievable) goal for the systems designer. For example, the system's being able to answer the question "Is individual X insurable?" appears to be a realistic goal for a computer application. The quality assurance group would have to determine that there is enough quantitative data to be evaluated to ascertain if an individual is insurable. However, should the goal be to accept only good risks, and there are neither adequate rules nor enough quantitative data to define a good risk, the goal could be easily determined to be unachievable. We could define an achievable goal as one that can be accomplished with the data and rules available.

System Goals Are Achievable. The established goals should be achievable with the existing technology and resources. For example, if the system goal is to put 500 terminals on-line with an average response time of one second or less, and a maximum response time of five seconds, the QA group could readily determine if this was achievable for their organization.

System Goals Are Compatible with the Goals of the Organization. This presupposes that the goals of the organization are documented. The goals of any one application system must be subservient to the goals of the organization. For example, if a goal of an organization is to compete without the use of bribes and kickbacks, then a system goal that allows for bribes and kickbacks is incompatible with the goals of the organization.

System Goals Are Compatible with the Goals of the User. The goals of the application and the goals of the user should be compatible. For example, if the user has the goal of shipping product within 24 hours after the receipt of the order, the system should be supportive of that goal. To design a system that takes more than 24 hours to process the paperwork before an order can be shipped would be incompatible with the desires of the user. Data processing personnel often make decisions affecting user goals without considering the impact of those decisions on the goal.

The third level of review is also aimed at reviewing documented established goals. It cannot be overemphasized that quality assurance is reviewing conformance to previously established criteria and statements. The more measurable those goals, statements, or criteria, the more successful quality assurance can be in the performance of its goal review function. The more subjective the judgment that has to be made by quality assurance, the more difficult the task. Bear in mind that the quality assurance function is a type of peer group review. The more objective the review, the better will be the working relationship with data processing personnel. Data processing management should want very specific systems goals, and where they exist quality assurance can do an effective job in reviewing conformance to those goals.

Each level 2 item can be further subdivided by a series of level 3 items. Let us first discuss the level 3 items and then show how they relate to the level 2 items. The level 3 items are as follows.

Business Problem Solution Is Compatible with System Goals. The project team has the task of developing a system that will solve the business problem. This is the goal of the system. The quality assurance group should look at this solution from the viewpoint of whether it does or does not solve the business problem.

Users Can Comprehend and Use the System. The solution to the business problem should be at a level comprehensible by the users of the system. The rules of the system must not be so complex that the people who have to work with them cannot understand them. Also, the data and results produced by the system should be readily understandable and usable by the users of the system. The system must not produce results that require higher competency than is available. The information in the system must be organized and presented in such a format that it is readily usable for the intended purpose.

User Personnel Want the System. The system as explained to the user is well received by the user. In other words, the user is not fighting the implementation of the system as proposed.

Adequate Resources Are Available to Implement the System. Resources refers to hardware and software, quantity of people and dollars, as well as caliber of personnel.

System Will Be Ready When Needed. The schedules as proposed are realistic within the resource constraints. The quality assurance group should also go one step further and see that the dates proposed for implementation are compatible with the needs of the user for that system.

System Will Have a Reasonable Lifespan. Based on the QA group's understanding of technology and the plans of the data processing department, the proposed system will have a life equivalent to that proposed when the project was approved by management.

Implemented System Can Run with Existing Technology for a Reasonable Period. The quality assurance group should have an appreciation of both the technological improvements in hardware and software and the plans of the organization to utilize that technology. These considerations need to be raised and evaluated by the QA group if the project team has not already contemplated these events.

System Technology Is Understood by the Organization. Technology in this instance refers primarily to that used by the system designers and programmers. If they are unfamiliar with the technology used in this application, the project is in jeopardy.

A Plan Exists to Meet Goals. In the early phases of the system development process, QA needs to examine the plan for achieving the goals. While the other items are the criteria to be included in the plan, they are not the plan itself.

Goals Are Achieved. Prior to implementation, the QA group should ascertain that the goals are actually achieved.

As you study the three levels of system review, keep in mind that each has a different impact on the project. Level 1 discusses the area itself. For example, in reviewing goals, level 1 is specific project goals. If the application has 15 goals, then there are 15 level 1 items to be covered by the QA. Level 2 discusses the approach taken by the project team for each of the level 1 items. The QA group can now begin to subdivide each goal into its review components for purposes of analysis. The level 2 questions are further subdivided by level 3 items. Some level 3 items listed in Figure 5.6 are more appropriate than others.

The Goals Evaluation Matrix (Figure 5.7) shows the relationship between level 2 items and level 3 items. The level 2 items are listed across the top and the level 3 items down the left-hand side of the matrix. The legend of the matrix shows how appropriate each level 3 item is to the level 2 items.

Examining Figure 5.7 we see the first level 3 item (Business problem solution is compatible with system goals.) is appropriate to whether the goal is realistic. A number "2" in the "realistic" column states that it is appropriate. In other words, a "realistic" goal should be compatible

REVIEW CRITERIA	Realistic	Achievable	Compatible with organization goals	Compatible with user goals	
1. Business problems is compatible with systems goals.	2	1	3	3	
2. Users can comprehend and use the system.	3	2	2	3	
3. User personnel want the system.	2	2	1	3	
4. Adequate resources available to implement the system.	3	3	1	1	
5. System will be developed when needed.	3	3	3	3	
6. System will have a reasonable life.	3	1	3	3	
7. Implemented system can run with existing technology for a reasonable period.	3	1	3	3	
8. System technology is understood by the organization.	2	2	2	2	
9. A plan exists to meet goals.	3	3	3	3	
10. Goals are achieved.	2	3	3	3	

Legend:
3 = very appropriate
2 = appropriate
1 = unappropriate

Figure 5.7. Goals evaluation matrix.

with the business problem solution. Thus, a number "2" in the "realistic" column indicates appropriateness of the level 2 item to the level 3 item.

On the other hand, for the goal to be achievable, it does not have to be compatible with the business problem solution. Thus, the "achievable" column is noted as inappropriate or a number "1" in the "achievable" column. However, the business problem solution must be compatible with systems goals for the level 2 items of "compatible with user goals." Each of these two is marked with a number "3" showing a very appropriate item.

Using Figure 5.6 and Figure 5.7, the QA group should be able to determine what it should accomplish in reviewing application goals.

REVIEW OF METHODS

The main part of any review will be the review of methods. (See Figure 5.8.) The one task almost universally requested of QA groups is to provide assurance that policies, procedures, and standards are being followed. This is a detailed and time-consuming but essential task.

In the case of methods, level 1 review has a single item. Project implementation conforms to the organization's policies and procedures. These policies and procedures should be incorporated into standards. Here again, as with its review goals, the quality assurance group needs objective items for review. When data processing management has adequately instructed personnel in the methods they are to utilize, adherence to those standards may be reviewed. On the other hand, if the quality assurance group is being asked to act as both judge and jury (to develop standards for each application and then review adherence to those standards), its function will be argumentative and probably ineffective.

Level 2 items are divided among the phases of the systems development life cycle. Each of the five phases of the system development life cycle of interest to quality assurance is a level 2 item.

1. *Conforms to system justification standards.* The standards developed for the feasibility or justification phase have been or will be followed.

2. *Conforms to system design standards.* The policies and procedures of the department relating to specification of the system have been or will be followed.

Level 1
- Implementation conforms to the organization's policies and procedures (standards).

Level 2
- Conforms to system justification standards.
- Conforms to system design standards.
- Conforms to system program standards.
- Conforms to system test standards.
- Conforms to system conversion standards.

Level 3
- Standards are realistic for this system.
- An adequate plan is developed and followed for implementing the standards.
- The designers understand the standards.
- The standards will be in effect when the system becomes operational.
- System standards do not conflict with organization, industry, or government standards.
- Procedures are taken to assure that standards will be followed.
- Users are trained to use the system.
- System is adequately documented.

Figure 5.8. Review of methods.

---

3. *Conforms to system program standards.* The method by which programmers must specify and code programs has or will be followed.

4. *Conforms to system test standards.* The methods and extent to which systems and programs are to be tested have been or will be followed.

5. *Conforms to system conversion standards.* All the procedures to be followed in the conversion process have been or will be followed.

Level 3 takes on more importance in methods review because it is within level 3 that the review gets specific. Moreover, the level 3 items for a methods review apply to most of the level 2 items. In the review of methods, there are nine level 3 items, which are briefly explained below:

Standards Are Realistic for This System. Just as a law does not apply in every situation, neither does a standard. Both the project team and the review group must take a realistic approach to the application of standards. If following a standard would be detrimental to the system and not following the standard would not incur any present or future hardship on others, procedures should be available to get an exception from the standard. In many organizations, QA has the authority to waive the standard for a particular situation.

An Adequate Plan Is Developed and Followed for Implementing the Standards. People tend to do what they are instructed and that on which they are evaluated. If the project team considers following standards important to the project, standards probably will be followed. This can be made even more likely by having data processing management use adherence to standards as a criterion for review of project members.

Most Data Processing Departments Have High Personnel Turnover. This means that new members to the department must be continually instructed in the use of standards. Also, in the course of their assignments, members of the project team may come in contact with specific standards only infrequently and irregularly. Thus, an important part of the review process is to determine that the standards are known and understood by the project team.

The Standards Will Be in Effect When the System Becomes Operational. Changes to hardware, software, and implementation methodology necessitate a continual revision to standards. If a project is being developed today, and a new set of standards will be in place when the system becomes operational, the project team must work with the new standards.

Systems Standards Do Not Conflict with Organization, Industry, or Government Standards. The QA group cannot be expected to be "all knowing." However, they do have an obligation to ask questions that would indicate any potential conflict between data processing standards and other standards. This conflict might have occurred after the data processing standards were developed, or the standards may have been developed in ignorance of other standards. In either case the QA group has an obligation to be alert to trends in the literature, trade press, and organization publications regarding potential conflicts.

Procedures Are Available to Assure That Standards Will Be Followed. QA cannot be expected to look at every line of code or documentation to determine that every standard was followed. They should ascertain that the project team, through project supervision, will be performing this type of review. This then permits the quality assurance group either to evaluate only that plan or make a few tests to determine if the plan is functioning as developed.

Users Are Trained to Use the System. "Users" in this context include personnel in data processing control, operations, and input preparation, as well as the users of the system and data.

System Is Adequately Documented. Documentation requirements cover all phases of the system development life cycle. The quality assurance group requires documentation for their review; and second, and more important, documentation is needed to protect the organization when systems problems occur. An organization with inadequate documentation is perhaps most vulnerable during the systems development phase. Without adequate documentation, loss of one or two key people at that time can necessitate the system being completely redesigned. Once the system becomes operational, there is at least enough documentation so that the system can be run. However, during the development phase, many of the ideas and approaches are within people's minds.

Figure 5.9 shows the interrelationship between the level 2 and level 3 items for methods review. Note the appropriateness of most level 3 items to the level 2 items.

REVIEW OF PERFORMANCE

The review of performance implies that there are established measurable levels of performance. Again, QA cannot be asked to be both judge and jury; it cannot be asked to establish levels of performance for each project and then review adherence to those levels of performance. What it can do is review adherence to predetermined criteria or levels of performance.

Many approaches can be taken to performance review. The level 1 criterion suggests that a realistic performance expectation is that the system is being implemented and operated at a reasonable cost. What the department

REVIEW CRITERIA / GOALS	System is in conformance with				
	Justification Standards	Design Standards	Program Standards	Test Standards	Convert Standards
1. Standards are realistic for this system.	3	3	3	3	3
2. An adequate plan is developed and followed for implementing the standards.	3	3	3	3	3
3. The designers understand the standards.	3	3	3	3	3
4. The standards will be in effect when the system becomes operational.	1	2	3	1	1
5. System standards do not conflict with organization, industry, or government standards.	3	3	3	3	3
6. Procedures are taken to assure that standards will be followed.	3	3	3	3	3
7. Users are trained to use the system.	1	1	1	1	1
8. System is adequately documented.	2	3	3	2	2

Legend:
3 = very appropriate
2 = appropriate
1 = unappropriate

Figure 5.9. Methods evaluation matrix.

or organization considers reasonable should be documented in performance standards.

Members of QA may participate in the setting of performance standards, and when this is done department wide, it is a good assignment for them. They can still review all projects against those performance standards and not be criticized for bias against one project. It is important to emphasize that in a peer group situation the review must be made in accordance to well-recognized and previously determined standards.

For review of performance, there are five level 2 items. These, plus the level 1 and level 3 items, are listed in Figure 5.10. The level 2 items are outlined below.

System Is Cost-Effective. The key element in this is that the system does the job well. It may be more costly than other means of doing the job, but in total it is more effective because of considerations such as time, customer service, or ease of use.

System Optimizes People and Machines. A total system is a combination of people effort and machine effort. The system should utilize people for what they do best and machines for what they do best. Obviously, you do not want to stop a computerized run for a small piece that can be better performed by people than machines. However, in the general context of the system, extremely cumbersome and complex routines should not be developed if that function can be readily performed by people without interruption to the system flow.

System Optimizes Hardware and Software. This is a design function focused on getting software to maximize hardware usage. On the other hand, another piece of hardware may be required to maximize a particular software package. This is a technical aspect of system design, but one that requires attention.

System Meets System Criteria. It has been said that nothing is more futile than to do a job well if the job need not be done at all. If the system does not solve the business problems, performance is irrelevant.

System Conversion Is Economical. One must not underestimate the impact of a system conversion. Many major problems have occurred in organizations because they underestimated the importance of performing the conversion well. The conversion process is a system within a system and must be so performed.

There are 10 level 3 items for review of performance. Consider as you review these that there is a continual conflict between effectiveness and economy, hardware and software utilization, and people versus machine utilization. The ideal system optimizes the trade-offs needed to resolve each of these conflicts. The level 3 items are explained briefly below:

Standards of Performance Have Been Established. Performance cannot be evaluated unless standards of performance have been established and the people involved understand the level of performance expected of them. Performance frequently is a trade-off between resources, time, abilities, etc. Therefore, to achieve a level of performance, the system designer must recognize these trade-offs and work them to his advantage.

People Know What Level of Performance Is Expected. An important aspect of quality is advising people what is expected from them. Quality is achieved by specifying quality, telling people what is expected from them, and then monitoring to be assured the expected level of quality was achieved.

Criteria Are Established to Evaluate Performance. The standards of performance must be interpreted into criteria for each specific system. These then become the level of performance the system designer tries to achieve or exceed.

Meeting Performance Levels Will Result in Rewards for Individuals. If the only criteria for evaluating project personnel is getting the system in on time and within budget, then performance will be secondary. If, on the other hand, performance is considered important, people must be evaluated and rewarded for meeting or exceeding expected levels of performance.

Schedules Have Been Established. Schedules are a category of performance in that it is an objective for the system designer to achieve.

Budgets Have Been Developed. Budgets, like schedules, are a level of performance which the system designer must meet.

Level 1
- System is implemented and operated at a reasonable cost.

Level 2
- System is cost-effective.
- System optimizes people and machines.
- System meets system criteria.
- System conversion is economical.

Level 3
- Standards of performance have been established.
- People know what level of performance is expected.
- Criteria are established to evaluate performance.
- Meeting performance levels will result in rewards for individuals.
- Schedules have been established.
- Budgets have been developed.
- Support systems are evaluated.
- Users are pleased with system performance.
- Design is changed frequently during design phase.
- System optimization alternatives are evaluated.

Figure 5.10. Review of performance.

Support Systems Are Evaluated. The performance of the computerized portion of a system must not degrade the performance of the total system. It is necessary to look at the total system, the computerized segment plus all the support segments. In evaluating performance, the total system needs to be considered.

Users Are Pleased with Systems Performance. There are many subtleties to be considered in performance which are difficult to quantify. One subjective judgment that should be considered is user evaluation of performance.

Design Is Changed Frequently During Design Phase. The project team should be evaluated on performing the project's tasks in an economical and effective manner. If the team's approach and plans are continually changing direction, performance must be judged as poor.

System Optimization Alternatives Are Evaluated. Effectiveness and efficiency, even with standards, can be difficult to review. Quality assurance can review adherence to standards, but cannot review whether all alternatives have been adequately evaluated. Thus, a quality assurance group has to assume the project team has considered alternatives and picked a reasonable one to implement.

The relationship between the level 2 and level 3 performance items is given in Figure 5.11. A review of this matrix begins to show some of the differences between effectiveness and economy, and optimization of people and machines, and optimization of hardware and software.

SUMMARY

In reviewing applications, the quality assurance group can consider goals, methods, and performance. Whether they review each area or some combination, this is basically a review of adherence or conformance to the policies and procedures of the organization. The data processing policies and procedures must be put in perspective with those of the entire organization. The group must also determine that the policies and procedures are reasonable and applicable to the particular application being reviewed.

The application review should be done with a top-down approach. The end result of the review is to advise the data processing manager whether to implement the application. This advice will be based on a review of such items as efficiency, economy, proper systems design, whether or not the application solves the business problems, and other factors. The top-down review approach never loses sight of the reason for undertaking the review. In other words, the means never become more important than the end.

This chapter was designed to explain "what" QA should accomplish during the review of an application. A three-level review was suggested. The first level is very broad, and related to the objectives of the review. A second level is oriented toward reviewing the approach taken by the project team to achieve its goals and objectives. The third level deals with the design and implementation of the computer system.

In this approach, levels 1 and 2 are oriented to whether or not the business problems were solved. The third level examines the implementation to the problem, which is the computerized application.

REVIEW CRITERIA	System cost-effective	Optimizes people and machines	Optimizes hardware and software	Meets system criteria	Conversion economical
1. Standards of performance have been established.	3	1	1	3	3
2. People know what level of performance is expected.	3	1	1	3	3
3. Criteria is established to evaluate performance.	3	3	3	3	3
4. Meeting performance level will result in rewards for individual.	3	3	3	3	3
5. Schedules have been established.	3	1	1	1	3
6. Budgets have been developed.	3	1	1	1	2
7. Support systems are evaluated.	1	1	1	3	2
8. Users pleased with system performance.	2	3	1	3	1
9. Design is changed frequently during design phase.	3	3	3	3	3
10. System optimization alternatives evaluated.	2	3	3	1	2

Legend:
3 = very appropriate
2 = appropriate
1 = unappropriate

Figure 5.11. Performance evaluation matrix.

Initiating Systems Review

Quality assurance groups should develop a plan for utilizing their resources each year (or more frequently). The plan should identify which computer application projects will be reviewed during the planning period and must be compatible with the data processing department's plan. When changes occur in the data processing department plan, the QA plan should be modified accordingly.

The initiation of a review is important because it establishes the ground rules and sets the tone of the review. Work must be completed prior to the review. This preparatory work encompasses gaining an understanding of the system and its implementation plan, determining at which point(s) in the development process reviews should be made, and developing the plan and staffing necessary to accomplish those reviews. Time expended in planning will result in a more efficient and effective review.

The review of an application begins with an entrance conference that provides an opportunity for members of the project team and the QA group to get to know one another and to discuss what will be involved during the review. The entrance conference permits QA to explain their function and objectives. They can also present the merits and advantages to the project team of having a review for their project. It is also the time to explain to the project team what is expected of them during the review process so that each group is aware of the commitment and responsibilities of the other parties.

PREPARATION FOR A QUALITY ASSURANCE GROUP

The first step in a review is authorizing the commitment of resources to conduct the review. To limit dissipation of resources on unauthorized reviews, this should be a formal step. The control over the start and stop of reviews is an important step in controlling the use of QA resources.

Preparation for a review is designed to provide the QA team with enough information to plan its review strategy. Six types of information are to be obtained.

1. *Comprehension of the system objectives.* QA needs to understand what the system is trying to accomplish so that it can estimate the risk the organization is subjected to by this system.

2. *Identification of the implementors.* The caliber and experience of the staff is an important factor in determining the depth of QA involvement.

3. *How the system is to be implemented.* Which techniques are to be used for implementation.

4. *Other parties involved in reviewing this system.* If internal or external audit is involved, that will affect the extent of the review.

5. *Characteristics of the system.* QA needs to know the volumes of transactions, types of master data needed, impact on other computerized applications, and so on.

6. *Schedules and budget.* These are evaluated to indicate the magnitude of the project together with the project team's conception of its timetable.

The aim of preparing for a review is to gain as much information about that system as possible, normally from sources other than the project team. That does not mean information is not requested of the project team. However, meetings, interviews, or conferences do not take place with the project team at this time. The objective is to gather information to prepare the review team to discuss the project intelligently at the first meeting with the project team.

There are many sources of information about a new project that do not require consultation with the project team (see Figure 6.1).

- System's formal documentation
- User manuals
- Correspondence
- Budgets
- Meeting notes
- Discussions with current system users
- Discussions with current system MIS personnel
- Discussions with current third-party users
- Industry reports
- Government reports
- Current system operating statistics
- Internal auditors

Figure 6.1. Sources of information for review planning.

System's formal documentation. The volume of letters and memorandums and/or more formalized feasibility reports will vary greatly depending upon the point at which QA becomes involved.

User manuals. Policies and procedures of the user department that relate to the application, but not necessarily to the computerized system.

Correspondence. These can be any type of correspondence relating to either the existing or new application. Letters may outline problems, justify the need for a new system, or discuss problems or areas of concern.

Budgets. Data processing annual budgets can contain extensive information about new projects.

Meeting notes. The project team may have had one or more meetings relating to the new system. Within these notes can be the thinking, planning, and alternatives considered.

Discussions with users of current system. Much information can be obtained from people working with the outputs of an existing system, if there is one. While this will not describe the new application, it will help describe the user's needs.

Discussions with MIS system personnel working with current system. The problems, shortcomings, and unfulfilled needs within the existing system provide background information to review the adequacy of a new application.

Discussions with current third party users. Third party users are customers of the organization as well as staff groups and management. While not as directly associated with the system as the user having responsibility for input to the system, these third party users frequently can provide insight into the problems and needs of the system.

Industry reports. Trends in industrial problems are often reported in trade literature. This can provide quality assurance personnel with some insight into long-term considerations for the application.

Government reports. Many government agencies do in-depth studies on industries, applications, and other topics which can provide background material helpful in preparing to review an application.

Current system operating statistics. If the application being reviewed is replacing or enhancing an existing system, operating statistics are a valuable input. Systems such as IBM's System Management Facility have extensive information on transactions, number of inquiries, and so on that are helpful when hardware and software considerations are involved.

Internal auditors. Auditing continually evaluates the main operating divisions of an organization. At the end of each of these audits, the auditors prepare a report which lists in detail problems encountered during that audit. A review of those reports and discussions with the auditors who perform them, will make quality assurance personnel aware of the control weaknesses that exist in the user department(s) and/or current application.

Is it worth looking at all of this wide variety of information sources. The answer is yes. No one source can provide all the information needed. The reviewer needs to build a complete picture, and this requires examining all the individual pieces. It is like assembling a jigsaw puzzle; once the individual pieces begin to fit together, solutions become much more obvious.

During this fact-finding process, QA personnel should make notes summarizing the odd bits of information collected. These notes should contain topical headings. At the end of the preparation process, the individual can sort and then review all the notes relating to each topic. At that time, bits of isolated information begin to fit into a pattern. For example, the trade literature on electronic funds transfer systems shows problems with user acceptance. If the project team indicated high user acceptance, the QA could deduce unrealistic estimates on user acceptance.

The manager of the QA function is responsible for controlling the review process. The initial quality control review point occurs when a project is authorized for review. Authorization for review should include allocation of resources (both people and dollars), assignment of personnel, and a tentative schedule.

Figure 6.2 provides a potential project review control sheet. QA groups can use this model to prepare one sheet for each project. The sheet becomes the authorization document to review a project. It also provides some statistical data to be recorded about the review as it progresses. To complete this form, the following is necessary:

1. Project name — title used by the data processing department.

2. Project number — accounting number for accumulating project costs and for control purposes.

3. Date began — date on which the quality assurance review started.

4. Project budget — both dollars and days allocated for the review.

5. Project team — individuals assigned to the team.

6. Review process — a list of estimated starting dates for all the phases of the review plus budget allocated to each of these review phases. As the project commences, the actual starting date for each review phase can be entered as well as the actual cost to complete each phase of the review. Space is provided to indicate that working documents of the review have been analyzed by a supervisor, who initializes the "reviewed by" column for each phase.

7. Review authorized by — signed and dated by the member of management who authorizes the review.

This simple form can be kept in a notebook by the manager of quality assurance. It provides a quick source of information about the work that has been, is, and will be performed.

QUALITY ASSURANCE REVIEW POINTS

The QA review process parallels the systems development process. QA will make reviews at those points during the systems development process when management will be making a decision or wants information about

Project Name: _____

Project Number: _____ Date Begin: _____

Project Budget: _____ Days: _____

Review Team: _____ In Charge: _____

Assistant: _____

Assistant: _____

Review Process								
Phase	Dates				Cost		Hours	
	Est. Start	Card No.	Actual Start	Com-plete	Budget	Actual	Budget	Actual	Reviewed By
Preparation									
Feasibility									
Design Program									
Test									
Conversion									
Other: _____ _____									

Review Authorized by: _____

Date: _____

Figure 6.2. Project review control sheet.

systems progress. On systems critical to the organization, it may be on a full-time basis. However, this is an exception rather than the rule.

Most QA groups perform reviews close to the completion of each of the five phases in a systems development life cycle:
1. Feasibility
2. System design
3. Programming
4. Testing
5. Conversion or implementation

Some systems, because of size, complexity or importance, may require more than one review at each phase. Other systems of lesser importance, complexity, or cost may only require one review for the entire development process. When one review is made, it normally occurs at the end of the design phase.

Some groups also review the system after installation. This review occurs a short time after the computer system becomes operational. In other organizations, the postimplementation review is performed by internal audit.

The value of a computerized application is the result from operations. If the application fails to produce the desired results, the design process, even though it complies with all the organization's policies and procedures, is a failure. QA can learn from problems or errors that occur in systems when they become operational and use this knowledge to prevent the same problem from occurring again, This postinstallation review may not be a formal review. It may only involve informal discussions with the project team or internal auditors.

At the end of each systems development life cycle phase, the QA group normally provides the data processing manager with an opinion as to the adequacy of the design process up to that point. Management can then use that as input in making its decision as to whether to progress to the next phase. If the next phase is not approved, the decision could involve cancelling the system, redoing the previous phase, modifying and enhancing the work done in the previous phase, or moving ahead but with extra work to be accomplished in the next phase to compensate for weaknesses in the previous phase. The five systems development phases are discussed below with the review criteria for each phase.

Feasibility Study

The primary objective of the feasibility study is to evaluate alternatives and recommend a course of action to management to solve a specific business problem. The feasibility study is a time to "blue sky" new ideas and approaches. QA may be called during this time as consultants to discuss the practicality of alternative techniques.

The feasibility study evaluates solutions to a business problem. Emphasis is placed on solving the business problem as opposed to the computer system design for solving the business problem. The individuals involved in analyzing the feasibility of various solutions may or may not be computer design personnel; however, most have a familiarity with the computer.

Cost considerations are extremely important during the feasibility phase. While management does not expect a high degree of accuracy on cost estimates, they do want reasonable estimates. These estimates and evaluations are outside the normal scope of work of QA. Again, they may be called in as a consultant, but do not have a responsibility to review cost estimates.

QA should become involved at the end of the feasibility phase. The prime concern at this point is whether the feasibility team followed the organization's procedures in developing a proposal for management. In addition, if the feasibility report proposes computerized solutions, the quality assurance group should review and comment on only those aspects of the proposal.

Design Phase

The design phase includes first the design of the solution to the business problem, and second, the design to implement the solution on a computer. In some organizations, the two design efforts are combined into one systems development life cycle phase. Unless the business system is a separate phase, it is implied that the solution to the business problem will be implemented on a computer. Other organizations treat the two design efforts as independent systems development life cycle phases. In that case, the QA group performs separate reviews on each.

The business problem systems design does not take into account is *how* the problem will be resolved. It is concerned with what the system will do to solve the problem. This phase does not deal with the method of processing the data. It will deal with the information needs of a user department(s). For example, a user problem in a merchandising organization is the prompt processing of customers' orders and the collection of funds for those orders. The business problem concerns itself with shipment of the right product to the right location, invoicing on a timely basis at the right price, handling of back orders, good customer relations, efficient processing in the distribution areas, etc. The computer system design is concerned with the data contained in the customer orders, its transition to machine-readable data, the processing rules, and the master data needed to do the processing, and so forth.

The QA group has a lesser role in reviewing the solution to the business problem than with the solution to the computer system problem. The solution to the business system problem is normally not subject to the same standards as is the computer design solution. As the phases become more specific, the QA group has a greater role. They can comment on the practicality of the business solution if it is to be processed by a computer. They should not be arguing for or against the proposed solution but, rather, reviewing the procedures by which that solution was determined.

Each phase gets more specific on cost. The evaluation of cost estimates and arguments is primarily the function of management. Should the business solution problem discuss costs of computer systems, these costs can be reviewed by QA. Also, they can review the method of accumulating costs as it conforms to the policies and procedures of the organization.

The computer system design phase is an extremely critical phase for the QA group. It is at this time that they can make the greatest impact on the design. The group wants to have an impact on the design without actually participating in the design process. Many organizations divide the review of computer systems design into two phases. The first is informal, the second formal. The first occurs after a rough preliminary design has been established. This is merely a brief, "discussion only" review. Rarely are any reports forwarded to management based on this review. It requires a good working relationship to have the project team discuss its preliminary thinking; reports to management at this time could damage this relationship. In very large applications, there may be two or three reviews during the design phase.

A formal review must occur at the end of the computer systems design phase. The design is normally fixed at this point, and ensuing phases make only minor changes to that design. The quality assurance group can review conformance to systems goals, compliance to procedures, and compliance to performance criteria. From the viewpoint of data processing management, this review will provide the best input as to whether the project is meeting the objectives and the performance criteria.

Program Phase

The program phase can be broken into program design and program coding. Many organizations combine those two phases into one. By doing this, the thought process and documentation achieved through a separate program design phase may be lost. Unless program design is a distinct step, the programmer may go into the coding before carefully developing the program design. While this appears to be a shortcut, it can result in insufficient program design documentation and program design problems.

To force formal program design, the QA group should insist on a review after program design, but before program coding. This will also give them the opportunity to review compliance to program design procedures and standards before coding occurs.

The program phase review should occur at the end of the programming phase to let QA make an assessment on compliance to procedures. Operating procedures include the proper use of program code, use of operating system facilities, conformance to programming and system standards, compliance to the computer operating department requirements, etc. If the data processing department is to have compliance with its procedures and standards, this review phase must be detailed. QA must look at program code, operating system instructions (in IBM systems, this would be Job Control Language), file structures, and other aspects that affect the operation of the computer system.

System Test Phase

The project team and the user have responsibility to test the system and review the adequacy of the test results. The QA group is concerned that an adequate test plan has been prepared, that it conforms to the standards of the organization, and that it has been followed. The QA group itself is normally not involved in the detailed testing. In other words, it does not prepare test data, process it, and review the results of testing. It may examine sample results from testing, however, to determine adherence to standards.

The testing plan should be prepared during either the system design or programming phase. Ideally, the plan will be prepared during the system design phase, and modified and enhanced during the programming phase. Part of the review of system testing occurs in the previous phases.

At the completion of the system testing, QA should perform a review to determine the system has been tested adequately. This involves conformance to the organization's testing policy. QA does not try to determine that every task has been tested but, rather, that the plan which they consider to be acceptable was followed.

The users have primary responsibility for the accuracy and completeness of processed data. Therefore they must attest that the system has performed according to their specifications. During its review, QA wants to know that the users are satisfied with the system.

Conversion Phase

Conversion is the process of either replacing an existing system or installing a totally new system. The primary concern of the quality assurance group is that an adequate conversion plan has been established and is being followed. As with the testing phase, this plan should be developed during the systems design phase, and then enhanced during the programming phase. The QA will review that conversion plan during the systems design and programming phases. At that point, they will review the adequacy of the plan, and its conformance to the organization's conversion procedures.

At the completion of the conversion phase, QA will make a final review that the procedures were, in fact, followed. Again, the user has the primary responsibility for the accuracy and completeness of the data converted during the conversion process. The QA group is concerned that the necessary technical steps are performed in the proper sequence to achieve a successful conversion.

STAFFING THE QUALITY ASSURANCE REVIEW

When the manager of quality assurance has decided at which points the review will be made, the next step is to determine who will perform that review and for how long. Previous chapters have discussed methods of determining the hours to be allocated to the review. They have also discussed how to divide those hours among the system development life cycle phases. The previous section in this chapter discussed some of the considerations regarding conducting reviews during each of those phases.

The quality assurance manager needs to select individuals to perform the review at each phase. The following factors should be considered when selecting individuals for a review team.

Objectivity. The reviewer should not have been involved in designing or programming the system being replaced or have a close personal relationship with key members on the project team being reviewed.

Time availability. The individual assigned should have sufficient time available to perform the review at the appropriate review points.

Background and experience. The reviewer should have sufficient technical experience to perform the review. For example, individuals should not be assigned to review an on-line database system when all their previous experience has been with tape batched systems.

Project duration. The key individuals assigned to review the project should be available throughout the project. For example, if individuals are known to be leaving QA within two months, they should not be assigned to review a project that will be in development for an 18-month period.

PLANNING THE QUALITY ASSURANCE REVIEW

There are three types of planning involved when preparing for a review. The first is administrative and includes staffing, budgeting, and scheduling. The second is general, preparing for the tasks that occur in all application reviews. Third is application planning, which covers the steps unique to the specific application being reviewed.

Administrative Planning

The successful utilization of QA resources depends on adequate administrative planning. It is important to get the right reviewer, at the right point, at the right time. This administrative planning can be accomplished with a few simple procedures.

The information contained on the Project Review Control Sheet (Figure 6.2) can provide the manager of quality assurance with planning information. This information can be used to schedule and control the project. This involves the following steps:

1. *Transcribe information from the project review control sheet to a project tickler card* (Figure 6.3). One tickler should be made for each phase being reviewed. If the QA manager determines there should be two or more reviews during one phase, two or more tickler cards are prepared for that phase. The data that gets transcribed is:

a. Action date — the estimated start date for each phase.

b. Assignment number — project number.

c. Action required — brief synopsis of review objective.

d. Hours allocated — the number of hours involved in the review of this phase.

e. Individual assigned — staff member in charge of the review.

f. Project contact — name of individual with whom the review is coordinated.

g. Action resolution — brief synopsis of the results of the review (taken from the review report).

h. Next project action data — estimated starting date of next review phase (or indicate at the end that this is the last step in the review).

2. *File the cards by a reminder date one to two weeks prior to the action date.* When this reminder date arrives, someone from the quality assurance group should contact the project team to determine that the action date is still appropriate. When a review is complete, the remaining review dates should be reconfirmed with the project team and the tickler card(s) refiled under new reminder dates. The project team manager should be asked to notify quality assurance if there is a delay in a future checkpoint.

3. *Develop a chart of individual assignments for quality assurance personnel using the tickler cards.* When making the assignments consider all of the project tickler cards for the period being scheduled, including all the cards whose action date has passed, but on which action is not yet complete. For example, if the assignment period is the last quarter of the year, October through December, then the cards wanted would be all of those with an action date of December 31 or earlier.

Sort the tickler cards by individual. The cards should now be in piles by individual. Because several names are on each card, the cards will have to be sorted as many times as there are names on the cards. The first sort is for the person in charge.

QUALITY ASSURANCE TICKLER CARD

Card No. _____

Action Date _____ Assignment No. _____

Action Required _____

_____

_____

Hours Allocated _____

Individual Assigned:

     In charge: _____

     Assistant: _____

     Assistant: _____

Project Contact: _____

Review Phase Complete   ☐ Yes

Action Resolution: _____

_____

Next Project Action Date: _____

Card No. _____

Figure 6.3. Project tickler card.

The assignments are then posted onto a Gantt assignment chart. (Figure 6.4). This chart shows the reviewer's name and each assignment for the three-month period. The person preparing the Gantt chart must use discretion when dividing the hours available over the assignment period. Generally for this type of chart, it is assumed the individual will be on the assignment full time once the assignment starts. Once the posting has been done for the person in charge, the cards can be resorted for the first assistant, and then again for the second assistant, etc. When the process is done, all of the assignments will be posted on the assignment chart. Next, nonreview time, such as vacation or training, must be posted on the chart. The completed chart will give the manager of quality assurance an overview of the QA group's assignments as well as individual assignments and will show overlaps and problems.

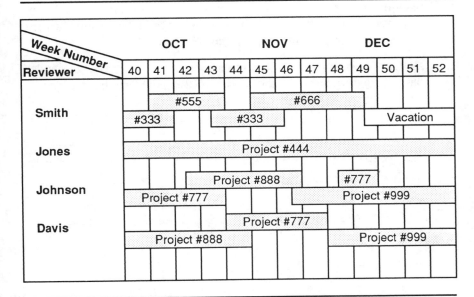

Figure 6.4. Gantt assignment chart.

Use of Gantt Chart

The Gantt chart is used to control personnel resources. When special jobs occur, or new assignments originate, the quality assurance manager can readily determine who is available and for how long. Assignment dates can change because of unexpected requests by management or users, delays or acceleration on the implementation of existing projects, and special assignments. Using a Gantt chart, assignments are made on a realistic basis and not by chance.

For larger groups, it is helpful to have weekly status reports. These are used to track progress and update Gantt chart scheduling. Figure 6.5 shows a typical weekly status report for a quality assurance group. This report includes:

a.   Project name — name of project.

b.   Week ended — the last day of the week covered by this report.

c.   Project phase — the phase or subsection of that phase under review.

d.   Review status — brief synopsis of the review to date.

e.   Review concern — any actual or potential problem perceived by the reviewers which, in their opinion, should be brought to the attention of management at the current time.

f.   Budget information — the number of hours budgeted, expended and needed to complete the review of this phase so that the quality assurance manager will know whether the project is over or under budget.

Project Name: _____   Week Ended : _____

Project Phase: _____

Review Status: _____

Review Concerns:

Budget Information:

 Budget for this phase   _____

 Actual to date for this phase: _____

 Needed to complete this phase: _____

 Estimate over (under) budget: _____

                                      _____
                                      Reviewer in Charge

Figure 6.5. Weekly status report.

Project Control

Some quality assurance groups maintain the status of MIS projects for the entire department. Keeping project status for QA reviews duplicates the project control administration function. This duplication can be avoided by centralizing the function within the quality assurance function.

Automating Scheduling

Quality assurance groups can obtain software to schedule computer reviews. Automating scheduling eliminates the need to hand schedule QA reviews and permits easy modification of schedules.

General Planning

The general plan covers those steps in a review that are executed on all application reviews:

1. Ascertain that all review personnel needed have been assigned to the project and will be available on the needed dates.

2. If the review is out of town, make travel and hotel arrangements.

3. If the review is conducted in another work location, make arrangements for work stations.

4. If questionnaires, procedures, etc. will be needed, obtain copies.

5. Requisition necessary supplies for the review.

6. If this is the first review for any of the group members, brief them on review procedures.

7. If assistants are assigned to the project, divide the work among the review team.

8. Obtain and review any information needed for preparatory understanding of the application.

9. Develop work schedules.

Application-Oriented Planning

Prior to commencing the review, the QA team needs to brief itself on the application. To become familiar with the application for review purposes, the team should do the following.

1. Review information relating to the application.

2. Make arrangements with the project team to hold an entrance conference (this will be discussed in the next section).

3. If assistants are assigned to the review, brief them on the application.

4. If previous phases of the project have been completed, review the results of those phases.

5. Prepare working papers for the review (this will be covered later in this chapter).

6. If internal auditing is involved in this review, coordinate the review with them.

ENTRANCE CONFERENCE

The entrance conference is the formal start of the review. The project team and the review team meet to discuss the review. This is one of the important parts of each review and provides an opportunity for two things to happen other than the instructions. First, QA have a chance to explain the quality assurance and promote their function. Second, they can outline their requirements. The QA group will need time, documentation, and information from the project team. These requests can be outlined so there will be no surprises, and the project team can schedule those tasks into its schedule. The planning steps previously outlined in this chapter should be completed prior to the entrance conference. It is important that QA be familiar with the project, and their needs and requirements determined before this conference.

An entrance conference is held prior to each review. Thus, if there are five review points, there will be five entrance conferences. The first entrance conference will be the most important. However, it is possible that the project team performing the feasibility study will be different from the one doing the systems design phase. People will change for other phases of the system development life cycle. New project personnel may not understand QA and its needs, so an entrance conference provides an opportunity to reestablish working relationships. If project personnel are relatively stable, the conferences after the first one can be much more informal and shorter. Where personnel change, the conferences should be more formal.

Entrance Conference Objectives

The entrance conference helps set the tone for the review and should be attended by the full review team as well as all the key people from the application project team. Ideally, the full project team should be there. The initial entrance conference should last about one hour. A second or later entrance conference can involve fewer people and be for a shorter period of time. However, if project team personnel have changed, the conference should revert to the initial meeting format.

The entrance conference should not be held until the QA group has adequately prepared for the conference. The following objectives should be accomplished at the entrance conference:

1.   Review objectives and what should be accomplished by the review.

2.   Explain and review the types of reports that will be prepared as a result of the review and who will receive them.

3.   Determine certain aspects of the project the QA group will review.

4.   Gain information from the project team about the project.

5.   Discuss in detail how the review team will conduct the review.

6.   Request the information the quality assurance team will need during the review.

7.   Determine the role of the project team during the review.

8.   Establish tentative review schedules showing the tasks for each group and the individuals involved. Discuss and agree upon key review dates.

9.   Assess the competence and effectiveness of the project team.

10.   Probe the project team on questions raised during their preparatory planning.

The first objective of the entrance conference is familiarization of both parties with the tasks and problems relating to the review. A second objective is to outline review requirements. The project team may not be able to commit to all requests. For uncommitted requests, an action plan needs to be developed. For example, the project team may not be able to state immediately when certain pieces of information will be available, but should be able to state on what date it can commit the availability of that information.

The review team leader should prepare an agenda for the entrance conference in order to limit the conference to about one hour. He or she should also be in charge of conducting the conference to ensure that all topics are covered.

Conducting the Entrance Conference

A typical agenda for an entrance conference would be:

1.   Introduce participants of the conference.

2.   Explain the objectives of QA.

3.   Explain what will be the results of the review, who will see them, and how they will be used.

4.   Discuss objectives of the review.

5.   Outline needs and requirements of QA.

6.   Have project team explain objectives of computer application.

7.   Have project team ask questions of QA.

8.   Discuss schedule of work.

9.   Discuss housekeeping matters.

Quality Assurance Documentation

There is a need for written documentation of the review process. The complete review process will occur over a period of months. There may be gaps of several months between review points. It is possible that there will be changeover in quality assurance or on the project team during the review of a system application.

Workpapers prepared by a quality assurance group comprise a major part of its review. Most groups keep these workpapers in notebooks, by project, in order to have:

1.   A chronological record of what has happened, when it has happened, and who did it.

2.   Reference material from which a report will be developed on the review.

3.   Supporting information to substantiate the conclusions in the report.

4.   Reference material so that the quality assurance team can review previous work.

5.   A means by which a supervisor can review the quality and extent of the work performed during the review.

6.   A training document for new individuals assigned to the review.

7.   A training document for individuals conducting similar reviews.

Workpaper Format. Workpapers should be organized for easy reference purposes. An indexing scheme enables each aspect of the review to be easily located.

There are four different types of workpapers. These are:

1. The report(s) issued as a result of the review.

2. Background and reference information collected during the review process.

3. Review programs accomplished during the review process.

4. Notes and other documents prepared by members of the review team.

The workpapers do not need to be organized in any specific manner but should be filed in the section to which they apply. In addition, each workpaper should contain the following basic identification 1) the section to which it belongs, 2) the subject of the workpaper, 3) the individual who prepared the paper, 4) the data on which it was prepared, 5) the source from which the data in the workpaper was obtained.

Contents of Workpapers. The workpapers need to be referenced for ease of location. Figure 6.6 outlines a suggested table of contents for review workpapers. Section A, which is the first section in the workpapers, is the completed report(s). Each statement in the report would be cross referenced to the detail workpaper that supports that statement. The report is the last section to be completed. However, if one looks at the workpapers as evidence to support the report, then it makes logical sense to have the report first.

Section B includes the background information on the project. Background information would include project objectives, policies, and procedures relating to the project. It might include organizational charts of the user department, background material on customers of the system, or federal regulations pertaining to the application. This is the type of information that the project review team can use to familiarize itself with the breadth and scope of the project. If data relates to one specific phase, it would be filed in that section. Data pertaining to the feasibility study is filed in the feasibility section and so forth.

Section C outlines the project approach. It is the program and instructions to the project team telling what it must do to complete the project. This will outline the key review points. This section would also include any special instructions given to the project team by the user or executive management regarding what the user or manager would like done during this review. For example, executive management may have some reservations about the hardware the project team is proposing and want a special study made on that hardware.

Section D outlines the administration of the review. It includes the plans, personnel, schedules and budgets for this project. The administrative details included in this section, are project oriented and should be in great detail.

Section E is generally a chronological filing of correspondence, including memorandums and letters both received and sent by the review team. If the correspondence is extensive, some organization of the correspondence other than chronological may be desirable. For example, it may be decided to file correspondence by addressee, department, or subject as opposed to a chronological filing.

Section F provides information on the project team. It includes the team plans, personnel, schedules, and budgets. This is the type of information the quality assurance group needs in order to plan the use of its resources.

Section G begins a series of similar sections covering the different reviews. The previous section related to the project in total. Section G relates only to the review of the feasibility study. Within the feasibility study, and all other reviews, are the following sections:

1.   Review conclusion/report — the report or conclusion issued from the feasibility study.

2.   Review questionnaire applicable to the feasibility study review. (This will be covered in Chapter 7.)

3.   Project documentation — information obtained from the project team relating to the feasibility study of the project.

4.   Correspondence — any memorandums, correspondence, or notes sent to other parties or received from them relating to the feasibility study review.

5.   Review notes — all the workpapers prepared by the quality assurance team during the feasibility study review. These should be supportive of the program/questionnaire included in this section. If notes or workpapers are developed as a result of that question asked or program step executed, it should be referenced to the question or program step.

6.   Miscellaneous — information collected during the review process not appropriate to other sections. For example, this could include information obtained from a vendor that was used as background material in this phase.

Sections H, I, J, and K all use the same format as Section G. The sections are for the systems design review, program review, test review, and conversion review. If the quality assurance group adds additional review steps, they should add more sections to the workpapers. For example, if there were two review points for the systems design phase, these would require two sections.

For larger reviews, Sections A – F are filed in one notebook. Each other section would be filed in an individual notebook. This would permit each review point to be filed separately.

Workpaper Retention. There are no legal requirements for maintaining review workpapers. The procedures of each organization govern the length of time the documentation is maintained. Workpapers from a project should be retained throughout the life of the project and then, at a minimum, until the application has been successfully implemented.

The QA group may desire to save review workpapers as a training vehicle for new quality assurance personnel, who can refer to a full set of working papers. Workpapers are also useful as reference and background material for a postimplementation review. Internal auditors making a postimplementation audit may wish to review the workpapers. Finally, if case management disregards quality assurance advice and quality assurance suspects problems in the new system, QA may wish to save the workpapers until it is satisfied about the resolution of those problems.

SUMMARY

Planning is needed prior to a QA review. Planning includes administrative, general, and application planning. Administrative planning includes personnel assignment, schedules, and budgets. General planning includes those aspects that relate to the application being reviewed. This planning prepares a quality assurance group for the entrance conference.

WORKPAPER	
Subject Reference	
Reference report (to workpapers)	A
Background information	B
— project objectives	B-100
— policies, procedure on project	B-200
Review program and instructions	C
Administrative (review team)	D
— plans	D-100
— personnel	D-200
— schedules	D-300
— budgets	D-400
Correspondence	E
Project team	F
— plans	F-100
— personnel	F-200
— schedules	F-300
— budgets	F-400
Feasibility study review	G
— review conclusions/report	G-100
— review program/questionnaire	G-200
— project documentation	G-300
— correspondence	G-400
— review notes (referenced to report and questionnaire)	G-500
— miscellaneous	G-600
Systems design review	H
— review conclusions/report	H-100
— review program/questionnaire	H-200
— project documentation	H-300
— correspondence	H-400
— review notes (referenced to report and questionnaire)	H-500
— miscellaneous	H-600

Figure 6.6. Workpaper table of contents.

WORKPAPER (cont'd)	
Subject Reference	
Program Review	I
— review conclusions/report	I-100
— review program/questionnaire	I-200
— project documentation	I-300
— correspondence	I-400
— review notes (referenced to report and questionnaire)	I-500
— miscellaneous	I-600
Test	J
— review conclusions/report	J-100
— review program/questionnaire	J-200
— project documentation	J-300
— correspondence	J-400
— review notes (referenced to report and questionnaire)	J-500
— miscellaneous	J-600
Conversion	K
— review conclusions/report	K-100
— review program/questionnaire	K-200
— project documentation	K-300
— correspondence	K-400
— review notes (referenced to report and questionnaire)	K-500
— miscellaneous	K-600

Figure 6.6. Workpaper table of contents. (cont'd)

The review personnel need to gain an understanding of the system during the planning process. Once the system is understood, the group can select the points at which it wants to review the system under development. These review points normally coincide with the end of the key phases in the development process. These phases are the feasibility, systems design, test, and conversion phases. Depending on the organization's development process and the complexity of the system, there may be more or fewer review points.

The official beginning of a review is an entrance conference. At this point, QA and the project team can get together and discuss the review process and requirements. Because this entrance conference sets the tone of the review, it is essential for the QA personnel to be adequately prepared.

The entrance conference accomplishes three objectives. First, it is a mechanism for the QA group and the project team to meet. Second, it offers QA the opportunity to explain and promote its function. Third, it is the means by which QA can outline its schedule, needs, and requirements with the project team. This will enable the project team to fit those needs and requirements into its implementation schedule.

7

Conducting a Quality Assurance Review

The quality assurance review can begin when the planning and preparatory work is complete. The type, frequency, and extent of the review will be determined during the preparatory stages. The type of review will depend upon the importance of the system to the organization as well as resources available to conduct the review.

Each of the twelve points from the feasibility study to the end of conversion covers a different aspect of the application system. Many systems may not warrant all twelve reviews because they may be small or potential exposure to the organization may be minimal, or personnel are not available to conduct reviews. In those instances, two or more of the review points will be consolidated into one review.

This chapter includes a checklist for each of t he recommended twelve review points. Each list concentrates on a different aspect of the application system. The reviewer should conduct tests and make evaluations based on the answers to the questions in the checklists. Chapter 8 explains how to conduct the tests. The checklists included in this chapter are cross-referenced to the tests explained in Chapter 8. Chapter 9 provides guidance on how to evaluate the results of the review and compare that evaluation to other application reviews. Chapters 7–9 provide the methodology for conducting a review.

QUALITY ASSURANCE REVIEW POINTS

The five phases of the system development life cycle are the justification phase, systems development phase, programming phase, testing phase, and conversion phase. Each of these phases normally concludes with the completion of a product. (We have discussed these phases in previous chapters.)

To assure a quality system, twelve review points have been selected during the five systems development life cycle phases. The twelve are considered to be the optimum number of reviews for a major application, so that QA can not only review but also influence system design. The twelve recommended review points are:

1. Mid-justification phase

2. End of justification phase

3. Business system solution phase

4. Computer equipment selection

5. Computer system design

6. Program design

7. Testing and conversion planning

8. Program coding and testing

9. Detailed test plan

10. Test results

11. Detail conversion planning and programs

12. Conversion results

Reviews occurring during the five system development phases should assist project personnel in the accomplishment of their task. Frequently with a few hours' consultation, quality assurance can save project personnel hours or days of wasted effort. This valuable consultation service can normally be accomplished while QA personnel are fulfilling their review requirements.

Twelve reviews do not require much more time than a smaller number of reviews. The items to be reviewed are split among several short reviews rather than consolidated into major reviews that could be held at the end of each of the five system phases.

If fewer than twelve reviews are desired, the checklists for the two or more reviews included in a phase should be consolidated in the one review. In a few cases, the same questions are included in two reviews during one system development life cycle phase, but that is the exception. The consolidation of two or more checklists is not difficult.

Review Point	Quality Assurance Review Point	Percent of QA Time Expended
1	Mid-justification review	5%
2	End of justification review	5%
3	Review of the business system solution	10%
4	Review of computer equipment selection	10%
5	Review of computer system design	20%
6	Review of program design	20%
7	Review of testing and conversion planning	5%
8	Review of program coding and testing	5%
9	Review of detail test plan	5%
10	Review of test results	5%
11	Review of detail conversion planning and programs	5%
12	Review of conversion results	5%

CONDUCTING THE REVIEW

During a review, the reviewer should maintain a helpful, cooperative attitude. Because reviews are peer group reviews, it is important to maintain a good working relationship both during and after each review. The review itself should not create tension and competition. Outstanding work performed by project personnel as well as deviations from departmental standards should be recognized.

Each review point has a checklist. The questions included on any of the checklists highlight the areas that should be addressed at that particular review. The questions included on the checklist are broad in scope. They are not meant to be answered yes or no but, rather, to indicate the degree of compliance to the departmental standards achieved by the project team. Because each organization has different standards, a general issue is raised but it must be supported by a series of very specific questions. This means that the quality assurance group will have to develop a series of questions which focus on the standards that need to be followed by the programmers.

In some cases, the degree of compliance will be a matter of judgment; in others, a more scientific approach can be taken. (Rating the quality of work of the project team will be discussed in Chapter 9.)

The amount of time allocated to the entire review must be split among the twelve review points. Figure 2.7 suggested a breakdown of time among the five phases of the system development life cycle. Listed in Figure 7.1 is a further breakdown of those items for the twelve review points: if two or more review points are consolidated into one review, the time for the reviews should be consolidated. For example, if Review Point 11 (the review of detail conversion planning and programs) and Review Point 12 (the review of conversion results) are combined into one review point, then the total of the time for the two reviews (i.e., 5 percent plus 5 percent) or 10 percent of the time expended should be spent on that consolidated review. Whether the total time spent on twelve reviews is longer than the time spent on fewer reviews will depend upon the experience of the quality assurance group and the proficiency of the individual reviewers.

Each review point will be discussed in detail in this chapter. Prior to that discussion, the objectives of the project team during the system development life cycle phase will be reviewed. This should put each phase of the systems development life cycle into perspective for the reviewer.

SYSTEM JUSTIFICATION PHASE

The recognition of a business problem will lead to the organization of a study designed to develop a proposed solution. The feasibility study will result in justifying what action should occur to solve the business problem.

The recommendation may be to live with the existing system, modify the existing system, or build a new system. Figure 7.1 shows the elements of this phase. Two review points are illustrated in this figure.

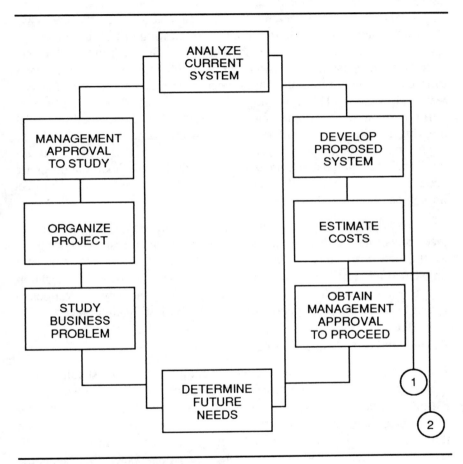

Figure 7.1. System justification phase.

During the justification phase, a team will be organized to study the business problem. For example, in a merchandising organization, a business problem may be excessive stockouts of merchandise. It is this type of a business problem that needs to be solved now and not studying how the computer should be involved. The study team should examine the present system to help determine future needs.

The study team will propose a solution to the business problem based on analyzing the business problem and the needs of various users. In the example of the merchandising organization with the excessive stockouts, the proposed solution may be monitoring orders and inventory levels to determine stock replenishment points. Such a solution does not necessarily propose that the computer be involved, as it may be too early to make that determination. That aspect is normally handled in the system design phase. This does not mean that the justification study team will not recommend a computer system but, rather, the method of implementing the solution is still flexible. Cost estimates may be developed for a range of solutions giving a probable cost for each. Many organizations feel that the cost estimates produced during the justification phase need only be accurate within plus or minus 50 percent of actual project implementation costs.

Even though they are primarily computer oriented, QA personnel can make a contribution during this phase. The study team assigned during the justification phase may be unaware of some of the newer technology for problem solving or how to determine the costs for the use of that technology as a potential solution. Therefore, certain solutions may be overlooked without skilled technical people involved in the justification phase.

Review Point 1: Mid-Justification Phase

The basic intent of a review is to verify compliance to the standards and procedures desired by data processing management. This can be done by listing the concerns of data processing management and then verifying that appropriate action has been taken regarding those concerns. The term "concern" is used in the context of what is needed to build a well-controlled, efficient, and effective data processing system that meets the needs of the user. If the data processing department has formalized standards and procedures, the concerns should be cross-referenced to those procedures and standards.

The early phases of the systems development life cycle have less formal and demanding MIS standards and procedures. This is because there is more creativity and ingenuity during the early phases of system development than during the later phases such as programming. It is more of an art to determine which solution is best for the organization than to perform the function of programming.

The intent of the mid-justification phase review is to verify first that the appropriate fact gathering has occurred according to departmental procedures and second that the plans of the justification team will permit its work to be completed on time and within budget. Because the costs are merely low during this phase, it is normally sufficient to merely verify that there are plans and budgets which are being followed.

Figure 7.2 outlines eight concerns for the QA group to consider during the mid-justification phase review. Associated with each of the concerns

	QUALITY ASSURANCE CONCERN	REVIEW TECHNIQUE
1	Are there a sufficient number of capable people assigned to the justification phase?	Project documentation Fact finding Judgment
2	Have good and bad parts of the current system been determined?	System documentation Fact finding Simulation modeling
3	Have the new information needs been determined?	System documentation Fact finding Checklist
4	Have data processing procedures and standards been followed?	System documentation Fact finding Checklist
5	Are there adequate alternatives available to meet the user's needs without building a new system?	System documentation Fact finding Judgment Consultants Confirmation
6	Will justification phase be completed on time?	Project documentation Fact finding
7	Will justification phase be completed within budget?	Project documentation Fact finding
8	Are goals and objectives to be solved clearly stated?	Project documentation System documentation

Figure 7.2. Review point 1: mid-justification phase review.

are the review practices recommended to the reviewer for determining to what degree the concern has been satisfied by the project team. Note that the concerns listed are not meant to be complete but merely representative of the type of concerns that the QA group should address.

The concerns listed normally cannot be answered by a simple yes or no. For example, the first question asks if there are "a sufficient number of capable people assigned to the justification phase." The reviewer might not want to ask this question directly of the justification phase project leader. The reviewer would want to examine the project documentation to determine who had been assigned to the justification phase, then through fact finding and interviewing determine the qualifications of the individuals assigned. Once this information has been accumulated, the reviewer can judge whether a sufficient number of people have been assigned to the justification phase, and whether or not those people are capable of completing the assignments given to them. Once the review has been conducted, the reviewer is in the position to answer the concern. Concerns must be based on MIS department standards or procedures. The QA group does not probe into areas unless that area is within the QA group charter.

Review Point 2: End of Justification Phase

Management of the organization must decide at the end of the justification phase whether to adopt the recommendation of the justification phase team, reject that recommendation, or accept it in a modified form. Many organization now only approve the funding of a project one phase at a time. That means that while the recommendation for the solution is accepted, only the funds and resources to complete the next systems development life cycle phase would be approved. The process is followed for each of the phases.

The evaluation of a completed phase by QA should be an input to management for its decision-making process. It is recommended that the QA group neither approves nor disapproves the work of computer department personnel, it is merely trying to assess compliance by the project team to departmental standards and procedures. These standards and procedures can be considered in the broad sense to be the goals and objectives of the system; QA is limited to reviewing methods. Most organizations begin by reviewing methods, and then expand to goals.

The justification phase will normally have fewer standards than the later phases. Most organizations have procedures that require justification teams to consider various criteria during their study. The typical criteria include:

1. The impact of the new system on people, computer hardware and software, existing systems, supporting systems and cost.

2. The expected life of the new system.

3. The user reaction to the new system.

4. The availability of resources, including people, to implement the new system.

5. Schedules for implementation.

6. Risks and exposures associated with the new system.

7. Various alternatives evaluated and the reasons for rejecting the various alternatives in favor of the recommended system.

Figure 7.3 lists twelve concerns for the review conducted at the end of the justification phase. Associated with each of these are recommended review practices. The review should be conducted so that management has the evaluation before it must make a decision on the justification team recommendation.

SYSTEMS DESIGN PHASE

The systems design phase includes both functional specification of the business system solution and the computer system solution phase. In some organizations these are separate phases; in others they are combined. If the business system solution phase is not a separate process, all solutions will include the computer as part of the solution. Therefore, it is desirable to have a review involved in the decision regarding whether or not the computer is to be part of the solution of the business problem.

When it has been objectively determined that the computer is to be part of the solution, then the computer system should be designed. QA personnel are normally quite familiar with the processes from the point where a computer becomes part of the solution to the business problem. If the organization has a different group working on business system solutions than that working on computer systems design, it may be advisable to have people with both backgrounds in the QA group.

	QUALITY ASSURANCE CONCERN	REVIEW TECHNIQUE
1	Have data processing costs been estimated?	System documentation
2	Have the user costs and benefits been estimated?	System documentation
3	Has conceptual system design been prepared?	System documentation
4	Have the data processing procedures and standards been followed?	System documentation Fact finding Checklist
5	Was the proposed system selected by a reasonable method from among the various alternatives?	System documentation Fact finding Judgment Quantitative analysis
6	Are the assumptions made in arriving at a solution valid?	System documentation Fact finding Judgment Simulation modeling Consultants Quantitative analysis
7	Does the proposed solution solve the business problem?	Project documentation System documentation Judgment Simulation modeling Confirmation
8	Does the user want the proposed system?	Fact finding
9	Does the proposed system have a reasonable life expectancy?	Judgment Simulation modeling Consultants Quantitative analysis Confirmation
10	Have the standards of performance for the new system been established?	System documentation Fact finding
11	Are the standards of performance documented and in the hands of the system designers?	System documentation Simulation modeling
12	Have criteria been established to evaluate performance after the system is operational?	System documentation

Figure 7.3. Review point 2: end of justification phase review.

At the completion of the system design phase, enough information should be documented to begin designing programs. This documentation includes the design of input data, files, and output reports. The long-range information needs of the user must be considered during the system design phase. As system designs move into distributed processing and large centralized databases, the use of information becomes an ever-increasing part of the system design phase. In batch-oriented systems, and simple disk systems, data can be accumulated exclusively for use by that application. However, when multiple applications begin to use the same database, the structure of the database should be based on the needs of the information users. It is a responsibility of QA to determine that files are structured to maximize the use of information.

Figure 7.4 outlines the main parts of the system design phase. Within the system design phase are three review points. The first (Review Point 3) occurs after the business system solution has been determined. At this point, the decision on whether to use the computer as part of the solution will be made. QA should make a review prior to that. The second review point (Review Point 4) involves the computer equipment selection process. Some organizations make the decision that all applications will run on centralized hardware. In that case, the computer equipment selection process is minimal. All the reviewer would want to do is to determine whether the available resources are sufficient to handle the new application. In other organizations, this is a very important review. The third review point (Review Point 5) comes just prior to the completion of the computer system design phase. It is the evaluation from this review that will be used by management in deciding whether to proceed to the next systems development life cycle phase.

Review Point 3: Review of the Business Systems Solutions

The business systems solutions phase determines the detailed solution to the business problem. This includes defining the information to be obtained and processed so that the desired results are obtained. The method of processing does not have to be determined, but the feasibility does. Determining the processing feasibility will decide the need for the computer. For example, certain inventory replenishment algorithms could not be hand processed on a daily basis to determine when new inventory is required. However, by using a computer, such processing becomes feasible. Similarly, in systems where interactive processing is required,

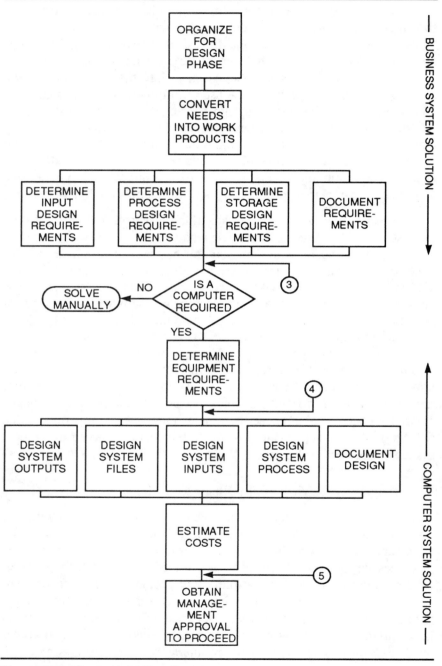

Figure 7.4. System design phase.

it may not be feasible to solve the business problem except by computer. It is in this part of the business systems solution phase that QA can be most helpful.

As systems progress through the developmental process, flexibility for considering alternatives decreases. Therefore, it is important that as many alternative solutions as possible be considered during the justification phase. When the justification phase is complete, the system course is charted and it may be difficult to deviate from the course. Because the most maneuverability exists in the early phases, QA should be involved in those phases.

Figure 7.5 lists nine concerns to be considered during the review of the business systems solution phase. While the objective of QA is compliance to departmental standards and policies, there should be time during the review of the business systems solution phase to determine that all logical alternatives were given consideration.

Review Point 4: Review of Computer Equipment Selection

Usually project leaders build systems within restrictions designed to maximize performance on existing hardware. When applications cause either new hardware to be ordered or extensions to existing hardware, a detailed equipment evaluation process occurs. However, this may be done by computer operations personnel instead of application project personnel.

Figure 7.6 lists six concerns during the review of computer equipment selection. The questions are of a general nature and assume there is existing computer hardware. If no hardware is in place, the equipment selection process is much more extensive. With existing equipment, new hardware normally must be compatible with that existing equipment. When no equipment exists, then the process of evaluating equipment from multiple vendors increases the complexity of the review.

Review Point 5: Review of Computer Systems Design

The review of the computer systems design phase is the most time-consuming part of the review. During this phase, the QA personnel can make their greatest contribution since the computer systems design phase will determine the performance level of the computer application.

	QUALITY ASSURANCE CONCERN	REVIEW TECHNIQUE
1	Have a sufficient number of capable people been assigned to the systems?	Project documentation Fact finding Judgment
2	Has the business problem been solved and are the needed work products?	System documentation Checklist
3	Has the source of the needed data been determined?	System documentation Checklist
4	Have the data storage (file) needs been determined?	System documentation Checklist
5	Has the required processing been determined?	System documentation Checklist
6	Do the various functions of the proposed system fit together?	System documentation Fact finding Judgment Confirmation
7	Does the proposed solution solve the business problem?	Judgment Simulation modeling Quantitative analysis
8	Will the system be implemented when needed?	System documentation Fact finding Judgment Simulation modeling
9	Will performance standards be achieved?	System documentation Fact finding Judgment Consultants

Figure 7.5. Review point 3: review of the business systems solution.

Reviewers should examine all parts of the computer system design. Look at how the system initiates transactions, transmits data from the initiation point to the computer, authorizes data, processes data, stores data, and produces reports from computerized data. It is important that the results of processing meet the needs of the user.

Most organizations have stringent standards covering the computer design phase. These standards include how data is specified, how output reports are specified, computer file specification, as well as processing specification. The reviewer must ascertain that these specifications are followed. QA personnel will be particularly interested in whether the computer system design can meet performance standards. This is critical because meeting operating cost specifications is dependent upon developing a good system design.

	QUALITY ASSURANCE CONCERN	REVIEW TECHNIQUE
1	Have the equipment requirements been determined?	System documentation Checklist
2	Has it been determined whether or not additional hardware will be required?	System documentation Fact finding
3	Has it been determined whether or not additional software will be required?	System documentation Fact finding
4	Has it been determined whether or not any special hardware or software installation will be required?	System documentation Fact finding Consultants
5	Have the MIS department and the project team determined the level of experience necessary to use the specified hardware and software?	Fact finding Judgment
6	Does the hardware provide for sufficient growth for the proposed system?	System documentation Fact finding Judgment

Figure 7.6. Review point 4: review of computer equipment selection.

At the end of the computer systems design phase, traditionally there is little flexibility remaining to make major system design changes. However, the majority of the cost to implement the computerized application is yet to come, so management can still abort the system at relatively minor expense. Therefore, the quality assurance evaluation at Review Point 5 should be extremely important input to management.

Figure 7.7 lists 20 concerns to be included in this review. The extent of these concerns illustrates the depth of the review that should be made at this point. Much of the work and time will be spent examining project and system documentation. Project documentation covers project scheduling, project organization, budgets, approaches, alternatives considered and rejected, and other information relating to managing the project. Systems documentation relates to the application being implemented. This is a permanent documentation although it needs to be updated throughout the life of the application. On the other hand, project documentation has little long-term use and probably will not be retained after the project becomes operational.

	QUALITY ASSURANCE CONCERN	REVIEW TECHNIQUE
1	Do the file specifications meet MIS standards?	System documentation Checklist
2	Do the input specifications meet MIS standards?	System documentation Checklist
3	Do the output specifications meet MIS standards?	System documentation Checklist
4	Do the process specifications meet MIS standards?	System documentation Checklist
5	Is the computer system design properly documented?	System documentation Checklist
6	Is the computer system design complete?	System documentation Judgment Consultants
7	Does the system as designed meet the needs of the user(s)?	Simulation modeling
8	Will the system as designed operate on the planned hardware and software?	System documentation Judgment Consultants
9	Have the costs been developed in accordance with MIS procedures?	System documentation

Figure 7.7. Review point 5: review of computer system design.

	QUALITY ASSURANCE CONCERN	REVIEW TECHNIQUE
10	Does the system design provide the capacity for reasonable growth?	Judgment Simulation modeling Consultants
11	Were other design alternatives considered and rejected for valid reasons?	Project documentation Fact finding Judgment
12	Does the system design impose undue restrictions on the user?	System documentation Fact finding Simulation modeling
13	Is the audit trail sufficient to reconstruct transactions?	System documentation Fact finding Checklist
14	Will the computer systems design phase be completed on time?	Project documentation Fact finding Judgment
15	Will the computer systems design phase be completed within budget?	Project documentation Fact finding Judgment
16	Are the MIS system standards realistic for this system?	Judgment Consultants
17	Are the current MIS system standards appropriate for the time when this system will be operational?	Judgment Simulation modeling Consultants
18	Can performance standards be achieved?	System documentation Judgment Consultants Quantitative analysis Confirmation
19	Is the system of internal control adequate to ensure the accurate and complete processing of transactions?	System documentation Fact finding Checklist
20	Is the system of internal control adequate to ensure the accuracy and integrity of the computer files and/or database?	System documentation Fact finding Checklist

Figure 7.7. Review point 5: review of computer system design. (cont'd)

PROGRAMMING PHASE

The systems design phase provides the information necessary to design programs. If the systems design has been thoroughly documented, the individuals responsible for program design can accomplish their task with little interaction with the user.

There are three aspects of the program design phase, each of which can be associated with a review. These are program design, planning testing and conversion, and coding. If these three are not broken apart, experience has shown they will not receive the proper attention. Program design should be a step separate from coding. When it is not a separate step, much of the program design is done concurrently with coding. Experience has shown this not to be the best way to develop programs.

When a review comes after the program design is complete, but before coding, management can be assured formal program design will occur. The planning for system testing and conversion should commence when programs are being designed. This may occur prior to the completion of the program design phase. The timing is optional. However, when the programs have been designed, the steps required for conversion and system testing are known. Because changes occur between the systems design and the program design, these changes can affect system testing and conversion.

Figure 7.8 illustrates the programming phase. Included within this phase are three QA review checkpoints. The first (Review Point 6) occurs after the programs have been designed. The second (Review Point 7) occurs after the testing and conversion procedures have been planned, and the third (Review Point 8) occurs after the programs have been coded and tested. Data processing management should be involved in deciding when systems are ready for system testing. Premature testing can be expensive. Therefore, a QA review prior to testing will be an important factor for data processing management to consider before they give the go-ahead on systems testing. If adequate program testing has not occurred, the cost of systems testing will be considerably higher.

Review Point 6: Program Design

QA should be sure that the program design has been executed prior to coding. Frequently systems design leaves a number of unanswered questions that do not become obvious until the programming phase. A formal program design methodology, such as structured design, will uncover these problems. It is easier to analyze program logic from design documentation

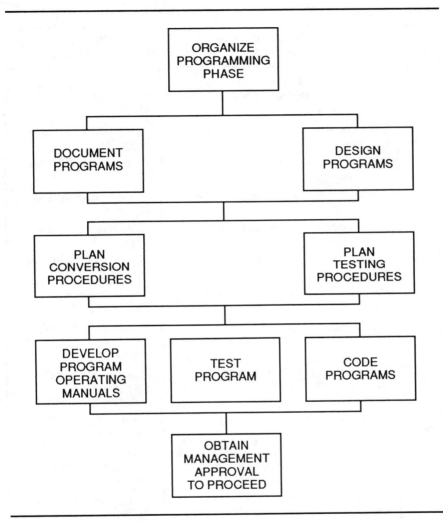

Figure 7.8. Testing phase.

than from program compiler listings. The review can be done by scanning program design documentation, or having the program designers explain briefly program logic. The reviewers should concentrate on the critical programs. Figure 7.9 lists twelve concerns for the review of program design. The program design function is one of the most standardized by organizations. Therefore, the review of program design should focus on a heavy compliance review to standards.

	QUALITY ASSURANCE CONCERN	REVIEW TECHNIQUE
1	Have a sufficient number of capable people been assigned to the program design phase?	Project documentation Fact finding Judgment
2	Does the program design meet MIS standards?	System documentation Checklist
3	Has the program design been properly documented?	System documentation Checklist
4	Has provision been made for restart procedures?	System documentation Checklist
5	Has provision been made for recovery procedures?	System documentation Checklist
6	Has provision been made to protect sensitive data?	System documentation Checklist
7	Is there a programming schedule?	Project documentation Fact finding
8	Will the program design phase be completed on time?	Project documentation Fact finding Judgment
9	Will the program design phase be completed within budget?	Project documentation Fact finding Judgment
10	Are the MIS program standards realistic for this system?	Judgment Consultants
11	Are the current MIS program standards appropriate for the time when this	System documentation Simulation modeling Consultants
12	Will performance standards be achieved?	System documentation Judgment Consultants Quantitative analysis Confirmation

Figure 7.9. Review point 6: review of program design.

Review Point 7: Testing and Conversion Planning

Problems not covered during the testing phase or poor conversions can be disastrous for organizations. One large organization almost went bankrupt when the conversion of its accounts receivable system destroyed all existing copies of the accounts receivable file. These types of problems should become apparent to qualified reviewers.

Systems development may take many months or years during which individuals are writing and debugging program code. It is only at the end of these processes that systems testing occurs, and many times the user takes a lead role in systems testing. Because many data processing personnel perform system testing infrequently, they are not familiar with the types of problems that can occur.

Most data processing personnel develop test data to test the system as they wrote it. The concern of the user is to test the system for conditions as they will happen during the operational status of the system. These two types of testing may be considerably different. It is the role of QA to determine that the testing is as near "real life" as possible. Many data processing personnel fail to adequately test error conditions and unusual circumstances that will occur when the system is put in production.

Figure 7.10 lists eight concerns for the review of testing and conversion planning. Concern number 3 — "Has a plan been established to test the new system?" — is the one requiring the most investigation. It is because of concerns like this that there should be a continuity of reviewer personnel. If the same reviewers have been assigned to an application since the justification phase, they will be in a much better position to assess this concern than will someone newly assigned to the review.

Review Point 8: Program Coding and Testing

Many organizations have established program coding standards and yet fail to ensure that those standards are followed. This determination of compliance is the logical task for QA. There is a natural tendency to follow standards when they are being enforced, and QA should determine whether or not the standards are followed.

	QUALITY ASSURANCE CONCERN	REVIEW TECHNIQUE
1	Has a plan been established to convert from the old to new system?	Project documentation Fact finding
2	Is the conversion plan in accordance with MIS standards?	Project documentation Fact finding
3	Has a plan been established to test the new system?	Project documentation Fact finding
4	Is the test plan in accordance with MIS standards	Project documentation Checklist
5	Have sufficient resources been allocated for the conversion?	Project documentation Judgment Consultants
6	Have sufficient resources been allocated for the system test?	Project documentation Judgment Consultants
7	Is there a testing schedule?	Project documentation Fact finding
8	Is there a conversion schedule?	Project documentation Fact finding

Figure 7.10. Review point 7: review of testing and conversion planning.

In any case, the review of program coding and testing should determine compliance to departmental standards. These standards should be put on detailed checklists so the reviewer can easily make the compliance determination. Appendix A gives a good illustration as to the type of questions one organization asks in support of the more general list of concerns in this chapter.

Figure 7.11 lists four concerns for the reviewer of program coding and testing. This review point is one used by many QA groups to train new personnel. Less judgment is involved in review of program code than in many of the other phases. Also, many QA personnel are more familiar with coding than other aspects of the systems development life cycle.

	QUALITY ASSURANCE CONCERN	REVIEW TECHNIQUE
1	Are programs coded in accordance with MIS standards?	Observation Checklist
2	Are programs adequately tested?	Observation Checklist
3	Is the program code maintainable by the average programmer?	Observation Judgment
4	Has the system of internal control been implemented according to specifications?	System documentation Checklist

Figure 7.11. Review point 8: review of program coding and testing.

TESTING PHASE

The testing phase should involve both data processing and user personnel. The two groups should work together as a team to design the system test plan, create test data, and develop training material for the people who will be using the system. The personnel from the data processing department should be those who were involved in the system design, program design, and coding. Personnel from the user department should be those individuals who will be involved in the use of the production system when it becomes operational.

The test data used to test the system should be normal input-type data. User personnel should fill out input forms with as many transactions as possible. Ideally, all paths through the computer application would be tested. Some organizations use test data generators in an attempt to test as many computer paths as possible.

Test data should include both valid and invalid transactions. When the various processing conditions are discussed during the systems design phase, they should be documented. This list will then serve as a guide as to the types of conditions that should be tested during the test phase. The organization's internal auditors frequently can be helpful in suggesting unusual error conditions.

System testing should continue until the test team is satisfied with the results. Frequently the results of a systems test will cause modifications to be made to the systems design and programs. This necessitates going back into the systems development life cycle. Systems tests should not be conducted again until the project team is satisfied that the system design has been adequately corrected, documented, and tested.

Figure 7.12 shows the main parts of the system test phase. Within the test phase are two review points. One (Review Point 9) occurs after the test data has been created and the user has been trained. At this point, QA can make an assessment as to the adequacy of test data. The second review (Review Point 10) occurs after the tests have been run and the results evaluated. QA will then make an evaluation of test results. However, rarely does QA actually prepare, enter, and run tests.

At the conclusion of the system test phase, management must make a decision whether to put the application into production. During the previous phases, there was time to compensate for previous problems. This is not true with the testing phase. When the testing phase is over, the system may go into production, at which time systems problems become user problems. If errors are not uncovered and corrected during testing, numerous transactions initiated by users may be wrong and have to be corrected along with the system when the problem is discovered. Therefore, it becomes important that the QA review is thorough and that resulting evaluation can be relied upon by management. It would be unusual for data processing management to authorize a system to go into production when QA has warned that it was not ready for that status.

Review Point 9: Detailed Test Plan

The detailed test plan includes the steps to be followed during the systems testing process. The test plan includes the criteria that must be met for the system to be acceptable for production. It identifies which tasks will be performed, who will perform them, when they will be performed, and who will verify the results.

The most important part of the test plan is the criteria which, when met, make this system acceptable. Many DP personnel fail to document these criteria and as a result incur high initial systems maintenance. Test

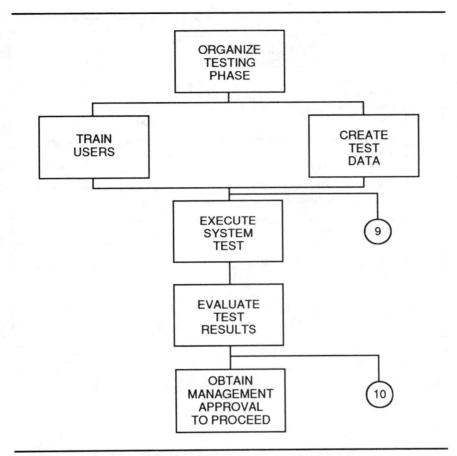

Figure 7.12. Testing phase.

data must be designed to test that the criteria are met. Criteria can include performance, for example, a defined response time in on-line systems or the proper handling of specified situations, such as rejecting certain types of transactions. Criteria can include the level of competence on the part of user personnel. The user should specify what criteria must be met.

Figure 7.13 lists six concerns for the review of the detailed test plan. This review depends heavily on the judgment of the QA team for five out of six concerns. This is indicative of the fact that we still have much to learn about how to test systems efficiently and effectively.

	QUALITY ASSURANCE CONCERN	REVIEW TECHNIQUE
1	Have a sufficient number of capable people been assigned to the system test phase?	Project documentation Fact finding Judgment
2	Will comprehensive test data be prepared?	Project documentation Checklist Judgment
3	Will users be adequately trained to evaluate test results?	Project documentation Fact finding
4	Will the planned test data test the system controls?	Project documentation Fact finding Judgment
5	Will the test phase be completed on time?	Project documentation Fact finding Judgment
6	Will the test phase be completed within the budget?	Project documentation Fact finding Judgment

Figure 7.13. Review point 9: review of detailed test plan.

Review Point 10: Test Results

The final responsibility to determine that the system meets specifications resides with the user. The data processing department has taken the user's needs and converted them into a system. The system has been built on the understanding of the data processing personnel as to what the user said was wanted. Based on that understanding, they wrote programs and debugged them. Prior to the system going into production, the user must make an evaluation as to whether or not data processing people truly understood his needs. This is done through detailed evaluation of test results.

Systems test evaluation is a detailed, tedious, time-consuming task. There is no easy way to perform a systems test and evaluation. The results of processing normally must be manually calculated and then compared against computer-produced results. If the new and old systems have the same or similar records, the testing technique of parallel processing can be utilized. Parallel processing means running the same data through both systems and comparing results. Unfortunately this only applies to a small number of system test situations.

Figure 7.14 lists five concerns for the review of test results. QA primarily reviews the evaluations of user and DP systems test personnel. Where additional test transactions are needed, those should have been specified by QA during the system test planning phase. QA should be more concerned with the test process than the test itself. For example, knowing how user personnel will manually calculate results and then compare them to computer-produced results is more important than QA actually making those comparisons.

	QUALITY ASSURANCE CONCERN	REVIEW TECHNIQUE
1	Does the system meet the needs of users as specified in the design?	Fact finding Observation Simulation modeling Testing Test data Base case
2	Does the system conform to MIS standards?	System documentation Observation Checklist
4	Is the user adequately trained to handle the day-to-day operational problems of the system?	Fact finding Observation Judgment
5	Have performance standards been achieved?	System documentation Judgment Testing Test data Base case

Figure 7.14. Review point 10: review of test results.

CONVERSION PHASE

All systems undergo a conversion of some type. Even if there is no existing system, a conversion occurs when data processing converts from no system to a new system. This involves the building of master files, special first-run problems, and problems associated with inexperienced operating and user personnel.

The conversion of files from an old system to a new one involves all the steps in a systems development life cycle. The steps are condensed, but they all exist. The problems occur because data processing personnel frequently shortcut good systems practices during the conversion phase. For example, where special programs are needed to convert files, they are done with "quick and dirty" techniques. The normal processes of systems design, program design, and documentation do not occur. These traditional safeguards are ignored because they are not considered important. Shortcuts frequently cause serious problems.

QA must determine that the traditional good system safeguards are followed during the conversion process. When conversion standards do not exist, QA should check for compliance to normal systems development standards and procedures in the building of conversion systems and programs.

Problems occurring during the conversion phase can be more difficult to correct than normal production problems. Production systems normally have built-in procedures for correcting data, based on normal data entry procedures. Conversion systems seldom are that elaborate, and problems can occur during conversion that cannot be corrected by traditional means. For example, if a field is designated numeric, the system itself prevents other than numeric data from entering that field. If during the conversion process alphabetic data gets into that field, it may not be correctable because the new system may prevent any change in that field.

Figure 7.15 shows the major steps in the conversion phase. Within conversion are two QA review points. The first (Review Point 11) reviews the detailed conversion planning and program development step. The second (Review Point 12) is the review of the results of the conversion process.

Review Point 11: Detail Conversion Planning and Programs

QA reviewers are concerned that there are sufficient controls during the conversion phase to protect the system's data. These controls may not be

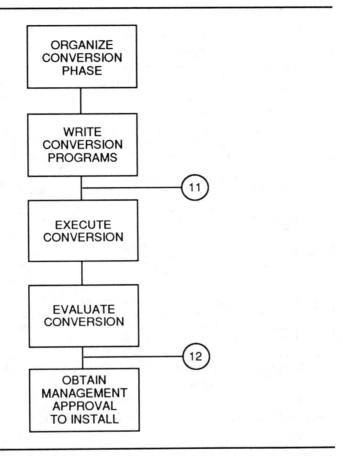

Figure 7.15. Conversion phase.

departmental standards and procedures. Because conversion occurs in-frequently, many data processing departments have not bothered to de-velop conversion standards.

Figure 7.16 lists six QA concerns with the review of detailed conver-sion planning and program development. When conversion standards are not documented, QA should attempt to develop some general procedures and guidelines for the conversion process. When QA develops detailed checklists for reviewing the conversion process, those same checklists can be used by project personnel as they go through the process.

	QUALITY ASSURANCE CONCERN	REVIEW PRACTICE
1	Have a sufficient number of capable people been assigned to the system conversion phase?	Project documentation Fact finding Judgment
2	Are conversion programs coded and tested in accordance with MIS standards?	System documentation Observation Checklist
3	Has a contingency plan been made in case the conversion is unsuccessful?	Project documentation Fact finding
4	Will the conversion phase be completed on time?	Project documentation Fact finding Judgment
5	Will the conversion phase be completed within budget?	Project documentation Fact finding Judgment
6	Are the controls over the conversion process adequate to ensure an accurate and complete conversion?	System documentation Fact finding Checklist

Figure 7.16.   Review point 11: review of detail conversion planning and programs.

Review Point 12: Review of Conversion Results

The final step for QA is to determine that the conversion process has been successfully completed. These steps parallel very closely the steps for verifying test results. Final responsibility for the accuracy and completeness of the conversion process rests with the user, who must mandate use of tests to be sure the conversion process has been successfully completed.

If files need to be converted, or new files created, the user must examine a sufficient number of records on those files to assure himself of the successful conversion of the data. This also includes totaling the key amount fields to assure that the totals of the old file agree with the totals in the converted file. Small errors, even in nonmoney fields, have been known to cost organizations dearly. In one example, the last digit in a post office box number was deleted on an accounts payable master file. Checks in the amount of several hundred thousand dollars were sent to the wrong post office box and cashed by the holder. The funds were never recovered.

Figure 7.17 lists two concerns for the review of conversion results. While the steps are limited, the process is difficult, time-consuming, and very important. The primary responsibility will be to see that the user and data processing personnel have followed the plan in sufficient detail to be sure the conversion process is successful.

	QUALITY ASSURANCE CONCERN	REVIEW PRACTICE
1	Was the conversion performed in accordance with conversion standards?	System documentation Checklist
2	Have the results of the conversion process been verified?	Fact finding Observation Checklist

Figure 7.17. Review point 12: review of conversion results.

Conversion Checklist

The conversion process may be difficult to execute within the time constraints. For example, many system conversions are performed over the weekend. If the conversion cannot be successfully completed within the two-day weekend period, the organization may face serious operational problems Monday morning. For this reason, many organizations have adopted a fail-safe method. They pick a point in time at which the new system must be successfully installed, and if it is not finished by then, they revert back to the old system. This process has saved many organizations from serious operational problems.

Because this is a high-risk phase, of very short duration, a conversion phase checklist follows for use in facilitating it. This conversion phase checklist can be used by the quality assurance analyst, or it can be given to computer operations to verify that the appropriate procedures have been followed during the conversion phase.

The checklist is designed so that yes responses are desirable and no responses require further investigation. A comments column is available to clarify no responses. The not applicable (N/A) column is included for those items in the checklist that are not applicable for your organization.

	YES	*NO*	*N/A*	*COMMENTS*
1. Have the files that need to be converted been identified?				
2. Have the records that require changes been identified?				
3. Have procedures been developed and implemented to verify the accuracy and completeness of data changes?				
4. Do procedures verify that the new data entered during conversion is authorized?				
5. Can the individual be identified who authorized new data during the conversion process?				
6. Is the addition of new account entities, such as employees, customers, etc., prohibited during the conversion process?				
7. Have the file integrity totals been documented?				
8. Have the files that will be modified prior to use with the new systems been identified?				
9. Will a simple accounting proof (i.e., old file balance, plus additions, minus deletions, equals new file balance) be used to verify the integrity of the new version of the file?				
10. Will the old version of the production files be maintained after the conversion phase?				

RESPONSE

RESPONSE

	YES	NO	N/A	COMMENTS
11. Will the old computer programs be saved?				
12. Will an audit trail of changes made to production files be retained?				
13. Have the programs for the previous system been retained in such a way that they can be reactivated if needed?				
14. Have the operating instructions for the previous system been retained in such a way that they can be reactivated if needed?				
15. Have the master files for the previous system been retained in such a way that they can be reactivated if needed?				
16. Has each step of the conversion plan been documented in the sequence in which it should be performed?				
17. Has a time estimate been assigned to each step of the conversion plan?				
18. Has a plan been developed to revert to the old system in the event the conversion is unsuccessful?				
19. Have the security requirements of the application system been defined and made known to the conversion team?				

	RESPONSE			
	YES	NO	N/A	COMMENTS
20. Are procedures invoked to protect the security of the data in programs during the conversion process?				
21. Is one individual responsible for security during the conversion process?				
22. Has a budget for the conversion process be established?				
23. Is the conversion budget adequate to develop and execute a well-controlled conversion phase?				
24. Does the conversion budget provide for security?				
25. Has user management appointed an individual from their area responsible for the conversion process, and is the responsible individual knowledgeable in the application and allotted sufficient time to monitor the conversion?				
26. Have criteria been established to ascertain when the conversion is successful?				
27. Has a procedure been developed to communicate conversion problems to the user area?				
28. Does the data processing department have conversion procedures?				

RESPONSE

	YES	NO	N/A	COMMENTS

29. Has the user prepared procedures for the conversion of the application?

30. Do the conversion procedures ensure that the new versions of programs will be in production at the appropriate time?

DETERMINING IF CONCERNS HAVE BEEN ADEQUATELY ADDRESSED BY THE PROJECT TEAM

A concern is normally a broad area which requires investigation to determine whether or not the project team has adequately addressed that area. For example, one concern is whether or not the project team has developed an adequate test plan. To ask the question "Have you developed an adequate test plan?" would not produce a meaningful answer because the answer would be an opinion.

What is needed to evaluate a concern is a list of criteria, which if met, would mean the concern has been adequately addressed. In our test plan example some of the criteria that should be included in the test plan are:

1. Error conditions are tested.

2. Null input and 1 record file are tested.

3. Backup/recovery procedures are tested.

4. Manual interface procedures are tested.

5. File limits are tested.

6. Error correction and reentry procedures are tested.

7. Audit trails are tested.

8. Etc., etc., etc.

If all these criteria are met then the QA group could conclude the test plan was adequate. The review would provoke no argument. However, these criteria must be developed and agreed upon by involved parties prior to conducting a review using those criteria.

SUMMARY

The QA review is a continuing process during the entire systems development life cycle. QA should become involved in as many points as practical for a system under development. This will provide data processing management with the continual monitoring of the health and well-being of all projects as they are being developed.

Twelve QA review points are recommended. Making reviews at these twelve points will involve quality assurance personnel at the major decision points and at the times when they can most easily influence the system design process.

QA can perform two functions during reviews. The first and most important is to provide an evaluation of the development process to data processing management. The second is to provide assistance and counsel to the project team. While the main responsibility is evaluation, the major contribution can be recommendations and suggestions to project personnel on design dilemmas.

Management of user organizations is faced with "go – no go" decisions at several points during the systems development life cycle. Depending on the point, and the value of the system, the decision may be made by executive management, user management, data processing management, or a combination thereof. Normally, the go – no go decisions during the early phases are made by executive management, during the middle phases by user management, and end phases by either data processing or user management. While QA is solely a data processing advisory group, data processing management may wish to pass the QA evaluation on to other management as an input to them in the decision making process. In other cases, data processing management may use QA input as a factor in making its decision on the advisability of continuing system application development.

This chapter has provided a list of QA concerns for each of the twelve review points. The reviewers should use these in formulating their review methodology for each of the twelve review points. With each concern is listed one or more review practices that can be used by the reviewer in determining how the project personnel or DP department handled that concern. Once the reviewers have considered each concern, they are in a position to make an evaluation of the application. The review practices are covered in the following chapter, and the evaluation methodology in Chapter 9.

8

Reviewing the Adequacy of Application Controls

One of the major responsibilities of quality assurance groups is to review the adequacy of application controls. For many QA groups, this involves three tasks:

1. Review the controls in application systems.

2. Recommend controls in application systems.

3. Develop control standards for application systems.

A system of internal controls is a structured grouping of controls. Controls are not independent of each other but are an integrated system. Internal controls must be developed and assessed as a system. Internal control should be developed and implemented as a hierarchical structure or system. Internal control policy is established at the highest organizational level and expanded, amplified, implemented, and enforced throughout the entire organization. Control is too often viewed as an independent segment within each business system. This often leads to a duplication of controls and an excessive expenditure for control.

INTERNAL CONTROL DEFINED

Internal control can be defined in both a broad and narrow sense. When defined narrowly it usually is referred to as *internal accounting control*, and when referred to in a broad sense it is referred to as *internal control*. Quality assurance personnel should look at control in the broad sense.

An early and broad definition by the American Institute of Certified Public Accountants appears to be closely tied to management's needs:

Internal controls comprise the plan of organization and all methods and procedures that are concerned mainly with, and related directly to, the safeguarding of assets and the reliability of the financial records. They generally include such controls as the system of authorization and approval, separation of duties concerned with record keeping, and accounting reports from those concerned with operations or asset custody, physical controls over assets, and internal accounting.*

The objective of internal accounting control as defined in the Foreign Corrupt Practices Act deals with the four areas:

1.   *Authorization.* Transactions are executed in accordance with management's general or specific authorization.

2.   *Recording.* Transactions are recorded as necessary to permit preparation of financial statements in conformity with generally accepted accounting principles or any other criteria applicable to such statements, and to maintain accountability for assets.

3.   *Access to assets.* Access to assets is permitted only in accordance with management's authorization.

4.   *Asset accountability.* The recorded accountability for assets is compared with the existing assets at reasonable intervals and appropriate action is taken with respect to any differences. Internal control is divided into environmental controls and application controls. The environmental controls govern the methods by which work is performed and apply to everybody in an organization. Examples include selected programming languages, system development life cycle, and data security systems. Application controls deal exclusively with a single application such as payroll.

Environment Control Objectives

Environmental controls are developed in support of the organization's internal control policy. Environmental controls include the plan of organization and all the methods and procedures that are concerned with operational

---

* Section 320.10, Statement on Auditing Standard No. 1, copyright 1973, American Institute of Certified Public Accountants.

efficiency and adherence to managerial policies. Environmental controls usually relate only indirectly to the financial records. Public accountants frequently refer to environmental controls as administrative or general controls. The internal control environment established by management has a significant impact on the selection and effectiveness of the company's application control procedures and techniques.

Application Control Objectives

More effort has gone into defining application control objectives than environmental control objectives. This is because the emphasis traditionally has been on application controls.

The three application control objectives are *accuracy, completeness,* and *authorization.* These are supplemented by other control objectives of lesser importance. The importance given to these objectives depends upon whether the evaluator's perspective is financial or operational.

Approaches to control design are as different as approaches to application design. It has been established that there are 50,000 different payroll applications in the United States. If organizations can develop that many different approaches to an application, they can develop an equal number of approaches to control.

High-volume transactions tend to be processed accurately, completely, and are authorized. It is the unusual or nonrecurring transactions that tend to cause the most problems. In many organizations the documented procedures on how to handle unusual/nonrecurring transactions are not as extensive as for high-volume transactions. Therefore, when designing application controls, attention should be paid to these unusual and/or nonrecurring transactions.

The application control objectives of the major accounting associations were studied in developing a set of application control objectives that could be used to explain application control design and assessment. The control objectives were chosen to illustrate the use of controls in applications as discussed below.

Accurate Data. Accurate data implies need for correction of inaccuracies associated with data preparation, conversion to machine-readable format, processing by the computer, or in the output preparation and delivery processes.

Complete Data. Completeness of processed data requires that data is not lost during preparation, in transit to the computer, during processing, between interrelated computer systems, and/or in transit to users of that data.

Timely Data. The timely processing of data ensures that management has the necessary information to take action in time to avert avoidable losses.

Authorized Data. Controls should ensure that any unauthorized data is detected prior to and during processing.

Processed According to GAAP. Financial data should be processed in accordance with generally accepted accounting procedures. Controls should ensure that these procedures are followed.

Compliance with Organization's Policies and Procedures. Organizations establish policies and procedures for handling transaction data. Controls should ensure that the data is processed according to those policies and procedures.

Compliance with Laws and Regulations. Regulatory agencies establish laws and regulations regarding the processing of transaction data. In today's business environment, many of these regulated transactions are highly visible, such as misuse of organizational funds on officers' expense accounts. Improper transactions can result in immediate repercussions to both individuals and their organization. Controls should ensure that laws and regulations are followed.

Adequate Supporting Evidence. Controls should ensure that sufficient evidence exists to reconstruct transactions and pinpoint accountability for processing. This evidence may also be used for restart and recovery purposes in computerized business applications. The evidence should enable tracing from source documents to control totals, and from control totals back to the supporting transactions. The methods for achieving these application control objectives are set forth in later sections of this manual.

ACCEPTABLE LEVEL OF RISK

Data processing organizations are continually subjected to the probability of loss due to risk. The primary purpose of controls is to reduce the amount of probable loss. If there is no risk, there need be no controls. Thus, in designing controls, the controls should always cost less to install than the savings achieved due to reducing losses.

Figure 8.1 illustrates the relationship of the cost of controls to the loss due to risk. At the leftmost side of the chart, we see that probable loss is maximized and there are no controls. As controls are added, the cost of controlling the risk situation increases, but the probable loss due to risk is reduced. At some point, these lines cross, which is normally the most cost-effective point for controls. On the right side of the chart we see that while the risk continues to drop, the cost of controls escalates. The total cost of any risk situation is the total of the probable loss due to the risk plus the cost of controlling that risk.

Most users of computer applications recognize that it is not cost-effective to reduce losses to zero. Therefore, application system users need to accept that there will be loss situations. For example, invoices will be mispriced, payroll will be miscalculated, checks will be processed for the wrong amount, etc., etc. The question that needs to be answered is, "How much loss is acceptable?" The answer to that question determines the level of controls to be designed.

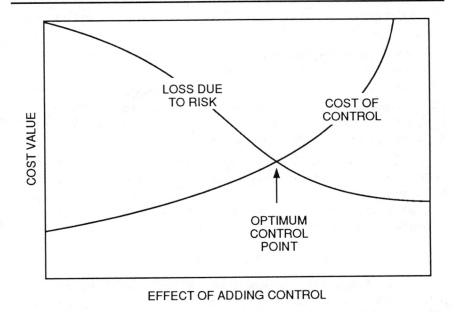

Figure 8.1. Cost-effectiveness curve of control.

Let's look at a banking example. When a teller in a bank cashes a check, the teller is faced with two risks: first, the account holder will have insufficient funds to cover the amount of the check; and second, the individual presenting the check is doing so illegally.

The bank has several decisions to make in addressing this risk in their application systems. The system includes both manual and automated segments. The bank could reduce losses to zero by implementing controls which verify the account balance, immediately reduce the account balance, obtain positive identification that the person presenting the check is authorized, verify the signature against a signature card, and so on. Unfortunately, this level of control would be very time-consuming and would substantially reduce the number of customers the bank teller could handle in a given period of time. On the other hand, without any control, the losses from bad checks may be so significant that the bank would go out of business.

The question the bank must answer is, "What is a reasonable amount of bad checks that a teller should accept?" For example, the bank might decide that each teller would be operating effectively if the bad checks he or she accepted did not exceed $500 per year. This becomes a systems requirement, and controls are designed to reduce the number of bad checks to that level.

Obviously, the effectiveness of control must be measured. If the bank managers find that with the implemented controls losses are approximately $500 per teller per year, they can be satisfied that the controls are achieving the risk requirements. On the other hand, if losses exceed $500 per teller per year, controls need to be tightened; and if losses are negligible, controls might be too tight and should be loosened.

You can see from this example that there are a lot of considerations in determining what level of loss is acceptable. This process is not followed by many organizations. This section is designed to help quality assurance analysts help systems analysts and users understand risk, and develop controls that will reduce that risk to an acceptable level.

METHODS FOR REDUCING LOSSES

Controls are designed to reduce the loss associated with risk. When the risk is high, controls should be strong, and when the risk is low only minimal controls may be needed. In some instances, the user may be willing to accept the risk, and thus no controls are needed.

The probable loss due to risk can be determined through either historical information or risk analysis. Historical information tells us what the expected losses will be in a given situation. We then use that experience in estimating losses in new situations.

Risk analysis is a methodology for determining the expected loss in a risk situation. The risk analysis algorithm involves two factors:

1.   The frequency of occurrence of a loss situation

2.   The average dollar loss per occurrence

The probable loss due to risk is calculated by multiplying the frequency of occurrence times the average loss per occurrence (see Figure 8.2).

There are four methods for reducing loss in a risk situation. The frequency of occurrence of loss due to risk can be reduced by reducing the frequency of occurrence of loss situations and reducing the opportunity for loss. The average loss per occurrence can be reduced by reduc-

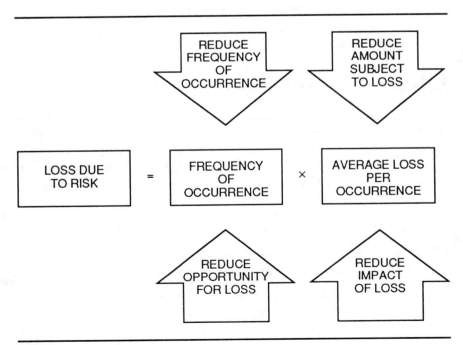

Figure 8.2. Reducing risks.

ing the amount subject to loss and reducing the impact of the loss. Each of these four methods of reducing risk is accomplished through the implementation of controls. However, it is helpful in discussing these controls to understand how they can reduce loss. Therefore, each of the methods will be discussed individually.

REDUCE THE FREQUENCY OF OCCURRENCE

The most effective way to reduce losses is to reduce the events that lead to losses. For example, if 100 data entry errors occur per day there is probability of 100 individual losses per day. If the frequency of data entry errors can be reduced to 50 per day, the probability of loss is equally reduced.

The following are just some of the methods that are effective in reducing the frequency of occurrence of loss events.

1.   Verify the correctness of input.

2.   Identify problems and search them out before they occur.

3.   Enter data only once into computer applications.

4.   Reduce the amount of data entered (i.e., use codes rather than alphabetic descriptions).

REDUCE OPPORTUNITY FOR LOSS

The conditions that lead to loss can be monitored to detect problems before they result in losses. Once the frequency of occurrences has been reduced as far as practical, monitoring of those events can help control the opportunity for error, and thus loss. Some of these controls can exist within computer applications, but many are external to the automated segment of the application.

The methods that can be used to reduce the opportunity for loss include:

1.   *Manual monitoring.* People oversee events to look for errors before computer results are released for action.

2.   *Anticipation audits.* Problem situations are anticipated, such as might occur when a customer orders a significantly larger amount of product than normally ordered, so that potential errors can be investigated.

3.   *Authorization*. The approval process usually involves verifying compliance and reasonableness of the event.

4.   *Training*. Employees are taught how to look for and anticipate problems in the normal course of their job.

REDUCE AMOUNT SUBJECT TO LOSS

Information systems can be structured so that the amount subject to loss is minimized. For example, in automated accounts payable systems, the value of a check produced by the system can be limited to a fixed amount, such as $1,000. This is imprinted on the check, and thus the loss due to any erroneously produced checks is limited to $1,000.

Two of the methods to reduce the amount subject to loss are

1.   Divide property between two or more locations (e.g., backup data libraries).

2.   Teach two or more people (e.g., programmers) to perform the same function.

REDUCE IMPACT OF LOSS

The impact of the loss can be reduced by recouping all or part of the loss. Minimizing the impact involves taking corrective action after the loss has occurred. Normally, the quicker the action, the more the impact can be minimized.

Among the methods that help reduce the impact of loss are

1.   Insuring the loss through an insurance company or a self-insurance procedure.

2.   Maintaining backup data to reconstruct processing in the event of problems, or when erroneous output is produced.

3.   Creating audit trails that enable systems to substantiate and/or reconstruct processing.

TYPES OF CONTROLS

Four different methods for reducing losses through controls have been presented in this chapter. These methods use one or more of the following types of controls:

1.   Preventive controls stop an undesirable event from occurring.

2. Detective controls uncover an undesirable event as it occurs.

3. Corrective controls provide the means for restoring a situation to normal after an unacceptable event.

The three types of controls can be illustrated in a fire situation. Fire is a risk that can result in loss to an organization. Preventive controls such as fire-resistant materials and firewalls stop the fire from occurring. Detective controls such as smoke detectors and fire alarms identify and announce that a fire has occurred. Corrective controls provide the means of putting out the fire; these include sprinkler system, fire department, and fire extinguishers.

The implementation and operation of preventive, detective, or corrective controls can be in one of the following two manners:

1. *Discretionary controls.* The execution and effectiveness of the control is left to the option of the implementer. For example, a guard may decide to challenge or not challenge a visitor; a supervisor may decide to verify for compliance or not to verify an event prior to approving it. Discretionary controls are normally associated with people controls. For example, an automobile seat belt is a discretionary control. People can decide whether or not they want to use the control when they get in an automobile.

2. *Nondiscretionary controls.* Controls whose use is mandatory are considered nondiscretionary controls. Normally, nondiscretionary controls are automated controls in either a manual or computerized environment. For example, air bags in an automobile activate on impact automatically, and computer system data validation routines operate on all input data. Nondiscretionary controls are dependable and consistent.

The effectiveness of the various types of control is illustrated in Figure 8.3. This figure shows that nondiscretionary controls are more effective than discretionary controls. In addition, the figure shows that the coupling of detective and corrective controls are important. Detective controls without corrective action may be of little value. For example, a fire alarm ringing serves no purpose unless corrective action is taken to put out the fire.

METHOD OF IMPLEMENTATION	TYPE OF CONTROL		
	PREVENTIVE	DETECTIVE	
		with corresponding CORRECTIVE	without CORRECTIVE
DISCRETIONARY	Least effective, generally manual controls applied at front end of processing. However, moderately efficient.	Moderately effective, manual controls probably least efficient controls.	Least effective and possibly dangerous since users rely improperly on them. Very inefficient.
NONDISCRETIONARY	Moderately effective, generally MIS controls, applied at front end of processing. Probably most efficient controls.	Most effective, generally controls which are computerized are applied before processing can take place. Moderately efficient.	May have some remote effectiveness but probably little. Highly inefficient.

Figure 8.3. Effectiveness and efficiency of controls.

REVIEWING CONTROLS *

Controls should be reviewed throughout the systems development process. The control design process parallels the systems design process. Controls are specified as needs, designed, implemented, documented, and tested.

The adequacy of control for a given application depends upon both the environmental and application controls. However, because environmental

---

* Audit Guide for Assessing Reliability of Computer Output, U.S. General Accounting Office, May 1978.

controls are common to most applications the quality assurance function may need to review environmental controls only once for all applications. Based on this review, the review of application controls may need to be increased or decreased depending upon the strength of the environmental controls.

This chapter provides quality assurance analysts with both environmental and application control checklists. In addition, a summarization form is included for both parts of control to aid the quality assurance analyst in evaluating the adequacy of the controls. Prior to presenting the questionnaires, let's review the more common system vulnerabilities.

COMMON SYSTEM VULNERABILITIES*

The list of risks helps explain what are the new and possibly increased risks in a computerized environment. It is presented as a tool for quality assurance to use in the identification of what may be different, from a risk perspective, in a computerized environment.

Erroneous or Falsified Data Input

Erroneous or falsified input data is the simplest and most common cause of undesirable performance by an applications system. Vulnerabilities occur wherever data is collected, manually processed, or prepared for entry to the computer.

- Unreasonable or inconsistent source data values may not be detected.

- Keying errors during transcription may not be detected.

- Incomplete or poorly formatted data records may be accepted and treated as if they were complete records.

- Records in one format may be interpreted according to a different format.

- An employee may fraudulently add, delete, or modify data (e.g., payment vouchers, claims) to obtain benefits (e.g., checks, negotiable coupons) for himself or herself.

---

* U.S. Nation Bureau of Standard, FIPS Pub. 65, pp. 2–17 to 2–21.

- Lack of document counts and other controls over source data or input transactions may allow some of the data or transactions to be lost without detection — or allow extra records to be added.

- Records about the data entry personnel (e.g., a record of a personnel action) may be modified during data entry.

- Data that arrives at the last minute (or under some other special or emergency condition) may not be verified prior to processing.

- Records in which errors have been detected may be corrected without verification of the full record.

Misuse by Authorized End Users

End users are the people who are served by the MIS system. The system is designed for their use, but they can also misuse it for undesirable purposes. It is often very difficult to determine whether their use of the system is in accordance with the legitimate performance of their job.

- An employee may convert information to an unauthorized use; for example, he may sell privileged data about an individual to a prospective employer, credit agency, insurance company, or competitor; or he may use statistics for stock market transactions before their public release.

- A user whose job requires access to individual records in a file may manage to compile a complete listing of the file and then make unauthorized use of it (e.g., sell a listing of employees' home addresses as a mailing list).

- Unauthorized altering of information may be accomplished for an unauthorized end user (e.g., theft of services).

- An authorized user may use the system for personal benefit (e.g., theft of services).

- A supervisor may manage to approve and enter a fraudulent transaction.

- A disgruntled or terminated employee may destroy or modify records — possibly in such a way that backup records are also corrupted and useless.

- An authorized user may accept a bribe to modify or obtain information.

Uncontrolled System Access

Organizations expose themselves to unnecessary risk if they fail to establish controls over who can enter the MIS area, who can use the MIS system, and who can access the information contained in the system.

- Data or programs may be stolen from the computer room or other storage areas.

- MIS facilities may be destroyed or damaged either by intruders or employees.

- Individuals may not be adequately identified before they are allowed to enter the MIS area.

- Remote terminals may not be adequately protected from use by unauthorized persons.

- An unauthorized user may gain access to the system via a dial-in line and an authorized user's password.

- Passwords may be inadvertently revealed to unauthorized individuals. A user may write his password in some convenient place, or the password may be obtained from card decks, discarded printouts, or by observing the user as he types it.

- A user may leave a logged-in terminal unattended, allowing an unauthorized person to use it.

- A terminated employee may retain access to an MIS system because his name and password are not immediately deleted from authorization tables and control lists.

- An unauthorized individual may gain access to the system for his own purposes (e.g., theft of computer service, data, or programs, modification of data, alteration of programs, sabotage, denial of services).

- Repeated attempts by the same user or terminal to gain unauthorized access to the system to a file may go undetected.

Ineffective Security Practices for the Application

Inadequate manual checks and controls to ensure correct processing by the MIS system or negligence by those responsible for carrying out these checks result in many vulnerabilities.

- Poorly defined criteria for authorized access may result in employees not knowing what information they, or others, are permitted to access.

- The person responsible for security may fail to restrict user access only to those processes and data which are needed to accomplish assigned tasks.

- Large funds disbursements, unusual price changes, and unanticipated inventory usage may not be reviewed for correctness.

- Repeated payments to the same party may go unnoticed because there is no review.

- Sensitive data may be carelessly handled by the application staff, by the mail service, or by other personnel within the organization.

- Postprocessing reports analyzing system operations may not be reviewed to detect security violations.

- Inadvertent modification or destruction of files may occur when trainees are allowed to work on live data.

- Appropriate action may not be pursued when a security variance is reported to the system security officer or to the perpetrating individual's supervisor; in fact, procedures covering such occurrences may not exist.

Procedural Errors at the MIS Facility

Both errors and intentional acts committed by the MIS operations staff may result in improper operational procedures, lapsed controls, and losses in storage media and output.

Procedures and Controls

- Files may be destroyed during database reorganization or during release of disk space.

- Operators may ignore operational procedures; for example, by allowing programmers to operate computer equipment.

- Job control language parameters may be erroneous.

- An installation manager may circumvent operational controls to obtain information.

- Careless or incorrect restarting after shutdown may cause the state of a transaction update to be unknown.

- An operator may enter erroneous information at CPU console (e.g., control switch in wrong position, terminal user allowed full system access, operator cancels wrong job from queue).

- Hardware maintenance may be performed while production data is on-line and the equipment undergoing maintenance is not isolated.

- An operator may perform unauthorized acts for personal gain (e.g., make extra copies of competitive bidding reports, print copies of unemployment checks, delete a record from journal file).

- Operations staff may sabotage the computer (e.g., drop pieces of metal into a terminal).

- The wrong version of a program may be executed.

- A program may be executed twice using the same transactions.

- An operator may bypass required safety controls (e.g., write rings for tape reels).

- Supervision of operations personnel may not be adequate during nonworking hour shifts.

- Due to incorrectly learned procedures, an operator may alter or erase the master files.

- A console operator may override a label check without recording the action in the security log.

Storage Media Handling

- Critical tape files may be mounted without being write protected.

- Inadvertently or intentionally mislabeled storage media are erased. In a case where they contain backup files, the erasure may not be noticed until it is needed.

- Internal labels on storage media may not be checked for correctness.

- Files with missing or mislabeled expiration dates may be erased.

- Incorrect processing of data or erroneous updating of files may occur when card decks have been dropped, partial input decks are used, write rings mistakenly are placed in tapes, paper tape is incorrectly mounted, or wrong tape is mounted.

- Scratch tapes used for jobs processing sensitive data may not be adequately erased after use.

- Temporary files written during a job step for use in subsequent steps may be erroneously released or modified through inadequate protection of the files or because of an abnormal termination.

- Storage media containing sensitive information may not get adequate protection because operations staff is not advised of the nature of the information content.

- Tape management procedures may not adequately account for the current status of all tapes.

- Magnetic storage media that have contained very sensitive information may not be degaussed before being released.

- Output may be sent to the wrong individual or terminal.

- Improperly operating output or postprocessing units (e.g., bursters, decollators, or multipart forms) may result in loss of output.

- Surplus output material (e.g., duplicates of output data, used carbon paper) may not be disposed of properly.

- Tapes and programs that label output for distribution may be erroneous or not protected from tampering.

Program Errors

Application programs should be developed in an environment that requires and supports complete, correct, and consistent program design, good programming practices, adequate testing, review, and documentation, and proper maintenance procedures. Although programs developed in such an environment will still contain undetected errors, programs not developed in this manner will probably be rife with errors. Additionally, programmers can deliberately modify programs to produce undesirable side effects, or they can misuse the programs they are in charge of.

- Records may be deleted from sensitive files without a guarantee that the deleted records can be reconstructed.

- Programmers may insert special provisions in programs that manipulate data concerning themselves (e.g., a payroll programmer may alter his own payroll records).

- Data may not be stored separately from code with the result that program modifications are more difficult and must be made more frequently.

- Program changes may not be tested adequately before use in a production run.

- Changes to a program may result in new errors because of unanticipated interactions between program modules.

- Program acceptance tests may fail to detect errors that only occur for unusual combinations of input (e.g., a program that is supposed to reject all except a specified range of values actually accepts an additional value).

- Programs, the content of which should be safeguarded, may not be identified and protected.

- Code, test data with its associated output, and documentation for certified programs may not be filed and retained for reference.

- Documentation for vital programs may not be safeguarded.

- Programmers may fail to keep a change log, maintain back copies, or formalize record-keeping activities.

- An employee may steal programs he is maintaining and use them for personal gain (e.g., sale to a commercial organization, hold another organization for extortion).

- Poor program design may result in a critical data value being initialized twice. An error may occur when the program is modified to change the data value — but only changed in one place.

- Production data may be disclosed or destroyed when it is used during testing.

- Errors may result when the programmer misunderstands requests for changes to the program.

- Errors may be introduced by a programmer who makes changes directly to machine code.

- Programs may contain routines not compatible with their intended purpose, which can disable or bypass security protection mechanisms. For example, a programmer who anticipates being fired inserts code into a program which will cause vital system files to be deleted as soon as his name no longer appears in the payroll file.

- Inadequate documentation or labeling may result in wrong version of program being modified.

Operating System Flaws

Design and implementation errors, system generation and maintenance problems, and deliberate penetrations resulting in modifications to the operating system can produce undesirable effects in the application system. Flaws in the operating system are often difficult to prevent and detect.

- User jobs may be permitted to read or write outside assigned storage area.

- Inconsistencies may be introduced into data because of simultaneous processing of the same file by two jobs.

- An operating system design or implementation error may allow a user to disable audit controls or to access all system information.

- An operating system may not protect a copy of information as thoroughly as it protects the original.

- Unauthorized modification to the operating system may allow a data entry clerk to enter programs and thus subvert the system.

- An operating system crash may expose valuable information such as password lists or authorization tables.

- Maintenance personnel may bypass security controls while performing maintenance work. At such times the system is vulnerable to errors or intentional acts of the maintenance personnel, or anyone else who might also be on the system and discover the opening (e.g., microcoded sections of the operating system may be tampered with or sensitive information from on-line fields may be disclosed).

- An operating system may fail to record that multiple copies of output have been made from spooled storage devices.

- An operating system may fail to maintain an unbroken audit trail.

- When restarting after a system crash, the operating system may fail to ascertain that all terminal locations which were previously occupied are still occupied by the same individuals.

- A user may be able to get into monitor or supervisory mode.

- The operating system may fail to erase all scratch space assigned to a job after the normal or abnormal termination of the job.

- Files may be allowed to be read or written without having been opened.

Communications System Failure

Information being routed from one location to another over communication lines is vulnerable to accidental failures and to intentional interception and modification by unauthorized parties.

Accidental Failures

- Undetected communications errors may result in incorrect or modified data.

- Information may be accidentally misdirected to the wrong terminal.

- Communication nodes may leave unprotected fragments of messages in memory during unanticipated interruptions in processing.

- Communication protocols may fail to positively identify the transmitter or receiver of a message.

Intentional Acts

- Communications lines may be monitored by unauthorized individuals.

- Data or programs may be stolen via telephone circuits from a remote job entry terminal.

- Programs in the network switching computers may be modified to compromise security.

- Data may be deliberately changed by individuals tapping the line (requires some sophistication, but is applicable to financial data).

- An unauthorized user may "take over" a computer communication port as an authorized user disconnects from it. Many systems cannot detect the change. This is particularly true in much of the currently available communication protocols.

- If encryption is used, keys may be stolen.
- A terminal user may be "spoofed" into providing sensitive data.
- False messages may be inserted into the system.
- True messages may be deleted from the system.
- Messages may be recorded and replayed into the system.

REVIEWING ENVIRONMENTAL CONTROLS*

Environmental controls should be reviewed prior to reviewing application controls. The review should be performed by an individual who

1. Understands the data processing function's policies, procedures, and standards.
2. Understands how the operating environment functions.
3. Has had project management experience.
4. Understands operating system software.
5. Can identify the risks and controls in a computerized environment.

For the purpose of reviewing the environmental controls, the computerized environment has been divided into the following categories.

Organizational Controls. Adequate separation of duties provides an effective check to ensure the accuracy and propriety of system and program changes and the consistency of information flowing through the computerized system. The related questions should establish the degree of job segregation within a data processing facility.

Computer Operation Controls. The related questions should help the quality assurance analyst determine whether the computer facility operates in accordance with prescribed processing procedures. An analysis of the responses should help the quality assurance analyst determine whether operating personnel could alter computer data without user knowledge.

---

* Audit Guide for Assessing Reliability of Computer Output, U.S. General Accounting Office, May 1978.

Access Controls. These questions deal with access to the computer area, remote computer terminals, systems documentation, computer programs, and computer output. The quality assurance analyst should pay particular attention to the adequacy of documented security measures surrounding the entire system.

File Controls. These questions deal with maintenance, storage, and access to computer-processed tapes, disk packs, and other data storage media. The quality assurance analyst should pay particular attention to the adequacy of documented security measures for releasing, returning, and maintaining data files.

Disaster Recovery Controls. Disaster recovery controls are preventive procedures that help protect critical files, programs, and systems documentation from fire or other hazards. To the extent possible, the quality assurance analyst should examine the organization's preventive procedures to determine whether data processing could be continued in the event of a computer facility disaster.

The Environmental Control Review Questionnaire (see Figure 8.4) is divided into the above sections. The questionnaire is designed so that "no" answers should be considered a potential control deficiency. "No" answers require additional investigation. Space is included on the form to qualify or explain responses to the questions.

An MIS Department Controls Profile Worksheet (see Figure 8.5) should be used as a tool in assessing the adequacy of controls. The questionnaire probes a series of areas for the five environmental control characteristics (i.e., organizational, computer, access, file, and disaster recovery controls). You must use judgment in completing this profile. Based on the questionnaire responses relating to the control characteristics, how much risk (low, medium, high) do you believe is involved in relying on the computer-processed data? The information about controls requested on this form is designed to help you with this judgment.

ITEM	RESPONSE			
	YES	NO	N/A	OTHER
Organizational Controls				
1. Is the MIS function independent from other operations?				
2. Is each of the following functions performed by a different individual?				
a. Maintaining the operating system/ data management system, etc.				
b. Systems design				
c. Programming				
d. Acceptance testing				
e. Authorizing program changes				
f. Handling source documents (Keypunching, etc.)				
g. Hardware operations				
h. File maintenance (Librarian for data and files)				
i. Input data				
Computer Operation Controls				
1. Have documented procedures been established covering the operations of the data center? (If so, obtain copy.)				
2. Are daily equipment operating logs maintained?				
3. Is computer downtime shown and explained?				
4. Is there an abnormal termination of job log or report for each such run?				
5. Does an operator maintain a daily input/output log for each job processed?				
6. Are these logs reviewed daily by the MIS operations manager?				
7. Does the MIS operations manager initial each log to indicate that the review has been performed?				

Figure 8.4. Environmental control review questionnaire.

ITEM	RESPONSE			
	YES	NO	N/A	OTHER
Computer Operation Controls				
8. Are all operator decisions recorded in a daily log?				
9. Is the console typewriter used to list:				
a. Date?				
b. Job name and/or number?				
c. Program name and/or number?				
d. Start/stop times?				
e. Files used?				
f. Record counts				
g. Halts (programmed and unscheduled)?				
10. If the system does not have a console typewriter, does some other method afford adequate control and record the activities performed by both the computer and operator?				
11. Is all computer time accounted for from the time it is turned on each day until it is shut down?				
12. Are disposition notes entered on the console log showing corrective actions taken when unscheduled program halts occur?				
13. Are job reruns recorded on the console log?				
14. Is the reason for each rerun recorded?				
15. Are console log pages sequentially numbered?				
16. Is the console log reviewed and signed at the end of each shift by the supervisor and filed as a permanent record?				
17. Are console printouts independently examined to detect operator problems and unauthorized intervention?				

Figure 8.4. Environmental control review questionnaire. (cont'd)

ITEM	RESPONSE			
	YES	NO	N/A	OTHER
18. Are provisions adequate to prevent unauthorized entry of program changes and/or data through the console and other devices?				
19. Does some form of printout indicate every operating run performed?				
20. Is there a procedure to prevent superseded programs from being used by mistake?				
21. Does the data center use a formal mechanism for scheduling jobs?				
22. Has a formal method been established for prioritizing the work schedules for operations?				
Access Controls				
A. **Computer Area**				
1. Is access to the computer area limited to necessary personnel?				
2. Are all employees required to sign an agreement regarding their role and responsibility in the department and the ownership and use of processing equipment and information within the data center?				
3. Do combination locks, security badges, or other means restrict access to the computer room?				
4. Are combinations on locks or similar devices periodically changed?				
5. Are account codes, authorization codes, passwords, etc., controlled to prevent unauthorized usage?				
B. **Remote Computer Terminals**				
6. Are terminals adequately secured to prevent unauthorized usage?				

Figure 8.4. Environmental control review questionnaire. (cont'd)

ITEM	RESPONSE			
	YES	NO	N/A	OTHER
7. Are access passwords to remote terminals controlled to prevent unauthorized usage?				
C. Systems Documentation				
8. Are operators denied access to program and system documentation?				
9. Are program listings inaccessible to computer operators?				
10. Do documented procedures exist for controlling systems documentation?				
D. Computer Programs				
11. Are programs protected from unauthorized access?				
12. Are privileged instructions in operating and other software systems strictly controlled?				
13. Does the agency use automated methods (e.g. a program management system) to restrict access to application programs?				
E. Computer Output				
14. Is access to blank stock of critical forms (i.e., negotiable instruments, identification cards, etc.) restricted to authorized individuals?				
15. Have controls been established over the issuance of critical forms for jobs being scheduled for processing?				
16. Are copies of critical output that needs to be destroyed maintained in a secure location until the destruction process can be accomplished?				

Figure 8.4. Environmental control review questionnaire. (cont'd)

ITEM	RESPONSE			
	YES	*NO*	*N/A*	*OTHER*
File Controls				
1. Is the responsibility for issuing and storing magnetic tapes and/or disk packs assigned to a tape librarian?				
2. Is the duty the librarian's chief responsibility?				
3. Are library procedures documented? (If so, obtain a copy.)				
4. Is access to the library limited to the responsible librarian(s)?				
5. Does the agency use automated methods (e.g., a file management system) to restrict access to computerized files?				
6. Are all data files logged out and in to prevent release to unauthorized personnel?				
7. Are tape and disk inventory records maintained?				
8. Are tape and disk status records maintained?				
9. Have external labeling procedures been documented? (If so, obtain a copy.)				
10. Are external labels affixed to active tapes and/or disks? Do labels tie in with inventory records?				
11. Are work or scratch tapes or disk packs kept in a separate area of the library?				
Disaster Recovery Controls				
1. Has the computer system operated without major malfunction within the last year?				

Figure 8.4. Environmental control review questionnaire. (cont'd)

ITEM	RESPONSE			
	YES	NO	N/A	OTHER
2. Is the data center backed up by an uninterruptible power source system?				
3. Have procedures been established to describe what action should be taken in case of fire and other hazards involving the data center, data files, and computer programs?				
4. Are these procedures implemented as defined?				
5. Are there provisions for retaining and/or copying master files and a practical means of reconstructing a damaged or destroyed file?				
6. Are sufficient generations of files maintained to facilitate reconstruction of records (grandfather-father-son routine)?				
7. Is at least one file generation maintained at a location other than the tape storage area?				
8. Are copies of critical files stored at a remote location and restricted from unauthorized access?				
9. Are copies of operating programs stored outside the computer room?				
10. Are duplicate programs maintained at a remote location and restricted from unauthorized access?				
11. Have documented backup procedures been established with another compatible data center for running the agency's programs in the event of a natural disaster or other emergency situation?				
12. Are backup procedures periodically tested at the backup data center?				

Figure 8.4. Environmental control review questionnaire. (cont'd)

PREPARER: _____   DATE: _____

REVIEWER: _____   DATE: _____

PART I

You must use judgment in completing this profile. Based on the question-naire responses relating to the control characteristics, how much risk (low, medium, high) do you believe is involved in relying on the computer-processed data? The information about controls requested on this form is designed to help you with this judgment.

CONTROL

Control Charac-teristic	Organiza-tional	Computer Operation	Access	File	Disaster Recovery
Is the control in place?					
Is the control effective?					
Is some alternate control in place?					
Is the alternate control effective?					
Level of potential risk					
COMMENTS					

Figure 8.5. MIS department controls profile worksheet.

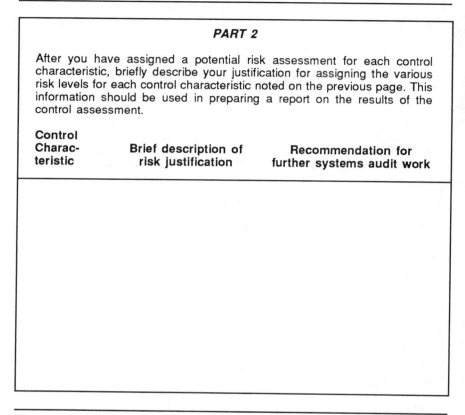

Figure 8.5. MIS department controls profile worksheet. (cont'd)

After you have assigned a potential risk assessment for each control characteristic, briefly describe your justification for assigning the various risk levels for each control characteristic noted on the previous page. This information should be used in preparing a report on the results of the control assessment.

REVIEWING APPLICATION CONTROLS

The objectives of control do not change in a computerized environment. The same control objectives that are applicable to a manual system are equally applicable to a computerized system. What changes are the methods of control needed to achieve the control objectives.

The impact of the computer on the control objectives is limited to the activities that occur in a computerized environment. Many of the controls in a computerized environment occur outside the computer segment. These controls are not directly impacted by the computer. For example, an accounts receivable application system should include all the controls needed to assure that the receipt of cash and the control over those cash receipts are outside the computer system. Examples of appropriate controls within the computer system include the following.

1. The proper version of the program is in operation.

2. Data written on computer media can be fully retrieved.

3. Integrity of data is maintained as it is passed between programs. The control objectives in a computerized application are as follows:
    a. data is accurate
    b. data is complete
    c. data is authorized
    d. data is timely
    e. data is supportable

Data Is Accurate*

The risk of greater reliance on a single source of information makes inaccurate data a higher concern. If data is inaccurate, it will be used inaccurately by all applications that use that particular data element. For example, if a product price is wrong, it will result in inaccurate customer billing, inventory value, credits, sales commission and bonuses, etc.

Errors affecting the accuracy of data may not be detected due to the fact that people are not monitoring the data and details may not be balanced to totals after processing. For example, if an element of information is entered as $69 as a detail record, but $89 is added to the control total, that condition will not be detected until a reconciliation has been made. At that point, the cost of correcting the inaccuracy may exceed the value of the error.

---

* Draft, December 17, 1980, Guideline on Computer Security Audit for the General Auditor, Center for Programming Science and Technology, Institute for Computer Sciences and Technology, National Bureau of Standards, Washington, D.C. 20234.

The greater accessibility to data makes the possibility of intentional and unintentional manipulation greater. People interfacing with the computer may change the value of individual records, values between records, or take small amounts from many records and place them into an account under their control. All these manipulations affect the accuracy of data in the database.

To achieve accuracy, an organization must make sure of the following.

1.   Data is not truncated.

2.   Data is entered correctly.

3.   Data is accumulated correctly.

4.   Data is identifiable to the user.

5.   Data is not misrepresented through electronic limitations such as overflow.

Data Is Complete

Because of the greater reliance on data as a source of information, the risk associated with incomplete data is increased. In a manual application, if data is incomplete only a single transaction may be affected. In a computerized environment, every application using the incomplete data is affected.

An incomplete data condition may not be detected until it is too late to take corrective action because the details may not be regularly balanced to the totals. If extended periods of time occur between reconciliations, data can be lost, and the cost of searching for that data could exceed its value.

The centralization of data in a computer provides greater accessibility to that data. This greater accessibility provides an opportunity to manipulate the data for the advantage of a particular individual. In this manipulation, data (i.e., organizational assets) can be lost.

In a database environment, data can be lost due to simultaneous updating. Two programs may attempt to update the same element of data simultaneously. Without proper controls, one of the two updates will be lost when the data is returned to the database. Data can also be lost if a pointer chain is broken.

To assure completeness of data, an organization would want to check the following.

1. Transactions are not lost.

2. All transactions are entered.

3. Transactions are entered in the proper accounting period.

4. Lost transactions can be identified.

5. Detailed records support the control totals.

Data Is Authorized

The main impact of the computer on the authorization of data is the changing methods of authorization. The primary control over data authorization has been with the user level. This is not part of the computer environment. However, this is changing, as authorization is being automated. For example, inventory is being automatically replenished.

Because there is greater accessibility to data, the possibility exists that unauthorized data will be entered. Access controls in a computer system can lessen this possibility. The data in most organizations is not equally accessible to all users. Restrictions are imposed for a variety of reasons. Access to raw data is often restricted because interpretation of the raw data cannot be made without specialized knowledge or information which is not stored with the data. Some data is viewed as private and given special protection because the information could be used to the disadvantage of the person or organization. Sometimes aggregated data is viewed as worthy of protection, while the individual components are considered to have no special value (e.g., individual sales data may be accorded only minor protection, but total sales figures are severely restricted).

The authority to enter data by means of source transactions or maintenance activities is usually much more controlled than the authority to access it. To protect the organization from defalcation, the authority to enter and access data is enforced in various ways. The ability to change data is often restricted to transactions which automatically provide a complete audit trail. This is analogous to the accounting requirement that no erasures are permitted in accounting journals: corrections require an adjusting transaction in the journal of transactions, rather than a simple change to an existing entry.

The authorization of data can be controlled using security profiles of users. These profiles have the capability to control data in the following manners:

1.   Use (e.g., read only, update, delete, etc.).

2.   Control use at field level.

3.   Limit use by values (e.g., update pay rate field for fields with a value of up to $199.99).

4.   Limit rate of change (e.g., change pay rate field by no more than plus or minus 10 percent).

To achieve the authorized audit objective, an organization would want to make sure of the following.

1.   Improperly authorized data is not accepted.

2.   Data that is not authorized is not accepted.

3.   Authorization is verified.

4.   Practices to avoid proper authorization, such as issuing two small purchase orders rather than one large, are identified.

Data Is Timely

Information from application systems should be available at the time of decision or action. The information needs to be available for the appropriate individual at the correct location. In many cases, failure to provide information will result in improper decisions or actions.

Timeliness is dependent on the application and type of information. In some applications, information is not critical to the process and thus the timely control objective assumes minimal importance. In other applications, such as on-line status systems, action cannot be taken until the needed information is available.

To assure timeliness of data, an organization would need to make sure that

1.   Information is sent to the right place.

2.   Information is delivered to the right person.

3.   Information is delivered on time.

4.   The needed information is identified.

Data Is Supportable

The *audit trail* is a control used for providing evidence for problems that have been detected or verifying the propriety of processing. If an authorization violation is detected and the audit trail is incomplete, the necessary corrective action may not be ascertainable. Thus, anything that affects the completeness of the audit trail has an effect on data authorization.

The adequacy of an audit trail can be viewed from two perspectives: first that it is complete; and second that the data needed is easily obtained. The computerized environment has a minor impact on the type of data retained for audit trail purposes. In actual practice, the movement to computerized environments usually increases the amount of data available for audit trail purposes. This is because the operating environment also retains data that can be used for audit trail purposes. There is a risk that the audit trail will be split into many segments. One part of the audit trail is located with all the application data, and the second part is retained in the operating environment as part of the recovery activity. Without proper planning, it may be extremely difficult, and probably impractical, to piece together all the segments of the audit trail. Thus, while the audit trail data may exist, for practical purposes the audit trail is incomplete.

The operating environment audit trail is often destroyed within a brief time because of the extensiveness of the audit trail. Some organizations use a utility program to condense the amount of data retained for audit trail purposes. Others retain the information only as long as is needed to recover from hardware and software failures. In most organizations, the operating audit trail information is retained in a time sequence so it can be used to recover operations. This may make it impractical to locate the needed information for the more traditional purposes of substantiating processing.

To make sure data is supportable, an organization would be concerned that

1. Transaction processing can be supported.
2. The support is adequate.
3. Transactions can be traced to control totals.
4. Control totals can be supported by detailed transactions.
5. Support information is readily retrievable.

Application Control Review

For the purpose of reviewing the application controls, the application has been divided into several categories:

Application System Overview. This questionnaire should be completed for each computerized application; although the data gathered is not directly related to data reliability, it will provide the quality assurance analyst with useful systems information. This document should be kept in the permanent file and updated during subsequent reviews.

System Documentation and Program Modification. Comprehensive and current documentation is necessary to describe how a computer application operates. In assessing the adequacy of a system's documentation, the quality assurance analyst should determine not only that the documentation reflects the application's current status, but also that the documentation is complete and in accordance with established standards. Although comprehensive documentation is normally prepared when an application is initially implemented, subsequent changes may be inadequately documented and should be given special attention.

Data Input. Input controls are established to verify that data is accurately transferred from an external document into a machine-readable format. The quality assurance analyst should try to make sure that source data reaches the processing programs without loss, unauthorized additions, or error.

Data Error. Data error controls involve the detection, correction, and resubmission of erroneous data. Adequate controls over rejected data are necessary for establishing a reliable database and reliable computer-processed products. The quality assurance analyst should carefully review the handling of data errors and rejected data to ensure that corrected data is promptly reentered into the system without loss or unnecessary manipulation.

Batch Process. Computer programs should develop control totals after processing data. These control totals should be compared with totals previously developed in the data initiating or transcribing departments. Control totals should also be compared to help make sure that data is properly processed through the entire system, i.e., run-to-run totals and trailer label checking.

Telecommunications. These questions are concerned with two remote data entry categories — remote batch systems and on-line systems. Remote batch systems permit access to the computer system at prearranged times. On-line inquiry and updating systems permit almost immediate access to the computer system. The quality assurance analyst should determine whether

- Access to the system, application programs, and files is limited to authorized personnel.

- Job scheduling procedures are used so that data is processed according to some priority.

- Logs are maintained showing that transactions were entered into the system.

Data Output. Output controls help make sure that data processing results are reliable and that no unauthorized alterations have been made to transactions and records while they are in the custody of the data processing facility. The quality assurance analyst should make sure that output control totals are compared against those originally established and reports distributed to appropriate users.

The Application Review Questionnaire (see Figure 8.6) is divided into the categories described above. The questionnaire is designed so that "no" answers should be considered a potential application deficiency. "No" answers require additional investigation. Space is included on the form to qualify or explain responses to the questions.

A Computer Application Profile Worksheet (see Figure 8.7) should be used as a tool in assessing the adequacy of applications. The questionnaire probes a series of areas for the seven application characteristics (i.e., application system overview, system documentation and program modification, data input, data error, batch process, telecommunications, and data output).

You must use judgment in completing this profile. Based on the questionnaire responses relating to the application characteristics, how much risk (low, medium, high) do you believe is involved in relying on the computer-processed data? The information about applications requested on this form is designed to help you with this judgment.

ITEM	RESPONSE			
	YES	NO	N/A	OTHER
Major Application(s) System				
1. System name and agency's ID number?				
2. Date of initial implementation?				
3. Is the system a vendor-designed system or an agency-designed system?				
4. What is system type (administrative, engineering, process control, scientific, other)?				
5. Type of processing: batch or on-line?				
6. Number of programs?				
7. Size of largest program (bytes of storage)?				
8. Programming language used?				
9. Was system tested with test data, live data, or not at all?				
10. Are system test results available?				
11. Number of system modifications in the last two years?				
12. Date last modification was tested?				
13. Date of last audit or evaluation? (Obtain report.)				
14. Processing frequency?				
15. Total monthly processing hours?				

Figure 8.6. Application review questionnaire.

ITEM	RESPONSE			
	YES	NO	N/A	OTHER
System Documentation and Program Modification				
A. System Documentation				
1. Does a procedures manual cover the preparation of source documents? (If so, obtain a copy.)				
2. Does this manual:				
a. Include control procedures?				
b. Define data preparation responsibility?				
3. Is there a user's data entry/conversion manual? (If so, obtain a copy.)				
4. Does this manual:				
a. Include instructions for entering data?				
b. Identify all records/fields which are subject to verification?				
5. Is there an overall narrative description of the application system?				
6. Is there an overall flowchart of the application system?				
7. Is each application program documented separately?				
8. Does program documentation include:				
a. Request for program development/ changes?				
b. General narrative description of the program?				

Figure 8.6. Application review questionnaire. (cont'd)

ITEM	RESPONSE			
	YES	NO	N/A	OTHER
8. c. System specification — both original and modifications?				
d. Detailed narrative description of the program?				
e. Detailed logic diagram or decision table?				
f. Input record formats?				
g. Input record descriptions?				
h. Output record format?				
i. Output record descriptions?				
j. Master file formats?				
k. Master file descriptions?				
l. Lists of constants, codes, and tables used?				
m. Source program listing?				
n. Object program listing?				
o. Operating instructions?				
p. Description of test plan and data used to test program?				
q. Detailed history of program failures?				
9. Do computer operators' run manuals exist?				
10. Are these run manuals provided to computer operators?				
11. Do operators' run manuals:				
a. Define input data, data source, and data format?				
b. Describe setup procedures?				
c. Characterize all halt conditions and actions to be taken?				

Figure 8.6. Application review questionnaire. (cont'd)

	RESPONSE			
ITEM	*YES*	*NO*	*N/A*	*OTHER*
d. Delineate expected output data and format?				
e. Delineate output and file disposition at completion of run?				
f. Include copies of normal console sheets?				
12. Do operators' run manuals exclude:				
a. Program logic charts or block diagrams?				
b. Copies of program listings?				
13. Is all documentation reviewed to ensure its completeness and adherence to established standards?				
14. Are copies of all documentation stored off the premises?				
15. If "yes," is the stored documentation periodically compared and updated with the documentation being used?				
16. Is there written evidence of who performed the systems and programming work?				
B. Program Modification				
17. Are all program changes and their effective dates recorded in a manner which preserves an accurate chronological record of the system?				
18. Are programs revised only after written requests are approved by user department management?				

Figure 8.6. Application review questionnaire. (cont'd)

	RESPONSE			
ITEM	YES	NO	N/A	OTHER
19. Do these written requests describe the proposed changes and reasons for them?				
20. Are changes in the master file or in program instructions authorized in writing by initiating departments?				
21. Are departments that initiate changes in master files or program instructions furnished with notices or listings showing changes actually made?				
22. Are changes reviewed to see that they were made properly?				
23. Do major users approve initial system design specifications?				
24. Is approval for each new application program supported by a cost/benefit analysis?				
25. Have program testing procedures been established?				
26. Does the test plan include cases to test: a. Mainline and end-of-job logic? b. Each routine? c. Each exception? d. Abnormal end-of-job conditions? e. Combinations of parameter cards and switch settings? f. Unusual mixtures and sequence of data (i.e., multiple transactions following deleted masters)?				

Figure 8.6. Application review questionnaire. (cont'd)

ITEM	RESPONSE			
	YES	*NO*	*N/A*	*OTHER*
Data Input				
1. Have procedures been documented to show how all source data is entered and processed?				
2. Is there an input/output control group?				
3. Do the initiating departments independently control data submitted for processing using:				
a. Turnaround transmittal documents?				
b. Record counts?				
c. Predetermined control totals?				
d. Other? (describe) _____				
4. Are duties separated in the initiating to make sure that one individual does not perform more than one phase of input data preparation (e.g., establishing new master records)?				
5. Are source documents retained in a manner which enables tracing all documents to related output records?				
6. Is information transcribed from the source document to some other document before being sent to the MIS department?				
7. Does the transcribing department, if separate from other offices, independently control data submitted for processing using:				
a. Turnaround transmittal documents?				
b. Record counts?				
c. Predetermined control totals?				
d. Other? (describe) _____				

Figure 8.6. Application review questionnaire. (cont'd)

ITEM	RESPONSE			
	YES	NO	N/A	OTHER
8. Are control totals developed in the transcribing department balanced with those of initiating departments and are all discrepancies reconciled?				
9. Are coding, keypunching, and verifying the same document performed by different individuals?				
10. Does the transcribing department have a schedule, by application, that shows when data requiring transcription will be received and completed?				
11. Is responsibility separated to make sure that one individual does not perform more than one of the following phases of a transaction: a. Inititating data? b. Transcribing data? c. Inputting data? d. Processing data? e. Correcting errors and resubmitting? f. Distributing output?				
Data Error				
1. Are controls in place covering the process of identifying, correcting, and reprocessing data rejected by the computer programs?				
2. Are record counts and predetermined control totals used to control these rejected transactions?				
3. Are corrections and resubmissions performed in a timely manner?				

Figure 8.6. Application review questionnaire. (cont'd)

ITEM	RESPONSE			
	YES	NO	N/A	OTHER
4. Are error corrections reviewed and approved by persons outside the data processing department?				
5. Do initiating departments review error listings affecting their data?				
6. Are erroneous and unprocessable transactions (i.e., no master record corresponding to transaction record or vice versa) rejected and written to an automated suspense file?				
7. Does the automated suspense file include: a. A code indicating error type? b. Date, time, and some sort of indicator ID?				
8. Are periodic printouts of suspense file entries produced?				
Batch Processing				
1. Does the data processing department independently control data submitted and processed using: a. Turnaround transmittal documents? b. Record counts? c. Predetermined control totals? d. Other? (describe) _____				
2. Are control totals balanced with those of the initiating department and are all discrepancies reconciled?				
3. Are run-to-run control totals used to check for completeness of processing?				

Figure 8.6. Application review questionnaire. (cont'd)

ITEM	RESPONSE			
	YES	*NO*	*N/A*	*OTHER*
4. Do the computer operating instructions for each program identify which data files are to be used as input?				
5. Do the operating instructions for each program clearly identify output files and storage requirements?				
6. Do all programs include routines for checking file labels before processing?				
7. Are there controls in place to prevent operators from circumventing file label routines?				
8. Are internal trailer labels containing control totals (e.g., record counts, dollars totals, hash totals, etc.) generated for all magnetic tapes and tested by the computer program to determine that all records have been processed?				
9. Do computer programs include the following type of tests for validity: a. Code? b. Character? c. Field? d. Transaction? e. Combinations of fields? f. Missing data? g. Check digit? h. Sequence? i. Limit or reasonableness test? j. Sign? k. Crossfooting of quantitative data?				

Figure 8.6. Application review questionnaire. (cont'd)

ITEM	RESPONSE			
	YES	*NO*	*N/A*	*OTHER*
Telecommunications				
1. Are there documented procedures for using the telecommunications network? (If so, obtain a copy.)				
2. Are authorization codes required to: a. Access the computer system? b. Access the applications program? c. Perform transactions?				
3. Are different authorization codes required to perform different transactions?				
4. Are authorization codes controlled to restrict unauthorized usage?				
5. Are authorization codes periodically changed?				
6. Is a nonprinting/nondisplaying or obliteration facility used when keying in and acknowledging authorization codes?				
7. Is a terminal identification check performed by the computer so that various transaction types can be limited to authorized data entry stations?				
8. If any answers to questions 2-7 are "yes," do these security measures work as designed?				
9. Is there a computer program used to: a. Send acknowledgments to the terminal? b. Periodically test line and terminal operating status with standardized test messages and responses?				

Figure 8.6. Application review questionnaire. (cont'd)

ITEM	RESPONSE			
	YES	NO	N/A	OTHER
10. Is the message header used to identify: a. Source, including proper terminal and operator identification code? b. Message sequence number, including total number of message segments? c. Transaction type code? d. Transaction authorization code?				
11. Is the message header validated for: a. Proper sequence number from the identified terminal? b. Proper transaction code or authorization code for terminal or operator? c. Number of message segments received equal to count indicated in header? d. Proper acknowledgment from terminal at end of transmission? e. Balancing of debit/credit totals derived from adding all message segments and comparing with corresponding totals in message header?				
12. Are there either accumulators in the terminal for keeping input totals or terminal-site logging procedures that record details of transactions?				
13. Are error messages returned to originating terminal, indicating type of error detected and requesting correction?				

Figure 8.6. Application review questionnaire. (cont'd)

ITEM	RESPONSE			
	YES	NO	N/A	OTHER
14. Is a block of characters automatically retransmitted when an error is detected?				
15. Does an end-of-transmission trailer include: a. Message and segment counts? b. Value totals, including debit and credit? c. An ending symbol?				
16. Is a transaction log of sequence-numbered and/or time-of-day-noted transactions maintained in addition to a periodic dump/copy of the master file?				
17. Is the transaction data log used to provide: a. Part of the audit trail, including originating terminal and message ID, transaction type code, time of day that the transaction is logged, and copy of transaction record? b. A transaction record for retrieval from terminal?				
18. At the end of the processing day, is the master file balanced, via programmed routine, by subtracting current totals from start-of-day totals and comparing the remainder to transaction log values?				
19. Are all master file records periodically processed to balance machine-derived totals against control trailer record totals?				

Figure 8.6. Application review questionnaire. (cont'd)

	RESPONSE			
ITEM	*YES*	*NO*	*N/A*	*OTHER*

20. Is the master file data log used to provide:
  a. File restructuring capability?
  b. Restart points and indicators of valid data flow?
  c. Storage for partial dump of vital tables, including message queue allocation, polling table contents, transaction routine tables, etc.?				

Data Output				
1. Does the initiating department balance control totals generated during computer processing with those originally established and reconcile discrepancies?				
2. Can transactions be traced forward to a final output control?				
3. Can transactions be traced back to the original source document?				
4. Is there some means of verifying master file contents: e.g., are samples periodically drawn from those records being printed and reviewed for accuracy?				
5. Is there an input/output control group?				
6. Is the input/output control group assigned to review output for general acceptability and completeness?				
7. Is a schedule maintained of the reports and documents to be produced by the MIS system?				

Figure 8.6. Application review questionnaire. (cont'd)

ITEM	RESPONSE			
	YES	NO	N/A	OTHER
8. Are there documented control procedures for distributing reports?				
9. Is responsibility separated to make sure that one individual does not perform more than one of the following phases of a transaction:				
a. Initiating data?				
b. Transcribing data?				
c. Inputting data?				
d. Processing data?				
e. Correcting errors and resubmitting data?				
f. Distributing output?				

Figure 8.6. Application review questionnaire. (cont'd)

PREPARER: _____   **DATE:** _____

REVIEWER: _____   **DATE:** _____

You must use judgment in completing this profile. Based on the questionnaire responses relating to the following control characteristics, how much
risk (low, medium, high) do you believe is involved in relying on the agency's
computer-processed data?

Control Character-istic	Is the control in place?	Is the control effective?	Is some alternate control in place?	Is the alternate control effective?	Level of potential risk
Application system documentation and program modification controls					
Data input controls					
Data error controls					
Batch processing controls					
Telecommunications processing controls					
Data output controls					
COMMENTS					

Figure 8.7. Computer application controls profile worksheet.

After you have assigned a potential risk assessment for each application characteristic, briefly describe your justification for assigning the various risk levels for each application characteristic noted. This information should be used in preparing a report on the results of the application assessment.

SUMMARY

The computer has substantially altered the methods by which data processing systems operate and are controlled and audited. The opportunities for personal review and clerical checking have declined as the collection and subsequent uses of data are changed. The changes are the result of moving from manual procedures performed by individuals familiar with both the data and the accounting process to high-volume, automated techniques performed by individuals unfamiliar with both the data and accounting practices.

The introduction of data processing equipment frequently requires that the recording and processing functions be concentrated in departments that are separate from the origin of the data; it may, however, eliminate the separation of some of the responsibilities that previously characterized the record-keeping function. A trend toward the integration of operating and financial data into organization-wide information systems of databases also eliminated independent records that might previously have provided a source of comparative data. At the same time, such integrated information systems can become the basis for more vital and timely management decisions.

Computerization has reduced substantially the time available for the review of transactions before their entry into the accounting records. As a result, in poorly controlled systems the opportunity for discovering errors or fraud before they have an impact on operations may be reduced, especially in the case of real-time and database systems. This has increased the importance of internal control procedures. It also affects the work the quality assurance analyst must perform. An important aspect of this work is reviewing the adequacy of computer controls.

9

Quality Assurance Review Techniques

Quality assurance reviews can be improved by the use of effective review techniques. These include the methods and procedures used by QA when conducting reviews, the means by which information is gathered, the techniques used to confirm and validate the accuracy of the information, and methods used to evaluate that information.

This chapter will cover thirteen QA review techniques. They are listed in Figure 9.1. Each will be described, an example provided, and an evaluation given as to where the practice can be used most effectively. The skills necessary to use the techniques will show the caliber of QA reviewer needed for the different parts of the review.

Effective QA groups must conduct reviews that are consistent in approach. It is important that application A be subjected to the same rigorous review as application B. The ongoing nature of QA requires maintaining good working relationships with data processing systems and programming personnel. Knowing that all projects will be reviewed the same way helps maintain these good working relationships.

QUALITY ASSURANCE REVIEW TECHNIQUES

A quality assurance reviewer's function is broken into three segments. These are: first, gathering information about the system being reviewed; second, confirming or validating that the information gathered is correct; and third, evaluating the system based on the information gathered.

Information gathering occurs both while planning for and conducting the QA review. Five vehicles are used in obtaining information about application systems. These are:

1. *Project documentation.* Use of the documentation about the management of the project, such as budgets, assignments, schedules, etc.

2. *System documentation.* All the documentation about the computer application relating to data, its processing, use, storage, operation, control, etc.

3. *Interviews.* Interviews with appropriate, involved people.

4. *Observation.* A means of understanding a system or determining the form in which information about it exists.

5. *Checklist.* A series of questions to be asked about a topic being investigated.

> **Information-Gathering Techniques**
> - Project documentation
> - System documentation
> - Fact finding (interview)
> - Observation (examination)
> - Checklist
>
> **Confirmation/Validation Techniques**
> - Testing (verification)
> - Test data
> - Base case
> - Confirmation
>
> **Evaluation Techniques**
> - Judgment
> - Simulation modeling
> - Consultants (advice)
> - Quantitative analysis

Figure 9.1. Quality Assurance review techniques.

If the information is erroneous, the evaluation is subjected to error. Error can occur from using false information, or using the wrong criteria in evaluating a situation. For example, a reviewer can be told that the current system has approximately 20 errors per day. The person providing this believes it to be true, but in actual practice the number of errors is closer to 100 per day. Evaluations based on this type of information will probably be erroneous. Therefore, it becomes necessary for the reviewer to confirm and validate whenever practical information is obtained and evaluations made. Some confirmation techniques are quite simple while others are time-consuming. However, the value of being sure is worth the time. Reviewers use various practices:

1. *Testing.* Verify that something exists, something works, or determine what the results will be if certain conditions happen.

2. *Test data.* Prepare transactions which can be used in testing.

3. *Base case.* Prepare an exhaustive set of test data for utilization in testing.

4. *Confirmation.* Validate with the individual who knows whether or not the condition or event has, will, or can occur.

The value QA provides data processing management is in evaluating the data obtained. The data gathered will contain bias, personal opinions, one-sided viewpoints and other interpretations by the person giving or documenting that data. The QA reviewers must sift and evaluate various pieces of information to arrive at conclusions. Evaluations range from highly quantitative to intuitive. The most common techniques for evaluations used by reviewers are these four:

1. *Judgment.* Use intuition and evaluation to arrive at a conclusion based primarily on the reviewer's own training and experience.

2. *Simulation/Modeling.* Mathematically construct the system or event to study in advance the probable results.

3. *Consultant (advice).* Use the judgment and experience of "experts" in the area of concern.

4. *Quantitative analysis.* Use mathematics to assist in arriving at judgments by giving weights or scores to the criteria included in decision making.

This list of techniques is not meant to be comprehensive but, rather, representative of the approaches used by QA in performing the function. QA reviewers can learn additional practices and techniques from auditors and visits with other QA groups.

APPLICATION OF TECHNIQUES

Each of the twelve review points requires different techniques. The early reviews rely heavily on information-gathering techniques. The middle review points use both information gathering and evaluation. The later reviews make more use of the confirmation/validation practices. This is logical because it closely parallels the system development process. Figure 9.2 shows which techniques are used for each of the review points. The most common review technique is the checklist: it is the only one used in all twelve review points. The checklist provides an organized approach to conducting a review. But the person making the review should not rely completely on the checklist; rather, he or she should use it as a guide in conducting the review. The checklist should be the initiating document for using the other review techniques.

Testing is rarely used by QA review groups. It is only in the analysis of system testing that QA gets into testing and test data practices. Testing practices are primarily utilized by the systems development team. When utilized by QA it is done mostly by piggy-backing QA tests with the project system tests. When QA needs to verify a condition or event the two most commonly used techniques are observation and confirmation.

An analysis of the review techniques matrix (Figure 9.2) shows that the majority of time spent by the QA group is in information gathering, the most common practice for making an evaluation judgment. From this we can begin to see that the ideal person for the QA group is one skilled in gathering facts who has enough experience and ability to make sound judgments about the status of application systems.

SKILLS NEEDED FOR QA REVIEW TECHNIQUES

Eight different skills and/or knowledge areas are necessary to execute effectively all the audit techniques.
1.   Project management
2.   General systems design

QA REVIEW POINT	Project Documentation	System Documentation	Fact Finding (interview)	Observation (examination)	Checklist	Testing	Test Data
1. Mid-Justification Phase	✔	✔	✔		✔		
2. End of Justification Phase	✔	✔	✔		✔		
3. Business Systems Solution Phase	✔	✔	✔		✔		
4. Computer Equipment Selection		✔	✔		✔		
5. Computer Systems Design	✔	✔	✔		✔		
6. Program Design	✔	✔	✔		✔		
7. Testing and Conversion Planning	✔		✔		✔		
8. Program Coding and Testing		✔		✔	✔		
9. Detailed Test Plan	✔		✔		✔		
10. Test Results	✔	✔	✔	✔	✔	✔	✔
11. Detail Conversion Planning and Programs	✔	✔	✔	✔	✔		
12. Conversion Results		✔	✔	✔	✔		

Figure 9.2. Quality Assurance review points/review techniques matrix.

QA REVIEW POINT	Base Case	Confirmation	Judgment	Simulation Modeling	Consultants (advice)	Quantitative Analysis
1. Mid-Justification Phase		✔	✔	✔	✔	
2. End of Justification Phase		✔	✔	✔	✔	✔
3. Business Systems Solution Phase		✔	✔	✔	✔	✔
4. Computer Equipment Selection			✔		✔	
5. Computer Systems Design		✔	✔	✔	✔	✔
6. Program Design		✔	✔	✔	✔	✔
7. Testing and Conversion Planning			✔		✔	
8. Program Coding and Testing			✔			
9. Detailed Test Plan			✔			
10. Test Results	✔	✔	✔			
11. Detail Conversion Planning and Programs			✔			
12. Conversion Results						

(Column heading: **REVIEW TECHNIQUES**)

Figure 9.2. Quality Assurance review points/review techniques matrix. (cont'd)

3.   Computer systems design

4.   Computer hardware

5.   Computer software

6.   Programming

7.   Computer center

8.   General business experience

It is not necessary to be a master of all eight skills. In some cases, the area in which the technique is used determines which skills are necessary. For example, to use the checklist on economic evaluations of computerized applications requires a general business experience but not a knowledge of the operation of the computer center. For some cases, the same skills are needed each time the technique is utilized. For example, to make use of automated packages for simulation and modeling routines, the systems analyst must have an understanding of automated packages for programming.

The eight skills and/or knowledge areas are explained below, as is the difference between basic and advanced mastery of the skills.

Project Management. Possessing the ability to organize and supervise the implementation of an application system project. This includes preparation of budgets, selection of personnel, organization of work, planning and scheduling the implementation process, directing individuals on their assignments, and controlling and evaluating their work. Basic project management includes skills involving managing one application system project. Advanced skills come after managing two or more application system projects.

General Systems Design. General systems design involves solving business problems. General systems design usually occurs during the feasibility study. The system may or may not require the use of a computer. General systems design skills include the ability to make an economic evaluation of alternative solutions for the business problem. Basic skills in general systems design come from working on those systems whose obvious solution is a computerized application. Advanced skills include general systems for which the use of the computer may or may not be all or part of the solution.

Computer Systems Design. The process of designing a computer system includes the definition of input, output, processing, and file design. A designer might have basic computer systems design skills with five years or less in computing systems and programming work. Advanced skills come with more of that kind of experience.

Computer Hardware. Computer hardware skills include the ability to select and configure computer hardware. It includes working with representatives of the computer vendors. The skill assumes a knowledge of conversion problems from one type of hardware to another, as well as economic considerations in hardware planning. Advance skills generally mean working with more than one computer vendor, or with more than one line of computers from a specific vendor. Skills include the ability to use one of the hardware evaluation manuals or services.

Computer Software. Skills in understanding the functions of computer software probably require the highest technical knowledge of all the skills. Skills include the ability to generate new versions of software systems. The features and economics of the software system must be known, as well as the control language and the means to link computer software to application systems. Basic skills include a comprehension of software packages, together with the ability to use control information to link computer software with application programs. Advanced skills include the ability to select among various software packages as well as the skill to generate the software system.

Programming. Programming knowledge and skills include the ability to design, code, and debug programs. The basic skills involve up to two years of actual programming experience. Advanced skills require over two years of programming experience.

Computer Center. Computer center skills include a knowledge of computer operations. This includes scheduling of computer runs, restart, recovery, data library and backup, telecommunication operation if applicable, as well as security of the computer center. Basic skills include an understanding of the operation of the computer center, while advanced skills can come with one year or more of experience in the operation of a computer center.

General Business Experience. General business experience means experience working in the business areas of an organization. Examples of business areas would be the payroll department, accounts receivable department, sales department, marketing, accounting or other segments of the general business operation of an organization. The experience should be that of a user of a computerized application. Basic skills include two years or less experience, advanced skills involve over two years of experience. General business experience also can be obtained in the management aspects of the data processing department. However, the experience should be other than managing the development of computer systems. An understanding of these skills and/or knowledge areas provides some additional insight into the background necessary for QA. As we examine each of the thirteen QA techniques, we will see which of these skills are needed for the various techniques.

QUALITY ASSURANCE TECHNIQUES

This section describes the thirteen QA techniques. Each write-up contains a brief overview and then a detailed description, an example of its use, and an evaluation of the future potential. Each write-up also contains a matrix showing the skills needed to use that particular technique. The skills matrix lists the eight skills described in the previous section.

Project Documentation Review Technique

One of the major sources of information is the documentation used in managing the project: the more formal the documentation, the more useful it is for QA purposes.

Description: Project documentation provides the reviewer with information on budgets, schedules, personnel assignments, technical decisions, user relationships, project implementation plans, project team organizational structure, as well as the current status of project implementation. Project documentation should be studied extensively during each review. Special emphasis should be placed on status of project implementation. Because many project leaders do not consolidate project documentation, it may be necessary for the reviewer to ask for some specific pieces of information.

Example: In an effort to determine whether a phase of the project will be completed within budget, the reviewer can check both the budget status and project schedule status. If the schedule shows the phase to be 30 percent complete, approximately 30 percent of the budget should be expended. Obviously certain expenses should be excluded from the calculation such as one-time costs for purchases of software. Based on a simple analysis the reviewer can make a judgment as to whether or not the phase under review will be completed within budget. Without project documentation this evaluation could be very time-consuming.

Evaluation: Project documentation is one of the two prime sources for gathering information. This is an essential element in QA reviews. Figure 9.3 illustrates the skills and/or knowledge needed to use project documentation in a QA review.

TECHNIQUE: Project Documentation			
Skill/Knowledge	*Skill Needed*	*Advanced Skill Needed*	*N/A*
Project Management		✔	
General Systems Design		✔	
Computer Systems Design	✔		
Computer Hardware			✔
Computer Software			✔
Programming			✔
Computer Center	✔		
General Business Experience		✔	

Figure 9.3. Skills needed to use Quality Assurance technique.

Systems Documentation Quality Assurance Technique

A major segment of every QA review includes a thorough study and analysis of system documentation.

Description: System documentation includes all input and output documentation, processing rules, and file organization. The documentation will include control techniques, operating instructions, training instructions and manuals for the personnel who will use the system, and program listings.

The reviewer studies the documentation to gain an understanding not only of what the system is supposed to accomplish, but how it functions.

Example: To determine the adequacy of the system's file organization, the reviewer studies both the input data elements and the output reports. This will provide the reviewer with insight as to what information is in this system and how it is entered, as well as the information needs of the user as expressed in output reports. This type of information is necessary in making an assessment as to the adequacy of file structure.

Evaluation: System documentation is, and will continue to be, the major source of information for the QA reviewer. Figure 9.4 shows the skills and/ or knowledge needed by quality assurance reviewers to use and understand system documentation.

Interviewing QA Techniques

Fact finding through interviews provides raw information to the reviewer. The data collected through fact finding should be subject to further evaluation and analysis.

Description: Information gathered through interviews should be considered to contain personal bias and opinion. Data reported by an individual normally reflects his point of view. In medical terms, perhaps it should be considered more of a symptom rather than the true cause or result of an event. The individual doing the fact finding must make an effort to get the viewpoint of all interested parties. It is only through the accumulation of full information that the proper evaluation can be performed.

Example: After an automobile accident involving two cars, each driver would probably present a totally different story. It is quite possible each version would show the other driver at fault. When the two versions are documented and other supportive facts collected, the true cause of the accident becomes more obvious than if all the data had been collected from only one driver.

Evaluation: Fact-finding skills can be learned and improved. Reviewers should study fact finding and interviewing methods to improve their skills. This is one of the basic tools of a reviewer. Figure 9.5 illustrates the skills and/or knowledge needed to use the quality assurance fact-finding (interviews) practice.

TECHNIQUE: System Documentation			
Skill/Knowledge	Skill Needed	Advanced Skill Needed	N/A
Project Management			✔
General Systems Design		✔	
Computer Systems Design		✔	
Computer Hardware	✔		
Computer Software	✔		
Programming			✔
Computer Center			✔
General Business Experience	✔		

Figure 9.4. Skills needed to use Quality Assurance technique.

Observation (Examination) QA Technique

A picture has been said to be worth ten thousand words. This is frequently true in the case of the reviewer observing and/or examining some event or condition important to the application system.

Description: Observation or examination involves witnessing events as they occur, or examining documents and other physical evidence. This need not be a time-consuming process. It has proven to be much more informative than verbal explanations of a process. Frequently, observation involves going to the user's place of business and examining an operation or process from start to finish. This may be coupled with fact finding. In that case the reviewer will discuss job functions with each person as the reviewer observes a process in action. After a few hours a reviewer should have a very good understanding of how a system or process works.

Example: Assume the application system under review is a payroll system. The reviewer, in an effort to understand the system, decides to observe the entire payroll process. This would start with the addition of an individual on the payroll. Perhaps this step is done through the personnel department with a series of forms which then go to the payroll department to update the payroll master file. The QA person observes people clocking in in the morning, clocking in and out for lunch, and then out at the end of the shift. The reviewer next may observe the problems that occur with individuals trying to get to time stations to report in and out, and problems occurring because of illness or other personal problems. Observing the process of preparing the payroll and making adjustments might involve going to each individual who is part of the process in the payroll department. Once the checks have been prepared, the reviewer would want to observe the distribution methods, and perhaps the reconciliation and control procedures used to assure that the proper person receives the proper pay for that work period.

TECHNIQUE: Fact Finding (Interviews)			
Skill/Knowledge	*Skill Needed*	*Advanced Skill Needed*	*N/A*
Project Management	✔		
General Systems Design	✔		
Computer Systems Design	✔		
Computer Hardware			✔
Computer Software			✔
Programming			✔
Computer Center	✔		
General Business Experience	✔		

Figure 9.5. Skills needed to use Quality Assurance technique.

Evaluation: Observation can be an extremely powerful technique to familiarize the reviewer with what is actually happening in the organization. Many times people describe the procedure as it should happen, or as they perceive it to happen, but only when the reviewer gets out into the user's place of business and observes the process can he or she fully understand what is actually happening. Observation is a practice that should be used by reviewers on each application reviewed. It may be possible to use observations made in early stages of a review throughout all the review point reviews. Figure 9.6 illustrates the skills and/or knowledge needed to use the observation (examination) technique.

TECHNIQUE: Observation (Examination)			
Skill/Knowledge	Skill Needed*	Advanced Skill Needed	N/A
Project Management	✔		
General Systems Design	✔		
Computer Systems Design	✔		
Computer Hardware	✔		
Computer Software	✔		
Programming	✔		
Computer Center	✔		
General Business Experience	✔		

* Varies depending on what is being observed (about 4 skills needed)

Figure 9.6. Skills needed to use Quality Assurance technique.

Note: The asterisk on the skills chart indicates that all the skills checked are not needed to use the observation technique. What is implied is that the area in which the observation will occur is the skill which the reviewer should have to use the technique effectively. For example, if the computer center is being observed, the reviewer should possess the skill being monitored. It is suggested that about four skills are necessary to effectively use any practice. For example, to observe in the computer center it is helpful if the reviewer has skills in the areas of 1) computer hardware, 2) computer software, 3) programming, and 4) computer center operations. This may not always be necessary, but it is a reasonable guideline. The same logic applies to all the following skill charts where the skills are dependent on where the technique is used.

Checklist QA Review Technique

The checklist is the most commonly used of all the review techniques. It provides the reviewer an organized and standardized approach for each of the review points.

Description: Checklists provide a series of questions which guide the reviewer through each checkpoint review. Many organizations believe that each item on the checklist should be reviewed with data processing management to determine if it is fair, since data processing personnel should not be asked to perform at a level beyond reasonable expectations; this also helps maintain a good working relationship.

While common questionnaires can be used as a base, they should be modified to meet the standards and procedures of the data processing department conducting the reviews. The questions should be supportive of the standards and procedures of the data processing department. While questions are normally asked in a yes/no mode, the answers are seldom all yes or all no. Reviewers need to apply judgment to the answers to determine the level of adherence to the desires of data processing management.

Example: The following questions are from a checklist for system design specifications. The questions, actually used by a QA group, deal with data validation and error messages.

1. For validation routines, have the editing rules been specified for:

   a. field format and content (data element description)?

   b. interfield relationships?

   c. intrafield relationships?

   d. interrecord relationship?

   e. sequence?

   f. duplicates?

   g. control reconciliation?

2. Has the rejection criterion been indicated for each type of error situation, as follows:

   a. warning message but transaction is accepted?

   b. use of the default value?

   c. outright rejection of record within a transaction set?

   d. rejection of an entire transaction?

   e. rejection of a batch transaction?

   f. program abort?

3.   Have the following validation techniques been included in the specifications:

    a.   validation of entire transaction before any processing?

    b.   validation to continue regardless of the number of errors on the transaction unless a run abort occurs?

    c.   provides information regarding an error so the user can identify the source and determine the cause?

Note that these questions are much more specific then those in Chapter 7. An extensive checklist may be required to support one of the concerns included in one of the review point's list of concerns included in Chapter 7.

Evaluation: Checklists are the major technique of the reviewer. They should continually be improved through the experiences gained conducting reviews. Figure 9.7 illustrates the skills and/or knowledge needed to use the checklist technique.

TECHNIQUE: Checklist			
Skill/Knowledge	*Skill Needed**	*Advanced Skill Needed*	*N/A*
Project Management	✔		
General Systems Design	✔		
Computer Systems Design	✔		
Computer Hardware	✔		
Computer Software	✔		
Programming	✔		
Computer Center	✔		
General Business Experience	✔		

* Varies depending on what is being observed (about 4 skills needed)

Figure 9.7. Skills needed to use Quality Assurance technique.

Testing (Verification) QA Technique

Testing is the process of verifying that conditions are as stated. It involves performing whatever steps are necessary to verify statements or conditions are correct.

Description: Testing can be used to verify the existence or effectiveness of physical properties, events, conditions, and internal control, or used to verify the accuracy and completeness of both data and totals. Testing should be performed by the reviewer. If other than the QA reviewer performs the test, the technique should be confirmation of something rather than testing. Testing implies work being done by the reviewer. In computer applications, tests can be performed with either live or fictitious data. In conducting tests the reviewer will have to calculate the results manually and then compare them to actual results.

Example: A project leader made a statement that the audit routines in the application being developed were so stringent that it was impossible for erroneous data to enter the system. The QA reviewer was skeptical of this statement and decided to make a test. The application under question used card input. The reviewer took two boxes of cards at random and fed them into the audit program of the application: seventeen "transactions" got through. As a result of this test additional audit routines were added in the computer application.

Evaluation: Testing is a very valid QA technique but should be used only where necessary. QA should encourage the project team and user to do extensive testing. However, where it is concerned over the adequacy of testing or the adequacy of evaluating test results, QA may wish to make a test itself. Figure 9.8 illustrates the skills and/or knowledge needed to use the quality assurance testing technique.

Test Data QA Technique

Test data is a series of transactions prepared for a computer system to see whether proper transactions are processed correctly and the improper transactions identified and rejected.

TECHNIQUE: Testing (Verification)			
Skill/Knowledge	*Skill Needed**	*Advanced Skill Needed*	*N/A*
Project Management			✔
General Systems Design	✔		
Computer Systems Design	✔		
Computer Hardware	✔		
Computer Software	✔		
Programming	✔		
Computer Center	✔		
General Business Experience	✔		

* Varies depending on what is being observed (about 4 skills needed)

Figure 9.8. Skills needed to use Quality Assurance technique.

Description: Test data helps to determine whether the computer programs process data accurately and whether the controls in the system can prevent improper results, such as exorbitant payroll checks. Test data should represent both expected and conceivable conditions that could happen during actual data processing operations. Before the transactions are run, expected processing results are calculated manually by the individuals conducting the tests so that actual results can be compared with these predetermined results. To design adequate test data, the reviewer must be familiar with input and output formats for all types of transactions being processed as well as the data processing system procedures. To be effective, test data should use transactions. Valid data is used for testing normal processing operations, and invalid data is used for testing programmed controls. Only one test transaction need be processed for each condition.

Example: A payroll computer application was designed for a maximum of 99 pay hours per week. To test that condition, the reviewer entered test data which showed 90 hours of work by an employee during the week. When this was processed by the computer the 50 hours of overtime were converted into 75 pay hours. The 75 pay hours should be added to the 40 hours of regular pay equaling 115 paid hours. The system only paid the employee for 15 hours.

While the audit programs prevented over 99 hours of work from entering the application, the systems analyst did not provide for regular plus overtime pay hours that would exceed 100. Based on this test the system was modified.

Evaluation: In most instances the reviewer will propose test transactions rather than actually prepare the test data. The experience of reviewers can help evaluate the thoroughness of the test plan. QA should concentrate test data recommendations on error conditions and unusual processing conditions. This is because data processing people tend to test for those conditions which have been provided for by the system: they do not try to think up test data for conditions which the system is not designed to process. Figure 9.9 illustrates the skills and/or knowledge needed to use test data.

TECHNIQUE: Test Data			
Skill/Knowledge	*Skill Needed*	*Advanced Skill Needed*	*N/A*
Project Management			✔
General Systems Design			✔
Computer Systems Design	✔		
Computer Hardware	✔		
Computer Software	✔		
Programming	✔		
Computer Center	✔		
General Business Experience			✔

Figure 9.9. Skills needed to use Quality Assurance technique.

Base Case QA Technique

Base case is an exhaustive group of test data designed to test all possible paths through a computer application.

Description: The base case test technique has proved very effective in organizations utilizing it. It is also a very costly testing technique which can cost up to 20 percent of the total system cost. Each organization must weigh the merits versus the cost of using the technique. It is not a QA technique per se but, rather, a technique which QA can advocate, and one in which they can participate.

Example: An organization developed an on-line entry system. This system was critical to the operation of the organization. All orders were entered and processed by this system. Thus 100 percent of the sales went through this system. It was determined that it was worth the cost to develop a base case testing system. The base case was also used anytime the system was modified. This double use justified the cost of the test approach.

Evaluation: Base case is probably the most effective testing technique known to organizations. In those critical systems where processing accuracy is essential the base case should be recommended by QA. Figure 9.10 illustrates the skills and/or knowledge needed to use the base case QA technique. Confirmation Quality Assurance Technique Confirmation is the process of verifying with a knowledgeable party that a condition or event is true.

TECHNIQUE: Base Case			
Skill/Knowledge	*Skill Needed*	*Advanced Skill Needed*	*N/A*
Project Management			✔
General Systems Design	✔		
Computer Systems Design	✔		
Computer Hardware	✔		
Computer Software	✔		
Programming	✔		
Computer Center	✔		
General Business Experience			✔

Figure 9.10. Skills needed to use Quality Assurance technique.

Description: Confirmation starts with a written or verbal request to a knowledgeable party for information. The item in question could be a policy clarification, a procedure interpretation, clarifying the accuracy of data or percentages used in processing, or the correctness of master data to be used during processing. Confirmation is used when the reviewer has a question regarding the authenticity of a condition or data. In most instances the confirmation is made by telephone. In some instances, however, it may be advisable to document the confirmation so the reviewer will get the confirmation in writing. This is particularly true when an outside party is involved, such as a customer, a governmental agency, or a supplier.

Example: In a payroll application the reviewer was uncertain of the algorithm being used for pension deduction. The systems project team was using information obtained from a discussion with the personnel department of the organization. The reviewer felt there might be a misinterpretation and sent a letter explaining the deduction algorithm being used to the insurance company handling the pension plan. The confirmation asked the insurance company to state whether the algorithm was correct. In this case it was, and the program was installed with assurance on the part of all that the algorithm was correct.

Evaluation: Confirmation is a technique available to the QA when the authenticity of an event or condition is essential. It is a seldom used technique but one that can be very valuable when needed. Figure 9.11 illustrates the skills and/or knowledge needed to use this technique.

TECHNIQUE: Confirmation			
Skill/Knowledge	*Skill Needed**	*Advanced Skill Needed*	*N/A*
Project Management	✔		
General Systems Design	✔		
Computer Systems Design	✔		
Computer Hardware	✔		
Computer Software	✔		
Programming	✔		
Computer Center	✔		
General Business Experience	✔		

* Varies depending on what is being confirmed (about 4 skills needed)

Figure 9.11. Skills needed to use Quality Assurance technique.

Judgment QA Technique

Judgment is the combined use of experience, intellect, and reasoning to arrive at a conclusion based on analysis of available information. It is the reviewer's judgment that is the main ingredient in making the function successful.

Description: Judgment is the hardest technique to teach and yet is the most valuable. A major ingredient in judgment is extensive experience in data processing systems and programming. Many judgmental decisions are made using the experience gained by many years of practice. Knowing the pitfalls that have occurred in one's personal experience, an individual can guide others away from making the same mistake. Other judgments are more intuitive in nature. The reviewer analyzes the facts available and, mixing this with personal experience, makes a judgment as to the best course of action. Many of these judgments will involve adherence to data processing standards and procedures.

Example: The data processing department standards state that all program modules are to be limited to 40K of computer storage. A frequently used module needs a 28K array for optimum efficiency. This will bring the total program module size to 56K. The module will be on-line frequently during the day and including the full 28K array would substantially increase the module's performance. The reviewer must make a judgment as to whether increased performance warrants deviation from the 40K program module size standard. The reviewer should not be a policeman but, rather, apply judgment to situations.

Evaluation: Without judgment, quality assurance is a clerical function. The prime reason organizations put senior data processing personnel into quality assurance is to gain the benefit of their judgment in problem situations. Figure 9.12 illustrates the skills needed to use this technique.

Simulation/Modeling QA Technique

When the technology is uncertain, or the application calls for some involved interrelated processing between modules, simulation/modeling provides greater assurance that the application will work when placed into production.

Description: Simulation or modeling is the use of one or more specially written computer programs to process data files in order to simulate

TECHNIQUE: Judgment			
Skill/Knowledge	Skill Needed	Advanced Skill Needed*	N/A
Project Management		✔	
General Systems Design		✔	
Computer Systems Design		✔	
Computer Hardware		✔	
Computer Software		✔	
Programming		✔	
Computer Center		✔	
General Business Experience		✔	

* Varies depending on what is being confirmed (about 4 skills needed)

Figure 9.12. Skills needed to use Quality Assurance technique.

normal computer application processing. A model may be built that can be used to simulate the processing of the entire application. However, in actual practice this is a very time-consuming process, and therefore modeling or simulation is used primarily on limited parts of the application. Simulation serves two purposes. First it determines how a system will function before it is built. For example, if an organization wanted to check response time in a teleprocessing system they could build a model and simulate processing. Second, simulation can be used to verify the correctness of the processing routine. The logic can be simulated in a program and the live or test data run through both the live and the simulated program. The comparison of results will determine the accuracy of the production version of the system.

Example: If a reviewer wanted to verify the accuracy of the FICA calculation in a payroll application, a simulation program could be written to duplicate that logic. The test data used to system test the production version could be run through the simulation program. The data used by the simulation program would be extracted from an interim input file because it would come from the middle of the production system. The simulation program would only calculate the FICA deduction. The results of the two runs are compared as a means of verifying the processing logic for the FICA calculation. If the results are the same, the calculation logic would be proven correct.

Evaluation: Simulation/modeling has limited use for the reviewer. The primary use would be in new complex data processing applications where the reviewer wanted to estimate the processing times. A more logical approach might be for the reviewer to recommend to the systems project team that they build a model to simulate the processing in question. Figure 9.13 illustrates the skills needed to use this technique.

TECHNIQUE: Simulation/Modeling			
Skill/Knowledge	Skill Needed	Advanced Skill Needed	N/A
Project Management	✔		
General Systems Design		✔	
Computer Systems Design		✔	
Computer Hardware	✔		
Computer Software	✔		
Programming		✔	
Computer Center	✔		
General Business Experience	✔		

Figure 9.13.   Skills needed to use Quality Assurance technique.

Consultants (Advice) QA Technique

It is not possible in the highly technical environment of data processing for one individual or one group to know everything. Where the reviewers lack technical expertise they should be able to call upon outside help for advice.

Description: Consultants are normally called upon to answer highly technical questions. They may also be used, for example, to obtain legal advice, answer questions regarding legislation, or explain Internal Revenue Service regulations. If the reviewer suspects a problem but is uncertain of the consequences of that problem, he should take that problem to consultants. Consultants already associated with the organization such as certified public accountants or resources available from computer vendors or software firms are an excellent and normally free source of advice. Most questions can be answered very quickly and may possibly be handled with a phone call.

Example: One QA group was uncertain about retention of computer files as outlined in the Internal Revenue Service Regulation 71-20. The reviewer called the organization's certified public accountants and obtained a quick answer regarding the Internal Revenue Service File Retention Policy. Figure 9.14 illustrates the skills needed to use consultants.

TECHNIQUE: Consultants (Advice)			
Skill/Knowledge	*Skill Needed**	*Advanced Skill Needed*	*N/A*
Project Management	✔		
General Systems Design	✔		
Computer Systems Design	✔		
Computer Hardware	✔		
Computer Software	✔		
Programming	✔		
Computer Center	✔		
General Business Experience	✔		

* Varies depending on what area consultants are used in (about 4 skills needed)

Figure 9.14. Skills needed to use Quality Assurance technique.

Quantitative Analysis QA Techniques

Quantitative analysis techniques provide a mathematical approach to decision-making.

Description: Quantitative analysis involves assigning of weights or ranking to the criteria used in the decision-making process. The individual using quantitative analysis techniques must first determine the criteria that will be used in the decision making process, and then either rank or weight those criteria. Normally weighting is the method used. Each of the criteria will then be scored and a total score arrived at by using the weighting factors. The score can be used to state mathematically the current state of a condition or event, or it can be used to compare two or more like alternatives, conditions, statuses, or events.

Example: The reviewer was evaluating an equipment selection decision. Discussions with the project team brought out the criteria that were to be considered. Included in the criteria were cost, available software, delivery dates, service, systems engineer support, and upward compatibility. The equipment from the various vendors considered were scored on each of these criteria and a total score for each vendor's equipment was determined. This readily showed one piece of equipment far superior to the others for that organization. The organization selected that piece of equipment.

Evaluation: Quantitative analysis is a very powerful practice available to reviewers. QA should be urging project teams to use quantitative analysis in their decision-making process. Chapter 10 shows how to apply this practice to quality assurance reviews. Figure 9.15 illustrates the skills needed to use this technique.

TECHNIQUE: Quantitative Analysis			
Skill/Knowledge	*Skill Needed*	*Advanced Skill Needed*	*N/A*
Project Management	✔		
General Systems Design		✔	
Computer Systems Design		✔	
Computer Hardware	✔		
Computer Software	✔		
Programming			✔
Computer Center	✔		
General Business Experience		✔	

Figure 9.15. Skills needed to use Quality Assurance technique.

An analysis of skills necessary to use QA practices provides some interesting information on the makeup of QA personnel. This analysis shows which skills are the most important to members of the group and which practices should be used by the more senior QA people. The analysis also provides us some insight as to where the emphasis should be placed in reviews. Figure 9.16 is a matrix showing the relationship between QA skills/knowledge and QA techniques. This matrix is the basis for the analysis of skills.

The matrix is an accumulation of the skill charts shown for each of the thirteen quality assurance techniques. The eight skills are listed across the top and the thirteen quality assurance techniques are listed down the left-hand margin of the matrix. Within the matrix a number "1" shows a basic skill is needed for the technique listed. A number "2" indicates an advanced skill is needed. A blank space indicates that the skill is not required for that particular technique. A numerical "1/2" indicates that the skill is required if it is applied in that area. For example, in the checklist technique the programming skill is required in checklists which examine programming. As previously explained, approximately 4 skills at the basic level are required to use the checklist technique effectively. The score adds up to 4 using a "1/2" in each skill column. The score for all techniques in which the skill required varies by use of the technique is calculated in this manner.

By accumulating the skills/knowledge, we can see which are most needed by QA personnel. Listing them in order of importance, we find the requirements are:

Rank	Skill/Knowledge
1	Computer systems design
2	General systems design
3	General business experience
4	Computer center
5	Computer software
6	Computer hardware
7	Project management
8	Programming

QA/TECHNIQUES	Project Management	General Systems Designs	Computer Systems Design	Computer Hardware	Computer Software	Programming	Computer Center	General Business Experience	Score
Information Gathering Techniques									
Project Documentation	2.0	2.0	1.0				1.0	2.0	8.0
System Documentation		2.0	2.0	1.0	1.0			1.0	7.0
Fact Finding (interview)	1.0	1.0	1.0				1.0	1.0	5.0
Observation (examination)	.5	.5	.5	.5	.5	.5	.5	.5	4.0
Checklist	.5	.5	.5	.5	.5	.5	.5	.5	4.0
TOTALS	4.0	6.0	5.0	2.0	2.0	1.0	3.0	5.0	28.0
Evaluation Techniques									
Judgment	1.0	1.0	1.0	1.0	1.0	1.0	1.0	1.0	8.0
Simulation/Modeling	1.0	2.0	2.0	1.0	1.0	2.0	1.0	1.0	11.0
Consultants (advice)	.5	.5	.5	.5	.5	.5	.5	.5	4.0
Quantitative Analysis	1.0	2.0	2.0	1.0	1.0		1.0	2.0	10.0
TOTALS	3.5	5.5	5.5	3.5	3.5	3.5	3.5	4.5	33.0
Confirmation/Validation Techniques									
Testing (verification)			1.0	1.0	1.0	1.0	1.0		5.0
Test Data			1.0	1.0	1.0	1.0	1.0		5.0
Base Case	.5	1.0	1.0	1.0	1.0	1.0	1.0		6.5
Confirmation		.5	.5	.5	.5	.5	.5	.5	3.5
TOTALS	.5	1.5	3.5	3.5	3.5	3.5	3.5	.5	20.0
GRAND TOTALS	8.0	13.0	14.0	9.0	9.0	8.0	10.0	10.0	81.0

Figure 9.16. Skills/techniques matrix.

From this, we see that the two most important are those relating to system design and general business experience. The two least important are programming and project management. This coincides with previous discussions indicating that the main area of QA involvement is in the area of compliance to systems methods, goals, and performance. While programming and project management skills are desirable, they tend to be outside the main review objectives of QA.

Analyzing the individual techniques, we see the ones that are most difficult to execute. Listing the scores from high to low, we can determine the difficulty of use. The first listed is the most difficult technically to execute, and the last is the least difficult technically to execute.

Rank	Technique	Area of Technique
1	Simulation/modeling	Evaluation
2	Quantitative analysis	Evaluation
3	Judgment	Evaluation
4	Project documentation	Information gathering
5	System documentation	Information gathering
6	Base case	Confirmation/validation
7	Test data	Confirmation/validation
8	Testing	Confirmation/validation
9	Fact finding	Information gathering
10	Observation	Information gathering
11	Checklist	Information gathering
12	Consultants	Evaluation
13	Confirmation	Confirmation/validation

Analyzing this listing, we see that the techniques that require programming and analytical knowledge are the most difficult. These include simulation/modeling and quantitative analysis. This is followed quite logically by judgment and project documentation. Both of these techniques deal with management-oriented concepts and require extensive experience to perform effectively. At the bottom of the list are those that primarily involve getting information from other people. These include observation, checklists, consultants, and confirmation. In these cases the QA person is merely utilizing the knowledge and experience and information of other people.

This matrix shows us some of the intricacies of the quality assurance process. We note that the highest skills are for the techniques involved in the evaluation of application systems (i.e., simulation/modeling, quantitative analysis, and judgment). This is the main objective of QA so it should be no surprise that the most skill is needed in performing this aspect of QA. Evaluation techniques are followed in skill level by information-gathering practices. Because QA expends so much effort in gathering information, the skills are for confirmation/validation techniques. This is probably because QA does minimal tasks in this area. It does not mean that validation and confirmation techniques are necessarily easy but, rather, that these are the easier techniques in this category.

AUTOMATING THE QUALITY ASSURANCE FUNCTION

Most quality assurance groups do the majority of their work with pencil and paper. Few QA groups use the power of the computer to improve the quality of computerized applications in their organization. This appears to be an area of need.

The techniques described in this chapter are primarily manual techniques, since those are the techniques being used. However, some QA groups are using the computer to fulfill their function. The results have been rewarding, and QA groups can expect this trend to accelerate.

Use of the computer by QA groups is the key to increased productivity. For example, a QA analyst can review a program listing to determine if improper source statement or combinations of source statement have been used — in other words, standards have been violated. In this process one analyst examines one program at a time. On the other hand, the QA group could write a program to analyze the program source master library and within minutes review all the programs for violations of standards.

Examples of how quality assurance groups are using the computer to improve quality are

•   Write special program to analyze:
    data dictionary
    source program library
    object program library
    logs

- Use test data generator to create test data.

- Analyze programs using program analyzers to identify both highly used and unused source statements.

- Evaluate completeness of data documentation using the data dictionary analysis routines.

These types of computer analysis multiply the effectiveness of the QA function.

SUMMARY

QA groups utilize many techniques in the performance of their work. This chapter identifies thirteen, categorized into three areas. The first are techniques used for gathering information; the second are used for evaluating application systems; and the third are designed to confirm or validate information or conditions.

Different skills/knowledge are needed to effectively utilize these. Eight are identified. These result from experience in project management, general systems design, computer systems design, computer hardware, computer software, programming, computer center operations, and general business. The explanation of each of the thirteen indicates which skills/knowledge are needed to utilize that technique effectively. The skill levels needed are either basic or advanced.

We learn much about the QA function by analyzing the skills required and techniques utilized. Of the three general areas of involvement, the highest skills/knowledge were needed for evaluation. Next were those needed for information gathering with the least required for confirmation/validation. The two most valuable are general systems design and computer systems design experience. The least needed were project management and programming.

The effective QA reviewer has advanced skills in general systems design and computer systems design, as well as general business experience. In addition, that individual understands project documentation and systems documentation as well as being effective in making judgments about problems in data processing application systems. The techniques requiring the highest skill level were those involving mathematics and analysis (i.e., simulation/modeling and quantitative analysis). The lowest skills were required for the techniques aimed at gathering information and opinions from other people. The techniques that showed high skill levels were those dealing with understanding systems and projects as well as judgmental evaluations.

Reporting Quality Assurance Results

Effective quality assurance reviews require competent reporting of results. Reports must convince data processing personnel that their recommendations are sound and should be incorporated into the application system. The written reports prepared by QA personnel affect the function. The more professional and useful the reports, the greater the acceptance of the QA function by both management and project personnel. The reports can do a lot to help "sell" the function to DP personnel.

Effective reporting requires extensive time and effort. A rule of thumb for successful QA is for the group to spend one-third of its time on planning, one-third on fact finding, and the remaining third on analysis and report writing. While this formula will not fit all situations, it does emphasize the importance of developing and presenting conclusions.

This chapter will provide guidance on how to prepare effective QA reports from application reviews. However, many of the lessons can be utilized in preparing narratives on the objectives of quality assurance, as well as writing requirements and procedures for data processing systems personnel to follow in developing good application systems.

RESULTS EXPECTED FROM QA REVIEWS

Simply stated, the objective of quality assurance is to improve the organization's data processing applications. This theme should be included in all QA reports. The group should be a very positive force in

the data processing organization; its reports should be designed to
1.   Help build better data processing systems
2.   Develop a uniform approach to systems development
3.   Share good system and control practices

The objective of QA should become obvious to the reader of the reports. All three goals above deal with methods of building quality application systems. However, MIS goals and performance should be considered a part of these methods. Before they write a report, QA personnel must ask themselves what they want to promote as a result of writing that report.

Better data processing systems occur because better methods are used which help achieve the goals and needs of the user. Effectiveness and efficiency are attributes of a good data processing system. Thus, developing better data processing systems includes the three general quality assurance concerns, which are methods, goals, and performance.

A uniform approach to systems development has proven to be a basic building block for developing better data processing systems: it provides a methodology for data processing systems personnel to follow. Multiple review points by QA personnel give data processing management confidence that the uniform approach is being implemented. Sharing of good system and control practices can be fostered by QA personnel. They obtain this knowledge first from their own personal experience, and second from the experiences of others which are learned through performance of the quality assurance function. As they move from system to system, they can carry with them the better systems development and control practices. Good system and control practices involve both methods and performance. When good system and control practices are followed, experience has shown that performance increases.

QA personnel can convey these concepts to MIS management and project personnel by the way in which reports explain the need for incorporating quality assurance recommendations. An essential element in reporting results is the organization and presentation of findings and recommendations.

WRITING QUALITY ASSURANCE REPORTS

Writing an effective report requires the same thoroughness of planning and execution as any other aspect of data processing. Because many data processing people dislike report writing, they tend to shortcut that aspect of a QA review. Understanding the basic aspects of any report is essential and will help to organize the material to be presented in the report. These elements are explained below:

1. *Who.* What individual or audience will receive the report? Knowing this, the report can be written in the style, language, and size appropriate for that audience.

2. *What.* What type of information does the recipient want? If the report is written for a programmer, the information should be useful in the performance of the programming function. However, if the report is written for executive managers, it should focus on the concerns of that level of management.

3. *Why.* Why is the report being written? To stop a data processing system? Shift it to other pieces of hardware or software? Or to praise the systems personnel for an outstanding job? The objective must be known before the report is written.

4. *When.* When is the report needed? A report submitted too late to be valuable in a decision-making process is a wasted report. If a recipient needs the information today, that is when the report should be ready.

5. *How.* How should the information be presented to best meet the needs of the recipient? The report can be oral (informal or formal) or written in a variety of formats. If the same individual will be receiving QA reports on a regular basis, a standard format is advisable. This will reduce the amount of time needed by the user of the report because the format will be familiar. Personal idiosyncrasies and desires of the report recipient(s) should be considered when deciding on how the material will be presented.

Let us examine the five elements as they occur in the report writing process. First we must look at the factors to be considered prior to writing the report. This includes the "who," "why," and "when." Next we will discuss what is meant by providing information needed by the report recipient. This is primarily the information needs of management and answers the "what" question. Lastly, a report organization will be presented which answers the question "how."

PLANNING FOR WRITING A REPORT

There are many different ways to write a good report. The following approach may prove valuable:

1. Decide for whom the report will be written and when it is needed.

2. Write out the objectives you want to accomplish by writing the report.

3. Write out the recommendations you want to make as a result of the review.

4. Outline the various parts of the report and jot down brief notes of what you want to include in those segments. (A proposed organization follows in a later part of this chapter.)

5. Cross-reference the findings and recommendations in the outline to the QA workpapers. This will provide you with the assurance that you can support each finding and recommendation. It will also show what has not been included so those items can be considered for the outline.

6. Write out a first draft of the report as quickly as possible, using the outline. If it is an oral report, rehearse the talk.

7. Read the report to see if it achieves the objectives you set out in step 2. Make any changes necessary to be sure you achieve those objectives.

8. Ask another member of the QA group, or someone else you respect, to read the report and tell you where the intent or wording is not clear.

9. Make the necessary improvements and have the report typed and presented to management. If it is to be an oral report, steps 6 through 8 will be rehearsal steps prior to presenting the report orally to management.

Step 1. For Whom and When Needed. It should be clear in the mind of the person writing the report for whom the report is being prepared. The distribution may be widespread, or to people with diverse backgrounds, but the report must be written for one person. Know the style with which that person is familiar, the concerns of the person, and then compose the report specifically for that person. Forget about all the others who will see the report.

Also, know the date when the report is needed. DON'T BE LATE. A less polished report on time is valuable; a polished report received late may be worthless.

Step 2. Objectives. For the report to be effective, the objectives must be clear in the mind of the person preparing the report. The following criteria should prove helpful:

• The report objectives should be consistent with the concerns of the person receiving the report. For example, objectives aimed at improving the computer center should not be in a report going to an application system project leader.

• The objectives covered in the report should be consistent with those of the review.

• The objectives of the report should be positive. For example, to improve a situation, increase performance, increase efficiency, etc.

Step 3. Recommendations. Recommendations included in QA reports should be presented from a management perspective. Reports which are written for the data processing manager should be written with the data processing manager's concerns addressed. A common mistake of QA groups is to write highly technical reports which the data processing manager can neither understand nor take much interest in. The data processing manager is a manager and, as such, has a manager's concern. The more the quality assurance function and its reports address those concerns, the more successful the function will be.

The data processing manager is responsible for planning, organizing, directing, and controlling the data processing function in the organization. It is on those concerns that the QA group should build its reports. Recommendations should help alleviate those concerns. Let's address these four concerns one at a time.

Planning is a management function. QA wants to determine that plans have been developed according to the organization's procedures, and not second-guess whether the plans are correct or not. Planning includes the development of detailed schedules for implementing the phase under review, and the project in total. The plans should include providing sufficient resources to perform the job. QA can make an assessment as to whether enough, too few, or too many resources have been allocated to the application system. Management is just as concerned that too many resources have been allocated as too few. Quality assessment can make some of these assessments by comparing plans, schedules, and budgets against actual usage. For example, falling behind on the schedule is indicative of either too few resources or resources of too low caliber for individuals to perform the job within the time available. Providing recommendations that address these types of management concerns can be a very valuable input to the DP manager.

Organizing the application system project team will usually be the task of the project manager, although the DP manager is responsible. The assessment as to the effectiveness of this organization by quality assurance again is compliance to the desires of data processing management. For example, if the project should be organized to include hardware and software consultants from a central group, QA should determine that that has happened. It can also make an assessment as to whether individuals are competent to perform the assignments which they have been given. While this is an argumentative part of the function, there can be no argument that it is valuable input to data processing management. Again, management has the responsibility for the successful completion of the project, and early warning of potential problems is highly appreciated by members of data processing management.

Directing the implementation of an application system implies compliance to the plans, policies, and procedures of the total organization. This must be the number one priority of quality assurance. Obviously, management is not looking for minor violations where the best interests of the company are served through a deviation from normal policies and procedures. What management is concerned about is serious violations which are not in the best interest of the organization. Recommendations should be addressed to problem areas and not to specific minor violations.

Management normally establishes *control mechanisms* to determine that the implementation process is functioning correctly. These include progress reports, time and budget reporting, and the use of accounting systems to record utilization of resources. For example, job accounting resource systems collect data on use of computer hardware and software facilities. QA wants to determine that these control mechanisms are being used. Management is also concerned that there is a reasonable control over the use of resources, so any input QA can provide management on more efficient use of resources is appreciated. This includes suggesting better ways to perform work, means of eliminating unnecessary hardware, software, or systems, as well as warning about inefficient systems design on the part of the user. Savings in the user department can be a valuable recommendation from QA reviewers.

Recommendations should encompass management concerns. Some suggestions:

- The recommendations in the report should be positively stated.
- Substantiating data to support the conclusions and recommendations should be available.
- Significant facts or events that occurred after the QA review should be contained in the report if they affect recommendations and conclusions. However, it should be clearly stated that they occurred after the report and thus were not subject to the same scrutiny as conditions that existed before and during the review.
- The desired action you want to be taken should be clearly stated.

Step 4. Report Outline. Reports from QA should be organized to make it easy for the reader to obtain the important points quickly. The size and content will fluctuate depending on the importance of the system, the extent of the review, and the frequency of reviews. But consistency of format permits management to get the essential information out of the report quickly. Quality assurance and data processing management should work together to improve upon the organization and content of quality assurance reports.

Effective QA reports can be organized as follows:

1. *Management Summary.* A one- or two-page synopsis, including summarized background information, findings, and recommendations.

2. *Background Information.* Enough data to orient the reader to the issues being discussed in the report. This includes the application under review, the phase being reviewed, the time of the review, the scope and objectives of the review, as well as other pertinent data relating to the application system.

3. *Findings.* The factual results of the review. This should include significant information only. It is specifically within the findings section that QA should present information from the perspective of the reader.

4. *Recommendations.* The specific recommendations that the QA group is recommending based on its findings. If the project team has already agreed to implement any of the recommendations, that should be noted so that the recipient of the report knows what management action is required.

5. *Effect of the Recommendation on Resources.* The anticipated effect on people, on hardware, on software, and dollar implications if the recommendations are implemented, should be clearly spelled out.

6. *Appendixes.* Include those items which are not essential to the report, but which are supportive of findings and/or recommendations, and could prove valuable to the recipient.

This organization structure is appropriate for reports of any size. The significance of the findings and recommendations will determine the size of the report. The management summary should never exceed two pages, as this provides data processing management with a quick overview of the situation, and also provides something to forward to upper management.

Listed below are some guidelines to be followed in preparing each of these sections:

1. *Management Summary*

   Is the objective of the quality assurance review clearly stated?

   Is the background information concisely summarized?

   Are the findings concisely summarized?

   Are the recommendations concisely summarized?

   Are the resource implications of the recommendations concisely summarized?

2. *Background Information*

   Are the application and review point clearly stated?

   Has the time when the review occurred as well as who made the review been stated?

Are the objectives of the review stated?

When personal opinions are included in the report, are they clearly identified as opinions?

If critical comments are made about the project team, have they been put into the proper perspective recognizing that unusual circumstances may have occurred which caused the problems?

Have the views of the project team been considered and presented in the report?

Is the material in the report factual and presented fairly?

Is sufficient information contained to explain wherever possible the causes of problems?

Has the factual material used as background information been substantiated by reviewing the contents of the review team working papers?

3. *Findings*

Have the findings been presented fairly and objectively?

Are the findings presented from a positive and not from a negative viewpoint?

Are the findings supportive of the system project personnel wherever possible? That is, if the project team is doing an outstanding job, it should be so stated.

Is enough detailed information contained in the findings to support the findings?

Are major exceptions to the organization's standards, policies, plans, and procedures noted in the findings?

4. *Recommendations*

Are recommendations clearly stated so there is no question in people's minds as to what is wanted?

Do the recommendations state who should execute the recommendations?

Are unresolved issues and questions needing further study stated as recommendations for further study, and not avoided in the report?

Are recommendations supported by the findings?

5. *Resource Implications*

Is the effect of the recommendations on people stated?

Is the effect of the recommendations on hardware and software stated?

Is the effect of the recommendations on schedules stated?

Is the effect of the recommendations on cost stated?

Is the effect of the recommendations on controls stated?

Is the effect of the recommendations on other systems stated?

Is the effect of the recommendations on the organization's plans, standards, policies, and procedures stated?

6. *Appendixes*

Do the appendixes include the information that will be helpful to the recipient of the report, but not necessary to read as support for the recommendations?

Step 5. Cross-Reference Findings to Workpapers. Working papers should be organized to reference information from detailed to general and vice versa. Problems uncovered should be summarized on lead sheets in the working papers. These lead sheets are then used by QA personnel in developing recommendations.

A copy of the report outline should be cross-referenced to the summarized lead sheets in the working papers. Each finding and recommendation should be cross-referenced. There may be several references to any one finding or recommendation.

The lead sheet should be cross-referenced to the outline. This will point out any finding uncovered or recommendation made that did not get into the report. Experience has shown this to be a very valuable exercise.

This procedure will enable QA personnel to answer questions about the report or to review it quickly. It also provides assurance that any finding or recommendation given in the report is supportable by work done during the review.

Step 6. Write a Report Draft. The quickest way to write a report is to do a rough first draft, review and modify it yourself, have it reviewed by an outside party, and then rewrite the report incorporating the review comments. The first step of this process is to complete, as quickly as possible, the first draft of the report. The draft report should be written according to the outline.

Step 7. Report Writer's Review of Report. The writer of the report should ask himself or herself:

1.   Have the objectives been achieved with this report?
2.   Is the report readable (i.e., do the ideas flow easily, are sentences short and words small)?
3.   Is it written in a style appropriate to the recipient of the report and does it address the concerns?
4.   Is the report a professional report?
5.   If I received this report, would I be moved to take action on the recommendation?

Step 8. Outside Review of Report. Once the writer is satisfied with the report, one or more outside opinions should be obtained. The outside reviewer can be the QA manager in a larger QA group. Other potential reviewers are respected friends or DP colleagues. The comments and recommendations received should be evaluated and the worthwhile ideas incorporated in the report.

If oral presentations are used, the presentation should be critiqued by giving the presentation to a small group. Because most oral presentations are not written out, they cannot be adequately reviewed by the person preparing the presentation. Therefore, the dress rehearsal is important.

Step 9. Prepare Final Report. The final report should incorporate the thinking gained from steps 1–8. The report should be the best effort possible with available resources.

The report in its physical format should be one in which the preparer can take pride. The following checklist provides suggestions to avoid some of the traps which have caused problems to other QA groups:

- The report should be neat and clean, identified, and dated.

- The preparer's name should be on the report.

- The report should not contain any grammatical or spelling errors.

- The final report should be checked before being presented to management to assure all pages are present, etc.

The reviewer's job is not complete when the report has been prepared. The contents of the report must be reviewed with the project team and then presented to management. In addition, the QA group should follow up to determine that the recommendations have been given proper consideration, and implemented wherever practical.

POSTREVIEW CONFERENCE

The best method for discussing review findings and recommendations with the project team is at an exit conference. At that time, the review personnel can discuss their findings and support them with information gathered during the review. In most cases, the recommendations would have been discussed informally during the review.

The exit conference provides the project team the opportunity to rebut, comment on, or concur with the findings and recommendations. The conference should be an open and free discussion held in an atmosphere of developing the best possible application system. Many times, when presented with findings and recommendations, the project team will have very valid arguments for not adopting certain recommendations. When arguments are valid, the quality assurance team may wish to withdraw those findings or recommendations from the final report.

The main purpose of the quality assurance report is to resolve any application system problems, and to correct any procedural misunderstandings on the part of the application system project team. This is most readily done with the cooperation of the project team. Therefore, it becomes important for the QA reviewers to review the report with the project team. Ideally, all recommendations will be resolved at the exit conference. This resolution can be that the project team has accepted the recommendation, the QA group has withdrawn the recommendation, or some compromise achieved. In these situations, the report going to management is informative rather than action oriented. Such a situation is desirable from both the viewpoint of quality assurance and the project team. QA has demonstrated that its function has provided a valuable service, and the project team has gained from that advice in a very positive professional manner by either accepting or modifying and then accepting worthwhile recommendations.

The exit conference should be conducted as soon after the review is complete as possible. Many QA groups conduct the conference on the last day of their review. This means that the report has been completed. This also has proven to be a good quality assurance practice.

Listed below are some guidelines for consideration in holding an exit conference:

1. The exit conference should be held at a time when there is sufficient time to discuss in detail the findings and recommendations.

2. The QA team leader should conduct the exit conference.

3. The quality assurance team leader should explain the objectives of the conference.

4. The project team should be given an opportunity to read the quality assurance report before the conference and to comment on it during the meeting.

5. The project team should be asked specifically if it agrees with all the findings (facts) presented in the report.

6. When a disagreement occurs regarding facts, a follow-up investigation should be made to determine if the facts presented were true and presented fairly.

7. Differences of opinion between the project team and the quality assurance review group should be noted, and included in the final report where practical.

8. The QA group should ask the project team if any material events have occurred or conditions changed between the end of the review and the exit conference.

9. The QA team leader should sum up the conclusions of the conference at the end of the conference.

The review can result in many findings and recommendations. It may not be appropriate to discuss all of these with any one of the parties interested in the findings. Depending on the type of finding and/or recommendation, it may be advisable to direct that finding or recommendation to only one of the recipients of the review results. The normal recipients of information from a review are data processing management and the project team. In addition, some QA groups give copies of the report to other groups such as users, internal auditors and external auditors.

WHO GETS QUALITY ASSURANCE RESULTS?

QA personnel should direct their comments and findings to the individual in the best position to take action on those recommendations. Occasionally, it is not in the best interest of the QA group, and the organization, to present certain findings or recommendations to specific people. Comments may be critical of an individual's performance, for example. Many times these opinions are judgmental and may or may not be supported by management. In cases where the judgments are not supported, it is better for all parties concerned that the statements be kept as confidential as possible.

In those instances when a fraud or embezzlement against the organization is suspected, it should be investigated by groups knowledgeable in frauds. It is not in the best interest of the organization for quality assurance people to confront data processing personnel with these facts because they are not familiar with dealing with frauds and may adversely affect the case against the person who committed the fraud. Individuals need to have an understanding of the legal implications of confronting someone about any sort of criminal activity before they do it.

Listed below are some of the groups interested in QA reports and the types of information that should be addressed to that group:

1. Application System Project Team
   All findings and recommendations dealing with methods
   All findings and recommendations dealing with goals
   All findings and recommendations dealing with performance

2. MIS Department Management
   Significant findings and recommendations dealing with methods
   Significant findings and recommendations dealing with goals
   Significant findings and recommendations dealing with performance
   Project team member performance
   Project team management performance
   Suspected fraud or embezzlement
   Misuse of resources
   Significant under- or overrun of budget

Significant schedule deviations

Poor working relationship with the user or other outside parties

3.   Departments Outside MIS Department

Full reports to internal audit when requested

Full or extracted reports to users with MIS department agreement for areas of interest to the users

Full or extracted reports to executive management with MIS department agreement for areas of interest to executive management.

QA personnel should have the concurrence of MIS department management before sending reports to outside groups. Sending reports to groups outside of the MIS department may reduce the effectiveness of the QA group when reviewing application projects. While quality assurance wants to maintain organizational independence of the group they are reviewing, its effectiveness is built on the belief that quality assurance is an internal MIS department function with the goal of supporting the project team. Sending negative comments about a project to the user of that application can cause hard feelings.

SUMMARY

Professional reports can greatly enhance the effectiveness of quality assurance. Management tends to judge staff groups on the quality of their reports. Quality assurance groups must spend the time and effort necessary to produce effective reports.

Effective reports to management are reports which address management concerns. Management has the responsibility for planning, organizing, directing, and controlling the data processing function. They are vitally interested in findings and recommendations which address these topics. Minor findings and recommendations should be resolved with project personnel. Findings and recommendations passed to management are those which are of interest or require the attention of management. Quality assurance personnel should discuss freely with management the organization, content, frequency, and scope of quality assurance reports.

Prior to issuing reports, quality assurance should meet with the project team to review the findings and recommendations of the report.

This conference should verify the authenticity of the facts and findings stated in the report. There should be an open and frank discussion of the recommendations in an effort to reach agreement on the recommendations. It is important for the QA group to know the reactions of the project team to its findings and recommendations before presenting them to data processing management.

Part 3

Quality Assurance Responsibilities and Methods

Verification, Validation, and Testing

QUALITY ASSURANCE THROUGH VERIFICATION

Testing is the traditional technique used to determine and assure the quality of products. For many items procured by the Government, the definition or description of a quality product and the testing methods used to ensure that quality are well established. These tests are usually physical tests based on both industry and Government standards (such as dimensions for fittings, strength for materials, power for motors, etc.). The success of these methods depends upon the definition of what constitutes a quality product, the determination of measurable properties that reflect the quality, the derivation of meaningful test criteria based on the measurable quantities, and the formulation of adequate tests to ensure the quality.

Unfortunately, software does not fit into the traditional framework of quality assessment. One reason is that software, in general, is a "one of a kind" product especially tailored for a particular application. There is often no standard product or specification to use as a model to measure against. Secondly, analogies to physical products with applicable dimensional, strength, etc. standards do not exist. Of greatest importance, the concept of what constitutes quality in software is not as well formulated. There is no universally accepted definition of software quality.

Attributes of Quality Software

There have been many studies directed toward the determination of appropriate factors for software quality. A number of attributes have been proposed; the set given by Figure 11.1 is representative. Most of these factors are qualitative rather than quantitative.

In Figure 11.1, the top level characteristics of quality software are reliability, testability, usability, efficiency, transportability, and maintainability. In practice, efficiency often turns out to be in conflict with other attributes, e.g. transportability, maintainability, and testability. As hardware costs decrease, efficiency of machine use becomes much less an issue and consequently a less important attribute of software quality. At present, a reasonable software development methodology will support the creation of software with all these qualities. While a piece of code may not be locally as efficient as a skilled programmer can write it disregarding all other factors, it must be designed to be as efficient as possible while still exhibiting the other desired qualities.

For the purpose of this document, two qualities stand out, reliability and testability. The others are equally important, but less related to testing and verification issues, and perhaps more qualitative than quantitative. Reliable software must be adequate; that is, it must be correct, complete, consistent, and feasible at each stage of the development life cycle. An infeasible set of requirements will lead to an inadequate design and probably an incorrect implementation. Given that the software meets these adequacy requirements at each stage of the development process, to be reliable it must also be robust. Robustness is a quality which represents the ability of the software to survive a hostile environment. We cannot anticipate all possible events, and we must build our software to be as resilient as possible.

At all stages of the life cycle, software should be testable. To accomplish this it must be understandable. The desired product (the requirements and design) and the actual product (the code) should be represented in a structured, concise, and self-descriptive manner so that they can be compared. The software must also be measurable, allowing means for actually instrumenting or inserting probes, testing, and evaluating the product of each stage.

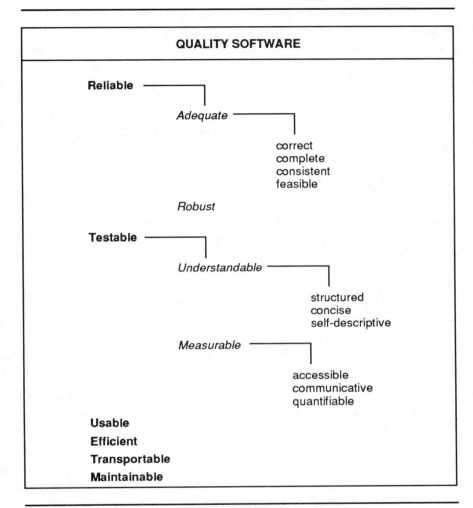

Figure 11.1. A hierarchy of software quality attributes.

Emphasis on particular quality factors will vary from project to project depending on application, environment, and other considerations. The specific definition of quality and the importance of given attributes should be specified during the requirements phase of the project.

Even if good quality is difficult to define and measure, poor quality is glaringly apparent. Software that is error prone or does not work is obviously poor quality software. Consequently, discovery of errors in the software has been the first step toward quality assurance. Program testing, executing the software using representative data samples and comparing the actual results with the expected results, has been the fundamental technique used to determine errors. However, testing is difficult, time-consuming, and inadequate. Consequently, increased emphasis has been placed upon insuring quality through the development process.

The criticality of the problem determines the effort required to validate the solution. Software to control airplane landings or to direct substantial money transfers requires higher confidence in its proper functioning than does a carpool locator program since the consequences of malfunction are more severe. For each software project not only the product requirements but also the validation requirements should be determined and specified at the initiation of the project. Project size, uniqueness, criticality, the cost of malfunction, and project budget all influence the validation needs. With the validation requirements clearly stated, specific techniques for verification and testing can be chosen. This document surveys the field of verification and testing techniques. The emphasis is upon medium and large size projects but many of the individual techniques have broader applicability. Verification and testing for very small projects are discussed elsewhere.

The following terms are sufficiently important to warrant definition in the test. It should be noted that some of these terms may appear with slightly different meanings elsewhere in the literature.

1. *Validation:* Determination of the correctness of the final program or software produced from a development project with respect to the user's needs and requirements. Validation is usually accomplished by verifying each stage of the software development life cycle.

2. *Certification:* Acceptance of software by an authorized agent usually after the software has been validated by the agent, or after its validity has been demonstrated to the agent.

3. *Verification:* In general the demonstration of consistency, completeness, and correctness of the software at each stage and between each stage of the development life cycle.

4.   *Testing:* Examination of the behavior of a program by executing the program on sample datasets.

5.   *Proof of Correctness:* Use of techniques of logic to infer that an assertion assumed true at program entry implies that an assertion holds at program exit.

6.   *Program Debugging:* The process of correcting syntactic and logical errors detected during coding. With the primary goal of obtaining an executing piece of code, debugging shares with testing certain techniques and strategies, but differs in its usual ad hoc application and local scope.

Verification Throughout Life Cycle

Figure 11.2 presents a traditional view of the development life cycle with testing contained in a stage immediately prior to operation and maintenance. All too often testing is the only verification technique used to determine the adequacy of the software. When verification is constrained to a single technique and confined to the latter stages of development, severe consequences can result. It is not unusual to hear of testing consuming 50 percent of the development budget. All errors are costly but the later in the life cycle that the error discovery is made, the more costly the error. Consequently, if lower cost and higher quality are the goal, verification should not be isolated to a single stage in the development process but should be incorporated into each phase of development. Barry Boehm has stated that one of the most prevalent and costly mistakes made on software projects today is to defer the activity of detecting and correcting software problems until late in the project. The primary reason for early investment in verification activity is that expensive errors may already have been made before coding begins.

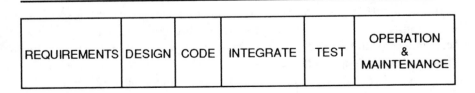

REQUIREMENTS	DESIGN	CODE	INTEGRATE	TEST	OPERATION & MAINTENANCE

Figure 11.2. The software development life cycle.

Figure 11.3 presents an amended life cycle chart which includes verification activities. The success of phasing verification throughout the development cycle depends upon the existence of a clearly defined and stated product at each development stage. The more formal and precise the statement of the development product, the more amenable it is to the analysis required to support verification. Many of the new software development methodologies encourage a firm product from the early development.

We will examine each stage of the life cycle and discuss the relevant activities. The following activities should be performed at each stage:

1.   Analyze the structures produced at this stage for internal testability and adequacy.

2.   Generate test sets based on the structures at this stage.

In addition, the following should be performed during design and construction:

3.   Determine that the structures are consistent with structures produced during previous stages.

4.   Refine or redefine test sets generated earlier.

Throughout the entire life cycle, neither development nor verification is a straightline activity. Modifications or corrections to structures at one stage will require modifications and reverification of structures produced during previous stages.

Requirements

The verification activities that accompany the problem definition and requirements analysis stage of software development are extremely significant. The adequacy of the requirements must be thoroughly analyzed and initial test cases generated with the expected (correct) responses. Developing scenarios of expected system use may help to determine the test data and anticipated results. These tests will form the core of the final test set. Generating these tests and the expected behavior of the system clarifies the requirements and helps guarantee that they are testable. Vague or untestable requirements will leave the validity of the delivered product in doubt. Late discovery of requirements inadequacy can be very costly. A determination of the criticality of software quality attributes and the importance of validation should be made at this stage. Both product requirements and validation requirements should be estimated.

Life Cycle Stage	Verification Activities
Requirements	Determine verification approach Determine adequacy of requirements Generate functional test data

Design	Determine consistency of design with
	    requirements
	Determine adequacy of design
	Generate structural and functional
	    test data

Construction	Determine consistency with design Determine adequacy of implementation Generate structural and functional test data Apply test data
Operation & Maintenance	Retest

Figure 11.3. Life cycle verification activities.

Some automated tools to aid in the requirements definition exist. Examples include Information System Design and Optimization System, The Software Requirements Engineering Program, Structured Analysis and Design Technique, and Systematic Activity Modeling Method. All provide a disciplined framework for expressing requirements and thus aid in the checking of consistency and completeness. Although these tools provide only rudimentary validation procedures, this capability is greatly needed and it is the subject of current research.

Design

Organization of the verification effort and test management activities should be closely integrated with preliminary design. The general testing strategy, including test methods and test evaluation criteria, is formulated; and a test plan is produced. If the project size of criticality warrants, an independent test team is organized. In addition, a test schedule with observable milestones is constructed. At this same time, the framework for quality assurance and test documentation should be established.

During the detailed design, validation support tools should be acquired or developed and the test procedures themselves should be produced. Test data to exercise the functions introduced during the design process as well as test cases based upon the structure of the system should be generated. Thus as the software development proceeds, a more effective set of test cases is built up.

In addition to test organization and the generation of test cases to be used during construction, the design itself should be analyzed and examined for errors. Simulation can be used to verify properties of the system structures and subsystem interaction, design walkthroughs should be used by the developers to verify the flow and logical structure of the system while design inspection should be performed by the test team. Missing cases, faulty logic, module interface mismatches, data structure inconsistencies, erroneous I/O assumptions, and user interface inadequacies are items of concern. The detailed design must be shown internally consistent, complete, and consistent with the preliminary design and requirements.

Although much of the verification must be performed manually, the use of a formal design language can facilitate the analysis. Several different design methodologies are in current use. Top Down Design proposed by Harlan Mills of IBM, Structured Design introduced by L. Constantine, and the Jackson Method are examples. These techniques are manual and facilitate verification by providing a clear statement of the design. The Design Expression and Configuration Aid, the Process Design Language, High Order Software and SPECIAL are examples of automated systems or languages which can also be used for analysis and consistency checking.

Construction

Actual testing occurs during the construction stage of development. Many testing tools and techniques exist for this stage of system development. Code walkthrough and code inspection are effective manual techniques. Static analysis techniques detect errors by analyzing program characteristics such as data flow and language construct usage. For programs of significant size, automated tools are required to perform this analysis. Dynamic analysis, performed as the code actually executes, is used to determine test coverage through various instrumentation techniques. Formal verification or proof techniques are used to provide further quality assurance. These techniques are discussed in detail under "Verification Techniques."

During the entire test process, careful control and management of test information is critical. Test sets, test results, and test reports should be catalogued and stored in a database. For all but very small systems, automated tools are required to do an adequate job, for the bookkeeping chores alone become too large to be handled manually. A test driver, test data generation aids, test coverage tools, test results management aids, and report generators are usually required.

Maintenance

Over 50 percent of the life cycle costs of a software system are spent on maintenance. As the system is used, it is modified either to correct errors or to augment the original system. After each modification the system must be retested. Such retesting activity is termed *regression testing*. The goal of regression testing is to minimize the cost of system revalidation. Usually only those portions of the system impacted by the modifications are retested. However, changes at any level may necessitate retesting, reverifying and updating documentation at all levels below it. For example, a design change requires design reverification, unit retesting and subsystem and system retesting. Test cases generated during system development are reused or used after appropriate modifications. The quality of the test documentation generated during system development and modified during maintenance will affect the cost of regression testing. If test data cases have been catalogued and preserved, duplication of effort will be minimized.

We will emphasize testing, verification, and validation during software development. The maintenance and operation stage is very important, but generally outside the scope of this report. The procedures described here for software development will, if followed correctly, make the task of maintaining, upgrading, evolving, and operating the software a much easier task.

AN OVERVIEW OF TESTING

Concepts

The purpose of this section is to discuss the basic concepts and fundamental implications and limitations of testing as a part of software verification. There are many meanings attributed to the verb "to test" throughout the technical literature. Let us begin by looking at the Oxford English Dictionary definition:

> **Test** — That by which the existence, quality, or genuineness of anything is, or may be, determined.

The objects that we test are the elements that arise during the development of software. These include modules of code, requirements and design specifications, data structures, and any other objects that are necessary for the correct development and implementation of our software. We will often use the term "program" in this document to refer to any object that may be conceptually or actually executed. A design or requirements specification can be conceptually executed, transforming input data to output data. Hence, remarks directed toward "programs" have broader application.

We view a program as a representation of a function. The function describes the relationship of an input (called a *domain element*) to an output (called a *range element*). The testing process is then used to ensure that the program faithfully realizes the function. For example, consider the function $1/x$. Its domain is the set of all floating point numbers excluding 0. Any program that realizes the function $1/z$ must, when given a floating point value r (r nonzero), return the value $1/r$ (given the machine dependent precision). The testing problem is to ensure that the program does represent the function.

Elements of the function's domain are called *valid inputs*. Since programs are expected to operate reasonably on elements outside of a function's domain (called "robustness"), we must test the program on such elements. Thus any program that represents $1/x$ should be tested on the value 0 and perhaps also on meaningless data (such as strings) to ensure that the program does not fail catastrophically. These elements outside of the function's domain are called *invalid inputs*. How to choose these and other test input values is discussed in detail in "Functional Testing Techniques."

The essential components of a program test are a description of the functional domain, the program in executable form, a description of the expected behavior, a way of observing program behavior, and a method of determining whether the observed behavior conforms with the expected behavior. The testing process consists of obtaining a valid value from the functional domain (or an invalid value from outside the functional domain to test for robustness), determining the expected behavior, executing the program and observing its behavior, and finally comparing that behavior with the expected behavior. If the expected and the actual behavior agree, we say the test instance succeeds, otherwise we say the test instance fails.

Of the five necessary components in the testing process, the most difficult to obtain is a description of the expected behavior. Often ad hoc methods must be used to determine expected behavior. These methods include hand calculation, simulation, and other less efficient solutions to the same problem. What is needed is an *oracle*, a source which for any given input description can provide a complete description of the corresponding output behavior. We will discuss this process later.

Dynamic Testing

We can classify program test methods into *dynamic* and *static analysis* techniques. Dynamic analysis requires that the program be executed and, hence, involves the traditional notion of program testing; i.e. the program is run on some test cases and the results of the program's performance are examined to check whether the program operated as expected. Static analysis does not usually involve actual program execution. Common static analysis techniques include such compiler tasks as syntax and type checking. We will first consider some general aspects of dynamic analysis within a general discussion of program testing.

A complete verification of a program, at any stage in the life cycle, can be obtained by performing the test process for every element of the domain. If each instance succeeds, the program is verified; otherwise an error has been found. This testing method is known as *exhaustive testing* and is the only dynamic analysis technique that will guarantee the validity of a program. Unfortunately, this technique is not practical. Frequently functional domains are infinite, or if not infinitive very large, so as to make the number of required test instances infeasible.

The solution is to reduce this potentially infinite exhaustive testing process to a finite testing process. This is accomplished by finding criteria for choosing representative elements from the functional domain. These criteria may reflect either the functional description or the program structure.

The subset of elements used in a testing process is called a *test dataset* (test set for short). Thus the crux of the testing problem is to find an adequate test set, one that "covers" the domain and is small enough to perform the testing process for each element in the set. The paper of Goodenough and Gerhart presents the first formal treatment for determining when a criterion for test set selection is adequate. In their paper, a criterion C is said to be *consistent* provided that test sets T1 and T2 chosen by C are such that all test instances of T2 are successful. A criterion C is said to be *complete* provided that it produces test sets that uncover all errors. These definitions lead to the fundamental theorem of testing which states:

If there exists a consistent, complete criterion for test set selection for a program P and if a test set satisfying the criterion is such that all test instances succeed, then the program P is correct.

Unfortunately it has been shown to be impossible to find consistent, complete test criteria except for the simplest cases. The above just confirms that testing, especially complete testing, is a very difficult process. Examples of criteria that are used in practice for the selection of test sets include:

1. The elements of the test set reflect special domain properties such as extremal or ordering properties.

2. The elements of the test set exercise the program structure such as test instances ensuring all branches or all statements are executed.

3. The elements of the test set reflect special properties of the functional description such as domain values leading to extremal function values.

Structural Versus Functional Testing

The properties that the test set is to reflect are classified according to whether they are derived from a description of the program's function or from the program's internal structure. Test data generation based on *functional analysis* and on *structural analysis* is described in the sections on functional and structural testing techniques. Classifying the test data inclusion criteria given above, the first and the third are based on functional analysis criteria while the second is based on structural analysis criteria. Both structural and functional analysis should be performed to ensure adequate testing. Structural analysis-based test sets tend to uncover errors that occur during "coding" of the program, while functional analysis-based test sets tend to uncover errors that occur in implementing requirements or design specifications.

Although the criterion for generating a structure-based test set is normally simple, the discovery of domain elements that satisfy the criterion is often quite difficult. Test data is usually derived by iteratively refining the database on the information provided by the application of structural coverage metrics. Since functional analysis techniques often suffer from combinatorial problems, the generation of adequate functional test data is no easier. As a result, ad hoc methods are often employed to locate data which stresses the program.

Static Testing

The application of test data and the analysis of the results are dynamic testing techniques. The class of static analysis techniques is divided into two types: techniques that analyze consistency and techniques that measure some program property. The consistency techniques are used to ensure program properties such as correct syntax, correct parameter matching between procedures, correct typing, and correct requirements and specification translation. The measurement techniques measure properties such as error proneness, understandability, and well-structuredness.

The simplest of the consistency checking static analysis techniques is the syntax checking feature of compilers. In modern compilers, this feature is frequently augmented by type checking, parameter matching (for modules), cross-reference tables, static array bounds checking, and aliasing. Two advanced static analysis techniques are symbolic execution and program proving. The latter proves the consistency of stated relations between program variables before and after program segments. Symbolic execution performs a "virtual" execution of all possible program paths. Since an actual execution does not occur, the method is considered a static analysis technique. Both are described in detail in the next section.

Manual Versus Automated Testing

A final classification of methods can be made upon the basis of whether the method is a *manual* method such as structured walkthrough or code inspection, or whether the method is *automated*.

In Table 11.1 we list the verification methods that will be discussed throughout the rest of this report. We provide a classification according to whether the method is dynamic or static, structural or functional, manual or automated.

Technique	Manual/ Automatic	Static/ Dynamic	Structural/ Functional
Correctness proof	both	static	both
Walkthroughs	manual	dynamic	both
Inspections	manual	static	both
Design Reviews and Audits	manual	static	both
Simulation	automated	dynamic	functional
Desk Checking	manual	both	structural
Peer Review	manual	both	structural
Executable Specifications	automated	dynamic	functional
Exhaustive Testing	automated	dynamic	functional
Stress Testing	manual	dynamic	functional
Error Guessing	manual	dynamic	functional

Table 11.1. Summary of testing techniques.

Technique	Manual/ Automatic	Static/ Dynamic	Structural/ Functional
Cause-Effect Graphing	both	dynamic	functional
Design-Based Functional Testing	manual	dynamic	functional
Coverage-Based Metric Testing	automated	both	structural
Complexity-Based Metric Testing	automated	both	structural
Compiler-Based Analysis	automated	static	structural
Data Flow Analysis	automated	static	structural
Control Flow Analysis	automated	static	structural
Symbolic Execution	automated	static	structural
Instrumentation	automated	dynamic	structural
Combined Techniques	automated	both	both

Table 11.1. Summary of testing techniques. (cont'd)

VERIFICATION TECHNIQUES

A description of verification, validation, and testing techniques can be arranged in several different ways. In keeping with the emphasis on verification throughout the life cycle, we first present general techniques which span the stages of the life cycle. The remaining sections are organized along the lines of the usual testing plan, providing discussion of test data generation, test data evaluation, testing procedures and analysis, and the development of support tools. Each procedure will be briefly discussed, with emphasis given to its role in the validation process and its advantages and limitations.

General Verification Techniques

Techniques that can be used throughout the life cycle are described here. The majority of the techniques involve static analysis and can be performed manually. They can be utilized without a large capital expenditure, although for analysis of large systems automated aids are advised. These include traditional informal methods of desk checking and review, disciplined techniques of structured walkthroughs and inspections, and formal methods of proof of correctness. In addition, the role simulation plays in validation and verification is described.

Desk Checking and Peer Review

Desk checking is the most traditional means for analyzing a program. It is the foundation for the more disciplined techniques of walkthroughs, inspections, and reviews. In order to improve the effectiveness of desk checking, it is important that the programmer thoroughly review the problem definition and requirements, the design specification, the algorithms and the code listings. In most instances, desk checking is used more as a debugging technique than a testing technique. Since seeing one's own errors is difficult, it is better if another person does the desk checking. For example, two programmers can trade listings and read each other's code. This approach still lacks the group dynamics present in formal walkthroughs, inspections, and reviews.

Another method, not directly involving testing, which tends to increase overall quality of software production is peer review. There are a variety of implementations of peer review, but all are based on a review of each programmer's code. A panel can be set up which reviews sample code on a regular basis for efficiency, style, adherence to standard, etc. and which provides feedback to the individual programmer. Another possibility is to maintain a notebook of required "fixes" and revisions to the software and indicate the original programmer or designer. In a "chief programmer team" environment, the librarian can collect data on programmer runs, error reports, etc. and act as a review board or pass the information on to a peer review panel.

Walkthroughs, Inspections, and Review

Walkthroughs and inspections are formal manual techniques which are a natural evolution of desk checking. While both techniques share a common philosophy and similar organization, they are quite distinct in execution. Furthermore, while they both evolved from the simple desk check discipline of the single programmer, they are very disciplined procedures aimed at removing the major responsibility for verification from the developer.

Both procedures require a team, usually directed by a moderator. The team includes the developer, but the remaining 3–6 members and the moderator should not be directly involved in the development effort. Both techniques are based on a reading of the product (e.g. requirements, specifications, or code) in a formal meeting environment with specific rules for evaluation. The difference between inspection and walkthrough lies in the conduct of the meeting. Both methods require preparation and study by the team members, and scheduling and coordination by the team moderator.

Inspection involves a step-by-step reading of the product, with each step checked against a predetermined list of criteria. These criteria include checks for historically common errors. Guidance for developing the test criteria can be found elsewhere. The developer is usually required to narrate the reading of the product. Many errors are found by the developer just by the simple act of reading aloud. Others, of course, are determined as a result of the discussion with team members and by applying the test criteria.

Walkthroughs differ from inspections in that the programmer does not narrate a reading of the product by the team, but provides test data and leads the team through a manual simulation of the system. The test data is walked through the system, with intermediate results kept on a blackboard or paper. The test data should be kept simple given the constraints of human simulation. The purpose of the walkthrough is to encourage discussion, not just to complete the system simulation on the test data. Most errors are discovered through questioning the developer's decisions at various stages, rather than through the application of the test data.

At the problem definition stage, walkthrough and inspection can be used to determine if the requirements satisfy the testability and adequacy measures as applicable to this stage in the development. If formal requirements are developed, formal methods, such as correctness techniques, may be applied to insure adherence with the quality factors.

Walkthroughs and inspections should again be performed at the preliminary and detailed design stages. Design walkthroughs and inspection will be performed for each module and module interface. Adequacy and testability of the module interfaces are very important. Any changes which result from these analyses will cause at least a partial repetition of the verification at both stages and between the stages. A reexamination of the problem definition and requirements may also be required.

Finally, the walkthrough and inspection procedures should be performed on the code produced during the construction stage. Each module should be analyzed separately and as integrated parts of the finished software.

Design reviews and auditors are commonly performed as stages in software development. The Department of Defense has developed a standard audit and review procedure based on hardware procurement regulations. The process is representative of the use of formal reviews and includes:

1. *System Requirements Review* is an examination of the initial progress during the problem definition stage and of the convergence on a complete system configuration. Test planning and test documentation are begun at this review.

2. *System Design Review* occurs when the system definition has reached a point where major system modules can be identified and completely specified along with the corresponding test requirements. The requirements for each major subsystem are examined along with the preliminary test plans. Tools required for verification support are identified at this stage.

3. *The Preliminary Design Review* is a formal technical review of the basic design approach for each major subsystem or module. The revised requirements and preliminary design specifications for each major subsystem and all test plans, procedures and documentation are reviewed at this stage. Development and verification tools are further identified at this stage. Changes in requirements will lead to an examination of the test requirements to maintain consistency.

4. *The Critical Design Review* occurs just prior to the beginning of the construction stage. The complete and detailed design specifications

for each module and all draft test plans and documentation are examined. Again consistency with previous stages is reviewed, with particular attention given to determining if test plans and documentation reflect changes in the design specifications at all levels.

5. Two audits, the *Functional Configuration Audit* and the *Physical Configuration Audit* are performed. The former determines if the subsystem performance meets the requirements. The latter audit is an examination of the actual code. In both audits, detailed attention is given to the documentation, manuals and other supporting material.

6. A *Formal Qualification Review* is performed to determine through testing that the final coded subsystem conforms with the final system specifications and requirements. It is essentially the subsystem acceptance test.

Proof of Correctness Techniques

Proof techniques as methods of validation have been used since von Neumann's time. These techniques usually consist of validating the consistency of an output "assertion" (specification) with respect to a program (or requirements or design specification) and an input assertion (specification). In the case of programs, the assertions are statements about the program's variables. The program is "proved" if whenever the input assertion is true for particular values of variables and the program executes, then it can be shown that the output assertion is true for the possibly changed values of the program's variables. The issue of termination is normally treated separately.

There are two approaches to proof of correctness: formal proof and informal proof. A formal proof consists of developing a mathematical logic consisting of axioms and inference rules and defining a proof either to be a proof tree in the natural deduction style or to be a finite sequence of axioms and inference rules in the Hilbert-Ackermann style. The statement to be proved is at the root of the proof tree or is the last object in the proof sequence. Since the formal proof logic must also "talk about" the domain of the program and the operators that occur in the program, a second mathematical logic must be employed. This second mathematical logic is usually not decidable.

Most recent research in applying proof techniques to verification has concentrated on programs. The techniques apply, however, equally well to any level of the development life cycle where a formal representation or description exists. The GYPSY and HDM methodologies use proof techniques throughout the development stages. HDM, for example, has as a goal the formal proof of each level of development.

Heuristics for proving programs formally are essential but are not yet well enough developed to allow the formal verification of a large class of programs. In lieu of applying heuristics to the program, some approaches to verification require that the programmer provide information, interactively, to the verification system in order that the proof be completed. Such information may include facts about the program's domain and operators or facts about the program's intended function.

A typical example of a program and its assertions is given below. The input assertion states that the program's inputs are respectively a nonnegative integer and a positive integer. The output assertion states that the result of the computation is the smallest nonnegative remainder of the division of the first input by the second.

Input Assertion $\{a > = 0$ and $d > 0$ and integer (a) and integer $(b)\}$

Program   integer r, dd;
                 $r : = a; dd: = d$;
                 while $dd < = r$ do $dd: = 2 * dd$;
                 while $dd~ = d$ do
                     begin $dd: = dd/2$;
                         if $dd < = r$ do $r: = r - dd$
                 end

Output Assertion $\{0 < = r < d$ and a congruent to r modulo $d\}$

Informal proof techniques follow the logical reasoning behind the formal proof techniques but without the formal logical system. Often the less formal techniques are more palatable to the programmers. The complexity of informal proof ranges from simple checks such as array bounds not being exceeded, to complex logic chains showing noninterference of processes accessing common data. Informal proof techniques are always used implicitly by programmers. To make them explicit is similar to imposing disciplines, such as structured walkthrough, on the programmer.

Simulation

Simulation is most often employed in real-time systems development where the "real-world" interface is critical and integration with the system hardware is central to the total design. There are, however, many non-real-time applications in which simulation is a cost effective verification and test data generation technique.

To use simulation as a verification tool several models must be developed. Verification is performed by determining if the model of the software behaves as expected on models of the computational and external environments using simulation. This technique also is a powerful way of deriving test data. Inputs are applied to the simulated model and the results recorded for later application to the actual code. This provides an "oracle" for testing. The models are often "seeded" with errors to derive test data which distinguish these errors. The datasets derived cause errors to be isolated and located as well as detected during the testing phase of the construction and integration stages.

To develop a model of the software for a particular stage in the development life cycle a formal representation compatible with the simulation system is developed. This may consist of the formal requirement specification, the design specification, or separate model of the program behavior. If a different model is used, then the developer will need to demonstrate and verify that the model is a complete, consistent, and accurate representation of the software at the stage of development being verified.

The next steps are to develop a model of the computational environment in which the system will operate, a model of the hardware on which the system will be implemented, and a model of the external demands on the total system. These models can be largely derived from the requirements, with statistical representations developed for the external demand and the environmental interactions. The software behavior is then simulated with these models to determine if it is satisfactory.

Simulating the system at the early development stages is the only means of determining the system behavior in response to the eventual implementation environment. At the construction stage, since the code is sometimes developed on a host machine quite different from the target machine, the code may be run on a simulation of the target machine under interpretive control.

Simulation also plays a useful role in determining the performance of algorithms. While this is often directed at analyzing competing algorithms for cost, resource, or performance trade-offs, the simulation under real loads does provide error information.

Test Data Generation

Test data generation is the critical step in testing. Test datasets must contain not only input to exercise the software, but must also provide the corresponding correct output responses to the test data inputs. Thus the development of test datasets involves two aspects: the selection of data input and the determination of expected response. Often the second aspect is most difficult. As discussed previously, hand calculation and simulation are two techniques used to derive expected output response. For very large or complicated systems, manual techniques are unsatisfactory and insufficient.

One promising direction is the development of executable specification languages and specification language analyzers. These can be used, as simulation is used, to act as an oracle providing the responses for the test datasets. Some analyzers such as the REVS system include a simulation capability. An executable specification language representation of a software system is an actual implementation of the design, but at a higher level than the final code. Usually interpreted rather than compiled, it is less efficient, constructed with certain information "hidden." This implementation would be in Parnas' terms an "abstract program," representing in less detail the final implementation. The execution of the specification language "program" could be on a host machine quite different from the implementation target machine.

Test data can be generated randomly with specific distributions chosen to provide some statistical assurance that the system, when tested, is error free. This is a method often used in high density LSI testing. Unfortunately, while errors in LSI chips appear correlated and statistically predictable, this is not true of software. Until recently the domains of programs were far more intractable than those occurring in hardware. This gap is closing with the advances in VLSI.

There is another statistical testing procedure for hardware that applies to certain software applications. Often integrated circuits are tested against a standard "correct" chip using statistically derived test sets. Applications of this technique include testing mass produced firmware developed for microcomputers embedded in high volume production devices such as ovens, automobiles, etc. A second possibility is to use this concept to test "evolving" software. For the development of an upwardly compatible operating system, some of the test sets can be derived by using a current field tested system as an oracle. Compiler testing employs a similar test set for each different compiler tested. However, since most software is developed as a "one of a kind" item, this approach generally does not apply.

Due to the apparent difficulty of applying statistical tests to software, test data is derived in two global ways, often called "black box" or functional analysis and "white box" or structural analysis. In functional analysis, the test data is derived from the external specification of the software behavior. No consideration is usually given to the internal organization, logic, control, or data flow in developing test datasets based on functional analysis. One technique, design-based functional analysis, includes examination and analysis of data structure and control flow requirements and specifications throughout the hierarchical decomposition of the system during the design. In a complementary fashion, tests derived from structural analysis depend almost completely on the internal logical organization of the software. Most structural analysis is supported by test coverage metrics such as path coverage, branch coverage, etc. These criteria provide a measure of completeness of the testing process.

Functional Testing Techniques

The most obvious and generally intractable functional testing procedure is exhaustive testing. As was described earlier, only a fraction of programs can be exhaustively tested since the domain of a program is usually infinite or infeasibly large and cannot be used as a test dataset. To attack this problem, characteristics of the input domain are examined for ways of deriving a representative test dataset which provides confidence that the system will be fully tested.

As was stated earlier, test data must be derived from an analysis of the functional requirements and include representive elements from all the variable domains. This data should include both valid and invalid inputs. Generally, data in test datasets based on functional requirements analysis can be characterized as *extremal, non-extremal,* or *special* depending on the source of their derivation. The properties of these elements may be simple *values,* or for more complex data structures they may include such attributes as *type* and *dimension.*

Boundary Value Analysis

The problem of deriving test datasets is to partition the program domain in some meaningful way so that input datasets which span the partition can be determined. There is no direct, easily stated procedure for forming this partition. It depends on the requirements, the program domain, and the creativity and problem understanding of the programmer. This partitioning, however, should be performed throughout the development life cycle.

At the requirements stage a coarse partitioning is obtained according to the overall functional requirements. At the design stage, additional functions are introduced which define the separate modules allowing for a refinement of the partition. Finally, at the coding stage, submodules implementing the design modules introduce further refinements. The use of a top-down testing methodology allows each of these refinements to be used to construct functional test cases at the appropriate level.

Once the program domain is partitioned into input classes, functional analysis can be used to derive test datasets. Test data should be chosen which lies both inside each input class and at the boundary of each class. Output classes should also be covered by input which causes output at each class boundary and within each class. This data is the extremal and non-extremal test sets. Determination of these test sets is often called *boundary value analysis* or *stress testing.*

The boundary values chosen depend on the nature of the data structures and the input domains. Consider the following FORTRAN example:

INTEGER X
REAL A(100,100)

If X is constrained, $a < X < b$, then X should be tested for valid inputs $a + 1$, $b - 1$, and invalid inputs a and b. The array should be tested as a single element array $A(1,1)$ and as a full 100×100 array. The array element values A(I, J) should be chosen to exercise the corresponding boundary values for each element.

Error Guessing and Special Value Analysis

Myers suggests that some people have a natural intuition for test data generation. While this ability cannot be completely described nor formalized, certain test data seems highly probable to catch errors. Some of these are in the category Howden calls special, others are certainly boundary values. Zero input values and input values which cause zero outputs are examples. For more complicated data structures, the equivalent null data structure such as an empty list or stack or a null matrix should be tested. Often the single element data structure is a good choice. If numeric values are used in arithmetic computations, then the test data should include values which are numerically very close and values which are numerically quite different. Guessing carries no guarantee for success, but neither does it carry any penalty.

Cause-Effect Graphing

Cause-effect graphing is a technique for developing test cases for programs from the high level specifications. A high level specification of requirements states desired characteristics of behavior for the system. These characteristics can be used to derive test data. Problems arise, however, of a combinatorial nature. For example, a program that has specified responses to eight characteristic stimuli (called causes) given some input has potentially 256 "types" of input (ie. those with characteristics 1 and 3, those with characteristics 5,7, and 8, etc.). A naive approach to test case generation would be to try to generate all 256 types. A more methodical approach is to use the program specifications to analyze the program's effect on the various types of inputs.

The program's output domain can be partitioned into various classes called effects. For example, inputs with characteristic 2 might be subsumed by those with characteristics 3 and 4. Hence it would not be necessary to test inputs with just characteristic 2 and also inputs with characteristics 3 and 4, for they cause the same effect. This analysis results in a partitioning of the causes according to their corresponding effects.

A limited entry decision table is then constructed from the directed graph reflecting these dependencies (i.e., causes 2 and 3 result in effect 4, causes 2, 3, and 5 result in effect 6, etc.). The decision table is then reduced and test cases chosen to exercise each column of the table. Since many aspects of the cause-effect graphing can be automated, it is an attractive tool for aiding in the generation of functional test cases.

Design-Based Functional Testing

The techniques described above derive test datasets from analysis of functions specified in the requirements. Howden has extended functional analysis to functions used in the design process. A distinction can be made between requirements functions and design functions. Requirements functions describe the overall functional capabilities of a program. In order to implement a requirements function it is usually necessary to invent other "smaller functions." These other functions are used to design the program. If one thinks of this relationship as a tree structure, then a requirements function would be represented as a root node. All functional capabilities represented by boxes at the second level in the tree correspond to design functions. The implementation of a design function may require the invention of other design functions. The successive refinement during top down design can then be represented as levels in the tree structure, where the $n + 1$st level nodes are refinements or subfunctions of the nth level functions.

To utilize design based functional testing, the functional design trees as described above are constructed. The trees document the functions used in the design of the program. The functions included in the design trees must be chosen carefully. The most important selection feature is that the function be accessible for independent testing. It must be possible to apply the appropriate input values to test the function, to derive the expected values for the function, and to observe the actual output computed by the code implementing the function.

Each of the functions in the functional design tree, if top down design techniques are followed, can be associated with the final code used to implement that function. This code may consist of one or more procedures, parts of a procedure, or even a single statement. Design-based functional testing requires that the input and output variables for each design function be completely specified. Given these multiple functions to analyze, test data for extremal, non-extremal, and special values should be selected for each input variable. Test data should also be selected which results in the generation of extremal, non-extremal, and special output values.

Structural Testing Techniques

Structural testing is concerned with ensuring sufficient testing of the implementation of a function. Although used primarily during the coding phase, structural analysis should be used in all phases of the life cycle where the software is represented formally in some algorithmic, design, or requirement language. The intent of structural testing is to stress the implementation by finding test data that will force sufficient coverage of the structures present in the formal representation. In order to determine whether the coverage is sufficient, it is necessary to have a structural coverage metric. Thus the process of generating tests for structural testing is sometimes known as *metric-based test data generation.*

Metric-based test data generation can be divided into two categories by the metric used: complexity-based testing or coverage-based testing. In the latter, a criterion is used which provides a measure of the number of structural units of the software which are fully exercised by the test datasets. In the former category, tests are derived in proportion to the software complexity.

Coverage-Based Testing

Most coverage metrics are based on the number of statements, branches, or paths in the program which are exercised by the test data. Such metrics can be used both to evaluate the test data and to aid in the generation of the test data.

Any program can be represented by a graph. The nodes represent statements or collections of sequential statements. The control flow is represented by directed lines or edges which connect the nodes. A node with a single exiting edge to another node represents a sequential code segment. A node with multiple exiting edges represents a branch predicate or a code segment containing a branch predicate as the last statement.

On a particular set of data, a program will execute along a particular *path*, where certain *branches* are taken or not taken depending on the evaluation of branch predicates. Any program path can be represented by a sequence, possibly with repeating sub-sequences (when the program has backward branches), of edges from the program graph. These sequences are called *path expressions*. Each path or each dataset may vary depending on the number of *loop iterations* caused. A program with variable loop control may have effectively an infinite number of paths. Hence, there are potentially an infinite number of path expressions.

To completely test the program structure, the test data chosen should cause the execution of all paths. Since this is not possible in general, metrics have been developed which give a measure of the quality of test databased on the proximity to this ideal coverage. Path coverage determination is further complicated by the existence of *infeasible paths*. Often a program has been inadvertently designed so that no data will cause the execution of certain paths. Automatic determination of infeasible paths is generally difficult if not impossible. A main theme in structured top down design is to construct modules which are simple and of low complexity so that all paths, excluding loop iteration, may be tested and that infeasible paths may be avoided.

All techniques for determining coverage metrics are based on graph representations of programs. A variety of metrics exist ranging from simple statement coverage to full path coverage. There have been several attempts to classify these metrics; however, new variations appear so often that such attempts are not always successful. We will discuss the major ideas without attempting to cover all the variations.

The simplest metric measures the percentage of statements executed by all the test data. Since coverage tools supply information about which statements have been executed (in addition to the percentage of coverage), the results can guide the selection of test data to insure complete coverage. To apply the metric, the program or module is instrumented by hand or by a preprocessor. A post processor or manual analysis of the results reveal the level of statement coverage. Determination of an efficient and complete test dataset satisfying this metric is more difficult. Branch predicates that send control to omitted statements should be examined to help determine input data that will cause execution of omitted statements.

A slightly stronger metric measures the percentage of *segments* executed under the application of all test data. A segment in this sense corresponds to a *decision-to-decision path (dd-path)*. It is a portion of a program path beginning with the execution of a branch predicate and including all statements up to the evaluation (but not execution) of the next branch predicate. Segment coverage guarantees statement coverage. It also covers branches with no executable statements; e.g., an IF-THEN-ELSE with no ELSE statements still requires data causing the predicate to be evaluated as both true and false. Techniques similar to those need for statement coverage are used for applying the metric and deriving test data.

The next logical step is to strengthen the metric by requiring separate coverage for both the exterior and interior of loops. Segment coverage only requires that both branches from a branch predicate be taken. For loops, segment coverage can be satisfied by causing the loop to be executed one or more times (interior test) and then causing the loop to be exited (exterior test). Requiring that all combinations of predicate evaluations be covered requires that each loop be exited without interior execution for at least one dataset. This metric requires more paths to be covered than segment coverage requires. Two successive predicates will require at least four sets of test data to provide full coverage. Segment coverage can be satisfied by two tests, while statement coverage may require only one test for two successive predicates.

Implementation of the above metric is again similar to that for statement and segment coverage. Variations on this metric include requiring at least "k" interior iterations per loop or requiring that all $2**n$ combinations of Boolean variables be applied for each n variable predicate expression. This latter variation has led to a new path testing technique called *finite-domain testing*.

Automated tools for instrumenting and analyzing the code have been available for a few years. These tools are generally applicable to most of the coverage metrics described above. Automation of test data generation is less advanced. Often test data is generated by iterating the use of analyzers with manual methods for deriving tests. A promising but expensive way to generate test data for path testing is through the use of symbolic executors. More on the use of these tools will be discussed in a later section.

Complexity-Based Testing

Several complexity measures have been proposed recently. among these are cyclomatic complexity, software science, and Chapin's software complexity measure. These and many other metrics are designed to analyze the complexity of software systems. Most, although valuable new approaches to the analysis of software, are not suitable, or have not been applied to the problem of testing. The McCabe metrics are the exception.

McCabe actually proposed three metrics: *cyclomatic, essential,* and *actual complexity.* All three are based on a graphical representation of the program being tested. The first two are calculated from the program graph, while the third is a runtime metric.

McCabe uses a property of graph theory in defining cyclomatic complexity. There are sets of linearly independent program paths through any program graph. A maximal set of these linearly independent paths, called a basis set, can always be found. Intuitively, since the program graph and any path through the graph can be constructed from the basis set, the size of this basis set should be related to the program complexity. From graph theory, the cyclomatic number of the graph, $V(G)$, is given by:

$$V(G) = e - n + p$$

for a graph G with number of nodes n, edges e, and connected components p. The number of linearly independent program paths though a program graph is $V(G) + p$, a number McCabe calls the cyclomatic complexity of the program. Cyclomatic complexity, $CV(G)$, where:

$$CV(G) = e - n + 2p$$

can be easily calculated from the program graph.

A proper subgraph of a graph, G, is a collection of nodes and edges such that if an edge is included in the subgraph, then both nodes it connects in the complete graph, C, must be in the subgraph. Any flow graph can be reduced by combining sequential single entry, single exit nodes into a single node. Structured constructs appear in a program graph as a proper subgraph with only one node which is single entry and whose entering edge is not in the subgraph, and with only one node which is single exit and whose exiting edge is not included in the subgraph. For all other nodes, all connecting edges are included in the subgraph. This single entry, single exit subgraph can then be reduced to a single node. Essential complexity is based on counting these single entry, single exit proper subgraphs of two nodes or greater. Let the number of these subgraphs be m, then essential complexity EV(G) is defined:

$$EV(G) = CV(G) - m$$

The program graph for a program built with structured constructs will obviously have all proper subgraphs as single exit, single entry. The number of proper subgraphs of a graph G of more than one node is CV(G) - 1. Hence the essential complexity of a structured program is one. Essential complexity is then a measure of the "unstructuredness" of a program.

Actual complexity, AV, is just the number of paths executed during a run. A testing strategy can be based on these metrics. If for a test dataset, the actual complexity is less than the cyclomatic complexity and all edges have been executed, then either there are more paths to be tested or the complexity can be reduced by CV(G) - AV by eliminating decision nodes and reducing portions of the program to in-line code. The cyclomatic complexity metric gives the number of linearly independent paths from analysis of the program graph. Some of these paths may be infeasible. If this is the case, then the actual complexity will never reach the cyclomatic complexity. Using a tool which derives the three complexity metrics, both a testing and a programming style can be enforced.

Test Data Analysis

After the construction of a test dataset it is necessary to determine the "goodness" of that set. Simple metrics like statement coverage may be required to be as high as 90 percent to 95 percent. It is much more difficult to find test data providing 90 percent coverage under the more complex coverage metrics. However, it has been noted that methodologies based on the more complex metrics with lower coverage requirements have uncovered as many as 90 percent of all program faults.

Statistical Analyses and Error Seeding

The most common type of test data analysis is statistical. An estimate of the number of errors in a program can be obtained from an analysis of the errors uncovered by the test data. In fact, as we shall see, this leads to a dynamic testing technique.

Let us assume that there are some number of errors, E, in the software being tested. There are two things we would like to know, a maximum likelihood estimate for the number of errors and a level of confidence measure on that estimate. The technique is to insert known errors in the code in some way that is statistically similar to the actual errors. The test data is then applied and errors uncovered is determined. If one assumes that the statistical properties of the seeded and original errors are the same and that the testing and seeding are statistically unbiased, then

estimate $E = IS/K$

where S is the number of seeded errors, K is the number of discovered seeded errors, and I is the number of discovered unseeded errors. This estimate obviously assumes that the proportion of undetected errors is very likely to be the same for the seeded and original errors.

How good is this estimate? We would like to ascertain the confidence level for the various predicted error levels. Assuming that all seeded errors are detected (K = S), the confidence that number of errors is less than or equal to E is given by:

$$0 \qquad ; I > E$$

$$\frac{S}{S + E + 1} \qquad ; I < = E$$

Note that when $E = 0$ and no errors are detected other than seeded errors ($I < = E$) when testing, the confidence level is very high (for $S = 99$, confidence = 99 percent). Testing for the error free case can be accomplished with high confidence as long as no errors are uncovered. On the other hand, if nonseeded errors are discovered and the estimate for E is higher, our confidence in the estimate also decreases. If the $E = 10$, then with $S = 100$, our confidence drops to 90 percent. When the number of actual errors approaches or exceeds the number of seeded errors, then the confidence in our estimates decreases dramatically. For example, if $E = 10$ and $S = 9$, then the confidence is only 45 percent.

A strategy for using this statistical technique in dynamic testing is to monitor the maximum likelihood estimator, and perform the confidence level calculation as testing progresses. If the estimator gets high relative to the number of seeded errors, then it is unlikely that a desirable confidence level can be obtained. The errors should then be corrected and the testing resumed. If the number of real errors discovered remains small or preferably zero as the number of seeded errors uncovered approaches the total seeded, then our confidence level for an error-free program increases.

Tausworthe discusses a method for seeding errors which has some hope of being similar statistically to the actual errors. He suggests randomly choosing lines at which to insert the error, and then making various different modifications to the code introducing errors. The actual modifications of the code are similar to those used in mutation testing as described below.

Mutation Analysis

A relatively new metric developed by DeMillo, Lipton, and Sayward is called mutation analysis. This method rests on the *competent programmer hypothesis* which states that a program written by a competent programmer will be, after debugging and testing, "almost correct." The basic idea of the method is to seed the program to be tested with errors, creating several mutants of the original program. The program and its mutants are then run interpretively on the test set. If the test set is adequate, it is argued, it should be able to distinguish between the program and its mutants.

The method of seeding is crucial to the success of the technique and consists of modifying single statements of the program in a finite number of "reasonable" ways. The developers conjecture a *coupling effect* which implies that these "first order mutants" cover the deeper, more subtle errors which might be represented by higher order mutants. The method has been subject to a small number of trials and so far has been successfully used interactively to develop adequate test datasets. It should be noted that the method derives both branch coverage and statement coverage metrics as special cases.

It must be stressed that mutation analysis, and its appropriateness, rests on the competent programmer and coupling effect theses. Since neither is provable, they must be empirically demonstrated to hold over a wide variety of programs before the method of mutations can itself be validated.

Static Analysis Techniques

As was described earlier, analytical techniques can be categorized as static or dynamic. The application and analysis of test data is usually described as dynamic activity, since it involves the actual execution of code. Static analysis does not usually involve program execution. Many of the general techniques discussed earlier, such as formal proof techniques and inspections are static analysis techniques. In a true sense, static analysis is part of any testing technique. Any analysis to derive test data, calculate assertions, or determine instrumentation breakpoints must involve some form of static analysis, although the actual verification is achieved through dynamic testing. As was mentioned earlier, the line between static and dynamic analysis is not always easily drawn. For example, proof of correctness and symbolic execution both "execute" code, but not in a real environment.

Most static analysis is performed by parsers and associated translators residing in compilers. Depending upon the sophistication of the parser, it uncovers errors ranging in complexity from ill-formed arithmetic expressions to complex type incompatibilities. In most compilers, the parser and translator are augmented with additional capabilities that allow activities such as code optimization, listing of variable names, and pretty printing, all such activities being useful in the production of quality software. Preprocessors are also frequently used in conjunction with the parser. These may perform activities such as allowing "structured programming" in an unstructured programming language, checking for errors such as mismatched common areas, and checking for module interface incompatibilities. The parser may also serve in a policing role. Thus software shop coding standards can be enforced, quality of code can be monitored, and adherence to programming standards can be checked.

Flow Analysis

Data and control flow analysis are similar in many ways. Both are based upon graphical representation. In control flow analysis, the program graph has nodes which represent a statement or segment possibly ending in a branch predicate. The edges represent the allowed flow of control from one segment to another. The control flow graph is used to analyze the program behavior, to locate instrumentation breakpoints, to identify paths, and in other static analysis activities. In data flow analysis, graph nodes usually represent single statements, while the edges still represent the flow of control. Nodes are analyzed to determine the transformations made on program variables. Data flow analysis is used to discover program anomalies such as undefined or unreferenced variables. The technique was introduced by Cocke and Allen for global program optimization.

Data flow anomalies are more easily found than resolved. Consider the following FORTRAN code segment.

SUBROUTINE HYP (A,B,C,)
$$U = 0.5$$
$$W = 1/V$$
$$Y = A ** W$$
$$Y = E ** W$$
$$Z = X + Y$$
$$C = Z ** (V)$$

There are several anomalies in this code segment. One variable, U, is defined and never used while three variables, X, V and E, are undefined when used. It is possible that U was meant to be V, E was meant to be B, and the first occurrence of Y on the left of an assignment was a typo for X. The problem is not in detecting these errors, but in resolving them. The possible solution suggested may not be the correct one. There is no answer to this problem, but data flow analysis can help to detect the anomalies, including ones more subtle than those above.

In data flow analysis, we are interested in tracing the behavior of program variables as they are initialized and modified while the program executes. This behavior can be classified by when a particular variable is *referenced, defined,* or *undefined* in the program. A variable is referenced when its value must be obtained from memory during the evaluation of an expression in a statement. For example, a variable is referenced when it appears on the right-hand side of an assignment statement, or when it appears as an array index anywhere in a statement. A variable is defined if a new value for that variable results from the execution of a statement, such as when a variable appears on the left-hand side of an assignment. A variable is unreferenced when its value is no longer determinable from the program flow. Examples of unreferenced variables are local variables in a subroutine after exit and FORTRAN DO indices on loop exit.

Data flow analysis is performed by associating, at each node in the data flow graph, values for tokens (representing program variables) which indicate whether the corresponding variable is referenced, unreferenced, or defined with the execution of the statement represented by that node. If symbols, for instance u, d, r, and 1 (for null), are used to represent the values of a token, the *path expressions* for a variable (or token) can be generated beginning at, ending in, or for some particular node. A typical path expression might be drllllrrlllllldllrllu, which can be reduced through eliminating nulls to drrrdru. Such a path expression contains no anomalies, but the presence of ... dd ... in an expression, indicating a variable defined twice without being referenced, does identify a potential anomaly. Most anomalies, ... ur ..., r ..., etc. can be discovered through analysis of the path expressions.

To simplify the analysis of the flow graph, statements can be combined as in control flow analysis into segments of necessarily sequential statements represented by a single node. Often, however, statements must be represented by more than one node. Consider,

$$IF (X .GT. 1) X = X - 1$$

The variable X is certainly referenced in the statement, but it may be defined only if the predicate is true. In such a case, two nodes would be used, and the graph would actually represent code which looked like

```
        IF (X .GT. 1) 100,200
100     X = X - 1
200     CONTINUE
```

Another problem requiring node splitting arises at the last statement of a FORTRAN DO loop after which the index variable becomes undefined only if the loop is exited. Subroutine and function calls introduce further problems, but they too can be resolved.

Symbolic Execution

Symbolic execution is a method of symbolically defining data that forces program paths to be executed. Instead of executing the program with actual data values, the variable names that hold the input values are used. Thus all variable manipulations and decisions are made symbolically. As a consequence, all variables become string variables, all assignments become string assignments and all decision points are indeterminate. To illustrate, consider the following small pseudocode program;

```
        IN a,b;
        a := a*a;
        x :=a + b;
        IF x=0 THEN x :=0 ELSE x :=1;
```

The symbolic execution of the program will result in the following expression.

if $a*a + b = 0$ then $x := 0$ else if $a*a + b \sim= 0$ then $x := 1$

Note that we are unable to determine the result of the equality test, for we only have symbolic values available.

The result of a symbolic execution is a large, complex expression. The expression can be decomposed and viewed as a tree structure where each leaf represents a path through the program. The symbolic values of each variable are known at every point within the tree and the branch points of the tree represent the decision points of the program. Every program path is represented in the tree, and every branch path is effectively taken.

If the program has no loops, then the resultant tree structure is finite. The tree structure can then be used as an aid in generating test data that will cause every path in the program to be executed. The predicates at each branch point of the tree structure for a particular path are then collected into a conjunction. Data that causes a particular path to be executed can be found by determining which data will make the path conjunction true. If the predicates are equalities, inequalities, and orderings, the problem of data selection becomes the classic problem of trying to solve a system of equalities and orderings.

There are two major difficulties with using symbolic execution as a test set construction mechanism. The first is the combinatorial explosion inherent in the tree structure construction. The number of paths in the symbolic execution tree structure may grow as an exponential in the length of the program leading to serious computational difficulties. If the program has loops, then the symbolic execution tree structure is necessarily infinite. Usually only a finite number of loop executions is required enabling a finite loop unwinding to be performed. The second difficulty is that the problem of determining whether the conjunct has values which satisfy it is undecidable even with restricted programming languages. For certain applications, however, the method has been successful.

Another use of symbolic execution techniques is in the construction of verification conditions from partially annotated programs. Typically, the program has attached to each of its loops an assertion, called an invariant, that is true at the first statement of the loop and at the last statement of the loop (thus the assertion remains "invariant" over one execution of the loop).

From this assertion, an assertion true before entrance to the loop and assertions true after exit of the loop can be constructed. The program can then be viewed as "free" of loops (i.e., each loop is considered as a single statement) and assertions extended to all statements of the program (so it is fully annotated) using techniques similar to the backward substitution method described above for symbolic execution.

Dynamic Analysis Techniques

Dynamic analysis is usually a three-step procedure involving static analysis and instrumentation of a program, execution of the instrumented program, and finally, analysis of the instrumentation data. Often this is accomplished interactively through automated tools.

The simplest instrumentation technique for dynamic analysis is the insertion of a turnstyle or a counter. Branch or segment coverage and other such metrics are evaluated in this manner. A preprocessor analyzes the program (usually by generating a program graph) and inserts counters at the appropriate places. Consider

```
          IF (X) 10,10.15
          •

          •
10        Statement i
          •

          •
15        Statement j
          •

          •
          DO 20 I = J,K.L
          •

          •
20        Statement k
```

A preprocessor might instrument the program segment as follows:

```
          IF (X) 100,101,15
          •

          •
100       N(100) = N (100) + 1
          GO TO 10
```

```
101        N(101) = N(101) +1
           Statement i
           •
           •
           I = J
           IF ( I .GT. K) THEN 201
20         N(20) = N(20) + 1
           •
           •
           Statement k
           I = I + L
           IF (I .LE. K) THEN 20
201        N(201) = N(201) +1
```

For the IF statement, each possible branch was instrumented. Note that we used two counters $N(100)$ and $N(101)$ even though the original code branches to the same statement label. The original code has to be modified for the DO loop in order to get the necessary counters inserted. Note that two counters are used, $N(20)$ for the interior execution count and $N(201)$ for the exterior of the loop.

Simple statement coverage requires much less instrumentation than branch coverage or more extensive metrics. For complicated assignments and loop and branch predicates, more detailed instrumentation is employed. Besides simple counts, it is interesting to know the maximum and minimum values of variables (particularly useful for array subscripts), the initial and last value, and other constraints particular to the application.

Instrumentation does not have to rely on direct code insertion. Often calls to runtime routines are inserted rather than actual counters. Some instrumented code is passed through a preprocessor/compiler which inserts the instrumentation only if certain commands are set to enable it.

Stucki introduced the concept of instrumenting a program with *dynamic assertions*. A preprocessor generates instrumentation for dynamically checking conditions often as complicated as those used in program proof techniques [STUC77]. These assertions are entered as comments in program code and are meant to be permanent. They provide both documentation and means for maintenance testing. All or individual assertions are enabled using simple commands and the preprocessor.

There are assertions which can be employed globally, regionally, locally, or at entry and exit. The general form for a local assertion is:

ASSERT LOCAL (extended-logical-expression)[optional qualifier] [control]

The optional qualifiers are ALL, SOME, etc. The control options include LEVEL, which controls the levels in a block structured program; CONDITIONS, which allows dynamic enabling of the instrumentation; and LIMIT, which allows a specific number of violations to occur. The logical expression is used to represent an expected condition to be dynamically verified. For example:

ASSERT LOCAL (A(2:6,2:10) .NE. 0) LIMIT 4

placed within a program will cause the values of array elements A(2,2),A(2,3),...,A(2,10),A(3,2),...,A(6,10) to be checked against a zero value at that locality. After four violations during the execution of the program, the assertion will become false.

The global, regional, and entry-exit assertions are similar in structure. Note that similarity with verification conditions, especially if the entry-exit assertions are employed. Furthermore, symbolic execution can be employed to generate the assertions as it can be used with proof techniques. Some efforts are currently underway to integrate dynamic assertions, proof techniques, and symbolic evaluation. One of these is described below.

There are many other techniques for dynamic analysis. Most involve the dynamic (under execution) measurement of the behavior of a part of a program, where the features of interest have been isolated and instrumented based on a static analysis. Some typical techniques include expression analysis, flow analysis, and timing analysis.

Combined Methods

There are many ways in which the techniques described above can be used in concert to form a more powerful and efficient testing techniques. One of the more common combinations today is the merger of standard testing techniques with formal verification. Our ability, through formal methods, to verify significant segments of code is improving, and moreover there are certain modules, which for security or reliability reasons, justify the additional expense of formal verification.

Other possibilities include the use of symbolic execution or formal proof techniques to verify segments of code, which through coverage analysis have been shown to be most frequently executed. Mutation analysis, for some special cases like decision tables, can be used to fully verify programs. Formal proof techniques may be useful in one of the problem areas of mutation analysis, the determination of equivalent mutants.

Osterweil addresses the issue of how to combine efficiently powerful techniques in one systematic method (combining data flow analysis, symbolic execution, elementary theorem proving, dynamic assertions, and standard testing) As has been mentioned, symbolic evaluation can be used to generate dynamic assertions. Here, paths are executed symbolically so that each decision point and every loop has an assertion. The assertions are then checked for consistency using both data flow and proof techniques. If all the assertions along path are consistent, they can be reduced to a single dynamic assertion for the path. Theorem proving techniques can be employed to "prove" the path assertion and termination, or the path can be tested and the dynamic assertions evaluated for the test data.

The technique allows for several trade-offs between testing and formal methods. For instance, symbolically derived dynamic assertions are more reliable than manually derived assertions, but cost more to generate. Consistency analysis of the assertions using proof and data flow techniques adds cost at the front end, but reduces the execution overhead. Finally there is the obvious trade-off between theorem proving and testing to verify the dynamic assertions.

Test Support Tools

Testing, like program development, generates large amounts of information, necessitates numerous computer executions, and requires coordination and communication between workers. Support tools and techniques can ease the burden of test production, test execution, general information handling, and communication. General system utilities and test processing tools are invaluable for test preparation, organization, and modification. A well organized and structurable file system and a good text editor are a minimum support set. A more powerful support set includes data reduction and report generation tools. Library support set includes data reduction and report generation tools. Library support systems consisting of a database management system and a configuration control system are as useful during testing as during software development since data organization, access, and control are required for management of test files and reports. Documentation can be viewed as a support technique. In addition to the general purpose support tools and techniques, specific test support tools exist. Test drivers and test languages are in this category. The following paragraphs will discuss these test specific support tools and techniques.

Test Documentation

The NIST guideline for software documentation during the development phase recommends test documentation be prepared for all multipurpose or multiuser projects and for other software development projects costing over $5,000. It recommends the preparation of a test plan and a test analysis report. The test plan should identify test milestones and provide the testing schedule and requirements. In addition, it should include specifications, descriptions, and procedures for all tests; and the test data reduction and evaluation criteria. The test analysis report should summarize and document the test results and findings. The analysis summary should present the software capabilities, deficiencies, and recommendations. As with all types of documentation, the extent, formality, and level of detail of the test documentation are functions of agency ADP management practice and will vary depending upon the size, complexity, and risk of the project.

Test Drivers

Unless the module being developed is a stand-alone program, considerable auxiliary software must be written in order to exercise and test it. Auxiliary code which sets up an appropriate environment and calls the module is termed a *driver* while code which simulates the results of a routine called by the module is a *stub*. For many modules both stubs and drivers must be written in order to execute a test.

When testing is performed incrementally, an untested module is combined with a tested one and the package is then tested. Such packaging can lessen the number of drivers and/or stubs which must be written. When the lowest level of modules, those which call no other modules, are tested first and then combined for further testing with the modules that call them, the need for writing stubs can be eliminated. This approach is called *bottom-up testing*. Bottom-up testing still requires that test drivers be constructed. Testing which starts with the executive module and incrementally adds modules which it calls, is termed *top-down testing*. Top-down testing requires that stubs be created to simulate the actions of called modules that have not yet been incorporated into the system. The testing order utilized should be coordinated with the development methodology used.

Automatic Test Systems and Test Languages

The actual performance of each test requires the execution of code with input data, an examination of the output, and a comparison of the output with the expected results. Since the testing operation is repetitive in nature, with the same code executed numerous times with different input values, an effort has been made to automate the process of test execution. Programs that perform this function of initiation are called *test drivers*, *test harnesses*, or *test systems*.

The simplest test drivers merely reinitiate the program with various input sets and save the output. The more sophisticated test systems accept data inputs, expected outputs, the names of routines to be executed, values to be returned by called routines, and other parameters. These test systems not only initiate the test runs but compare the actual output with the expected output and issue concise reports of the performance. TPL/2.0 which uses a test language to describe test procedures is an example of such a system. In addition to executing the tests, verifying the results and producing reports, the system helps the user generate the expected results.

PRUFSTAND is an example of a comprehensive test system. It is an interactive system in which data values are generated automatically or are requested from the user as they are needed. The system is comprised of a:

- Preprocessor to instrument the code
- Translator to convert the source data descriptors into an internal symbolic test data description table
- Test driver to initialize and update the test environment
- Test stubs to simulate the execution of called modules

- Execution monitor to trace control flow through the test object
- Result validator
- Test file manager
- Post processor to manage reports

A side benefit of a comprehensive test system is that it establishes a standard format for test materials, which is extremely important for regression testing. Currently automatic test driver systems are expensive to build and consequently are not in widespread use.

SUMMARY

In the previous sections we have surveyed many of the techniques used to validate software systems. Of the methods discussed, the most successful have been the disciplined manual techniques, such as walkthroughs, reviews, and inspections, applied to all stages in the systems life cycle. Discovery of errors within the first stages of development (requirements and design) is particularly critical since the cost of these errors escalates significantly if they remain undiscovered until construction or later. Until the development products at the requirements and design stages become formalized and hence amenable to automated analysis, disciplined manual techniques will continue to be key verification techniques.

For the construction stage, automated techniques can be of great value. The ones in widest use are the simpler static analysis techniques (such as type checking), automated test coverage calculation, automated program instrumentation, and the use of simple test harnesses. These techniques are relatively straightforward to implement and all have had broad use. Combined with careful error documentation, they are effective validation methods.

Many of the techniques discussed have not seen wide use. The principal reasons for this include their specialization (simulation), the high cost of their use (symbolic execution), and their unproven applicability (formal proof of correctness). Many of these techniques represent the state of the art in program validation and are in areas where research is continuing.

The areas showing the most commercial interest and activity at present include automated test support systems and increased use for automated analysis. As more formal techniques are used during requirements and design, an increase in automatic analysis is possible. In addition, more sophisticated analysis techniques are being applied to the code during construction. More complete control and automation of the actual execution of tests, both in assistance in generating the test cases and in the management of the testing process and results, are also taking place.

We reemphasize the importance of performing validation throughout the life cycle. One of the reasons for the great success of disciplined manual techniques is their uniform applicability at requirements, design, and coding phases. These techniques can be used without massive capital expenditure. However, to be most effective they require a serious commitment and a disciplined application. Careful planning, clearly stated objectives, precisely defined techniques, good management, organized record keeping, and strong commitment are critical to successful validation. A disciplined approach must be followed during both planning and execution of the verification activities.

We view the integration of validation with software development as so important that we suggest that it be an integral part of the requirements statement. Validation requirements should specify the type of manual techniques, the tools, the form of project management and control, the development methodology, and acceptability criteria which are to be used during software development. These requirements are in addition to the functional requirements of the system ordinarily specified at this stage. Thus embedded within the project requirements would be a contract aimed at enhancing the quality of the completed software.

A major difficulty with a proposal such as the above is that we have neither the means of accurately measuring the effectiveness of validation methods nor the means of determining "how valid" the software should be. We assume that it is not possible to produce a "perfect" software system; the goal is to try to get as close as required to perfect. In addition, what constitutes perfection and how important it is for the software to be perfect may vary from project to project. Some software (such as nuclear reactor control systems) needs to approach perfection more closely than other software (such as an address labeling program). The definition of "perfect" (or quality attributes) and its importance should be part of the validation requirements. However, validation mechanisms written into the requirements do not guarantee high quality software, just as the use of a particular development methodology does not guarantee high quality software. The evaluation of competing validation mechanisms will be difficult.

A second difficulty with specifying as collection of validation methods in the requirements is that most validation tools do not exist in integrated packages. This means that the group performing the verification must learn several tools that may be difficult to use in combination. This is a problem that must receive careful thought. For unless the combination is chosen judiciously, their use can lead to additional costs and errors. The merits of the tool collection as a whole must be considered as well as the usefulness of any single tool.

Future work in validation should address the above issues. One possible course of action is to integrate the development and validation techniques into a "programming environment." Such an environment would encompass the entire software development effort and include verification capabilities to:

1. Analyze requirements and specifications.

2. Analyze and test designs.

3. Provide support during construction (e.g. test case generation, test harnesses).

4. Provide a database sufficient to support regression testing.

The use of such environments has the potential to improve greatly the quality of the completed software and also to provide a mechanism for establishing confidence in the quality of the software. At present the key to high quality remains the disciplined use of a development methodology accompanied by verification at each stage of the development. No single technique provides a magic solution.

A description of the more commonly used testing tools and techniques is presented in Appendix B. The techniques and tools covered in Appendix B with the testing objective are listed in Table 11.2.

Technique/Tool	Technique/Tool Objective
Algorithm Analysis	algorithm efficiency amount of work (CPU operations) done computational upper bound, how fast amount of space (memory, disk, etc.) used accuracy analysis
Analytic Modeling of Software Designs	system performance prediction bottlenecks
Assertion Generation	formal specifications data characteristics physical units loop invariants expected inputs, outputs and intermediate results
Assertion Processing	assertion violations dynamic testing of assertions
Cause-Effect Graphing	test case design using formal specification requirements specification analysis
Code Auditor	standards checker portability analyzer
Comparator	regression testing expected versus actual results
Control Structure Analyzer	call graph hierarchical interrelationships of modules module invocation branch and path identification
Cross-Reference Generators	inter-module structure variable references

Table 11.2. Testing techniques and tools.

Technique/Tool	Technique/Tool Objective
Data Flow Analyzer	uninitialized variables unused variables file (or other event) sequence errors
Execution Time Estimator/Analyzer	program execution characteristics
Formal Reviews	go/no go decisions status reviews
Formal Verification	proof of correctness
Global Roundoff Analysis of Algebraic Processes	numerical stability rounding error propagation
Inspections	checklist
Interactive Test Aids	selective program execution variable snapshots/tracing
Interface Checker	correspondence between actual and formal parameters type checking global information flow
Mutation Analysis	test data generation completeness of test data
Peer Review	technical review code reading round-robin reviews walkthroughs inspections
Physical Units Testing	consistency in computation
Regression Testing	retesting after changes

Table 11.2.   Testing techniques and tools. (cont'd)

Technique/Tool	Technique/Tool Objective
Requirements Analyzer	functional interrelationships information flow consistency performance analysis requirements walkthrough
Requirements Tracing	requirements indexing requirements to design correlation
Software Monitors	execution sampling execution monitoring program execution characteristics
Specification-based Functional Testing	test data generation boundary test cases
Symbolic Execution	evaluation along program paths verification of algebraic computation
Test Support Facilities	test harness execution support environment simulation
Test Coverage Analyzers	branch testing statement testing statement coverage path testing testing thoroughness
Test Data Generators	test case preparation (definition and specification)
Walkthroughs	manual simulation

Table 11.2. Testing techniques and tools. (cont'd)

12

Improving Software Maintenance

There is a growing interest in software maintenance, as evidenced by the number of articles, reports, and textbooks on the subject. This interest has been spurred by estimates that more resources are required to maintain existing systems than to develop new ones. Federal managers responsible for software application systems estimate that 60 to 70 percent of the total application software resources are spent on software maintenance.

Two of the major causes of this software maintenance burden are the growth of the inventory of software that must be maintained and the failure to adopt and utilize improved technical and management methods and tools. The issue that must be addressed is not one of reducing the absolute cost of software maintenance, but rather of improving the quality and effectiveness of software maintenance and thus reducing the relative or incremental costs.

In order to improve quality and effectiveness, it is necessary not only to improve software maintenance techniques, methodologies, and tools, but also to improve the management of software maintenance. This Guide discusses the problems associated with managing software maintenance and software maintainers, and examines management methods that can reduce those problems.

Informal discussions were held with selected federal agencies and private sector organizations to gain a better understanding of the current state of software maintenance. These discussions provided background information on current practices, procedures, and policies. This information, along with additional research, is the basis for this report.

The major topic areas addressed in these discussions were:

1.   Definition of software maintenance

2.   Methods and techniques in coordinating and performing software maintenance

3.   Major maintenance problems

4.   Types of applications being maintained

5.   Developmental history of existing software

6.   Maintenance staff profiles

7.   Management of maintenance activities

8.   Utilization of maintenance tools

It was expected that there would be some commonality in the information provided by these discussions. In fact, while each organization has problems peculiar to its environment, there was an extremely high degree of consistency in the comments made and the problems cited.

The primary difficulties and deficiencies encountered in software maintenance fall into five categories: software quality, environment, management, users, and personnel. Specific problems that were consistently mentioned are listed in Table 12.1.

As can be seen from Table 12.1, there are both technical and management problems. It appears, however, that many of the technical problems are often the result of inadequate management control over the software maintenance process. These problems arise for at least two different reasons. First, there is a great deal of code that was not developed with maintenance in mind. Indeed, the emphasis has often been to get the program up and running without being "hindered" by guidelines, methodologies, or other controls. Second, over the life cycle of a software system, the code and logic that may have been well designed and implemented often deteriorate due to an endless succession of "quick-fixes" and patches that are neither well designed nor well documented. Thus, in today's vast inventory of application systems, there are many programs that at the time of their development were considered "state-of-the-art," but today are, in fact, virtually unmaintainable.

Software	• program quality
	– software design
	– software coding
	– software documentation
	– programming languages used
	• lack of common data definitions
	• increasing inventory
	• excessive resource requirements
Environment	• growth
	• evolving/change
	• new hardware
Management	• maintenance controls
	• maintenance techniques and proce-dures
	• maintenance tool usage
	• standards enforcement
Users	• demanding more capabilities
Personnel	• lack of experience
	• image/morale problems
	• view of maintenance: unchallenging, unrewarding

Table 12.1. Software maintenance problems.

The need to maintain old, outdated, poorly documented systems was consistently cited as a primary problem in software maintenance. There appears to have been some improvement in the quality of software over the last four to five years, but these improvements have come mainly on an individual basis where a programmer, analyst, or line manager has introduced one or more modern programming practices (e.g., structured code, top-down design and development, peer review). There usually has not been a systematic adoption of these practices at a higher level within an agency, nor has there been extensive institutional introduction of standards and guidelines for software development and maintenance.

DEFINITION OF SOFTWARE MAINTENANCE

Software maintenance is a commonly "understood" term for which there is no single definition. This lack of a standard definition often results in confusion for those attempting to address the problems of software maintenance.

The following definition of software maintenance is used throughout this report.

> Software maintenance is the performance of those activities required to keep a software system operational and responsive after it is accepted and placed into production.

Software maintenance, then, is the set of activities that result in changes to the originally accepted (baseline) product set. These changes consist of modifications created by correcting, inserting, deleting, extending, and enhancing the baseline system. Generally, these changes are made in order to keep the system functioning in an evolving, expanding user and operational environment.

Functional Definition

Functionally, software maintenance activities can be divided into three categories, which were originally proposed by E. B. Swanson: perfective, adaptive, and corrective. Many software managers consider requirements specification changes and the addition of new capabilities to be software maintenance. Although these areas were not addressed by Swanson, the definition of perfective maintenance has been expanded to include them. The three maintenance categories are defined in the following manner:

- *Perfective maintenance* includes all changes, insertions, deletions, modifications, extensions, and enhancements made to a system to meet the evolving and/or expanding needs of the user.

- *Adaptive maintenance* consists of any effort initiated as a result of changes in the environment in which a software system must operate.

- *Corrective maintenance* refers to changes necessitated by actual errors (induced or residual "bugs") in a system.

Perfective	:	changes, insertions, deletions, modifications, extensions, and enhancements
Adaptive	:	adapting the system to changes in the environment
Corrective	:	fixing errors

Table 12.2. Functional definition of software maintenance.

Perfective Maintenance

Perfective maintenance refers to enhancements made to improve software performance, maintainability, or understandability. It is generally performed as a result of new or changing requirements, or in an attempt to augment or fine-tune the software. Activities designed to make the code easier to understand and to work with, such as restructuring or documentation updates (often referred to as "preventive" maintenance), are considered to be perfective. Optimization of code to make it run faster or use storage more efficiently is also included in the perfective category. Estimates indicate that perfective maintenance comprises approximately 60 – 70 percent of all software maintenance efforts.

Perfective maintenance is required as a result of both the failures and successes of the original system. If the system works well, the user will want additional features and capabilities. If the system works poorly, it must be fixed. As requirements change and the user becomes more sophisticated, there will be changes requested to make functions easier and/or clearer to use. Perfective maintenance is the method usually employed to keep the system "up-to-date," responsive, and germane to the mission of the organization.

There is some disagreement over whether the addition of new capabilities should be considered maintenance or additional development. Since it is an expansion of the existing system after it has been placed into operation, and is usually performed by the same staff responsible for other forms of maintenance, it is appropriately classified as maintenance.

Fine-tuning existing systems to eliminate shortcomings and inefficiencies and to optimize the process is often referred to as "preventive maintenance." It can have dramatic effects on old, poorly written systems both in terms of reducing resource requirements and in making the system more maintainable and thus easier to change or enhance. Preventive maintenance may also include the study and examination of a system prior to occurrence of errors or problems. Fine-tuning is an excellent vehicle for introducing the programmer to the code, while at the same time reducing the likelihood of serious errors in the future.

Adaptive Maintenance

Adaptive maintenance refers to modifications made to a system to satisfy or accommodate changes in the processing environment. These environmental changes are normally beyond the control of the software maintainer and consist primarily of changes to the following:

- Rules, laws, and regulations that affect the system.

- Hardware configurations, e.g., new terminals, local printers.

- Data formats, file structures.

- System software, e.g., operating systems, compilers, utilities.

Changes to rules, laws, and regulations often require the performance of adaptive maintenance on a system. These changes must often be completed in a very short time in order to meet the dates established by the laws and regulations. If rules and their actions are implemented modularly, the changes are relatively easy to install. Otherwise, they can be a nightmare.

Changes to the computer hardware (new terminals, local printers, etc.) that support the application system are usually performed to take advantage of new and/or improved features that will benefit the user. They are normally performed on a scheduled basis. The usual goal of this maintenance is to improve the operation and response of the application system.

Changes to data formats and file structures may require extensive maintenance on a system if it was not properly designed and implemented. If reading or writing of data is isolated in specific modules, changes may have less impact. If data descriptions are embedded throughout the code, the effort can become very lengthy and costly.

Changes to operating system software (compilers, utilities, etc.) can have varying effects on the existing application systems. These effects can range from requiring little or no reprogramming, to simply recompiling all of the source code, to rewriting code that contains nonsupported features of a language that are no longer available under the new software.

Maintenance resulting from changes in the requirements specifications by the user, however, is considered to be perfective, not adaptive, maintenance.

Corrective Maintenance

Corrective maintenance consists of activities normally considered to be error correction required to keep the system operational. By its nature, corrective maintenance is usually a reactive process where an error must be fixed immediately. Not all corrective maintenance is performed in this immediate response mode, but all corrective maintenance is related to the system's not performing as originally intended.

There are three main reasons why systems are required to undergo corrective maintenance:

1.   Design errors

2.   Logic errors

3.   Coding errors

Design errors are generally the result of incomplete or faulty design. When a user gives incorrect, incomplete, or unclear descriptions of the system being requested, or when the analyst/designer does not fully understand what the user is requesting, the resulting system will often contain design errors.

Logic errors are the result of invalid tests and conclusions, faulty logic flow, incorrect implementation of the design specifications, etc. Logic errors are usually attributable to the designer or previous maintainer. Often, the logic error occurs when unique or unusual combinations of data, which were not tested during the development or previous maintenance phases, are encountered.

Coding errors are the result of either incorrect implementation of the detailed logic design or the incorrect use of the source code. These errors are caused by the programmer. They are usually errors of negligence or carelessness and are the most inexcusable but usually the easiest to fix.

THE SOFTWARE MAINTENANCE PROCESS

The life cycle of computer software extends from its conception to the time it is no longer available for use. There are a number of definitions of the software life cycle, which differ primarily in the categorization of activities or phases. One traditional definition is: *requirements, design, implementation, testing,* and *operation and maintenance.*

The *requirements phase* encompasses problem definition and analysis, statement of project objectives, preliminary system analysis, functional specification, and design constraints. The *design phase* includes the generation of software component definition, data definition, and interfaces, which are then verified against the requirements. The *implementation phase* entails program code generation, unit tests, and documentation. During the *test phase,* system integration of software components and system acceptance tests are performed against the requirements. The *operations and maintenance phase* covers the use and maintenance of the system. The maintenance phase of the life cycle usually begins at the delivery and user acceptance of the software product set.

The process of implementing a change to a production system is complex and involves many people in addition to the maintainer. Table 12.3 outlines the software maintenance process, which begins when the need for a change arises and ends after the user has accepted the modified system and all documentation has been satisfactorily updated.

Although the process is presented in a linear fashion, there are a number of steps where iterative loops often occur. The change request may be returned to the user for additional clarification; the results of the design review may necessitate additional design analysis or even modification of the change request; testing may result in additional design changes or recoding; the standards audit may require changes to the design documents, code, and/or documentation; and the failure of users to accept the system may result in return to a previous step or the cancellation of the task.

1. Determination of need for change
2. Submission of change request
3. Requirements analysis
4. Approval/rejection of change request
5. Scheduling of task
6. Design analysis
7. Design review
8. Code changes and debugging
9. Review of proposed code changes
10. Testing
11. Update documentation
12. Standards audit
13. User acceptance
14. Post-installation review of changes and their impact on the system
15. Completion of task

Table 12.3. Software maintenance process.

One way of describing the activities of software maintenance is to identify them as successive iterations of the first four phases of the software life cycle, i.e., *requirements, design, implementation,* and *testing.* Software maintenance involves many of the same activities associated with software development with unique characteristics of its own, some of which are discussed in the following paragraphs.

Maintenance activities are performed within the context of an existing framework or system. The maintainer must make changes within the existing design and code structure constraints. This is often the most challenging problem for maintenance personnel. The older the system, the more challenging and time-consuming the maintenance effort becomes.

A software maintenance effort is typically performed within a much shorter time than is a development effort. A software development effort may span one, two, or more years, while corrective maintenance may be required within hours and perfective maintenance in cycles of one to six months.

Development efforts must create all of the test data from scratch. Maintenance efforts typically take advantage of existing test data and perform regression tests. The major challenge for the maintainer is to create new data to adequately test the changes to the system and their impact on its environment.

SOFTWARE MAINTENANCE PROBLEMS

The responses to the ICST survey of selected federal and private-sector ADP organizations consistently cited a common set of software maintenance problems. Generally, these problems can be categorized as technical and management; most of them, however, can be traced to inadequate management control of the software maintenance process. This section presents an overview of the technical aspects of the maintenance problems identified in the survey. Management control issues are addressed in subsequent sections of this report.

Software Quality

Modern programming practices, which utilize a well-defined, well-structured methodology in the design and implementation of a software system, address at least one major software maintenance problem — poor program quality. The importance of these methodologies, whether they are formal or informal, is to give structure and discipline to the process of developing and maintaining software systems. While this may alleviate some of the software maintenance problems for systems developed using these methodologies, it does not solve the problem of existing systems that were designed, developed, and maintained without utilizing a disciplined structure.

A lack of attention to software quality during the design and development phases generally leads to excessive software maintenance costs. It should be clearly understood during the design and development phases that the maintainability of the system is directly affected by the quality of the software.

Poor Software Design

The design specifications of a software system are vital to its correct development and implementation. Poor software design can be attributed to:

- A lack of understanding by the designer of what the user requested.
- Poor interpretation of the design specifications by the developers.

- The use of convoluted and complex logic to meet a requirement.
- Disjointed segments that do not fit together into a nicely integrated whole.
- A lack of discipline in design that results in inconsistent logic.
- Large, unmodular systems (or, worse yet, one large system with no component segments) that are bulky, unwieldy, and very difficult to understand.

Poorly Coded Software

A great deal of existing software contains poorly written code. As computer programming evolved, much of the code development was performed in a undisciplined, unstructured manner. This resulted in a great deal of software that does not effectively utilize the programming language in which it is coded. Poor programming practices exhibited by this lack of discipline include:

- Unmeaningful variable and procedure names
- Few or no comments
- No formatting of the source code
- Overuse of logical transfers to other parts of the program
- Use of nonstandard language features of the compiler
- Very large, poorly structured programs

The task of understanding poorly written code becomes even more arduous for the maintainer when the program has been modified by different individuals and there is a multiplicity of programming styles. Often, such code simply does not do what it was intended to do. Even if this code produces expected results, it is sometimes harder to use than anticipated; it is not suited for the skill level available to use it; or it is slow and unresponsive. Attempting to change such code without the aid of up-to-date specifications or other documentation is often a time-consuming effort.

Software Designed for Outdated Hardware

There are many problems associated with maintaining software designed to run on previous-generation, outdated hardware. Oftentimes, the investment in the software is such that it cannot be discarded or rewritten and must be kept functioning as efficiently as possible. The first difficulty is in finding maintainers who are ready, able, and willing to maintain these systems. Few "good" programmers will be willing to work on hardware that is unique and for which the acquired skills are not relevant to other potential work. The career advancement opportunities from working on such a system are minimal to nonexistent. Additionally, most systems of this type are very difficult to maintain.

Lack of Common Data Definitions

An application system (whether it is large or small) should have common data definitions (variable names, data types, data structures, etc.) for all segments of the system. These common definitions involve the establishment of global variable names used to refer to the same data values throughout the system. In addition, the structure of any data array or record should be defined and used for all programs in the system. Problems invariably arise when two or more programmers independently create data names and structures that conflict or do not logically associate with one another.

More Than One Programming Language Used

The use of more than one programming language in an application system (for example, assembly language subroutines to perform specific processes in a COBOL program) is often the cause of many software maintenance problems. If the maintainer is not proficient in the use of each of the specific languages, the quality and consistency of the maintenance can be affected. Changes to any of the languages or corresponding compilers may also necessitate changes to the application system.

Increasing Inventory

Rapidly changing technology, and its impact on the practices, procedures, and requirements in many organizations, has resulted in a substantial growth in the number of new application systems. In addition, the average life expectancy of a software system has increased from about three years a decade ago to seven to eight years today.

Excessive Resource Requirements

While some types of maintenance (especially enhancements) may legitimately result in increased resource requirements, other maintenance often results in needless increases. This occurs primarily because of the maintainer's inability to correctly and quickly determine the optimum solution for the required change. The changes are accomplished by making a "patch" to the source code (or worse, to the object code) that does not fit well and is not carefully integrated into the system. Subsequent maintenance efforts may compound this problem until the resource requirements become excessive.

Documentation

One of the major problems in software maintenance can be summarized in the single phrase, "a failure to communicate." The maintainer who receives the assignment to perform maintenance on the system must first understand what the program is doing, how it is doing it, and why. This job is greatly simplified if the original requester, the designer, the developer, and the previous maintainers have communicated all the pertinent information about the system. This communication should include design specifications, code comments, programmer notebooks, and other documentation.

Too often, the maintainer receives little, conflicting, or incorrect communication, or none at all, from those who have previously handled the system. There is often inadequate documentation; no detailed record of the original request and subsequent updates; no explanation of existing code and changes that have been made to the code; a weak understanding of new user requests; and no explanation concerning why seemingly complex or convoluted logic and coding structures were selected over a more simple implementation.

Thus, the problems of software maintenance begin simply with a breakdown in communication among those involved with ensuring that the system does what it is supposed to do. This communication is hampered by the inability of those involved to speak the same language (jargon), the inability to understand the basic requirements (users not understanding computing; programmers not understanding user requirements, and, most important, the time frame in which the actions occur. There may be months or years between the original development of a system and each subsequent maintenance activity. When a problem occurs, none of the individuals involved with the original design, implementation, and previous maintenance may be available. The only source of information may be the documentation and the code. Thus, good documentation is the only means for good communication. The more complete, clear, and concise this communication is, the greater the chance that maintenance can be performed in a timely, efficient, and accurate manner.

Users

Users are often unable to concisely specify what they want from an application system. The initial requirements definition and design often lack the detailed specificity that enables the developer to create a system that accurately performs all of the functions the user needs. Thus, an incomplete system is placed into production. The maintainer must enhance the system using the initial, inadequate specifications and the new, sometimes vague, sometimes conflicting, often incomplete, change requests from the user.

If a system is well specified, well designed, and well implemented, and does what the user needs, the user will often think of things to add. The old adage that "nothing succeeds like success" holds true for software development and maintenance. The more successful a system is, the more additional features the user will think of. If the system works well, the user will be constantly demanding more features. If it does not work well, there will be a constant demand for remedial action to make it function properly. Therefore, it is essential that management establish and enforce controls to ensure that the change requests are justified and do not interfere with the maintenance workload.

User requests for changes and enhancements that are excessive, conflicting, or vague have a major impact on the maintenance of an application system. Much of the difficulty in this area stems from the fact that the user is often unaware of the impact that one change can have on both the system and the maintenance workload. The number of user requests for a specific system is usually directly proportional to the success of the original system and the previous maintenance efforts. A careful and thorough management review of user change requests is essential for controlling the level of software maintenance and ensuring adequate feedback to the user on the cost and consequences of each request.

Personnel

A common and widespread complaint by maintenance personnel is that software maintenance is considered to be unimportant, unchallenging, unrewarding, uncreative work that is not appreciated by the user or by the rest of the ADP organization. Software maintenance requires the efforts of experienced, well-qualified, dedicated professionals. It should not be the sole responsibility of the new or junior staff. With the development of more multi-purpose, complex software systems, there is a greater need for software maintainers who can readily understand the entire system.

Traditionally, management has not rewarded personnel who perform software maintenance as generously as they have those who perform software development. It was generally thought that systems analysts, designers, and developers were responsible for the most difficult, challenging tasks and therefore must be more capable.

While this attitude is still common, there is an increasing awareness by management of the importance of software maintenance to the successful, smooth operation of an organization. Many technical personnel, however, still view software maintenance as an assignment to be avoided at all costs. There is too often a general lack of recognition that a good maintainer must be a highly skilled, competent programmer and analyst concerned both with making the actual changes and with assessing the impact of those changes on the system and its environment.

THE IDEAL MAINTAINER

Software maintenance is the lifeblood of an ADP organization. Persons assigned to perform maintenance must effectively meet the challenge of maintaining a software system while keeping the user satisfied, costs down, and the system operating efficiently.

The characteristic qualities of this ideal maintainer include:

Flexible — the ability to adapt to different or changing styles of coding, user requests, and priorities.

Self-motivated — the ability to independently initiate and complete work after receiving an assignment.

Responsible — reliability; performance of assigned tasks in a dependable, timely manner.

Creative — the ability to apply innovative and novel ideas that result in practical solutions.

Disciplined — the ability to be consistent in the performance of duties and not prone to trying haphazard approaches.

Analytic — the ability to apply well thought out analysis to a problem.

Thorough — the ability to address even the smallest detail to ensure that all aspects of the problem are understood and nothing is left untested.

Experienced — prior exposure to a variety of applications and programming environments.

The ideal maintainer should be a senior, experienced professional who can perform all of the functional activities that occur during the software life cycle. Equally important from a maintenance standpoint, the maintainer should be extremely knowledgeable about the existing system before attempting to change it.

The maintainer must be able to analyze the problem and the impact on the program, determine the requirements and design changes necessary for the solution, test the solution until the desired results are obtained, and then release the revised software to operations or the user. The maintainer's task is both intellectually and technically difficult. Maintenance is an activity where everything that can go wrong eventually does. The problems will continue to surface, and enhancements will be requested as long as the system is used. It is a function that must be anticipated and planned for. It is also a function for which there may be an unending succession of emergencies for which staff must be taken away from other "more important" work.

The maintainer is also an intermediary between the application systems support staff and the users. Maintenance, unlike development, cannot start with a clean slate and be unaffected by previous decisions and work. It often takes a great deal of time and patience to analyze both the users' needs and the existing system, and then to carefully and adequately implement the existing changes.

In the final analysis, the most important function of an application system software support activity is software maintenance. Maintenance and the response to the user problems that arise are always in the spotlight. Unfortunately, there is usually far less attention paid to maintenance when it is done well and the users are pleased. Maintenance is an ongoing, almost always intense, effort which should be spotlighted for its successes, as well as its failures.

SYSTEM MAINTENANCE VERSUS SYSTEM REDESIGN

Although maintenance is an ongoing process, there comes a time when serious consideration should be given to redesigning a software system. A major concern of managers and software engineers is how to determine whether a system is hopelessly flawed or can be successfully maintained. Admittedly, the thought of software redesign may not be a comfortable one. Nevertheless, the costs and benefits of the continued maintenance of software that has become error-prone, ineffective, and costly must be weighed against those of redesigning the system.

While there are no absolute rules on deciding when to rebuild rather than maintain the existing system, some of the factors to consider in weighing such a decision are discussed in this section. These characteristics are meant to be general "rules of thumb" that can assist a manager in understanding the problems in maintaining an existing system and in deciding whether or not it has outlived its usefulness to the organization.

1.	Frequent system failures
2.	Code between 7 and 10 years old
3.	Overly complex program structure and logic
4.	Code written for outdated hardware
5.	Running in emulation mode
6.	Very large modules or unit subroutines
7.	Excessive resource requirements
8.	Hard-coded parameters that are subject to change
9.	Difficulty in keeping maintainers
10.	Seriously deficient documentation
11.	Missing or incomplete design specifications

Table 12.4. Characteristics of systems that are candidates for redesign.

When a decision has been reached to redesign or to stop supporting a system, the decision can be implemented in a number of ways. Support can simply be removed and the system can die through neglect; the minimum support needed to keep it functioning may be provided while a new system is built; or the system may be rejuvenated section by section and given an extended life. How the redesign is affected depends on the individual circumstances of the system, its operating environment, and the needs of the organization it supports.

The potential for redesign as opposed to continued maintenance is directly proportional to the number of characteristics listed in Table 12.4. The greater the number of characteristics present, the greater the potential for redesign.

Frequent System Failures

A system in virtually constant need of corrective maintenance is a prime candidate for redesign. As systems age and additional maintenance is performed on them, many become increasing fragile and susceptible to changes. The older the code, the more likely frequent modifications, new requirements, and enhancements will cause the system to break down.

An analysis of errors should be made to determine if the entire system is responsible for the failures or if a few modules or sections of code are at fault. If the latter is found to be the case, then redesigning those parts of the system may suffice.

Code Over Seven Years Old

The estimated life cycle of a major application system is 7 to 10 years. Software tends to deteriorate with age as a result of numerous fixes and patches. If a system is more than 7 years old, there is a high probability that it is outdated and expensive to run. A great deal of the code in use today falls into this category. After 7 to 10 years of maintenance, many systems have evolved to where additional enhancements or fixes are very time-consuming. A substantial portion of this code is probably neither well structured nor well written. While this code was adequate and correct for the original environment, changes in technology and applications may have rendered it inefficient, difficult to revise, and in some cases obsolete.

However, if the system was designed and developed in a systematic, maintainable manner, and if maintenance was carefully performed and documented using established standards and guidelines, it may be possible to run it efficiently and effectively for many more years.

Overly Complex Program Structure and Logic Flow

"Keep it simple" should be the golden rule of all programming standards and guidelines. Too often, programmers engage in efforts to write a section of code in the least number of statements or utilizing the smallest amount of memory possible. This approach to coding has resulted in complex code that is virtually incomprehensible. Poor program structure contributes to complexity. If the system being maintained contains a great deal of this type of code, and the documentation is also severely deficient, it is a candidate for redesign.

Complexity also refers to the level of decision making present in the code. The greater the number of decision paths, the more complex the software is likely to be. Additionally, the greater the number of linearly independent control paths in a program, the greater the program complexity. Programs characterized by some or all of the following attributes are usually very difficult to maintain and are candidates for redesign:

- Excessive use of DO loops
- Excessive use of IF statements
- Unnecessary GOTO statements
- Embedded constants and literals
- Unnecessary use of global variables
- Self-modifying code
- Multiple entry or exit modules
- Excessive interaction between modules
- Modules that perform the same or similar functions

Code Written for Previous-generation Hardware

Few industries have experienced as rapid growth as has the computer industry, particularly in the area of hardware. Not only have there been significant technological advances, but the cost of hardware has decreased tenfold during the last decade. This phenomenon has generated a variety of powerful hardware systems, and software written for earlier generations of hardware is often inefficient on newer systems. Attempts to superficially modify the code to take advantage of the newer hardware is generally ineffective, time-consuming, and expensive.

Running in Emulation Mode

One of the techniques used to keep a system running on newer hardware is to emulate the original hardware and operating system. Emulation refers to the capacity of one system to execute a language written for another machine. In effect, it extends the architecture (hardware and software) of the host machine to include the range of the machine being emulated. This is normally done when resources are not available to convert a system or the costs would be prohibitive. These systems run a very fine line between functional usefulness and total obsolescence. One of the major difficulties in maintaining them is finding maintainers who are familiar with the original hardware and who are willing to maintain it. Since the hardware is outdated, the specific skills developed in maintaining the system have little applicability elsewhere. Thus, the career development potential of supporting such a system is not very promising.

Very Large Modules or Unit Subroutines

"Mega-systems" that were written as one or several very large programs or sub-programs (thousands or tens of thousands of lines of code per program) can be extremely difficult to maintain. The size of a module is usually directly proportional to the level of effort necessary to maintain it. If the large modules can be restructured and divided into smaller, functionally related sections, the maintainability of the system will be improved.

Excessive Resource Requirements

An application system that requires a great deal of CPU time, memory, storage, or other system resources can place a very serious burden on all ADP users. These "resource hog" systems, which prevent other jobs from running, may not only require the addition of an extra shift, but may degrade the service to all users. Questions to be answered when deciding what to do about such a system include:

• Is it cheaper to add more computer power or to redesign and reimplement the system?

• Will a redesign reduce the resource requirements? If it won't, then there is no use in redesigning.

Hard-coded Parameters That Are Subject to Change

Many older systems were designed with the values of parameters used in performing specific calculations "hard-coded" into the source code rather than stored in a table or read in from a data file. When changes in these values are necessary (withholding rates, for example), each program in the system must be examined, modified, and recompiled as necessary. This is a time-consuming, error-prone process that is costly both in terms of the resources necessary to make the changes and in the delay in getting the changes installed.

If possible, the programs should be modified to handle the input of parameters in a single module or to read the parameters from a central table of values. If this can't be done, serious consideration should be given to redesigning the system.

Difficulty in Keeping Maintainers

Programs written in low-level languages, particularly assembler, require an excessive amount of time and effort to maintain. Generally, such languages are not widely taught or known. Therefore, it will be increasingly difficult to find maintainers who already know the language. Even if such maintainers are found, their experience with low-level languages is probably dated.

Seriously Deficient Documentation

One of the most common software maintenance problems is the lack of adequate documentation. In most organizations, the documentation ranges from nonexistent to out-of-date. Even if the documentation is good when delivered, it will often steadily and rapidly deteriorate as the software is modified. In some cases, the documentation is up to date but still not useful. This can result when the documentation is produced by someone who does not understand the software or what is needed.

Perhaps the worst documentation is that which is well structured and well formatted but incorrect or outdated. If there is no documentation, the maintainer will be forced to analyze the code in order to try to understand the system. If the documentation is physically deteriorated, the maintainer will be skeptical of it and verify its accuracy. If it looks good on the surface but is technically incorrect, the maintainer may mistakenly believe it to be correct and accept what it contains. This will result in serious problems over and above those that originally necessitated the initial maintenance.

Missing or Incomplete Design Specifications

Knowing "how and why" a system works is essential to good maintenance. If the requirements and design specifications are missing or incomplete, the task of the maintainer will be more difficult. It is very important for the maintainer to understand not only what a system is doing but how it is implemented and why it was designed. Missing or incomplete design specifications often result in end-products that do not perform as intended. The user must then request new changes and enhancements.

CONTROLLING SOFTWARE CHANGES

The key to controlling software maintenance is to organize it as a visible, discrete function and, to the extent possible, plan for it. It is not enough for the software manager to manage the budget, people, and schedules. It is equally important that the software changes be managed and controlled.

Controlling Perfective Maintenance

Perfective maintenance comprises an estimated 60 percent of the total maintenance effort. It deals primarily with expanding, extending, and enhancing a system to give it greater power, more flexibility, additional capabilities, or greater reliability. Requests for perfective maintenance are initiated by three different groups: the user, upper management, and the maintenance staff.

The user is almost never completely satisfied with a system. Either it does not perform up to expectations, or, as the user gains confidence in the system, additional features become desirable and the maintenance staff is asked to add them. This is a normal evolution in all software systems and must be planned for when developing budget requests and resource allocation schedules.

1. Require formal (written) requests for all changes.

2. Review all change requests and limit changes to those approved.

3. Analyze and evaluate the type and frequency of change requests.

4. Consider the degree to which a change is needed and its anticipated use.

5. Evaluate changes to ensure that they are not incompatible with the original system design and intent. No change should be implemented without careful consideration of its ramifications.

6. Emphasize the need to determine whether a proposed change will enhance or degrade the system.

7. Approve changes only if the benefits outweigh the costs.

8. Schedule all maintenance.

9. Enforce documentation and coding standards.

10. Require that all changes be implemented using modern programming practices.

11. Plan for preventive maintenance.

Table 12.5. Suggested policies for controlling software changes.

Upper management drives the perfective maintenance process by requesting new and enhanced features which must be incorporated into existing application systems. Once again, this is a normal part of the functioning of any organization and must be planned for in the maintenance budget.

Finally, the maintenance staff drives the perfective maintenance process by discovering inefficiencies and potential problems as it works with a system. These problems, while not requiring immediate attention, are such that at some point in time they could have a significant impact on either the functioning of the system or the ability to maintain it. Thus, the "cleaning up" of code (often referred to as "preventive maintenance") is an important perfective maintenance process that should be planned for and included in the resource allocation schedule. The proverbial "stitch in time" of preventive maintenance can often prevent minor problems in a system from becoming major problems at some later date. This undoubtedly will make future maintenance easier as a result of the "cleaning up" of the code.

The management of perfective maintenance deals primarily with maintaining an orderly process in which all requests are formally submitted, reviewed, assigned a priority, and scheduled. This does not mean that unnecessary delays should be built into the process, or that in small organizations these steps are not consolidated. Rather, it defines a philosophical approach that can help the maintenance manager bring order to the maintenance environment.

There should be a centralized approval point for all maintenance projects. This may be the maintenance project manager or, for larger systems or organizations, a review board. Changes should not just happen to a system. When the need for a change or enhancement arises, a formal written request should be submitted. Each request should be evaluated on the basis of resource requirements, time to complete the work, impact on the existing system and other maintenance efforts, and justification of need. The centralized approval process will enable one person or group to have knowledge of all the requested and actual work being performed on the system. If this is not done, there is the likelihood that two or more independent changes to the system will be in conflict with one another, and as a result, the system will not function properly. Additionally, different users will often request the same enhancements to a system, but will have small differences in the details. By coordinating these requests, details can be combined and the total amount of resources required can be reduced.

If the system requires maintenance as a result of changes in policy or procedures in the organization, an evaluation of the cost and effects of the changes should be prepared for upper management. Ideally, this should be prepared prior to the decision to institute the changes, but even if it is not, management *and* the users must be aware of the costs. Users often request enhancements to a system because it "would be nice to have" or another system has a similar feature. These requested enhancements should be evaluated and the estimated costs reported to the user. Regardless of whether the users are responsible for funding the work, it is important to keep them aware of the actual costs of their requests. Doing so will help to minimize the amount of unneeded or marginally needed enhancements that must be installed on the system. In addition, this type of interchange with the user will help the maintenance manager in evaluating and assigning priorities to the work requests.

In many organizations, there is a significant backlog of maintenance work requests. Users need to understand the level of effort required to meet their requests and the relative priority of the work in relationship to other user requests. This can only be accomplished by involving all parties in the discussions and keeping everyone informed of the schedules and actual progress.

Controlling Adaptive Maintenance

Adaptive maintenance comprises approximately 20 percent of the maintenance burden. It consists of any effort required to keep a system functioning as a result of changes in the environment in which the system must operate, and it is, to a great degree, beyond the control of the software maintenance manager. Changes to the operating system, system utilities, terminal devices, and the rules, laws, and regulations that the software must incorporate are the primary causes of adaptive maintenance. The maintenance efforts required are usually nonproductive in terms of improving the application system.

There is little that the software maintainer can do to control changes to rules and legislation. These changes, to the extent possible, should be anticipated and the code structured in a manner that facilitates the needed adaptations. This type of adaptive maintenance usually must be performed whenever it is required. Management should always be given feedback regarding the impact that changes in policies and regulations have on the maintenance of a system, especially the cost. Such feedback will improve the future decision-making process and may reduce the level of adaptive maintenance.

In many organizations, the application support group functions independently of the computer facility group. As a result, there is inadequate communication and understanding between the two regarding the impact of each's decisions and work on the other. Thus, changes may be made to the environment and announced to the user community without giving the application support function an opportunity to analyze the impact of the changes and the effect on the application system. Similarly, changes or additions to an application system that increase the computer resource requirements may cause serious problems with the functioning of all applications using the computer.

Therefore, it is very important that the facilities group and the applications support group work closely to minimize the impact of one's work on the other. There are times when a choice simply does not exist, but usually, through adequate planning and evaluation, both organizations can accomplish their objectives with a resulting net improvement for each.

The application support manager is responsible for knowing what changes to the environment are being planned or considered. He or she is also responsible for keeping management informed of such changes' potential impact (both negative and positive), so that management can review their total costs and the implications. Decisions can then be made regarding which organization should bear the costs of the resulting required adaptive maintenance of the application systems.

Controlling Corrective Maintenance

Corrective maintenance is primarily the identification and removal of errors, bugs, and other code defects that either reduce the effectiveness of the software or render the product useless. This category of maintenance is concerned with returning the code to an operational state. Controls are needed to ensure that the occurrence of errors or bugs is the exception rather than the rule.

Most of the cost of software maintenance is often assumed to be the result of poor workmanship during development and prior maintenance phases of the system. While this is a contributing cause, it is very rare for even a "perfect" system not to require significant maintenance during its lifetime. While software does not "break" in the sense that a piece of hardware can fail, it can become nonfunctional or faulty due to changes in the environment in which it must operate, the size or sophistication of the user community, the amount of data it must process, or damage to code resulting from other maintenance efforts on other parts of the system. Corrective maintenance is necessitated by discovery of a flaw that has always existed in the system or was introduced during prior maintenance.

Difficulties encountered during corrective maintenance can be reduced significantly by the adoption and enforcement of appropriate standards and procedures during the development and maintenance of the software. While it is probably not possible to eliminate corrective maintenance, the consistent and disciplined adherence to effective design and programming standards can, and will, significantly reduce the corrective maintenance burden.

IMPROVING SOFTWARE MAINTENANCE

Maintainability is the ease with which software can be changed to satisfy user requirements or can be corrected when deficiencies are detected. The maintainability of a system must be taken into consideration throughout the life cycle of that system. Many techniques and aids exist to assist the system developer, but there has been little emphasis on aids for the maintainer. However, since the processes occurring in the maintenance phase are similar to those of the development phase, there is considerable overlap in the applicability of the development aids in the maintenance environment.

The philosophies, procedures, and techniques discussed in this section should be utilized throughout the life cycle of a system in order to provide maintainable software. Software systems that were not developed using these techniques can also benefit from their application during major maintenance activities. In other words, if a system must be maintained, its maintainability can be improved by applying the ideas discussed in this section to the parts of the system that are modified during the maintenance process. While the effect will not be as pronounced as when programs are "developed with maintenance in mind," future maintenance efforts can be made easier by utilizing the techniques described in this section to "maintain systems with future maintenance in mind."

---

1. Use of a single high-order language
2. Coding conventions for variable names, structures, format, grouping, etc.
3. Structure and modularity
4. Standard data definitions
5. Meaningful comments in the code
6. Avoidance of compiler extensions

Table 12.6. Factors that affect source code maintainability.

Source Code Guidelines

Source code guidelines and standards aid maintainability by providing a structure and framework within which systems can be developed and maintained in a common, more easily understood manner.

Use a Single High-Order Language

The use of more than one programming language or the use of machine, assembler, or outdated languages, when it is not absolutely necessary to do so, can seriously impact the maintainability of a system. When more than one language is employed, the potential for communication problems between modules is increased. Systems written in low-order or outdated languages are difficult to maintain because they generally require more source code to perform the same amount of work. Wherever possible, a single high-order language (HOL) should be used. Advantages of using an HOL include the following:

- HOLs resemble English and are easy to learn, read, and understand.

- There are standards for the commonly used HOLs (COBOL and FORTRAN).

- There are a substantial number of programmers who can understand and use HOLs effectively.

- Many of the older machine languages are no longer supported by the manufacturer.

- Few programmers understand machine languages, and fewer still can use them effectively.

- HOLs are self-documenting to a large degree.

- It is easier to move from one environment to another with an HOL.

Coding Conventions

The first obstacle a maintainer must conquer is the code itself. Unfortunately, a great deal of the source code written by developers and maintainers is not written with the future maintainer in mind. Thus, the readability of source code is often very poor.

Source code should be self-documenting and be written in a structured format.

Regardless of the programming language(s) used, simple rules regarding the use of the language(s) and the physical formatting of the source code should be established. Code standards do not have to be lengthy or complex in order to be effective. In fact, like the code itself, the best standards are simple and short. The following techniques can improve program readability and should be used as the basis for a code standard.

- *Keep it simple.* Complicated, fancy, exotic, tricky, confusing, or "cute" constructions should be avoided whenever a simpler method is available. Use common sense and write code as if you had to pick it up and maintain it without ever having seen it before.

- *Indentation,* when properly utilized between sections of code, serves to block the listing into segments. Indentation and spacing are both ways to show subordination. It is very difficult to follow code that continues line after line without a break or change in form.

- *Extensively comment the code* with meaningful comments. Do not comment for comment's sake. Rather, comment in order to communicate to subsequent maintainers not only what was done and how it was done, but why it was done in this manner.

- Use of *meaningful variable names* is one of the most important coding principles to follow when developing and maintaining programs. The name of a variable should convey both what it is and why it is used.

- *Similar variable names* should be avoided. Each variable name should be unique in order to prevent confusion.

- When *numerics* are used, they should be placed at the end of the variable. Some of the more common errors are caused by mistaking variable names that begin with the numerics 0,1,2,5 for O,I,Z,S, respectively. Numbers used as program tags or labels should be sequential.

- *Logically related functions should be grouped together* in the same module or set of modules. It is extremely difficult to analyze the program flow when execution jumps in and out of different portions of code. To the extent possible, the logic flow should be from top to bottom of the program.

- *Avoid nonstandard features* of the version of the language being used unless absolutely necessary. Failure to do so will exacerbate problems of conversion or movement of the program to another machine or system.

Structured, Modular Software

While there has been considerable debate regarding structured programming, the consensus is that, generally, such code is easier to read. A structured program is constructed with a basic set of control structures, each of which has one exit and one entry point. Structured programming techniques are well-defined methods that incorporate top-down design and implementation and strict use of structured programming constructs. Whether the strict definition or a more general approach (which is intended to organize the code and reduce its complexity) is used, structured programming has proven to be useful in improving the maintainability of a system.

Modularity refers to the structure of a program. A program comprising small, hierarchical units or sets of routines, where each performs a particular, unique function, is said to be modular. It is not, as is often though, mere program segmentation. A module is said to have two basic determinants: cohesiveness and coupling.

Cohesion refers to the degree to which the functions or processing elements within a module are related or bound together. It is the intra-module relativeness. The greater the cohesion, the less impact changes will have on the software.

Coupling refers to the degree that modules are dependent upon each other. The less dependency or interaction there is between modules, the better, from both a functional and a maintenance standpoint. A high degree of cohesion almost always assures a lower degree of coupling. Controlling cohesion and coupling are very effective techniques in the design and maintenance of structured, modular software.

One of the most obvious advantages of designing and coding structured modules is that if it is determined that a function is no longer needed, only that module is affected. The size of a module is dependent upon its function, but it should be kept as small as possible. Modules should be constructed using the following basic design principles:

- Modules should perform only one principal function.

- Interaction between modules should be minimal.

- Modules should have only one entry and one exit point.

Standard Data Definitions

It is very important not only that individual modules of a system be able to communicate with one another, but that the maintainer understand what is being communicated. A typical problem in a large multi-module system is that one person will use a set of names for data items that do not match the names used by another person on the team. Even more serious is the use of the same names to represent two different data items. Thus, it is imperative that a standard set of data definitions be developed for a system. These data definitions will define the name, physical attributes, purpose, and content of each data element utilized in the system. They should be as descriptive and meaningful as possible. If this is consistently and correctly done, the task of reading and understanding each module and ensuring correct communication between each module is greatly simplified.

Well-commented Code

Good commentary increases the intelligibility of source code. In addition to making programs more readable, comments serve two other vital purposes. They provide information on the purpose and history of the program, its origin (the author, creation, and change dates), the name and number of subroutines, and input/output requirements and formats. They also provide operation control information, instructions, and recommendations to help the maintainer understand aspects of the code that are not clear.

Maintainers (and managers) often mistake quantity for quality when writing comments. The purpose of comments is to convey information needed to understand the process and the reasons for implementing it in that specific manner, not how it is being done. Comments should be thought of as the primary form of documentation. They should include the following:

- What the code is doing

- Why a process is being performed

- Why it is implemented in the specific manner

- How this section of code affects and interacts with other sections of code
- Any known or potential problems
- When the changes were made
- Who made the changes
- What specific code was modified
- Any other information which might help a future maintainer in understanding and modifying the code

Avoid Compiler Extensions

The use of nonstandard features of a compiler can have serious effects on the maintainability of a system. If a compiler is changed or the application system must be transported to a new machine, there is a very great risk that the extensions of the previous compiler will not be compatible with the new compiler. Thus, it is best to refrain from language extensions and to stay in conformance with the basic features of the language. If it is necessary to use a compiler extension, its use should be well documented.

Documentation Guidelines

The documentation of a system should start with the original requirements and design specifications and continue throughout the life cycle of the system. Good software documentation is essential to good maintenance.

---

1. Keep it simple and concise.
2. The maintainer's first source of documentation is the source code.
3. The manager's first source of documentation is the design specifications and implementation reports.
4. The user's first source of documentation is the users guide and the maintainer.
5. Do not underdocument. Do not overdocument.
6. Documentation cannot be "almost correct." Either it is up to date or it is useless.
7. Documentation maintenance is a vital part of system maintenance.
8. Documentation should be available to the maintainer at all times.

Table 12.7. Documentation guidance.

The documentation must be planned so that a maintainer can quickly find the needed information. A number of methodologies and guidelines exist that stress differing formats and styles. While preference may differ on which methodology to use, the important thing is to adopt a documentation standard and to then consistently enforce adherence to it for all software projects.

The success of a software maintenance effort is dependent on how well information about the system is communicated to the maintainer. Documentation should support the usable transfer of pertinent information. Documentation guidelines should include instructions on what information must be provided, how it should be structured, and where the information should be kept. In establishing these guidelines and standards, keep in mind that the purpose is to communicate necessary, critical information, not to communicate all information.

Basically, the documentation standards should require the inclusion of all pertinent material in a documentation folder or notebook. This material should cover all phases of the software life cycle and must be kept fully updated. Management must enforce documentation standards and *not* permit shortcuts. There should be a requirement to complete and/or update documentation before new work assignments are begun.

The key to successful documentation is recording all necessary information and making it easily and quickly retrievable by the maintainer. On-line documentation that has controlled access and update capabilities is the best form of documentation for the maintainer. If the documentation cannot be kept on-line, a mechanism must exist to permit access to the hardcopy documentation by the maintainer at any time.

If documentation guidelines, or any other software guidelines or standards, are to be effective, they must be supported by a level of management high enough within the organization to ensure enforcement by all who use the software or are involved with software maintenance. Such guidelines, when supported by management, will help direct attention toward the need for greater discipline in the software maintenance process.

Coding and Review Techniques

The techniques listed in this section have been found to be very effective in the generation of maintainable systems. Not all techniques are generally applicable to all organizations, but it is recommended that they be considered.

---

1. Top-down/Bottom-up design and implementation
2. Peer reviews
3. Walkthroughs
4. Chief programmer team

Table 12.8. Coding and review techniques.

Top-down/Bottom-up Approach

A top-down design approach (development or enhancements) involves starting at the macro or overview level and successfully breaking each program component or large, complex problem into smaller less complicated segments. These segments are then decomposed into even smaller segments until the lowest-level module of the original problem is defined for each branch in the logic flow tree.

In general, top-down implies that major functions are considered first. Once it is clear how they fit together, the next, lower-level, functions are designed. During the first phase, the lower-level functions are often created as empty black boxes or modules that simply return control to the major level or calling functions.

The bottom-up design approach begins with the lowest level of elements. These are combined into larger components, which are then combined into divisions, and finally, the divisions are combined into a program. A bottom-up approach emphasizes designing the fundamental or "atomic" level modules first and then using these modules as building blocks for the entire system.

Both of these approaches are valid and superior to a random "seat-of-the-pants" approach. In most situations, a combination of top-down and bottom-up can be utilized to develop a clear, concise, maintainable system. The adoption of and adherence to either approach provides a structure or methodology that enables persons working on a system to communicate with one another in a consistent and understandable manner.

Peer Reviews

Peer review is a quality assurance method in which two or more programmers review and critique each other's work for accuracy and consistency with other parts of the system. This type of review is normally done by giving a section of code developed by one programmer to one or more peer programmers who are charged with identifying what they consider to be errors and potential problems. It is important to establish and to keep clearly in the participants' minds that the process is not an evaluation of a programmer's capabilities or performance. Rather, it is an analysis and evaluation of the code. As stated in the name, such reviews are performed on a peer basis (programmer to programmer) and should never be used as a basis for employee evaluation. Indeed, project managers should not, if possible, be involved in the peer reviews.

Walkthroughs

Walkthroughs of a proposed solution or implementation of a maintenance task can range from informal to formal, unstructured to structured, and simple to full-scale. The principle involved in walkthroughs is simply that "two heads are better than one." In its simplest form, a walkthrough can be two maintainers sitting down and discussing a task one of them is working on. In its more complex forms, there may be a structured agenda, report forms, and a recording secretary. Managers may or may not participate in walkthroughs, although this is an excellent way for a manager to keep informed about the work being performed by the team.

The basic format of a walkthrough is for the person whose work is being reviewed to describe in detail the proposed solution or the draft of the code. The reviewers ask questions to clarify areas where questions arise and point out any errors or potential problems they spot. The goal, as in peer reviews, is to minimize the number of design, logic, and/or coding flaws that remain in the system. Walkthroughs are similar to peer reviews, but differ in that the manager may be present; the reviewers meet as a group to discuss the work under consideration, and there are often formal recording and reporting mechanisms.

Two important points should be stressed regarding the manager's role in a walkthrough:

1. Walkthroughs should never be used as part of an employee evaluation. The goal is an open, frank dialogue resulting in the refinement of good ideas and the changing or elimination of bad ones.

2. The manager's role should only be as active as his or her technical expertise regarding the subject matter permits. The manager must recognize that the other members of the walkthrough team probably have greater technical knowledge about the specific subject being discussed. Participating in a passive manner can be an excellent means to attain an understanding of the maintenance effort and to improve the manager's technical understanding of the system.

Chief Programmer Team

The chief programmer team is based on the premise that an experienced programer, supported by a team of programmers, can produce computer programs with greater speed and efficiency than a group of programmers working within the traditional line and staff organization. The size of the team can range from 3 to 10 members, with the chief programmer being responsible for overall design, development, review, and evaluation of the work performed by the team. This can include the establishment and enforcement of rules regarding programming style, control, and the integrity of the programs.

The chief programmer functions as the focal point of the maintenance team and is required to be aware of and familiar with all work it performs. There is an enormous amount of administrative and technical responsibility placed on the chief programmer. This person must have impeccable leadership abilities, a strong technical capability, and the ability and willingness to delegate work and responsibility.

Change Control

Change control is necessary to ensure that all maintenance requests are handled accurately, completely, and in a timely manner. It helps assure adherence to the established standards and performance criteria for the system and facilitates communication between the maintenance team members and the maintenance manager.

Change Request

All changes considered for a system should be formally requested in writing. These requests may be initiated by the user or maintainer in response to discovered errors, new requirements, or changing needs. Procedures may vary regarding the format of a change request, but it is imperative that each request be fully documented in writing so that it can be formally reviewed. The review may be performed by the project manager or a change review board; however, there must be a formal, well-defined mechanism for initiating a request for changes or enhancements to a system. Change requests should be carefully evaluated and decisions to proceed should be based on all the pertinent areas of consideration (probable effects on the system, actual need, resource requirements versus resource availability, budgetary considerations, priority, etc.). The decision and reasons for the decision should be recorded and included in the permanent documentation of the system.

---

1. Change request
2. Code audit
3. Review and Approval

Table 12.9. Controlling changes.

The change request should be submitted on forms that contain the following information:

- Name of requester
- Date of request
- Purpose for request (error reported, enhancement, etc.)
- Name of program(s) affected
- Section of code/line numbers affected
- Name of document(s) affected
- Name of data file(s) affected
- Date request satisfactorily completed
- Date new version operational
- Name of maintainer
- Date of review
- Name of reviewer
- Review decision

Code Audit

The code review or audit is a procedure used to determine how well the code adheres to the coding standards and practices and to the design specifications. The primary objective of code audits is to guarantee a high degree of uniformity across the software. This becomes a critical factor when the software must be understood and maintained by someone other than the original developer. Audits are also concerned with such program elements as commentary, labeling, paragraphing, initialization of common areas, and naming conventions. Someone besides the original author should perform the audit. Questions addressed during an audit should include:

- Are comments well constructed?

- Do the comments provide meaningful information?

- Are the comments consistent throughout the code?

- Are the constants centrally defined and locally initialized?

- Are the statement labels descriptive and sequential?

- Is the code formatted in a readable manner?

- Are indentation and paging used to make the code easier to read and understand?

Review and Approval

Review and approval is the final phase of the software change control process. Prior to installation, each change (correction, update, or enhancement) to a system should be formally reviewed. In practice, this process ranges from the review and sign-off by the project manager or user to the convening of a change review board to formally approve or reject the changes. The purpose of this process is to ensure that all of the requirements of the change request have been met; that the system performs according to specifications; that the changes will not adversely impact the rest of the system or other users; that all procedures have been followed and rules and guidelines adhered to; and that the change is indeed ready for installation in the production system. All review actions and findings should be added to the system documentation folder.

Testing Standards and Procedures

Testing, like documentation, is an area of software maintenance that is often not done well. Whenever possible, the test procedures and test data should be developed by someone other than the person who performed the actual maintenance on the system. The testing standards and procedures should define the degree and depth of testing to be performed and the disposition of test materials upon successful completion of the testing.

Testing is a critical component of software maintenance, so the test procedures must be consistent and based on sound principles. Whether the testing is performed on the entire system or on a single module within the system, the same principles are required. They include the following:

- The test plan should define the expected output.

- Whenever possible, the test data should be prepared by someone other than the tester.

- The valid, invalid, expected, and unexpected cases should be tested.

- The test should examine whether or not the program is doing what it is supposed to.

- Testing is done to find errors, not to prove that errors do not exist.

SOFTWARE MAINTENANCE TOOLS

Software tools are computer programs that can be used in the development, analysis, testing, maintenance, and management of other computer programs and their documentation. This section discusses some tools that can be useful in maintaining a software system. Generally, these tools can be divided into two categories: technical and management. The technical tools can be further subdivided into those that process, analyze, and test the system and those that help the maintainer manipulate and change the source code and the documentation. The management tools assist the maintenance manager in controlling and tracking all of the maintenance tasks. Table 12.10 lists some of the tools available to the maintainer and the maintenance manager.

Technical tools
    Processing tools
        Compilers
        Cross-referencer
        Comparator
        Traces/dumps
        Test data generator
        Test coverage analyzer
        Preprocessor
        Verification/validation

    Clerical tools
        On-line editor
        Documentation library
        Archival capabilities
        Reformatter
        Data dictionary

    Management tools
        Problem reporting
        Status reporting
        Scheduling
        Configuration management

Table 12.10. Software maintenance tools.

Cross-referencer

One of the single most useful aids to the maintainer is the cross-reference list that accompanies the compiler source listing. It usually provides a concise, ordered analysis of the data variables, including the location and number of times the variables are used as well as other pertinent information about the program.

In large systems, it is often difficult to determine which modules are called or used by other programs, and where within the system a specific module or parameter is used. What is often needed too is the capacity to produce and develop a cross-reference listing on an interprogram rather than on an intraprogram basis. This information can be obtained from some of the available cross-reference generators. To the maintainer, such information is useful when attempting to backtrack to determine where an error occurred.

Comparators

Comparators are software tools that accept two (or more) sets of input and generate a report listing the discrepancies between the input datasets. This tool can be used for finding changes in the source code, input data, program output, etc. It is extremely useful to the maintainer who must ascertain if a change made to the system caused it to fail or work differently. It can also be used to ensure that one set of test results is identical to a previous set, or to identify where the results have changed. Most comparators are developed for a specific system. They may be general in nature or work on specific parts of the system and perform specific functions. They are relatively simple to build and are very valuable tools in the maintainer's tool box.

Diagnostic Routines

Diagnostic routines assist the maintainer by reducing the amount of time and effort required for problem resolution. Some of the more commonly used routines include:

- *Trace*, which generates an audit trail of actual operations during execution.

- *Breakpoint*, which interrupts program execution to initiate debug activities.

- *Save/restart*, which salvages program execution status at any point to permit evaluation and reinitiation.

- *Dumps*, which give listings (usually unformatted or partially formatted) of all or selected portions of the program memory at a specific point in time.

Compilers often provide diagnostic capabilities that can be optionally selected to assist the programmer in analyzing the execution flow and to capture a myriad of data at predetermined points in the process. In the hands of a skilled maintainer, these diagnostics can help identify the sections of code that caused the error as well as what is taking place there. While these aids are extremely useful, they are usually "after the fact" tools used to help determine what has gone wrong with an operational system. Far more useful are diagnostic capabilities designed and implemented within the source code as it is developed. This latter type of diagnostic is normally disabled, but can be turned on through the use of one or more control parameters.

Application Utility Libraries

Most operating systems provide support and utility libraries that contain standard functional routines (square roots, sine, cosine, absolute values, etc.). In addition, HOL compilers have many built-in functions that can be utilized by the programmer to perform standard functions. Just as these libraries provide standardized routines to perform processes common to many applications systems, large application systems should have a procedure library that contains routines common to various segments of the application system. These functions and utility routines should be available to all persons working on the system, from the developer to the maintainer. Application support utility libraries assist by:

- Saving time (the programmer does not have to reinvent the wheel).

- Simplifying the changing of common code (changes all programs that utilize a module). This usually requires relinking or recompiling each affected program, but it eliminates the need to change lines of code in each of the programs.

- Enabling wider use of utility procedures, developed by one person or group, by all persons working on the system.

- Facilitating maintenance of the system by keeping the code in a central library or set of libraries.

In addition to the stored library routines, all the source code for the applications system should be stored in a centralized, on-line library. Access to this library should be controlled by a librarian who has the duty of maintaining the integrity of the library and the code.

On-line Documentation Libraries

System documentation normally consists of one or more folders or files in hardcopy form, which are stored at a central location. The need for the maintainers to have access to the information in these documentation folders and the need to keep the documentation up-to-date and secure are sometimes at cross-purposes. Thus, it is recommended that as much documentation as practical also be kept on-line in documentation libraries the maintainer can access at any time. Updating of this library should be controlled by a librarian.

On-line/Interactive Change and Debug Facilities

Interactive debugging provides significant advantages over the batch method because of the convenience and speed of modification. With interactive processing, the maintainer can analyze the problem area, make changes to a test version of the system, and test and debug the system immediately. The alternative, to submit a batch job to perform the testing, requires much more time to complete. While in some instances this may be necessary because of system size or resource requirements, most maintenance activities (including perfective maintenance) are highly critical problems that must be addressed and solved as quickly as possible. Interactive processing provides a continuity that enables greater concentration on the problem and quicker response to the tests. Although the estimates of the increase in productivity vary widely, it is clear that there is a substantial improvement when the maintainer has on-line interactive processing capabilities.

Generation and Retention of Test Data

Standardized procedures (often developed in-house) for generating and retaining test data are recommended. One of the perennial problems in software maintenance is the lack of test data. While in most instances, test data is generated by the maintainer, studies have found that more errors and inconsistencies are uncovered when test data is prepared by the user, and testing is more effective if samples of the actual data are included in the test data.

Once a test dataset has been generated and the system successfully run against it, the data should be retained for use in future maintenance regression testing. Regression testing is the selective retesting of the system to detect any faults that may have been introduced and to verify that the maintenance modifications have preserved the functionality of the system. The system testing verifies that the system produces the same results and continues to meet the requirements specifications. In addition, the results of the testing should be saved in machine-readable form so that the results of future maintenance testing can be compared with the previous test results through the use of a comparator.

Although some test dataset generators are commercially available, most are developed either as part of the original development effort of a large system or as part of the maintenance effort. A test data generator is usually built for a specific system and designed to test the system to a selected level of detail.

MANAGING SOFTWARE MAINTENANCE

The effective use of good management techniques and methodologies in dealing with scheduling maintenance, negotiating with users, coordinating the maintenance staff, and instituting the use of the proper tools and disciplines is essential to a successful software maintenance effort. Software maintenance managers are responsible for making decisions regarding the performance of software maintenance; assigning priorities to the requested work; estimating the level of effort for a task; tracking the progress of work; and assuring adherence to system standards in all phases of the maintenance effort. A software maintenance manager must be not only a good technician but also a good manager. While this may seem to be an obvious point, it is, in actual practice, far too often ignored.

There appears to be a common failure to recognize the importance of the word "management" in the phrase "software maintenance management." In many instances, technical persons are promoted to positions of management within an organization on the assumption that technical expertise is all that is required to effectively manage a software maintenance operation. On the contrary, a software maintenance function has the same organizational needs and managerial problems as any other function.

The primary duties of a software maintenance manager include:

1. Evaluate, assign, prioritize, and schedule maintenance work requests.
2. Assign personnel to scheduled tasks.
3. Track progress of all maintenance tasks and ensure that they are on or ahead of schedule.
4. Adjust schedules when necessary.
5. Communicate progress and problems to the user.
6. Communicate progress and problems to upper management.
7. Establish and maintain maintenance standards and guidelines.

8. Enforce standards and make sure that the software maintenance is of high quality.

9. Deal with problems and crises as they arise.

10. Keep the morale of the maintenance staff high.

This list is not complete, but it is sufficient to illustrate the point that if the words "software maintenance" were deleted, it would simply be a list of management duties for any other organizational function. Thus, it is imperative that a software maintenance manager be qualified both technically and managerially to hold such a position. If he or she is not qualified, the ability to be an effective maintenance manager will be severely diminished.

Just as the importance of management skills has not been recognized in the selection of many software maintenance managers, in other instances, neither has the need for technical maintenance expertise been addressed. While many of the required skills involve dealing with and coordinating people, the software maintenance manager also has the responsibility to control the technical aspects of the process. Without a strong technical background and actual experience in performing software maintenance, the manager may not be able to deal with the conflicting needs and requirements of many maintenance tasks.

The software maintenance manager should be aware of, and familiar with, all of the work being performed by the software maintenance staff. While this is not always practical or possible in large organizations, each specific application system must have a central authority who is responsible for controlling and coordinating the maintenance of that system. Too often, a form of anarchy exists in software maintenance organizations. The maintainers are not adequately coordinated and are permitted to address problems as they arise, without adhering to established standards and procedures. In the short term, this may be the most effective manner of addressing immediate problems, but the long-term consequences are usually a decreased level of maintainability for the system and an increased need for maintenance. This section discusses standards, guidelines, procedures, and policies that will facilitate the management of the software maintenance function and improve the capability to maintain application systems.

Goals of Software Maintenance Management

The goal of software maintenance management is to keep all systems functioning and to respond to all user requests in a timely and satisfactory manner. Unfortunately, given the realities of staffing limitations, computer resource limitations, and the unlimited needs and desires of most users, this goal is very difficult to achieve. Thus, the realistic goal is to keep the software maintenance process orderly and under control. The specific responsibility of the software maintenance manager is to keep all application systems running and to facilitate communication between the three groups involved with software maintenance.

The user must be kept satisfied that everything possible is being done to keep each system running as efficiently and productively as possible.

---

1. Keep the maintenance process orderly and under control.
2. Keep the application systems running.
3. Keep the users satisfied.
4. Keep the maintainers happy.
5. Keep maintenance viewed as a positive aspect of ADP — one that contributes to the meeting of the goals of the organization — not something that has to be done because the ADP staff just can't do it right the first time.

Table 12.11. Goals of software maintenance.

Upper management must be kept informed of the overall success of the software maintenance effort and how software maintenance supports and enhances the organization's ability to meet its objectives. In dealing with upper management, one of the primary responsibilities of the software maintenance manager is to keep maintenance viewed in a positive perspective. Software maintenance is an important effort that supports and contributes to the ability of the organization to meet its goals. Too many of the problems encountered in software maintenance are the result of a negative attitude that it exists because the software support staff can "never do it right." Rather, the emphasis should be on the idea that software maintenance enables an organization to improve and expand its capabilities using existing systems.

Finally, the software maintenance manager has the responsibility for keeping the maintenance staff happy and satisfied. Software maintenance must be thought of as the challenging, dynamic, interesting work it can be.

Establish a Software Maintenance Policy

A software maintenance policy should employ standards that describe in broad terms the responsibilities, authorities, functions, and operations of the software maintenance organization. It should be comprehensive enough to address any type of change to the software system and its environment, including changes to the hardware, software, and firmware. To be effective, the policy should be consistently applied and must be supported and promulgated by upper management to the extent that it establishes an organizational commitment to software maintenance. When supported by management, the standards and guidelines help to direct attention toward the need for greater discipline in software design, development, and maintenance.

The software maintenance policy must specifically address the need and justification for changes, the responsibility for making the changes, the change controls and procedures, and the use of modern programming practices, techniques, and tools. It should describe management's role and duties in regard to software maintenance and define the process and procedures for controlling changes to the software after the baseline has been established. (Baseline refers to a well-defined base or configuration to which all modifications are applied.) Implementation of the policy has the effect of enforcing adherence to rules regarding the operating software and documentation, from initiation through completion of the requested change. Once this is accomplished, it is possible to establish the milestones necessary to measure software maintenance progress. Plans, however, are of little use if they are not followed. Reviews and audits are required to ensure that the plans are carried out.

The primary purpose of change control is to assure the continued smooth functioning of the application system and the orderly evolution of that system. The key to controlling changes to a system is the centralization of change approval and the formal requesting of changes. The software maintenance surveys found that each successful organization had a formal trouble report/change request process, with a single person or a change review board approving all changes/enhancement requests prior to the scheduling of work. When this is not done, the confusion that results from independent maintenance efforts is usually disastrous.

Everything done to software affects if quality. Thus, measures should be established to aid in determining which category of changes is likely to degrade software quality. Care must also be taken to ensure that changes are not incompatible with the original system design and intent. The degree to which a change is needed and its anticipated use should be a major consideration. Consideration should also be given to the cost/benefit of the change: "Would a new system be less expensive and provide better capabilities?" The policies establishing change control should be clear, concise, well publicized, and strictly enforced.

---

1. Review and evaluate all requests for changes
   - The change must be fully justified.
   - The impact on other work and users should be taken into consideration.

2. Plan for and schedule maintenance.
   - Each change request should be assigned a priority.
   - Work should be scheduled according to priority.
   - The schedule should be enforced and adhered to.

3. Restrict code changes to the approved/scheduled work.

4. Enforce documentation and coding standards through reviews and audits.

Table 12.12. Establishing a software maintenance policy.

Review and Evaluate All Requests for Changes

All user and staff requests for changes to an application system (whether enhancements, preventive maintenance, or errors) should be requested in writing and submitted to the software maintenance manager. Each change request should include not only the description of the requested change but a full justification for it. These change requests should be carefully reviewed and evaluated before any actual work is performed on the system. The evaluation should take into consideration, among other things, the staff resources available versus the estimated workload of the request; the estimated additional computing resources that will be required for the design, test, debug, and operation of the modified system; and the time and cost of updating the documentation. Of course, some flexibility must be built into the process with some delegation of authority to initiate critical tasks. However, each request should be reviewed and judged by either the software maintenance manager or a change review board. This will reduce the amount of unnecessary and/or unjustified work which is often performed on a system.

Plan for and Schedule Maintenance

The result of the review of all change requests should be the assignment of a priority to each request and the updating of a schedule for meeting those requests. In many ADP organizations, there are simply more work requests than staff resources to meet those requests. Therefore, all work should be scheduled and every effort made to adhere to the schedule rather than constantly changing course in response to the most visible crisis.

Restrict Code Changes to the Approved Work

In many cases, especially when the code was poorly designed and/or written, there is a strong temptation to change other sections of the code as long as the program has been "opened up." The software maintenance manager must monitor the work of the software maintenance staff and ensure that only the authorized work is performed. In order to monitor maintenance effectively, all activities must be documented. This includes everything from the change request form to the final revised source program listing.

Permitting the software maintenance staff to make changes other than those authorized can cause schedules to slip and may prevent other, higher-priority work from being completed on time. It is very difficult to limit the work done on a specific program, but it is imperative to the overall success of the maintenance function to do so.

Enforce Documentation and Coding Standards

Some programmers do not like to document, and some are not good at it, but primarily, documentation suffers because of too much pressure and too little time in the schedule. Proper and complete communication of necessary information between all persons who have worked, are currently working, and who will work on the system is essential. The most important media for this communication is the documentation and the source code.

It is not enough to simply establish standards for coding and documentation. Those standards must be continually enforced via technical review and examination of all work performed by the software maintenance staff. In scheduling maintenance, sufficient time should be provided to fully update the documentation and to satisfy established standards and guidelines before a new assignment is begun.

Staffing and Management of Maintenance Personnel

Selecting the proper staff for a software maintenance project is as important as the techniques and approaches employed. There is some debate on whether an organization should have separate staffs for maintenance and development. Many managers have indicated that separate staffs can improve the effectiveness of both functions; however, the realities of size, organization, budget, and staff ceilings often preclude this.

Management must apply the same criteria to the maintainers that are applied to software and systems designers or other highly sought after professional positions. If an individual is productive, consistently performs well, has a good attitude, and displays initiative, it should not matter whether the project is development or maintenance. Recent studies on the motivation of programmers and analysts indicate that three major psychological factors can impact an individual's attitude, morale, and general performance:

- The work must be considered worthwhile according to a set of values accepted by the individual as well as the standards employed by the organization.

- The individual must feel a responsibility for his or her performance. There is a need to feel personally accountable for the outcome of an effort.

- The individual must be able to determine on a regular basis whether the outcome of his or her efforts is satisfactory.

When these factors are high, the individual is likely to have a good attitude and be motivated.

Some organizations have attempted to improve maintainers' morale simply by renaming the maintenance function. This is a superficial approach that does nothing to change what is in fact being done or the way it is perceived by the maintainer and supported by management. A more positive approach is to acknowledge the importance and value of good maintenance to the organization through career opportunities, recognition, and compensation.

Often, a maintainer is responsible for large amounts of code, much of which was developed and previously maintained by someone else. This code is generally old and unstructured, has received numerous patches, and is inadequately documented. The potential for errors, delays, and unhappy users is considerable. Praise, thanks and recognition are often as important as salary and challenging assignments in keeping good analysts and programmers.

It is essential that work assignments offer growth potential. Continuing education is required at all levels to ensure that not only maintainers but users, managers, and operators have a thorough understanding of software maintenance. Training should include programming languages, standards and guidelines, operating systems, and utilities.

There is a common misperception that maintenance is dull, tedious, noncreative work offering little chance for reward or advancement. This view can only be changed through management initiatives. The maintainer is a critical part of the process — the key to delivery of the product both promised by management and desired by users. Indeed, the maintainer is one of the most important members of the application software staff. Therefore, the importance of maintenance must be acknowledged in terms of both position value and function.

Some points to keep in mind when managing a software maintenance function are outlined in Table 12.13.

1. Maintenance is as important as development and just as difficult and challenging.

2. Maintainers should be highly qualified, competent, dedicated professionals. The staff should include both senior and junior personnel. Do not short-change maintenance. Don't isolate the maintenance staff.

3. Maintenance should *not* be used as a training ground where junior staff are left to "sink-or-swim."

4. Staff members should be rotated so they are assigned to both maintenance and development. It takes a good developer to be a good maintainer, and, conversely, it takes a good maintainer to be a good developer.

5. Good maintenance performance and good development performance should be equally rewarded.

6. There should be an emphasis on keeping the staff well trained. This will keep performance at an optimum level and help to minimize morale problems.

7. Rotate assignments. Do not permit a system or a major part of a system to become someone's private domain.

Table 12.13. Managing the software maintenance function.

13

Reuse of Software

One of the most effective means of improving the productivity of software development is increasing the proportion of software that is reused. Reusable software not only increases productivity but also improves the reliability of software and reduces development time and cost. However, there are many technical, organizational, economic, cultural, and legal issues to be resolved before widespread reuse of software can become a reality.

The basic causes of increased software costs include the explosive growth in size, complexity and increasing criticality of modern software systems, and rising personnel costs. Software costs for both development and maintenance are largely related to the labor-intensiveness of the process and the inadequate use of available technology.

Before addressing the technical and economic reasons why software should be reused, it is important to gain a perspective on recent advances in the state of the practice. It is often argued that software reuse is feasible since hardware reuse has been successful. However, this analogy is not as straightforward as it may appear. Hardware tends to be relatively simple, consisting of replicated logic elements, while software must deal with substantially more complex application issues. In addition, hardware primitive components have had a much longer time to stabilize. There are years between the initial engineering release of a hardware component and its subsequent widespread commercial use. Software has yet to gain the benefit of this maturing process and thus still displays a higher degree of variability.

Current software management concerns have focused on how to reduce software development and maintenance costs, the need for a standard operating system interface, an automated programmers' support environment, automatic programming by a computerized software factory, reusable software libraries, and organization-wide software development and configuration management guidelines and standards. Each of these represents promising innovations with major payoff potential over the next five to ten years. However, immediate software cost savings and software programmer productivity improvements can be gained simply through small changes in the way software projects and knowledge are managed.

A common conception of software reuse is that it is limited to existing source code. However, it should be more broadly defined as the reuse of any information that may be collected and later used to develop other software. This definition includes reuse of available software requirements, specifications, system design, source code, modules, operating systems, documentation, analysis data, test information, maintenance information databases, and software development plans and methodologies. The reuse of automated tools for generating software, a well-designed reusable software library for classifying and retrieving various error-free software components, and an integrated software support environment to improve software life cycle processes are also part of the scope of software reuse efforts.

THE SOFTWARE CRISIS

The problems in the development and maintenance of software have increased rapidly over the past decade. This is due to the explosive growth in size, complexity, and critical nature of modern software applications, as well as to the lack of an integrated software development environment for supporting the software life cycle process. The inability to manage the complexity of software often results in insufficient definition of requirements and specifications, extended development time, and software cost overruns.

The software problem entails not only the high cost of software development but also the poor quality. In fact, many organizations spend 60 to 70 percent of their resources in maintaining old software, which includes eliminating bugs and incorporating changes in requirements.

"A Management Overview of Software Reuse," published by the National Bureau of Standards, gave the following reasons that software is costly:

1. Requirements of new software systems are more complex than before. Almost every national defense system contains embedded computer software that performs mission-critical functions. These software systems have high performance expectations that require the software to be highly flexible and reliable.

2. There is a lack of professional training. The need to train software professionals and end-users in new technology is often overlooked. Training programs can serve as a feedback mechanism for collecting information from users about their experiences in adapting and using these rapidly changing, modern programming techniques and practices.

3. The demand for qualified software professionals exceeds the number available. There is a growing shortage of software professionals, and the United States Air Force (USAF) Scientific Advisory Board has estimated that the demand for software professionals will continue to exceed available resources unless remedial measures are taken. As a result, the difficulty of developing quality software will continue to rise.

4. There is only limited use of software development tools and methodologies to develop and maintain software. Many software managers do not know what information is currently available for improving the traditional software life cycle processes. It is difficult for them to identify the information needed for selecting the right tools and methods without the appropriate information management techniques. As a result, software productivity has only increased an estimated 3 to 8 percent per year.

THE NATURE OF SOFTWARE REUSABILITY

A common misconception of software reuse is that it is limited to existing source code. There are, however, many approaches that address software reusability. Reusable software includes any information that may be collected and later used to develop other software; available software development methodologies; software requirements; specifications and designs; source code; modules; documentation; analysis data; test information; and maintenance information databases. The reuse of automated tools for generating software and a software support environment for improving software life cycle processes is also part of the software reuse effort.

The use of subroutine libraries and off-the-shelf software is the most common example of reusing existing software. For many commercial applications, modestly priced packages are available that can be incorporated into a software system. Similarly, well-developed existing packages for scientific, government, aerospace, and mission-critical applications are available.

Some good examples of software reuse are:

1. A study done by the Missile System Division of the Raytheon Company reported that 40 to 60 percent of actual source code was reused in more than one software system.

2. Reuse factors of 85 percent have been reported in Japanese software factories.

3. Sixty percent of the design and code on all business applications is reusable.

4. One reason for the wide and rapidly growing popularity of AT&T's UNIX™ system is that its design philosophy is based on reusability. UNIX succeeds in reusability because of the low perceived complexity of its interface (i.e., files and pipes). The actual interface is complicated because most of the details are hidden away in the environment.

5. Seventy-five percent of the program functions are common to more than one application, and only 15 percent of the source code found in most programs is unique and novel to a specific application.

6. Reuse has a place in the creation of some very complex systems; 12 of 16 software programs involving satellites were based on 68 to 95 percent of the existing software that has potential for reusability at NASA's Goddard Space Flight Center.

While these examples indicate the possibilities of successful reuse, the state of the practice has not adequately taken advantage of these opportunities in order to make widespread software reuse a reality.

THE SOFTWARE REUSE PROCESS

Software reuse is the use of previously acquired concepts or objects in a new situation. Actually, reuse is a continuous matching process between new and old situations and, when matching succeeds, duplication of the same actions. The iterative refinement process of a software development life cycle can be viewed as another effective way of reusing existing software. In this notion, reusability evolves as an iterative process of refining requirements, specifications, design, programming, testing, and implementation throughout the software life cycle to meet the users' needs. The software development life cycle process must become fully automated in the future, so that the rapid prototyping approach to software development through reuse and maintenance can become truly feasible. This automation-based software development environment approach will provide an integrated set of tools that directly supports software programmers with the "corporate memory" of knowledge as well as system requirements and specifications, design, testing, implementation, and maintenance processes.

Levels of Reusable Software Information

It is important software reuse be viewed as the use of any information that has already been collected to develop other software. This definition includes reuse of available software requirements, specifications, design, source code, modules, operating systems, documentation, analysis data, test information, maintenance information databases, software development plans, and methodologies. The reuse of automated tools for creating software and an integrated software support environment to improve software life cycle processes are also considered part of the reusable information. This software reuse information can be separated into three different levels, some more amendable to reuse than others. Figure 13.1 summarizes these levels of reusable software information.

Reuse of Ideas. In civil engineering, reuse of ideas consists of applying engineering concepts, such as standard design equations for determining the dimensions and materials of a beam. An example of how components are reused is selecting the beam that best meets design criteria from a set of standard beam shapes, cross-sections, and materials. In software engineering, software requirements, specifications, design, development methodologies, and techniques are ideas that can be reused to build a new system.

If the process of transforming a system specification into an executable implementation can be recorded and replayed, then when the requirements and specifications change, the implementation can be generated by reusing the previous development with slight changes. In order to effectively use this approach, the software development process must be systematically automated.* **

---

1. Reuse of ideas (e.g., specification, design, development methodologies, and techniques).

2. Reuse of domain knowledge (e.g., documentation, technical textbooks, plans, personnel, analysis data, test and maintenance information database).

3. Reuse of particular components (e.g., source code, subroutines, modules, operating system, packages, programming languages, tools).

Figure 13.1. Three levels of reusable software information.

Reuse of Domain Knowledge. At present, the reuse of domain knowledge or domain information is not widely recognized. Some identify reuse of domain knowledge with Artificial Intelligence (AI) technologies (e.g., knowledge-based systems). However, domain knowledge residing in a software programmer's head gets reused frequently in every software application that is developed or modified. Reuse of software personnel is a common way of reusing domain knowledge.

Domain knowledge can also be embedded in the architecture of functional collections of a reusable software library, an example is the set of libraries available on the X-Windows System. The subroutines in these libraries are arranged in a distinct hierarchy, covering four levels of programming functionality such as dialogs (the highest level), field editors, intrinsics, X library primitives (the lowest level). Developers of software applications using X-Windows reuse not only the subroutines in the X and X-Ray libraries,

---

* Balzer, R., "Evolution as a New Basis for Reusability" *Proceedings Workshop on Reusability in Programming*, ITT Programming, September, 1983.

** Neighbors, J.M., "The Draco Approach to Constructing Software from Reusable Components", *Proceedings of ITT Workshop on Reusability in Programming*, September, 1983.

they also reuse a systematic technique for building windows which is enforced by the architecture of the libraries.*

The creators of the libraries have succeeded in taking the results from their domain analysis (i.e., the key concepts and methods for developing an effective windowing system) and embedding them in the structure of the libraries so that they encourage the reuse of the results of the analysis.

Application generators can also be viewed as examples of the use of domain knowledge. For well-established domains such as report generation and language parsers, the basics of generating applications in that domain are captured in a tool (i.e., the applications generator), and only the application-specific details need to be supplied to use the tool to generate the software.

Reuse of Particular Components. The use of subroutine libraries and off-the-shelf software is the most common example of reusing existing software components. For software component reuse to be attractive and successful, the overall effort must be less than the effort to create new software. Before a software component is reused, it must be:

1. *Identified, located, and retrieved* — candidate software for reuse must be found among all the reusable components that are archived in the "software database management system (SDMS)." The SDMS must present users with a lucid classification scheme that appeals to their intuition. Each candidate software component must be specified in such a way that the software developer is likely to find it. A complete or a close match is made between component need and a software component available in SDMS. The major contributors are good specifications for identifying an existing software component and an SDMS with a good classification scheme.

2. *Understood* — understanding a software component means knowing what it does, how it does it, and how it can be reused. What is the software component's function? How reliable is its operational behavior, and what are the performance characteristics? What are the environmental requirements and the interface through which the component is modified and incorporated into the software under development?

---

* Coron, H.M., Marden, J., Wong, E., "FULCRUM: A Reusable Code Library Toolset", *Proceedings of Fifth Annual Pacific Northwest Software Quality Conference*, Portland, Oregon, October, 1987.

3.   *Adapted* — when the software component is being reused, it must be able to be tailored or modified. Two typical modifications are:

   a.   Making new entities (types) from old by modifying them — for example, making a binary sort routine from a binary search routine by adding functionality to the search.

   b.   Making new instances of types — for example, instantiating or making specific Ada™ (registered by the U.S. Government, AJPO) generics with parameters that particularize it for the software in which it is included. Changing parameters to make a new entity or new instance is preferable to changing source code. Source code should be tailored from the outside using parameters.

Reusable Software Classification

The effectiveness of software reuse depends on the ability to locate and retrieve an appropriate software component from a large collection of components in a well-designed and well-documented reusable software library. A classification scheme is a domain knowledge structure that organizes collections of items to satisfy the needs of the software developers to be able to reuse an existing component for building a new system.

Classification is the act of grouping like things together. All members of a group or class share at least one characteristic that members of other classes do not possess. Classifications display the relationships between things and between classes of things, and the result is a network or structure of relationships that may be used for many purposes. Classification is a fundamental tool for the organization of knowledge. A library is an example of classification where a collection of reusable information has been organized for easy access and retrieval.

Reusable software can be classified by size, life cycle phase product, the domain of applications in which the software will be reused, or the originating organization. The amount of successful reuse is dependent upon the users' awareness of its existence and the domain of its applicability. Thus, it is important for the reusable software library developer to provide the capability of retrieving various software components in different applications. The developer must not only build wide applicability into the library, but also must communicate this attribute to the users of the library system.

Below are some of the obvious pitfalls that can diminish the economic benefit of software reuse:

1.   Wide applicability is built into the library, but that attribute is not communicated to the user through the library classification system.

2.   A library is designed with wide applicability over a narrow domain of applications, but could have been designed to cover other application areas.

3.   A library is designed with narrow applicability, but could have been designed with wider applicability either over a single application area or over many application areas.

Proper design and classification is imperative. Narrowing the domain of applicability will lead to the proliferation of software modules, with a resulting increase in cost along with unnecessary complication of the reusable software retrieval system.

If a software package is classified as application-specific, the likelihood of its being applied outside that domain is small. For example, software classified in the accounting domain will likely be used only for accounting. As reusable software libraries are established, it is important that software placed into these libraries be designed with as large a domain of applicability as possible.

Software Commonality

The more times a software component is used, the more economic benefit can be gained. The degree of reuse depends on the domain of applicability. The wider the applicability, either across many different applications or within a single application, the greater the possibilities for reuse. Classification systems for application software reuse can be applied across two domains:

1.   Degree of commonality within an application area

2.   Degree of commonality across application areas

An application area is a distinct business or industrial grouping — for example, missiles, aircraft, spacecraft, weapons, ships, lasers, command/control, radar, business accounting, finance, education, payroll, medicine, etc. Software in any of these domains is a good candidate for software reuse. Since the objective is to design software packages that will increase the amount of software reuse, the design process should explore the possibility of expanding the software's domain so that it can be reused across many application areas. Figure 13.2 presents an example of a software package commonality index for a spacecraft system. The higher the index, the greater the predicted domain of applicability. The scale goes from 0 to 6, with 0 yielding the least commonality (i.e., degree of reuse is low) and 6 yielding the most (i.e., degree of reuse is high).

Function	Degree of Commonality	Function	Degree of Commonality
sort	6	telemetric functions	4
data structure	6	computer languages	4
abstract processes	6	software design	4
computer system	6	software development	4
software maintenance	6	software verification	4
math functions	5	mission function	2
geometric functions	5	input routines	2
matrix functions	5	output routines	2
vector functions	5	system functions	0
process functions	5	warhead control	0
communications	5	system inputs	0
guidance functions	4	system outputs	0
navigation functions	4		

Figure 13.2. Software package commonality index.

ADVANTAGES OF SOFTWARE REUSE

The benefits arising from software reuse depend on the complexity and size of the software product and the differences between the old and new applications — the more complex a software system, the higher the anticipated cost to reuse it. Because a significant effort will be required to understand the structure and function of the system, modifications required to reuse a complex system will be more difficult and debugging the modifications will be costly. Systems based on well-designed, well-tested, and well-documented reusable software, in principle, should cost less and contain fewer defects because the software has been successfully tested and used. If a software component is reused frequently, the incremental cost of creating and cataloging it can be amortized over the number of times it is used. Similarly, there is benefit in reusing well-developed specifications, designs, tools, analysis data, and support environments. Efforts to achieve software reusability can be seen as a capital investment, and improved productivity and quality are two of its main returns.

Productivity

Reusing well-designed, well-developed, and well-documented software improves productivity and reduces software development time, costs, and risks. Examples of productivity improvement include:

1. Software reuse "amplifies" programming capabilities, allowing concentration of resources on improving the software product. The programmer has less work to do in developing a piece of software when large portions of the software or design are reused.

2. Software reuse reduces the amount of new documentation and testing required, because the software component that is known to reliable decreases the potential of unforeseen errors.

3. When the system is developed with reusable components, it becomes easier to maintain and modify because the software developers are more familiar with the reusable components from which it is constructed and they can more rapidly understand the complete system design.

4. It often takes less time and effort to use an existing well-designed, well-tested, and well-documented software component than to attempt to rewrite it.

Quality

Improvements in the quality of software developed from well-designed, well-tested, and well-documented reusable software components can be attributed to:

1. Software components that are designed to be reused.

2. Documentation that is developed according to established organization-wide software standards. This results in well-understood software that is likely to be used appropriately.

3. Software components that are well tested and certified for reuse. The more software is reused, the greater the probability that errors will already be found and corrected. It can also reduce future maintenance efforts.

4. Software development based on well-designed, well-tested, and well-documented reusable software offers opportunities for increased system performance when frequently used software components are transported into new systems.

DIFFICULTIES IN SOFTWARE REUSE

Although the concept of reusable software appears attractive from both economic and technical viewpoints, it represents a major deviation from the traditional approach to software development. Effective software reuse may involve substantial up-front investment in order to lay the basis for future gains, and thus it may be initially difficult to implement in an organization. As previously indicated, many technical, organizational, cultural, and legal issues make reusing software difficult. These issues include:

1. The specifications of the software are either nonexistent or sufficiently ambiguous to make it impossible to determine exactly what the software does without understanding all of the source code.

2. The cost of changing the software to perform the specific function is greater than the cost of writing new software.

3. Although the software to perform the specific function may exist, nobody on the project knows about it or those who know of its existence don't know how to find it.

4. Software that can perform the required task is available, but it is so general that it is too inefficient for the task.

5. Lack of organization-wide standardization makes it extremely difficult to share software with confidence.

6. Lack of a standard data interchange format limits both sharing data among applications and systems reusability.

7. Organizational liabilities and data rights are significant issues influencing software reusability. If reused software is not classified

and managed properly, legal concerns regarding data rights and liabilities may strongly affect software life cycle management and development.

A Software Professional Viewpoint

This section addresses both the technical and cultural biases that lead software programmers to resist using someone else's code or design. The technical issues focus on the lack of good reusable software component libraries and the lack of an integrated software engineering environment to support software development efforts throughout the entire software life cycle. The cultural issues focus on the lack of confidence in reusing someone else's code and the doubt that software developed by another person or organization, for another system, can be reused in a new system without any modifications. These issues include:

1. It is easier to write it yourself than to try to locate it, figure out what it does, and find out if it works. If it has to be modified, then it also might be faster to write it from scratch.

2. There are few tools to help find components or to compose a system from the reusable parts.

3. There are few software development methodologies that stress reusing code, let alone reusing a design or a specification.

4. It is more fun to write it yourself.

5. It would imply a sign of weakness not to be able to do it yourself.

6. "It's not my code." This is part of the "Not Invented Here" (NIH) syndrome.

7. There was no consideration by the system analyst who specified the system that portions of an existing system could be salvaged and reused.

8. There is little emphasis and little taught in academia on reusing software.

9. The source code or tool in question is not supported. If a bug is found, no one will take the responsibility of fixing it.

A Software Managerial Viewpoint

Managers often make decisions based on more than just technical issues. Organizational and cultural issues are part of the policy-making process. Many managers have little incentive to reuse existing software because they feel threatened by potential cuts in budgets and resources resulting from the payoffs of software reusability. Reasons for not adopting a reusable software approach include:

1. If no tools or components exist, then it will take time and manpower to create the tools and components and to gain expertise in their use. Such costs are generally not within the budget of a single project.

2. If special tools (e.g., application generators or preprocessors) are used to create a program, then a customer might expect these tools to be delivered along with the product for maintenance purposes.

3. If the tools do exist for making programmers more productive, then this will make the project dependent on fewer personnel. Any reduction in staff might be perceived as reducing the manager's "empire."

4. If a defect appears in a program developed using reused components, who is legally responsible for damages?

5. If there are no standards to control what is entered into the reusable components library, then time and money must be spent setting and maintaining the standards for the library.

A Cognition/Cultural Viewpoint

Computer programming is simply one form of problem solving. Understanding the merits of existing programming paradigms from the perspective of cognitive psychology has provided valuable insight in dealing with complexity. There is a strong need for a proper software development environment to facilitate the reusable software engineering paradigm. Tools and training must be available to deal with system complexity and assist the software developer in finding and understanding what reusable software components exist. A summary of the evidence gathered as it applies to reusable software follows:

1. The data a person can manipulate consciously at one moment in time is limited to five to nine pieces of information. This limit on complexity can be overcome by proper integration or modularization

of components (i.e., by collecting units of information into seman-
tically meaningful pieces or packages). This argument also supports information hiding and object-oriented design.

2. Experienced programmers develop applications through the recur-
    sive mental process of matching pieces of the problem with famil-
    iar solution segments. Therefore, portions of designs are reused
    each time a piece of software is written.

3. Internal conceptualization of the knowledge base in which program/
    design segments reside tends to evolve toward a uniform content for
    all programmers. In other words, experienced programmers tend to
    think alike and express their solutions in similar forms.

4. Programmers cannot reuse something they don't understand. Further-
    more, expert programmers follow certain explicit rules of discourse
    regarding naming conventions and programming style, which enhance
    program readability and comprehension. This implies that for some-
    thing to be reused, it has to be designed, developed, and documented
    according to an accepted set of software development standards.

FEASIBILITY OF SOFTWARE REUSE

During the last several years, interest in making software reusable has
increased, but due to a number of factors, only limited success has been
achieved. Managerial and cultural problems are the major stumbling
blocks. On the technical side, part of the issue centers around the large
differences between "code reusability in the small" and "code reusability
in the large," including programming practices, location of reusable
components, standard design, and the strong protection of proprietary
software.

Even if the reuse of a software component is desirable, it may not be
feasible. In considering the feasibility of software reuse, both technical and
organizational aspects should be examined; management incentives must be
provided, problem areas defined, sufficient personnel supported, and the
viability of reuse among differing versions of the same system considered.

Reuse of a component in successive versions of an evolving program
appears to be a more important source of increased productivity than reuse
of code in different applications. Components are rarely portable between
applications and even if they are, the incremental benefit of using a component in two applications is only a factor of two. But the number of

versions of a system over its lifetime can number in the hundreds or thousands.*

It is important to recognize the basis for concern about the viability of component (source code) reuse across applications. Across applications in this context means applications that are at least somewhat dissimilar, as opposed to derivative versions of an application, such as a specific version of an accounting system tailored to a particular customer.

It is generally agreed that application generators are capable of developing custom-tailored programs within a well-defined application area, such as business accounting systems. The problem with component reuse arises as the application areas become complex and ill-defined, and as organizational boundaries are crossed. Complexity makes it difficult to specify exactly what is needed from each component with sufficient precision to ensure that a reused component is, in fact, what was needed. Crossing organizational boundaries makes the "reuse" of project personnel who are familiar with the software components, and their roles and limitations, important.

Source code reuse is much more difficult than the reuse of high-level software (i.e., requirements, specifications and high-level design). Source code is usually closely related to hardware and operating system characteristics, which makes it, consequently, much more difficult to describe and reuse.

> Previous implementations will not be the basis for reusability. They will not be gathered into libraries to be reused. All such attempts (with the exception of mathematical subroutine libraries) have failed and continue to fail because even with our most sophisticated forms of parameterization, the implementations are far too instantiated to mesh with the potential uses. We have no technology to characterize the set of "small" changes to functionality and/or environment that arise in these potential uses.

A survey of reusability identifies instances of feasible software reuse:

1. Most of the successful instances of software reuse in industry involved similar, well-defined application problems that used the same operating system and hardware. Some identified projects were

---

* Wegner, P., "Varieties of Reusability", *Proceedings of ITT Workshop on Reusability in Programming*, September, 1983.

able to reuse entities even though the applications were substantially different. In most situations, the functions or program units tended to be too closely linked to the specific application to be reusable across different applications.

2. Most instances of reusability were achieved on the specification level (by matching interfaces) and on design level (by expressing the design in a sufficiently abstract design language).

3. It was easier to achieve reuse at the application level than within the operating system. Application reuse was amplified considerably by common operating system and common hardware.

4. In many cases, reusability across projects was achieved because all or some of the key people worked on both projects.

The observations made above are summarized in Figure 13.3.

---

1. Software reuse across organizational boundaries should be confined to a well-defined problem area.

2. Software reuse among different versions of the same system is more viable than reuse among different application areas.

3. The wider the application area, the higher the level of reuse (e.g., reuse across organizational boundaries should probably be higher than the code level).

4. An integrated development environment must be common among those who reuse the same components.

5. Reusability across project boundaries is often only possible when some or all of the key people have worked on both projects.

Figure 13.3. Feasibility of software reuse.

Factors that affect software reusability include:

1. *Size and complexity of the software component* — as the size and complexity of the software component increase, the feasibility of reusability decreases. Small, simple software components are usually easier to design, test, and maintain than large, complex components.

2. *The life cycle phase that the component represents* — as the life cycle phase of the component approaches implementation, the feasibility of reuse usually decreases. It is likely easier to reuse a requirements document than to reuse source code. Source code has more elements associated with it (e.g., operating system, utilities, parameter, interfaces, standards routines) than just the high-level abstractions used in a requirements document.

3. *Domain of application* — the domain of applications in which the software is to be reused determines how well-defined and how flexible the software component must be. If the software component is used within a narrow domain of applications, where terminology and assumptions are well understood, the definition of the software component need not be exceptionally rigorous. However, when the domain of applications is broad, the software component must be very rigorously defined, since the terminology and assumptions will be more varied and less well known.

4. *Organizational boundaries* — the number of "organizational layers" that separate the person who reuses a software component from the person who initially developed the component can affect software reuse. Example of this boundary include "within the same division in an organization," "between sections of the same organization," or "between different organizations." In general, the more organizational layers between the software component creator and the reuser, the greater the difficulty in reusing that software.

Circumstances under which software has been successfully reused include:

1. *Small software project* — most of the software developed in an organization is written by individuals or small teams of software programmers associated with a single project. Software is reused for the following reasons:
   a. It was written by a person who is reusing it.
   b. It was written by another person in the project.
   c. An application is being developed where a previous version or a similar program is available.
   d. The software is for a function that:

  – is well understood;
  – has only a few data types;
  – relies on a stable underlying technology; and
  – has standards within the problem domain (scientific subroutines are examples of this type of software).

2. *Software factory approach* — the Japanese have taken a different approach to programming. They view software development as software production and cite programming productivity increases because:

  a. They have established a critical mass in the number of reusable components and programmers available to use and develop them.

  b. They have taken the separate phases of the software development process and assigned them to different organizations within the software factory.

  c. They have developed an integrated set of tools and standards to support reuse in the software development life cycle. Because of the large number of software programmers using the tools, the initial development cost of the tools can be economically justified.

  d. Software reuse is part of their training process. One software factory gives programming exercises each month to all its software programmers. These exercises require referencing the reusable software components library in order to complete an exercise with a minimum of effort.

3. *Reusable software components library* — a well-designed reusable software components library can substantially improve software productivity and quality by increasing the efficient reuse of error-free code for both new and modified software systems. However, there are difficulties inherent in selecting and effectively integrating reusable software into new or existing software systems. Many critical issues must be addressed in developing large libraries of reusable software components, such as configuration and change control, quality assurance, cataloging, documentation, data rights and liability.

THE ROLE OF PROTOTYPING IN SOFTWARE REUSE

Prototyping is an iterative process for developing and refining software requirements and specifications. It is the building of trial, immature versions of software systems that can be used as the basis for assessment of ideas and decisions in preparation of a complete and deliverable product. Prototyping offers a number of attractive advantages, such as the early resolution of high-risk issues and the flexibility to adapt to changing environmental characteristics or perceptions of users' needs. Two major approaches to prototyping are referred to as specification-driven and components-driven.

In specification-driven approaches, prototypes serve to make requirements and design notions visible to system users and software developers. The major objective is to improve and refine the users' requirements and specifications. Evolving a prototype to an operational system is a secondary objective, but must not be mandated unless mature software component repositories exist. The prototype is often thrown away after the feasibility assessment is complete.

At the other end of the spectrum, the components-driven prototype is expected to be an experimental model of the full-scale development system. The prototype is assembled with as many existing components from a library and off-the-shelf packages as possible. The objective is to determine what modifications to the collection of components are needed in order to make the production system acceptable to the users.

In practice, any software prototype development effort is between these two extremes. Prototypes have multiple objectives in terms of reusability. Rapid prototyping should be used if a significant amount of the new software can be derived from the reuse of existing software components. It can validate the current functional requirements and examine the system to see where payoffs can be realized through optimization of high-frequency paths. Furthermore, there may be several iterations of prototypes to address feasibility of the sought-after system, to assess the attributes of components from libraries, to analyze the interaction of reusable components, to specify off-the-shelf software packages, and to determine the shortfall of requirements to meet the users' needs.

An example of prototyping, describing the prototyping practice of one Chicago bank, provides a good illustration of a throwaway prototype:

End users spent an average of 250 hours developing each throw away prototype (primarily requirements definition) for a group of six large applications. They then invested an average of 45 hours more per prototype on working with system developers to add other procedures. The system development group itself expended between 75 and 225 hours reusing what had already been done in the prototype. Thus, the bank supported efforts that were between 30% and 90% redundant.*

Employing evolutionary prototyping for software development, coupled with proper planning, tools, Very High Level Languages (VHLLs), discipline, methodology, and user interfaces, can substantially improve software productivity and quality.

REUSABILITY AND SOFTWARE ACQUISITION

The primary objective of software acquisition is to identity commonality among available software components and to be able to use these components to develop timely, cost-effective, reliable new software systems. The introduction of well-designed, well-developed, and well-documented reusable software into the software acquisition and development life cycle will change the current views and practices of the acquisition and procurement processes. Software management and software developers can take advantage of existing components and then concentrate on the unique requirements for developing new software systems. This should result in better systems and shorten the software development cycle.

Incentives are required in order to successfully acquire and adapt existing software. If the benefits of reuse are to be realized, a "sustaining" software development environment must be created that promotes the concept of reuse and encourages the use of available components. Explicit policy support of and references to software reuse in a Request For Proposal (RFP) and a Software Contract are necessary to address potential long-term reuse benefits. The RFP should require developers to identify the reusable software appropriate for the target system within acceptable development cost, schedule, and risk levels.

Major issues influencing current software acquisition and procurement practices include:

1.   The RFP and Software Contract must be structured so that software reusability is explicitly addressed and encouraged.

---

* Guimaraes, T., "Prototyping: Orchestrating for Success", *Datamation*, December, 1987.

2. Software developers must show how development costs and risks will be minimized by the selection of reusable software in developing new systems in an RFP.

3. Contract review and monitoring of reusability activities must be provided. Status review of software reuse must be addressed throughout the entire software development life cycle.

4. Data rights and liability issues must be addressed and managed properly between users and software developers.

5. Software developers should be encouraged and rewarded when they meet software reuse goals and objectives.

SOFTWARE PORTABILITY

Software portability refers to the ease with which a piece of software can be transported to and reused in a different environment without any modification. Software adaptability is defined by the ease with which a component's properties can be modified.

A software component is portable if the effort required to transport it is much less than the effort required in its initial implementation, and if it retains its initial qualities after the transport. Software users are increasingly demanding that specific software be portable because software has become more and more expensive in comparison with hardware costs. It should also be noted that the increasing complexity of software systems has more often required that they be written in Very High Level Languages (VHLLs), which has contributed greatly to software portability.

Obviously, software portability increases flexibility and reusability. Portability considers environmental factors such as hardware, operating system, programming languages, interface with other software components, etc. It is very expensive, in time and resources, to recreate software for every new machine. It is important to know how to design and build a piece of software so that it can be transported to other environments in order to facilitate reuse.

The advantages of designing and building portable software include:

1. As software developers build and sell portable software, they can appeal to a much wider market. Instead of building new software

for each possible computer environment, it is in the developer's own interest to reduce the effort needed to change from one environment to another. The overall cost of developing portable software, and then transporting and reusing it, is less than the cost of rewriting the same software several times.

2. Since software is becoming more expensive than hardware, its life cycle must be made longer; that is, it must be designed and developed to survive hardware changes.

3. Anticipating that a piece of software will be portable is likely to have beneficial effects on its programming. The coding will have to be cleaner, more systematic, more disciplined, and more readable. Hence, the reliability, reusability, maintainability, and overall quality of the software will be improved.

SUMMARY

Software reusability can provide substantial economic benefits. Initial reusability efforts should emphasize understanding the concept of software reuse and encouraging the use of existing well-developed software specifications, designs, methods, techniques, tools, and other information. Reusing well-designed, well-developed, well-documented software can significantly enhance the ability to develop timely, cost-effective, reliable software systems.

Reusability is attractive from both technical and economical standpoints. However, it may be initially difficult to implement in an organization without resolving certain technical, organizational, legal, and cultural issues. Management must recognize the increasingly critical and pervasive role of software, its characteristics, and the software information management problems that must be addressed. These major issues include:

1. Current views and practices of the software acquisition and procurement processes must be changed so that software reuse is explicitly addressed and encouraged.

2. Incentives must be provided to encourage reuse of existing software.

3. Organizational liabilities and data rights issues significantly influence the concept of software reuse. If not classified and managed

properly, legal concerns regarding data rights and liabilities may affect software life cycle development and management.

4. Most software programmers and managers tend to view software reusability simply from the perspective of source code, whereas reuse of other programming artifacts (e.g., requirements, specifications, designs, plans, tests, and methodologies) leads to more productivity. Other reusability paradigms (e.g., application generators, translation systems, Very High Level Languages (VHLLs), automated tools, and automation-based software support environment) have proven successful.

5. Meaningful, properly designed, tested, and verified standard guidelines and classified reusable software components need to be developed before they can be reused.

6. Tools and training must be available to deal with system complexity and assist software programmers in finding and understanding what software components are available from a reusable software components library.

7. The feasibility of software reuse has been demonstrated by the Japanese software factories, partly because of the concentration of software programmers (critical mass) that maximizes their return on tool investment.

8. Many software applications are common and generic and thus are a logical target for standard functions and reusable modules.

9. Software can be transportable only if standardization and reusability are goals and objectives in the original design.

10. Criteria for accepting and retaining a software entity for a reusable software components library (e.g., frequency of reuse and degree of reusability) must be established.

11. Characteristics that promote reuse of software (e.g., generality, portability, modularity, independence, maintainability, self-descriptiveness, and verifiability) should be the basis for developing standards, techniques, and measurements.

Effective software reuse requires a substantial investment up front in order to establish the basis for future gains. While there is no magic solution to the problem of achieving the goals of software reuse, this chapter provides some general management guidance. Managerial problems should be considered with technical concerns when an organization attempts to reuse existing software. No matter how good the software development methodology, managerial issues will often determine the effectiveness and viability of a particular approach. Therefore, software management and software professionals must recognize the substantial economic benefits of software reuse, and properly address and resolve the issues in order to make widespread reuse of software a reality.

14

Special Quality Assurance Group Tasks

QA groups are frequently asked by data processing management to undertake special assignments, covering all aspects of data processing. Examples are developing standards, evaluating software and hardware, and performing special cost/benefit analyses for the data processing manager.

Rarely will postponing a QA review impact on meeting schedules for implementing application systems. The quality of systems might be affected, but rarely the schedule. This permits the data processing manager to pull QA groups from their normal work to handle special assignments.

Quality assurance groups should welcome special assignments. They do not substantially affect the members' performance of their regular reviews and the experience gained in the special assignments may well assist the individual in the performance of later (QA) application review.

The different types of assignments should be considered and prioritized by QA groups so that if and when assignments occur, the group has developed a position. Some assignments are very supportive of QA functions while others may best be done by other groups or other people in data processing.

QA groups have the obligation to inform the data processing manager of the consequences of undertaking a special assignment. If in their opinion a special assignment will adversely affect the review function of the group, this should be brought to the attention of the data processing manager.

Undertaking special assignments makes maximum use of quality assurance experience. In conducting reviews, personnel have the opportunity to see many systems. They are able to discuss a variety of approaches with various members of the data processing department. They are involved in the newer technology, as it is normally first used by systems under development. QA personnel have the time and opportunity to study problems and look for solutions. They approach evaluation from a management viewpoint. When special assignments occur, this background, experience, and approach are what data processing management wants in the individual conducting the special task.

Because they do not have any application systems line responsibility, QA personnel can approach a special assignment from an independent viewpoint. They are not biased by special needs that will make "their" application more efficient. QA group members are charged with maintaining and improving quality on all application systems. This perspective makes them ideal candidates for special assignments.

Many special assignments are a result of a departmental problem, a user request, or an inquiry by a member of executive management of the organization. Answering these needs and requests permits QA personnel to delve into problems and potential solutions to those problems. This type of experience can prove very beneficial when they are evaluating the goals, methods, and performance of application system implementation.

Executing special assignments is a vehicle for training QA personnel. This adds a new dimension and a new challenge for a group member. Having to conduct these assignments will broaden one's background and experience. Many times the assignments will involve new technology and will help prepare the QA person to review applications that use that technology at a later time.

In most cases the QA group is performing the review function that a data processing manager would do in a smaller organization. The administrative challenge of a larger department does not permit the data processing manager to do quality assurance type assignments. From this perspective, special assignments are an extension of the QA function. Those tasks that the data processing manager does not have time to undertake are logical tasks for quality assurance personnel.

There are some strong reasons why QA personnel should reject some assignments. These should be weighed heavily because the primary responsibility of quality assurance is to assure quality on installed application systems. The major disadvantage for a QA group to undertake a special assignment is that it dilutes their primary tasks. If a review effort is reduced, delayed, or consolidated due to special assignments, the effectiveness of the group may suffer. Project leaders will begin to view QA as a group organized to do special assignments for the DP manager. When this happens, the function will be viewed as less important in the eyes of the project personnel.

Conducting many special tasks can also cause groups to lose objectivity in conducting reviews. Many special assignments involve the setting of standards and procedures to be followed by project personnel. Because QA has established those procedures, they may not be able to view them from an independent viewpoint when conducting a review. For example, when project personnel argue that a procedure or standard is unrealistic because of unique circumstances of that application, the person who developed that procedure or standard may be blinded by his or her own logic in developing it.

Some special assignments can lead to conflict with project personnel. The type of assignment that can lead to conflict is one in which the QA is making judgments about the performance and competency of project personnel. When quality assurance takes on the role of a supervisor, it no longer is a peer group review and a cooperative attitude on the part of project personnel will probably be lost.

The advantages and disadvantages discussed for the tasks may not apply to any given assignment involving that task. The group must examine the types of assignments that may be offered to quality assurance. During this examination, each of the above advantages and disadvantages must be put into the perspective of their own data processing department. If the group is given an option of whether or not to accept an assignment, they will have a position because of having previously analyzed the advantages and disadvantages of that assignment. This will enable them to present a very logical reason to the data processing manager as to why they want to accept or reject that assignment.

TYPICAL QUALITY ASSURANCE SPECIAL TASKS

The number and broad range of tasks quality assurance groups are asked to do indicates that there are gaps in many data processing organizations. There appears to be a need for a group in data processing to conduct special studies and no such group exists, so the assignments go to QA.

When the assignments given to a QA group begin to occupy a significant amount of resources — more than 20 percent of available time, for example — the group should rethink those assignments. When special tasks become an integral part of the QA function, management might consider revising the charter of the group and adding personnel to undertake those tasks. Many assignments are recurring; for example, developing systems and programming standards. The group should be adequately staffed to perform those recurring functions.

Developing Control Standards

The single most beneficial step that most data processing departments could undertake is formalizing control standards. Many of the problems occurring in data processing occur because technology has outpaced the ability to control applications. Data processing departments work on technology years in advance of its use, but they only worry about control after problems have occurred. Development of control standards may be one of the most fruitful areas for quality assurance involvement.

Controls can be subdivided into those that prevent problems, those that detect problems, and those that provide information to correct problems once they occur. Controls are further organized by system functions such as recording, authorizing, transmitting, processing, storage, and output. Control standards include both the type of control the organization believes necessary for an application system and the process to select the controls. Many organizations include in their control standards a list of actual controls to select from.

Most controls used by organizations are there due more to happenstance than to planning. Many project leaders select controls based on their own personal experience rather than on training. For example, one of the major problems in data processing is control of the accounting period cutoff. This involves synchronizing manual and computerized operations. In many organizations, they use a different control mechanism. Quality assurance personnel having experience in reviewing and working with many applications are in the best position in data processing to develop a control standard for a procedure such as the accounting period cutoff procedure.

Hardware Selection Analysis

Hardware analysis involves comparing hardware alternatives in order to obtain the best piece of equipment for the job and may range from selecting major pieces of equipment to minor upgrading or downgrading of existing hardware. The assignment usually involves working with representatives of hardware vendors.

Quality assurance groups can maintain manuals that provide comparison between various hardware units. Even when quality assurance does not do the actual selection, they can provide material to the group doing it and then review the selection process.

Because quality assurance personnel are continually reviewing new applications, they are in a good position to make an assessment of future hardware needs. Quality assurance should be involved in the hardware selection process, either doing the selecting or reviewing the selection process.

Software Selection Analysis

Software selection analysis involves determining which piece of software optimizes both the hardware and the application systems. Software analysis can occur for both new and existing software packages. Frequently features of existing software are not properly utilized. Packages and/or features must be analyzed using a knowledge of the hardware, the software package, and the application system. Few people have a knowledge of all three.

Selecting and generating software systems is a highly technical function. In most organizations, the individuals performing that function have only a minimal appreciation of the goals and objectives of application systems. This is because their specialty does not permit the time to work on applications from a user viewpoint. Therefore, they tend to optimize hardware and software without regard for the needs of the application system. Quality assurance personnel involved in this process bring to the selection process a wide background in application systems.

Involving quality assurance personnel in software selection benefits systems programmers as well since they gain an appreciation of the needs of both current and future application systems. This will put software in a better perspective for them. Quality assurance personnel become more familiar with the capabilities of software, and are then better able to advise application systems and programmers on the capabilities and shortcomings of software systems.

Develop Systems and Programming Practices

Systems and programming practices are the methods by which application systems are implemented. Systems practices include the process for developing systems, documentation procedures, organization of project teams, data documentation, and progress reporting procedures. Programming practices include program documentation, programming conventions, testing procedures, program change procedures, and status reports.

The major responsibility of QA is to review compliance with systems and programming practices. In this review, weaknesses in the practices are readily discernible. Areas where systems and programming practices should be strengthened become apparent. Quality assurance people are in an ideal position to develop and/or improve systems and programming practices because they have seen them used over many applications.

Training MIS Personnel in Control, System, and Programming Practices

New personnel and changing technology make it essential to train data processing personnel continually. Vendors provide training in their hardware and software packages. However, organizations must train their personnel in their own systems and control practices. It is not enough to develop standards and procedures; these must be taught to the people who will use them during systems implementation.

Quality assurance experience in review of application systems puts them in an ideal position to conduct these training sessions. From the reviews, they become aware of the problems systems and programming personnel are having in using the organization's control and systems practices. This enables them to emphasize the areas that are causing trouble. Also, by having reviewed many diverse applications, QA personnel have the experience necessary to answer questions in terms of applications familiar to the students.

By teaching, QA personnel learn themselves. In order to teach control and systems practices, personnel must have a thorough understanding of those practices. This teaching experience also makes them better reviewers because the classroom teaching experience has shown them the students' areas of concern and areas where misunderstandings are most likely to occur.

Providing Systems Consultant Services

In today's complex technology, it is unrealistic to expect a project team to possess all the knowledge and disciplines necessary to adequately implement a computer application. A successful project team requires the combined experiences of many data processing specialists. In addition to technological problems, the project team may need advice in organizational policies and procedures, general business advice, government or industry regulations, plus other business disciplines.

In forming a QA group, data processing management should try to draw from diverse backgrounds. For example, the group may include software specialists, hardware specialists, telecommunication specialists, programming specialists, etc. When a project team member has need for expertise in one of these areas, it is logical to call upon quality assurance to help them with a particular difficult system problem.

QA personnel keep their skills up-to-date by working with project personnel on real-life problems. There is value in reading manuals and attending sessions in an area of skill, but the real value comes in applying those skills to an application problem. It is also to the advantage of the data processing department to make as many uses of specialized skills as possible.

Resolving the Technical Problems of Application Systems

Many application systems run into technical problems during the implementation phases of an application system. The project personnel decide on an approach, may or may not discuss it with consultants, and then begin implementing that approach. When they begin to move from the general specifications to the specific implementation, problems arise. In the latter stages of implementation, this may be a hang-up on the computer. In earlier stages, they can reach a point where they cannot work out the details for a general solution.

Technical problems can occur because of the lack of planning or because people are too close to the problem to see an obvious solution. Other times people cause their own problem. For example, a programmer may misuse a program language instruction but be convinced the misinterpretation is correct. The use of an outside party to make an assessment may save project personnel considerable time.

QA personnel are in an ideal position to make this independent assessment. Working with multiple systems, they may have seen the same technical problem previously, and either have solved the problem or been aware of the solution to the problem. The experience gained in working out technical problems can be used by them in solving similar problems when they occur in other systems.

Bridging the Gap Between Systems and Operations Personnel

One of the major problems which has plagued data processing from its inception is the language barrier. One group develops one set of jargon and another group adopts another set. When they begin discussing a problem, not only do the different perspectives cause problems, but so does terminology. For example, application systems personnel tend to use the jargon of their application and user, while operations personnel will use the jargon of the hardware and software vendors.

Without a full appreciation of the other group's needs and problems, operations and systems groups can develop procedures which are not mutually supportive. For example, operations personnel can select operating systems options which make systems work more difficult. On the other hand, systems personnel can build systems which are ineffective to operate. Neither group may be aware of the impact of their work on the other.

Quality assurance groups working with both systems personnel and operations personnel can gain a good understanding of the concerns and problems of each group. Using quality assurance personnel as mediators to resolve differences of opinions between the two groups is a valuable service. Because of its independent position in data processing, QA's opinions and recommendations will not be taken to be self-serving in most situations.

Developing More Effective MIS Methods

Data processing management continually looks for new and better ways of performing that data processing function. These methods can be better ways to develop systems, more effective programming techniques, better use of hardware and software, or better training and use of personnel. Because data processing is a production environment, it is frequently difficult for project personnel and data processing management to step back and objectively view the department, its policies and procedures.

Quality assurance is in the unique position of independently reviewing the implementation of application systems. During these reviews, they observe the good and bad points of different implementation methods. After several reviews, they begin to determine which methods are the most efficient and which are the least efficient. They also begin to get an appreciation between methods and the caliber of people using those methods.

Charging QA with the responsibility for developing more effective MIS methods is a logical assignment for the group. As an ongoing special assignment, they can transfer the knowledge gained from the better implemented systems to the less skilled systems and programming personnel. This special assignment is highly recommended as one which quality assurance should seek, and one which should be assigned to them by data processing management.

Reviewing Data Center Operations

Data center operations include input preparation, job scheduling, computer operations, data storage, security, and output distribution. If telecommunications are used, data processing has a responsibility for the outlying terminals. The operations responsibility includes making sure that the right program is run at the right time using the right data.

QA can review the data center operations for compliance to procedures, as well as effectiveness, efficiency, and economy of operations. The review can be concentrated in one area (for example, the data library), or it can be broad in nature and cover all facets of the data center.

A review of data center operations is also beneficial to QA in its application systems review process. Having a better appreciation of the problems and procedures in the data center equips QA better to assess implementation plans on new applications. This provides sufficient background information to make an adequate evaluation as to whether or not the planned implementation of an application system will cause operating difficulties.

Evaluation of Operational Application Systems

After the system has become operational, it is advisable to compare the actual systems results against the planned systems results. For example, if the system specifications called for responding to a user terminal request within three seconds, it should be determined whether or not the system in production meets that three-second response as specified.

QA personnel have the application background needed to conduct such a review. This is because they have worked throughout the systems development life cycle. They have built up an extensive background about the project and know its strengths and weaknesses. By having quality assurance personnel make an evaluation of an operational system, they can provide data processing management with a judgment based on full knowledge of the application, and do it more efficiently than probably any other group could.

Few QA groups perform evaluations of application systems once they are operational. This function is normally done by internal auditors. Evaluation of operational systems normally is done for executive management and user departments. This would put quality assurance in the position of evaluating data processing for outside departments. While quality assurance may be in a good position to do it, it tends to undermine their relationships with data processing personnel.

Advantages and Disadvantages of Special Assignments

The unique situations and needs of each organization make accepting or rejecting special assignments by QA a very personal decision. The actual decision may be based on factors unique to that organization such as utilizing one individual's extensive personal experience. There are some general guidelines a QA group can use in evaluating special assignments and these are illustrated in Figure 14.1, the Special Assignment/Advantages-Disadvantages Matrix.

The matrix lists the advantages and disadvantages of special assignments. Checkmarks in the rows beside each special assignment indicate which advantages and disadvantages are appropriate for that special assignment. Organizations may wish to change some of these based on unique situations.

The two columns on the right-hand side of the matrix state whether or not the quality assurance group should undertake that special assignment. The four assignments not recommended are:

1. *Hardware selection analysis.* While this is a good training assignment, it does take a lot of time. Also, it may require more specialized knowledge than possessed by quality assurance personnel. This assignment may be done by QA in smaller organizations because no one else is better qualified.

2. *Software selection analysis.* Again, while this is a good training assignment, it does take a lot of time. Also, it may require more specialized knowledge than possessed by quality assurance personnel. This assignment may be done by QA in smaller organizations because no one else is better qualified. If the QA group is included, software selection is more appropriate than hardware selection.

3. *Reviewing data center operations.* When done by QA, as opposed to auditing, this tends to become more of a performance review and as such can cause personality conflicts.

4. *Evaluation of operational application systems.* This assignment is best done by auditing because it is more of a performance review than a compliance review unless system performance has been specified in detail. Most organizations leave this assignment for auditing. A major reason is that reports should go outside data processing to the user and executive management.

The other assignments are supportive of quality assurance and should be done by them unless it interferes too much with their regular reviews.

Special Assignment	Special Assignments Has These									Quality Assurance Should Perform This Special Assignment	
	Advantages to QA							Disadvantages to QA			
	Maximizes Experience	Independent Viewpoint	Implementation Schedule Not Affected	Increases QA Awareness of Needs	QA Training Vehicle	Helps DP Manager	Dilution of QA Effort	Loss of Objectivity	Causes Conflict With Project personnel	Yes	No
Developing control standards	✓	✓	✓	✓	✓	✓	✓			✓	
Hardware selection analysis	✓		✓	✓	✓	✓	✓				✓
Software selection analysis	✓		✓		✓		✓				✓
Develop system and programming practices	✓	✓	✓	✓	✓	✓	✓			✓	
Training MIS personnel in control and systems programming practices	✓		✓		✓					✓	
Providing systems consultant services	✓		✓	✓	✓					✓	

Figure 14.1. Special assignment/advantages-disadvantages matrix.

Special Assignment	Maximizes Experience	Independent Viewpoint	Implementation Schedule Not Affected	Increases QA Awareness of Needs	QA Training Vehicle	Helps DP Manager	Dilution of QA Effort	Loss of Objectivity	Causes Conflict With Project personnel	Quality Assurance Should Perform This Special Assignment — Yes	No
Resolving the technical problems of application systems	✓	✓	✓	✓	✓					✓	
Bridging the gap between systems and operational personnel	✓	✓	✓	✓	✓					✓	
Developing more effective MIS methods	✓		✓		✓		✓			✓	
Reviewing data center operations	✓		✓	✓	✓	✓		?			✓
Evaluation of operational application systems	✓		✓	✓	✓			✓			✓

Figure 14.1. Special assignment/advantages-disadvantages matrix. (cont'd)

EVALUATING THE MERITS OF SPECIAL TASKS

Each special assignment should be evaluated on its own merits. Given the choice, QA needs a method of determining whether or not to undertake a special assignment. There will be some special assignments that most QA groups would like to do, and others that would be preferable not to perform. However, rather than making the choice on personal preference, some logic should be applied to the decision.

Listed below are questions that QA should be asking about each of the special assignments. An honest and fair evaluation of the special assignment based on these questions will determine the merits of doing or not doing the special assignment. The questions are:

1. Is there a choice about doing the special assignment? If not, do it.

2. If QA performs the special assignment, will it have an effect on the regularly scheduled reviews? If the answer is yes, then a judgment must be made as to which is the most important for the department and the organization.

3. Will performing the special assignment help the QA in either reviews or in developing QA procedures? If the answer is yes and the assignment will not adversely affect review schedules, the assignment probably should be undertaken.

4. Will the special assignment provide some needed training for one or more of the people in QA? If the answer is yes and the special assignment will not adversely affect the review schedules, the assignment probably should be performed.

5. Will conducting the special assignment cause QA personnel to lose objectivity in future reviews? This question implies that the assignment would bias the quality assurance reviewer's opinion on a future review. For example, an in-depth study of a special piece of hardware might convince a person that all systems should use that piece of hardware. If conducting a review on a system where the project team selected an alternative piece of hardware, it may be difficult for that reviewer to accept the project team's judgment as the best choice.

SUMMARY

The quality assurance group is in a unique position to receive special assignments from the data processing manager. Their experience is broad, they become involved in most of the new applications in the data processing department, and they are frequently the more senior people in the data processing department. In addition, they are not tied to a strict production schedule, where a week or two on a special assignment would adversely affect that schedule.

This chapter was designed to alert QA to the types of assignments being given their counterparts in other organizations. Quality assurance groups should do some planning as to which types of assignments are valuable and which are not prior to being asked about special assignments. Making assessments as to the worth of conducting each of these types of assignments puts quality assurance in a very strong position to try to obtain assignments which would be helpful to the group, and to avoid assignments which would dilute their primary responsibility.

15

Quality Assurance and the Personal Computer

INTRODUCTION

Designers and users of large electronic data processing (MIS) systems have long been aware of the need to provide security and privacy for these systems. However, the number of such people who must worry about these matters has been relatively limited in the past. This situation has changed dramatically with the rapid introduction of personal computers (PCs) into the workplace. Now, literally millions of people are (or soon will be) using personal computers for either business or personal needs.

Along with the obvious benefits available through the use of personal computers, there are some significant dangers that are now being recognized. As more people begin to use PCs, it becomes vital that these dangers and the need for protection be understood. Both equipment and data must be protected, and the protection needs of each are different.

This chapter is intended to provide both managers and users of personal computers with an understanding of the information security threats involved in using such systems, and it describes approaches to reducing the associated risks.

BASIC SECURITY CONCERNS

Before discussing specific security considerations for personal computers, it will be useful to define the basic information security problem we are attempting to solve.

Information Security Objectives

Regardless of the size or nature of an MIS system or application, the following major *security objectives* must be met:

- *Confidentiality* of personal, proprietary, or otherwise sensitive data handled by the system

- *Integrity* and accuracy of data and the processes that handle the data

- *Availability* of systems and the data or services they support

If these objectives are met, then other assets that are involved with or dependent upon the information being protected will also be protected. For example, meeting these goals will, in general, ensure that the physical equipment itself is protected from unauthorized access or damage.

Threats

A wide range of accidental or intentional events can threaten information resources. These threats include:

- Environmental hazards

- Hardware and equipment failure

- Software failure

- Errors and omissions

- Disgruntled or dishonest personnel

The potential manifestations of each type of threat are endless and depend upon the specific characteristics of the system, data, and operational environment.

THE NATURE OF THE PC SECURITY PROBLEM

The preceding discussion of information security objectives and threats applies, in general, to systems of any size. Personal computers and other small systems, however, have unique security problems that must be understood if rational and effective security measures are to be implemented. The following is a general discussion of the nature of the security problem as it relates to personal computers.

Although personal computers provide essentially the same services as large systems (i.e., they permit the rapid manipulation and examination of large amounts of text and data), there are some characteristics that present special security problems. In general, the differences are in:

- Physical accessibility
- Built-in security mechanisms
- Nature of data being handled
- Users

Each is discussed below.

Physical Accessibility

Basic physical protection of a computer system is required to ensure operational reliability and basic integrity of hardware and software. Other security mechanisms (e.g., those implemented in systems hardware and software) rely on this underlying level of protection.

A large-scale, multi-user computer system represents a sizable investment and is usually provided with considerable physical and environmental protection. The exposure of the system to damage or unauthorized access can, therefore, be limited, and the cost of such protection is a relatively small proportion of the overall investment.

With personal computers, however, physical accessibility is not as easily controlled — indeed, accessibility is inherent in the concept of "personal." It is seldom feasible to build a protective "shell" around an individual personal computer, which means that protection against damage, hardware modification, or unauthorized access is difficult. Since many technical security mechanisms (e.g., access control software and cryptographic routines) are often dependent on the integrity of the underlying hardware and software, these security mechanisms may no longer provide the intended degree of protection.

Built-in Security Mechanisms

A second security problem with most personal computers is the lack of built-in hardware mechanisms needed to isolate users from sensitive, security-related system functions. For example, the typical personal computer does not support the following important security mechanisms that have long been available on larger systems:

- *Multiple processor states* — enabling separate "domains" for users and system processes.

- *Privileged instructions* — limiting access to certain functions (e.g., reading and writing to disk) to trusted system processes.

- *Memory protection features* — preventing unauthorized access to sensitive parts of the system.

Without such hardware features it is virtually impossible to prevent user programs from accessing or modifying parts of the operating system and thereby circumventing any intended security mechanisms.

Nature of Data Being Handled

The information processed and stored on personal computer systems often can be more sensitive and accessible than that found on larger, multi-user systems. This is due primarily to the fact that the information on a given machine is often associated with one person or a well-defined group. This information is likely to be in the form of memoranda, reports, spreadsheets, or simple lists which are readily accessible using software tools familiar to all personal computer users. Finally, such data will tend to be in relatively "final" form rather than being a mass of unanalyzed or unprocessed raw data. All of this may make the job of searching for specific information much easier than on a large system with thousands of users and data files.

The personal computer has been called the electronic equivalent of the desk or file cabinet. This is a useful analogy, since users of personal computers should have an inherent understanding of the nature and need to protect items in their desks.

Users' Responsibilities

In the past, many of the operational and security-related tasks associated with the use of computer systems were performed by relatively small and well-trained groups of systems and support personnel. This enabled economies of scale, standardization, and general consistency in the execution of such tasks. One of the perceived benefits of personal computers is the reduction of users' dependence on (and, perhaps, frustrations with) a central data processing facility. Along with that independence, however, come many of the responsibilities that previously were assumed by the central facility. The problems of providing adequate training, assuring consistent procedures (security and otherwise), and minimizing duplication of effort (while retaining necessary separation of duties) are significant issues that make the personal computer environment unique.

IS THERE REALLY A SECURITY PROBLEM?

It may be argued that a "personal" computer does not need sophisticated security mechanisms and that users need only remove and lock away any diskettes containing sensitive data. Indeed, this concept of the single-user system has resulted in the general lack of security features in personal computers. In the "real world," however, most personal computer systems often are too expensive to be sitting idle on someone's desk and therefore must be shared among several users. To complicate matters, the introduction of fixed ("hard") disks for data storage and multi-user systems makes it difficult or impractical for a user to remove all sensitive data from the system. In addition, there may well be a valid concern for integrity of common software shared by several users (e.g., word processors, spreadsheet software, or database management systems).

Thus, personal computers do, indeed, present data sharing and, therefore, real security problems. However, as will be discussed later, the problem should not be viewed as a *PC* security problem. Rather, the security of information on personal computers is just a part of the overall information security issue that management must address. Nevertheless, both managers and users should understand the special security considerations that affect their use of personal computers.

PROTECTING THE EQUIPMENT

Before considering sophisticated data security mechanisms, it is first necessary to ensure basic physical and environmental protection of the equipment itself. If the computer system is damaged, stolen, or simply not working, most other security concerns are moot. This section describes control measures to provide a safe physical environment for personal computer systems.

Theft and Damage Protection

Protecting the PC (and associated equipment) from theft and physical damage is not a new problem; it has been necessary to protect office equipment for years. The only new factors are the relatively high unit value of PC equipment and the somewhat greater concern for environmental controls. Otherwise, the physical protection needs of PCs are the same as for other valuable equipment in the workplace. Indeed, if an organization has not addressed such problems prior to introducing personal computers, management should rethink its overall loss protection posture.

Area Access Control

In general, personal computers should not be placed in areas that have no basic physical access controls (e.g., locks on the doors and people present during working hours). This is only prudent, since the value of a typical PC may well be in excess of $2,000. Providing such simple and inexpensive controls will not only minimize the theft risk, it will also help reduce exposures to some of the more sophisticated technical problems discussed later.

Equipment Enclosures

In situations where it is not feasible to secure an entire area, the equipment can be placed in special workstation enclosures that can be closed and locked when the equipment is not in use. This can provide protection for other valuable items such as documentation, diskettes, and peripherals.

Equipment Lockdown Devices

Several types of equipment lockdown devices are available to prevent theft of PCs (and other types of office equipment). These may be used to secure the equipment to a table or other fixed object. Some devices also prevent access to the system power switch and thus can help prevent unauthorized equipment use.

Equipment Cover Locks

It is becoming increasingly important to prevent unauthorized access to the inside of the PC itself to ensure component theft protection and configuration control. Many systems contain valuable expansion boards (e.g., additional memory, modems, graphics interfaces, etc.), which have become a popular theft target. In addition, system security mechanisms (e.g., cryptography) may be dependent on certain components, and their integrity must also be protected. Equipment lockdown devices often provide additional protection against access to the interior of the equipment; devices are available for some systems that simply lock the equipment cover.

Environmental Controls

Personal computers are designed to operate in the "typical" office environment (i.e., without special air conditioning, electrical power quality control, or air contamination controls). In general, it can be argued that "if the people are comfortable, the PCs will be comfortable." Nevertheless, special attention should be given to minimizing the environmental hazards to which such equipment is exposed.

Electrical Power Quality

The typical PC is sensitive to the quality of its electrical power source. It may be helpful to place PC equipment on isolated power sources, although this is not always necessary. Inexpensive devices are available to protect against power surges (spikes) short of a direct lightning strike. If the local power supply quality is unusually poor (e.g., large fluctuations in voltage or frequency, voltage spikes, or frequent outages), then more extensive power conditioning, battery backup, or uninterruptible power supply (UPS) systems should be considered. In most cases, however, it will be sufficient to just keep the computer equipment on a power source separate from appliances or office equipment.

Heat and Humidity

The temperature and relative humidity found in the typical office are well within the operating limits of most personal computer systems. However, if equipment is used in other environments (e.g., on a factory floor or an outside location), users should refer to manufacturer specifications. Care should be taken with portable systems to avoid drastic changes in temperature or humidity (e.g., transporting a system from the outside into an office). Before operation, sufficient time should be allowed for the equipment to adjust to the new environment.

Air Contaminants

The general cleanliness of the area in which personal computer equipment operates has an obvious effect on reliability — both of equipment and magnetic media. It should be recognized that electronic equipment (including PCs) will naturally attract charged particles in the air. Eliminating such contaminants as smoke and dust will certainly have a beneficial effect on equipment and magnetic media (not to mention people).

Fire and Water Damage

Personal computers do not represent any more of a significant fire hazard than does any other office equipment, so it is unnecessary to install extensive fire and water protection systems similar to those required for major computer facilities. However, the value of the equipment, data, and other items in the area may be sufficient reason for a re-examination of fire detection and suppression facilities.

To protect equipment from possible water leaks (e.g., from overhead piping), consideration should be given to inexpensive plastic equipment covers. Such covers will also provide protection from dust and other airborne contaminants.

Other Environmental Hazards

Static Electricity. Static electrical charges can build up in a person, especially around carpeting, causing a discharge when he or she touches the PC equipment. Such a discharge could cause damage to integrated circuit components or semiconductor memory. This problem can be minimized through the use of anti-static spays, carpets, or pads. In addition, personnel can be instructed to discharge any built-up static charge by simply touching a grounded object (other than the computer). It may be worthwhile to post signs on each machine to remind users.

Radio Frequency Interference. In some isolated situations, radio frequency (RF) interference from other electronic equipment can cause computer equipment to malfunction. However, unless there are major nearby sources of such radiation, this should not be a problem.

Magnetic Media Protection

Particular attention should be given to the protection of magnetic media, not only because they are the primary repository of each user's information, but also because they are the system component perhaps most vulnerable to damage. The following discusses hazards affecting the two primary types of magnetic storage media found in personal computer systems — fixed and flexible disk — and some general hazards that can affect all types of magnetic media.

Fixed Disk Devices

Fixed or rigid disk devices (also known as "hard disks") usually are self-contained sealed units that are relatively well protected from environmental contaminants. However, care must be exercised when moving these units because of the potential damage to read/write heads or other internal components.

Flexible Diskettes

Virtually every personal computer system has at least one "floppy" disk drive. Flexible diskettes are the most prevalent medium for distributing software and data, and the handling of diskettes is an integral part of using almost any PC. The actual magnetic disk is contained within a protective jacket. However, there must be openings in the jacket for access by the read/write heads of the drive mechanism. These surfaces are particularly vulnerable to damage. Smaller ("microfloppy") diskettes employ a rigid plastic casing with a retractable access cover, thus reducing their vulnerability to rough handling and contaminants.

Potential dangers and proper handling techniques for flexible disks should be well known to all users; however, a summary of general precautions is worth repeating:

- Always store in the protective jacket.
- Protect from bending or similar damage.
- Insert carefully into the drive mechanism.
- Maintain an acceptable temperature range (50 – 125° F).
- Avoid direct contact with magnetic fields.
- Do no write directly on diskette jacket or sleeve.

Most of these precautions are simply common sense. Nevertheless, many PC users are quite careless with magnetic media, and management has the responsibility of providing proper handling instructions.

General Hazards

Exposure to ordinary contaminants (smoke, hair, doughnut crumbs, coffee, etc.) is probably the major reason for failures in magnetic media. Therefore, particular care should be exercised to minimize such exposures through as little direct contact as possible with magnetic devices. It is worth noting that airport x-ray devices and magnets (kept six or more inches away from magnetic media) pose no danger, despite considerable concerns to the contrary.

Since simple wear is another cause of failures, it is important that backup copies be made of all important disks. Indeed, day-to-day operation should be conducted with a backup copy and not the master copy of such diskettes.

Maintaining Perspective

While physical protection is certainly important, it is also important that a sense of perspective be maintained. The typical personal computer installation cannot and, generally, should not be treated like a large data center with respect to physical and environmental protection needs. The amount of protection provided must be determined by the value of equipment and the value of the processing capability (i.e., the system criticality). Depending on the size of the organization and the nature of the processing, the system's criticality may dictate extraordinary physical protection measures.

In most cases, absolute prevention of unauthorized physical access cannot be achieved with reasonable cost constraints. However, it should be possible to ensure that such access is at least detected. For example, a simple cover lock or lockdown device will not prevent a determined thief from stealing the equipment, but it will make it virtually impossible for a person to steal or even gain access to the interior of the equipment without being observed or detected. This usually will provide sufficient deterrence and protection.

On the assumption that basic physical and environmental protections have been provided, it is now possible to look at several other categories of system and data security measures.

SYSTEM AND DATA ACCESS CONTROL

Although there is considerable value in computer equipment, the purpose for having it is to handle information. Information and the ability to produce, store, and analyze it ultimately have more value to the organization than the equipment itself, and protecting that information is considerably more challenging. This should be a major concern to management.

The problem of controlling access to systems and information consists of the following elements:

- *Authorization* — establishing the *rules* that determine who may access which systems and information.
- *Identification* — of users and the systems or data they are permitted to access.
- *Access Control* — enforcement of the specified authorization rules.

Each of these is discussed below.

Authorization Rules

Access control implies that some rules exist for specifying which users are authorized to access which system resources (normally programs or data). Such rules must be established by the "owners" of the resources to be controlled, and they may consist of nothing more than a statement that only members of a given group or department are to have access to a given computer or application system. On the other hand, they may consist of formal definitions of information classifications and rules for accessing each. They type of authorization rules adopted will depend on the needs of each organization. It is important, however, that there be *some* type of authorization process.

Most automated access control mechanisms (on personal computers and on large-scale systems) are designed to address the former situation, where lists of systems or files and authorized users are developed and subsequently enforced. Enforcement of access control based on classifications of information (sometimes called "mandatory" access controls) is considerably more difficult to implement because of differing classification schemes and the need to provide unchangeable labels on the data to be protected. The mechanisms discussed below for personal computers fall into the first category.

Identification

For authorization rules to be enforceable, it is necessary that users and resources (usually data) be identified. The following is a discussion of this process in the context of personal computers.

User Identification

In a personal computer environment, user identification may be implicit or explicit. In a typical situation, a user establishes "authority" to use the system simply by being able to turn it on. If such implied identification is to mean anything at all, the system must be a true "personal" (i.e., single-user) system and there must be adequate physical controls to ensure that only that user can gain access. Locked offices or equipment enclosures can provide some degree of assurance in this area. If a system is shared, then such simple procedures may not be adequate.

Initial Authentication. For most situations in which PCs are shared, user identification should be authenticated in some manner. This requires an explicit interaction between the system and the user that should be accomplished with some type of system "logon" process in which the user provides a nonsecret identifier (e.g., name or account number) and some sort of evidence to authenticate that claim (e.g., a password). User logon (authentication) should occur whenever the system is powered up or a new user needs to use the system.

It is worth noting that many user identification mechanisms for personal computers (both commercial products and user-developed systems) often require only a single (presumably secret) code rather than separate identifier and authentication codes. This is not a good practice, since it does not provide a nonsecret identifier for audit and accountability purposes. In addition, it may make it easier for an intruder to guess a valid password, since any of the passwords valid for the system will permit access.

Authentication at power-up (and after "system reset") is usually accomplished by a program that interrupts the system initialization process and requires the user to complete a logon process. Most personal computer operating systems provide a facility for an automatically executing ("AUTOEXEC") program to be invoked upon system power-up or reset. The actual program, however, must be provided by the user organization. Logon procedures can be developed "in-house," or commercially available products can be installed. Since an effective mechanism requires relatively detailed technical knowledge, commercial products are often used. Some products involve additional hardware (e.g., expansion boards) that can trap key system events (e.g., power-up or system reset) and take control of the user authentication process. This can reduce the exposure of the authentication process to unauthorized modification, since the necessary hardware and software are often independent of the rest of the computer system.

Reauthentication. User reauthentication should also take place whenever it is likely that the user has changed. This is most easily accomplished in single-user systems simply by having each user turn off the machine after use, which requires each new user to go through the standard user authentication process. However, this is difficult to enforce and is often unacceptable when a machine must be used often, since the power-up process may require a significant amount of time. Alternative techniques include the following:

• *Manual system reset* — require each user to perform a "system reset" (often called a "system reboot") before leaving the machine. This will cause reinvocation of the logon process.

• *Automatic system reset* — set up the application program (or the AUTOEXEC file) to perform a system reset upon completion of processing.

• *Automatic timeout* — modify the operating system to cause a system reset after a predetermined period of system inactivity.

It user identification is established through a logon procedure, then that identification can be used for subsequent access control decisions. However, most single-user systems do not have mechanisms for retaining such identification for the duration of a computer session. Therefore, repeating the authorization process may be necessary during the course of a user's session at the personal computer.

Resource (Data) Labels

In addition to identifying the user, there must be some means of identifying the resources to be protected. These "resources" are usually files containing data or programs; however, they could also include the ability to perform a certain function within a given application. For the purpose of this discussion, we shall focus on data labeling.

External Labels. It has long been accepted practice to label sensitive documents and other materials with clear external indicators. Typically, the front cover (and often each page) of such documents must have a standard marking to indicate classification and handling requirements. Although such labeling is not always as easy to accomplish with the various forms of magnetic media used with personal computers, it is not difficult for floppy disks, the most common form of data storage medium. Diskettes containing sensitive information can be marked with special labels or brightly colored jackets, which will enable personnel to readily identify those materials that require special protection. This also makes sensitive materials obvious to a would-be thief, so it must be assumed that users will provide appropriate protection for all such materials.

Internal Labels. If the operating system or programs are to recognize files containing sensitive information, internal (i.e., machine-readable) labels must be present. The standard file management facilities of most personal computer systems provide only basic file identification capability — the file name. However, it is often possible to store files in specific "directories," which permits segregating files associated with each user or by data sensitivity.

Logical Access Controls

Two basic approaches are available for protecting data. The first is to prevent unauthorized persons from gaining access in the first place. The second is to deny effective use of information even if access is gained. Logical access controls provide the first type of protection; cryptography provides the second. Often, both types of protection are necessary.

The problems of controlling logical access to data on removable media are different from those associated with data stored on fixed media.

Removable Media Protection

If the data is resident on removable media, then the simple lock-and-key approach will probably provide the most cost-effective solution. If diskettes containing sensitive data cannot be protected in this manner (e.g., during shipment), then encryption may be appropriate.

Nonremovable Media Protection

If data resides on nonremovable media (e.g., a hard disk), then preventing access requires controlling access to the machine itself (user identification) and then to the data available to the user.

Physical System Access Control. There are several commercial products available to control physical access and use of personal computer equipment. If a given machine must be available for access by several users or cannot be physically locked when not in use, procedural controls may be a solution. It is usually possible to provide effective access control to the equipment during working hours because people are present. However, it is often necessary to place equipment in areas that cannot be monitored at all times.

Internal Access Control. If equipment must be shared by several users and cannot be monitored at all times, then hardware- or software-based security mechanisms should be considered. Such mechanisms can limit the type of access available to each user. The AUTOEXEC type of facilities available on most personal computers can be used to set up special menu-oriented user interface environments that will limit what each user can do. A more comprehensive approach is to embed access control mechanisms in the operating system to reduce the opportunities for circumventing them. An example of such a control is intercepting all file open requests to check for proper user authorization. There are commercial products designed for this purpose, or users may develop such software themselves.

Potential Problems. However, when such technical access control mechanisms are employed, it must be remembered they are vulnerable to attack if a user has the opportunity to make modifications to the equipment (e.g., by removing or substituting circuit boards) or to the software (e.g., through programming or debugging facilities). Nevertheless, such modifications often require certain technical skills and "unusual" actions (e.g., opening up the cabinet) that only alert employees may notice. If users require only predetermined functional capabilities (e.g., routine entry of transaction data), then these types of controls should be fully satisfactory.

It should also be recognized that the type of constrained environment suggested above, except for certain well-defined and restricted applications, may negate the benefits for which the personal computer was originally acquired. It may be easier, cheaper, and more effective in the long-run to put sensitive applications (i.e., those requiring special protection) on different computers.

Cryptography

Cryptography is the process of transforming information (cleartext) into an unintelligible form (ciphertext) so that it may be sent over insecure channels. The transformation process is controlled by a data string ("key"). Anyone intercepting the ciphertext while it is in the insecure channel must have the appropriate key to decrypt (convert back to cleartext) the information. The intended receiver is assumed to have that key.

Cryptography not only provides protection against unauthorized disclosure, it also ensures the detection of unauthorized modifications of information, since any change to encrypted data (without the necessary key) will prevent successful decryption by the intended recipient. It should be clear, however, that cryptography does nothing to *prevent* modification or destruction; it simple ensures the *detection* of such events. Thus, critical data cannot be protected simply by encryption.

Although the primary application of cryptography is in data communications, it has other important applications in a personal computer environment. In effect, personal computers and their storage media can be considered "insecure channels" because of their physical accessibility. The following discusses only personal computer (versus communications security) applications.

General Cryptographic Facilities

There are several commercially available software- and hardware-based products that provide personal computer users with cryptographic capabilities. These products, in general, enable the user to perform the following cryptographic functions.

- Enter or change cryptographic keys

- Encrypt a block of data

- Decrypt a block of data

In some cases, facilities are provided for the generation and management of keys. Normally, however, this is left to the user. Indeed, this can be one of the major problems in the effective use of cryptography, since the randomness and secrecy of keys are critical to the protection provided by cryptography.

Bulk File Encryption

The normal manner in which cryptography is used in a personal computer environment is to encrypt and decrypt entire files. Typically, a user prepares a file (presumably containing sensitive information) and then runs an encryption utility to produce the file's ciphertext version. The original file should then be overwritten. (See the discussion below on data residue). Before using the file again, the utility program must decrypt it and produce a cleartext version. The user is usually responsible for selecting, entering, and remembering the key used for the encryption and decryption process. Commercial cryptographic products usually provide utility programs for bulk file encryption and decryption as well as a utility to overwrite old files.

Integral File Cryptography

Problems with bulk encryption and decryption of data files include general inconvenience, the need to erase cleartext files, and the need for personnel training. An alternative to file encryption is to use a cryptographic facility that is integral to the file input/output subsystem. Basically, each block of data to be written to disk is first encrypted, and each block read from disk is decrypted before it is passed to the requesting program. This makes the entire cryptographic process almost transparent to the user and eliminates the inconvenience and dangers associated with bulk file procedures. Users with sufficient technical expertise can implement such a capability themselves. In addition, there are commercial hardware and software products that may be considered.

Selection Considerations

In selecting cryptographic products, three basic considerations are important:

- Private versus public key systems

- Cryptographic algorithm

- Hardware versus software implementation

It is beyond the scope of this guide to deal with these subjects in detail. However, the following paragraphs address their basic issues.

Private Versus Public Key Systems. There are two basic types of cryptographic systems in common use. A "private key" cryptosystem requires that the sending and receiving parties share a common cryptographic key, which must be kept secret (private) to ensure the security of the encrypted information. This requires special precautions and protocols for the distribution of keys, which, indeed, has long been one of the obstacles to the widespread application of cryptography to large communications networks. In situations involving small numbers of users, this is generally not a significant problem, however.

A "public key" cryptosystem involves pairs of keys, one for encrypting and another for decrypting. The encrypting key is public, so anyone wishing to send a message to a given user can use anyone else's encrypting key. Only the recipient, however, has the (secret) decryption key. This type of cryptosystem can reduce certain key management problems and can be attractive for large networks of interconnected users.

In both types of system, the selection and protection of keys (even public keys) is critical to the overall security of the system. It is possible to combine the two systems to provide very effective security with relatively little administrative overhead.

Cryptographic Algorithms. All cryptosystems require a well-defined process (algorithms) by which information is transformed from cleartext to ciphertext and back to cleartext. It is an accepted principle of cryptology (the design and analysis of codes and ciphers) that the strength of a cryptosystem should *not* be dependent on the secrecy of the algorithm itself. This enables the exchange of information necessary for design and manufacture of systems incorporating the algorithm. It also permits critical analysis of the algorithm itself and eliminates the need to provide physical protection for devices and documentation.

The Data Encryption Standard (DES) is the cryptographic standard for nonclassified federal government applications. A private key cryptosystem, it is described in *Federal Information Processing Standards Publications 46* (FIPS46). Since DES has undergone extensive critical analysis, the level of protection it provides is well understood. It is important to note that federal government agencies are, in general, required to use the DES for cryptographic applications involving nonclassified information.

Although there is no standard public key cryptosystem, algorithms have been published in the open literature. Like DES, they also have received considerable critical review. Several commercially available cryptographic products incorporate either the DES or the openly available public key algorithms.

A number of commercial cryptographic products (both private and public key systems) use proprietary (secret) cryptographic algorithms, which are often designed to operate at higher speeds than algorithms like the DES. However, since these algorithms are not made public, it is difficult to obtain an objective evaluation of their cryptographic strength, so the user must make the necessary determination.

Hardware Versus Software. Cryptographic algorithms can, in general, be implemented in either hardware or software. The former implementation usually results in much faster operation and better integrity protection, while the latter is often cheaper and more flexible. Hardware implementations of the DES on a single integrated circuit chip are available and are used in a number of cryptographic products. Full compliance with the DES requires hardware implementation, although software versions of the DES algorithm are available.

Residue Control

Another aspect of access control that often is overlooked is the data "residue" left on disk or in memory. This is data stored in areas of disk or memory that have been released for reuse. Such information can often be read by subsequent users. A common example of the disk residue problem is the "erasing" of disk files (e.g., with the ERASE or DELETE commands), which usually results only in the setting of a "file deleted" indicator in the file directory — not the physical erasure or overwriting of the actual data. It is often a simple matter to reset the "file deleted" indicator and thereby "unerase" the file. In fact, there are many software utilities designed for exactly this purpose. It is dangerous, therefore, to pass files to other users on diskettes that contain "erased" files of sensitive data.

The problem also exists for hard disks, since the data remains potentially accessible to subsequent users of the system. Users should also recognize that many common programs (e.g., word processors) create and delete "scratch" files that the user never sees. These files could contain sensitive information and are exposed to the same vulnerability.

The problem of residue can be solved with a program that "purges" (i.e., overwrites) all file data as part of the deletion process. Think of it as the electronic equivalent of the traditional "burn bag" used to discard sensitive information. Although such programs are relatively easy to write, they are usually not offered as standard features of personal computer operating systems. Therefore, users must acquire or write them themselves. If such a utility is not available, then sensitive disk media should not be shared among users. If a fixed disk is used for such data, users have three options: use an overwrite utility, encrypt sensitive files, or do not share the system with other users.

Placement of Controls

In general, it is desirable to place control mechanisms as "low" in the system as possible to reduce the number of alternate paths available for circumventing them. The levels at which such controls can be placed, from "lowest" to "highest," are the hardware, the operating system, the application program, and the user "environment."

Controls placed at lower levels (e.g., hardware or operating system) tend to be stronger, but designing and implementing such controls are often beyond the capabilities of most users and, moreover, changes made at this level may affect system reliability and compatibility. Therefore, such controls usually must be provided by the system supplier or other vendors. It is easier for user organizations to implement controls within application systems or to establish limited user "environments" through the use of automatically executing programs. Unfortunately, controls at this level are often easy to circumvent.

Summary

Personal computers do not, in general, have the type of hardware and operating system support mechanisms necessary for sophisticated security and access control. However, since these systems usually are used to handle large numbers of users, such mechanisms often constitute needless overhead. Nevertheless, many opportunities exist for providing technical access control mechanisms over personal computers and the data they contain. These mechanisms can be developed by the user or can be acquired commercially. It is important, however, for the user to determine first the type of control actually necessary for a given system, rather than arbitrarily installing sophisticated (and often costly) access controls.

SOFTWARE AND DATA INTEGRITY

It has long been recognized that software and data integrity are critical in almost all phases of data processing. In most organizations, information produced on computer systems (usually large-scale systems) and the software used to handle such information has been subject to extensive critical review and error-checking, both during system development and during normal processing. This has enabled a great deal of confidence to be placed in the quality of resulting information and other "products" of computer systems.

The personal computer has made powerful computational and analytical tools available to users throughout many organizations. Increasingly important decisions are being made based on information processed by such systems. Unfortunately, there may be a reluctance to apply the same degree of care (and cost) to integrity assurance as is routinely applied to larger systems. Nevertheless, the formal and "official" appearance of printed materials that can be produced easily by any personal computer can lead to unwarranted confidence in the substance of such materials.

To the extent that personal computers are used for routine personal work and are not being used for critical decision-making functions, the lack of formal quality and integrity controls may not be a significant problem. However, for applications that are critical to the organization, there must be commensurate quality controls.

Formal Software Development

In situations where important functions are being performed on personal computers, management should consider placing formal controls over software development, testing, and data integrity. This applies not only to situations where systems are being designed and programmed in traditional programming languages (e.g., BASIC or Pascal); there is increasing use of generic software tools (e.g., spreadsheet and database management systems) to build complex applications. Even though many of the typical programming problems may be reduced in these situations, the need for careful analysis and control is just as important. This may very well require additional training of personnel or the use of specially trained personnel, since system development skills are not a normal part of professional training.

Data Integrity Controls

Even a properly functioning application program is of little value if the data it handles is corrupted. Most generic software tools do not provide built-in facilities for checking the integrity of input data. Therefore, it becomes the responsibility of the user to build in such checks. These should include data format and range checks and other redundant cross-checks of results. Managers should require supporting information and evidence necessary to ensure that calculations and other data handling operations have been performed properly. It is perhaps most important for managers to require individual accountability and auditability of results before relying on information generated by PC systems.

Operational Controls

When a major data processing application is implemented on a PC, formal operational procedures are as critical as they are for a large-scale system. An important application is important regardless of where or how it is processed. Operation procedures should include:

- Data preparation and input handling procedures

- Program execution procedures

- Media (probably diskette or tape) procedures

- Output handling and distribution procedures

These are, of course, the same types of procedures needed for large-scale system applications. It is important to recognize, however, that the personnel performing such procedures probably will not have extensive data processing or operations training and will be performing these duties along with their other responsibilities.

Documentation

Documentation of all aspects of any repetitive activity is critical to its on-going operation. Again, the use of generic software tools makes some believe that there is less need for documentation. In addition, it is often more difficult to prepare documentation for such systems, since the user interface is often not as simple and straightforward as specially designed application programs. Rather, the user often must first understand how to use the generic application and then must learn procedures for each specific application. This problem can be alleviated somewhat with the use of facilities in many generic software tools to "customize" an application and thereby simplify the user interface.

Additional Guidance

It is beyond the scope of this chapter to describe the many types of system and data integrity controls that apply to data processing applications in general. Nevertheless, most of these controls and procedures apply to the personal computer environment and should be understood by management.

BACKUP AND CONTINGENCY PLANNING

The problem of backup and contingency planning in a personal computer environment is essentially the same as in other data processing activities. Indeed, for organizations with both personal computers and large-scale systems, backup and contingency planning should be an integrated process. However, there are special considerations for personal computers due primarily to wide distribution of equipment and number of people now involved. This section discusses some of these considerations.

Elements of Contingency Planning

Contingency planning consists of activities undertaken in anticipation of potential events that could cause serious adverse effects. This, of course, could apply to individual users and their applications as well as to organizations. In a personal computer environment, one of the key elements in the contingency planning process is the individual user, since there is no central staff to perform many of the important functions.

Contingency plans should consist of emergency procedures, resource (hardware, software, data, etc.) backup preparations, and backup operation plans. In addition, comprehensive contingency plans will include recovery and test procedures. This section will focus primarily on the first three areas.

Emergency Procedures

In general, the introduction of personal computers into an office environment should not require significant changes in emergency preparations. Any area in which people work and important information is handled should have basic emergency procedures, including:

- Alarm activation and deactivation procedures
- Evacuation plans
- Lockup procedures
- Medical emergency supplies and procedures
- Fire detection and extinguishing equipment
- Bomb threat procedures

If such precautions are not in place, then the introduction of the personal computers may emphasize the need for them, if for no other reason than to protect the investment in equipment.

File Backup

With a personal computer "on every desk," there is obviously a need to encourage regular and systematic backup of files, since such backup can no longer be done centrally and systematically as is possible with a large-scale system. Unfortunately, it often takes the loss of an important file to convert most users to regular backup.

Backup Approaches

The method and frequency of backup must be determined by each user, based on the storage media and the volatility of the data involved.

Full-volume Backup. For data stored on diskettes or other removable media, it is often easiest to make a backup copy of the entire volume (e.g., diskette) after each use or at the end of each day if a given volume is used frequently during the day. This approach eliminates the need to keep track of individual files. If the original volume is damaged, the backup copy can be used.

For large-capacity, nonremovable storage devices, such as fixed disks, it is usually impractical (and unnecessary) to perform full disk copies on a daily basis. In this situation, two basic alternative approaches should be considered: incremental backup and application-based backup.

Incremental Backups. In an incremental backup, only those files that have been modified since the last full or incremental backup are copied to the backup medium. This, of course, requires a mechanism in the file system to set an indicator whenever a file is opened for writing. Most personal computer operating systems designed to handle hard disk systems have such facilities. It should be noted, however, that full backups are still required (e.g., monthly), since no single incremental backup will contain all files.

Recovery from minor problems (e.g., a single file error) involves locating the latest incremental backup containing the affected file. Recovery from major file loss, however, requires first reloading from the last full backup and then reloading each successive incremental backup. This can be a very time-consuming, error-prone process if there are too many incremental backups between full backups. A reasonable schedule might be a full backup each month and an incremental backup each week. However, the specific schedule must be determined for each system.

Application-based Backup. Because of the potential complexity of incremental backups and the impracticality of full-volume backup for large capacity volumes, it may be more appropriate to perform backups based on each application or file grouping, for example, individual file subdirectories. Certain file groups (e.g., generic software, which never changes) need only one initial backup. Software associated with locally maintained applications needs to be backed up only when the software is changed. Data files can be backed up whenever updated. Although this approach may require more backup volumes (e.g., diskettes) it will generally be easier to organize them and to locate files for restoration than with incremental or full-volume backups.

Backup Media

The most common backup medium is floppy disk, since virtually every personal computer has a floppy disk drive. For systems with hard disks, however, a full file backup may require more than 20 diskettes. Alternatives, such as streaming cassette backup systems, should be considered if incremental backups to diskette are too difficult or time-consuming.

Errors on backup copies can obviously have disastrous consequences. The typical backup utilities available on personal computer systems are basically file copy functions; they do not contain redundancy mechanisms found in some larger-scale systems. Therefore, regardless of the type of backup, only high-quality media should be used. Additional assurance of successful backup can be achieved by performing file comparison of original and backup copies. Most personal computer systems provide disk and file comparison utility programs. In addition, some operating systems provide a write-verification option (which usually may be turned on or off as desired) that will read each disk record immediately after it is written to verify its accuracy. Most backup, file copy, or file comparison utilities will provide a display of files processed. This information should be directed to the printer and stored with the backup media.

Storage

It is important for users to understand the threats addressed by backup procedures. The obvious reason for backing up files is to enable recovery of data after loss from media or hardware problems or accidents (e.g., unintentional erasure of files). This is why users should store backup copies in a convenient, nearby location. The other threat, however, is loss resulting from a fire, theft, or other event that might involve an entire office or building. In these situations, locally stored backup copies would be lost along with the originals. Therefore, careful consideration should be given to storing periodic archival copies at some location unlikely to be affected by "common" emergencies such as fire or flooding. In situations where personal computers are connected to a data communications network (e.g., a local area network), it may be possible to establish procedures to make backup copies on a separate device, such as a remote host or a file server. This may provide the physically separate storage needed for disaster recovery purposes.

Other Backup Considerations

Data files are not the only things that can be lost, damaged, or destroyed. Indeed, without the necessary equipment, personnel, and documentation, the data files themselves may be useless. Therefore, users must identify all elements that make up their personal computer applications.

Equipment and Facilities

One advantage of the widespread use of personal computers is built-in equipment backup — if one machine is damaged or lost, it may be easy to find a replacement. However, not all systems are compatible. As application systems on personal computers become more complex, it becomes more difficult simply to move from one computer to another. Different equipment options, installation variations, and piracy protection mechanisms used in many popular software packages can make "portability" extremely difficult. It should also be recognized that a major disaster (e.g., a fire or water damage) may affect much more than a single machine or area. Therefore, advanced planning is critical.

Software

Application software should be protected in the same manner as data files. Backup considerations may differ, depending on the source of the application software.

Commercial Software. Applications on personal computers are often built around mass-marketed "generic" software, such as database management systems, spreadsheet programs, or word processing systems. Licensed software is often costly to replace if not properly registered with the supplier. Much commercially available software is distributed with piracy protection mechanisms that link the software to a given machine or "system" disk. This may cause considerable difficulties in backup operations on different equipment or with alternate versions of the software.

Locally Maintained Software. For locally developed or maintained applications, backup should include source program files and, optionally, loadable versions of all software. The required compiler or interpreter programs should, of course, also be backed up. (See the discussion above on application-based file backup).

Personnel, Procedures, and Documentation

Personal computer applications, especially those involving only one machine and only one person (or a small group), are often unique. Moreover, they are often developed in a much less structured environment than are "traditional" data processing applications. Nevertheless, they often require a detailed knowledge of procedures that may not be documented. If such applications are to have any long-term value, their operation should not be dependent on individuals or small groups. In emergency situations, others should be able to understand and use the applications, which requires specific efforts to document procedures and, perhaps, cross-train personnel.

Summary

Backup and contingency planning is difficult because it concerns nonimmediate problems and considerable speculation regarding future events. In a personal computer environment, because of the many users who may be involved, these problems become even more difficult. Nevertheless, management must ensure that users are aware of the need for regular backup activities and that they have the necessary tools and training to perform those activities in an effective and consistent manner.

MISCELLANEOUS CONSIDERATIONS

Effective information security involves more than the issues and measures discussed in detail in the previous sections. This section discusses several of these additional areas of concern.

Auditability

Designers of important applications, whether on small or large systems, will require reliable audit trails. Organizations also may wish to monitor use of personal computers by employees. A single-user personal computer may need special audit trail facilities as an historical record and to aid in recovery from errors. The placement and use of audit trails in personal computer systems, however, requires special consideration.

Placement of Audit Trails

Audit trail information can be recorded as part of an access control process such as any of those discussed earlier. However, designers should avoid dependence on the personal computer to provide a safe environment for the storage of such data, because such data may be too easy for a user to modify or delete. If it is important enough to keep audit trail information on the personal computer, the system should be provided with appropriate physical and access control safeguards to protect the data's integrity. If access to a host system is involved, the *host* is the proper location for the placement of audit data capture mechanisms.

Usage Monitoring

Organizations with substantial investment in personal computer equipment may wish to monitor its uses. Although not primarily a security concern, effective monitoring can have security benefits. The types of event that may be of interest include:

- System startup

- User session initiation and completion

- Program initiation and completion

- Access to certain data files

It is, of course, possible to require that users maintain manual logs of such activities, but this is likely to be ineffective. It is also possible to develop or acquire software that will record basic system usage information. This requires, at minimum, the use of AUTOEXEC-type routines and may involve modifications to operating system functions to ensure that all relevant activity is logged. In addition, it requires a reliable source of date and time information (e.g., an internal clock-calendar) and methods to protect the log information from modification or destruction. Management must decide if the user constraints needed to meet these requirements are justified by the usage information that will be obtained.

Multi-user Personal Computers

An increasing number of microprocessor-based systems are capable of supporting multiple users. Some of these systems have advanced hardware with multiple processor states, virtual memory addressing, and other features that are needed to provide adequate user isolation and security. Such systems, despite their size, are the functional equivalent of multiuser minicomputer and mainframe systems; as such, if they will be supporting users with security requirements, they must be provided with appropriate administrative and physical protection to enforce the system security features they contain.

Most multi-user microprocessor systems, however, simply allow one or more processors and memory segments to be shared, making no attempt to ensure security (i.e., user isolation and access control). Such systems are not appropriate for groups of users who have a need to control data access among themselves, since any control mechanisms are likely to be ineffective.

Communications Environments

In most organizations, the personal computer is but one of several types of data processing devices used. Increasingly, there is a need to connect personal computers as terminal devices to larger host systems or to connect two or more personal computers in networks. The security issues in each of these situations are basically the same as have always existed in multi-user host systems and data communications networks, respectively. However, there are some sharing issues unique to the personal computer that should be addressed by managers.

Terminal Emulation

When a personal computer is connected to a host system, the basic requirements for security and access control remain with the host — as far as the host is concerned, there is just another terminal out there. Even so, the personal computer has the ability to upload (send to the host) and download (receive from the host) large amounts of data at rates often exceeding those possible with ordinary terminals. This may be possible even with the same speed communication lines because the personal computer's disk drives may be used, eliminating the printer or keyboard. The amount and types of data that can be downloaded, however, are still under control of the host.

Communications software for personal computers often provides the facility to store telephone numbers and logon sequences for frequently called host systems. A significant potential problem can arise when users store passwords or other sensitive information in this manner. In effect, the security of the host is now dependent on the physical security provided over the personal computer and its files. Users should be instructed never to store host system passwords or other sensitive information in communication software control files.

The Personal Computer as Host

Personal computers are often used as single-user host systems. For example, a personal computer and an auto-answer modem permits a user to access the system remotely. A simple logon protocol is appropriate in this situation. A simple (well-selected) password should suffice if only one person is to use the system. However, if several users are to be allowed access, and there is a need to monitor and control the system, a traditional user identifier and password logon process should be used.

Personal Computer Networks

When two or more personal computers (or similar devices) are connected in a network, communication security becomes a problem. Remember that in most local area network (LAN) systems, all nodes have the ability to read all traffic on the network. Therefore, privacy cannot be assured without cryptographic protection. Most commercially available data encryption devices will work with personal computers as well as with other devices. Also available are devices that can be incorporated into the personal computer (i.e., expansion boards) that include complete communications and cryptographic protocol functions.

Electromagnetic Emanations

All electronic equipment emanates electromagnetic signals. For some equipment (e.g., computers, communication lines, and data terminals), these emanations may carry information that can be detected by appropriately placed monitoring devices. Security measures to prevent detection are known as "Tempest" controls. Classified applications involving national security generally must be processed on on equipment that has been specially shielded or modified to minimize emanations. Although the technical requirements for such shielding are classified, Tempest-certified equipment can be purchased by nondefense users — at a considerable premium. It is management's responsibility to determine if the extra cost is justified.

The Micro as an Accomplice

The danger posed to host systems from increasing availability of personal computers (i.e., the potential of the personal computer as an "accomplice") has received considerable attention in the news and entertainment media. This is perhaps the greatest security concern expressed by managers regarding personal computers.

Although there is certainly some reason for concern, it is important to recognize that almost no new host system security threats result directly from the use of personal computers. The personal computer presents the same type of threat as does a "dumb" terminal, and adequate security measures for terminal access have been available for a long time. Even such seemingly exotic threats as programming a personal computer to automatically generate thousands of telephone numbers and passwords are easily defeated with available mechanisms — if they are used. If security problems exist for an organization's remotely accessed host systems, the fault probably lies with inattentive or imprudent management, not with the introduction of personal computers.

Additional Issues

There are many other issues involving the rapidly expanding use of personal computers that must be faced by management. These include controlling licensed software, personal use of equipment, and employees working from home. Each of these issues has some clear security implications. However, most of them involve policy and administrative considerations that are outside the scope of this book.

MANAGING THE SECURITY PROBLEM

The preceding sections have described the security exposures facing the users of personal computer systems and some of the specific control measures that can be used to reduce those exposures. This section provides an overall management perspective to the problem and an approach to effectively managing information security in a personal computer environment.

Information Security Management — An Overview

Information security management involves more than just security for various computer systems. The following is a brief overview of the process.

Protection Strategies

There are three basic strategies for protecting information resources from threat:

- *Prevent* threats from striking

- *Detect* that threats have struck

- *Recover* from damaging effects

Any security measure will fall into one or more of these basic strategy categories. The objective of security management is to select cost-effective control measures that involve *all* of the above protection strategies, not just one or two.

A General Approach to Security Management

It should be obvious that the above strategies are not, in themselves, of much value to a manager or user concerned with protecting information. A systematic approach to identifying and implementing security requirements is needed. In general, such an approach should include the following activities:

- *Asset identification* — identifying and classifying the information and other assets that require protection.

- *Risk assessment* — identifying and evaluating the threats, specific vulnerabilities, and degree of exposure (risk) to information assets.

- *Control selection and implementation* — selecting control measures that provide cost-effective reduction of exposure.

- *Audit and evaluation* — ongoing activities to review the continued effectiveness and appropriateness of controls.

The underlying objective of these activities (and, indeed, the challenge to management) is the selection and implementation of *cost-effective* control measures. With unlimited resources, virtually any level of security can be achieved. However, no rational organization should commit resources in excess of the risks involved. The key is *risk management.*

Risk Analysis and Risk Management

The concepts of risk analysis and risk management are central to any well thought out information security program. The purpose of risk *analysis* is to determine the exposure to loss (usually expressed in expected dollar loss per year) for a given system. Risk *management* is concerned with reducing those risks to an acceptable level, determined by balancing the cost of alternative control measures against their risk reduction characteristics. Basically, the risk manager must minimize total security-related costs, which consist of expected losses plus the cost of controls.

Focusing on Information Assets. When analyzing risk, it is important to view it as an *information* security problem, not a *computer* security problem. This is particularly true as the personal computer becomes just another office tool, like the typewriter, dictating machine, or telephone. Risks are related primarily to *information* and only secondarily to the physical devices on which that information may be stored or processed.

Risk Analysis Activities. In general, risk analysis consists of the following steps:

- *Potential loss analysis* — determining the potential losses to be suffered *if* various adverse events were to occur.

- *Threat analysis* — identifying the source and likelihood (e.g., occurrences per year) of adverse events actually occurring.

- *Exposure evaluation* — combining estimates of potential loss and frequency of occurrence to obtain estimates of *expected loss* (usually expressed in dollars per year).

In concept, this process involves the use of quantitative estimates of potential loss, occurrence rates, and loss expectancies. For large, centralized data processing activities involving many applications and users, formal risk analysis may be costly and time-consuming. Nevertheless, such a relatively complex environment requires a careful and systematic analysis. In a small systems environment, however, the risks and the associated need for detailed analysis are probably less.

Except for the obvious need to provide physical protection for the equipment, the security concern (particularly in a small systems environment) should be only with the *application*, not with the equipment. If a system is not being used for sensitive or critical applications (which, in many cases, it will not be), then a formal (i.e., quantitative) risk analysis is not necessary. If, on the other hand, a highly sensitive or critical application is being run on the small system, a detailed risk assessment must be performed *regardless of the value of the computer equipment itself.*

Security Management Program Elements

There are many possible ways to structure effective security management. The key requirement is to *establish a formal program.* This is of particular importance in a small systems environment because of the large number and relative autonomy of people who are likely to be using such systems in a typical organization. Without some formal security management structure and associated guidance, these various users cannot be expected to apply consistent and effective controls.

Responsibility. There should be a formal assignment of authority and responsibility for information security management for the entire organization. This applies to information in *any form*, whether on a personal computer, on a mainframe system, or on paper. However, the basic operational responsibility should be with the people who "own" the information, have the incentive to protect it, and have the necessary authority and resources — the *user* group. Therefore, except in developing policy and guidance, a single point of responsibility for personal computer security is probably inappropriate.

Personnel Screening. Many security controls ultimately depend on trust in individuals. Therefore, there should be some process to screen personnel who are authorized to access sensitive information systems. This does not imply, however, that special screening is needed simply because a person will be using a computer system. Most organizations have pre-employment screening procedures and, if needed, security background investigations. If such screening is considered sufficient for the employee's position, it should be irrelevant whether or not a computer is used as part of the job.

Management Control Procedures. Management should establish formal control procedures over the development and use of information systems. This is more easily done when such information systems are relatively well structured and distinct. Many of the ad hoc uses of personal computers are not, however, well defined or structured. Nevertheless, if important decisions are based on the results of personal computer applications, management must establish procedures to ensure the accuracy and integrity of the information generated.

Risk Analysis. There should be periodic, formal assessments of the threats and risk associated with sensitive information systems. This is required as a basis for selecting cost-effective control measures for those systems.

Contingency Plans. The continued availability of many information systems is important or even critical to the organization. Therefore, management should establish formal plans and procedures to respond to emergency or disaster situations that would disable or make such systems unavailable.

Procurement Procedures. In general, it is more difficult and costly to "retrofit" security measures into systems after they have been implemented. Therefore, it is important the security requirements be specified early in the design or procurement process. There should be policies and procedures for ensuring that security requirements are specified in all procurements of systems and equipment.

Audit and Evaluation. Systems, organizations, and environments change, and the changes often result in changes in risk. There should be a program of regular audits and evaluations of sensitive systems to ensure the continued adequacy, effectiveness, and appropriateness of security measures.

The elements listed above do not, in themselves, ensure appropriate protection. Rather, they provide a consistent framework within which to build an effective information security program.

Management's Role

As with any security program, it is management's responsibility to take the lead in ensuring security for personal computer systems. This is all the more important due to the growing number of people in any organization who are or will soon be involved in the use of such systems. Management should focus on a) protecting *information*, not computers; b) emphasizing the use of a risk management approach to protection decisions; and c) assigning responsibility (and necessary authority) for security to the actual "owners" and users of the information resources.

Information Versus Computer Security. Perhaps the most important thing that management can do in addressing the personal computer security problem is *not* to view it as a personal computer problem. Since personal computers represent only a tool (albeit a ubiquitous one) in the organization's overall information handling process, management should address the *overall* automated information security problem. This approach will help ensure consistency of policies and procedures and the involvement of everyone in the organization. Although the technology and economics of security have changed, the basic objectives have not — confidentiality, integrity, and availability of information resources must be protected.

Adopting a Risk Management Approach. Because valuable and potentially sensitive information resources are increasingly being handled throughout the typical organization, it is all the more important that management adopt a risk management approach to implementing security measures. This approach requires that three elements be analyzed: the value of assets being protected, the nature and likelihood of threats facing those assets, and the cost-effectiveness of existing or potential safeguards. This does not necessarily dictate the use of highly formal, quantitative risk analysis procedures in all situations, although such procedures are often still appropriate. For a single personal computer application, a less formal, qualitative analysis might well be sufficient. However, for applications involving multiple PCs, networking, or host systems, the analysis should be considerably more rigorous.

Individual Responsibility. Despite efforts to convince them otherwise, users of large, centralized MIS applications seldom consider themselves individually responsible for the security of those systems. With personal computers, users (and their management) can no longer avoid those responsibilities. Therefore, it is important for management to ensure that policies and procedures are made clear to all personnel and that necessary resources are provided to enable compliance.

A Plan of Action

No "cookbook" approach to information security can be provided for managers and users of personal computers. However, the following is a recommended plan of action that may at least get the process started.

Establish an Information Security Policy

A formal information security policy (not a *computer* security policy) is a prerequisite to a workable security program. This requires, at a minimum, identifying the types of information requiring protection (e.g., personal, trade secret, etc.) and specifying the control measures that apply to each type of information (e.g., storage, transmittal, disposal). If such a policy exists, then *all* information in the organization — not just that in a specific format (e.g., paper) — will be addressed in a consistent manner.

Many organizations have security policies that apply to traditional (e.g., hardcopy) documents. In general, these policies need only be reviewed and, where necessary, modified to include information in other forms, such as that on magnetic media. This again makes the "electronic desk" concept a useful analogy.

Develop an Inventory of Applications

Most organizations in which personal computers are used find out quickly that it is useful, indeed necessary, to maintain an inventory of equipment and software. Similarly, it is important to develop an inventory of "applications." Each component should attempt to identify various applications and the associated information processed on the component's computer systems. For personal computers, it may be easiest to start with each hardware system and document the following:

- System identification, location
- Responsible user (i.e., "owner")
- Other users
- General categories of sensitive information handled
- Specific, identifiable applications
- General description of access controls and other security measures currently in place

This is the first step in developing an understanding of the extent of any potential security problems and needs.

Conduct a Risk Assessment

The first step will provide an overall assessment of basic risks, but for those systems or applications that process sensitive or critical applications, a more detailed assessment should be performed. The risk assessment process was described earlier.

Select Control Measures

For those systems or applications for which risks are determined to be unacceptable, additional control measures must be implemented. In general, such controls will fall into one of the following categories.

- *Physical protection* — as noted earlier, traditional physical control measures (e.g., locks) will prove to be the most cost-effective approach.

- *Administrative procedures* — policies and procedures will play a significant role in the control structure.

- *Self-development software* — in many cases, simple programs or automated procedures ("batch files") can be used to provide a controlled environment for users. It may also prove worthwhile to make certain modifications to the operating system or key application programs to provide additional access controls.

- *Commercial security products* — in addition to all the steps described above, management will find a growing number of security-enhancing products available on the commercial market. Some of these were described in earlier sections of this report.

Since the "basic" personal computer generally provides very little in the way of security mechanisms, it is the user's responsibility to provide whatever controls deemed necessary. There may be a temptation to favor the fourth category above (commercially available products). It is important to note, that security cannot be achieved simply by installing gadgets. Without physical and administrative controls, such devices can usually be circumvented with little effort.

When considering technical security products (e.g., access control packages, password schemes, etc.), an additional caution is appropriate. Because of the two fundamental security weaknesses of personal computers that were discussed earlier (physical accessibility and lack of hardware security mechanisms), users should be wary of products (particularly software) that claim to provide "absolute" security. Without certain physical controls and limits on what users are permitted to do once in the system, such claims are meaningless.

Audit and Monitor the Results

After selecting and implementing appropriate security measures for personal computer systems (and, it is hoped, other information systems), management should conduct some type of post-implementation review and subsequent periodic audits. These are needed to ensure that control measures are, indeed, in place and in operation and that they remain appropriate as the organization and its information environment change.

Opportunities

Despite the potential problems, one should not be left with the impression that personal computers represent unreasonable security risks. Clearly, the benefits of personal computers will continue to outweigh most perceived risks, and so they will continue to be introduced at a rapid pace. Indeed, it is possible to minimize most of the risks discussed above. And there are some unique security advantages offered by personal computers.

Using Existing Security Technology

Most control measures that have been used for large-scale systems (e.g., administrative controls, separation of duties, physical and environmental controls, etc.) apply to personal computers as well. The primary difference is one of scale; it is difficult to justify an expensive access control system for a single personal computer. On the other hand, simple physical controls, such as a lock on the door or the equipment itself, can be both cheap and effective. Similarly, since relatively few people must share data on a given machine, the controls over data access can be relatively simple (e.g., keeping sensitive data on removable diskettes or selective encryption of such files).

New microprocessor technology will continue to provide personal computers with more of the hardware features previously available only in larger systems (e.g., virtual memory addressing and multiple processor states). This, too, will enable current security technology to be applied to smaller systems.

Isolating Sensitive Systems

A unique opportunity offered by the relative low cost and high availability of personal computers is the ability to completely isolate a particularly sensitive application. Rather than applying strict controls over every user of a large multi-user system, it may be less expensive and more effective to implement a sensitive application on its own dedicated hardware. This offers isolation and security without the usual overhead necessary in a resource-sharing environment.

PERSONAL COMPUTER SELF-ASSESSMENT QUESTIONNAIRE (Figure 15.1)

Evaluation of information security risks is often a complex process. Risk is dependent upon many factors, including the sensitivity and criticality of the information involved and the operational environment (physical, organizational, technical, and so forth). It is not a situation that lends itself well to checklists or other "cookbook" approaches.

Nevertheless, it is often helpful for an individual manager or user to conduct a relatively simple self-audit of potential information security risks. This questionnaire is intended to help them do that. The questions are intentionally general in nature, since the adequacy of control measures is dependent on many factors that cannot be ignored, including the operational requirements and sensitivity of information on each system. In situations where a personal computer is used for a relatively well-defined and understood set of applications, this self-audit process may provide a good evaluation of the associated risks. However, if the personal computer is part of one or more larger applications (e.g., part of a network), the questionnaire must be used with care.

Generally, it is not possible to answer each question for the organization as a whole. If this were possible, the honest answers would always be "no." Questions must be addressed to individual systems or organizational components. It should also be noted that this is by no means a comprehensive list of issues that should be addressed. No attempt has been made to include traditional data security and integrity control practices that should be considered regardless of the nature or size of equipment involved.

PERSONAL COMPUTER SECURITY PRODUCTS

The basic personal computer often has little in the way of protection features. Users with specific security needs must first determine an acceptable balance between the risk they face and the cost of additional control measures. The main body of this chapter has described the types of control measures that should be considered. This section provides an outline of several types of commercially available protection products. This list focuses on products designed specifically for personal computers and does not include other security and environmental control products such as locks, fire detection and suppression equipment, alarm systems, shredders, and a wide range of other products and services.

	RESPONSE			
ITEM	*YES*	*NO*	*N/A*	*COMMENTS*
Organizational and Policy				
1. Are there organizational policies and procedures that address the handling of sensitive and proprietary information?				
2. Are the procedures for the protection of sensitive information handled on PCs consistent with those for other types of sensitive information in the organization?				
3. Are policies regarding personal use of PC equipment and software clearly stated?				
User Awareness and Training				
1. Are users provided with adequate training and awareness of organizational information security policies and their individual responsibilities?				
2. In each of the areas discussed in this questionnaire, are users provided adequate training in the performance of required procedures and the use of necessary equipment or systems?				
Physical and Environmental Protection				
1. Is equipment provided with adequate protection from theft, damage, and unauthorized use?				

Figure 15.1. Personal computer self-assessment questionnaire.

	RESPONSE			
ITEM	*YES*	*NO*	*N/A*	*COMMENTS*
2. Is electrical power quality satisfactory? If not, are surge suppressors or other power quality enhancement equipment used?				
3. Are temperature and relative humidity maintained within acceptable limits?				
4. Is equipment protected adequately from airborne contaminants (smoke, dust, etc.)?				
Control of Storage Media				
1. Are there procedures for external labeling of sensitive materials?				
2. Are there adequate storage facilities for security sensitive media (hardcopy, removable magnetic media, etc.)?				
3. Are there procedures to ensure the proper handling and storage of magnetic media (to minimize physical or magnetic damage)?				
4. Are there procedures for the proper disposal of sensitive media (e.g., shredding paper, degaussing diskettes)?				
Data and System Integrity				
1. Is common use (shared) software protected from undetected modification?				

Figure 15.1. Personal computer self-assessment questionnaire. (cont'd)

ITEM	RESPONSE			
	YES	*NO*	*N/A*	*COMMENTS*
2. In situations where important decisions are based on data produced by a PC, are there adequate procedures to validate results?				
3. Are users provided with adequate training in the use of the software tools they are using?				
4. Are major PC application systems subjected to formal system development controls?				
System and Data Access Controls				
1. If a system is intended for use only by specific users, are there adequate methods (physical or otherwise) to prevent unauthorized use?				
2. If multiple users of a system are using a fixed disk, are there adequate mechanisms to provide needed file access control?				
3. If access control hardware or software is used:				
a. Is the user interface sufficiently constrained to prevent users from circumventing the control mechanisms?				
b. Is there a method to prevent users from using an unauthorized copy of the operating system?				

Figure 15.1. Personal computer self-assessment questionnaire. (cont'd)

ITEM	RESPONSE			
	YES	*NO*	*N/A*	*COMMENTS*
4. If cryptography is used, are there adequate key selection and management procedures?				
5. Are users provided with utilities (and training) to overwrite sensitive disk files or system memory?				
Contingency Planning				
1. Are there adequate procedures and equipment for handling emergency situations (e.g., fire, flooding, emergency evacuation, bomb threat, etc.)?				
2. Are routine backup procedures for data and software adequate for the sensitivity, criticality, and volatility of such information?				
3. Are critical materials (data, software, equipment, documentation, etc.) needed for backup operation stored and available at offsite or otherwise safe locations?				
4. Are there formal plans for the backup operation of critical functions and for eventual recovery from contingency situations?				
5. Is readiness to respond to contingency situations tested and reviewed periodically?				

Figure 15.1. Personal computer self-assessment questionnaire. (cont'd)

	RESPONSE			
ITEM	*YES*	*NO*	*N/A*	*COMMENTS*
Auditability 1. If audit trails are needed for a PC application, is the user interface sufficiently constrained to prevent unauthorized modification or destruction of audit trail data?				
PC to Host Connections 1. Are measures taken to prevent the practice of storing sensitive host logon information (e.g., passwords) in PC terminal emulation software? If not, are such PC systems provided with adequate controls to prevent unauthorized access (and thereby access to associated host systems)?				
2. If a PC is used to prepare and preedit transactions for submission to a host-based system, are there redundant edits and audit trail mechanisms at the host to protect against corruption of transactions prior to receipt at the host?				
3. Are host system security mechanisms adequate to:				
a. Prevent unauthorized access to system facilities and data?				
b. Monitor and, if necessary, limit the type and volume of data that may be downloaded to a remote device?				

Figure 15.1. Personal computer self-assessment questionnaire. (cont'd)

	RESPONSE			
ITEM	*YES*	*NO*	*N/A*	*COMMENTS*
PC Networks				
1. If PC systems are connected to a local area network and message security is required, are there adequate cryptographic or other communications security measures?				
2. If a PC is accessible for remote use, are there adequate user identification and authentication mechanisms in the PC to prevent unauthorized access?				
Miscellaneous Issues				
1. Is there adequate monitoring, control, and accountability of PC equipment and software?				
2. Are there policies and procedures to monitor and control the use of PC-related devices, software, and supplies?				
3. Are there procedures to ensure compliance with licensed software and proprietary information protection agreements?				

Figure 15.1. Personal computer self-assessment questionnaire. (cont'd)

The list of security products below describes only *types* of products that are available rather than specific vendors or products. It should also be noted that the mention of a specific type of product does not imply any direct or indirect endorsement by the National Bureau of Standards.

Physical Access Control and Theft Protection

Products in this category provide physical protection of equipment from damage, theft, and general physical access. Thus, they also provide a first line of control over system and file access.

- Lockable equipment enclosures and workstations
- Equipment lockdown devices
- Power switch locks
- Equipment cabinet or enclosure locking devices
- Equipment removal detection devices

Electrical Power Quality Control

This class of product provides protection from variations in electrical power that could damage or impair the reliability of equipment.

- Surge suppressors
- Power "conditioning" systems
- Uninterruptible power supply (UPS) systems

Environmental Protection

These products are intended to maintain acceptable environmental conditions for equipment.

- Fire detection and suppression equipment
- Water detection alarms
- Temperature and relative humidity monitors
- Dust covers
- Static mats, sprays, or grounding devices
- Dust filters, fans, etc.

Magnetic Media Protection

- Lockable storage devices
- Color-coded labels and jackets
- Protective containers and mailers

- Degaussing and destruction equipment
- File encryption systems

System and File Access Control

This category of product provides user control over access to system facilities or individual files and programs. User identification and authentication may also be provided.

- *User authenticators* — devices or software that require users to identify themselves before access to the system is granted. These usually require the entry of a password to gain access.

- *Card or badge readers* — devices that read information from magnetically coded cards (e.g., credit cards) for entry to the system and use for access control decisions.

- *Authentication code devices* — devices that work in conjunction with system software to generate a session-unique authentication code to be input by the user.

- *File access control systems* — modifications to operating system service routines that limit which files or directories a user may access.

- *Port protection devices* — devices that control remote access to a system. These devices normally are inserted between the computer system and the modem. They require remote users to provide user authentication (usually a password or code). Some systems provide a call-back option in which the line is disconnected and the user is called back at a predetermined telephone number.

Cryptographic Systems

These products use cryptographic protection for various operational requirements. Cryptographic systems may have any or a combination of the following characteristics or features:

- Hardware or software implementation of the cryptographic algorithm
- Hardware or software implementation of supporting functions
- Private or public key cryptographic approach
- Automatic or manual key generation, entry, storage, and distribution
- Proprietary or public (e.g., DES) algorithms

It should be noted that some of the products listed under System and File Access Control also use cryptographic protection.

- *General-purpose cryptographic facilities* — hardware or software that provides basic crypto functions (set key, encrypt, and decrypt). Users must build specific applications around these products.

- *Bulk file encryption utilities* — programs that enable a user to encrypt or decrypt a specified data file. The user normally is required to enter the cryptographic key. Some systems act directly on the original file (thus destroying its original contents), while other systems produce a separate file (requiring use of an overwrite utility to prevent access to the original file).

- *Integral disk encryption systems* — usually hardware and software that cause all disk write (or read) operations to be encrypted (decrypted), thus eliminating cleartext on disk while not changing the application interface.

- *Communications encryption systems* — devices that provide integral communications and cryptographic facilities to enable secure communications among PC systems.

Miscellaneous

- *System utilities* — software designed to enable use of write-protect, "hide" files, and other system facilities that can be used for additional protection.

- *CRT privacy screens* — covers for CRT screens that limit screen viewing to a narrow angle of view, normally sufficient only for the user.

SUMMARY

This chapter has discussed some of the security issues that must be addressed by any organization using or contemplating the use of personal computers.

Personal computers offer tremendous opportunities for improved productivity, and their introduction into the office environment will continue to grow. It would be hopeless (indeed, counterproductive) for over-zealous auditors or security officers to try to stop this process. However, this does mean more people and more points of potential security exposure with which management must deal. These are not insurmountable problems, but they do require an extra degree of attention and creativity on the part of both management and users.

Part 4

Measurements/
Metrics

16

Quantitative Analysis of System Reviews

The more precise a quality assurance evaluation, the more valuable that evaluation is to data processing management. Statements like "The system looks good" or "They might have some trouble with that system" are too nebulous to be of much value to anyone. While it may be of some value to management to say that system A is better than system B, managers want to know how much better. Data processing management desires a precise measurement of the efficiency of a computer application.

This chapter provides the QA reviewer with methodology for quantifying the evaluation of computer application system review. The result will be a numerical score which can be evaluated and compared to other evaluations. Each review point can be rated and the continuum of ratings plotted to determine whether the work on the project is improving or declining. This trend evaluation can be extremely valuable to management if it has any reservation about continuing the development of a particular application. If definite improvement can be shown from one review to another, management's confidence in that project team will increase. While judgment must still be applied to any quantitative evaluation, scoring a system review is an excellent tool for describing the status of an application system and comparing current to prior status.

VALUE OF RATINGS

The concerns addressed in the checkpoint reviews should not be answered yes or no even though the concerns are worded so that it appears a yes or no answer would be appropriate. In practice, this is not practical. For example, one of the concerns stated is "whether or not the system development life cycle phase being reviewed will be completed within budget." If the answer is yes, does this mean it will be completed exactly for the budgeted amount, $1 less, $1,000 less, $10,000 less, or whatever? On the other hand, does a no answer mean it will run $1 over budget, $1,000 or $10,000 over budget? While a yes answer is comforting, and a no answer discouraging, it is possible the difference is $2 or less. Therefore, we need to be able to provide a more definitive response than yes or no.

The method given in this chapter is to answer each concern on a five-point rating scale. The midpoint on the scale is considered an average implementation or resolution of a concern. The lower end of the scale would be a poor implementation or resolution of a concern, with the bottom of the scale being very poor. The ratings on the upper end of the scale would be good and very good. This now permits the reviewer to avoid a black or white answer, and to work instead with shades of gray. The scale can be used in a variety of ways, but all are designed to provide a wider range of responses than yes/no.

The objective of the rating is to be able to accumulate the responses to the concerns to determine a total rating score for the review point. If the answer to every concern was that the MIS system project team had implemented or resolved the concern to an average degree, then the total rating for the review point would be average. However, it would be unusual if all concerns were handled at the same level.

The unweighted accumulation of the various points on the scale at first appears logical, but further analysis shows us that some of the concerns are much more important than others. For example, in the mid-justification phase review, it is important that the good and bad points of the current system have been determined, but this concern is not nearly as important as the concern that new information needs have been determined. With an unweighted system, if the reviewer were to rate the project team as very poor on determining the good and bad parts of the current system, but very good on determining the new information needs, the total rating of the work based on those two concerns would be average. That is unfair since one concern was much more important than the other. The overall rating should be above average because the more important concern scored very good.

The resolution is to weight each of the concerns by a factor of 1, 2, or 3. The weight is a measure of importance of a concern. In our previous example, the new information needs being determined might be given a weighting factor of 3, and determining the good and bad parts of the current system is given a weighting factor of 1. The logic of this is that if you can satisfy all the current needs of the user, it is not too important whether or not you are aware of all the good and bad parts of the current system. This does not diminish the value of learning from existing experience but, rather, explains the need to compare the importance of different concerns.

The evaluation of a concern can be a very time-consuming and detailed task. QA personnel may have to develop extensive questionnaires to arrive at an evaluation for each of the concerns, and these questionnaires themselves may have to be given a rating scale so that at the conclusion of the review a quantitative score can be calculated.

RATING CONSIDERATIONS

The QA group must determine how ratings will be given for a particular concern. For example, to evaluate whether or not the project was implemented within budget, the group needs to establish guidelines for rating. Let us assume that the organization involved states that a project manager should be able to complete a project within plus or minus 5 percent of the stated budget amount. Since completing the project with a 5 percent tolerance is expected, achieving that performance can be considered average. Working with DP management, the quality assurance group could extrapolate that if the project manager can complete the project within plus or minus 15 percent of the stated budget, that is an acceptable performance. If costs exceed 115 percent of budget, performance is very poor, while if the project leader can complete it in less that 85 percent of the budget, the performance is very good. Using these guidelines, we can now rate the answer to the concern about implementation within the budget dollars. The rating would be as follows:

Ratings	Criterion
Very good	Project complete within 85 percent of budget or less
Good	Project complete within 85.1 – 94.9 percent of budget
Average	Project complete within 95 – 105 percent of budget
Poor	Project complete within 105.1–114.9 percent of budget
Very poor	Project complete for over 115 percent of budget

This type of evaluation must be done for each of the concerns within each review point review. Some of the concerns fit very easily into a quantitative analysis while others do not. For example, the concern that the proposed system will have a reasonable life expectancy is difficult to quantify. If we can determine what a reasonable life expectancy is, we can then develop a five-point rating for that life expectancy.

Concerns that are difficult to rate quantitatively are those that deal with subjective judgments such as feelings, preference, likings, etc. For example, consider the concern of whether or not the user wants the proposed system. Rarely will a user respond "Yes, I want it," or "No, I do not want it." Most times the response to the question if asked as stated would be "Yes, BUT ..." The interpretation of "Yes, BUT" answers can be difficult. Therefore, either the reviewer must pin down the user to a quantitative response or convert the user's response into a quantitative response.

This conversion of subjective responses into quantitative answers is not as difficult as it first appears. There are a number of methods that seem to work very well. One way is to ask the user to pick the one from the five-point scale which appears most appropriate. For example, for the question "Does the user want the proposed system?" we could give the user the following five choices and ask which is most appropriate. The five choices might be

1. Do you very much want the proposed system to be installed?

2. Do you want the new system to be installed?

3. Is it unimportant to you whether or not the new system is installed?

4. Would you prefer that the new system is not installed?

5. Do you desire very much not to have the new system installed?

The reviewer may not feel comfortable asking user personnel to pick among five different choices. Alternatives to this are to merely discuss the general topic area, such as the user's feeling about the new system, and then let the reviewer make a judgment as to what the user has said. Obviously, this has some interpretation and bias on the part of the reviewer, but may prove to be a better method of collecting information than to have the user try to pick among five responses to a concern.

When picking a specific response is difficult for a user, or if the approach is awkward for the reviewer, another method can be used to arrive at an evaluation. Rather than ask for a specific response to a question, the reviewer can ask one or more questions related to a concern and then rate the answer on a five-point scale. In the example above, he can ask questions relating to whether the system will be easy to work with, whether the system does the job the user hoped it would do, and whether the user's job will be easier or harder after the new system is installed. For instance, in determining whether or not the user wants the new system, a good question might be "Will your job be easier when a new system is installed?" From the answer given by the user the reviewer can create a rating scale:

1.   The job will be much easier when the new system is installed. (Rate very good.)

2.   The job will be easier when the new system is installed. (Rate good.)

3.   The job will be about the same when the new system is installed. (Rate average.)

4.   The job will be harder when the new system is installed. (Rate poor.)

5.   The job will be much harder when the system is installed. (Rate very poor.)

The reviewer uses a series of questions and then, based on the totality of all the answers, makes a judgment as to the quantitative rating for that review concern.

Another method of getting quantitative opinions to subjective concerns is to probe the user's response. Again, if we wanted to determine if the user wanted the proposed system, the reviewer could ask a question such as "Do you feel that the proposed system is going to be valuable to your department?" The user would probably respond "Yes, but" and give some reasons. The reviewer can then probe the "Yes, buts" as to whether it will be helpful, very helpful, not helpful, etc. This might be done in a casual conversation that is more relaxing and easier for the user than probing for a specific answer.

REVIEW POINT EVALUATION FORMS

The QA group concerns as given in Chapter 7 become the basis for evaluating quantitatively each review point. The reviewer must make an evaluation for each of the concerns. Figures 16.1 through 16.12 are worksheets for evaluating each concern for each checkpoint.

The factor column on the worksheet shows suggested weights for every concern using a three-point scale proposed earlier. A factor of 3 is used to show the concern of most importance, and a factor of 1 to show the concern of least importance. During the evaluation process for a concern by the quality assurance reviewer, the factor is not used. However, the factor is used in arriving at a weighted score for a concern for that particular review point.

The reviewer checks the column showing his rating of how well each concern has been handled. There is also room on the worksheet to indicate if the concern is not applicable to that specific project. For example, if the organization in question does not have budgets, then the concern regarding "implementing the project within the budget" is not applicable (N/A) for that particular review point.

The worksheet includes a column for comments. For example, if the reviewer is about to begin review point 9, that individual should review the results of the previous eight reviews. Comments included can be very helpful in explaining why a particular rating was given. This is especially true if the rating could almost be determined by a toss of a coin between two categories. Therefore, a comment that indicates a borderline decision will be helpful to the next person reviewing the project.

When the reviewer has completed the entire review point review, the next step is to calculate the score for that review point.

SCORING THE QA REVIEW

There are three steps to follow in scoring each review. First, each concern must be rated by the five-point scale. Second, the rating must be translated in a quantitative score and accumulated for the review. Third is the interpretation of the score. The reviewer must rate each concern at the end of each review point. In review point 1, there are eight concerns. Assuming all eight are applicable to the application under review, each of the eight concerns would be rated within the five-point scale (i.e., very good, good, average, poor, or very poor).

		MIS SYSTEMS PROJECT TEAM IMPLEMENTATION/RESOLUTION OF CONCERN					
QUALITY ASSURANCE CONCERN	Factor	Very Good	Good	Aver-age	Poor	Very Poor	N/A
1. A sufficient number of capable people have been assigned to the justification phase.	1						
2. The good and bad parts of the current system have been determined.	1						
3. The data processing procedures and stan-dards have been fol-lowed.	3						
4. There are no adequate alternatives available to meet the user's needs without building a new system.	2						
5. The justification phase will be completed on time.	3						
6. The justification phase will be completed within budget.	1						
7. The goals and objec-tives to be solved are clearly stated.	1						
8. The goals and objec-tives to be solved are clearly stated.	3						
Comments							

Figure 16.1. Quality Assurance review point #1: mid-justification phase review.

QUALITY ASSURANCE CONCERN	Factor	MIS SYSTEMS PROJECT TEAM IMPLEMENTATION/RESOLUTION OF CONCERN					
		Very Good	Good	Aver-age	Poor	Very Poor	N/A
1. The data processing costs have been esti-mated.	1						
2. The user costs and benefits have been estimated.	1						
3. A conceptual system design has been pre-pared.	2						
4. The data processing procedures and stan-dards have been fol-lowed.	2						
5. The proposed system was selected by a reasonable method from among the various alternatives.	2						
6. The assumptions made in arriving at a solution are valid.	2						
7. The proposed solution solves the business problem.	3						
8. The user wants the proposed system.	3						
Comments							

Figure 16.2. Quality Assurance review point #2: end of justification phase review.

QUALITY ASSURANCE CONCERN	Factor	MIS SYSTEMS PROJECT TEAM IMPLEMENTATION/RESOLUTION OF CONCERN					
		Very Good	Good	Aver-age	Poor	Very Poor	N/A
9. The proposed system has a reasonable life expectancy.	3						
10. The standards of per-formance for the new system have been established.	2						
11. The standards of per-formance are docu-mented and in the hands of the system designers.	2						
12. Criteria have been estab-lished to evaluate per-formance after the system is operational.	2						
Comments							

Figure 16.2. Quality Assurance review point #2: end of justification phase review. (cont'd)

QUALITY ASSURANCE CONCERN	Factor	MIS SYSTEMS PROJECT TEAM IMPLEMENTATION/RESOLUTION OF CONCERN					
		Very Good	Good	Aver-age	Poor	Very Poor	N/A
1. A sufficient number of capable people have been assigned to the systems design phase.	1						
2. The business problem has been solved and the needed work products (report, etc.) are defined.	3						
3. The source needed data has been determined.	3						
4. The data storage (file) needs have been determined.	2						
5. The required processing has been determined.	2						
6. The various functions of the proposed system fit together.	2						
7. The proposed solution solves the business problem.	3						
8. The system will be implemented when needed.	2						
9. Performance standards will be achieved.	2						
Comments							

Figure 16.3. Quality Assurance review point #3: review of business systems solution phase.

QUALITY ASSURANCE CONCERN	Factor	MIS SYSTEMS PROJECT TEAM IMPLEMENTATION/RESOLUTION OF CONCERN					
		Very Good	Good	Aver-age	Poor	Very Poor	N/A
1. The equipment require-ments have been deter-mined.	2						
2. It has been determined whether or not addi-tional hardware will be required.	2						
3. It has been determined whether or not addi-tional software will be required.	2						
4. It has been determined whether or not any special hardware or software installation will be required.	2						
5. The MIS department and the project team have the level of experi-ence necessary to use the specified hardware and software.	2						
6. The hardware provides for sufficient growth for the proposed system.	2						
Comments							

Figure 16.4. Quality Assurance review point #4: review of equipment selection.

QUALITY ASSURANCE CONCERN	Factor	MIS SYSTEMS PROJECT TEAM IMPLEMENTATION/RESOLUTION OF CONCERN					
		Very Good	*Good*	*Aver-age*	*Poor*	*Very Poor*	*N/A*
1. The file specifications meet MIS standards.	2						
2. The input specifications meet MIS standards.	2						
3. The output specifications meet MIS standards.	2						
4. The process specifica-tions meet MIS standards.	2						
5. The computer system design is properly documented.	2						
6. The computer system design is complete.	2						
7. The system as designed meets the needs of the user(s).	3						
8. The system as designed will operate on the planned hardware and software.	3						
9. The costs have been developed in accor-dance with MIS procedures.	2						
Comments							

Figure 16.5. Quality Assurance review point #5: review of computer system design.

QUALITY ASSURANCE CONCERN	Factor	MIS SYSTEMS PROJECT TEAM IMPLEMENTATION/RESOLUTION OF CONCERN					
		Very Good	*Good*	*Aver- age*	*Poor*	*Very Poor*	*N/A*
10. The system design provides the capacity for reasonable growth.	1						
11. Other design alterna- tives were considered and rejected for valid reasons.	2						
12. The system design does not impose undue re- strictions on the user.	2						
13. The audit trail is suffi- cient to reconstruct transactions.	3						
14. The computer systems design phase will be completed on time.	1						
15. The computer systems design phase will be completed within budget.	1						
16. The MIS system stan- dards are realistic for the system.	1						
Comments							

Figure 16.5. Quality Assurance review point #5: review of computer system design. (cont'd)

QUALITY ASSURANCE CONCERN	Factor	MIS SYSTEMS PROJECT TEAM IMPLEMENTATION/RESOLUTION OF CONCERN					
		Very Good	*Good*	*Aver- age*	*Poor*	*Very Poor*	*N/A*
17. The current MIS systems standards are appropriate for the time when this system will be operational.	1						
18. Performance standards can be achieved.	2						
19. The system of internal control is adequate to ensure the accurate and complete processing of transactions.	3						
20. The system of internal control is adequate to ensure the continued integrity of the computer files and/or databases.	3						
Comments							

Figure 16.5. Quality Assurance Review point #5: review of computer system design. (cont'd)

QUALITY ASSURANCE CONCERN	Factor	MIS SYSTEMS PROJECT TEAM IMPLEMENTATION/RESOLUTION OF CONCERN					
		Very Good	Good	Aver-age	Poor	Very Poor	N/A
1. A sufficient number of capable people have been assigned to the program design phase.	1						
2. The program design meets MIS standards.	2						
3. The program design has been properly documented.	2						
4. Provision has been made for restart procedures.	1						
5. Provision has been made for recovery procedures.	2						
6. Provision has been made to protect sensitive data.	2						
7. There is a programming schedule.	1						
8. The program design phase will be completed on time.	1						
Comments							

Figure 16.6. Quality Assurance review point #6: review of program design.

QUALITY ASSURANCE CONCERN	Factor	MIS SYSTEMS PROJECT TEAM IMPLEMENTATION/RESOLUTION OF CONCERN					
		Very Good	Good	Aver-age	Poor	Very Poor	N/A
9. The program design phase will be completed within budget.	1						
10. The MIS program standards are realistic for this system.	1						
11. The current MIS program standards are appropriate for the time when this system will be operational.	1						
12. Performance standards will be achieved.	2						
Comments							

Figure 16.6. Quality Assurance review point #6: review of program design. (cont'd)

QUALITY ASSURANCE CONCERN	Factor	MIS SYSTEMS PROJECT TEAM IMPLEMENTATION/RESOLUTION OF CONCERN					
		Very Good	Good	Aver-age	Poor	Very Poor	N/A
1. A plan has been estab-lished to convert from the old to the new system.	2						
2. The conversion plan is in accordance with MIS standards.	2						
3. A plan has been estab-lished to test the new system.	2						
4. The test plan is in accordance with MIS standards.	2						
5. Sufficient resources have been allocated for the conversion.	1						
6. Sufficient resources have been allocated for the system test.	1						
7. There is a testing schedule.	1						
8. There is a conversion schedule.	1						
Comments							

Figure 16.7. Quality Assurance review point #7: review of testing and conversion planning.

QUALITY ASSURANCE CONCERN	Factor	MIS SYSTEMS PROJECT TEAM IMPLEMENTATION/RESOLUTION OF CONCERN					
		Very Good	Good	Aver- age	Poor	Very Poor	N/A
1. Programs are coded in accordance with MIS standards.	2						
2. Programs are ad- equately tested.	2						
3. The program code is maintainable by the average programmer.	2						
4. The system of internal control has been imple- mented according to specifications.	3						
Comments							

Figure 16.8. Quality Assurance review point #8: review of program coding and testing.

QUALITY ASSURANCE CONCERN	Factor	MIS SYSTEMS PROJECT TEAM IMPLEMENTATION/RESOLUTION OF CONCERN					
		Very Good	*Good*	*Aver-age*	*Poor*	*Very Poor*	*N/A*
1. A sufficient number of capable people have been assigned to the system test phase.	1						
2. Comprehensive test data will be prepared.	2						
3. Users will be adequately trained to evaluate test results.	2						
4. The planned test data will test the system controls.	2						
5. The test phase will be completed on time.	1						
6. The test phase will be completed within budget.	1						
Comments							

Figure 16.9. Quality Assurance review point #9: review of detailed test plan.

QUALITY ASSURANCE CONCERN	Factor	MIS SYSTEMS PROJECT TEAM IMPLEMENTATION/RESOLUTION OF CONCERN					
		Very Good	*Good*	*Average*	*Poor*	*Very Poor*	*N/A*
1. The system does meet the needs of the user as specified in the design.	3						
2. The system does conform to MIS standards.	2						
3. The test was performed according to MIS test standards.	2						
4. The user is adequately trained to handle the day-to-day problems of the system.	3						
5. Performance standards have been achieved.	2						
Comments							

Figure 16.10. Quality Assurance review point #10: review of test results.

QUALITY ASSURANCE CONCERN	Factor	MIS SYSTEMS PROJECT TEAM IMPLEMENTATION/RESOLUTION OF CONCERN					
		Very Good	*Good*	*Aver-age*	*Poor*	*Very Poor*	*N/A*
1. A sufficient number of capable people have been assigned to the system conversion phase.	1						
2. Conversion programs are coded and tested in accordance with MIS standards.	2						
3. A contingency plan has been made in case the conversion is unsuccessful.	2						
4. The conversion plan will be completed on time.	1						
5. The conversion phase will be completed within budget.	1						
6. The controls over the conversion process are adequate to ensure an accurate and complete conversion.	3						
Comments							

Figure 16.11. Quality Assurance review point #11: review of detail conversion planning and programs.

QUALITY ASSURANCE CONCERN	Factor	EDP SYSTEMS PROJECT TEAM IMPLEMENTATION/RESOLUTION OF CONCERN					
		Very Good	Good	Aver-age	Poor	Very Poor	N/A
1. The conversion was performed in accordance with conversion standards.	2						
2. The results of the conversion process have been verified.	3						
Comments							

Figure 16.12. Quality Assurance review point #12: review of conversion results.

The next step is to translate the rating into quantitative scores. The Review Score Sheet (Figure 16.13) is used for this purpose. The Review Score Sheet is divided into three rating sections. Each rating section is used for one of the three factor numbers. The first rating section is for factor 1 rated concerns, the second section for factor 2 rated concerns, and the third section for factor 3 rated concerns.

The best method to accumulate the total score for a review is to quantify the rating for each concern in order by its factor weight. The reviewer looks first at the concerns weighted by factor number 1. For these concerns, the reviewer adds up all the check marks in each column. This means the number of checks in the very poor column, poor column, average column, etc. In review point 1, there are 4 concerns weighted with a factor number 1. The ratings for these must now be transcribed to the factor number 1 section of Figure 16.13. For example, if 2 of those were checked not applicable, the reviewer would put a number 2 in the "number of questions rated" for the not applicable (N/A) rating. If 1 of the 4 was scored average, the reviewer would put a 1 in the "number of questions rated" column for the average rating for factor number 1. If the other concern was rated good, the reviewer would then put a 1 in the "number of questions rated" column for the good score.

Then the reviewer would move to the factor 2 and look at all the concerns that were weighted by a factor number 2. In the Review Score Sheet, this grading would be put in the factor 2 section. For review point number 1, there are three concerns weighted by factor number 3. This means in section three of the Review Score Sheet the three ratings would be transcribed to the section 3 ratings with the number of questions rated put in the "number of questions rated" column.

Review Point # _____ **Date Completed** _____

Reviewer's Name _____

Factor Number	Rating	Number of Questions Rated	Times This Constant	Equals This Score
1	Not Applicable (N/A)		0	
	Very Poor		1	
	Poor		2	
	Average		3	
	Good		4	
	Very Good		5	
2	Not Applicable (N/A)		0	
	Very Poor		2	
	Poor		4	
	Average		6	
	Good		8	
	Very Good		10	
3	Not Applicable (N/A)		0	
	Very Poor		3	
	Poor		6	
	Average		9	
	Good		12	
	Very Good		15	———
	Total Score			═══
	N/A Score			═══

Figure 16.13. Review score sheet.

When the ratings for all the concerns for the review point being scored have been transcribed to the Review Score Sheet, it is time to calculate the score. To do this, the number in the "number of questions rated" column is multiplied by the constant in the "times this constant" column. For example, we said there was one question rated average for factor 1. In this example, we multiply the 1 times 3 to get a total score of 3 for the average rating for factor 1. The score of 3 is put in the "Equals this score" column. This process is continued until each number in the "Number of questions rated" column has been multiplied by the constant in the "times this constant" column to arrive at a score. The "Equals this score" column is accumulated to arrive at a total score for the review point.

Next, the not applicable (N/A) score must be calculated. This is done by multiplying the number of questions rated times the factor number for each of the three factors. The following table illustrates how this can be accomplished.

Factor Number	Number of N/A Questions Checked for Factor Number	Times This Constant	Equals the N/A Score for This Review Point
1	_____	× 1	= _____
2	_____	× 2	= _____
3	_____	× 3	= _____

Total N/A score is _____

Note: This total N/A score is put at the bottom of the Review Score Sheet (see Figure 16.13).

The review score has now been calculated for the completed review point. The top of the form should be completed, which shows the review point number, the date the review was completed, and the lead reviewer's name.

This calculation has produced a raw score which must be adjusted so that it can be compared to other reviews. The adjusted score is calculated by dividing the number of questions times their weight into the total score. This will produce an adjusted score between zero and five. Figure 16.14 is a form to be used in developing the adjusted scores. This adjusted score can then be used for comparative purposes between all twelve review points and other systems.

Assuming all concerns are applicable to the review point, the "total score" from the Review Score Sheet (Figure 16.13) is moved to the "total score" column of Figure 16.14 for the applicable review point. This "total score" is then divided by the constant in the "divided by this constant" column. The result, which is the adjusted score (should be calculated to two decimal places), is put in the adjusted score column.

If some of the concerns are not applicable (N/A) to the review point, the "Divided by this constant" constant must be adjusted. The adjustment is made by subtracting from the constant in the "Divided by this constant" (Figure 16.14) the "N/A score" calculated in the Review Score Sheet (Figure 16.13). For example, if one question with a weighting of factor 1 was not applicable, the N/A score would be 1. This is calculated by multiplying the number of not applicable questions times the factor number. If this was for review point 1, then 1 would be subtracted from the constant 15 to arrive at a new constant of 14. Fourteen would then be divided into the total score for review point 1 to arrive at an adjusted score.

Once the adjusted score has been determined, it can then be compared to scores for the other twelve review points, and other application system reviews for the same review point number.

EVALUATING THE SCORE

At the completion of each review point, the reviewer will calculate an adjusted score. This is a score between 1.0 and 5.0 and it represents a quantitative evaluation by the reviewer for the application system for the phase under review.

The adjusted score can be compared to other review points, as well as to other application system reviews. However, like any quantitative evaluation score, it must be interpreted. The score is a very viable indicator of the health of the application system. For example, an adjusted score of 3.5 would be considered above average. This still needs interpretation. For example, a score of 3.5 that has dropped from 4.0 in the previous review point may be of more concern than a score which stayed consistent at 3.5 from review point to review point or one which has moved up from 3.0 to 3.5 at this review point.

The score can vary depending on the reviewers — some are "hard markers" and others are "easy." Some organizations assign factors to the reviewers themselves. For example, they may multiply the reviewer's score by a 1.2 for a hard marker and by a .8 for an easy marker to equate scores. A better method might be just an explanation of the mark itself. For example, an adjusted score of 3.0 from one reviewer may be equivalent to a score of 3.5 from another reviewer. This is something that must be learned from experience at each organization.

The following is a guide for interpreting adjusted scores. The final interpretation should take into account the characteristics of application systems, the caliber of people working on the system, the "hardness" or "easiness" of the individual arriving at the adjusted score, and other organization-related factors which can affect the score. The following is given as a guideline to be used on some of the early reviews.

Adjusted Score/Explanation of Adjusted Score

1.0 – 1.99 The implementation and/or resolution of concerns by the systems project team is poor. In this range, the reviewer should consider recommending substantial additional work on this systems development life cycle phase before the system is advanced. The project appears to be in trouble.

2.0 – 2.75 The project needs either additional work or more direction or both. Possibly the project should move to the next stage, but only with extra resources allocated to the project. A score in the 1.0 – 2.75 range for the final three review points flags the system as one in serious trouble.

2.76 – 3.25 The project implementation appears to be adequate. The implementation and/or resolution of concerns is at an acceptable level. Within this range, the quality assurance function can play an important role. It is important that projects in this range maintain adequate quality throughout the remaining phases of the systems development life cycle.

3.26 – 4.0 This is the ideal range for an implemented project. Projects in this range should require little attention and concern of data processing management. The caliber of implementation and/or resolution of concern is above average and should result in a cost-effective, well-controlled system that meets the needs of the user. Quality assurance personnel should be able to cut back some of their effort in reviewing application systems in this range.

4.01 – 5.0 Applications in this range should be considered superior in implementation. However, the implementation effort may be excessive and as such may not be cost-effective. Frequently, systems analysts or programmers have more time allocated than necessary to implement the project. With that time they put in the extra "bells and whistles" which make the project ideal from an implementation viewpoint, but may utilize more resources than necessary.

The trend shown by plotting the adjusted score from review point to review point is a valuable tool for analysis of the implementation process. Ideally, the adjusted score should stay within a small range (e.g., within half a point) throughout all the review points. Wide fluctuations may indicate that work is being shifted from phase to phase. For example, a score that drops during the program design can mean that the project leader is transferring that aspect of the application system development to the programming phase.

Reviewers should try to understand and explain to data processing management fluctuations in adjusted score. Whenever adjusted score fluctuates more than half a point, the difference should be investigated and explained to management. It indicates that a problem has occurred, or has been corrected, and management should be advised of this situation.

EXAMPLE OF REVIEW POINT EVALUATION

Assume that you have been assigned to review an application and that you are at the first review point.

Referring back to Figure 7.2, there are eight concerns which are listed below. The quality assurance reviewer rating for these concerns is also listed.

#	*Quality Assurance Concern*	*Rating*
1	A sufficient number of capable people have been assigned to the justification phase.	Average
2	The good and bad parts of the system have been determined.	Poor
3	The new information needs have been determined.	Good

#	*Quality Assurance Concern*	*Rating*
4	The data processing procedures and standards have been followed.	Average
5	There are no adequate alternatives available to meet the user's needs without building a new system.	Very Good
6	The justification phase will be completed on time	N/A
7	The justification phase will be completed within budget.	N/A
8	The goals and objectives to be solved are clearly stated.	Average

The reviewer's ratings are then transcribed to the Review Score Sheet. Figure 16.15 shows a Review Score Sheet scored for this review. There are two not applicable ratings, one poor rating, three average ratings, one good rating, and one very good rating. Each of these has been transcribed to Figure 16.15 in the appropriate factor number section. Refer back to Figure 16.1 for the factor number.

After the rating from the review sheet has been transcribed, the total score can be calculated. The total score for this review point is 47. Two questions were answered not applicable (N/A). The N/A score is 2.

When the total score for the review point has been accumulated, an adjusted score needs to be calculated. From Figure 16.14, we see that the constant to divide by is 15. Because there is an N/A score, this must be adjusted. The calculation for adjusted score for this review point 1 example is shown below:

Step	*Explanation*	*Score*
1	Determine the "divided by constant" for review point one (see Figure 9.14)	15
2	Determine the "N/A score" for review point 1 (for example)	2
3	Subtract "N/A score" from constant to obtain new "divided by constant."	13

Step	*Explanation*	*Score*
4	Determine "total score" for review point one.	47
5	Divide new "divided by constant" into "total score" for review point 1 to obtain adjusted score (i.e., 47 divided by 13 equals 3.62.)	3.62

Review Point Decimal Number	Review Point Name	Total Score	Divided By This Constant (Less N/A Score)	Adjusted Score (2 Decimal Places)
1	Mid-Justification Phase		15	
2	End of Justification Phase		25	
3	Business Systems Solution Phase		20	
4	Computer Equipment Selection		12	
5	Computer System Design		40	
6	Program Design		17	
7	Testing and Conversion Planning		12	
8	Program Coding and Testing		9	
9	Detailed Test Plan		9	
10	Test Results		12	
11	Detail Conversion Planning and Programs		10	
12	Conversion Results		5	

Figure 16.14. Adjusted score for comparative purposes.

The adjusted score is 3.62, which can be interpreted to mean this project should require little attention and concern of data processing management. The caliber of implementation is above average and should result in a cost-effective, well-controlled system.

Review Point # _____   *Date Completed* November 18

Reviewer's Name ___I.M. Reviewer_____

Factor Number	Rating	Number of Questions Rated	Times This Constant	Equals This Score
1	Not Applicable (N/A)	2	0	—
	Very Poor		1	
	Poor	1	2	2
	Average	1	3	3
	Good		4	
	Very Good		5	
2	Not Applicable (N/A)		0	
	Very Poor		2	
	Poor		4	
	Average	1	6	6
	Good		8	
	Very Good		10	
3	Not Applicable (N/A)		0	
	Very Poor		3	
	Poor		6	
	Average	1	9	9
	Good	1	12	12
	Very Good	1	15	15
	Total Score			47
	N/A Score			2

Figure 16.15. Review score sheet.

OTHER METHODS FOR EVALUATING QUALITY

A quantitative review of project concerns produces a mathematical score representing quality. It should be used as an indicator of quality and not as a precise measurement of quality. The advantage to scoring quality is that it forces the QA analyst to make a positive statement about quality and then be prepared to defend that score. However, scoring is only one of several evaluation methods. The three most common methods of evaluating the quality of computerized applications are:

1. *Judgment.* The QA analyst, using his or her experience, draws a conclusion on the quality of the application being reviewed. This method is most successful when the reviewers are the most senior and most respected individuals in the data processing department.

2. *Missing criteria.* The QA analyst reviews the application looking for the presence of specific criteria. The evaluation then states which criteria are present and which are missing.

3. *Metrics.* The QA analyst quantitative measure of predetermined quality characteristics. Metrics are explained in Chapter 17.

SUMMARY

Determining a quantitative score for each review point serves two purposes. First, it enables both the reviewer and data processing management to evaluate the result of the review quantitatively. Second, it enables both QA and data processing management to compare different review points. These review points can be from the same or different applications. The comparison of a quantitative number enables data processing management to gain a better appreciation of the status of implementation of an application system.

To develop a comparable score, the reviewer must rate each of the QA concerns for a review point on a five-point scale. These concerns are then weighted by a factor so that the more important concerns have a greater impact on the final score. Once the concerns have been rated, a comparable adjusted score can be calculated.

The score for the quality assurance review needs to be interpreted. Variables in arriving at a score include the stringency of the individual quality assurance reviewer making the rating, the characteristics of the application system, the caliber of people working on the project, plus other unique characteristics of the project. A quantitative evaluation of an application system can be used to measure the level of success of a project implementation by all concerned parties.

17

Metrics — A Tool for Defining and Measuring Quality*

There has been an increased awareness in recent years of the critical problems that have been encountered in the development of large-scale application systems (i.e., application software). These problems include not only the cost and schedule overruns typical of development efforts, and the poor performance of the systems once they are delivered, but also the high cost of maintaining the systems, the lack of portability, and the high sensitivity to changes in requirements.

The potential of the metric concepts can be realized by their inclusion in quality assurance programs. Their impact on a quality assurance program is to provide a more disciplined, engineering approach to quality assurance and to provide a mechanism for taking a life cycle viewpoint of quality. The benefits derived from their application are realized in cost reductions over the life cycle of the system.

The purpose of this chapter is to present procedures and guidelines for introducing and utilizing current quality measurement techniques in a quality assurance program associated with large-scale system developments. These procedures and guidelines will explain how to identify and specify software quality requirements (set quality goals).

---

* This chapter is based on the results of research conducted in support of the United States Air Force Electronic Systems Divisions (ESD), Rome Air Development Center (RADC), and the United States Army Computer Systems Command's Army Institute for Research in Management Information and Computer Science (USACSC/AIRMICS).

QUALITY MEASUREMENT IN PERSPECTIVE

The evolution during the past decade of modern programming practices, structured, disciplined development techniques and methodologies, and requirements for more structured, effective documentation, has increased the feasibility of effective measurement of software quality. The metrics can be classified according to three categories: anomaly-detecting, predictive, and acceptance.

Anomaly-detecting metrics identify deficiencies in documentation or source code. These deficiencies usually are corrected to improve the quality of the software product. Standards enforcement is a form of anomaly-detecting metrics.

Predictive metrics are measurements of the logic of the design and implementation. These measurements are concerned with attributes such as form, structure, density, and complexity. They provide an indication of the quality that will be achieved in the end product, based on the nature of the application and design and implementation strategies.

Acceptance metrics are measurements that are applied to the end product to assess the final compliance with requirements. Tests are an acceptance-type measurement.

The measurements described and used in this chapter are either anomaly-detecting or predictive metrics. They are applied during the development phases to assist in the early identification of quality problems so that corrective actions can be taken when they are more effective and economical.

The measurement concepts complement current quality assurance and testing practices. They are not a replacement for any current techniques utilized in normal QA programs. For example, a major objective of quality assurance is to assure conformance with user/customer requirements. The software quality metric concepts described in this book provide a methodology for the user/customer to specify life-cycle-oriented quality requirements usually not considered, and a mechanism for measuring if those requirements have been attained. A function usually performed by quality assurance personnel is a review/audit of software products produced during software development. The software metrics add formality and quantification to these document and code reviews.

The metric concepts also provide a vehicle for early involvement in the development since there are metrics which apply to the documents produced early in the development.

Testing is usually oriented toward correctness, reliability, and performance (efficiency). The metrics assist in the evaluation of other qualities like maintainability, portability, and flexibility. A summarization of how the software metric concepts complement quality assurance activities is provided in Figure 17.1.

QUALITY ASSURANCE PROGRAM REQUIREMENTS	IMPACT OF SOFTWARE QUALITY METRIC CONCEPTS
• Assume conformance with requirements	• Adds software quality
• Identify software deficiencies	• Anomaly-detecting
• Provide configuration management	• No impact
• Conduct Test	• Assist in evaluation of other qualities
• Provide library controls	• No impact
• Review computer program design	• Predictive metrics
• Assure software documentation requirement conformation	• Metrics assist in evaluation of documentation as well as code
• Conduct reviews and audits	• Procedures for applying metrics (in form of worksheets) formalizes inspection process
• Provide tools/techniques/ methodology for quality assurance	• This chapter describes methodology of using metrics
• Provide subcontractor control	• No impact

Figure 17.1. How software metrics complement Quality Assurance.

IDENTIFYING QUALITY REQUIREMENTS

The primary purpose of applying software quality metrics in a quality assurance program is to improve the quality of the software product.

Rather than simply measuring, the concepts are based on achieving a positive influence on the product, to improve its development.

This section addresses the problem of identifying software quality requirements or goals. These requirements are in addition to the functional, performance, cost, and schedule requirements normally specified for a software development. The fact that the goals established are related to the quality of the end product should, in itself, provide some positive influence.

The vehicle for establishing the requirements is the hierarchical model of software quality. This model, shown in Figure 17.2, has at its highest level a set of software quality factors that are user/management-oriented terms and represent the characteristics which comprise software quality. At the next level for each quality factor is a set of criteria which are the attributes that, if present, provide the characteristics represented by the quality factors. The criteria, then, are software-related terms. At the lowest level of the model are the metrics which are quantitative measures of the software attributes defined by the criteria.

The procedures for establishing the quality requirements for a particular software system utilize this model and will be described as a

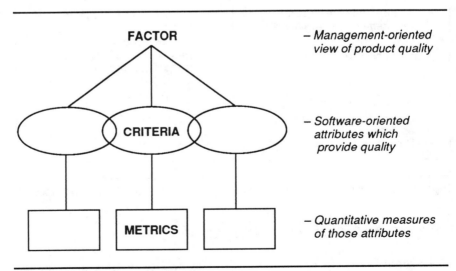

Figure 17.2. Framework for measuring quality.

three-level approach, the levels corresponding to the hierarchical levels of the software quality model. The first level establishes the quality factors that are important. The second level identifies the critical software attributes. The third level identifies the metrics which will be applied and establishes quantitative ratings for the quality factors.

Once the quality requirements have been determined by following the procedures described in the subsequent paragraphs, they must be transmitted to the development team. The quality requirements should be documented in the same form as the other system requirements and relayed to the development team. Additionally, a briefing emphasizing the intent of the inclusion of the quality requirements is recommended.

Procedures for Identifying Important Quality Factors

The basic tool to be utilized in identifying the important quality factors is the Software Quality Requirements Survey form shown in Figure 17.3. The formal definitions of each of the eleven quality factors are provided on that form.

It is recommended that a briefing be provided to the decision makers using the tables and figures which follow in this section to solicit their responses to the survey. The decision makers may include the acquisition manager, the user/customer, the development manager, and the QA manager. To complete the survey, the following procedures should be followed.

Consider basic characteristics of the application. The software quality requirements for each system are unique and are influenced by system or application-dependent characteristics. There are basic characteristics which affect the quality requirements, and each software system must be evaluated for its basic characteristics. Figure 17.4 provides a list of some of these basic characteristics. For example, if the system is being developed in an environment in which there is a high rate of technical breakthroughs in hardware design, portability should take on an added significance. If the expected life cycle of the system is long, maintainability becomes a cost-critical consideration. If the application is an experimental system where the software specifications will have a high rate of change, flexibility in the software product is highly desirable. If the functions of the system are expected to be required for a long time, while the system itself may change considerably, reusability is of prime importance in those modules which implement the major functions of the system. With the advent of more computer networks and communication capabilities, more systems are being required to interface with other systems; hence, the concept of interoperability is extremely important. These and other system characteristics should be considered when identifying the important quality factors.

Consider life cycle implications. The eleven quality factors identified on the survey can be grouped according to three life cycle activities associated with a delivered software product. These three activities are product operation, product revision, and product transition. The relationship of the quality factors to these activities is shown in Figure 17.5. This table also illustrates where quality indications can be achieved through measurement and where the impact is felt if poor quality is realized. The size of this impact determines the cost savings that can be expected if a higher quality system is achieved through the application of the metrics. These cost savings are somewhat offset by the cost to apply the metrics and the cost to develop the higher quality software product as illustrated in Figure 17.6.

A cost to implement versus life cycle cost reduction relationship exists for each quality factor. The benefit versus cost-to-provide ratio for each factor is rated as high, medium, or low in the right-hand column of Figure 17.5. This relationship and the life cycle implications of the quality factors should be considered when selecting the important factors for a specific system.

Perform trade-offs among the tentative list of quality factors. As a result of the previous two steps, a tentative list of quality factors should be produced. The next step is to consider the interrelationships among the factors selected. Figures 17.7 and 17.8 can be used as a guide for determining the relationships between the quality factors. Some factors are synergistic while others conflict. The impact of conflicting factors is that the cost to implement will increase. This will lower the benefit-to-cost ratio described in the preceding paragraphs.

Identify most important quality factors. The list of quality factors considered to be important for the particular system compiled in the preceding three steps should be organized in order of importance. A single decision maker may choose the factors or the choice may be made by averaging several survey responses. The definitions of the factors chosen should be included with this list.

1. The 11 quality factors listed below have been isolated from the current literature. They are not meant to be exhaustive, but to reflect what is currently
   thought to be important. Please indicate whether you consider each factor to
   be Very Important (VI), Important (I), Somewhat Important (SI), or Not Important (NI) as design goals in the system you are currently working on.

Response	*Factors*	*Definition*
	Correctness	Extent to which a program satisfies its specifications and fulfills the user's mission objectives.
	Reliability	Extent to which a program can be expected to perform its intended function with required precision.
	Efficiency	The amount of computing resources and code required by a program to perform a function.
	Integrity	Extent to which access to software or data by unauthorized persons can be controlled.
	Usability	Effort required to learn, operate, prepare input, and interpret output of a program.
	Maintainability	Effort required to locate and fix an error in an operational program.
	Testability	Effort required to test a program to ensure that it performs its intended function.
	Flexibility	Effort required to modify an operational program.
	Portability	Effort required to transfer a program from one hardware configuration to another.
	Reusability	Extent to which a program can be used in other applications — related to the packaging and scope of the functions that programs perform.
	Interoperability	Effort required to couple one system with another.

2. What type(s) of application are you currently involved in?

3. Are you currently in:
   ☐ 1. Development phase
   ☐ 2. Operations/Maintenance phase

4. Please indicate the title which most closely describes your position:
   ☐ 1. Program Manager
   ☐ 2. Technical Consultant
   ☐ 3. Systems Analyst
   ☐ 4. Other (please specify)

Figure 17.3. Software quality requirements survey form.

CHARACTERISTIC	QUALITY FACTOR
• If human lives are affected	Reliability Correctness Testability
• Long life cycle	Maintainability Flexibility Portability
• Real-time application	Efficiency Reliability Correctness
• On-board computer application	Efficiency Reliability Correctness
• Processes classified information • Interrelated systems	Integrity Interoperability

Figure 17.4. System characteristics and related quality factors.

Provide explanations for choices. Document rationale for the decisions made during the first three steps.

An Example of Factors Specification

To illustrate the application of these steps, consider an inventory control system. The inventory control system maintains inventory status and facilitates requisitioning, reordering, and issuing of supplies. The planned life of the system is ten years. Each step described previously will be performed with respect to the tactical inventory control system.

Consider basic characteristics of the application. Utilizing Figure 17.4 and considering the unique characteristics of the tactical inventory control system resulted in the following:

Characteristic	*Related Quality Factor*
Critical supplies	Reliability Correctness
Long life cycle with stable hardware and software requirements	Maintainability

Characteristic	*Related Quality Factor (cont'd)*
Utilized by supply personnel	Usability
Interfaces with inventory systems at other sites	Interoperability

Consider life cycle implications. Of the five quality factors identified in Figure 17.3, all provide high or medium life cycle cost/benefits according to Figure 17.5.

Factors Cost/Benefit	*Ratio*
Reliability	High
Correctness	High
Maintainability	High
Usability	Medium
Interoperability	High

Perform trade-offs among factors. Using Figure 17.7, there are no conflicts which need to be considered.

Identify most important quality factors. Using the survey form, Figure 17.3, and the guidance provided in the preceding paragraphs, the following factors are identified in order of importance. The definitions are provided.

- *Correctness.* Extent to which a program satisfies its specifications and fulfills the user's mission objectives.
- *Reliability.* Extent to which a program can be expected to perform its intended function with required precision.
- *Usability.* Effort required to learn, operate, prepare input, and interpret output of a program.
- *Maintainability.* Effort required to locate and fix an error in an operational program.
- *Interoperability.* Effort required to couple one system to another.

Provide explanation for choice.
- *Correctness.* The system performs critical supply function.
- *Reliability.* The system performs critical supply functions in remote environment.
- *Usability.* The system will be used by personnel with minimum computer training.
- *Maintainability.* The system life cycle is projected to be ten years and it will operate in the field where field personnel will maintain it.

- *Interoperability.* The system will interface with other supply systems.

Procedures for Identifying Critical Software Attributes

The next level of identifying the quality requirements involves proceeding from the user-oriented quality factors to the software-oriented criteria. Sets of criteria, which are attributes of the software, are related to the various factors by definition. Their identification is automatic and represents a more detailed specification of the quality requirements.

Identify critical software attributes required. Figure 17.9 should be used to identify the software attributes associated with the chosen critical quality factors.

Provide definitions. The definitions in Figure 17.10 should also be provided as part of the specification.

Example of Identifying Software Criteria

Continuing with the inventory example, the software criteria for the identified quality factors would be chosen.

Identify critical software attributes. Using the relationships provided in Figure 17.9, the following criteria would be identified:

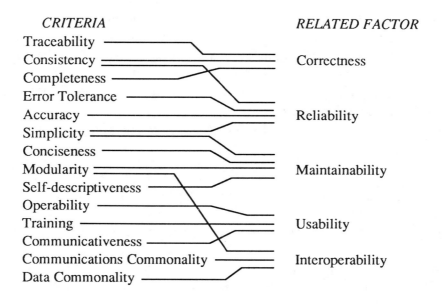

CRITERIA	*RELATED FACTOR*
Traceability	
Consistency	Correctness
Completeness	
Error Tolerance	
Accuracy	Reliability
Simplicity	
Conciseness	
Modularity	Maintainability
Self-descriptiveness	
Operability	
Training	Usability
Communicativeness	
Communications Commonality	Interoperability
Data Commonality	

LIFE-CYCLE PHASES / FACTORS	DEVELOPMENT			EVALUATION	POSTDEVELOPMENT			EXPECTED COST SAVED vs. COST TO PROVIDE
	REQUIRE-MENTS ANALYSIS	DESIGN	CODE & DEBUG	SYSTEM TEST	OPER-ATION	REVI-SION	TRANS-ITION	
CORRECTNESS	Δ	Δ	Δ	X	X	X		HIGH
RELIABILITY	Δ	Δ	Δ	X	X	X		HIGH
EFFICIENCY	Δ	Δ	Δ		X			LOW
INTEGRITY	Δ	Δ	Δ		X			LOW
USABILITY	Δ	Δ		X		X		MEDIUM
MAINTAINABILITY		Δ	Δ			X	X	HIGH
TESTABILITY		Δ	Δ	X		X	X	HIGH
FLEXIBILITY		Δ	Δ			X	X	MEDIUM
PORTABILITY		Δ	Δ				X	MEDIUM
REUSABILITY		Δ	Δ				X	MEDIUM
INTEROPERABILITY	Δ	Δ		X			X	LOW

LEGEND: Δ – where quality factors should be measured   X – where impact of poor quality is realized

Figure 17.5. The impact of not specifying or measuring software quality factors.

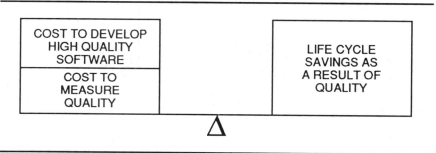

Figure 17.6. Cost versus benefit trade-off.

Provide definitions. The definitions for each of these criteria would be provided also.

Procedures for Establishing Quantifiable Goals

The last level, which is the most detailed and quantified, requires precise statements of the level of quality that will be acceptable for the software product. Mathematical explanations that would allow measurement at this level of precision do not yet exist for all of the quality factors. The mechanism for making the precise statement for any quality factor is a rating of the factor. The underlying basis for the ratings is the effort or cost required to perform a function such as to correct or modify the design or program. For example, rating for maintainability might be that the average time to fix a problem should be five man-days or that 90 percent of the problem fixes should take less than six man-days. This rating would be specified as a quality requirement. To comply with this specification, the software would have to exhibit characteristics which, when present, give an indication that the software will perform to this rating. These characteristics are measured by metrics which are inserted into a mathematical relationship to obtain the predicted rating.

In order to choose ratings such as the two mentioned above, data must be available which allows the decision maker to know what is a "good rating" or perhaps what is the industry average. Currently there is generally a lack of good historical data to establish these expected levels of operations and maintenance performance for software. The data utilized in this section is based on experiences applying the metrics to several large military command and control software systems and other experiences reported in the literature.

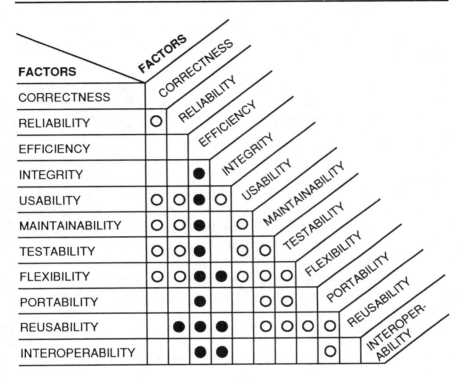

LEGEND

If a high degree of quality is present for factor,
what degree of quality is expected for the other:

○ = High   ● = Low

Blank = No relationship or application dependent

Figure 17.7. Relationships between software quality factors.

Specify rating for each quality factor. After identification of the critical quality factors, specific performance levels or ratings required for each factor should be specified. Figure 17.11 should be used as a guideline for identifying the ratings for the particular factors. Note that mathematical relationships have not been established for some of the factors. In those cases, it is advisable not to levy requirements for meeting a specific quality rating but instead specify the relative importance of the quality factor as a development goal. Note that the reliability ratings are provided in terms familiar to traditional hardware reliability. Just as in hardware reliability, there are significant differences between ratings of .9 and .99.

Identify specific metrics to be applied. The next step, or an alternative to the preceding step, is to identify the specific metrics which will be applied to the various software products produced during the development.

Specifications of metric threshold values. In lieu of specifying quality ratings or in addition to the ratings, specific minimum values for particular metrics may be specified. This technique is equivalent to establishing a standard which is to be adhered to. Violations to the value established are to be reported. When establishing these threshold values based on past project data, projects which have been considered successful (i.e., have demonstrated good characteristics during their life cycle) should be chosen. For example, a system which has been relatively cost-effective to maintain over its operational history should be chosen to apply the metrics related to maintainability and to establish threshold values.

Example of Metrics

Using the inventory example again the quality ratings would be specified as follows.

Specific quality factor ratings. Ratings for two of the five important quality factors can be established using Figure 17.11.

| Reliability | .99 | Require less than one error per 100 lines of code to be detected during formal testing. |
| Maintainability | .8 | Require 2 man-days as an average level of maintenance for correcting an error. |

These ratings can also be established at each measurement period during the development as follows:

	REQ	POR	CDR	IMPL	ACCEPTANCE
Reliability	.8	.8	.9	.9	.99
Maintainability	.7	.7	.8	.8	.8

The progressively better scores are required because there is more detailed information in the later phases of the development to which to apply the metrics and more confidence in the metrics' indication of quality. This is analogous to the concept of reliability growth.

Identify specific metrics to be applied. The metrics to be applied to assess the level of each important quality factor are chosen based on the favorable application system experiences of the organization. Some suggestions are listed below.

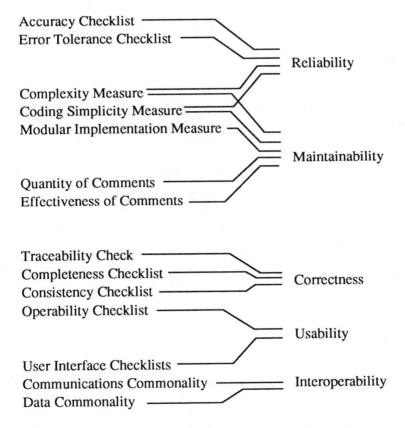

Specify threshold values. Threshold values are established based on past experience and to provide a goal for the quality factors that were not given ratings. They are derived by determining the average scores of past applications of the metrics.

INTEGRITY VERSUS EFFICIENCY	The additional code and processing required to control the access of the software or data usually lengthens run time and requires additional storage.
USABILITY VERSUS EFFICIENCY	The additional code and processing required to ease an operator's tasks or provide more usable output lengthens run time and required additional storage.
MAINTAIN-ABILITY VERSUS EFFICIENCY	Optimized code, incorporating intricate coding techniques and direct code, always provides problems to the maintainer. Using modularity, instrumentation, and well-commented high-level code to increase the maintainability of a system usually increases the overhead, resulting in less efficient operation.
TESTABILITY VERSUS EFFICIENCY	The above discussion applies to testing.
PORTABILITY VERSUS EFFICIENCY	The use of direct code of optimized system software or utilities decreases the portability of the system.
FLEXIBILITY VERSUS EFFICIENCY	The generality required for a flexible system increases overhead and decreases the portability of the system.
REUSABILITY VERSUS EFFICIENCY	The above discussion applies to reusability.
INTEROPERA-BILITY VERSUS EFFICIENCY	Again, the added overhead for conversion from standard data representations, and the user of interface routines decreases the operating efficiency of the system.
FLEXIBILITY VERSUS INTEGRITY	Flexibility requires very general and flexible data structures. This increases the data security problem.
REUSABILITY VERSUS INTEGRITY	As in the above discussion, the generality required by reusable software provides severe protection problems.
INTEROPERA-BILITY VERSUS INTEGRITY	Coupled systems allow more avenues of access to more and different users. The potential for accidental access of sensitive data is increased as well as the opportunities for deliberate access. Often, coupled systems share data or software which compounds the security problems as well.

Figure 17.8. Typical factor trade-offs.

REUSABILITY VERSUS RELIABILITY	The generality required by reusable software makes providing error tolerance and accuracy for all cases more difficult.

Figure 17.8. Typical factor trade-offs. (cont'd)

FACTOR	SOFTWARE CRITERIA	FACTOR	SOFTWARE CRITERIA
Correctness	Traceability Consistency Completeness	*Flexibility*	Modularity Generality Expandability
Reliability	Error Tolerance Consistency Accuracy Simplicity	*Testability*	Simplicity Modularity Instrumentation Self-descriptiveness
Efficiency	Storage Efficiency Execution Efficiency	*Portability*	Modularity Self-descriptiveness Machine Independence
Integrity	Access Control Access Audit	*Reusability*	Generality Modularity Software System Independence
Usability	Operability Training Communicativeness		
Maintainbility	Consistency	*Interoperability*	Modularity Communication Commonality Data Commonality

Figure 17.9. Software criteria and related quality factors.

CRITERION	DEFINITION
TRACEABILITY	Those attributes of the software that provide a thread from the requirements to the implementation with respect to the specific development and operational environment.
COMPLETENESS	Those attributes of the software that provide full implementation of the functions required.
CONSISTENCY	Those attributes of the software that provide uniform design and implementation techniques and notation.
ACCURACY	Those attributes of the software that provide the required precision in calculations and outputs.
ERROR TOLERANCE	Those attributes of the software that provide continuity of operation under non-nominal conditions.
SIMPLICITY	Those attributes of the software that provide implementation of functions in the most understandable manner. (Usually avoidance of practices which increase complexity.)
MODULARITY	Those attributes of the software that provide a structure of highly independent modules.
GENERALITY	Those attributes of the software that provide breadth to the functions performed.
EXPANDABILITY	Those attributes of the software that provide for expansion of data storage requirements or computational functions.
INSTRUMEN-TATION	Those attributes of the software that provide for the measurement of usage or identification of errors.
SELF-DESCRIP-TIVENESS	Those attributes of the software that provide explanation of the implementation of a function.

Figure 17.10. Criteria definitions for software quality.

CRITERION	DEFINITION
EXECUTION EFFICIENCY	Those attributes of the software that provide for minimum processing time.
STORAGE EFFICIENCY	Those attributes of the software that provide for minimum storage requirements during operation.
ACCESS CONTROL	Those attributes of the software that provide for control of the access of software and data.
ACCESS AUDIT	Those attributes of the software that provide for an audit of the access of software and data.
OPERABILITY	Those attributes of the software that determine operation and procedures concerned with the operation of the software.
TRAINING	Those attributes of the software that provide transition from current operation or initial familiarization.
COMMUNICATIVENESS	Those attributes of the software that provide useful inputs and outputs which can be assimilated.
SOFTWARE SYSTEM INDEPENDENCE	Those attributes of the software that determine its dependency on the software environment (operating systems, utilities, input/output routines, etc.).
MACHINE INDEPENDENCE	Those attributes of the software that determine its dependency on the hardware system.
COMMUNICATION COMMONALITY	Those attributes of the software that provide the use of standard protocols and interface routines.
DATA COMMONALITY	Those attributes of the software that provide the use of standard data representations.
CONCISENESS	Those attributes of the software that provide for implementation of a function with a minimum amount of code.

Figure 17.10. Criteria definitions for software quality. (cont'd)

QUALITY FACTOR	RATING EXPLANATION	RATING GUIDELINES			
RELIABILITY*	Rating is in terms of the number of errors that occur after the start of formal testing. Rating = 1 – Number of Errors/Number of Lines of source code excluding comments.	RATING	.9	.98**	.99	.999
		ERRORS 100 LOC	10	2	1	1
MAINTAIN-ABILITY*	Rating is in terms of the average amount of effort required to locate and fix an error in an operational program. Rating = 1 – .1 (Average number of man-days per fix)	RATING	.3	.5	.7**	.9
		Average Effort (Man-Days)	7	5	3	1
PORTABILITY*	Rating is in terms of the effor required to convert a program to run in another environment with respect to the effort required to originally implement the program. Rating = 1 – Effort to Transport/Effort to implement	RATING	.25	.5**	.75	.9
		% of Original Effort	75	50	25	10
FLEXIBILITY*	Rating is in terms of the average effort required to extend a program to include other requirements. Rating = 1 – .05 (Average number or man-days to change)	RATING	.3	.5**	.7	.9
		Average Effort (Man-Days)	14	10	6	2

Figure 17.11. Quality factor ratings.

QUALITY FACTOR	RATING EXPLANATION
CORRECTNESS	The function which the software is to perform is incorrect. The rating is in terms of effort required to implement the correct function.
EFFICIENCY	The software does not meet performance (speed, storage) requirements. The rating is in terms of effort required to modify software to meet performance requirements.
INTEGRITY	The software does not provide required security. The rating is in terms of effort required to implement proper levels of security.
USABILITY	There is a problem related to operation of the software, the user interface, or the input/output. The rating is in terms of effort required to improve human factors to an acceptable level.
TESTABILITY	The rating is in terms of effort required to test changes or fixes.
REUSABILITY	The rating is in terms of effort required to use software in a different application.
INTER-OPERABILITY	The rating is in terms of effort required to couple the system to another system.

Figure 17.11. Quality factor ratings. (cont'd)

Notes:

*   Data collected to date provides some basis upon which to allow quantitative ratings for these quality factors. These ratings should be modified based on data collected within a specific development environment. Data has not been collected to support ratings of the other quality factors.

**   Indicates rating which might be considered current industry average.

SUMMARY

Software developers have a tendency to view programs as static, finished products once they have gone into the operational phase of the life cycle. Most of us, however, are well aware of the fact that this is not true, that, in fact, software has a complete life cycle and goes through maintenance and enhancement phases before its final obsolescence.

Users of software systems have a different outlook. Software usually performs a service for the user, and developers then become the providers of the system that provides the needed service. Of particular importance in the MIS environment, however, is the fact that the development staff almost invariably acts as a support unit to the primary function of the organization. For the most part, the programs are not in themselves the products which the user organization ultimately produces. In this sense, the developer's staff performs a service for the rest of the organization, and so the task of the developer's staff is one of providing that service to the functional (user) components of the organization. User components are not in themselves interested in the technical aspects of programming or even in that of systems analysis; rather, they are interested in the systems provided to them and the way those systems serve their needs.

This is significant for the reason that the user will make systems decisions based on only one criterion from the developer's viewpoint. If the system adequately serves the needs of the user, even if the system is of low technical quality, the user will be hesitant to authorize expenditures for a replacement system whose quality is much higher, and which might provide better service. Similarly, if the system does not supply adequate service to the user, and will entail significant replacement costs as well as technical complexity, the user will more readily authorize the expenditure of funds in order to alleviate his immediate need for adequate service. Thus, while the developer sees the quality of the system in many lights, in terms of error rates, error tolerance, readability, ease of debugging, etc., the users perceive the system in only one way — how well it meets their needs.

To the developer, these characteristics obviously have a cumulative effect on the user's perception of the quality of the system, but for the most part users do not have this awareness since it requires that they have some experience in the technical aspects of systems development in order to be aware of the problems associated with the task. It is the responsibility of the developer to be aware of the users' needs, their perceptions of what a quality system is, and to develop the system in consonance with those perceptions. This often is not a simple task, since perceptions can change in time. Thus, a user may gain a more mature appreciation of systems if exposed to "user-friendly" systems, or may become less systems oriented after being exposed to systems which are difficult to work with.

At the highest level of our quality metric framework, some of the required translation between user and developer can be accommodated. The quality factors show relevancy of technical aspects of the software to the user's needs over the life cycle of the system. Utilizing the factors, the user can appreciate the impact of a system which is unreliable, or hard to maintain, or hard to change. The user sees this impact in terms of cost, the user's ultimate measure, and its effect on the service the system provides.

Thus, it is beneficial to organizations to view software developers as providers of services over long periods of time. Many management information systems are developed with planned life spans of ten years. The enhancement or rewrite of such systems is a large undertaking requiring the investigation of downstream processing impact. If one views software systems as services, then one can view such problems in light of their impact on the provision of service to users and customers, and thus on the entire organization, rather than on individual modules or subsystems. This enables managers to make more rational decisions based on an overall organizational viewpoint.

An important point to note, related to the nature of organizations, is that change is unavoidable. Organizations and systems change as their objectives and goals change, and it follows that information systems which they use must change with them.

A corollary to this is the fact that the tendency of software managers to engage in trying to avoid changing software systems if at all possible (while positive in some instances) can have a detrimental impact on the overall goals of the organization.

Products go away after a time. Sometimes the life span is long, as in the case of the B-52 or the Volkswagon "Beetle," but eventually they are replaced by new products. The need for specific services lasts a very long time. This long life span is a problem which an awareness of the service perspective gives in the application of quality metrics. The use of metrics throughout the life cycle gives us a method for effectively specifying and monitoring the delivery of service to the user during the operational/maintenance phase of the life cycle.

18

Measuring Computer System Reliability

Computer systems have become an integral part of most organizations. As the computer system and its services become more essential to the success of these organizations, the ability of the system to process information correctly and to provide continuous service becomes even more critical. However, recent trends such as decentralization of computing, inexperienced users, and larger, more complex systems have produced operational environments that thwart the attainment of these goals. Rising repair costs also make the reliability of the general-purpose computer system an important issue.

Historically, computing has been dominated by the large, general-purpose mainframe. Associated with this type of computer system is a certain set of reliability questions and answers. Although this environment is changing with the advent of microcomputers, distributed data processing, and distributed databases, many of the reliability concerns remain the same. Whatever the system configuration, reliability continues to be an important aspect of the computer system.

PURPOSE AND SCOPE

This chapter is intended to assist users in acquiring a basic understanding of computer system reliability and to identify areas for further examination. It presents an overview of the fundamental concepts and concerns associated with system reliability and identifies elements and activities involved in planning and implementing a reliability program.

The chapter provides general guidance and, as such, does not present an in-depth methodology for creating or maintaining a reliable computer system. The underlying theme is that a knowledge of reliability is important in the development of new system specifications as well as in the continual assessment of systems that now exist.

We are concerned here with the services and facilities of a general-purpose computer system in the multi-user environment. In general, this chapter can be applied to other types of computer systems (i.e., minicomputers, microcomputers, distributed systems, etc.). The size of the system, its complexity, and mission within an organization will dictate the set of applicable guidance. The system planner should analyze and evaluate this report with respect to the system and apply the appropriate subset.

The reliability of a computer system will be discussed in terms of a system's three major components: hardware, software, and human/machine interface (the human component).

FUNDAMENTAL CONCEPTS

Terminology

The term *system* is used to denote a collection of interconnected components designed to perform a set of particular functions. Within this definition, any component of the system may itself be regarded as a system: e.g., the central processing unit, memory, communications to and from the system, software programs, and computer system users.

For purposes of this report, the *failure* of the computer system will refer to the termination, disruption, corruption, or incorrect outcome of system components (e.g., hardware, software).

The *reliability* of a computer system is defined as the probability that the system will be able to process work correctly and completely without its being aborted or corrupted. Note that a system does not have to fail (crash) for it to be unreliable. The computer configuration, the individual components comprising the system, and the system's usage are all contributing factors in overall system reliability. As the reliability of these elements varies, so will the level of system reliability.

The *availability* of a system is a measure of the amount of time the system is actually capable of accepting and performing a user's work. The terms "reliability" and "availability" are closely related and often used (although incorrectly) synonymously. For example, a system that fails frequently but restarts quickly would have high availability, even though its reliability is low. To distinguish between the two, reliability can be thought of as the quality of service, availability as the quantity of service. Throughout this chapter, availability will be viewed as a component of reliability.

Reliability Distinctions

A computer system consists of a combination of hardware, software, and human components, each of which can cease functioning correctly, cause another component to malfunction, or help to increase the reliability of the other components. The reliability of this combination of components can be thought of as computer system reliability. Traditionally, the reliability of the computer system has concentrated on hardware. This approach leads to the assumption that software is 100-percent reliable. Since this is unlikely, it is necessary to include software in the system reliability calculations. Finally, the need for human interaction with a computer system (to detect and correct problems, restart the system, input key information, etc.) makes its inclusion in the determination of system reliability a necessity.

Reliability Requirements

The computer system (application) objectives and the environment in which it operates are major considerations in determining the level of reliability required of the system. An important question to be answered is: "How reliable must the system be?"

This section outlines several factors that contribute to answering this question. The discussion is in two parts: operational criteria — factors associated with the operational setting of the system and which are affected by the reliability of the system; and risk analysis — a method for balancing the degree of system reliability against acceptable levels of loss with a less reliable system.

Operational Criteria

Operational criteria are those characteristics of the system that make reliability more or less important. The identification of these factors and their relationship to reliability is necessary in evaluating system reliability. At least the following factors should be evaluated:

1. *Safety*. Reliability is critical to a system where there is a potential for loss of life, health, destruction of property, or damage to the environment. Examples: health care systems, scheduling of safety inspections, power system controls, air traffic control.

2. *Security*. Reliability is a fundamental element in the security of computer systems. A failure can decrease or destroy the security of the system. Undesirable events such as denial of information, unauthorized disclosure of information, or loss of money and resources can result from lack of reliability. Examples: military command and control, electronic funds transfer, management of classified information, inventory control.

3. *Access*. Reliability becomes a major concern to systems when it is unusually costly or impossible to access that system. Reliability techniques are used to minimize the potential failures that may render the system useless. These systems are usually very expensive, with reliability costs a fraction of the overall system expense. Examples: remotely operated/controlled systems (space shuttle, missiles, satellites).

4. *Mode of operation*. Reliability has varying levels of importance depending on the mode of operation. Failures affect real-time, on-line, and batch applications differently. Real-time applications are immediately affected by a failure. Similarly, a system that fails while supporting an on-line application will demonstrate a deviation from expected conditions sooner than the same system operating in exclusively batch mode. Examples: data management systems, centralized information systems, air traffic control, computer service bureau.

5. *Organizational dependency*. The importance of reliability increases as the organization's dependence on the computer system and its services becomes more critical to the organization's success. A failure can directly affect the organization by creating delays or disruptions to production schedules, administrative activities, management decision making, etc. Examples: all systems.

Risk Analysis

A balance between the application reliability requirements and the cost of designing and implementing a system needs to be struck. The system planner should be aware that for some applications, a failure and its recovery may cost less than achieving an increase in system reliability (prevention of a failure). A risk analysis approach should be used to determine the affect of a failure and its recovery and the level of reliability sufficient for that system. The three key elements to be considered in such an analysis are:

- The amount of damage which can result from a failure

- The likelihood of such an event occurring

- The cost-effectiveness of existing or potential safeguards

EVALUATING RELIABILITY

In order to ensure that the computer system meets or exceeds performance requirements, the system planner must be able to assess or specify the reliability of the computer system. This section describes system reliability data gathering, analysis, and assessment results. The data obtained about the system is used as input to the reliability metrics, which, in turn, are used to derive policies and performance criteria about the system's reliability.

Sources of Reliability Data

Reliability information can be obtained from a number of sources. The data can be derived from job accounting, system performance, error routines that are part of the operating system, diagnostic routines, operator logs, hardware and software monitors, and system users. A host of computer performance evaluation tools and capacity planning tools can also be used to acquire data about the system.

Whatever the source of reliability data, it is important to keep accurate, timely, and complete records. These records form the basis for assessing the reliability of the system. Typical data elements that should be recorded are:

- The date and time of any event evincing a reliability problem

- Type of event
- Amount of time lost (if any)
- The system and responsible component
- Average service and response time for a job
- Number of jobs and job mix at a given time
- The system resources used for these jobs

A continuous record of system performance and activity provides the system planner with historical data for evaluating reliability. This information will enable the planner to base future acquisition, current operation procedures, and maintenance decisions on past system reliability and performance.

The responsibility for recording and reporting the system reliability information should be clearly delineated. The recording and reporting procedure should be reviewed periodically for duplication and/or missing elements. It is suggested that records be maintained for at least six months. Actual time frames for maintaining these records should be determined by the system planner based on the system's reliability and performance, as well as on the usage of the records within the organization (e.g., to take contractual action against a vendor).

Accounting Logs

Accounting logs provide performance information along with billing information. Accounting logs usually contain data about individual programs as well as system usage. The type of data and depth of detail can vary among computer systems. A few examples of possible data elements are listed below:

- *Program data*: initiation and termination time, total service time for each used resource (e.g., CPU, disk), memory used, I/O counts, and user identification.

- *System data*: system configuration, software parameters, checkpoint records, and device errors.

Analysis programs use accounting logs to produce system performance reports. These reports enable the system planner to recognize deviations from normal system usage and to evaluate the impact of a failure by observing and contrasting the system performance prior to and subsequent to a failure. Figure 18.1 is an example of one type of report that can be generated.

Device Type: Magnetic Tape
Unit-Serial   Model vendor   Date
Tape 05-189 3420   Jul 10

NUMBER AND TYPE OF FAILURES

	This month to date			Previous Performance					
				Prior 5 Days				Prior month	
	Today	high	total	−1	−2	−3	−4	high	total
Hard Fails	3	3	13	0	1	0	0	3	18
Soft Fails	37	29	203	6	15	0	13	819	3505

- DAILY THRESHOLD LEVELS EXCEEDED: Hard = 0   Soft = 0
- DAILY FAILURE LOG:

Unit-serial	Jobname	Volser	MM/DD	HH.MM-HH.MM	Cpu	Failure	Record#	Density
Tape -05-1189	LMSPUOTD	000000	07/10	12.55-12.55	189	Eqpt-rd	003	6250
	00000000	MITSTP	07/10	11.42-11.42	189	Eqir-27	7098	1600
	Landumpe	010758	07/10	00.13-00.13	189	Data-wr	3914	6250

NOTE: − Used to identify devices exceeding threshold values.
        Includes device hard failure log for total picture

(a) DAILY DEVICE FAILURE REPORT

			FAILURE TYPE		USAGE DATA	RATIOS	
			#Hard	#Soft		Use/	Use/
	Device type	Model	fails	fails	Total	Hardfail	Softfail
this month	Disk storage	332	4	147	6400	1600.0	40.0
prior month			13	273	6200	407.6	22.8
this month	Disk storage	335	2	88	4104	2052.0	46.7
prior month			4	321	3625	906.2	11.3
this month	Magnetic tape	189	18	3505	4526	251.4	1.2
prior month			13	1597	5616	432.0	3.5

(b) MONTHLY DEVICE SUMMARY

Figure 18.1. System performance reports — examples of one type of accounting information analysis.

System Incident Reports (SIR)

System incident reports are generated by the operations staff whenever a problem occurs. The SIR calls for full information, including time of day, system status, tasks and jobs in the system, possible cause (relating it to hardware, software, or unknown), diagnostic messages, availability of core, etc. (Figure 18.2). The final disposition of the incident and routing information (if any) is also provided. The completed SIR and any supporting documentation is then circulated to appropriate technical personnel.

Console Operator Logs

Console operator logs are an operator-maintained account of the system's daily activity (Figure 18.3). Typical information recorded in these logs includes: operator actions (e.g., boots, mounts, backups), system configuration, outages, crashes, downtime, malfunction of peripherals, and routine and corrective maintenance repairs. The system planner, operator, and maintenance personnel can use the information contained in the operator logs to analyze daily activity, identify problem areas, track reliability control procedures, and evaluate reliability metrics. Summary reports, such as weekly log reports (Figure 18.4), efficiency reports (Figure 18.5), utilization statistics (Figure 18.6), and failure categorization reports (Figure 18.7) can be derived from the logs and used to evaluate the system.

System Error Messages

System error messages are automatically generated by the system and often provide clues to the source of an error. Relevant information pertaining to the error(s) is recorded. Such information may include: time of day, error type, control limits exceeded (exception reports), consistency checks, timers, and selected traces and dumps. Many systems automatically log the error messages and related data. Analysis programs, available from system vendors or other commercial sources, are used to extract the relevant reliability information.

Diagnostic Routines

Diagnostic routines provide information on the integrity of the system by identifying failures or indicating (by the absence of failures) that the system is operating correctly. The routines can be run periodically or subsequent to the occurrence of a problem. They can provide information about the problem type and location.

SYSTEM INCIDENT REPORT

Date _____   Down
Time _____   CPU _____
                                       Unit _____
                                       Subassembly ____

Reference   System   System
Mar _____   Avail _____   Return _____   Module _____

Description of Problem _____

_____

_____

_____

_____

_____

_____

_____

Corrective Action _____

_____

_____

_____

_____

_____

_____

_____

Diagnostic Routine _____   Service
Diag. Fail: Yes No   Person _____

Figure 18.2. System incident report.

```
%OPCOM,      29-Jun-19   12:28:28.72,   message from user NETAAP
NET shutting down
%OPCOM,      29-Jun-19   12:33:54.07,   operator disabled
%OPCOM,      29-Jun-19   12:35:15.47,   operator enabled
%OPCOM,      29-Jun-19   12:45:05.22,   operator status
PRINTER, TAPES, DISKS, DEVices
%OPCOM,      29-Jun-19   12:48:53.21,   request from user PUBLIC
Please mount volume KLAT in device MTAO:
%OPCOM,      29-Jun-19   12:50:02.11,   request satisfied
%OPCOM,      29-Jun-19   12:50:03.54,   message from user SYSTEM
Volume KLAT mounted, on physical device MTAO:
%OPCOM,      29-Jun-19   13:01:26.91,   device LPO is offline
%OPCOM,      29-Jun-19   13:31:15.63,   request from user PUBLIC
Mount new relative volume 2 () on MTA:
%OPCOM,      29-Jun-19   13:33:45.05,   message from user SYSTEM
MTA: in use, try later, mount aborted
%OPCOM,      29-Jun-19   13:46:21.67,   message from user SYSTEM
Current system parameters modified by process ID 001f003C
%OPCOM,      29-Jun-19   13:46:21.97,   device DSK4 is offline
Problems with DSK04
Problems with DSK04
%OPCOM,      29-Jun-19   13:47:01.30,   message from user SYSTEM
DSK04 has been remounted - back online
```

Figure 18.3. Sample operator log.

SYSTEM LOG REPORT FOR THE WEEK ENDING July 9

1. **System Utilization for the week**

Time sharing with operator coverage	128:18
Time sharing without operator coverage	16:35
Regular field service PM's	13:55
Extra field service	4:05
Computer operation – stand alone	3:09
Lost time	1:58
TOTAL HOURS	168:00

Figure 18.4. Weekly log report.

2. **Equipment**

   Hardware problems contributing to system downtime:
   MF10 – down, memory parity errors
   DF110-TM10 – problems occurred when using MTA drive

   Hardware problems not causing system downtime:
   LPA1 – replaced hammer module col. 35
   TU56 – tightened hub

3. **Reruns and Lost time**

   -246-
   Estimated lost time on system 246 was 20 hours and 25 min.

   -541-
   Estimated lost time on system 541 was 7 hours and 45 min.

4. **Monitor problems**

Name	Date	Problem	Detail
RF6B9N	5Jul	Hung	One job running, most other jobs swapped in Run state
RF6B9N	5Jul	Loop	On PI 4 interrupt chain
RF6B9N	7Jul	Loop	Dubious crash data
RF6B9N	8Jul	Hung	Most jobs waiting for disk monitor buffer or disk I/O wait

5. **Job Distribution (average number of jobs)**

	0700-0900	0900-1300	1300-1700	1700-1900	1900-2400
7/4	22.70	48.05	50.20	40.00	32.00
7/5	30.90	53.89	54.95	40.70	34.43
7/6	27.15	47.50	55.50	39.40	34.50
7/7	30.15	44.15	49.90	32.50	19.14
7/8	31.80	49.89	46.12	22.90	23.20

Figure 18.4. Weekly log report. (cont'd)

WEEKLY EFFICIENCY REPORT (July)

Date	System turned off	Performance during scheduled hours				Scheduled time (hours)	Actual system up time (hours)	Efficiency/ wk (% uptime)
		down due to soft-ware	down due to hard-ware	other	total num. of hours down			
1-3	7	1:51	1:03	:40	3:34	43:30	39:56	92%
5-10	7	1:48	:43	—	2:31	95:30	92:59	97.3%
12-17	8	:48	8:53	:57	10:38	95:30	84:52	88.8%
19-24	3	:27	6:25	—	6:52	95:30	88:38	92.8%
26-31	6	:30	:29	2:52	3:51	98:30	94:39	94.6%
total	31	5:24	17:33	4:29	27:26	428:30	401:04	94%

system operational 6 days/week, 24 hours/day

Figure 18.5. Efficiency report.

Hardware and Software Monitors

Hardware monitors are electronic devices physically attached to the computer system, and software monitors are software programs residing in and utilizing some or all of the host's resources. Both types of monitors make measurements on the system by recording, analyzing, and/or presenting data under real-time operation. The performance level of system resources, as well as any problems that might occur, can be pinpointed and tracked with respect to their cause and effect within the system. For example, in the data communications area, measurements of response time and communication line utilization can be used to identify and locate potential problem areas.

SYSTEM UTILIZATION STATISTICS (July)

Reloading System for Processing	Hours	Percent of Total
Down — System not operational due to hardware or software failure	22:57	4.2%
Site — Down due to electrical, air conditioning, water damage, etc.	3:31	.6%
P.M. — Scheduled preventive maintenance	20:00	3.6%
Unscheduled maintenance	0:00	0%
Off — System shut off	31:00	5.6%
Idle — Work to be processed, but no one available to process it	30:00	5.4%
Development — System up, but not for "public use"	42:34	7.7%
Public use — System operational for all users	401:04	72.8%

Figure 18.6.   Utilization statistics.

NUMBER OF FAILURES BY CAUSE (July)

	Total Number	% of Total
Hardware	212	44
Software	106	22
Application	10	2
Operations	29	6
Environmental	77	16
Unknown	10	2
Reconfiguration	39	8
	483	100

Figure 18.7.   Failure categorization.

User's Level of Satisfaction

User's level of satisfaction with the system's performance can provide an indication of the system reliability. User complaints and questions can aid the system planner (analyst, operator, etc.) in the identification of problem areas. Interaction with users may be a formal or informal procedure, including joint system staff/user meetings, surveys of the user community (e.g., ask about possible problem areas), or user requests for refund of purchased computer services (an indication of possible system problem areas).

System Performance Meetings

System performance meetings provide the opportunity for appropriate personnel (system managers, operators, analysts, technicians) to meet, discuss, and analyze the system performance. The reports and information obtained from the above sources, as well as any additional data, form the basis of the system reviews. Those attending the meeting try to identify the system components that fail most frequently, the cause of the failures, and solutions to minimize or eliminate future occurrences of such events.

Reliability Metrics

Reliability metrics provide a quantitative basis for the assessment of computer system reliability. The actual measurement is accomplished by applying data gathered about the system as input to the reliability metrics. The data can be obtained from the system planner's in-depth knowledge of the system's capacity and activity and formal inspection of the system components, as well as from the sources previously cited.

Numerous quantitative methods exist to measure the reliability of the computer system. Most metrics for system reliability are derived from a combination of hardware and software measurements. Because of the complexity of computer systems, a variety of reliability metrics should be chosen to describe the system adequately. The development/identification of appropriate metrics is not an easy task. Often it is necessary for a reliability expert to identify a set of metrics, develop mathematical models (algorithms) to describe the system in terms of probabilities, or do both.

A quantitative value, or threshold level, consisting of either a number, range, or percent should be established for each measurement. This value/level can be established in accordance with:

* Comparison with similar systems

* System specifications by vendors

* Specific application requirements

Comparisons of these prestated values with the actual derived measurement values will be helpful in assessing the reliability of the computer system. Note that it is not always possible to establish a mathematical value for all measurements. In these cases, it is advisable to develop a relative importance rating (priority factor) to indicate reliability of a computer system.

The remainder of this section presents an overview of system reliability metrics. The discussion will be divided into three categories: hardware, software, and human measurements. The objective is to identify the basic concepts and underlying attributes associated with the metrics of the various categories. Detailed analysis of specific metrics is beyond the scope of this document, but additional references are given for each category.

Hardware Measurements

There has been an abundance of information written on hardware reliability metrics. It is these metrics that are the most familiar and thought of as the "traditional" measurements. The metrics are used to assess the mechanical or electrical elements of the computer system and have been used as the original tools for the evaluation of total computer system reliability.

The hardware metrics are a means of evaluating the amount of processing time lost due to the failure of the computer system or a specific component. The calculation of the reliability measurement will vary with the complexity of the system configuration. Although the basic concepts will remain the same, the hardware reliability measurements for a single, nonredundant, nonrepairable system will differ from that of redundant, repairable, or distributed system configurations. Metrics for the latter must compensate for the special properties (e.g., replication of components) of the system.

There are two approaches to estimating hardware reliability: one is based on statistical probability distribution models, and the other is based on actual system performance. The probability model is the analytical basis for making reliability predictions. The determination of an appropriate model is necessary to achieve realistic predictions and should be developed by an expert.

Quantitative metrics based on an operational system can provide information on the processing time lost due to the failure of the computer system or a specific component. Among the measurements of interest are: the number of times the hardware ceases to function in a given time period (failure rate), the average length of time the hardware is functional (mean time between failures, MTBF), the amount of time it takes to resume normal operation (mean time to repair, MTTR), and the quantity of service (availability). Although a simplistic model, Figure 18.8 depicts some of these measurements.

Other measurement algorithms and analysis techniques might include calculations to determine:

- A level of confidence in the system's ability to survive a failure

- The number of instructions that could be processed before a failure

- The amount of time the system will be inoperable

- The response time delay

Software Measurements

There is a tendency to use hardware metrics to evaluate the software component of the computer system. Although use of these metrics may be appropriate in a few cases, it can limit the scope of the software evaluation because of differences between hardware and software failure origination and repeatability. For example, hardware failures are either transient or repeatable and result from design, development, and component fault; software failures are almost always repeatable and originate in design and development.

Software reliability calculations can be performed throughout the system life cycle to quantify the expected or actual reliability. In the early phases of development, the measurements can be applied to the

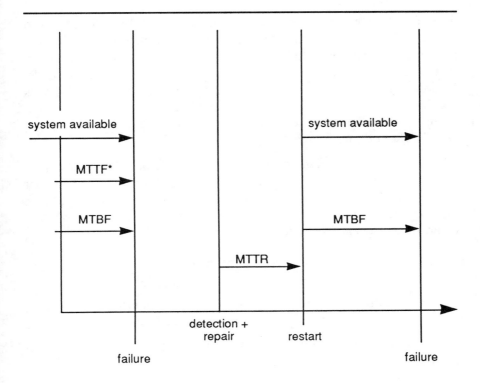

$$\text{MTTF*} = \text{the number of time units the system is operable before the first failure occurs}$$

$$\text{MTBF} = \frac{\text{sum of the number of time units the system is operable}}{\text{number of failures during the time period}}$$

$$\text{MTTR} = \frac{\text{sum of the number of time units required to perform system repair}}{\text{number of repairs during the time period}}$$

* MTTF applies to nonrepairable systems and is not applicable after the first failure. (Some experts consider MTTF to be a special case of the MTBF measure.)

Figure 18.8. Measures of MTTF, MTBF, MTTR, and availability.
(The time line illustrates the various measurements with respect to the recognition and repair of failure occurrences.)

documentation on the system concepts and design, and in later phases to both the documentation and the source code. The metrics should measure errors caused by deficiencies or the inclusion of extraneous functions in the system design specification, documentation, or source code. They should be limited to errors caused by software deviating from its specifications while the hardware is functioning correctly. Any error that occurs several times before detection and correction should be charged as a single error in the reliability calculations.

Software measurements are used to predict or quantify the software quality of the system. The measurement can be calculated by either the evaluation of past success or the prediction of future failure. One method of calculating software reliability might be to count the number of errors that occur in the source code, e.g.,

$$1 - \frac{\text{Number of Errors}}{\text{Total Number of Lines of Executable Code}}$$

(Rating is in terms of the expected or actual number
of errors that occur in a specified time interval.)

Other measurement algorithms or analysis techniques might include calculations to:

- Define the levels of error occurrence and tolerance
- Determine the percentage of errors during a time interval
- Identify error types and the modules in which they occur
- Identify deficiencies in the documentation or code

Human Measurements

Human reliability and its influence on the computer system is a developing discipline. Although new models are being developed, there has been a shortage of human reliability metrics, a general lack of understanding of the analysis required, and an absence of pertinent reliability data.

Human reliability metrics differ from those for hardware or software. These differences stem from the ability of the human to make decisions, to learn from the one's experiences, and to continue functioning in spite of a mistake ("failure"). Thus, the metrics need to model a human's ability to work under different situations. A recognized approach is to divide the metrics into two fundamental components:

- *The "performance" element* — a task is completed, with no decision required.

- *The "control" element* — a task consists of several parameters and requires a decision to be made.

The failures that should be assessed by the metrics include: incorrect diagnosis, misinterpretation of instructions, inadequate support or environmental conditions, and insufficient attention or caution. Algorithms and analysis techniques might include calculations to:

- Determine improper human (operator, user, etc.) performance

- Determine the amount of downtime caused by human/machine interaction

- Identify the number of errors that were manually detected and corrected

- Identify the errors caused by human alteration to the system

- Evaluate human/machine interaction — amount required, cost to implement, and time to accomplish

Assessing the Quality of the Computer System

The analyses of the information obtained from the reliability metrics (in the previous section) can be used individually, in combination, or in conjunction with historical system data to evaluate, estimate, or predict the reliability of the computer system. Specifically, the system planner can use this derived information to:

- Establish performance and acceptance criteria

- Formulate policies to reflect or achieve reliability goals

- Gather information on the effect of a failure on the system and organization

- Clarify and identify specific failures or problems

Examples of assessments that can be made about the system are given in the following paragraphs. A chart listing these examples and the measurement class that might be associated with them is given in Figure 18.9.

Performance/Acceptance Criteria							
Threshold Value Assessments	X	X	X	X	X	X	X
General System Stability		X	X				X
General System Availability		X	X	X			X
Policy Formulation							
Maintenance Policies	X	X	X		X	X	X
Acquisition Policies	X		X		X	X	
Information on the Impact of a Failure							
Productivity and Workload Scheduling	X	X	X	X			
Amount of "Backup" Work	X	X	X	X			
Clarification/Identification of Failures		X			X	X	X
EXAMPLES OF ASSESSMENTS	1	2	3	4	5	6	7
	INDEX TO CLASSES OF MEASUREMENTS						

Classes of Measurements: The following are possible classes of measurements that can be used in the evaluation of the assessment examples.

1 Measurements that indicate QUALITY of service
2 Measurements that indicate FREQUENCY of failure
3 Measurements that indicate LENGTH OF TIME the system is inaccessible
4 Measurements that indicate system ACTIVITY
5 Measurements that indicate the IDENTITY of the failure
6 Measurements that indicate the LOCATION of the failure
7 Measurements that indicate the RESULTING ACTION following a failure

Figure 18.9. Assessment examples and classes of measurements.

Performance/Acceptance Criteria

The following criteria can be used in the specification and evaluation of performance levels in contracts with vendors, in-house system policies, or both.

Threshold Value Assessment is the comparison of preestablished metric values with the actual derived value of the metric. The technique is used to indicate if the measurement exceeds, meets, or falls short of expected levels of performance. It is a method that can be applied to all measurement types and provides a means of specifying the minimum performance level that is to be achieved.

General System Availability is the amount of time the overall computer system is operational and usable. The achievement of a predetermined availability threshold can be used to indicate acceptable, substandard, or unacceptable performance levels. A chart should be developed to indicate the limits for acceptable, substandard, and unacceptable performance of the system, with values based on availability requirements. For existing systems, the derived metric values should be compared against the required levels listed in the chart. The chart below is a hardware-oriented example of system availability performance limits (using hours of downtime in a computer system).

HOURS OF SYSTEM DOWNTIME

Subsystem causing Downtime	Acceptable	Substandard	Unacceptable
CPU + memory	0–16.9	17.0–33.9	>34.0
Disk storage	0–16.9	17.0–33.9	>34.0
Magnetic tape	0–8.4	8.5–16.9	>17.0
Printer	0–8.4	8.5–16.9	>17.0

(Note: The ranges listed are for illustration purposes and are not meant to be recommended values for any particular system.)

General System Stability is the average amount of time the system is operational before user services are interrupted, loss of work results, or a system reboot is required. The determination of system stability can be derived from the number of system interruptions (e.g., measurements that indicate the number and length of time the system is unavailable for use). A malfunction or failure that does not result in system interruption is ignored for system stability determination. A chart should be developed to indicate the limits of performance of the system, with values based on stability requirements. For existing systems, the derived metric values should be compared against the required levels listed in the chart. For example, the chart below illustrates acceptable, substandard, and unacceptable performance levels for several subsystems during a 30-day period.

NUMBER OF SYSTEM INTERRUPTIONS

Subsystem causing Downtime	Acceptable	Substandard	Unacceptable
CPU + memory	0–9	10–19	>20
Disk storage	0–9	10–19	>20
Magnetic tape	0–4	5–9	>10
Software module 1	0–12	13–24	>25
Software module 2	0–12	13–24	>25

(Note: The ranges listed are for illustration purposes and are not meant to be recommended values for any particular system.)

General Survivability is the probability that the system will continue to perform after a portion of it becomes inoperable. A numerical value or importance level should be established and used to indicate the acceptable and/or required levels of survivability. Survivability can be derived from measurements that relate to the number of failures (both hard and soft failures) and the ability of the system to recover from the failure. In addition, measurements that indicate the system usage and the amount of damage that could result from a failure can influence the survivability rating and should also be considered. The following list is an example of levels of importance associated with various types (hardware, software, etc.) of subsystems. (Note: documentation survivability encompasses the scope, clarity, completeness, and correctness of the documentation that will enable a user to read, understand, and perform the activity described correctly).

IMPORTANCE LEVELS

Subsystem	Level of Importance	Comments
CPU	high	Level depends on the functional
Tape drive 1	low	importance and usage of the device
Software module 1	high	Level depends on the functional
Software module 2	moderate	importance and usage of the module
Documentation	moderate	Level depends on the subject importance and the usage of the documentation

(Note: The levels listed are for illustration purposes and are not meant to be recommended values for any particular system.)

Policy Formulation

The values obtained from the reliability measurements are used in the formulation and adjustment of reliability policies.

Maintenance Policies and Procedures should be examined and evaluated to reflect the reliability requirements of the computer system. The system planner can use the metrics to assess the effectiveness of the current maintenance policies and to adjust them accordingly. Almost all the reliability measurements can be used to indicate system problems and are helpful tools in the identification of potential and actual subsystem failures. In addition, the logistic delay — delays encountered while waiting for parts and/or service personnel — should be included in the considerations.

Acquisition Policies should be examined and evaluated to reflect the reliability requirements of the computer system. The reliability measurements are indications of the system activity and quality, and can be used as supporting factors in the justification and specification of new system acquisitions and/or system reconfiguration.

Information on the Impact of a Failure

The more dependent an organization is on the computer system, the greater the impact a failure would have on that organization. Reliability measurements that provide information about the frequency and identity of system failures and the performance level of the computer system are used in the assessment of the impact.

Productivity and Workload Scheduling is the scheduling of the amount of work that consumes computer resources. A system not functioning to its full capacity may delay or prevent the processing of user and system jobs. This interruption can affect productivity and product schedules and, as such, translates into a cost. With knowledge of the computer system's reliability, a system planner can adjust and forecast current and future workload requirements accordingly.

Amount of "Backup" Work is the amount of work performed in anticipation of a failure. This would include multiple copies of system and user programs and data, checkpoints for easy restart, and multiple runs of identical jobs. Efforts such as these are used to circumvent the effects of a failure or to facilitate recovery. In general, the less reliable a computer system is, the greater the amount of "backup" work performed.

Clarification and Identification of Failures

The combined analysis of reliability measurement results and accumulated historical system data is a means of identifying the occurrence of specific failures/problems or of obtaining early warning indicators of potential failures/problems. This knowledge enables the system planner to take the appropriate corrective action in a timely manner. Of particular value in pinpointing the cause of the failure/problem is the correlation of measurements that pertain to the type, location, and frequency of the failure/problem with the system's resultant action (e.g., crash, recovery — retry or warm start).

BASIC TECHNIQUES

Reliability techniques are incorporated into a computer system to reduce the errors and effects resulting from the corruption of data or the malfunction of the hardware during system operation. The techniques are implemented to prevent, offset, or correct the occurrence of one of the following fundamental categories of faults.

1. *Physical faults.* The disruption of the information processing function due to a hardware malfunction of the computer, its peripherals, or both. These failures result from the weakening and breakage of the components over a period of time and usage.

2. *Design faults.* The imperfections in the system due to mistakes and deficiencies during the initiation, planning, development, programming, or maintenance of the computer system.

3. *Interaction faults.* The malfunctions or alterations of programs and data caused by human/machine interactions during system operations.

The remainder of this section presents a general discussion of basic reliability techniques. The selection of techniques that are applicable to a given system will depend on the system objectives and configuration as well as the feasibility of implementing the technique. The discussion is divided into two parts: design features and implementation techniques. Design features are the reliability techniques designed into the hardware configuration or software source code by the system developer. Implementation techniques are those the system planner can adopt to improve the reliability of the system.

Design Features

A large range of reliability techniques is available to the designers of computer systems. The goal of these techniques is to keep the system operational either by eliminating faults or in spite of them. A combination of reliability-enhancing features may be used within a single system. The specific techniques used may vary among systems due to cost, performance, and reliability trade-offs.

Typically, the system planner cannot designate which design techniques are to be incorporated into the computer system. (The development of custom-designed system software may be an exception to this rule). Despite this inability, the system planner should be familiar with reliability design techniques in order to better specify and understand the system's reliability capabilities. A list of techniques is shown in Figure 18.10. A brief explanation of several of these follows.

Fault Avoidance

The goal of a fault avoidance approach is to reduce or eliminate the possibility of a fault through design practices such as component burn-in, testing and validation of hardware and software, and careful signal path routing. The approach assumes an a priori perfectibility of the system. To achieve fault avoidance, all components of the system (hardware and software) must function correctly at all times. Some fault avoidance techniques:

- *Environmental factors.* The elimination of faults caused by heat produced by the system's circuitry.

- *Quality components.* The acquisition and use of extremely reliable components.

- *Component and system integration.* The careful assembly and interconnection, and extensive testing and verification, of individual modules, subsystems, and the entire system.

- *Verification, validation, and testing.* The process of review, analysis, and testing employed throughout the software development life cycle to insure the correctness, completeness, and consistency of the final product.

Function	Technique
Fault Avoidance	Environment modification
	Quality components
	Component integration level
	Verification and validation
Fault Tolerance	
Fault detection:	Duplication
	Error detection codes
	M-of-N codes
	Parity
	Checksums
	Arithmetic codes
	Cyclic codes
	Self-checking and failsafe logic
	Watchdog timers and timeouts
	Consistency and capability checks
Masking redundancy:	NMR/voting
	Error correcting codes
	Hamming SEC/DED
	Masking logic
	Interwoven logic
	Coded-state machines
	Recovery Block
	N-version Programming
Dynamic redundancy:	Reconfigurable duplication
	Reconfigurable NMR
	Backup sparing
	Reconfiguration
	Recovery

Figure 18.10. Classification of reliability techniques.

Fault Tolerance

The goal of a fault tolerance approach is to preserve the continued correct execution of functions after the occurrence of a selected set of faults. This is achieved through redundancy: the addition of hardware or software or the repetition of operations beyond those minimally required for normal system operation. Fault tolerance techniques include:

- *Watchdog timers and timeouts.* A process must reset a timer or complete processing within a set time period. Inability to accomplish this task is an indication of possible failure. Neither timers nor timeouts can be used to check data for errors.

- *N=Module Redundancy (NMR)/voting.* The outputs of N identical modules are compared. By the use of majority voting, a fault can be detected, the correct output selected, and processing continued. The most common NMR technique is Triple Modular Redundancy (TMR) (Figure 18.11).

- *Error correction codes (ECC).* This is the representation of information by code sequences that will enable the extraction of original information despite its corruption.

- *Recovery block method.* Several independent programs are developed to perform a specific task. If a fault is detected in one program, an alternate program is selected to execute the task.

- *N-version programming.* The outputs of N independently coded and executed programs are compared. By majority voting or a

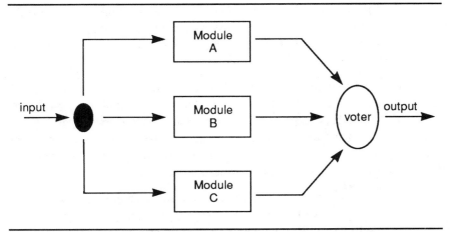

Figure 18.11. Triple modular redundancy (TMR) system with voting.

predetermined strategy, a "correct" result is identified. Since the programs are developed independently, it is assumed that the probability of a common error is close to zero.

Implementation Techniques

A variety of reliability-related techniques can be implemented by the system planner. Several of these techniques are simply variations of design features described above. They may require adjustments to current procedures, the system configuration, or management policies. The following are several examples of techniques a system planner can implement with the addition of hardware or software, or through the management of the facility. The first four techniques are based on principles of redundancy.

- *Duplication of systems.* The replication of the computer system, subsystem, software, or peripherals to provide a replacement capability should a failure occur. The ability to switch to an alternative system (subsystem, etc.) enables usage of the system to continue as repairs (corrections) are made to the failed unit.

- *Environmental backup.* The ability to use alternative sources of power, air conditioning, and communication lines in case an outage should occur. Battery backup, uninterrupted power supply (UPS), and frequency interference filters are examples of techniques to counter environmental interferences.

- *Reconfiguration.* The removal or disabling of a faulty module from the rest of the system. The system continues to function (without the faulty module) but at a degraded level — e.g., with limited capacity or capabilities.

- *Software archive.* The duplication of software to replace corrupted or inaccessible data or programs. These redundant copies of software should be kept current, on alternate storage media, and available for use should a failure occur. Because of the possible threat of damage or theft, consideration should be given to storing the software archive at an offsite location.

- *Maintenance policy.* The establishment of a preventive maintenance (PM) program to periodically check the system and correct potential faults. PM is a means of locating and correcting problems before they propagate through the system and cause major damage. A corrective maintenance program should also be provided, which is activated after the system ceases to function as originally intended. The system is returned to an error-free state.

- *Personnel.* Support personnel (operators, analysts, technicians) should be available while the system is operational and able to intercede if a problem occurs. For example, if an operator is required to boot a system, a provision should be made for having an operator on duty any time the system is operational. Staff schedules should be adjusted in order to curtail delay due to personnel unavailability. Proper training and complete documentation will help personnel act quickly when a problem occurs and prevent or minimize loss of information or loss of the system (i.e., crash).

- *Supplies.* Directly related to the hardware or software of the system, the use of quality printer ribbon, disks, tapes, etc., can eliminate many peripheral-related failures.

RECOVERY STRATEGY

Recovery is the process of restoring the system to a correctly functioning state from an erroneous one. The reliability objectives, the effects of a fault, and the system's tolerance of the resulting errors must be understood and considered in the determination of a recovery strategy.

Recovery Procedures

It is necessary for the system planner to establish procedures to recover from a failure and restart the system quickly. While many of the error recovery procedures pertain to methods imbedded in the system architecture (both hardware and software), others are a result of facility management practices or site-implemented techniques. Imbedded procedures are limited by the vendor design and need to be specified during the planning and acquisition of the system. Facility management and site-implemented techniques can be established at system initiation as well as during the operational stage.

Details of possible imbedded (design) techniques and implemention techniques were given in the previous section.

In choosing recovery techniques, the system planner needs to evaluate the system requirements with respect to:

1. The amount of time between the occurrence of a failure and the start of the recovery process.

2. The amount of time between the initiation of recovery and the restoration of the system.

3. The amount of human interaction (maintenance) required to restore the system. (Manual recovery techniques generally require more time than do automatic recovery techniques.)

Recovery Levels

The level of computing achieved through recovery procedures can be grouped into three classes.

•   Full recovery returns the system to the set of conditions existing prior to the failure. Hardware and software possess the same computing capability as before. Typically, failed components are replaced by spare equipment (hardware) or duplicate software modules. Data and information are returned to their prefailure state.

•   Degraded recovery means the system is returned to an operational state, but with a reduced computing capacity. Malfunctioning hardware and software and corrupted data and information are identified and excluded from the system.

•   Safe shutdown occurs when the system cannot maintain a minimum level of computing capacity. The system is shut down with as little damage and as much warning as possible. Diagnostic information and warning messages are given. Attempts to reduce the amount of damage to the remaining hardware, software, and data are made.

The objective of these recovery levels is to avoid a hard, complete crash of the system. If full recovery cannot be achieved, the alternatives are to continue processing in a degraded mode or shut down the system. To determine the appropriate recovery level, the system planner must answer the following questions:

1. *System application requirements:* can the application tolerate a shutdown or graceful degradation?

2. *Extent of damage to hardware and software:* can critical operations continue to be processed despite damage to system components?

3. *Speed with which the operation must be recovered:* is there sufficient time for the recovery process to complete without violating system operational (speed, safety, etc.) requirements?

4. *Technical capability to implement the recovery techniques:* is it possible to design or implement techniques to identify, locate, correct, and record a fault to the system or its components?

5. *Cost to implement the recovery process:* is the recovery level cost-beneficial?

6. *Amount of external assistance (manual intervention):* how much maintenance is required and will be available for recovery efforts after a failure occurs?

All the above questions should be examined with respect to the system as a whole and any critical or self-contained subsystems or components, or both.

THE RELIABILITY PROGRAM

Implementing a Reliability Program

A reliability program should be initiated with the conception of the system, continue through daily operation, and end only when the system is retired from use. It should be incorporated into the system life cycle as early as possible in order to maintain consistency with overall system objectives, as well as to minimize the difficulty and cost of implementation.

The tasks involved in implementing a successful reliability program require the participation of personnel from a variety of organizations (e.g., system planner, technical specialists, users, procuring personnel, and vendors). To ensure the success of the program, the system planner needs to understand the reliability engineering and management tasks and coordinate the efforts of the people required to perform them. The system planner must be able to:

- Understand reliability engineering terminology
- Specify reliability performance tasks

- Schedule the tasks to be performed
- Identify personnel to perform the tasks
- Understand the consequences of eliminating or curtailing the tasks
- Identify major alternatives with respect to cost and risks
- Locate additional information/consultants if needed

Financial Considerations

There are several fundamental costs associated with the implementation of a reliability program. Calculating the costs versus the benefits of such a program is not an easy task. The analysis should provide the system planner with the information needed to evaluate alternative approaches and make decisions about initiating, procuring, continuing, or modifying the reliability program.

The system planner should view the costs of a reliability program as an investment that is amortized over the life cycle of the system. It is important that the system planner consider not only the cost of implementation but also the cost of nonimplementation. A knowledge of these considerations can aid the system planner in assessing the effects of reliability on the costs of ownership.

Cost of Not Implementing a Reliability Program

As the organization becomes increasingly dependent on its computer systems, the impact of a failure needs to be examined and evaluated — interruption of service by any fully utilized system will eventually lead to a loss of money or time. It is not possible to generalize the cost of failing to implement a reliability program, since it is dependent on the system applications and the frequency with which the system fails. However, the greater the application's dependence on the computer system, the higher the cost of downtime. These costs are reflected by:

- A disruption or delay in production, development, and schedules
- The loss or corruption of information (data and programs)
- An increase in maintenance costs
- An increase in acquisition costs of spare (replacement) parts
- A decrease in user productivity and confidence in the system

Cost of Implementing a Reliability Program

Associated with the elements of a reliability program is the cost to implement and maintain those elements. These costs may be either one-time expenses or recurrent over the system's life cycle. Despite these costs, the deployment of a reliability program and its resulting reliability improvements will yield reductions in future operation and maintenance expenditures. The costs are reflected in the following reliability program elements and activities. (Further explanation of these elements can be found in previous chapters of this book.)

- Reliability specifications in the RFP (design techniques, reliability measures, controls, and thresholds)

- Site preparation (alternate power sources and communication lines)

- Redundancy of critical subsystems

- Hardware and software monitors

- Auditing and analysis software

- Auditing, analysis, and refinement of the reliability program

- Routine maintenance program (preventive maintenance)

- Spare parts inventory

- Trained support personnel (operators, analysts, technicians)

- Duplication and storage of software (programs and data)

Activities for Establishing and Maintaining Reliability

The successful evolution of a reliable computing system requires several important management decisions and actions. Outlined below are the major activities in the establishment and maintenance of a reliability program.

1. Establish reliability goals:
    - Determine the probability of a failure and its impact on the system.
    - Determine how much should be spent on reliability concerns (Remember, reliability affects other life cycle costs, e.g., maintenance).
    - Determine and integrate reliability concerns with overall system objectives.

2. Consider alternative ways of achieving reliability goals:
    - Consider the various design and implementation techniques.

- Determine the feasibility of implementing the targeted reliability techniques.
- Consider all options. For example, to provide backup computing ability, weigh the advantages of implementing a redundant computer system versus buying time-sharing services.

3. Select appropriate measures and controls:
- Include controls that provide early warning of reliability problems.
- Incorporate measures that can provide information on the performance objectives of the system.
- Include several complementary and overlapping measures in order to achieve realistic and complete reliability information.
- Establish an appropriate schedule (frequency) for collecting and assessing reliability data.

4. Establish clear contracts with system vendors:
- Alert internal procurement personnel to reliability needs.
- Define reliability requirements clearly and in detail.
- Amplify requirements and tasks in the RFP statement of work, technical specifications, data requirements list, data item descriptions, etc.
- Identify the responsible agent for each requirement and/or product (including groups or personnel internal to the organization).
- Specify penalties and contingency plans for failure to meet performance standards.

5. Define acceptance criteria:
- Specify levels of acceptable computing performance for the system and its subsystems.
- Define threshold levels and criteria for reliability measures.

6. Develop maintenance strategy:
- Provide for remedial maintenance to correct any problems on a timely basis.

- Determine the optimum schedule and scope of preventive maintenance.

- Determine if stockpiling of spare parts is cost-beneficial. If so, determine the type and quantity of equipment to store.

7.   Monitor the system:

- Implement quality control techniques to retard the deterioration of the system.

- Process and evaluate the reliability information.

- Plan and conduct periodic reviews of the system and adjust accordingly. Account for system aging and wearout (Figure 18.12) and initiate change when more reliable system components are available and cost-effective.

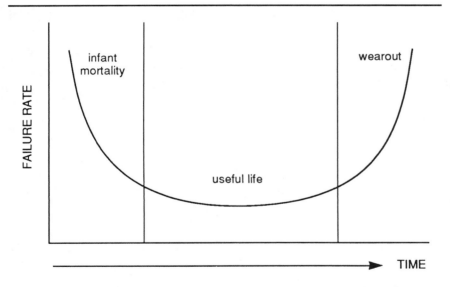

As the system gets older, more failures occur due to wearout of the components. The time to repair increases because of the difficulty in obtaining replacement parts and knowledgable repair personnel.

Figure 18.12. Bathtub curve — failure rate as a function of time.

Part 5

Relationships to Internal Audit

19

Relationship to Internal Auditing

Executive management has recognized the importance of data processing to its day-to-day operation. The proper functioning of data processing applications is becoming increasingly important in the ongoing functioning of an organization. Management, in exercising its control responsibility, is establishing groups to provide assurance that data processing systems are adequately implemented and controlled.

Both internal and external audits avoided heavy involvement in data processing until about 1970. Since then, auditing review of data processing has been increasing. A major study in systems auditability and control concluded that not enough emphasis was being placed on control. In that study, it was recommended that greater involvement by the internal audit function should occur in all phases of data processing.

In some organizations, internal audit had tried to fill the control gap by designing controls for computer applications, but this is a function that should be done by the data processing department and the user. The user has primary responsibility for application controls, and data processing for data center related controls. Internal audit should review controls, but not design them.

The establishment of the QA function in data processing permits internal audit to exercise its normal independent review function. Many internal audit groups are strongly recommending the establishment of a QA function in data processing. Where one is established, it should develop a close working relationship with internal auditing.

INTERNAL AUDIT RESPONSIBILITIES

With more than 15,000 members, the Institute of Internal Auditors is the only international organization dedicated to the advancement of the individual internal auditor and the profession. The Institute issued a Statement of Responsibility of the internal auditor in 1947 and three revisions in 1957, 1971, and 1978. The current statement embodies the concepts previously established and includes such changes as are deemed advisable in the light of the present status of the profession. It reads:

Nature

Internal auditing is an independent appraisal activity within an organization for the review of operations as a service to management. It is a managerial control which functions by measuring and evaluating the effectiveness of other controls.

Objectivity and Scope

The objective of internal auditing is to assist all members of management in the effective discharge of their responsibilities by furnishing them with analyses, appraisals, recommendations and pertinent comments concerning the activities reviewed. Internal auditors are concerned with any phase of business activity in which they may be of service to management. This involves going beyond the accounting and financial records to obtain a full understanding of the operations under review. The attainment of this overall objective involves such activities as:

1. Reviewing and appraising the soundness, adequacy, and application of accounting, financial, and other operating controls, and promoting effective control at reasonable cost.

2. Ascertaining the extent of compliance with established policies, plans, and procedures.

3. Ascertaining the extent to which company assets are accounted for and safeguarded from losses of all kinds.

4. Ascertaining the reliability of management data developed within the organization.

5. Appraising the quality of performance in carrying out assigned responsibilities.

6. Recommending operating improvements.

Responsibility and Authority

The responsibility of internal auditing in the organization should be clearly established by management policy. The related authority should provide the internal auditor full access to all of the organization's records, properties, and personnel relevant to the subject under review. The internal auditor should be free to review and appraise policies, plans, procedures, and records.

The internal auditor's responsibilities should be:

1. To inform and advise management, and to discharge this responsibility in a manner that is consistent with the Code of Ethics of the Institute of Internal Auditors.

2. To coordinate internal audit activities with others so as to best achieve the audit objectives of the organization.

In performing their functions, internal auditors have no direct responsibilities for nor authority over any of the activities under review. Therefore, the internal audit review and appraisal does not in any way relieve other persons in the organization of the responsibilities assigned to them.

Independence

Independence is essential to the effectiveness of internal auditing. This independence is obtained primarily through organizational status and objectivity.

1. The organizational status of the internal auditing function and the support accorded to it by management are major determinants of its range and value. The head of the internal auditing function, therefore, should be responsible to an officer whose authority is sufficient to assure both a broad range of audit coverage and the adequate consideration of an effective action on the audit findings and recommendations.

2. Objectivity is essential to the audit function. Therefore, internal auditors should not develop and install procedures, prepare records, or engage in any other activity which they would normally review and appraise and which could reasonably be construed to compromise the independence of the internal auditor. The internal auditor's objectivity need not be adversely affected, however, by determining and recommending standards of control to be applied in the development of the systems and procedures being reviewed.

CONTROL IN AN MIS ENVIRONMENT

One of the primary responsibilities of an auditor is to evaluate the adequacy of control. Over the past several hundred years control in a business environment has been slowly revolving. Prior to the advent of the computer, auditors understood good control practices. The computer changed control. Let's review what has happened to control in computerized business environment.

Most MIS departments are organized into two groups. One group runs the computer, while the other group designs and writes programs. Generally the MIS department takes direction for new assignments from prospective users who have little, if any, real knowledge of how to use or control a computer. In the old days when the computer read a card, sorted some data, and printed a report, the user could somehow relate to the data even though the user did not totally understand what was being done to it. The accepted control philosophy was that the user was responsible for defining the needs and controlling the data that flowed through the user's system. In small companies where minicomputers are being installed, we can still find this basic pattern of organization and control.

In larger companies, with large computer installations, we are finding increasing sophistication employing such new concepts as distributed network processing, database systems, virtual storage, transaction processing, and a whole lot of other buzzwords. Although the technology of computers and systems design has been changing at an unbelievable rate, many companies still retain the same organization they had in the early days of the computer or, worse, in the days of the unit record tab equipment.

To illustrate quickly what can happen, a bank recently installed an on-line teller systems linking a number of branches into a centrally controlled system. Prior to the change, each bank had a head cashier who was directly responsible for the direction and control of each teller. After the change, the computer performed most of the tasks previously performed by the head cashiers. The head cashiers, operating independently at each bank, did not design the system nor could they, as a group, direct or control the system effectively. Nor did they fully understand all that the computer was doing. Organizationally, the head cashiers were still held responsible for teller operations, but no one realized until later that the administrative responsibility for all of the bank's normal cash-handling functions had passed over to a programmer/analyst, who seized the opportunity to get rich. As a postscript, an auditor had approved the controls built into the system but failed to realize that no one was organizationally responsible for using them.

There is generally lack of control within many MIS installations, but the auditing profession may be trying to solve the wrong problem. Very little has been researched, written, or discussed relative to the impact the computer is having on traditional organization structures. Yet, weaknesses in the organizational structure may very well be the primary cause for the lack of control that exists in many MIS systems. To illustrate the situation, a president of a large corporation asked the payroll manager if he would do anything differently if he knew he would be fired if anyone connected with the MIS installation were found defrauding the company through the payroll system. His immediate response was a very audible "yes!" The president wanted to know why he wasn't presently doing those other things. The manager's response was "Today, I am not responsible if something goes wrong in there." The payroll manager's job description has since been rewritten and there have been dramatic improvements in control.

In many cases the technological advances in computers and their associated systems have outstripped the ability of the rest of the organization to keep up. As an illustration, there was a medium-sized company where many normal administrative procedures went from manual mode to a small card handling computer to a large mainframe transaction processing database-oriented computer within three years. Managers were just realizing the need for adequate batch controls when they had to start learning all over again. In this same company, the manual mode never worked well even before the computer made a mess of things. This situation created an environment where, admittedly, the organization was unable to change fast enough to keep up with the changing computer technology. Rather than slow down or change the organization, the attitude shifted to one of making the users look incompetent with the end result being a total takeover of most administrative responsibilities by the MIS group! Control almost disappeared. This company was, at one time, virtually being run by the MIS organization.

Control is a management function that requires an appropriate organization to be effective. To have control, one must be assigned a responsibility for control and be vested with appropriate authority which will assure getting it. The breakdown of control can usually be traced to an organizational efficiency where a responsibility was not spelled out or the person responsible was not granted sufficient authority to carry out his responsibilities. As in the earlier example of the president and payroll manager, the absence of control in MIS systems is often traceable to improperly defined responsibility.

THE AUDITOR AND CONTROL

In many companies, the MIS auditor has stepped into the breach, recognizing the lack of control, user ignorance, and a certain apathy toward control on the part of MIS personnel. He has chosen to improve the situation by demanding that certain basic controls be established and performing certain tests which provided assurance that the absence of these basic controls had not created as yet an undetected problem. There is little, if any, question that the auditor's input was both necessary and desirable. However, auditors who jump into the breach have often been so busy trying to "plug holes" they have not stepped back to determine what is causing the problem. If the cause can be identified, then it can be dealt with is such a way that the solution should reduce or eliminate the undesirable effects.

Internal auditing, through the MIS auditor, is trying to fill an organizational void by assuming the responsibility for control. Obviously, the responsibility has been properly defined in the organization and there is lack of control in most MIS systems. The lack of an assigned responsibility for control should be dealt with. However, the assumption of responsibility for control by an auditor, any auditor, is an impossible and illogical solution. Responsibility and authority must be granted in equal shares, organizationally. To be effective as an independent and objective observer, an auditor, by definition, must be denied, organizationally, any authority. Without authority there can be no responsibility. If auditors assume the responsibility, they must be granted or must seize the authority — at which point, they cease to be effective as auditors. This represents a very real "catch–22" and one which has not been faced up to very well.

The first step in improving the overall control of the computer resource is to recognize that there is probably no defined organizational responsibility for control. A lot of people probably recognize the need for control and are no doubt involved in some way in providing controls. This is not the same thing as being responsible for control.

The second step is to recognize that sophisticated systems require integration of function which, in most cases, involves the horizontal linkage of many organizational components. Historically, control, responsibility, authority, and communication were all channeled in a vertical organization structure. The imposition of a horizontal structure by the computer results in an absence of an organizational entity that is responsible for the system as a whole even though a number of persons may be assigned some responsibility for control of a portion of the total system. Internal auditing's role is not to provide the missing control elements on an ongoing basis but, rather, to apprise management that this defect in control exists and to request that it be remedied. The near absence of any written research or other material on organization structure indicates that the cause and effect relationship between the computer-imposed horizontal organization and an attendant lack of assigned responsibility for control of "The System" has not yet been widely recognized.

CONTROL AND MIS ORGANIZATION

It has been recognized that no one in an organization has an assigned responsibility for control of "The System" and that to be effective large, integrated systems must be based on a horizontal integration of function which imposes a strain on traditional vertical organization structures by complicating the assignment of a responsibility for control. Then what is the answer? In many companies there is an awareness that the installation of large-scale computers with highly integrated systems does, in fact, force the traditional organization structure to change. Many managers have the feeling that things are coming unglued and that they are no longer "in control." However, most of them can't define why they feel as they do. There is also a perception that the MIS group is increasingly gaining a bigger piece of the management pie. However, in most companies the change away from traditional concepts is not necessarily a planned change toward something better. The change just happens and out of the confusion something that works emerges. The something that works most often seems to be an assumption of responsibility by the MIS group for "The System" and an assumption of responsibility by the

MIS auditor for control of "The System." This is an assumption of responsibility because there is no assignment of appropriate authority, and it works only until disaster occurs. This is not necessarily the only or best solution. In most cases it is, in reality, the default solution which occurs because the effect of the computer-dictated horizontal integration of function on the corporate organization structure is not well understood in advance and management responsibility assignments are not appropriately planned or made in advance to support the change.

The solution to the problem must lie in creating new and different organizational structures, ones more suited to the horizontal structure imposed by the computer. There are two sides to the organizational question, the corporate organization itself which must relate to the conditions imposed by computer systems and the organization of the MIS group so that it can relate more effectively with the corporate organization.

Using the example of the on-line teller systems noted earlier, the bank could have created the position of "Vice President for On-Line Teller System" and assigned him total responsibility and authority for the planning, direction, organization, and control of the entire system. This course would have resulted in all head cashiers, tellers, and some MIS personnel reporting to this newly created position. In other words, he would have been given all the tools he needed to do the job. Recognizing that a horizontal integration-of-function type system does cross normal organization boundaries, then one answer might be to create a new organizational entity within the traditional vertical framework which is suitably chartered so that it has complete control over all of the entities that are horizontally connected by "The System." Quite obviously, to maintain appropriate management control via segregation of duties, this person would be part of the line organization and outside the MIS group.

Another way of assigning responsibility and authority might entail nothing more than amending a job description or providing some form of incentive-related control. The payroll manager is an example of what might happen just by expanding a job description and giving the manager more authority. Another example concerns a case where it was merely a case of oversight. A plant manager for a $20 million brass casting plant was allowing some of the inventory to be piled next to the fence which separated the storage yard from the parking lot. Many of the mill hands drove pickup trucks which were parked against the fence. Inventory write-offs were common but not of a material nature. The plant manager had argued, successfully, that the write-offs were small and that a lack of storage capacity, budget constraints, poor systems, and a whole lot of other problems prevented him from doing things differently. The auditors were never able to really prove that a problem existed or that the risk was greater than the cost of the control. The president toured the plant one day and saw the situation which the plant manager dutifully explained. Upon returning to his office the president learned that the plant manager's job description did not list as one of his responsibilities that he "... shall have responsibility for the security and protection of corporate owned assets." This was added to the plant manager's job description and along with it the incentive system was changed so that inventory write-offs caused a direct reduction of the manager's bonus. Suddenly, controls that had always been too difficult or expensive in the past became feasible almost overnight. In many large corporations, job descriptions, manager contracts, and policy charters do not make any reference to responsibility control, protection, or security.

The rapid growth in the complexity of computer systems has outpaced the ability of many organizations to alter their organizational structure into new forms required by these technical advances. Recognizing this, there needs to be a similar growth in the state of the art of management theory and organization structure. Little has been done or written in this area. New or different ideas should be explored such as managers or directors of systems. A careful evaluation of job descriptions and incentive systems should be made to determine if responsibilities for control of computer systems have been appropriately defined.

The absence of usable alternatives has resulted in many companies relying on the default solution whereby responsibility for "The System" is assumed by MIS auditing. The first area of worthwhile exploration lies in finding improved methods for restructuring the organization to improve areas within the MIS group itself.

Historically, neither the DP group responsible for writing the programs nor the group responsible for running the programs on the computer has been given any responsibility for control or authority to direct the installation of controls. As a point of fact, most controls are counterproductive to the whole idea behind using computers in the first place in that they create inefficiency, redundancy, and a lot of extra work. Whatever control does exist in most MIS installations has been forced upon them by outsiders such as internal auditors, CPA firms and executive management personnel who have become terrified by the horror stories in leading business publications.

NEED FOR QUALITY ASSURANCE

Establishing a quality assurance group is an approach to the organization of various functions to achieve a responsibility for the control of computer systems. This is not the only alternative, but it may be the best. It is almost a written law that the cashier cannot be general ledger bookkeeper. Auditors can identify with this element of internal control and have no difficulty expressing their concern in an audit report. However, most auditors, including the specialized breed of MIS auditors, run right past the fact that there is no independent responsibility in most MIS organizations for the control of computer systems. There is copious material on the appropriate organizational splits that are effective in achieving control over the accounting records, but very little has been written on how to organize functions within MIS organizations. Therefore, most MIS installations are organized to produce and run programs with an emphasis on volume or production. Controls, or any other administrative overhead, that tend to reduce the production rate are not going to be installed willingly by the MIS organization.

Somewhere along the line during the evolution of computer technology, the auditing profession went astray of its mission. Historically, if the organization structure did not provide for a sufficient segregation of duties a recommendation was made to correct the deficiency. However, if the deficiency was present, the auditor would not put himself into the position of chief accountant for an indefinite period in order to make sure everything was being done properly. With computer systems, however, MIS auditors have sensed an absence of control, have been unable to trace the problem to organizational weaknesses, and have put themselves into the middle of things as they assume the responsibility for instituting control. There is something very wrong about this, but for some reason the profession has not been particularly vocal about letting MIS auditors throw away their objectivity and independence.

One of the very real myths that exist in some aspects of MIS auditing may be in confusing a test of properly designed controls with providing control as a function. Test decks, for example, are a very necessary part of getting a new program released into production. Someone within the MIS group should be assigned specific responsibility for making sure any new program or program change is adequately tested before it can become operational. An MIS auditor should verify that this testing was done and done properly, but if the MIS auditor does it, the MIS auditor is, in fact, assuming a responsibility for executing a control procedure which the MIS auditor has not been authorized to do. In this latter case where test decks are a necessary control to make sure programs are functional before they are released, the auditor, if he creates or uses the test deck himself, is in reality providing the control rather than determining if an appropriate control is actually operational.

Auditors appear to be so busy concentrating on the detailed minutiae of MIS that they have overlooked the bigger picture. They keep checking for check digits, running test decks, bench tracing, checking logic loops, trying to defeat passwords, and testing a zillion other specific controls. When problems are noted, auditors have a tendency to take over and install control mechanisms or assume a responsibility for proving the control themselves. Admittedly, the conclusion, almost universally quoted by MIS auditors, is that there is an appalling lack of control in most MIS systems. Similarly, MIS auditors have been instrumental in providing some basic level of control to prevent abuses. However, the cause of the problem in the first place is not being adequately addressed.

Organizations have not recognized that the installation of sophisticated computer systems has substantially altered the traditional organizational structure. This has resulted in numerous breakdowns in the traditional management control systems primarily because of an absence of assigned responsibilities for control of computer systems. This problem of organizational structure obsolescence should be studied and dealt with in three different but related ways.

1. Attempt to define new acceptable organizational structures which reestablish the more traditional vertical lines of authority and responsibility by reaching out in unique ways to reconfine the horizontal integration of function that results from sophisticated computer systems.

2.   Redefine the organization structure within the data processing group to establish a separate quality assurance activity which is held responsible for the control of the quality of the computer product and which, if appropriately designed, will also strengthen the overall management control of the function by improving the segregation of duties within the MIS organization.

3.   Reinforce the essential mandate of the auditing profession, which is objectivity through independence.

WORKING RELATIONSHIPS WITH INTERNAL AUDITORS

Quality assurance and internal audit have different but overlapping functions. It is in the best interest of both groups to coordinate their efforts to avoid overlap. Internal audit is primarily concerned with the system of internal control that assures accurate and complete processing of financial transactions. They're also interested in protecting the assets of the organization, which includes the proper use of assets. While quality assurance is concerned with the financial accuracy of data, its concern is limited to processing within the computerized application. This perspective is considerably different than that of internal audit.

In an application review, the quality assurance responsibility is much broader than that of internal audit. Some organizations have had an internal auditor participate as a member of the quality assurance review team. In this capacity, the internal auditor can concentrate on the adequacy of internal control to assure accuracy and completeness of processing financial data. In a review in which the internal auditor does not participate, the quality assurance group may wish to get a checklist from the internal auditors to be used in reviewing the control aspect of the application system.

Internal auditing and quality assurance use many of the same practices in performing their respective functions. One group can learn from the experiences and techniques of the other. It may be advisable to hold joint meetings where the practices and problems of each can be openly discussed. This sharing of experiences will also promote a better working relationship between the groups.

Organizations having both a quality assurance group and internal audit department have developed practices which help their joint working relationship. These practices are in the following areas:

1. Working with auditors to perform the audit function

2. Using auditors on the quality assurance review team

3. Reliance by auditors on QA reviews

4. Cross-training

5. Exchange of reports

6. Internal audit support of quality assurance

The discussion of these experiences provided below should prove helpful in building good working relationships with internal auditors.

Working with Auditors to Perform the Audit Function

Many audits in the data processing department are conducted by auditors with minimal data processing experience. Obtaining internal auditors with sufficient data processing experience has been a major problem for internal audit departments. Recently internal audit departments have been using large numbers of data processing professionals in auditing. This has proven to be a stopgap measure and is not regarded as a long-term solution to the problem.

Quality assurance personnel have an objective outlook on the data processing function. This outlook makes them candidates to assist internal auditors in fulfilling their internal audit function. Internal audit assignments include audits of specific applications, developing extract programs to obtain data for audit purposes, participation in systems design, audits of security, and audits of the data center. Auditors frequently desire to have some party other than the one being audited to discuss some of the technical data processing problems. Quality assurance personnel can fill this need.

Quality assurance should initiate a policy to "Take an auditor to lunch." This provides an informal opportunity to discuss mutual problems and alternative solutions.

Using Auditors on the Quality Assurance Review Team

Many internal audit groups are involved in reviewing the systems during the development phase. Current internal auditing literature is strongly recommending audit involvement during systems development. This is based on the premise that if controls are not built in during the developmental phase the cost to add them after the system is live may be prohibitive. Thus, internal audit's involvement becomes a matter of economics, as well as control evaluation.

There are no standards of control in the data processing industry. Control of each computer application must be handcrafted. Some organizations have general guidelines, but very few state specific programming control standards. Without control standards, many internal audit groups spend much of their time working with data processing personnel to build controls into data processing applications. Most data processing people do not understand control from an accounting viewpoint and, therefore, much of the internal auditor's time must be spent on persuasion and instruction.

It may be advisable to have the internal auditor participate as a member of the quality assurance review group rather than have a project team work separately with both the internal audit group and the quality assurance group. Because the internal auditors must maintain an independent attitude, they cannot work under the direction of a quality assurance review team leader. However, it is reasonable to expect an internal auditor to work very closely with the QA team during a review.

When participating on the quality assurance team, the internal auditor will still need to prepare an independent report. This report may be attached to the quality assurance group's report, or it might be incorporated into the quality assurance report. Regardless of the method of distribution, the audit report will probably be seen by the same people who receive the quality assurance report.

Reliance by Auditors on QA Reviews

Quality assurance reviews properly performed can be used by internal auditors in the performance of their work. By relying on quality assurance, audit costs can be reduced two ways. First, there is the elimination of duplication of work by having two groups performing the same review.

Second, quality assurance personnel will probably be more proficient in the data processing than the average internal auditor and, therefore, can perform the review more efficiently.

Internal auditors will tend to rely more on the work of quality assurance when the quality assurance review procedures are formalized. The use of a quality assurance approach similar to that outlined in Chapters 7, 8, and 9 gives the proper assurance to internal auditing that an adequate review has been performed. A standardized approach, plus good working relationships with internal auditors, will enable internal auditing to reduce their effort in review systems under development. This reduction may also be extended to external audit costs as they, too, may rely on the quality assurance group.

Cross-Training

One of the dilemmas facing both quality assurance and internal audit is how to keep the members of their department current on technological developments. In addition, the problem of maintaining proficiency in data processing poses another problem. Cross-training the two groups can be helpful in staying current technically and in maintaining the proficiency of personnel in both groups.

Cross-training of the groups can be conducted in one of the following manners:

1. Assign a quality assurance member to work with auditing during one or more audits.

2. Assign an internal auditor to work with quality assurance during one or more reviews.

3. Hold joint meetings to discuss practices and problems.

4. Conduct joint training sessions for members of both groups.

5. Both groups participate in data processing training sessions.

6. Members of either group attend professional seminars and conferences and the report back to both groups.

Exchange of Reports

Quality assurance should make all its reports available to internal audit excluding from this distribution only special reports that deal with individual performance as distinct from the review of an application system. By receiving the quality assurance reports regularly, internal audit will be more willing to rely on the quality assurance work. This will help reduce audit costs.

Conversely, internal audit should make available to quality assurance reports and workpapers relating to applications under review. For example, if quality assurance is reviewing a new payroll system, workpapers of the internal audit department for the past few audits of payroll could prove very beneficial. As with the QA reports dealing with personnel performance, it may be necessary for internal audit to do some screening of confidential data in audit reports and workpapers, but most of the data should be accessible to QA personnel. If internal audit does not offer quality assurance its workpapers, QA should ask for them.

Internal Audit Support of Quality Assurance

Quality assurance is one of the best methods of assuring adequately controlled data processing applications, and most internal audit departments will support establishing the function. Quality assurance not only makes the internal audit function in data processing easier, but adds control that would not be possible with internal audits alone.

The data processing departments should solicit the support of the internal audit function regarding quality assurance. Strong recommendations by internal audit to executive management urging the formation of the group, strengthening the group, expanding the scope and responsibility of the group, and urging more independence within the data processing department for the group, are all supportive of effective quality assurance. The concept of "taking an internal auditor to lunch" may do more for quality assurance than any other single use of a lunch hour.

SUMMARY

It is advantageous to both internal audit and quality assurance to develop a good working relationship. Quality assurance personnel can help internal auditors perform their function. Internal auditors can participate in quality assurance reviews. They should work with each other to cross-fertilize practices and experiences. Quality assurance personnel should have access to internal audit workpapers and reports, where practical, to assist them in reviewing an application. The background information provided in the internal audit workpapers can prove very helpful in conducting quality assurance reviews.

Quality assurance and internal audit personnel can help each other with training. Training can be done by having personnel of one group participate in the work of another. There can be joint training sessions. Also, the exchange of reports and other information is a training mechanism.

Internal audit support of quality assurance can be very helpful in promoting quality assurance in an organization. It is advantageous to both groups to work for a strong quality assurance group. The quality assurance group, by performing its function diligently, can reduce audit effort and costs. Auditors should be able to reduce the number of data processing reviews conducted for systems under development by relying on the work of the quality assurance group.

Appendix A: Sample Quality Assurance Manual

Included in this appendix is a manual developed and used by a quality assurance group in a large organization. The QA group had been in existence for about two years when they developed this manual. The material comes from their actual review experiences and was developed by the manager of the QA group. Note that most of the material in this manual is quality control (i.e., an application system review process).

The text of this book discusses the reasons for establishing QA, how to establish it, areas to be reviewed by quality assurance, and methods of conducting those reviews. The scope of the book is broad and covers all the functions that are attributable to a mature QA group. In actual practice, there is probably no group whose scope is as broad as to encompass all the areas covered in this book. For this reason, it is felt that a "real-world" example would be helpful to organizations contemplating establishing a QA function.

The manual included in this appendix should be used as a guide to developing a manual for your organization. The topics included in the manual are those which need to be addressed. A major factor in the success of QA is performing consistent reviews. Manuals offer the standardized procedures which help ensure that the consistency of reviews is maintained. Also, the existence of a review manual will show project leaders the level of performance expected by their management.

Organization's Computer Philosophy

The organization which contributed this manual uses a structured approach to system design. The process begins with the examination of the general business problem. The philosophy of organization is that they solve business problems; their goal is not to develop computer systems. The solution to the business problem may or may not result in development of a computer application. Each step is completed and reviewed with management approval obtained prior to going to the next phase in the systems development life cycle. Management then allocates resources sufficient to complete the phase of the systems development life cycle and then reviews progress again. In such an environment, QA is a very valuable aid to management in making this phase-by-phase evaluation.

The organization is an IBM shop, using IBM hardware and software. The programming languages used are primarily COBOL and PL/1. Throughout the manual there will be references to these languages, as well as IBM software products. The abbreviations used throughout the manual (e.g., ISAM, DDNAME, etc.) are terms associated with the IBM operating system and its associated program products including compilers. These IBM terms are not defined in the appendix.

Abbreviations Used

MSP — Management Systems and Programming Department: The department responsible for all systems designs and programming.

BSD — Business System Design: Those aspects of system design that relate to solving the business problem.

CSD — Computer System Design: Those aspects of design work that relate to the development of the computer system.

QA — Quality Assurance: Abbreviation for quality assurance.

SAPP — Systems and programming Practices: The data processing department manual that includes system design and programming standards.

SDM — System Development Methodology: The step-by-step approach used by the organization during the systems development life cycle to develop new applications.

Quality Assurance Philosophy

The QA group that developed this manual was established primarily to verify compliance to the system development methodology and systems and programming procedures for the Management Systems and Programming Department of the organization. All questions included in the manual were reviewed by the management of the Management Systems and Programming Department. The questions have been judged by management to be fair questions. The systems analysts and programmers in the Management Systems and Programming Department have access to this manual. The general philosophy of the QA group is to be helpful to the systems analysts and programmers in fulfilling their function, while at the same time reviewing compliance to the systems and programming procedures.

How the Manual Is Used

Each question of the manual is cross-referenced to a paragraph or section within the Management Systems and Programming Department's system and programming procedural manual and system development methodology manuals. The development of the manual required a thorough review of all Management Systems and Programming Department procedures. Quality assurance helps assure the level of quality specified by the management of the Management Systems and Programming Department.

QUALITY ASSURANCE MANUAL
CONTENTS

Section   *Description*

   I. Introduction 624

  II. Summary 625

 III. MSP Quality Assurance Program (QA) Scope,
Objectives, and Constraints 626

 IV. QA Review and Evaluation Procedure 627

  V. Quality Assurance Project Selection 630

 VI. Phase Descriptions 632

 VII. Business System Design Checklist 637

VIII. Computer Systems Design (CSD) Checklist 643

 IX. Programming Checklist 654

  X. Feasibility Study Checklist 666

 XI. Installation Checklist 673

 XII. Staffing the Quality Assurance Function 675

I.   INTRODUCTION

    A.   Purpose

        The purpose of the Quality Assurance Program (QA) is to provide MSP management with another tool to assure that systems comply with existing MSP standards and guidelines.

    B.   Assumptions

        The Quality Assurance program will establish formal QA reviews to be conducted subsequent to these discrete phases of SDM:

        −   Feasibility Study

        −   Business System Design

        −   Computer System Design

        −   Programming

        −   Installation

        The tuned versions of the SDM phase being reviewed would be the standard against which the review would be made.

        Projects would not be delayed entering a subsequent phase pending the results of a QA review of the prior phase.

        The QA function will be a separate activity within MSP, reporting to the manager of the support group.

        The checklists for each phase must represent a consensus of views and be acceptable to all functional areas prior to their inclusion in the program.

    C.   Quality Assurance — Philosophy

        1.   Manufacturing and Other Disciplines

            Within Manufacturing as well as within other environments, the quality assurance of products has been considered a proper and normal procedure. It is commonly referred to as quality or production control. Products are tested in toto or by using statistical acceptance sampling techniques to measure performance to specifications.

        2.   MS Functions

            MS functions can be compared to manufacturing and other disciplines in that products (systems) are produced. Since systems are developed according to established standards and procedures, the role of quality assurance within MS becomes analogous to that of QA for manufacturing, namely assuring that the systems (products) produced have adhered to these standards and guidelines.

D.   Benefits

The QA Function would yield benefits to MSP as follows:

–   Provide management with a mechanism that will monitor adherence to existing standards and procedures.

–   Ensure a uniform approach to phase reviews.

–   Assure resolution of differences of interpretation by providing for more than one review.

II.   SUMMARY

In order to begin the Quality Assurance Program within MSP, the following tasks have been approved for implementation after reviews with management and/or their representatives from each functional area:

–   The scope, objectives, and constraints of the QA program as it will be implemented.

–   QA review and evaluation procedures.

–   Project selection procedures.

–   Checklists for the BSD, CSD, and programming phases of SDM.

–   Feasibility and installation.

The Quality Assurance Team will include:

–   QA project leader (from MSP Support).

–   Analysts from each functional area who will not be permanent team members at this time.

The mechanics of the QA review and evaluation procedure are described in detail in Section IV.

Checklists will be used for all reviews and they have been geared to those tasks and activities within a particular SDM phase. Provision has been made to indicate to the QA team any task or activity for the phase that was not addressed by the project team.

III. MSP QUALITY ASSURANCE PROGRAM (QA) SCOPE, OBJECTIVES, AND CONSTRAINTS

A. Introduction

The purpose of this write-up is to outline the MSP Quality Assurance (QA) program that will be established within MSP. The program provides MSP management with control information regarding adherence to established standards and guidelines for project development work within MSP.

B. Scope

1. The Quality Assurance Program would be applicable to all projects being developed within MSP.

2. The Quality Assurance Program will be structured according to various phases of the established systems development methodology (SDM).

C. Objectives

1. To establish a Quality Assurance Program for MSP compatible with the aims and goals of the department using current standards and guidelines.

2. Develop a core of analysts capable of performing QA reviews across a wide range of systems.

3. To assure that all projects which are budgeted over a stipulated amount, which impact profit or which involve a substantial risk factor are subject to Quality Assurance Review. In addition, to make sure that projects not included in the preceding groupings would be subject to a QA review.

D. Constraints

1. Projects will not require a QA sign-off in order to proceed to the next stage of development.

2. QA team personnel (other than the QA project leader from the Support Group) will not be permanently assigned to the QA function.

IV. QA REVIEW AND EVALUATION PROCEDURE

A.   Purposes

To establish guidelines and procedures to govern the conduct of Quality Assurance Reviews during various discrete phases of the system development cycle.

B.   Definition

A Quality Assurance Review is, by definition, a periodic and systematic review of system development efforts and their products to determine the adherence to existing standards or guidelines in use within the MSP community.

C.   Objective

The aim of the Quality Assurance Review is to assure that the system is being developed according to established policies, procedures, and standards.

D.   Scope

This procedure applies to selected system development efforts across the spectrum of MSP. Quality Assurance may be done on any project selected as a result of the Project Selection Procedure.

E.   Responsibilities

1.   Functional Area

Each functional area has the primary responsibility for the quality of its systems.

2.   Management — MSP

The manager of MSP has overall responsibility (using QA as a tool for assuring that existing standards have been adhered to during the development of systems by each functional area).

3.   The manager of MSP Support has staff responsibility for the Quality Assurance Program as well as the Quality Assurance Reviews.

F.   Concept

Quality Assurance is founded on the principle that a peer review of a project based upon agreed standards or guidelines will lead to a better product. It is not to be construed as a restrictive procedure or an attempt to direct department efforts. Quality Assurance should be approached with a spirit of assistance relying ultimately upon close cooperation and mutual professional confidence.

G.   Procedure

Responsibility	*Action*
QA Project Leader (Group Support)	1. Under the Direction of Manager of MSP Support: a. Develop and maintain sets of Quality Assurance checklists suitable for various systems and geared to discrete phases of systems development. 2. Provide copies of checklists to the MSQ QA team as directed by the Manager of MSP support.
Manager MSP Support	1. Notifies Functional Managers of a scheduled Quality Assurance Review for a particular SDM phase and indicates the documentation required for the Quality Assurance Review Team.
Functional Manager	1. Acknowledges the notification of the QA Review; may suggest different date. 2. Provides the required documentation and indicates any tasks and/or activities within tasks that have not been included and sends the requisite number of copies to the QA Project Leader.

QA Project Leader (Support Group)	1. Sets up and maintains QA project file. 2. Notifies members of the QA review team that a review has been scheduled and distributes the phase documentation to each team member. 3. Schedules each QA review meeting.
QA Team	1. Individually review phase documentation using the appropriate checklist. (The checklist may have been modified depending upon whether all tasks and activities are to be reviewed.) 2. In session, prepare the first version of the QA Evaluation Form(s).
QA Project Leader (Support Leader)	Schedules the second QA review to be held jointly with the project team.
QA Team Review	1. Discuss and review the QA evaluation with the project team. 2. Complete and distribute Quality Review Evaluation Form(s) for the phase reviewed to the Functional Department. The Evaluation Form(s) are cross-referenced to the QA phase checklist.
QA Project Leader	If required, informs Functional Manager and schedules the third and final QA review. Attendees would be the QA Team, the project team members, and the Functional Manager.

QA Team, Project Team, Function Manager	Discuss, review, and resolve outstanding items from the evaluation forms.
QA Project Leader	1. Prepares final version of the QA Evaluation Form(s).
	2. Prepares a QA report to management summarizing the findings of the review.
	3. Places all forms and reports in the QA project file.

V.   QUALITY ASSURANCE PROJECT SELECTION

The purpose of this phase is to set forth the criteria that will be used for selection of projects for QA review. In addition, a proposed procedure stating the mechanics is included for your consideration. Also included is a definition of the principles that would be considered standard for QA purposes.

   A.   Criteria

   1.   Effect on Financial Results
   Definition:

   Those projects which by their nature impact the financial results of the corporation. These would include such projects as modeling, cost minimization, profit maximization, allocation of raw materials, facilities planning, and inventory, among others.

   2.   Exposure to Fraud
   Definition:

   Those projects which by their classification are prone to fraud. These would encompass such projects as accounts payable, general ledger, purchasing payroll, petty cash, as well as some other peripheral applications.

   3.   Scope of the System
   Definition:

   Those projects which, because of their cost or by

virtue of interfacing with or impacting many other systems, can be defined as being large in scope.

4. Risk to the Company

Definition:

Those projects which influence decisions regarding large capital expenditures or because of the confidential nature of the data may require unique security considerations.

5. Impact on Future Systems

Definition:

Those projects that because they utilize new technology (Database Management Systems) may affect the design considerations of others which may interface with them. In addition, projects using "Improved Programming Techniques" (LPTs) would be in this category since they would influence other systems being developed.

6. Workload of the QA Team

Because of the large number of systems being developed, modified, and expanded throughout MSP, coupled with the fact that the QA team will only have one permanent full-time member, these criteria should be evaluated on a prioritized basis.

B. Proposed Selection Procedures

1. Priorities

Following for your consideration is the suggested ranking of priorities for project selection in descending sequence of priority.

a. Effect on Financial Results

b. Exposure to Fraud

c. Scope of System

d. Risk to Company

e. Impact on Future Systems

2. Procedure

Person(s) Responsible	*Action Required*
MGR, MSP Support and QA Team Leader	1. Review projects from various Functional Areas and based upon the priorities established select a project for Quality Assurance Review.
QA Team Leader	2. Inform Functional Manager of the project and SDM phase to be reviewed.
	3. Inform Project Manager of the QA review and the SDM phase to be reviewed.
	4. Inform the rotating members of the QA team of the project and SDM phase to be reviewed.
	5. Set up a QA file for the project.
Project Manager	6. Acknowledge notification of QA review notification and set up QA file for the project.

VI. PHASE DESCRIPTIONS

A. Feasibility Study

The intent of a Feasibility Study is to determine whether or not a solution or set of solutions can be applied to solve a business problem or to enhance an opportunity. In order to accomplish this, the following objectives should be pursued.

1. Identify solution alternatives considering business, operational, environmental, technical, and economic factors including costs.

2. Recommend a best alternative.

3. A clear definition or statement of the business problem and/or opportunity.

4. A description of the current system.

5. A clear statement regarding the viability of the solution(s) in light of the factors mentioned previously.

The primary and singularly most important deliverable of the Feasibility Study is the final report with supporting detail that would be used by management to decide whether or not to make the commitments required to proceed to the next phase.

B.   Business System Design

The objectives of the Business System Design phase are to:

1.   Furnish the user with a comprehensive functional description of the system proposed to solve the business problem or enhance the business opportunity. It should describe the components to be performed either by clerical or automated processes.

2.   Provide a basis for orderly development of a technical solution by defining the requirements for the resolution.

3.   Develop a test strategy which will assure that the requirements of the system can be met.

4.   Provide reasonable assurance that the solution can be developed and put into operation.

5.   Distill the financial analysis and time projections to a level where they can be construed as firm for the duration of the project.

C.   Computer System Design

The aim of the Computer System Design is to translate the set of requirements put forth in the BSD into a computer system which satisfies those requirements.

The key objectives of the Computer System Design are to:

1.   Develop the physical files (and/or database records).

2.   Develop the set of programs to process the data to produce the output.

3.   Develop the specifications for the programs by showing what each has to accomplish rather than how to achieve that.

D.   Programming

The computer system defined and subsequently designed during the Computer System and Program Design phases is programmed according to specific test plans during this phase.

E.   Installation

The purpose of this phase is to shift the system from test to production mode in the user and operations areas. Some of the objectives are:

1.   Where necessary, transform files and implement user operating procedures.

2.   Conduct user and Computer Operations acceptance tests and analyze the results.

3.   Ensure that user and operations documentation has been reviewed and update, if appropriate.

NOTIFICATION OF QUALITY ASSURANCE REVIEW

To: _____ From: _____ Date: _____

Project Name: _____

Project Mgr./Leader: _____

An: _____ Review has been scheduled:

The review is scheduled tentatively for Date: _____ Time: _____

Room #: _____

Indicate here a more convenient date if required: _____

Please send a copy of the phase document to_____ MSP Support

Indicate tasks and activities omitted by three-digit SDM Reference #:

_____

Please return this form (or copy) to the manager of MSP Support:

MSP representatives assigned to the Quality Assurance Review Team for this project:

Team Member	*Extension*
_____	_____
_____	_____
_____	_____

Mgr. MSP Support: _____ Date: _____

_____

QUALITY ASSURANCE REVIEW
NOTIFICATION TO PROJECT TEAM

To: _____ From: _____ Date: _____

Project Name:_____

Project Mgr./Leader: _____

A Quality Assurance Review for the:_____

Phase of this project has been completed: _____

The project team review is scheduled for: _____

Indicate here a more convenient date if required:_____

Please assign project team member(s) to take part:

QA Team Member(s)	Ext.	Project Team Member(s)	Ext.
_____	____	_____	____
_____	____	_____	____
_____	____	_____	____
_____	____	_____	____
_____	____	_____	____
_____	____	_____	____
_____	____	_____	____
_____	____	_____	____

Mgr. MSP Support: _____ Date: _____

MSP QUALITY ASSURANCE REVIEW
EVALUATION FORM

Project Name: _____ QA Review #: _____

Project #: _____ QA Proj. Ldr.: _____

Functional area: _____

Development Phase: _____

Checklist reference #: _____ QA Comment/Analysis: _____

_____

_____

Date prepared: _____

_____

_____

_____

_____

Recommendation: _____

_____

_____

_____

_____

Date prepared: _____

_____

Response: _____

_____

Date: _____

VII. BUSINESS SYSTEM DESIGN CHECKLIST

	YES	NO	N/A	REF.#
Systems Overview:				
1. Is there a brief description of interfaces with other systems?				
2. Is there an outline of the major functional requirements of the system?				
3. Are the major functions defined into discrete steps with no boundary overlapping?				
4. Have manual and automatic steps been defined?				
5. Has the definition of what data is required to perform each step been indicated and how the data is obtained?				
System Descriptions:				
6. Has a system structure chart been developed, showing the logical breakdown into subsystems and interfaces with other systems?				
7. Have the major inputs and outputs been defined as well as the functional processing required to produce the output?				
8. Is there a narrative description of the major functions of the system?				
9. Have subsystem functional flow diagrams been developed showing the inputs, processing, and outputs relevant to the subsystem?				

	YES	*NO*	*N/A*	*REF.#*
10. Has a subsystem narrative description been developed?				
11. Do the functional outlines follow the logical structure of the system?				
12. Are they hierarchical in nature, that is, by function and by steps within function?				
13. Has the data been grouped into logical categories (i.e. customer product, accounting, marketing, sales, etc.)?				

Design Input and Output Data:

Data Structure:

14. Has the data been categorized as follows:
    a. Static
    b. Historical data likely to be changed
    c. Transaction related?

15. Have standard data names (if possible) been used?

16. Has the hierarchical relationship among data elements been defined and described?

Design Output Documents:

17. Are there headings?

18. Do the headings include report titles, department, date, page, number, etc.?

19. Are the output dates, system identification, titles and page numbers shown?

	YES	NO	N/A	REF.#
20. Are processing dates, system identification, titles and page numbers shown?				
21. Has consideration been given to COM or other output devices?				
22. Is each data column identified?				
23. Where subtotals are produced (e.g. product within customer) are they labeled by control break?				
24. Are the date elements clearly indicated?				
25. Has the source of the data been defined (department and individual)?				
26. Have input requirements been documented?				
27. Is the purpose of the input document clear (e.g., enter orders, process salary action)?				
28. Is the sequence (if applicable) indicated?				

Design Computer Processing:

29. Has each function been described using functional terminology (e.g., if salary exceeds maximum, print message)?				
30. Has validity checking been defined with reference to the Data Element Dictionary?				
31. In cases where the same data may be coming from several sources, have the sources been identified as to priorities for selection by the system?				

	YES	NO	N/A	REF.#

32. Has processing been classified according to type of function (e.g., transaction, calculation, editing etc.)?

Define Non-Computer Processing:

33. Has the preparation of input been described?

34. Has the distribution of output been described?

35. Has an error correction procedure been described?

36. Have organizational controls been established?

37. Have controls been established across department lines?

38. Have the control fields been designed?

39. Are there control validation procedures prior to proceeding to the next step?

Overall System Controls:

40. Have controls been designed to reconcile data received by the computer center?

41. Have controls for error correction and re-entry been designed?

42. Have controls been designed that can be reconciled to those of another system (e.g., accounting transactions whose various categories should equal General Ledger totals)?

	YES	*NO*	*N/A*	*REF.#*

Input Controls:

43. Have some or all of the following criteria been used for establishing input controls?

   a. Sequence numbering

   b. Prepunched cards

   c. Turnaround documents

   d. Batch numbering

   e. By type of input

   f. Predetermined totals

   g. Self-checking numbers

   h. Field length checks

   i. Limit checks

   j. Reasonability checks

   k. Existence/nonexistence checks

Processing Controls:

44. Do controls and totals exist for:

   a. Each value column

   b. Where appropriate, cross-foot totals

   c. Counts of input transactions, errors, accepted transactions

   d. Input transactions, old master, new master?

45. Are the results of all updates listed for each transaction showing the before and after condition?

46. As the result of an update are the number of adds, deletes, and changes processed shown?

	YES	*NO*	*N/A*	*REF.#*
47. If relationship tests have been used, are they grouped and defined?				
48. If used, have control total records been utilized to verify that all records have been processed between runs?				

Output Controls:

49. Have output controls been established for all control fields?				
50. Is there a separate output control on errors rejected by the system?				

BSD System Test Plan:

51. Have acceptance criteria (user-defined conditions) been identified?				
52. Has a tentative User Acceptance Strategy been identified?				
53. Have test data requirements been defined?				

Complete BSD:

54. Have Data Element Dictionary forms been completed?				
55. Have organizational changes been defined (if required)?				
56. Have new organization charts or new positions been required?				
57. If required, have areas for special user procedures been identified?				
58. Has a timetable for operating the system been developed?				

	YES	NO	N/A	REF.#

59. Were separate timetables developed for different cycles (weekly, monthly)?

60. Has the documentation been gathered and organized?

Evaluate BSD:

61. Has a financial analysis been performed?

62. Have the scope, objectives and constraints for the CSD been developed?

63. Has a plan for CSD, user procedures, and conversion phases been completed?

64. Has the plan been broken down into approximate "work units" (days) to serve as a basis for a schedule for the other phases?

65. Have the resources and responsibilities been arranged (who is doing what?)?

66. Have schedules been prepared for the next phases?

67. Have appropriate budgets for the next phases been prepared?

68. Has a project authorization been properly prepared for remaining phases?

VIII. COMPUTER SYSTEMS DESIGN (CSD) CHECKLIST

Develop Outline Design:

1. Has a detailed review of the BSD resulted in requiring additional information or changes?

		YES	*NO*	*N/A*	*REF.#*
2.	Have revisions been reviewed by the analyst (BSD) and the user and used to update the BSD or the CSD?				
3.	Have existing sources of data been identified?				
4.	Has a data management alternative been considered because of the nature of the system?				
5.	Have the data elements been grouped by category of data?				
6.	Have the record layout forms been used for listing the data elements?				
7.	Has the file description form been used to show the characteristics of each file?				
8.	Have the access methods been determined?				
9.	Has use been made of blocking factors to reduce access for a sequential file?				
10.	If a database has been used, has the relationship between segments (views of the database) been included?				
11.	If new data elements have been required, have they been included as part of the data dictionary?				
12.	Has the description of processing (BSD) been translated into system flowcharts showing programs and their relationships as well as reports?				

	YES	NO	N/A	REF.#

13. Has the processing been isolated by frequency as well as function?

14. Does each file requiring updating have an associated unique transaction file?

15. Does each main file have a separate validation and update function?

16. Have the following been addressed in order to reduce excessive passing of files:
    a. Sort verbs (statements)
    b. Input procedure
    c. Output procedure
    d. Random updating?

17. Has a matrix been prepared showing which programs create, access, and update each file?

18. Has a separate program section been set up for each program in the system showing:
    a. Cover page showing the program name, systems and/or subsystem name, run number, and a brief description of the program
    b. Input/Output diagram
    c. Processing description?

19. Does the processing description contain a brief outline of the processing that the program is going to perform?

20. Have the content and format of each output been defined?

	YES	*NO*	*N/A*	*REF.#*
21. Conversely, have the same been completed for each input?				
22. Have data items been checked out to the rules specified in the data dictionary?				
23. Have transactions that update master files been assigned record types?				
24. For multirecord transactions have the following been done:				
a. Identifying the record types that define the records comprising one transaction				
b. Developing a sequence number if required				
c. Defining mandatory and optional records?				

Hardware/Software Configuration:

25. Has the hardware configuration been defined showing:				
a. CPU				
b. Minimum Core Storage				
c. Number and type of peripherals				
d. Special Hardware				
e. Numbers of tapes and/or disk packs				
f. Terminals, minicomputers, microfilm, microfiche, optical scanning, etc.?				
26. Has the software been defined specifically:				
a. Operating system				
b. Telecommunications (CICS, TSO, etc.)				

27. If telecommunications equipment is
involved, has a communications
analyst been consulted regarding
type, number, speed, etc.?

File Conversion Computer System:

28. If applicable, have the file conversion requirements been specified
(task 10.2 in BSD)?

29. If required, have program specifications for the file conversion programs been completed?

30. If applicable, can the main
program(s) be utilized to perform
the file conversion?

31. Has a schedule been established?

Design System Tests:

32. Has the user's role for testing been
defined, namely:

 a. Has the user described what he
expects from the system output?

 b. Has the user agreed to provide
system test data and to check
system output?

33. Have responsibilities and schedules
for preparing test data been agreed
to by the user?

34. Has the input medium been agreed
to (cards, on-line entry, other)?

35. Is special hardware/software required,
and if so, will programmers and/or
users require additional training?

	YES	NO	N/A	REF.#

36. Have turnaround requirements been defined?

37. Have testing priorities been established?

38. If an on-line system, has an investigation of required space as opposed to available space been made?

39. Has an analysis of the impact upon interfacing systems been made and have arrangements been made for acquiring required information and data?

Design System Test:

40. Have testing control procedures been established (logs, tapes, disks, etc.)?

41. Has the possibility of utilizing existing code (prewritten subroutines) been investigated?

42. Has a System Test Plan been prepared consisting of a description of each run (program or a number or programs) to be made and specifically does each show:
    a. Test run identification
    b. Test run description (program/ job title)
    c. Programs and utilities required for the test
    d. Dependencies (runs which must be completed prior to testing)
    e. Inputs and their sources

	YES	NO	N/A	REF.#

42. f. Outputs: content and destination

    g. List of conditions to be tested
(e.g., validation rules)

43. Has the user prepared the system
test data as defined by the conditions
to be tested in the System Test
Plan?

44. Has Computer Operations been
consulted regarding key-punching
and/or verification?

Revise and Complete Design:

45. Have all required forms from
previous phases as well as previous
tasks/activities in this phase been
completed?

46. Has the processing description for
program specifications been categorized by function (e.g., validation,
error handling, reports, updating end
of file)?

47. For validation routines have the
editing rules been specified for:

    a. Field format and content (data
element descriptions)

    b. Interfield relationships

    c. Intrafield relationships

    d. Interrecord relationships

    e. Sequence

    f. Duplicates

    g. Control reconciliation

48. Have the rejection criteria been indicated for each type of error situation, as follows:

    a. Warning message but transaction is accepted

    b. Use of the default value

    c. Outright rejection of record within a transaction set

    d. Rejection of an entire transaction

    e. Rejection of a batch of transactions

    f. Program abort

49. Have the following validation techniques been included in the specifications:

    a. Validation of entire transaction before any processing

    b. Validation to continue regardless of the number of errors on the transaction unless a run abort occurs

    c. Provide information regarding an error so the user can identify the source and determine the cause?

Revise and Complete Design:

50. If applicable, has a procedure been developed for correction of rejected input either by deletion, reversal or re-entry?

51. Do the specifications for each report (output) define:

    a. The origin of each time including the rules for the selection of optional items

	YES	NO	N/A	REF.#

51. b. The rules of governing calculations

     c. The rules for printing and/or print suppression?

52. Have the following been defined for each intermediate (work) file:

     a. Origins or alternative origins for each element

     b. Calculations

     c. Rules governing record types, sequence, optional records as well as inter and intra-record relationships?

53. Have the following audit controls been built in where applicable:

     a. Record counts (in and out)

     b. Editing of all source input

     c. Has totals on selected fields

     d. Sequence checking of input files

     e. Date checking

     f. Listing of errors and review

     g. Control records?

Determine Tentative Operational Requirements:

54. Has the impact of the system upon existing computer resources been evaluated?

55. Have the computer processing requirements been discussed with Computer Operations (e.g., volumes, timeframes, turnaround, etc.)?

	YES	*NO*	*N/A*	*REF.#*

56. Have backup procedures been developed?

On-Line Systems:

57. Have testing plans been discussed with Computer Operations to ensure that required resources (core, disk space) for "sessions" will be available?

58. Have terminal types been discussed with appropriate Technical Support personnel?

59. Have IMS considerations (if applicable) been coordinated with Computer Operations Technical Support and DBA representatives?

60. Has a user training program been developed?

61. Have run schedules been prepared to provide Computer Operations with the basic information necessary to schedule computer usage?

62. Have run flowcharts including narrative (where required) been prepared?

63. Have "first cut" estimates of region sizes, run times (using SAPP 15.02.13) etc. been provided on the flowcharts or some other documentation?

64. Has the following information been shown for either input or output tapes and disks:

    a. DDNAME, DSNAME, LABEL, UNIT, DCB, RECFM,

	YES	NO	N/A	REF.#

BLKSIZE, DISP, RETPD,
estimated volumes of records,
concatenation, source, destination

On-Line Systems:

    b. In addition to the above, for disk
        files:

        1. Input, output or input/output

        2. Space (number of blocks)

65. Where appropriate, have restart
procedures been described for each
step of the job?

66. If appropriate, have restart procedures been appended to the Security
and Backup section of the CSD
documentation?

Plan Program Design:

67. Has all relevant documentation for
each program been gathered?

68. Has the sequence in which programs
are to be developed been defined in
accordance to the System Test Plan?

69. Has the number of users and personnel (including outside vendors)
required been ascertained?

70. Has computer time required for
program testing (compiles, test runs)
been established?

71. Have data preparation requirements
been discussed with Computer
Operations regarding data entry?

	YES	*NO*	*N/A*	*REF.#*
72. Has a development cost worksheet been prepared for the next phase or phases?				
73. Have personnel been assigned and project work schedules been prepared?				
74. Has the project schedule and budget been reviewed and updated if required?				

Prepared Project Authorization:

75. If required, has a Project Authorization Form been completed?

IX.   PROGRAMMING CHECKLIST

A.   COBOL Checklist

General Principles:

1.   Does the program accomplish everything specified in the acceptance criteria?

2.   It is maintainable, i.e.:

   a.   It is clearly written

   b.   Is it formatted according to standards

   c.   Does each procedure/paragraph contain comments regarding function and purpose?

Identification Division:

3.   Have the following standards been incorporated into the program:

   a.   Program identification using the Panvalet naming standard

	YES	NO	N/A	REF.#

b. Has the name(s) been entered for AUTHOR

c. Has the data upon which coding commenced been entered for date written?

4. Are there remarks to indicate:

a. Function of the program

b. The name of the system of which it is a member

c. Date and author of any revisions?

Environment Division:

5. Do the source and object computer statements state the model number of any computer?

6. Has the IBM-370 been specified for the object computer?

7. For the Input/Output section have the following been adhered to:

a. Does the DDNAME used in the SELECT clause adhere to standards set forth in SAPP Data Dictionary Procedures?

8. For class:

a. Has UT been used for all QSAM datasets?

b. Has DA been used for only ISAM/VSAM and BDAM?

c. Has UR been used?

9. Has the use of RESERVE NO ALTERNATIVE AREAS been eliminated?

	YES	NO	N/A	REF.#

10. Has the APPLY WRITE-ONLY clause been used for variable mode files that use standard sequential organization?

11. Has APPLY CORE-INDEX clause been used for ISAM/VSAM files accessed randomly?

Data Division — General:

12. Do all record names begin with an 01 level?

13. Do all subsequent record fields begin with 05 and are they in turn incremented by factors of 05?

14. Have all level numbers greater than the preceding level number been indented four spaces?

15. Do the same level numbers appear in the same columns?

16. Where applicable, have COPY Techniques been used in instances when at least two modules are utilizing identical record descriptions?

Data Division — File Section:

17. Do the file and record names follow Data Dictionary specifications?

18. Has the LABEL RECORDS clause been used?

19. Has BLOCK CONTAINS 0 RECORDS been coded for all sequential files?

	YES	NO	N/A	REF.#
20. Do FD's for files containing spanned records indicate BLOCK CONTAINS 0 RECORDS?				
21. Has BLOCK CONTAINS n RECORDS been specified for all ISAM/VSAM files?				
22. Had BLOCK CONTAINS (n^1 TO n^2) CHARACTERS clause been used for documentation purposes, where applicable?				

Working Storage Section:

	YES	NO	N/A	REF.#
23. Has the use of "77" levels been eliminated?				
24. Have 01 levels and levels within the 01 groups been utilized to aggregate data?				
25. Wherever possible (codes, conditions) have 88 levels been used?				
26. Have meaningful data names been used consistent with Data Dictionary procedures?				
27. Has DISPLAY been specified for numeric data not being used for computation or subscripting?				
28. Has COMPUTATIONAL been used for subscripting and has the file been signed and synchronized?				
29. Has COMPUTATIONAL-3 been used to designate numeric fields used for comparisons and calculations, and have the fields been signed?				

	YES	*NO*	*N/A*	*REF.#*

30. Has the VALUE clause been used to establish initial values?

31. When the REDEFINES clause has been used does the redefined data name have an R suffix?

Procedure Division:

32. Is the program modular; i.e., does it consist of routines which can be:
    a. Performed paragraphs through an exit
    b. Performed sections
    c. Separately compiled called modules?

33. Is the program arranged in such a manner that it comprises blocks of code that accomplish specified functions (main line, initialization, input, match, output, etc.)?

34. Do the modules have one entry point and one exit?

35. Do the blocks comprise a reasonable amount of lines of code averaging 30–50 over the course of the program?

36. Are the section and paragraph names on separate lines?

37. Has the program been formatted for readability?

38. Has the use of literals been generally restricted to the working storage section of the data division?

	YES	NO	N/A	REF.#

39. Have GOTO's been restricted to forward movement within a paragraph or section or at most back to the immediate paragraph name?

40. Has the use of "called" separately compiled subprograms been kept to a minimum?

41. Have overlays and/or segmentation been avoided?

42. With the exception of performed sections, have all performs been written through exits?

43. Has all reference to the ALTER verb been eliminated?

44. Have all verbs used for debugging purposes been removed?

45. Has the COMPUTE verb been used for all calculations above the most rudimentary level?

46. If arithmetic verbs have been used, has the GIVING option been specified?

47. If applicable, have COPY techniques been used when at least two modules are using identical procedures?

48. Does the use of IF statements correspond to suggested standards regarding:
    a. Negative IF statements
    b. Complicated compound statements
    c. Number of levels of nesting
    d. Column alignment?

	YES	NO	N/A	REF.#

49. Has the program been terminated using the GOBACK rather than STOP RUN?

Program Logic Structure:

50. Does the program consist of a main block and a series of CALLED procedures, DO groups and BEGIN blocks?

51. Do each of the blocks (procedures) contain only one entry and one exit?

52. Does each block (sub-blocks may be nested within blocks) perform one function?

53. Have the blocks been coded according to the principles of structuring, namely using the constructs CALL, DO, WHILE, IF THEN ELSE, and implied CASE?

54. Have other ON units been used primarily for trapping I/O conditions (ON ENDFILE, ON ENDPAGE) or workspace overflow (ON AREA)?

55. Have other ON units (ZERO-DIVIDE, SUBSCRIPTRANGE, ERROR) been used and documented in the program?

56. Has the use of GOTO been minimized as follows:
    a. Restricted to forward use
    b. Raising error conditions
    c. As an aid for implementing the structured CASE facility?

	YES	*NO*	*N/A*	*REF.#*

57. Are standard PL/1 error features being utilized?

Formatting of Code:

58. Does each line of code within a block contain one statement?

59. Has use been made of indentation to indicate logic flow?

60. Have sub-blocks been indented within each higher level block?

61. Does the program contain initial comments specifying its name, purpose, function, inputs, outputs, program author, revision information, and a brief description of program flow?

62. Does each block of code contain comments regarding its purpose and function?

63. Have comments been used preceding CALLS describing the purpose and function?

64. Whenever possible, has the use of label variables been eliminated?

65. Are the variable and procedure (block) names meaningful?

66. Have all statements used as debugging aids been removed from the program?

67. Where "Built-in Functions" have been utilized, have they been adequately documented by comments?

	YES	NO	N/A	REF.#

68. Does the program contain the following comments:

   a. Program identification, including the Panvalet name, program name, system name, department number, project number, and CASE number

   b. Author(s) responsible

   c. Date written

   d. A brief description of what the program is to accomplish along with the I/O requirements and general logic

   e. Revision information showing the requester and the date along with a brief description of the revision

   f. External references showing the list of subroutines or CALLED functions

   g. A glossary showing a list of important variables along with a brief description of each?

69. For each subroutine within the program, have comments been included describing how subroutine was called along with the parameters?

70. Have the parameters been broken down and described?

71. Do the comments give an understanding of what the programming intended to accomplish?

	YES	NO	N/A	REF.#

Variable Names:

72. Do the selected variable names best identify the symbolic quantities they represent?

73. Has the use of variables in different contexts been eliminated within the program?

74. Has the use of the Fortran Standard comments as variable names been eliminated?

Statement Formatting:

75. Have parentheses been used to clarify mathematical expressions and/or to simplify the reading of a compound IF statement?

76. Has the use of splitting variable names over two lines been avoided?

77. Does the variable name appear subsequent to an operator?

78. Are blanks included in statements to enhance readability?

79. Have the lists in specification statement (INTEGER, REAL, DIMENSION, etc.) been arranged in alphabetical order?

80. Has the program been written in a neat, logical manner?

Statement Ordering:

81. Has the following pattern of statements been followed as closely as possible?

	YES	NO	N/A	REF.#

81. a. TYPE statements

      b. EXTERNAL statements

      c. DIMENSION statements

      d. COMMON statements

      e. EQUIVALENCE statements

      f. DATA statements

      g. Statement function statements

      h. Executable statements

      i. END Line?

82. Are the statement numbers in ascending order?

83. Have FORMAT statements been grouped together at the end of the program with numbers in the 9000 level?

Subscripting:

84. Has the use of subscripting adhered to SAPP standards?

85. Have scalars been used in lieu of vectors wherever possible?

86. Have N dimensional arrays been eliminated when an array of N-1 dimensions will suffice?

Subroutines:

87. Have subroutines been used to repeatedly execute common blocks of code?

88. If available, has use been made of vendor and corporate library subroutines?

	YES	NO	N/A	REF.#

Fortran Statements:

89. Have COMMON statements been stored to the source library and brought into the program using ++ INCLUDE statements?

90. Have verbs used primarily for debugging purposes been removed from the program?

91. Have separate statements for each DEFINE FILE been used?

92. Does every DO statement refer to a CONTINUE as the end of its range and does each DO refer to a different CONTINUE?

93. Has the use of GOTO's been minimized or, at the least, been restricted to forward references?

94. Has FORMAT been used to read cards, write to the printer, produce a print tape, and create files for input to non-Fortran programs?

95. Has the use of FORMAT been excluded for all other input/output transmissions?

96. Has the ERR = and END = option been used to transfer control upon an error or end-of-file condition?

97. Has the use of implied DO loops been avoided in I/O statements?

	YES	NO	N/A	REF.#

X.   FEASIBILITY STUDY CHECKLIST

Review Scope, Objectives and Constraints

1.   Have the scope, objectives and constraints been specifically defined?

2.   If applicable, have the Project and Personnel Work schedules been established?

3.   Have personnel assigned to the project been briefed about the system to be developed?

Analyze Business Functions and Environments:

4.   Have the relevant business functions been identified?

5.   Has the purpose of each function and the interrelationships between functions been described?

6.   Has an estimate of the volume of business transactions and the personnel required to process them been made?

7.   Have system interfaces been defined?

8.   Have the "key leverage points" (those impacting profits, costs, sensitivity) been analyzed with a view toward isolating those that are not affected by the objectives of the project?

	YES	NO	N/A	REF.#

9. Has the management environment been described functionally and administratively?

Describe Current Information Systems:

10. Has the information required to accomplish each function been described?

11. Has the output created by each function been described?

12. Has the source of information and the destination of output been described?

13. Have each of the functions been divided into component processes showing dependencies?

14. Has the flow of data been described and linked to either an input, process, or output function?

15. Have the existing controls been identified and categorized as follows?

   a. Management Controls (1)

   b. Data Security Controls (2)

   c. Organizational Controls (3)

   d. System Controls (4)

   1. Management Controls would include statistical information, such as average times to process transactions, peak load periods, etc.

   2. Data Security Controls would consist of those procedures required to

	YES	*NO*	*N/A*	*REF.#*

protect confidential and sensitive data.

3. Organizational Controls are those concerned with checks and balances required to safeguard assets (separation of duties).

4. System Controls are those used to control input (batch controls); control processing (checkpoints, cross-footing, etc.); file controls (pre-determined totals); output controls (total logs) and overall controls (trial balance).

16. Have interfaces with other systems been described showing data flow medium and scheduling?

17. Have transaction characteristics been defined showing anticipated volume by type, complexity and frequency?

18. Has an analysis been made of the possible growth of transaction volume?

Analyze Current Operating Costs:

19. Has the pattern of work been defined to reflect personnel costs as well as to serve as a basis for estimating operating costs and benefits of alternative solutions (if applicable)?

20. If the function is clerical, have standard rates been used to arrive at a unit cost per hour?

	YES	NO	N/A	REF.#

21. If the function is automated have the machine costs been shown?

22. Have Operating Cost Worksheets been completed showing time and cost per function.

23. Has an estimate been made of the cost to maintain the system?

Develop Alternative Solutions:

24. Have alternative solutions been developed on the business and technical levels?

25. Have the alternatives considered:
    a. The capability to satisfy system "musts" and "desirables"
    b. The probable cost of developing and, in turn, operating the system
    c. Time constraints
    d. Control requirements
    e. Risk factors
    f. Hardware/software requirements
    g. The impact on the users of other operations?

26. Have the broad system requirements been ascertained and described showing:
    a. Major input transactions
    b. Major output(s)
    c. Major functional processing elements

	YES	NO	N/A	REF.#

d. A description of the data (not to include attributes or editing considerations)

e. Timing and/or response time requirements

f. Controls, security, and backup requirements

g. Interfaces with existing or planned systems?

27. Have the high-volume, high-cost functions been isolated?

28. Have alternatives for getting information into and out of the system been described?

29. In the event new hardware/software or packages may be required, have the following questions been considered for further study and action:

a. Has the equipment been thoroughly tested?

b. Has the technology group been made aware of their possible consulting role?

c. Have or will estimates be increased to reflect the learning curve?

d. Does the package require modification prior to installation?

e. Are there other sources of supply?

f. Is the equipment (package) compatible with existing in-house equipment?

	YES	NO	N/A	REF.#

g. Is there anyone within the
organization experienced with
the technology?

h. Is the vendor reliable and
capable of providing support?

30. Has a Development Cost Worksheet
been prepared for the subsequent
phases? (NOTE: This is only a
guide.)

31. Has an estimate been made of the
cost to run or modify the new
solution(s)?

32. Has the user indicated the benefits to
be accrued including such items as:

a. Increased profits

b. Reduction of costs

c. Better data for strategic planning
(site selection, demand forecast-
ing, seasonality factors, etc.)

d. Improved customer service (new
order entry system)

e. More effective and timely
reporting to management and
governmental authorities

f. Improvement in data security

g. Better cost control?

Evaluate Alternative Solutions:

33. Has the solution been show to be
technically feasible?

34. If appropriate, has Computer Operations indicated that the proposed
solution(s) is compatible with the
existing or planned environment?

	YES	NO	N/A	REF.#

35. If appropriate, have cash flow worksheets been prepared for the current and proposed solution(s) using the Net Present Value (NPV) calculation formula as the criterion for economic evaluation?

36. If applicable, has an assessment of risks been made for considerations such as:

   a. Changing business environment

   b. Fluctuating volumes

   c. Organization changes

   d. Changing product lines?

37. Has a solution been recommended?

Plan Subsequent Phases:

38. Have the scope, objectives, and constraints for the next phase(s) been stated?

39. Have the tasks and activities to be done during the next phase(s) been selected?

40. Has a logical network or PERT network been developed for the next phase(s)?

41. Have the resources required for the next phase(s) tasks and activities been estimated?

42. Have work schedules and a budget for the next phase(s) been prepared?

43. Has a Development Cost Worksheet been prepared for the next phase(s)?

	YES	NO	N/A	REF.#

XI.   INSTALLATION CHECKLIST

Prepare for Acceptance Test:

1.   Have success criteria for system performance been stated specifically by the user?

2.   Has agreement been reached on how the acceptance test will be evaluated?

3.   When comparing old and new system results as a part of acceptance testing, has agreement with the user been obtained regarding the following:

   a.   The number of cycles to be run and the definition of what constitutes a cycle

   b.   Correctness of results?

4.   If current data is *required* for acceptance testing, has an alternative for that testing that may require cyclical processing been discussed with the user?

5.   If applicable, has all equipment to be installed at the user's location been put into place?

6.   If prior system procedures are to be eliminated by installation of the new system, has a backup procedure been provided in the event of system failure?

7.   Is input to the acceptance test based upon rules set forth in the BSD System Design Test Plan?

	YES	*NO*	*N/A*	*REF.#*

8. If required, have the appropriate files been converted?

9. Have the files been checked to verify counts, totals, etc?

10. Have listings of the old and new files been prepared for comparison, if required?

Conduct Acceptance Test:

11. Have the system outputs been verified according to the acceptance test plan and the user's criteria?

12. Has a checklist of problems encountered during acceptance testing been maintained?

13. If problems were encountered and corrected, was the documentation of appropriate prior phases changed?

14. If problems were uncovered, was a schedule prepared to estimate the amount of time required to make the appropriate changes?

15. If applicable, has Computer Operations tested the system?

16. Has Computer Operations evaluated the system for conformance to Computer Operations requirements, if applicable?

Documentation:

17. Is the documentation organized for ease of reference?

	YES	NO	N/A	REF.#
18. Have COM procedures for source program listings been included as a separate portion of documentation?				
Hand Over New System:				
19. Has the user signed off on the system by approving the documentation?				
20. Has Computer Operations signed off on the system?				

XII. STAFFING THE QUALITY ASSURANCE FUNCTION

The Quality Assurance Program will be administered by the MSP Support Department. The team, initially, will consist of one permanently assigned QA Project Leader with other team members participating as defined by MSP management. Team members, either permanently assigned, on rotation for a defined period of time, or assigned by project, should possess the appropriate training and systems experience to achieve maximum acceptance from their peer group.

Obviously, participation in terms of time (assuming the absence of a permanent group) of team members reviewing a phase of a project would vary depending upon the size of the project.

Appendix B: Testing Tools and Techniques

1.1. INTRODUCTION

Each technique and tool description is alphabetically presented in a standard format. The following describes the entries for each, where "n" is the technique tool and number.

n.1. Name. The accepted title or, when an appropriate one does not exist, an invented title.

n.2. Basic Features. A short description of the technique or tool.

n.3. Information Input. A description of the input required for use.

n.4. Information Output. A description of the results of the technique or the output of the tool.

n.5. Outline of Method. A brief list of the actions that a user is expected to perform.

n.6. Example. An example to illustrate the inputs, outputs, and method.

n.7. Effectiveness. A brief assessment of the effectiveness and usability, including underlying assumptions and difficulties that can be expected in practice.

n.8. Applicability. An indication of the situation in which the technique is likely to be useful.

n.9. Learning. An estimate of the learning time and training needed to use the technique or tool successfully.

n.10. Cost. An estimate of the resources needed.

2.1.   NAME. ALGORITHM ANALYSIS

2.2   BASIC FEATURES

Two phases of algorithm analysis can be distinguished: "a priori analysis" and "a posteriori testing." In a priori analysis, a function (of some relevant parameters) is devised that bounds the algorithm's use of time and space to compute an acceptable solution. The analysis assumes a model of computation such as: a Turing machine, RAM (random access machine), general-purpose machine, etc. Two general kinds of problems are usually treated: 1) analysis of a particular algorithm; and 2) analysis of a class of algorithms. In a posteriori testing, actual statistics are collected about the algorithm's consumption of time and space while it is executing.

2.3.   INFORMATION INPUT

a.   Specification of algorithm

b.   Program representing the algorithm

2.4.   INFORMATION OUTPUT

a.   A priori analysis
     Confidence of algorithm's validity
     Upper and lower computational bounds
     Prediction of space usage
     Assessment of optimality

b.   A posteriori testing
     Performance profile

2.5.   OUTLINE OF METHOD

a.   A priori analysis. Algorithms are analyzed with the intention of improving them, if possible, and choosing among several available for a problem. The following criteria may be used:

Correctness

Amount of work done

Amount of space used

Simplicity

Optimality

Accuracy analysis

Correctness. There are three major steps involved in establishing the correctness of an algorithm.

1. Understand that an algorithm is correct, if, when given a valid input, it computes for a finite amount of time and produces the right answer.

2. Verify that the mathematical properties of the method and/or formulas used by the algorithm are correct.

3. Verify by mathematical argument that the instructions of the algorithm do produce the right answer and do terminate.

Amount of Work Done. A priori analysis ignores all of the factors that are machine or programming language dependent and concentrates on determining the order of magnitude of the frequency of statement execution. For denoting the upper bound on an algorithm, the O-notation is used. The following notational symbols are used in the following description: ** = exponentiation; [ ] = subscription.

Definition, $f(n) = O(g(n))$ if and only if there exist two positive constants C and n[o] such that $f(n) \leq C\, g(n)$ for all $n \geq n[o]$.

The most common computing times for algorithms are: $O(1) < O(\log n) < O(n) < O(n\log\ n) < O(n**2) < O(n**3)$ and $O(2**n)$; $O(1)$ means that the number of executions of basic operations is fixed and, hence, that total time is bounded by a constant. The first six orders of magnitude are bounded by a polynomial. However, there is no integer such that n**m bounds 2**n. An algorithm whose computing time has this property is said to require exponential time. There are notations for lower bounds and asymptotic bounds. The term "complexity" is the formal term for the amount of work done, measured by some complexity (or cost) measure.

In general, the amount of work done by an algorithm depends on the size of input. In some cases, the number of operations may depend on the particular input. Some examples of size are:

Problem	*Size of input*
1. Find X in a list of names	The number of names in the list
2. Multiply two matrices	The dimensions of the matrices
3. Solve a system of linear equations	The number of equations and solution vectors

To handle the situation of the input affecting the performance of an algorithm, two approaches (average and worst-case) are used. The *average* approach assumes a distribution of inputs, then calculates the number of operations performed for each type of input in the distribution, and then computes a weighted average. The *worst-case* approach calculates the maximum number of basic operations performed on any input of a fixed size.

Amount of Space Used. The number of memory cells used by a program, like the number of seconds required to execute one, depends on the particular implementation. However, some conclusions about space usage can be made by examining the algorithm. A program will require storage space for the instructions, the constants, and variables used by the program, and the input data. It may also use some work space for manipulating the data and storing information needed to carry out its computations. The input data itself may be representable in several forms, some of which require more space than others. If the input data has one natural form — for example, an array of numbers or a matrix — then we analyze the extra space used aside from the program and the input. If the amount of extra space is constant with respect to the input size, the algorithm is said to work "in place."

Simplicity. It is often, though not always, the case that the simplest and most straightforward way of solving a problem is not the most efficient. Yet simplicity in an algorithm is a desirable feature. It may make verifying the correctness of the algorithm easier, and it makes writing, debugging, and modifying a program for the algorithm easier. The time needed to produce a debugged program should be considered when choosing an algorithm, but if the program is to be used very often, its efficiency will probably be the determining factor in the choice.

Optimality. Two tasks must be carried out to determine how much work is necessary and sufficient to solve a problem.

1.   Devise what seems to be an efficient algorithm; call it A. Analyze A and find a function such that, for inputs of size n, A does at most g(n) basic operations.

2.   For some function f, prove a theorem that for any algorithm in the class under consideration, there is some input of size n for which the algorithm must perform at least f(n) basic operations.

If the functions g and f are equal, then the algorithm A is optimal.

Accuracy Analysis. The computational stability of an algorithm is verified by determining that the integrity of roundoff accuracy is maintained. It is done manually at the requirements or specification level.

    b.   A posteriori testing. Once an algorithm has been analyzed, the next step is usually the confirmation of the analysis. The confirmation process consists first of devising a program for the algorithm on a particular computer. After the program is operational, the next step is producing a "performance profile," that is, determining the precise amounts of time and storage the program will consume. To determine time consumption, the computer clock is used. Several datasets of varying size are executed and a performance profile is developed and compared with the predicted curve.

    A second way to use the computer's timing capability is to take two programs that perform the same task whose orders of magnitude are identical and compare them as they process data. The resulting times will show which, if either, program is faster. Changes to a program that do not alter the order of magnitude but which purport to speed up the program also can be tested in this way.

2.6.   EXAMPLE

QUICKSORT is a recursive sorting algorithm. Roughly speaking, it re-arranges the keys and splits the file into two subsections, or subfiles, such that all keys in the first section are smaller than all keys in the second section. Then QUICKSORT sorts the two subfiles recursively (i.e., by the same method), with the result that the entire file is sorted.

    Let A be the array of keys and let m and n be the indices of the first and last entries, respectively, in the subfile that QUICKSORT is currently sorting. Initially, $m = 1$ and $n = k$. The PARTITION algorithm chooses a key K from the subfile and rearranges the entries, finding an integer j such that for $m \leq i < j$, $A(i) \leq K$; $A(j) = K$; and for $j < i \leq n$, $A(i) \geq K$. K is then in its correct position and is ignored in the subsequent sorting.

QUICKSORT can be described by the following recursive algorithm:

```
QUICKSORT (a, m, n)
if m < n then do          PARTITION (A, m, n, i, j)
                          QUICKSORT (A, m, j)
                          QUICKSORT (A, i, n)
                          end
```

Figure 2.6-1. QUICKSORT.

The PARTITION routine may choose as K any key in the file between $A(m)$ and $A(n)$; for simplicity, let $K = A(m)$. An efficient partitioning algorithm uses two pointers, i and j, initialized to m and $n + 1$, respectively, and begins by copying K elsewhere so that the position $A(i)$ is available for some other entry. The location $A(i)$ is filled by decrementing j until $A(j) \leq K$, and then copying $A(j)$ into $A(i)$ into $A(j)$, now $A(j)$ is filled by incrementing i until $A(i) \geq K$ and then copying $A(i)$ into $A(j)$. This procedure continues until the values of i and j meet; then K is put in the last place. Observe that PARTITION compares each key except the original in $A(m)$ to K, so it does $n - m$ comparisons.

Worst-Case Analysis. If when PARTITION is executed, $A(m)$ is the largest key in the current subfile (that is, $A(m) \geq A(i)$ for $m \leq i \leq n$), then PARTITION will move it to the bottom to position $A(n)$ and partition the file into one section with $n - m$ entries (all but the bottom one) and one section with no entries. All that has been accomplished is moving the maximum entry to the bottom. Similarly, if the smallest entry in the file is in position $A(m)$, PARTITION will simple separate it from the rest of the list, leaving $n - m$ items still to be sorted. Thus, if the input is arranged so that each time PARTITION is executed, $A(m)$ is the largest (or the smallest) entry in the section being sorted, then $p = n - m + 1$, the number of keys in the unsorted section being sorted, then let $p = n - m + 1$, the number of keys in the un-sorted section, then the number of comparisons done is

$$\sum_{p=2}^{k} (p-1) = \frac{k(k-1)}{2}$$

Average Behavior Analysis. If a sorting algorithm removes at most one inversion from the permutation of the keys after each comparison, then it must do at least $(n**2 - n)/4$ comparisons on the average. QUICKSORT, however, does not have this restriction. The PARTITION algorithm can move keys across a large section of the entire file, eliminating up to $n - 2$ inversions at one time. QUICKSORT deserves its name because of its average behavior.

Consider a situation in which QUICKSORT works quite well. Suppose that each time PARTITION is executed, it splits the file into two roughly equal subfiles. To simplify the computation, assume that $n = 2**p - 1$ for some p. The number of comparisons done by QUICKSORT on a file with n entries under these assumptions is described by the recurrence relation

$$R(p) = (2**p) - 2 + 2R\ (p - 1)$$

$$E(1) = 0$$

The first two terms in $R(p)$, $(2**p) - 2$, are $n - 1$, the number of comparisons done by PARTITION the first time. The second term is the number of comparisons done by QUICKSORT to sort the two subfiles, each of which has $(n - 1)/2$, or $(2**(p - 1)) - 1$, entries. Expand the recurrence relation to get

$$
\begin{aligned}
R(p) &= (2**p) - 2 + 2R(p-1) \\
&= (2**p) - 2 + 2(2**(p-1)-2) + 4R(p-2) \\
&= (2**p) - 2 + (2**p) - 4 + (2**p) - 8 + 8R(p-3)
\end{aligned}
$$

thus

$$
\begin{aligned}
R(p) &= \sum_{i=1}^{p-1} (2**p) - (2**i) = (p-1)(2**p) - \sum_{i=1}^{p-1} 2**i \\
&= ((p-1)2**p) - ((2**p) - 2) = \log\ n\ (n+1) - n + 1
\end{aligned}
$$

Thus, if $A(m)$ were close to the median each time the file was split, the number of comparisons done by QUICKSORT would be of the order (nlog n). If all permutations of the input data are assumed equally likely, then QUICKSORT does approximately 2nlog n comparisons.

Space Usage. At first glance, it may seem that QUICKSORT is an in-place sort. It is not. While the algorithm is working on one subfile, the beginning and ending indices (call them the borders) of all the other subfiles yet to be sorted must be saved cn a stack, and the size of the stack depends on the number of sublists into which the file will be split. This, of course, depends on n. In the worst case, PARTITION may split off one entry at a time in such a way that n pairs of borders are stored on the stack. Thus, the amount of space used by the stack is proportional to n.

n	1000	2000	3000	4000	5000
MERGESORT	500	1050	1650	2250	2900
QUICKSORT	400	850	1300	1800	2300

(Time is in milliseconds)

Figure 2.6-2. MERGESORT and QUICKSORT comparison.

Testing. The results of comparing QUICKSORT and MERGESORT are summarized in Figure 2.6-2.

2.7. EFFECTIVENESS

Algorithm analysis has become an important part of computer science. The only issue that limits its effectiveness is that a particular analysis depends on a particular model of computation. If the assumptions of the model are inappropriate, then the analysis suffers.

2.8 APPLICABILITY

An analysis of an algorithm can be limited by the current state of the art and the ingenuity of the analyst.

2.9. LEARNING

Algorithm analysis requires significant training in mathematics and computer science. Generally, it will be done by a specialist.

2.10. COSTS

The cost to analyze an algorithm is dependent on its complexity and the amount of understanding about algorithms of the same class.

3.1. NAME. ANALYTIC MODELING OF SYSTEMS DESIGNS

3.2. BASIC FEATURES

The purpose is to provide performance evaluation and capacity planning information in a system design. The process follows the top-down approach to design through hierarchical levels of resolution. It can be applied at early design stages when functional modules are relatively large and where knowledge of their execution behavior may be imprecise. As the design proceeds and the modules are further resolved, the estimates of their behavior and execution resource characterization become more precise. The approach is predicated on two representational bases: extended execution graph models of programs and systems, and extended queueing network models of computer system hardware resources and workloads.

3.3. INFORMATION INPUT

The information that is needed for this technique consists of functional design and performance specifications as follows:

a. Identification of the functional components of the software design to be modeled.

b. Identification of the execution characteristics (primarily, execution time estimate) of each functional component.

c. An execution flow graph giving the definition of the order of execution of the various functional components.

d. Execution environment specifications, which can include information such as operating system overhead and the workload on the system that could potentially impact the particular software under development.

e. System execution scenarios providing the definition of the external inputs to the model needed for each simulation of the model.

f. Performance goals for the total system and components (an example is an upper bound for the mean and variance of the response time for a specified execution environment and scenario).

3.4. INFORMATION OUTPUT

Output from the technique will consist of the following:

a.   A lower bound on the performance of the system.

b.   A comparison of the performance goals with the performance results.

c.   Identification of the functional components that had the greatest effect on system performance.

3.5. OUTLINE OF METHOD

Much of the effort in using this technique comes in the preparation of the necessary input information. Once this has been done, it is generally submitted to a computer that performs the simulation of the execution of the model and reports the results, which are then analyzed, and the model is revised as necessary. The specific steps in the technique are as follows:

a.   The structure of the software design is characterized in terms of its functional components. In that software designs are generally hierarchical in structure, a model may be modified to represent the system at different levels of detail, each being analyzed at different stages in the process.

b.   The order of execution of the components is determined and the execution graph is constructed.

c.   Resource requirements (e.g., hardware or operating system resources) of the functional components are identified, and a possible environment is studied with the specific resource workloads being determined. These workloads consist of the average wait and usage times for the resources controlled by the environment and used by the software (such as average disk access time).

d.   The workloads are then mapped into the model (as represented by the execution graph) based upon the identified environment resource requirements of the individual functional components.

e.   Next, the system execution scenarios are constructed. The external outputs comprising each scenario may be formulated, for example, in terms of the number of disk accesses required to find a needed data item within a particular component.

f.   Upon completion of the above steps, the model is driven, producing system and component performance results. (The "driving" of the model is usually done using a system simulation tool such as GPSS, General Purpose Systems Simulator, on a coded specification of the model.)

g.   The performance results are now compared with the performance goals of the system. If the goals are not met, performance-critical components are then analyzed in order to determine where improvements can be made. The design is modified and the technique repeated. This process continues until the performance is acceptable or until it can be determined that the goals are unreasonable.

3.6.   EXAMPLE

Finite element analysis is a technique for determining characteristics such as deflections and stresses in a structure (i.e., building, airplane, etc.) otherwise too complex for closed-form mathematical analysis. The structure is broken into a network of simple elements (beams, shells, or cubes depending on the geometry of the structure), each of which has stress and deflection characteristics defined by classical theory.

Determining the behavior of the entire structure then becomes a task of solving the resulting set of simultaneous equations for all elements.

The example developed below is a portion of a system that does a finite element analysis. Consider the software execution graph in Figure 3.6-1. Only the top level of the processing is illustrated here. The CPU time and I/O requirements for each component are shown in Table 3.6-1.

The elapsed time to complete an I/O operation is assumed to be 30 ms. Other specifications are unimportant in this example.

The average response time for this scenario is 3326 seconds (55.4 minutes), which is clearly unacceptable for an interactive transaction. The bottleneck analysis indicates that the CPU is the critical resource since it has a higher ratio to the elapsed time than the I/O ratio. Furthermore, the "find node location" component is the critical component.

The processing details of this collapsed model are not shown; however, close examination of the details indicates that a "find" database command is invoked for each of the three search keys, and then

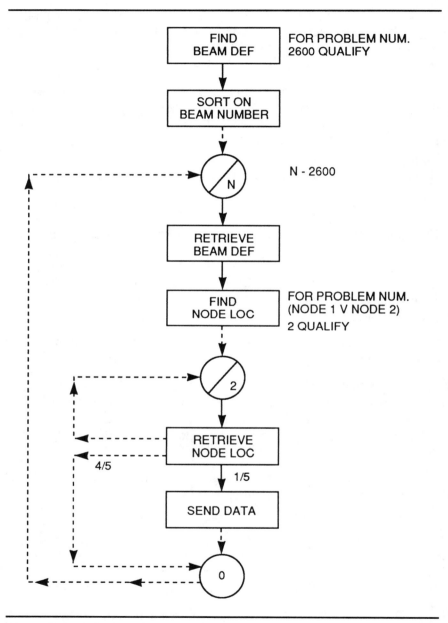

Figure 3.6-1. Optimization example.

Function	Disk Accesses	CPU Time (ms)
Find beam definition	7	111
Sort on beam number	72	32,644
Retrieve beam definition	72	88,832
Find node locations	21	3,018,726
Retrieve node locations	36	177,016
Send data	0	2,600
Total	208	3,319,929

Table 3.6-1. Resource requirements for optimization example.

takes the intersection of the records that qualify. Also, it is found that the result of the "find" for the problem number search key is invariant throughout the loop and need not be repeated. A knowledge of the nature of the problem leads to the observation that most of the time (85 percent) the "find" on the node 1 key yields the same result as the "find" on the node 2 key from the previous pass through the loop, and need not be repeated. The results of this analysis indicate changes that optimize the process.

These optimizations are reflected in the execution graph in Figure 3.6-2. This graph is more complex; however, the total processing requirements are reduced, as shown in Table 3.6-2.

The response time has been *reduced* by 3023 seconds, a substantial savings. The new response time (303 seconds) is still unacceptable for most on-line applications. Another optimization, storing the "beam def" data in beam number sequence, precludes the sort. The resulting response time is 269 seconds. This optimization process continues until a resulting response time of 82 seconds is obtained.

The performance is still only marginally acceptable, but it is a dramatic improvement over the original design. The bottlenecks are detected and corrected prior to actual coding, and, therefore, the modifications require minimal effort.

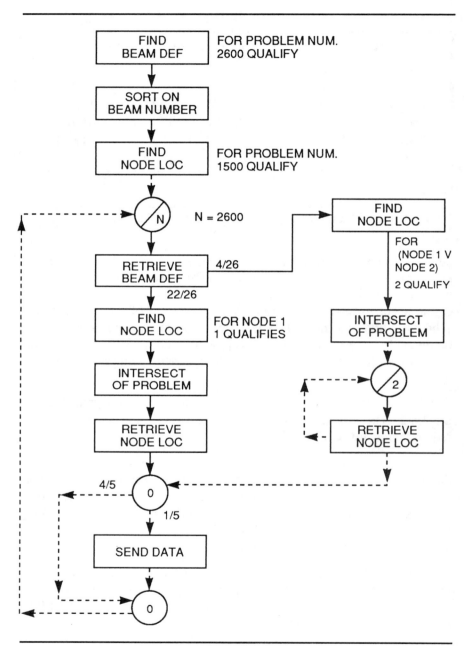

Figure 3.6-2. Revised optimization example.

Function	Disk Accesses	CPU Time (ms)
Find beam definition	7	111
Sort beam number	72	32,644
Find node location	4	1,075
Retrieve beam definition	72	88,832
Find node location:		
B-tree I/O	17	102
Find 2 nodes	–	44,000
Retrieve 2 nodes	–	27, 200
Find 1 node	–	26,000
Retrieve 1 node	–	71,800
Record I/O	36	216
Send data	0	2,600
Total	208	297,580 ms.

Table 3.6-2. Resource requirements for revised optimization example.

3.7. EFFECTIVENESS

The accuracy of the performance prediction is only as good as the quality of the performance specifications. The quality of the specifications usually improves during the design process. A simplified approach is used to analyze queueing network models. This results in approximation of the relationships between contending resources. Several compensating features are used to offset the approximations used.

3.8. APPLICABILITY

The technique is generally applicable to nondistributed systems.

3.9. LEARNING

The user of this approach needs to be familiar with the intricacies of the model techniques used.

3.10. COSTS

The preparation, analysis, and solution of the model costs approximately 5 percent to 15 percent of the total design costs.

4.1. NAME. ASSERTION GENERATION

4.2. BASIC FEATURES

Assertion generation is not so much a verification technique itself as it is foundational to a variety of other techniques. Assertion generation is the process of capturing the intended functional properties of a program in a special notation (called the assertion language) for insertion into the various levels of program specification, including the program source code. Other verification techniques utilize the embedded assertions in the process of comparing the actual functional properties of the program with the intended properties.

4.3. INFORMATION INPUT

A specification of the desired functional properties of the program is the input required for assertion generation. For individual modules, this breaks down, at a minimum, to a specification of the conditions that are "assumed" true on a module entry and a specification of the conditions desired on module exit. If the specifications from which the assertions are to be derived include algorithmic detail, the specifications will indicate conditions that are to hold at intermediate points within the module as well. Additionally, assertions can state data characteristics, e.g., loop invariants, physical units, or a variable, as input only (cannot be set).

4.4. INFORMATION OUTPUT

The assertions that are created from the functional or algorithmic specifications are expressed in a notation called the assertion language. This notation commonly includes higher-level expressive constructs that are found, for example, in the programming language. An example of such a construct is a set. Most commonly, the assertion language is equivalent in expressive power to the first order predicate calculus. Thus, expressions such as *forall* i *in* set S, A[i] A[i + 1]" or "*there exists* x *such that* f(x) = 0" are possible. The assertions that are generated, expressing the functional properties of the program, can then be used as input to a dynamic assertion processor, a formal verification tool, walkthroughs, specification simulators, and inspections, among other V&V techniques.

4.5. OUTLINE OF METHOD

Assertion generation proceeds hand in hand with the hierarchical elaboration of program functions. When, during development, a function is identified as being needed, it is usually first specified by what input it is expected to take and what the characteristics of the output are (outputs are often in terms of the input quantities). For such a function, it is possible to generate input and output assertions without any knowledge of how the function performs its task. The input assertion expresses the requirements on the data the function is to use during its processing. The output assertion expresses what is to be true on function termination.

Later, as the function is elaborated, the designer or coder will identify the necessary steps to be taken in order to accomplish what is required of the function. After each step, it can be said that a "part" of the task has been accomplished. That part is necessary for the proper operation of the next step, and so on, until the entire function has been realized. The character of each part can be captured by an assertion in the same way as the description of the entire function can. The output assertion for one step represents (at least part of) the input assertion for the following step. Such assertions are called intermediate assertions.

Each assertion, input, output, and intermediate is expressed using the assertion language and is placed into the specification of the function being implemented at the appropriate points. Thus, the program source test will include in it all the assertions developed during the requirements, design, and coding phases.

Some programming languages include facilities for expressing assertions in the source code but most do not. In such cases, it is customary to include the assertions within comments, for indeed they are documentation expressing the desired functional characteristics of the program. Subsequent V&V tools, such as dynamic assertion processors, are constructed to utilize these special comments during their processing. Dynamic assertion processors are able to check the validity of the source assertions during program execution. Thus, a method for dynamically verifying the program is behaving according to its intended specification is possible.

For programs that contain loops (which is just about all programs), it is often important to formulate assertions that are always true at specific points within the loops. Such assertions are termed *invariant* or *inductive* assertions.

4.6. EXAMPLE

Since assertion generation is so closely entwined with program development, only a brief example is presented here.

During program development the requirement arises for sorting the elements of an array or table. In order to support flexible processing in the rest of the system, the array is declared with a large, fixed length. However, only a portion of the array has elements in it. The number of elements currently in the array, when passed to the sort routine, is contained in the first element of the array, which is always to be sorted in ascending order. The sorted array is returned to the calling program through the same formal parameter.

The first specification of the sort routine may appear as:

```
                SUBROUTINE SORT (A, DIM)
C
C       A is the array to be sorted
C       DIM is the dimension of A
C
C       sort array
C
        RETURN
        END
```

Figure 4.6-1. Sort specification.

The characteristics of the subroutine may be partially captured by the following assertions. Notationally, v = "or" and & = "and."

ASSERT INPUT $(0 \leq A(1) \leq DIM)$, $(DIM \geq 2)$
ASSERT OUTPUT $(A(1) = 0 \text{ v } A(1) = 1 \text{ \& } true) \text{ v}$
$(A(1) > 1 \text{ \& FORALL I IN } [2 \ldots A(1)] \text{ } A(I) \text{ } A(I + 1))$

The input assertion notes the required characteristics of A(1) and DIM. The output assertion indicates that if there is 0 or 1 element in the array, the array is sorted by default. If there are at least two elements in the array, then the array is in ascending order.

The next level of the program may have the following appearance. An intermediate assertion is now shown.

```
            SUBROUTINE SORT (A, DIM)
C
C           A is the array to be sorted
C           DIM is the dimension of A
C
            ASSERT INPUT (0≤A(1) DIM), (DIM>2)
            IF (A(1) .LE. 1) GOTO 100
            ASSERT (2≤A(1)≤DIM)
C
C           Sort non-trivial array
C
100         ASSERT OUTPUT (A(1) = 0 v A(1) = 1 & true)   v
            (A(1)>1 & FORALL I IN [2 . . A(1)] A(I)≤A(I+1))
            RETURN
            END
```

Figure 4.6-2. Sort routine with assertions.

Suppose a straight selection sort algorithm is chosen for the non-trivial case (i.e., find the smallest element and place it in A(2), find the next smallest and place it in A(3), and so forth, where the original contents of A(1) is exchanged with the element that belongs in the Ith position in the sorted array). An appropriate intermediate assertion is included within the sorting loop.

```
C           PERFORM STRAIGHT SELECTION SORT
            DO 50 J = 2, A(1)
C
C               find smallest element in A(J) . . A(A(1)+2)
C               let that element be A(K)
C
            ASSERT (2≤J≤A(1))
            FORALL I IN [2 . . A(1)] A(1)≤A(I+1))
50          CONTINUE
```

Figure 4.6-3. Sort routine with an intermediate assertion.

A significant issue that we have not dealt with yet is asserting, on termination, that the sorted array is a permutation of the original array. In other words, we wish to assert that in the process of sorting, no elements were lost. To do this at the highest level, our first attempt at the program requires advanced assertion language facilities.

4.7. EFFECTIVENESS

Assertion generation, particularly when used in conjunction with allied techniques like dynamic assertion processing or functional testing, can be extremely effective in aiding V&V. Such effectiveness is only possible, however, where the assertions are used to capture the important functional properties of the program. Assertions such as the following are of no use at all:

$$I = 0$$
$$I = I + 1$$
$$\text{ASSERT } I > 0$$

Capturing the important properties can be a difficult process and is prone to error. Such effort is well rewarded, though, by increased understanding of the problem to be solved. Indeed, assertion generation is effective because the assertions are to be parallel to the program specifications. This parallelism enables the detection of errors, but effort is required.

A cost-effective procedure, therefore, is to develop intermediate assertions only for particularly important parts of the computation. Input assertions should always be employed, as should output assertions whenever possible.

4.8. APPLICABILITY

The technique is generally applicable in all development phases and for all programming languages.

4.9. LEARNING

Training and experience in writing assertions are the key to their effective use. Thoughtful consideration of the material contained in the references should enable a programmer to begin with useful assertions. Experience will sharpen the ability, especially if a dynamic assertion processor or other allied technique is also used.

4.10. COSTS

Assertion generation is generally a manual technique, i.e., no machine resources are required. Effective use requires thoughtful problem and solution consideration, but no more than is normally required in professional task performance. Tools do exist that use symbolic execution to automatically generate loop invariant assertions. The cost then becomes that of symbolic execution.

5.1. NAME. ASSERTION PROCESSING

5.2 BASIC FEATURES

Assertion processing is the process whereby the program's assertions (containing user-specified assertions as described in the previous section) are checked during program execution. As such, the techniques serve as a bridge between the more formal program correctness proof approaches and the more common "black box" testing approaches.

5.3. INFORMATION INPUT

Information input to this technique consists of a program that contains the assertions to be processed. The program can be written in any language, but may be restricted to a particular language if an automatic tool is used to perform the dynamic assertion processing. Moreover, if a tool is used, the format for specifying the assertions will be that defined by the particular tool. Generally, assertions are specified as comments in the source program.

5.4. INFORMATION OUTPUT

Output from a dynamic assertion process normally consists of a list of the assertion checks that were performed and a list of exception conditions with trace information for determining the nature and location of the violations.

5.5 OUTLINE OF METHOD

The assertions are generated by the developer as described in the "Assertion Generation" technique in the previous section. The assertions are then translated into host language program statements that actually perform the assertion checking at program execution time. The translation can be done manually or through the use of an automated dynamic assertion processor.

The translation process is shown in the following illustration. An assertion of the form:

(*ASSERT condition*)

is translated into:

IF NOT (condition) THEN

  process assertion violation;

The processing of the assertion violation will, minimally, keep track of the total number of violations for each assertion, print a message indicating that a violation of the assertion has occurred, and print the values of the variables referenced in the assertion. In addition, the location, i.e., statement number, and the number of times the assertion is checked may be kept and printed when a violation occurs.

Sufficient information should be reported upon violation of an assertion to assist the programmer in the specific nature of the error.

An automated dynamic assertion processor can be of great assistance by alleviating for the programmer the burden of hand-generating the source code necessary to perform the assertion checking. Not only will this save time, but it will also perform the translation more reliably.

Specifying assertions within comments is a valuable form of documentation and also ensures that the source program is kept free of nonportable, tool-specific directives.

It is important to note that dynamic assertion processing for non-real-time programs must not alter the functional behavior of a program. Use of a good automated tool will ensure this. Execution time, however, will be increased — by what amount will depend on the number of assertions that are processed. It is important to note that dynamic assertion processing can alter the functional behavior of a program by altering the execution timing.

In order to effectively utilize assertion processing, test data should be generated that will cause the execution of each assertion.

5.6.   EXAMPLE

The program segment in Figure 5.6-1 is taken from a Pascal program that calls on routine "sort" to sort array "A," consisting of "N" integer elements, in ascending order. The assertion following the call to sort asserts that the elements are indeed in ascending order upon return from the sort procedure. The numbers to the left are the line numbers from the original source.

```
                               •
                               •
    12    Var
    13                      N : integer;
    14                      A : array [1..MAXN] of integer;
                               •
                               •
    26    begin
                               •
                               •
    56                      sort (N,A);
    57    (*assert forall i in [1..N−1]:A[i]<=A[i+1]*);
```

Figure 5.6-1. Source program with untranslated assertion.

The program segment in Figure 5.6-2 is what results after all of the assertions have been translated into Pascal. Note that a rather large number of statements were used to implement the assertion. This is because of the rather involved checking required to implement an *"assert forall . . ."* Simpler assertions will require fewer statements. The spec could be reduced through the use of a common assertion violation procedure.

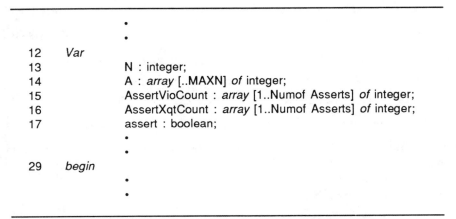

```
                          •
                          •
    12   Var
    13        N : integer;
    14        A : array [..MAXN] of integer;
    15        AssertVioCount : array [1..Numof Asserts] of integer;
    16        AssertXqtCount : array [1..Numof Asserts] of integer;
    17        assert : boolean;
                          •
                          •
    29   begin
                          •
                          •
```

Figure 5.6-2. Source program with translated assertions.

```
77              sort (N,A);
78              (*assert forall : in [1..N–1] : A[i]=A[i+1]*);
79                 AssertXqtCount[3]:=AssertXqtCount[3]+1;
80                 assert : = true;
81                 i : = 1;
82              while (i<=N) and (assert) do(*check assertion*)
83                    if A[i]>A[l+1] then
84                        assert : = false
85                    else
86                        i := i + 1;
87              if not assert then begin (*assertion violation*)
88                 AssertVioCount[3] : = AssertVioCount [3] = 1;
89                 Writeln ('violation of assertion 3 at statement 57');
90                 Writeln ('on execution', AssertXqtCount[3];
91                 Writeln ('array A = ', A)
92              end (*assertion violation *);
```

Figure 5.6-2. Source program with translated assertions. (cont'd)

During the testing, the following values of A were used in successive executions of the sort routine.

execution					array A					
1	0	3	12	27	53	171	201	251	390	501
2	0	12	3	53	27	201	171	390	251	501
3	501	390	251	201	171	53	27	12	3	0
4	0	0	0	0	0	0	0	0	0	0
5	0	0	0	100	100	100	999	999	999	1000

The resulting execution produced the following assertion violation:

violation of assertion 3 at statement 57 on execution: 3

array A = 3 12 27 53 171 201 251 340 501 0

This was the only violation that occurred.

Subsequent analysis of the sort procedure indicated that the error was due to an "add-by-one" error on a loop limit.

5.7. EFFECTIVENESS

The effectiveness of dynamic assertion processing will depend on the quality of the assertions included in the program being analyzed. Moreover, if the translation is being done by hand, the amount of time required to translate, coupled with the unreliability associated with the process, will reduce its effectiveness. Nevertheless, the technique can be of significant value in revealing the presence of program errors.

5.8. APPLICABILITY

The technique is generally applicable.

5.9. LEARNING

A functional understanding of assertions is all that is necessary in order to manually use this technique. If a tool is used, then an hour or so should be sufficient to learn the specification syntax for assertions acceptable to that tool. Of course, the generation of useful assertions (see "Assertion Generation" writeup) is necessary in order for this technique to be truly valuable.

5.10. COSTS

The costs associated with this technique almost entirely comprise the amount of time required to translate the assertions into source code. If done manually, this could amount to significant cost. If done automatically, the cost will be on the order of compilation (assertion processors are usually implemented as source language preprocessors). If a tool is not available, it may well be worth the cost to develop one in-house.

6.1. NAME. CAUSE-EFFECT GRAPHING

6.2. BASIC FEATURES

Cause-effect graphing is a test-case design methodology. It is used to select, in a systematic manner, a set of test cases that have a high probability of detecting errors that exist in a program. This technique explores the inputs and combinations of input conditions of a program in developing test cases. It is totally unconcerned with the internal behavior or structure of a program. In addition, for each test case derived, the technique identifies the expected outputs. The inputs and outputs of the program are determined through analysis of the requirement specifications. These specifications are then translated into a Boolean logic network or graph. The network is used to derive test cases for the software under analysis.

6.3. INFORMATION INPUT

The information that is required as input to carry out this technique is a natural language specification of the program that is to be tested. The specification should include all expected inputs and combinations of expected inputs to the program, as well as expected outputs.

6.4. INFORMATION OUTPUT

The information output by the process of cause-effect graphing consists of the following:

a.   An identification of incomplete or inconsistent statements in the requirement specifications.

b.   A set of input conditions on the software (causes).

c.   A set of output conditions on the software (effects).

d.   A Boolean graph that links the input conditions to the output conditions.

e.   A limited entry decision table that determines which input conditions will result in each identified output condition.

f.   A set of test cases.

g.   The expected program results for each derived test case.

The above outputs represent the result of performing the various steps recommended in cause-effect graphing.

6.5. OUTLINE OF METHOD

A Cause-effect graph is a formal language translated from a natural language specification. The graph itself is represented as a combinatorial logic network. The process of creating a cause-effect graph to derive test cases is described briefly below.

a.   Identify all requirements of the system and divide them into separate identifiable entities.

b.   Carefully analyze the requirements to identify all the causes and effects in the specification. A cause is a distinct input condition; an effect is an output condition or system transformation (an effect that an input has on the state of the program or system).

c.   Assign each cause and effect a unique number.

d.   Analyze the semantic content of the specification and transform it into a Boolean graph linking the causes and effects; this is the cause-effect graph.

* Represent each cause and effect by a node identified by its unique number.

* List all the cause nodes vertically on the left side of a sheet of paper; list the effect nodes on the right side.

* Interconnect the cause and effect nodes by analyzing the semantic content of the specification. Each cause and effect can be in one of two states: true or false. Using Boolean logic, set the possible states of the causes and determine under what conditions each effect will be present.

* Annotate the graph with constraints describing combinations of causes and/or effects that are impossible because of syntactical or environmental constraints.

e.   By methodically tracing state conditions in the graph, convert the graph into a limited entry decision table as follows. For each effect, trace back through the graph to find all combinations of causes that will set the effect to be true. Each such combination is represented as a column in the decision table. The state of all other effects should also be determined for each such combination. Each column in the table represents a test case.

f.   Convert the columns in the decision table into test cases. This technique to create test cases has not yet been totally automated. However, conversion of the graph to the decision table, the most difficult aspect of the technique, is an algorithmic process that could be automated by a computer program.

6.6.   EXAMPLE

A database management system requires that each file in the database have its name listed in a master index, which identifies the location of each file. The index is divided into 10 sections. A small system is being developed that will allow the user to interactively enter a command to display any section of the index at his terminal. Cause-effect graphing is used to develop a set of test cases for the system.

a. The specification for this system is as follows. To display one of the 10 possible index sections, a command must be entered consisting of a letter and a digit. The first character entered must be a D (for display) or an L (for list), and it must be in column 1. The second character entered must be a digit (0 – 9) in column 2. If this command occurs, the index section identified by the digit is displayed on the terminal. If the first character is incorrect, error message A is printed. If the second character is incorrect, error message B is printed. The error messages are:

A: INVALID COMMAND

B. INVALID INDEX NUMBER

b. The causes and effects have been identified as follows. Each has been assigned a unique number.

Causes

1. Character in column 1 is D.
2. Character in column 1 is L
3. Character in column 2 is a digit.

Effects

50. Index section is displayed.
51. Error message A is displayed.
52. Error message B is displayed.

c. Figure 6.6-1, a Boolean graph, is constructed through analysis of the semantic content of the specification.

Node 20 is an intermediate node representing the Boolean state of node 1 or node 2. The state of node 50 is true if the state of nodes 20 and 3 are both true. The state of node 20 is true if the state of node 1 or node 2 is true. The state of node 51 is true if the state of node 20 is *not* true. The state of node 52 is true if the state of node 3 in *not* true.

Nodes 1 and 2 are also annotated with a constraint that states that causes 1 and 2 cannot be true simultaneously (the exclusive constraint).

d. The graph is converted into a decision table, Figure 6.6-2. For each test case, the bottom of the table indicates which effect will be present (indicated by a 1). For each effect, all combinations of causes that will result in the presence of the effect are represented by the entries in the columns of the table. Blanks in the table mean that the state of the cause is irrelevant.

    e.   Each column in the decision table is converting into test cases, Table 6.6-1.

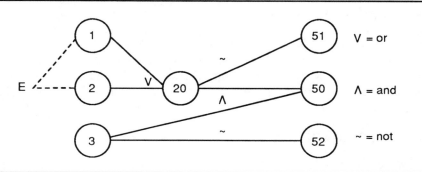

Figure 6.6-1. Boolean graph.

	Test Cases			
Causes	1	2	3	4
1	1	0	0	
2	0	1	0	
3	1	1		0
Effects				
50	1	1	0	0
51	0	0	1	0
52	0	0	0	1

Figure 6.6-2. Decision table.

Test Case #	Inputs	Expected Results
1	D5	Index section 5 is displayed
2	L4	Index section 4 is displayed
3	B2	INVALID COMMAND
4	DA	INVALID INDEX NUMBER

Table 6.6-1. Test cases.

6.7. EFFECTIVENESS

Cause-effect graphing is a technique used to produce a useful set of test cases. It has the added capability of pointing out incompleteness and ambiguities in the requirement specification. However, this technique does not produce all the useful test cases that can be identified. It also does not adequately explore boundary conditions.

6.8. APPLICABILITY

Cause-effect graphing can be applied to generate test cases in any type of computing application where the specification is clearly stated and combinations of input conditions can be identified. Manual application of this technique is a somewhat tedious, long, and moderately complex process. However, the technique could be applied to selected modules where complex conditional logic must be tested.

6.9 LEARNING

Cause-effect graphing is a mathematics-based technique that requires some knowledge of Boolean logic. The requirement specification of the system must also be clearly understood in order to successfully carry out the process.

6.10. COSTS

Manual application of this technique will be highly labor-intensive.

7.1. NAME. CODE AUDITOR

7.2. BASIC FEATURES

A code auditor is a computer program that is used to examine source code and automatically determines whether prescribed programming standards and practices have been followed.

7.3. INFORMATION INPUT

The information input to a code auditor is the source code to be analyzed and the commands necessary for the code auditor's operation.

7.4. INFORMATION OUTPUT

The information that is output by a code auditor is a determination of whether the code being analyzed adheres to prescribed programming standards. If errors exist, information is generated detailing which standards have been violated and where the violations occur. This information can appear as error messages included with a source listing or as a separate report. Other diagnostic information, such as a cross-reference listing, may also be output as an aid in making the needed corrections.

7.5. OUTLINE OF METHOD

Code auditors are fully automated tools that provide an objective, reliable means of verifying that a program complies with a specified set of coding standards. Some common programming conventions that code auditors can check for are given below.

- *Correct syntax* — do all program statements conform to the specifications of the language definition?

- *Portability* — is the code written so that it can easily operate on different computer configurations?

- *Use of structured programming constructs* — does the code make proper use of a specified set of coding constructs such as IF-THEN-ELSE or DO-WHILE?

- *Size* — is the length of any program unit not more than a specified number of statements?

- *Commentary* — is each program unit appropriately documented; e.g., is each unit preceded by a block of comments that indicates the function of the unit and the function of each variable used?

- *Naming conventions* — do the names of all variables, routines, and other symbolic entities follow prescribed naming conventions?

- *Statement labeling* — does the numeric labeling of statements follow an ascending sequence throughout each program unit?

- *Statement ordering* — do all statements appear in a prescribed order; e.g., in a FORTRAN program, do all FORMAT statements appear at the end and DATA statements before the first executable statement of a routine?

- *Statement format* — do all statements follow a prescribed set of formatting rules that improve program clarity; e.g., are all DO-WHILE loops appropriately indented?

As demonstrated by this list, code auditors vary in sophistication according to their function. Each auditor, however, requires that some form of syntax analysis be performed. Code must be parsed by the auditor and given an internal representation suitable for analysis. Because this type of processing is found in many static analysis tools, many code auditors are part of a more general tool having many capabilities. For example, a compiler is a form of code auditor that checks for adherence to the specifications of a language definition. PFORT, a tool used to check FORTRAN programs for adherence to a portable subset of American National Standard Institute (ANSI) FORTRAN 66, also has the capability of generating a cross-reference listing.

Code auditors are useful to programmers as a means of self-checking their routines prior to turnover for integration testing. These tools are also of value to software product assurance personnel during integration testing, prior to formal validation testing, and again prior to customer delivery.

7.6. EXAMPLE

a. Application. A flight control program is to be coded entirely in PFORT, a portable subset of ANSI FORTRAN 66. The program is to be delivered to a military government agency, which will install the software on various computer installations. In addition, the customer requires that each routine in the program be clearly documented in a prescribed format. All internal program comments are to be later compiled as a separate source of documentation for the program.

b. Error. A named common block occurs in several routines in the program. In one routine, the definition of a variable in that block has been omitted because the variable is not referenced in that routine. This is, however, a violation of a rule defined in PFORT, which requires that the total length of a named common block agree in all occurrences of that block.

c. Error discovery. A code auditor that checks FORTRAN for adherence to PFORT detects this error immediately. The programmer of this routine is informed that the routine is to be appropriately modified and that any confusion over the use of the variable is to be clarified in the block of comments that describe the function of each defined variable in the routine. A code auditor that checks for the presence of appropriate comments in each routine is used to verify that the use of the variable is appropriately documented. At the end of code construction, all such internal program documentation will be collated and summarized by another code auditor that processes machine readable documentation imbedded in source code.

7.7. EFFECTIVENESS

Code auditors are very effective tools in certifying that software routines have been coded in accordance with prescribed standards. They are much more reliable than manually performed code audits and are highly cost-effective, as they are less time-consuming than manual audits.

7.8. APPLICABILITY

Code auditors can be generally applied to any type of source code. However, each specific tool will be language-dependent (i.e., will operate correctly only for specified source languages) and will only accept input that appears in a prescribed format.

7.9. LEARNING

No special training is required to use code auditors. As they may be used by a wide variety of people (programmers, managers, quality assurance personnel, customers), ease in their use is an important attribute. In order to use code auditors effectively, however, some learning is required to gain familiarity with the standards upon which the auditor is based.

7.10. COSTS

Code auditors are generally very inexpensive to use, since their overhead is usually no more than the cost of a compilation.

8.1. NAME. COMPARATORS

8.2. BASIC FEATURES

A comparator is a computer program used to compare two versions of source data to establish that the two versions are identical, or to specifically identify where any differences in the versions occur.

8.3. INFORMATION INPUT

Input to comparators consists of two versions of source data to be compared and those commands necessary for the comparator to operate. The source data may be:

a. Source programs

b. Sets of program test cases or test results

c. Databases

d. Arbitrary data files

Many comparators provide various user options, such as whether blank lines are to be included in compare processing, to control comparison operation.

8.4. INFORMATION OUTPUT

The output from a comparator is a listing of the differences, if any, between the two versions of input. Various report writing options are usually supplied by the comparator to designate the desired format of the output, e.g., whether each difference found should be preceded by line numbers. Many general comparator utility programs installed in large text-editing systems can also create a file of text-editor directives that can be used to convert one input file into the other.

8.5. OUTLINE OF METHOD

Comparators are fully automated tools that serve to eliminate the tedious, time-consuming task of performing large numbers of comparisons. They are most useful during program development and maintenance. During program development, they provide a means of ensuring that only the intended portions of a program are changed when modifications are to be made to the latest version. When regression testing must be performed following software corrections or updates, comparators provide an efficient means of comparing current and past test cases and test results.

Most comparators are widely available and are often provided as general utilities in operating systems. Some comparators may be more specialized and require input files to be of a prescribed format in order to operate correctly.

Comparators are invaluable tools in assisting configuration management and change control as the software takes different forms during development.

8.6.   EXAMPLE

a.   Application.   A large command and control flight software system is being developed. During system testing, the generation of many different databases is required as a source of input data for each associated test case. Strict control of the databases, including identification of their similarities and differences, must be constantly maintained in order to properly verify test results.

b.   Error.   A bug in the software causes the execution of Test Case 3 to generate test results that are totally incompatible with the results of Test Case 1, though the input in both test cases is almost identical.

c.   Error discovery.   A comparator was used to compare the databases used in Test Case 1 and 3. The location of specific differences in the two files determined exactly which input data should be examined more closely, and when traced through the program, the error was found.

8.7.   EFFECTIVENESS

Comparators are most effective during software testing and maintenance, when periodic modifications to the software are anticipated. Their overall effectiveness is dependent upon the quality of their use.

8.8.   APPLICABILITY

This method is generally applicable.

8.9.   LEARNING

A minimal amount of effort is required to learn how to use comparators effectively. The tool's user documentation should provide sufficient information for its proper utilization.

8.10. COSTS

Comparators are generally inexpensive to use. Their cost is similar to that of performing two passes of read operations on one file.

9.1. NAME. CONTROL STRUCTURE ANALYZER

9.2. BASIC FEATURES

Application of an automated structure analyzer to either code or design allows detection of some types of improper subprogram usage and violation of control flow standards. It also identifies control branches and paths used by test coverage analyzers. A structure analyzer is also useful in providing required input to data flow analyzers and is related, in principle, to code auditors.

9.3. INFORMATION INPUT

Two input items are required by a structure analyzer. The first is the test of the program or design to be analyzed. Typically, the test is to be provided to the analyzer in an intermediate form, i.e., after scanning and parsing but not as object code. Often structure analyzers are incorporated within compilers.

The second input item is a specification of the control flow standards to be checked. These standards are often completely implicit in that they may be part of the rules for programming in the given language or design notation. An example of such a rule is that subprograms may not be called recursively in FORTRAN. Individual projects may, however, establish additional rules for internal use. Many such rules — for instance, limiting the number of lines allowed in a subprogram — can be checked by a code auditor. Others, however, can require a slightly more sophisticated analysis and are therefore performed by a structure analyzer. Two examples in this category are "All control structures must be well nested" and "Backward jumps out of control structures are not allowed."

Typically, this second input item is not directly supplied to a structure analyzer, but is incorporated directly in the tool's construction. Therefore, substantial inflexibility is common.

9.4. INFORMATION OUTPUT

Error reports and a program call graph are the most common output items of a structure analyzer. Error reports indicate violations of the standards that were input to the tool. Call graphs indicate the structure of the graph with respect to the use of subprograms; associated with each subprogram is information indicating all routines that call the subprogram and all routines that are called by it. The presence of cycles in the graph (A calls B calls A) indicates possible recursion. Routines that are never called are evident, as well as attempts to call nonexistent routines.

In checking adherence to control flow standards, the structure analyzer may also output a flow graph for each program unit. The flow graph represents the structure of the program, with each control path in the program represented by an edge in the graph. Additionally, structurally "dead" code within each module is detectable.

The flow graph and the call graph are items required as input by data flow analyzers, and it is common for the two analysis capabilities to be combined in a single automated tool.

9.5. OUTLINE OF METHOD

Since structure analysis is an automated static analysis technique, little user action is required. Aside from providing the input information, the user is only required to peruse the output reports and determine if program changes are required. Some simple manifestations of the tool may not provide detailed analysis reports; therefore, more responsibility is placed on the user, for example, to examine the call graph for the presence of cycles.

9.6. EXAMPLE

a.   An on-line management information systems program, Figure 9.6-1, calls a routine MAX to report the largest stock transaction of the day for a given issue. If MAX does not have the necessary information already available, RINPUT is called to read the required data. Since RINPUT reads many transactions for many issues, a sort routine is utilized to aid in organizing the information before returning it to the calling routine. Due to a keypunch error, the sort routine calls routine MAX (instead of the proper routine, MAXI) to aid in the sorting process. This error will show up as a cycle in the call graph and will be reported through use of a structure analyzer.

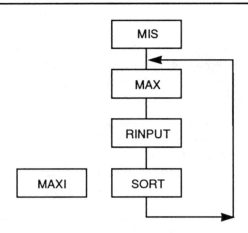

Figure 9.6-1. MIS flow chart.

b. As part of the programming standards formulated for a project, the following rule is adopted:

All jumps from within a control structure must be to locations after the end of the structure.

Figure 9.6-2, a segment of Pascal code, contains a violation of this rule, which would be reported by a suitably constructed structure analyzer.

```
100 :   X: = 100;
    while X > 70 do
        begin
          •
          •
        if Z = 5 then goto 100;
          •
          •
          •
        end;
```

Figure 9.6-2. Goto violation.

9.7. EFFECTIVENESS

The technique is completely reliable for detecting violations of the standards specified as input. The standards, however, only cover a small range of programming standards and possible error situations. Thus, the technique is useful only in verifying very coarse program properties. Its primary utility is in the early stages of debugging a design or code specification.

9.8. APPLICABILITY

The technique is generally applicable and may be applied in design and coding phases. Particular applicability is indicated in systems involving large numbers of subprograms and/or complex program control flow.

9.9. LEARNING

Minimal training is required for use of the technique. See "Outline of Method."

9.10. COST

Little human cost is involved, as there is no significant time spent in preparing the input or interpreting the output. For an average program, computer resources are small; the processing required can be done very efficiently, and only a single run is required for analysis. For large or complex programs, the cost can be quite high. A plotter, which produces the most readable structure diagrams, drives the cost up.

10.1. NAME. CROSS-REFERENCE GENERATORS

10.2. BASIC FEATURES

Cross-reference generators produce lists of data names and labels showing all of the places they are used in a program.

10.3. INFORMATION INPUT

Input to cross-reference generators consists of a computer program in either source or object format.

10.4. INFORMATION OUTPUT

Output from a cross-reference generator is an alphabetized list of variable names, procedure names, and statement labels showing where in the program they are defined and referenced. Other information, which is sometimes included, is data type, attributes, and usage information.

10.5. OUTLINE OF METHOD

Cross-reference generators provide useful information that can aid both program development and maintenance. They aid program development by helping identify errors such as misspelled identifiers and improperly typed variables. Program maintenance is aided by helping to locate, by variable or statement label, those portions that may be affected by a program change (e.g., a variable name needs to be changed).

Cross-reference generators are widely available and are usually provided with program source text analyzers such as compilers, standards checkers, and data flow analyzers.

Cross-reference listings should be checked in detail after a program change has been made to check for misspelled identifiers and incorrect usage, etc.

10.6. EXAMPLE

a. *Application.* A communication network controller manages the control of a network of high-speed communication lines connecting a large number of CRT terminals to an airline reservation system computer.

b. *Error.* A variable used to store message addresses is assigned an address that erroneously points to a location storing highly critical queue control information. A subsequent call to the device handler causes data to be read into the critical storage area, causing a system crash.

c. *Error discovery.* A quick study of the software's cross-reference listing showed all the locations where the offending variable was used, one of which clearly showed that the error was due to improper use of a pointer variable.

Figure 10.6-1 shows a sample program listing and corresponding cross-reference list. The program is a utility routine used by a large aerodynamic analysis program. The tool that generated the report is called PFORT, which performs various FORTRAN source analyses. The list shows, for each identifier, its type (e.g., integer or real), usage (e.g., variable or function), attributes (e.g., argument, whether the variable has been set, scalar or array), and the line numbers where it is referenced.

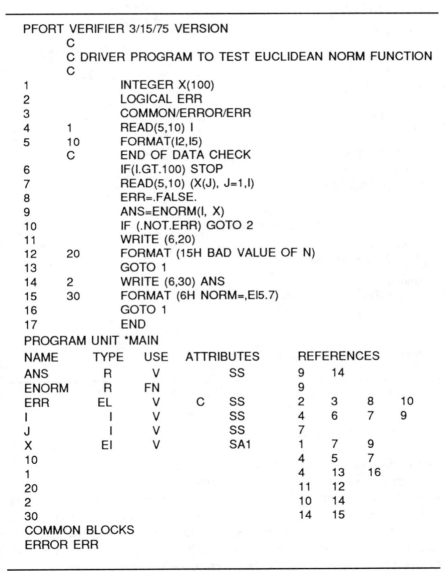

```
PFORT VERIFIER 3/15/75 VERSION
        C
        C DRIVER PROGRAM TO TEST EUCLIDEAN NORM FUNCTION
        C
1               INTEGER X(100)
2               LOGICAL ERR
3               COMMON/ERROR/ERR
4       1       READ(5,10) I
5       10      FORMAT(I2,I5)
        C       END OF DATA CHECK
6               IF(I.GT.100) STOP
7               READ(5,10) (X(J), J=1,I)
8               ERR=.FALSE.
9               ANS=ENORM(I, X)
10              IF (.NOT.ERR) GOTO 2
11              WRITE (6,20)
12      20      FORMAT (15H BAD VALUE OF N)
13              GOTO 1
14      2       WRITE (6,30) ANS
15      30      FORMAT (6H NORM=,EI5.7)
16              GOTO 1
17              END
```

PROGRAM UNIT *MAIN

NAME	TYPE	USE	ATTRIBUTES		REFERENCES			
ANS	R	V		SS	9	14		
ENORM	R	FN			9			
ERR	EL	V	C	SS	2	3	8	10
I	I	V		SS	4	6	7	9
J	I	V		SS	7			
X	EI	V		SA1	1	7	9	
10					4	5	7	
1					4	13	16	
20					11	12		
2					10	14		
30					14	15		

COMMON BLOCKS
ERROR ERR

Figure 10.6-1. Sample cross-reference examples.

Key to Figure 10.6-1

Type Key

column 1:
E explicitly typed

column 2:

I	INTEGER
R	REAL
D	DOUBLE PRECISION
C	COMPLEX
L	LOGICAL
H	HOLLERITH

Attribute Key

column 1:
C   in COMMON

column 2:
E   in an EQUIVALENCE statement

column 3:
A   dummy argument

column 4:
S   value set by program unit

column 5, 6:
S   scalar

An array with n dimensions

Use Key

columns 1, 2:

FA	arithmetic-statement function argument
FN	function name
E	external (function or subroutine)
GT	assigned goto variable
IF	intrinsic function
SF	arithmetic statement function
SN	subroutine name
V	variable

Figure 10.6-1. Sample cross-reference examples. (cont'd)

10.7.   EFFECTIVENESS

Cross-reference generators are most effective during the software maintenance phase to help determine where software errors are occurring, as seen in the previous example. Cross-reference generators are tools whose utility can often be taken for granted or even considered bothersome (e.g., "it produces too much paper"). Its lack of availability, however, will painfully demonstrate how necessary this seemingly basic capability is. Nevertheless, its true effectiveness is totally dependent upon the quality of its use.

10.8. APPLICABILITY

This method is generally applicable.

10.9. LEARNING

Minimal effort is required to learn how to effectively utilize cross-reference generators.

10.10. COSTS

Cross-reference programs are widely available, usually as a function provided by a larger system (e.g., a compiler) and add only an incremental amount to the total cost.

11.1 NAME. DATA FLOW ANALYZERS

11.2. BASIC FEATURES

Data flow analyzers are tools that can determine the presence or absence of data flow errors, that is, errors that are represented as particular sequences of events in a program's execution. The following description is limited to sequential analyzers, although efforts are under way to include synchronous and concurrent events.

11.3. INFORMATION INPUT

Data flow analysis algorithms operate on annotated graph structures that represent the program events and the order in which they can occur. Specifically, two types of graph structures are required: a set of annotated flowgraphs and a program invocation (or call) graph. There must be one flowgraph for each procedure. A flowgraph is a digraph whose nodes represent the execution units (usually statements) of the procedures, and whose edges are used to indicate the progression of execution units. Each node is annotated with indications of which program events occurred as a consequence of its execution. The program invocation (call) graph is also a digraph whose purpose is to indicate which procedures can invoke which others. Its nodes represent the procedures of the program, and its edges represent the invocation relation.

11.4. INFORMATION OUTPUT

The output of data flow analysis is a report on the presence of any specified event sequences in the program. If any such sequences are present, then the identity of each sequence is specified and a sample path along which the illegal sequence can occur is used. The absence of any diagnostic message concerning the presence of a particular event sequence is a reliable indicator of the absence of that sequence.

11.5. OUTLINE OF METHOD

Data flow analyzers rely basically upon algorithms from program optimization to determine whether any two particular specified events can occur in sequence. Taking as input a flowgraph annotated with all events of interest, these algorithms focus upon two events and determine: 1) whether there exists some program path along which the two occur in sequence, and 2) whether on all program paths the two must occur in sequence. If one wishes to determine illegal event sequences of length three or more, these basic algorithms can be applied in succession.

A major difficulty arises in the analysis of programs having more than one procedure, because the procedure flowgraphs often cannot be completely annotated prior to data flow analysis. Flowgraph nodes representing procedure invocations must be left either partially or completely unannotated until the flowgraphs of the procedures they represent have been analyzed. Hence, the order of analysis of the program's procedures is critical. This order is determined by a postorder traversal of the invocation graph in which the bottom-level procedures are visited first, then those that invoke them, and so forth, until the main-level procedure is reached. For each procedure, the data flow analysis algorithms must determine the events that can possibly occur both first and last and then make this information available for annotation of all nodes representing invocations of this procedure. Only in this way can it be ensured that any possible illegal event sequence will be determined.

11.6. EXAMPLE

The standard example of the application of data flow analysis is to the discovery of references to uninitialized program variables. In this case, the program events of interest are the definition of a variable, the reference to a variable, and the omission of a definition of a variable. Hence, all procedure flowgraphs are annotated to indicate which specific variables are defined, referenced, and undefined at which nodes. Data flow analysis algorithms are then applied to determine whether the definition omission event can be followed by the reference event for any specific variable without any intervening definition event for that variable. If so, a message is produced indicating the possibility of a reference to an uninitialized variable and a sample program path along which this will occur. A different algorithm is also used to determine if a specific variable definition omission must, along all paths, be followed by reference without intervening definition. For invoked procedures, these algorithms are also used to identify which parameters and global variables are sometimes used and always used as inputs and outputs. This information is used to annotate all nodes representing the invocation of this procedure, to enable analysis of these higher-level procedures.

Data flow analysis might also be applied to the detection of illegal sequences of file operations in programs written in languages such as COBOL. Here the operations of interest would be opening, closing, defining (i.e., writing), and referencing (i.e., reading) a file. Errors whose presence or absence could be determined would include: attempting to use an unopened file, attempting to use a closed file, and reading an empty file.

11.7. EFFECTIVENESS

As noted, this technique is capable of determining the absence of event sequence errors from a program, or their presence in a program. When an event sequence error is detected, it is always detected along some specific path. Because these techniques do not study the executability of paths, the error may be detected on an unexecutable path and hence give rise to a spurious message. Another difficulty is that this technique is unreliable in distinguishing individual elements of an array. Thus, arrays are usually treated as if they were simple variables. As a consequence, illegal sequences of operations on specific array elements may be overlooked.

11.8. APPLICABILITY

Data flow analyzers can be applied to any annotated graph. Therefore, the availability of this technique is only limited and restricted by the availability of the (considerable) tools and techniques needed to construct such flowgraphs and call graphs.

11.9. LEARNING

This technique requires only a familiarity with and understanding of the output messages. No input data or user interaction is required.

11.10. COSTS

This technique requires computer time, but the algorithms employed are highly efficient, generally executing in time that is linearly proportional to program size. Experience has shown that the construction of the necessary graphs can be a considerable cost factor, however. Potential users are warned that prototype tools exploiting this technique have proven quite costly to operate.

As noted above, no human input or interaction is required, resulting in only the relatively low human cost for interpretation of results.

12.1. NAME. EXECUTION TIME ESTIMATORS/ANALYZERS

12.2. BASIC FEATURES

Execution time estimators/analyzers are tools that provide information about the execution characteristics of a program. They may be considered validation tools in that they can be used to validate performance requirements and are part of the programming phase of the life cycle.

12.3. INFORMATION INPUT

The programs that are to have their execution performance monitored are, essentially, the input needed by the tool. Depending on the sophistication of the particular tool being used, the programs may be processed by a processor that automatically inserts probes to measure performance, or probes may need to be manually inserted. The probes usually consist of calls to a monitor that records execution information such as CPU and I/O time and statement execution counts.

12.4. INFORMATION OUTPUT

The output produced by execution time estimators/analyzers is reports that show either by statement or module the execution time distribution characteristics. For example, a tool will provide information showing, per module, the number of entries to the module, cumulative execution time, mean execution time per entry, and the percent execution time of the module with respect to the total program execution time.

12.5. OUTLINE OF METHOD

Execution time estimators and execution time analyzers both perform similar functions but in different ways. Execution time estimators function much in the same way as test coverage analyzers. A source program is instrumented with probes that collect statement execution counts when executed. Associated with each statement is a machine-dependent estimate of the time required to execute the statement. The execution time estimate is multiplied by the statement execution count to give an estimate of the total time spent executing the statement. This is done for all statements in a program. Reports showing execution time breakdowns by statement, module, statement type, etc., can be produced.

Execution time analyzers are not usually as sophisticated as execution time estimators. Probes to measure the actual execution time of modules or program segments are inserted (usually by hand) into the source program. When the program has completed its execution, but just before it terminates, a routine is called that prints a report showing the execution characteristics of the monitored portions of the program.

The value of the tool lies primarily in its use as a performance requirements validation tool. In order for the tool to be used to formally validate performance requirements, however, it is necessary for the performance requirements to have been clearly stated and associated with specific functional requirements. Moreover, the system should have been designed so that the functional requirements can be traced to specific system modules.

Assuming that the above conditions are met, the tool could be used in the following way. The program to be analyzed would be monitored by the execution time estimator/analyzer during testing. The execution times for the modules corresponding to specific functional requirements would be compared with the performance requirement for that function. Those modules that fail to satisfy their performance requirements would be studied in more detail for possible efficiency improvements. The tool results can also help to identify execution time critical sections of code. Once the necessary optimizations have been made, the program should be tested again using the tool to validate the performance requirements.

12.6. EXAMPLE

a. Application. A particular module in a real-time, embedded computer system is required to perform its function within a specific time period. If not, a critical time-dependent activity cannot be performed, resulting in the loss of the entire system.

b. Error. The module in question contained an error that involved performing unnecessary comparisons during a table look-up function, although the proper table entry was always found.

c. Error detection. The problem was discovered during system testing using an execution time analyzer that clearly indicated that the offending module was not able to meet its performance requirements. The specific error was discovered on further examination of the module.

12.7. EFFECTIVENESS

The use of execution time estimators/analyzers (as well as test coverage analyzers) has uncovered an interesting property of many programs. The majority of the execution time spent by a program is spent executing a very small percentage of the code. Knowledge gained of where this execution time critical code is located through the use of an execution time estimator/analyzer can be extremely helpful in optimizing a program in order to satisfy performance requirements and/or reduce costs.

12.8. APPLICABILITY

Execution time estimators/analyzers can be used in any application.

12.9. LEARNING

The learning required is simply what is necessary to execute the tool.

12.10. COSTS

The tool is automated and therefore does involve some cost. The amount will depend on the tool's sophistication, but generally will not be excessive.

13.1. NAME. FORMAL REVIEWS

13.2. BASIC FEATURES

Formal reviews constitute a series of reviews of a system, usually conducted at major milestones in the system development life cycle. They are used to improve development visibility and product quality and to provide the basic means of communication between the project team, company management, and user representatives. They must provide judgmental decisions made by a team of blue ribbon specialists with a proven knowledge of current system operations. Formal reviews are most often implemented for medium- to large-size development projects, although small projects often employ a less rigorous form of the technique.

The most common types of formal reviews are held at the completion of the Requirements, Preliminary Design, Detailed (Critical) Design, Coding, and Installation phases. Whereas names of these reviews may vary by company, some generally recognized names are: Requirements Review, Preliminary Design Review (PDR), Critical Design Review (CDR), Code Construction Review, and Acceptance Test Review.

13.3. INFORMATION INPUT

The input to a particular formal review will vary slightly depending on the stage of the life cycle just completed. In general, each formal review will require that some sort of review package be assembled and then distributed at a review meeting. This package commonly contains a summary of the requirements that are the basis for the product being reviewed. These and other common inputs to formal reviews fall into three main categories, described below.

a. Project documents. These are documents produced by the development team to describe the system. The specific documents required are dependent upon the life cycle phase just completed. For example: a review conducted at the conclusion of the requirements phase would necessitate availability of Functional Specifications or System/Subsystem Specifications.

b. Backup documentation. This type of input is documentation that is not usually contractually required, but which must be prepared to support systems development or otherwise record project progress. Specific types of backup documentation vary by the phase for which the review is performed. Rough drafts of user and maintenance manuals are examples of backup documentation examined during a design review to plan for continuation of the project. Program listings are an example of backup documentation utilized during a code construction review.

c.   Other inputs. All other inputs are primarily used to clarify or expand upon the project documents and backup documents. They may include viewfoils and slides prepared by project management for the formal review meeting, the minutes of the previous phase review meeting, or preliminary evaluations of the project documents under review.

13.4. INFORMATION OUTPUT

The information output associated with a formal review generally falls into the following categories.

a.   Management reports. These are written reports from the project manager to upper management describing the results of the review, problems revealed, proposed solutions, and any upper management assistance required.

b.   Outside reviewer reports.   These are written reports to the project manager from participants of the review who have not worked on the project. These reports provide outside reviewers an opportunity to express their appraisal of the project status and the likelihood of meeting project objectives. It also allows them to make suggestions for correcting any deficiencies noted.

c.   Action items. This is a list of all required post-review action items to be completed before a review can be satisfactorily closed out. With each item is an indication of whether customer or contractor action is required for resolution.

d.   Review minutes. This is a written record of the review meeting proceedings, which are recorded by a designee of the leader of the review team. The minutes of the review are distributed to each review team member after the completion of the review meeting.

e.   Decision to authorize next phase. A decision must be reached at any formal review to authorize initiation of the next life cycle phase.

f.   Understanding of project status. At the conclusion of any formal review there should be a common understanding of project status among the project personnel present at the review.

13.5. OUTLINE OF METHOD

a. Participants. The participants in a formal review are often selected from the following group of people:

- Project manager
- Project technical lead
- Other project team members — analysts, designers, programmers
- Client
- User representative(s)
- Line management or project manager
- Outside reviewers — quality assurance personnel, experienced people on other projects
- Functional support personnel — finance, technology personnel
- Subcontractor management, if applicable
- Others — configuration management representative, maintenance representative

b. The process. Formal reviews should be scheduled and organized by project management. Each review must be scheduled at a meaningful point during system development. The review effectively serves as the phase milestone for any particular phase.

There are five basic steps involved in every formal review.

1. Preparation. All documentation that serves as source material for the review must be prepared prior to the meeting. These materials may be distributed to each participant before the meeting in order to allow sufficient time to review and make appraisals of the materials. The location and time of the meeting must be established, participants must be identified, and an agenda planned.

2. Overview presentation. At the review meeting, all applicable Product and Backup Documentation is distributed and a high-level summary of the product is presented. Objectives are also given.

3. Detailed presentation. A detailed description of the project status and progress achieved during the review period is presented. Problems are identified and openly discussed by the team members.

4.   Summary.   A summary of the results of the review is given. A decision about the status of the product is made, a list of new action items is constructed, and responsibility for completion of each item is assigned.

5.   Follow-up.   The completion of all action items is verified. All reports are completed and distributed.

13.6. EXAMPLE

By contract agreement, two weeks prior to completion of the requirements document, the producer of a program receives notification from his client that a requirements review meeting is desired. The client notifies a preselected chairperson to conduct the meeting. For participants the chairperson has selected the project manager, project technical lead, a member of the requirements definition team, and a member of the requirements analysis team. The client also has indicated that he would like to include the following people in the review: a representative from the user shop, a reviewer from an independent computing organization, and a representative from his own organization.

The chairperson informs all review participants of the date, time, and location of the review. Ten days prior to the meeting, the chairperson distributes all documents produced by the requirements definition and analysis teams (requirements document, preliminary plans, other review material) to each participant. In preparation of the meeting, each reviewer critically inspects the documents. The user representative is puzzled over the inclusion of a requirement concerning the use of a proposed database. The reviewer from the outside computing organization notes that the version of the operating system to be used in developing the system is very outdated. A representative of the client organization has a question concerning the use of a subcontractor in one phase of the project. Each reviewer submits his comments to the chairperson before the scheduled review meeting. The chairperson receives the comments and directs each to the appropriate requirements team member to allow proper time for responses to be prepared.

The requirements review meeting begins with a brief introduction by the chairperson. All participants are introduced, review materials are listed, and the procedure for conducting the review is presented. A presentation is then given summarizing the problem that led to the requirements and the procedure that was used to define these requirements. At this time, the user representative inquires about the requirement concerning the use of a particular database as stated in the requirements document. The project technical lead responds to this question. The user representative accepts this response, which is so noted by the recorder in the official minutes of the meeting.

The meeting continues with an analysis of the requirements and a description of the contractor's planned approach for developing a solution to the problem. At this time, the questions from the client representative and the outside computing organization are discussed. The project manager responds to questions concerning the use of a subcontractor on the project. Certain suggestions have been made that require the approval of the subcontractor. These suggestions are placed on the action list. The technical lead acknowledges the problems that the independent computing organization has pointed out. He notes that certain system vendors must be contacted to resolve the problem. This item is also placed on the action list. A general discussion among all review team members follows.

At the end of the review, the chairperson seeks a decision from the reviewers about the acceptability of the requirements document. They agree to give their approval, providing that the suggestions noted on the action list are thoroughly investigated. All participants agree to this decision and the meeting is adjourned.

The chairperson distributes a copy of the minutes of the meeting, including action items, to all participants. The project manager informs the subcontractor of the suggestions made at the meeting. The subcontractor subsequently agrees with the suggestions. The project technical leader contacts the system vendor from which the current operating system was purchased and learns that the latest version can be easily installed before it is needed for this project. He notifies the project manager, who subsequently approves its purchase. The requirements document is appropriately revised to reflect the completion of these action items. The chairperson verifies that all action items have been completed. The project manager submits a Management Report to management, summarizing the review.

13.7. EFFECTIVENESS

Since the cost to correct an error increases rapidly as the development process progresses, detection of errors by formal reviews is an attractive prospect.

Some of the qualitative benefits attributable to the use of formal reviews are given below:

- Highly visible systems development
- Early detection of design and analysis errors
- More reliable estimating and scheduling
- Increased product reliability, maintainability
- Increased education and experience of all individuals involved in the process
- Increased adherence to standards
- Increased user satisfaction

Little data is available that identifies the quantitative benefits attributable to the use of formal reviews.

Experience with this technique indicates that it is most effective on large projects. The costs involved in performing formal reviews on small projects, however, may be large enough to consider lessening the formality of the reviews or even eliminating or combining some of them.

13.8. APPLICABILITY

Formal reviews are applicable to large or small projects following all development phases and are not limited by project type or complexity.

13.9. LEARNING

This technique does not require any special training. However, the success or failure of a formal review is dependent on the people who attend. They must be intelligent, skilled, knowledgeable in a specific problem area, and be able to interact effectively with other team members. The experience and expertise of the individual responsible for directing the review are also critical to the success of the effort.

13.10. COSTS

The method requires no special tools or equipment. The main cost involved is that of human resources. If formal reviews are conducted in accordance with the resource guidelines expressed in most references, the cost of reviews for average programs is not high. However, the cost of reviewing major programs can be significant. Most references suggest that formal review meetings should not require more than one to two hours. Preparation time can amount to as little as one half hour and should not require longer than one half day per review.

14.1. NAME. FORMAL VERIFICATION

14.2. BASIC FEATURES

The purpose of formal verification is to apply the formality and rigor of mathematics to the task of proving the consistency between an algorithmic solution and a rigorous, complete specification of the intent of the solution.

14.3. INFORMATION INPUT

The two inputs that are required are the solution specification and the intent specification. The solution specification is in algorithmic form — often, but not always, executable code. The intent specification is descriptive in form, invariably consisting of assertions, usually expressed in Predicate Calculus.

Additional inputs may be required depending upon the rigor and specific mechanisms to be employed in the consistency proof. For example, the semantics of the language used to express the solution specification are required and must be supplied to a degree of rigor consistent with the rigor of the proof being attempted. Similarly, simplification rules and rules of inference may be required as input if the proof process is to be completely rigorous.

14.4. INFORMATION OUTPUT

The proof process may terminate with a successfully completed proof of consistency, or a demonstration of inconsistency, or it may terminate inconclusively. In the former two cases, the proofs themselves and the proven conclusion are the outputs. In the latter case, any fragmentary chains of successfully proven reasoning are the only meaningful output. Their significance is, as expected, highly variable.

14.5. OUTLINE OF METHOD

The usual method used in carrying out formal verification is Floyd's Method of Inductive Assertions or a variant thereof. This method entails the partitioning of the solution specification into algorithmically straightline fragments by means of strategically placed assertions. This partitioning reduces the proof of consistency to the proof of a set of smaller, generally much more manageable lemmas.

Floyd's Method dictates that the intent of the solution specification be captured by two assertions. The first assertion is the input assertion, which describes the assumptions about the input. The second assertion is the output assertion, that describes the transformation of the input, which intended to be the result of the execution, of the specified solution. In addition, intermediate assertions must be fashioned and placed within the body of the solution specification in such a way that every loop in the solution specification contains at least one intermediate assertion. Each such intermediate assertion must express completely the transformations that are intended to occur or are occurring at the point of placement of the assertion.

The purpose of placing the assertions as just described is to ensure that every possible program execution is decomposable into a sequence of straightline algorithmic specifications, each of which is bounded on either end by an assertion. If it is known that each terminating assertion is necessarily implied by executing the specified algorithm under the conditions of the initial assertion, then, by induction, it can be shown that the entire execution behaves as specified by the input/output assertions and, hence, as intended. For the user to be assured of this, Floyd's Method directs that a set of lemmas be proven. This set consists of one lemma for each pair of assertions, which is separated by a straightline algorithmic specification and no other intervening assertion. For such an assertion pair, the lemma states that, under the assumed conditions of the initial assertion, execution of the algorithm specified by the intervening code necessarily implied the conditions of the terminating assertion. Proving all such lemmas establishes what is known as "partial correctness." Partial correctness establishes that whenever the specified solution process terminates, it has behaved as intended. In addition, total correctness is established by proving that the specified solution process must always terminate. This is clearly an undecidable question, being equivalent to the Halting Problem, and, hence, its resolution is invariably approached through the application of heuristics.

In the above procedure, the pivotal capability is clearly the ability to prove the various specified lemmas. This can be done to varying degrees of rigor, resulting in proofs of corresponding varied degrees of reliability and trustworthiness. For the greatest degree of trustworthiness, solution specification, intent specification, and rules of reasoning must all be specified with complete rigor and precision. The principal difficulty here lies in specifying the solution with complete rigor and precision. This entails specifying the semantics of the specification language and the functioning of any actual execution environment with complete rigor and precision. Such complete details are often difficult or impossible to adduce. They are, moreover, when available, generally quite voluminous, thereby occasioning the need to prove lemmas that are long and intricate.

14.6.   EXAMPLE

As an example of what is entailed in a rigorous formal verification activity, consider the specification of a bubble sort procedure. The intent of the bubble sort must first be captured by an input/output assertion pair. Next, observing that the bubble solution algorithm contains two nested loops leads to the conclusion that two additional intermediate assertions might be fashioned, or perhaps one particularly well-placed assertion might suffice. In the former case, up to eight lemmas would then need to be established — one corresponding to each of the (possible two) paths from the initial to each intermediate assertion, one corresponding to each of the two paths from an intermediate assertion back to itself, one for each of the (possibly two) paths from one intermediate assertion to the other, and finally one for each of the (possibly two) paths from intermediate to terminating assertion. Each lemma would have to be established through rigorous mathematical logic. Finally, a proof of necessary termination would need to be fashioned.

14.7.   EFFECTIVENESS

The effectiveness of formal verification has been attacked on several grounds. First and most fundamentally, formal verification can only establish consistency between intent and solution specification. Hence, inconsistency can indicate error in either or both. The same can be said for most other verification techniques, however. What makes this particularly damaging for formal verification is that complete rigor and detail in the intent specification are important, and this requirement for great detail invites error.

The amount of detail also occasions the need for large, complex lemmas. These, especially when proven using complex, detailed rules of inference, produce very large, intricate proofs that are highly prone to error.

Finally, formal verification of actual programs is further complicated by the necessity to express rigorously the execution behavior of the actual computing environment for the program. As a consequence of this, the execution environment is generally modeled incompletely and imperfectly, thereby restricting the validity of the proofs in ways that are difficult to determine.

Despite these difficulties, a correctly proven set of lemmas establishing consistency between a complete specification and a solution specification whose semantics are accurately known and expressed conveys the greatest assurances of correctness obtainable. This ideal of assurance seems best attainable by applying automated theorem provers to design specifications, rather than code.

14.8. APPLICABILITY

Formal verification is a technique that can be applied to determine the consistency between any algorithmic solution specification and any intent specification. As elaborated upon earlier, however, the trustworthiness of the results is highly variable depending primarily upon the rigor with which the specifications are expressed and the proofs are carried out. Formal verification is best employed on critical code where errors have severe consequences.

14.9. LEARNING

As noted, the essence of this technique is mathematical. Thus, the more mathematical sophistication and expertise practitioners possess, the better. In particular, a considerable amount of mathematical training and expertise is necessary for the results of applying this technique to be significantly reliable and trustworthy.

14.10. COSTS

This technique, when seriously applied, must be expected to consume very significant amounts of the time and effort of highly trained, mathematically proficient personnel. Hence, considerable human-labor expense must be expected.

As noted earlier, human effectiveness can be considerably improved through the use of automated tools such as theorem provers. It is important to observe, however, that such tools can be prodigious consumers of computer resources. Hence, their operational costs are also quite large.

15.1. NAME. GLOBAL ROUNDOFF ANALYSIS OF ALGEBRAIC PROCESSES

15.2. BASIC FEATURES

The technique involves the use of computer software to locate numerical instabilities in algorithms consisting of algebraic processes. Global roundoff analysis is the determination of how rounding error propagates in a given numerical method for many or all permissible sets of data. This technique has two areas of application: Case I — to decide whether an algorithm is as accurate as can be expected given the fundamental limitation of finite precision arithmetic; and Case II — to decide which of two competing algorithms is "more stable," i.e., less susceptible to rounding errors.

15.3. INFORMATION INPUT

a.   Case I — analysis of a single algorithm
    i.   algorithm described in a simple programming language
    ii.   dataset for algorithm
    iii. choice and type of rounding error measures
    iv.   stopping value for maximizer

b.   Case II — Comparison of two algorithms
    i.   each algorithm described in a simple programming language
    ii.   dataset for algorithms
    iii. choice of rounding error measure and mode of comparison
    iv.   stopping value for maximizer

15.4. INFORMATION OUTPUT

a.   Case I — analysis of a single algorithm
    i.   output computed for the initial dataset
    ii.   list of values found by the maximizer

    iii.   final set of data

    iv.   if instability diagnosed, then all arithmetic operations at the final set of data are listed

b.   Case II — comparison of two algorithms

    i.   output computed for the initial algorithms

    ii.   list of values found by the maximizer

    iii.   final set of data

15.5. OUTLINE OF METHOD

For an algorithm and a dataset, d, then:

a.   A function $w(\bar{d})$, called a Wilkinson number, has been defined that measures the effects of rounding errors. Large values for w are the sign of an unstable algorithm.

b.   Wilkinson number has been shown to be a "smooth" function of $\bar{d}$, i.e., as the original dataset values are altered in small increments, the values of w are correspondingly altered in small increments.

c.   An approximation to Wilkinson numbers has been developed that is straightforward to compute.

d.   The representation of the algorithm is analyzed.

e.   Using the initial dataset as a starting point, the global analysis program uses numerical maximization techniques to modify the dataset. The search is directed toward finding a dataset with a disastrously large value of $w(\bar{d})$.

15.6. EXAMPLE

Triangular Matrix Inversion. The better matrix inversion algorithms are known from experience to almost invariably produce satisfactory results. However, the question remains whether there is a guarantee that the results are *always* good. The question can be reformulated as: Is the traditional back substitution algorithm for inverting an upper triangular matrix numerically stable in the sense that there is a modest bound, depending on the matrix size, for w? To apply the technique, the algorithm is represented as a program in Figure 15.6-1. Note that the statement "TEST (N=4)" indicates that the search for numerical stability will be conducted in the domain of 4 x 4 matrices. An approximation to w, W_4, will be calculated.

```
C        TEST (N=4)
         COMPUTE S = (T INVERSE), WHERE T IS A NONSINGULAR,
         UPPER
C        TRIANGULAR MATRIX.
         DIMENSION (S(N,N),T(N,N))
C        INPUT T.
            FOR J = 1 to N BY 1
               FOR I = J to 1 BY −1
                  INPUT (T(I, J))
                  END (I)
               END(J)
C
C        COMPUTE S.
            FOR K = 1 TO N BY 1
               S(K,K) = 1.0/T(K,K)
               FOR I = K−1 TO 1 BY−1
                  S(I,K) = −SUMMATION(T(I,J)*S(J,K),J=I+I TO K)/T(I,I)
                  END (I)
               END(K)
C
C        OUTPUT S.
            FOR J=I TO 1 BY 1
               FOR I=J TO 1 BY −1
                  OUTPUT(S(I,J))
                  END(I)
               END(J)
STOP
```

Figure. 15.6-1. Triangular matrix inversion.

The compiler portion of the package checks the program for errors, then translates them into a form suitable for analysis.

The initial dataset for the search for numerical instability was:

$$T_0 = \begin{pmatrix} 1 & 0 & 0 & 0 \\ & 2 & 0 & 0 \\ & & 3 & 0 \\ & & & 4 \end{pmatrix}$$

The roundoff analysis program was told to seek a value of W in excess of 10,000. The maximizer located the following matrix:

$$T\infty \approx \begin{pmatrix} -0.001 & 5.096 & 5.101 & 1.853 \\ & 3.737 & 3.740 & 3.392 \\ & & 0.0006 & 5.254 \\ & & & 4.567 \end{pmatrix}$$

with $W_4(T_\infty) > 10,000$ in 6 seconds CPU time on a IBM 370/168.

The fact that W_4 can be large for data like T seems implicit in known results, e.g., verifying the ill behavior of triangular matrices with diagonal entries approaching zero.

15.7. EFFECTIVENESS

Failure of the maximizer to find large values of W does not guarantee that none exist. Thus, the technique tends to be optimistic; unstable methods may appear stable. However, experience indicates that this method is surprisingly reliable. At least, the failure of the maximizer to find large values of w can be interpreted as providing evidence for stability equivalent to a large amount of practical experience with low order matrices.

15.8. APPLICABILITY

The technique is intended for noniterative methods from numerical linear algebra.

15.9. LEARNING

Most algorithms should be able to be analyzed in two to eight hours of training and preparation assuming the software is available.

15.10. COSTS

The performance of the technique is related to the performance of the algorithm being checked.

16.1. NAME. INSPECTION

16.2. BASIC FEATURES

Informal reviews constitute a thorough inspection mechanism used to detect errors in system components and documentation. Several inspections are generally conducted for each item as it progresses through the life cycle. The most commonly recognized inspections are conducted during the design and programming stages and are referred to as design inspections and code inspections. However, the inspection concept may be applied to any functionally complete part of a system during any or all phases of the life cycle and is typified by utilization of checklists and summary reports. Another unique feature of an inspection is the use of data from past inspections to stimulate future detection of categories of errors.

16.3. INFORMATION INPUT

The input required for each inspection falls into three main categories: relevant project documents, backup documentation, and inspection checklists.

a. Project documents. These are documents produced by the development team to describe the system. The specific documents required are dependent upon the life cycle phase currently in progress. For example: an inspection conducted during the design phase would necessitate availability of Functional Specifications or System/Subsystem Specifications.

b. Backup documentation. This type of input is documentation that is not usually contractually required but must be prepared to support systems development or otherwise record project progress. Specific types of backup documentation vary by the phase in which the inspection is conducted. Data dictionaries and cross-reference tables are examples of backup documentation utilized during a design inspection. Program listings are an example of code inspection backup documentation.

c. Checklists. Each member of the inspection team uses a checklist for review preparation and during the course of the inspection itself. The checklist content may vary based upon the particular application being inspected and is updated from feedback of other recent inspections. For example, a checklist to be employed during a code inspection of a COBOL program component would contain items like:

- Are specialized printer controls used to enhance component readability (e.g., use of EJECT or SKIP commands)?
- Does each procedure have only one exit and entry?
- Are IF-THEN-ELSE statements indented in a logical fashion?
- Are file, record, and data names representative of the information they contain and do they conform to established naming conventions?
- Are comments explicit and accurate?
  -
  -
  -
- etc.

16.4. INFORMATION OUTPUT

The information output associated with an inspection is either related to inspection planning and scheduling or inspection results.

a. Inspection Schedule Memo. The memo is produced upon notification from management that an inspection should be forthcoming. The memo defines the roles and responsibilities of each inspection team member, estimated time required for each inspection task, and a summary of the status of the item being reviewed (including any previous inspections conducted).

b. Problem Definition Sheet/Error Description Summary. This form is used to record information about each detected error. It describes the location, nature, and classification of the errors.

c. Summary Report. A Summary Report is used to document correction of all errors reported during an inspection. Data recorded on the report is tabulated and becomes part of cumulative error statistics, which can be used to improve the development and inspection processes.

d. Management Reports. These reports are the means by which management is informed about the types of errors being detected and the amount of resources being expended to correct them. The information from these reports highlights frequent sources of errors, providing input to management for future updates to the inspection checklist.

16.5. OUTLINE OF METHOD

a. Roles and responsibilities. The group of people responsible for the inspection results are usually called an inspection team and are given responsibilities based upon their contribution to the item being inspected. The leader of the group is responsible for all process planning, moderating, reporting, and follow-up activities. The designer/implementer (person responsible for building the item) and the tester of the item being inspected are also members of the inspection team. Management does not normally participate in an inspection.

b. The process.   There are five basic steps involved in every inspection: planning, preparation, inspection meeting, rework and follow-up. The first inspection for a particular item contains another step: overview presentation. These steps are summarized below.

While these steps should not vary functionally for inspections conducted at different development phases, the responsibilities of the individuals on the inspection team will necessarily vary slightly. This occurs because the primary responsibility for the item shifts as the life cycle progresses. For example, during a design inspection, the designer is the focal point. However, during a code inspection or document inspection, the implementation is the focal point.

1. *Planning.* Set up inspection schedule and assemble inspection team.

2. *Overview presentation* (conducted only for the first inspection of the item during the development process). Distribute applicable Product and Backup Documentation and present a high-level summary of the item to be inspected.

3. *Preparation.* Team members read and review documentation and list any questions.

4. *Inspection Meeting.* Conduct detailed description of the item, noting all errors detected. Use checklists to ensure inspection completeness and Problem Definition Report to summarize errors.

5. *Rework.* Estimate time to correct errors and implement the corrections.

6. *Follow-up.* Verify that all errors have been corrected using Problem Definition Sheet as a checklist. Complete Summary and Management Reports.

16.6. EXAMPLE

The following is an example of a design inspection of a software component or item that defines the roles and responsibilities of the inspection team members. Upon decision of management to conduct a design inspection, the selected leader initiates process planning by identifying team members and their roles and responsibilities. If this is the first inspection for this item (i.e., there has been no requirements inspection), the leader next schedules an overview presentation. The project and backup documentation (i.e., Functions Specification, system flowcharts, etc.) are distributed and the item designer leads the team through a high-level description of the item.

After the presentation, each team member reads and reviews the distributed documentation and lists any questions. This list of prepared questions is often given to the leader and/or designer prior to the inspection meeting.

At the designer inspection meeting, the implementer leads the team through a detailed description of the design of the item being inspected. Backup documentation facilitates the description and clarifies points that may be brought up. The checklist is used by each team member to help identify errors and enforce standards. The problem definition sheet is prepared by the team leader at the end of the inspection. The item design will either be approved as-is, approved with modifications, or rejected. In the last two cases, the Problem Definition Sheet is given to the designer and the correction process begins.

At the start of this rework process, an estimate is made by the leader and designer specifying time required for correction. This estimate is entered on the Problem Definition Sheet and provided to management. Management can then make a judgment as to whether their project schedule will be affected. Necessary changes to the item are made, and the item is either reinspected or submitted to follow-up procedures.

During follow-up, the Problem Definition Sheet is used as a checklist for the leader and designer to verify that all errors have been analyzed and corrected. The leader then fills out the Summary and Management Reports and submits them to management.

16.7. EFFECTIVENESS

Since the cost to correct an error increases rapidly as the development process progresses, detection of errors by early use of inspections is an attractive prospect.

Studies have been carried out that indicate that inspections are an effective method of increasing product quality (reliability, usability, and maintainability). Experience with the technique indicates that it is effective on projects of all sizes. The best results are generally achieved when the inspection leader is experienced in the inspection process.

Some of the best quantitative results of the use of inspections have come from IBM, which has been studying the use of the technique for a number of years. One study, detailing and comparing the benefits of inspections and structured walkthroughs, indicated 23 percent higher programmer productivity with inspections than with walkthroughs. No data was available documenting the amount of increased programmer productivity attributable to inspections alone. The study also reported 38 percent fewer errors in the running code than if solely applying walkthroughs as an error detection mechanism.

The qualitative benefits attributable to the use of inspections are substantial. The following list is illustrative of some of these positive effects:

- Programs that are less complex

- Subprograms that are written in a consistent style, complying with established standards

- Highly visible systems development

- More reliable estimating and scheduling

- Increased education and experience of all individuals involved in the inspection process

- Increased user satisfaction

- Improved documentation

- Less dependence on key personnel for critical skills

16.8. APPLICABILITY

While the most commonly used inspections are for design and code, the technique is not limited to these phases and can be applied during all phases, for most types of applications (i.e., business, scientific, etc.) on large or small projects.

16.9. LEARNING

The experience of the inspection leader is essential to the success of the effort. A correct attitude about the process is essential to all involved, including the appropriate managers. Many excellent texts about inspections (and other types of reviews) exist that should supply the required level of detail as well as discuss some team psychology issues pertinent to inspection conduct.

16.10. COSTS

The method requires no special tools or equipment. The main cost involved is that of human resources. If inspections are conducted in accordance with the resource guidelines expressed in most references, the costs of inspections are negligible compared with the expected returns. It should be kept in mind that follow-up inspections to correct previously detected errors can increase the original cost estimation. Most references suggest that inspection meetings should last no longer than 2 hours, and can reasonably be kept to 15 minutes. Preparation time can amount to as little as one half hour and should not require longer than one half day per inspection.

17.1. NAME. INTERACTIVE TEST AIDS

17.2. BASIC FEATURES

Interactive test aids, debuggers, are tools used to control and/or analyze the dynamics of a program during execution. The capabilities provided by these tools are used to assist in identifying and isolating program errors. These capabilities allow the user to:

- Suspend program execution at any point to examine program status
- Interactively dump the values of selected variables and memory locations
- Modify the computation state of an executing program
- Trace the control flow of an executing program

17.3. INFORMATION INPUT

Interactive test aids require as input the source code that is to be executed and the commands that indicate which testing operations are to be performed by the tool during execution. Included in the commands are indications of which program statements are to be affected by the tool's operation. Commands can be inserted in the source code and/or entered interactively by the user during program execution at preselected break points.

17.4. INFORMATION OUTPUT

The information output by an interactive test aid is a display of requested information during the execution of a program. This information may include the contents of selected storage cells at specific execution points or a display of control flow during execution.

17.5. OUTLINE OF METHOD

The functions performed by an interactive test aid are determined by the commands input to it. Some common commands are described below.

BREAK: Suspend program execution when a particular statement is executed or a particular variable is altered.

DUMP: Display the contents of specific storage cells, e.g., variables, internal registers, other memory locations.

TRACE: Display control flow during program execution through printed traces of:
- statement executions (using statement labels or line numbers)
- subroutine calls
- alterations of a specified variable

SET: Set the value of a specified variable.

CONTENTS: Display the contents of certain variables at the execution of a specific statement.

SAVE: Save the present state of execution.

RESTORE: Restore execution to a previously SAVEd state.

CALL: Invoke a subroutine.

EXECUTE: Resume program execution at a BREAK point.

EXIT: Terminate processing.

These commands allow complete user control over the computation state of an executing program. It allows the tester to inspect or change the value of any variable at any point during execution.

The capabilities of special interactive testing aids can also be found in many implementations of interpreters and compilers for such languages as BASIC, FORTRAN, COBOL, and PL/I.

17.6. EXAMPLE

A critical section of code within a routine is to be tested. The code computes the values of three variables, X, Y, and Z, which later serve as inputs to other routines. To ensure that the values assigned to X, Y, and Z have been correctly computed in this section of code, an interactive testing aid is used to test the code.

Two BREAK commands are initially inserted into the code. A BREAK command is inserted immediately before the first statement and immediately after the last statement of the section of code being tested. To display the value of X, Y, and Z, a CONTENTS command is placed before the second BREAK command. The program containing the above mentioned code is executed. When the first BREAK command is encountered, execution is halted and a prompt is issued to the user requesting that a command be entered. A SAVE command is typed by the user in order to save the present state of execution. Then SET command is entered to set the values of two variables, A and B, which are used to compute the values of X, Y, and Z. The EXECUTE command is then issued to resume program execution.

At the end of execution of the relevant section of code, the preinserted CONTENTS command displays the computed values of X, Y, and Z. The second BREAK command allows time for these values to be examined and gives the user the opportunity to enter new commands. At this time, a RESTORE command is entered that will restore the computation state to the state that was previously saved by the SAVE command. For this example, the computation state returns to that which followed the first BREAK command, allowing the code under analysis to be tested with different input values. Different values for A and B are entered and the contents of X, Y, and Z are observed as before. This process is repeated several times using carefully selected values for A and B, and the corresponding values of X, Y, and Z are closely examined each time. If results of several computations look suspicious, their input and output values are noted and the code is more thoroughly examined. The program is finally terminated by entering the EXIT command at one of the two possible break points.

17.7. EFFECTIVENESS

To be an effective testing tool, an interactive test aid should be used with a disciplined strategy to guide the testing process. The tools can be easily misused if no testing methodology is combined with their use.

17.8. APPLICABILITY

Interactive test aids can be applied to any type of source code. Most existing tools, however, are language dependent (i.e., will operate correctly only for a specific language).

17.9. LEARNING

A minimal amount of learning is required to use these tools. It is comparable to the learning required in using a text editor. However, if the tool is to be used most efficiently, some learning is required in utilizing it with an effective testing strategy.

17.10. COSTS

Programs executing under an interactive test aid will require more computing resources (e.g., execution time, memory for diagnostic tables) than if executed under normal operation. The cost is dependent on the implementation of the tool. For example, those based on interpretive execution will involve costs different from those driven by monitor calls.

18.1. NAME. INTERFACE CHECKER

18.2. BASIC FEATURES

Interface checkers analyze the consistency and completeness of the information and control flow between components, modules, or procedures of a system.

18.3. INFORMATION INPUT

Information needed by interface checkers consists of:

a.   a formal representation of system requirements

b.   a formal representation of system design

c.   a program coded in a high-level language

18.4. INFORMATION OUTPUT

Module interface inconsistencies and errors are revealed. The information can be provided as error messages included with a source listing or as a separate report.

18.5. OUTLINE OF METHOD

Interface checkers are fully automated tools that analyze a computer-processable form of a software system requirements specification, design specification, or code. The method for each of the three representations — requirements, design, and code — will be illustrated below by examining the interface checking capabilities of three existing tools.

PSL/PSA (Problem Statement Language/Problem Statement Analyzer) is an automated requirements specification tool. Basically, PSL/PSA describes system requirements as a system of inputs, processes, and outputs. Both information and control flow are represented within PSL. Interface checking performed by PSA consists of ensuring that all data items are used and generated by some process and that all processes use data. Incomplete requirements specifications are, therefore, easily detected.

The Design Assertion Consistency Checker (DACC) is a tool that analyzes module interfaces based on a design that contains information describing, for each module, the nature of the inputs and outputs. This information is specified using assertions to indicate the number and order of inputs, data types, units (e.g., feet or radians), acceptable ranges, and so on. DACC checks module calls against the assertions in the called module for consistency. This produces a consistency report indicating which assertions have been violated.

PFORT is a static analysis tool that is primarily used for checking FORTRAN programs for adherence to a portable subset of the FORTRAN language, but it also performs subprogram interface checking. PFORT matches actual with dummy arguments and checks for unsafe references, such as constraints being passed as arguments.

Interface checking capabilities can also be included within a particular language's compiler as well. For example, Ada provides a parameter passing mechanism whereby parameters are identified to be input or output or input/output. Moreover, data type and constraints (e.g., range and precision) must match between the actual arguments and the formal parameters (in nongeneric subprograms).

In summary, interface checking tools will generally check for:

• Modules that are used but not defined

• Modules that are defined but not used

• Incorrect number of arguments

• Data type mismatches between actual and formal parameters

• Data constraint mismatches between actual and formal parameters

• Data usage anomalies

18.6. EXAMPLE

a. Application. A statistical analysis package written in FOR-TRAN utilizes a file access system to retrieve records containing data used in the analysis.

b. Error. The primary record retrieval subroutine is always passed a statement number in the calling program that is to receive control in case an abnormal file processing error occurs. This is the last argument in the argument list of the subroutine call. One program, however, fails to supply the needed argument. The compiler is not able to detect the error. Moreover, the particular FORTRAN implementation is such that no execution time error occurs until a return to the unspecified statement number is attempted, at which time the system crashes.

c. Error discovery. This error can easily be detected with an interface checker at either the design (e.g., DACC) or coding phase (e.g., PFORT) of the software development activity. Both DACC and PFORT can detect incorrect numbers of arguments.

18.7. EFFECTIVENESS

Interface checkers are very effective at detecting a class of errors that can be difficult to isolate if left to testing. They are generally more cost-effective if provided as a capability within another tool such as a compiler, data flow analyzer, or a requirements/design specification tool.

18.8. APPLICABILITY

The method is generally applicable.

18.9.   LEARNING

The use of interface checkers requires only a very minimal learning effort.

18.10.   COSTS

Interface checkers are quite inexpensive to use, usually much less than the cost of a compilation.

19.1.   NAME.   MUTATION ANALYSIS

19.2.   BASIC FEATURES

Mutation analysis is a technique for detecting errors in a program and for determining the thoroughness with which the program has been tested. It entails studying the behavior of a large collection of programs that have been systematically derived from the original program.

19.3.   INFORMATION INPUTS

The basic input required by mutation analysis is the original source program and a collection of test datasets on which the program operates correctly, and which the user considers to adequately and thoroughly test the program.

19.4.   INFORMATION OUTPUTS

The ultimate output of mutation analysis is a collection of test datasets and good assurance that the collection is in fact adequate to thoroughly test the program. It is important to understand that the mutation analysis process may very well have arrived at this final state only after having exposed program errors and inadequacies in the original test dataset collection. Hence, it is not unreasonable to consider errors detected, new program understanding, and additional test datasets to also be information outputs of the mutation analysis process.

19.5.   OUTLINE OF METHOD

The essential approach taken in the mutation analysis of a program is to produce from the program a large set of versions, each derived from a trivial transformation of the original, and to subject each version to testing by the given collection of test datasets. Because of the nature of the transformations, it is expected that the derived versions will be essentially different programs from the original. Thus, the testing regimen should demonstrate that each is in fact different. Failure to do so invites suspicion that the collection of test datasets is inadequate. This usually leads to greater understanding of the program and either the detection of errors or an improved collection of test datasets, or both.

A central feature of mutation analysis is the mechanism for creating the program mutations — the derived versions of the original program. The set of mutations that is generated and tested is the set of all programs that differ from the original only in a small number (generally 1 or 2) of textual details, such as a change in an operator, variable, or constant. Research appears to indicate that larger numbers of changes contribute little or no additional diagnostic power.

The basis for this procedure is the "Competent Programmer" assumptions, which states that program errors are not random phenomena, but rather result from lapses of human memory or concentration. Thus, an erroneous program should be expected to differ from the correct one only in a small number of details. Hence, if the original program is incorrect, then the set of all programs created by making a small number of the small textual changes just described should include the correct program. A thorough collection of test datasets would reveal behavioral differences between the original, incorrect program and the derived correct one.

Hence, mutation analysis entails determining whether each mutant behaves differently from the original. If so, the mutant is considered incorrect. If not, the mutant must be studied carefully. It is entirely possible that the mutant is in fact functionally equivalent to the original program. If so, its identical behavior is clearly benign. If not, the mutant is highly significant, as it certainly indicates an inadequacy in the collection of test datasets. It may, furthermore, indicate an error in the original program that previously went undetected because of inadequate testing. Mutation analysis facilitates the detection of such errors by automatically raising the probability of each such error and then demanding justification for concluding that each has not in fact been committed. Most mutations quickly manifest different behavior under exposure to any reasonable test dataset collection, and thereby demonstrate the absence of the error corresponding to the mutation by which they were created.

This forces detailed attention on those mutants that behave identically to the original and thus forces attention on any actual errors.

If all mutations of the original program reveal different execution behavior, then the program is considered to be adequately tested and correct within the limits of the "Competent Programmer" assumption.

19.6.   EXAMPLE

Consider the FORTRAN program, Figure 19.6-1, which counts the number of negative and nonnegative numbers in array A:

```
      SUBROUTINE COUNT (A, NEG, NONNEG)
      DIMENSION A(5)
      NEG=0
      NONNEG=0
      DO 10 I=1,5
      IF (A(I).GT.0) NONNEG=NONNEG+1
      IF (A(I).LT.0) NEG=NEG+1
10    CONTINUE
      RETURN
      END
```

Figure 19.6-1.   Subroutine count.

and the collection of test datasets produced by initializing A in turn to:

I	II	III
1	1	−1
−2	2	−2
3	3	−3
−4	4	−4
5	5	−5

Mutants might be produced based upon the following alterations:

a.   Change an occurrence of any variable to any other variable, e.g.:
A to I
NONNEG to NEG
I to NEG

.
.
.

    b.   Change an occurrence of a constant to another constant that is close in value, e.g.:

1 to 0

0 to 1

0 to −1

1 to 2

    c.   Change an occurrence of an operator to another operator, e.g.:

NEG + 1 to NEG * 1

NEG + 1 to NEG − 1

A(I).GT.0 to A(I).GE.0

A(I).LT.0 to A(I).NE.0

Thus, the set of all "single alteration" mutants would consist of all programs containing exactly one of the above changes. The set of all "double alteration" mutants would consist of all programs containing a pair of the above changes.

Clearly, many such mutations are radically different and would quickly manifest obviously different behavior. For example, in changing variable I to A (or vice versa) the program is rendered uncompilable by most compilers. Similarly, changing "NEG=0" to "NEG=1" causes a different outcome for test case I.

Significantly, changing A(I)GT.0 to A(I).GE.0 or A(I).LT.0 to A(I).LE.0 produces no difference in run-time behavior on any of the three test datasets. This rivets attention on these mutants, and subsequently on the issue of how to count zero entries. One rapidly realizes that the collection of test datasets was inadequate in that it did not include any zero input values. Had it included one, it would have indicated that:

IF (A(I).GT.0) NONNEG=NONNEG+1 should have been
IF (A(I).GE.0) NONNEG=NONNEG+l.

Thus, mutation analysis has pointed out both this error and this weakness in the collection of test datasets. After changing the program and collection, all mutants will behave differently, strongly raising our confidence in the correctness of the program.

19.7.   EFFECTIVENESS

Mutation analysis can be an effective technique for detecting errors, but it must be understood that it requires combining an insightful human with good automated tools. Even then it must be understood that it is a reliable technique for demonstrating the absence only if all possible mutation errors (i.e., those involving alteration, interchanging, or omission of operators, variables, etc.) are examined.

The need for good tools is easily understood when one realizes that any program has an enormous number of mutations, each of which must be generated, exercised by the test datasets, and evaluated. On the surface, this would appear to entail thousands of edit runs, compilations, and executions. Clever tools have been built, however, that operate off a special internal representation of the original program. This representation is readily and efficiently transformed into the various mutations, and also serves as the basis for very rapid simulation of the mutants' executions, thereby avoiding the need for compilation and loading of each mutant.

This tool set still does not bypass the need for humans, however. Humans must still carry out the job of scrutinizing mutants that behave identically to the original program in order to determine whether the mutant is equivalent or whether the collection of test datasets is inadequate.

At the end of a successful mutation analysis, many errors may have been uncovered, and the collection of test datasets has certainly been made very thorough. Whether the absence of errors has been established, however, must be considered relative to the "Competent Programmer" assumption. Under this assumption, clearly all errors of mutation are detectable by mutation analysis; thus, the absence of diagnostic messages or findings indicates the absence of these errors. Mutation analysis cannot, however, ensure the absence of errors that cannot be modeled as mutations.

19.8.   APPLICABILITY

Mutation analysis is apparently applicable to any algorithmic solution specification. As previously indicated, it can only be considered effective when supported by a body of sophisticated tools. Tools enabling analysis of FORTRAN and COBOL source text exist. There is, furthermore, no reason why tools for other coding languages, as well as algorithmic design languages, could not be built.

19.9.   LEARNING

This technique requires the potential mutation analyst to become familiar with the philosophy and goals of this novel approach. In addition, it appears that the more familiar the analyst is with the subject algorithmic solution specifications, the more effective the analyst will be. This is because the analyst may well have to analyze a collection of test datasets to determine how to augment it, and may have to analyze two programs to determine whether they are equivalent.

19.10.   COSTS

In view of the previous discussion, it is important to recognize that significant amounts of human analyst time are likely to be necessary to do mutation analysis. The computer time required is not likely to be excessive if the sophisticated tools described earlier are available.

20.1.   NAME.   PEER REVIEW

20.2.   BASIC FEATURES

A peer review is a process by which project personnel perform a detailed study and evaluation of code, documentation, or specification. The term peer review refers to product evaluations that are conducted by individuals of equal rank, responsibility, or of similar experience and skill. There are a number of review techniques that fall into the overall category of a peer review. Code reading, round-robin reviews, walkthroughs, and inspections are examples of peer reviews that differ in formality, participant roles and responsibilities, output produced, and input required.

20.3.   INFORMATION INPUT

The input to a particular peer review will vary slightly depending on which form of peer review is being conducted. In general, each of the forms of peer review requires that some sort of review package is assembled and distributed. This package commonly contains a summary of the requirement(s) that are the basis for the product being reviewed. Other common inputs are differentiated by the stage of the life cycle currently in process. For example, input to a peer review during the coding phase would consist of program listings, design specifications, programming standards, and a summary of results from the design peer review previously held on the same product. Common input to particular forms of peer review are described below.

a. Code reading review.
- Component requirements
- Design specifications
- Program listings
- Programming standards

b. Round-robin reviews.
- Component requirements
- Design or code specifications
- Program listings (if during coding phase)

c. Walkthrough.
- Component requirements
- Design or code specifications
- Program listings (if coding phase walkthrough)
- Product standards
- Backup documentation (i.e., flowcharts, HIPO charts, data dictionaries, etc.)
- Question list (derived by participants prior to review)

d. Inspections.
- Component requirements
- Design or code specifications
- Program listings (if during coding phase)
- Product standards
- Backup documentation
- Checklist (containing descriptions of particular features to be evaluated)

20.4. INFORMATION OUTPUT

The output from a peer review varies by form of review. One output common to each form of a peer review is a decision or consensus about the product under review. This is usually in the form of a group approval of the product as is, an approval with recommended modifications, or a rejection (and rescheduled review date).

Specific output from peer reviews are as follows:

a. Code reading review and round-robin review.

- Informal documentation of detected problems
- Recommendation to accept or reject reviewed product
- Discrepancy List

b. Walkthrough.

- Action List (formal documentation of problems)
- Walkthrough Form (containing review summary and group decision)

c. Inspection.

- Inspection schedule and memo (defining individual roles, responsibilities, agenda, and schedule)
- Problem definition set
- Summary report (documenting error correction status and related statistics on the errors)
- Management report (describing errors, problems, and component status)

20.5. OUTLINE OF METHOD

The peer review methodology and participant responsibilities vary by form of review. Summaries of these methodologies are provided in the later part of this section. However, there are a few features common to each methodology.

For example, most peer reviews are not attended by management. (An exception is made in circumstances where the project manager is also a designer, coder, or tester — usually on very small projects.) The presence of management tends to inhibit participants, since they feel that they personally are being evaluated. This would be contrary to the intent of peer reviews — that of studying the product itself.

Another common feature is the assembly and distribution of project review materials prior to the conduct of the peer review. This allows participants to spend some amount of time reviewing the data to become better prepared for the review.

At the end of most peer reviews, the group arrives at a decision about the status of the review product. This decision is usually communicated to management.

Most reviews are conducted in a group organization as opposed to individually by participants or by the project team itself. While this may seem an obvious feature, it bears some discussion. Most organizations doing software development and/or maintenance employ some variation of a team approach. Some team organizations are described below.

- *Conventional team* — A senior programmer directs the efforts of one or more less experienced programmers.

- *Egoless team* — Programmers who are of about equal experience share product responsibilities.

- *Chief programmer team* — A highly qualified senior programmer leads the efforts of other team members for whom specific roles and responsibilities have been assigned (i.e., backup programmer, secretary, librarian, etc.).

The group that participates in the peer review is not necessarily the same as the team organized to manage and complete the software product. The review group is likely to be composed of a subset of the project team plus other individuals as required by the form of review being held and the stage of the life cycle in process. The benefits of peer reviews are unlikely to be attained if the group acts separately, without some designated responsibilities. Some roles commonly used in review groups are described below. These roles are not *all* employed in any one review but represent a list.

- *Group/review leader* — the individual designated by management with planning, detecting, organizing, and coordinating responsibilities.

Usually has responsibilities after the review to ensure that recommendations are implemented.

- *Designer* — the individual responsible for the specification of the product and a plan for its implementation.

- *Implementer* — the individual responsible for developing the product according to the plan detailed by the designer.

- *Tester* — the individual responsible for testing the product as developed by the implementer.

- *Coordinator* — the individual designated with planning, directing, organizing, and coordinating responsibilities.

- *Producer* — the individual whose product is under review.

- *Recorder* — the individual responsible for documenting the review activities during the review.

- *User representative* — the individual responsible for ensuring that the user's requirements are addressed.

- *Standards representative* — the individual responsible for ensuring that product standards are conformed to.

- *Maintenance representative* — the individual who will be responsible for updates or corrections to the installed product.

- *Others* — individuals with specialized skills or responsibilities that contribute during the peer review.

While the forms of peer reviews have some similarities and generally involve designation of participant roles and responsibilities, they are different in application. The remainder of this section will summarize the application methods associated with the forms of peer reviews previously introduced.

a.   Code reading review.   Code reading is line-by-line study and evaluation of program source code. It is generally performed on source code that has been compiled and is free of syntax errors. However, some organizations practice code reading on uncompiled source listings or hand-written code on coding sheets in order to remove syntax and logic errors prior to code entry. Code reading is commonly practiced on top-down,

structured code and becomes cost-ineffective when performed on unstructured code.

The optimum size of the code reading review team is three to four.
The producer sets up the review and is responsible for team leadership.
Two or three programmer/analysts are selected by the producer based
upon their experience, responsibilities with interfacing programs, or other
specialized skill.

The producer distributes the review input (see Section 20.3) about
two days in advance. During the review, the producer and the reviewers
go through each line of code checking for features that will make the
program more readable, usable, reliable, and maintainable. Two types of
code reading may be performed: reading for understanding and reading
for verification. Reading for understanding is performed when the reader
desires an overall appreciation of how the program module works, its
structure, what functions it performs, and whether it follows established
standards. Assuming that Figure 20.5-1 depicts the structure of a program component, a reviewer reading for understanding would review the
modules in the the following order: 1.0, 2.0, 2.1, 2.2, 3.0, 3.1, 3.2, 3.3.

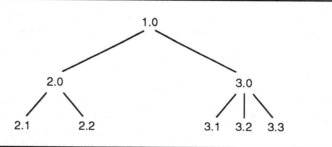

Figure 20.5-1. A program structure.

In contrast to this top-to-bottom approach, reading for verification
implies a bottom-up review of the code. The component depicted above
would be perused in the following order: 3.3, 3.2, 3.1, 3.0, 2.2, 2.1, 2.0,
1.0. In this manner, it is possible to produce a dependency list detailing
parameters, control switches, table pointers, and internal and external
variables used by the component. The list can then be used to ensure

hierarchical consistency, data availability, variable initiation, etc. Reviewers point out any problems or errors detected while reading for understanding or verification during the review.

The team then makes an informal decision about the acceptability of the code product and may recommend changes. The producer notes suggested modifications and is responsible for all changes to the source code. Suggested changes are evaluated by the producer and need not be implemented if the producer determines that they are invalid.

There is no mechanism to ensure that change is implemented or to follow up on the review.

b.   Round-robin review.   A round-robin review is a peer review where each participant is given an equal and similar share of the product being reviewed to study, present, and lead in its evaluation.

A round-robin review can be given during any phase of the product life cycle and is also useful for documentation review. In addition, there are variations of the round-robin review that incorporate some of the best features from other peer review forms, but continue to use the alternating review leader approach. For example, during a round-robin inspection, each item on the inspection checklist is made the responsibility of alternating participants.

The common number of people involved in this type of peer review is four to six. The meeting is scheduled by the producer, who also distributes some high-level documentation. The producer will either be the first review leader or will assign this responsibility to another participant. The temporary leader will guide the other participants (who may be implementers, designers, testers, users, maintenance representatives, etc.) through the first unit of work. This unit may be a module, paragraph, line of code, inspection item, or other unit of manageable size. All participants (including the leader) have the opportunity to comment on the unit before the next leader begins the evaluation of the next unit. The leaders are responsible for noting major comments raised about their piece of work. At the end of the review, all the major comments are summarized and the group decides whether or not to approve the product. No formal mechanism for review follow-up is used.

c.   Walkthroughs.   This type of peer review is more formal than the code reading review or round-robin review. Distinct roles and responsibilities are assigned prior to review. Prereview preparation is greater, and a more formal approach to problem documentation is stressed. Another key feature of this review is that it is presented by the producer. The most common walkthroughs are those held during design and code, yet recently they have been applied to specifications documentation and test results.

The producer schedules the review and assembles and distributes input. In most cases the producer selects the walkthrough participants (although sometimes this is done by management) and notifies them of their roles and responsibilities. The walkthrough is usually conducted with less than seven participants and lasts not more than two hours. If more time is needed, a break must be given or the product should be reduced in size. Roles usually included in a walkthrough are producer, coordinator, recorder, and representatives of user, maintenance, and standards organizations.

The review is opened by the coordinator, yet the producer is responsible for leading the group through the product. In the case of design and code walkthrough, the producer simulates the operation of the component, allowing each participant to comment based upon his area of specialization. A list of problems is kept, and at the end of the review each participant signs the list or other walkthrough form indicating whether the product is accepted as-is, accepted with recommended changes, or rejected. Suggested changes are made at the discretion of the producer. There is no formal means of follow-up on the review comments. However, if the walkthrough review is used for products as they evolve during the life cycle (i.e., specification, design, code, and test walkthrough), comments from past reviews can be discussed at the start of the next review.

d.   Inspections.   Inspections are the most formal, commonly used form of peer review. The key feature of an inspection is that it is driven by the use of checklists to facilitate error detection. These checklists are updated as statistics indicate that certain types of error are occurring more or less frequently than in the past. The most commonly held types of inspections are conducted on the product design and code, although inspections may be used during any life cycle phase. Inspections should be short, since they are often quite intensive. This means that the product component to be reviewed must be of small size. Specifications or design that will result in 50–100 lines of code are normally manageable. This translates into an inspection of 15 minutes to 1 hour, although complex components may require as much as 2 hours. In any event, inspections of more than 2 hours are generally less effective and should be avoided. Two or three days prior to the inspection the producer assembles input and gives it to the coordinator for distribution. Participants are expected to study and make comments on the materials prior to the review.

The review is led by a participant other than the producer. Generally, the individual who will have the greatest involvement in the next phase of the product life cycle is designated as reader. For example, a requirements inspection would likely be led by a designer, a design review by an implementer, and so forth. The exception to this occurs for a code inspection that is led by the designer. The inspection is organized and coordinated by an individual designated as the group leader or coordinator.

The reader goes through the product component, using the checklist as a means to identify common types of errors as well as standards violations. A primary goal of an inspection is to identify items that can be modified to make the component more understandable, maintainable, or usable. Participants (identified earlier in this section) discuss any issues that they identified in preinspection study.

At the end of the inspection an accept/reject decision is made by the group, and the coordinator summarizes all the errors and problems detected and provides this list to all participants. The individual whose work was under review (designer, implementer, tester, etc.) uses the list to make revisions to the component. When revisions are implemented, the coordinator and producer go through a minireview using the problem list as a checklist.

The coordinator then completes Management and Summary Reports. The summary report is used to update checklists for subsequent inspections.

20.6. EXAMPLE

The following is an example describing a code reading review.

Three days prior to estimated completion of coding, the producer of a program component begins preparation for a code reading review. The component is composed of 90 lines of FORTRAN code and associated comments. The producer obtains copies of the source listing and requirements and design specifications for the component and distributes them to three peers, notifying them of the review date and place.

Each reviewer reads the code for general understanding, reviewing a major function and its supporting functions prior to reviewing the next major function.

One reviewer notes an exception to the programming standards. Another thinks that the data names are not meaningful. The third has found several comments that inaccurately represent the function they describe. Each reviewer makes a note of these points as well as any comments about the structure of the component. Next, the requirements are studied to ensure that each requirement is addressed by the component. It appears that the requirements have all been met.

The code reading review is led by the producer. After a brief description of the component and its interfaces, the producer leads the reviewers through the code. Rather than progressing through the component from top to bottom, the decision is made to perform code reading from the bottom up. This form of code reading is used to verify the component's correctness.

As the code is being perused, one of the reviewers is made responsible for keeping a dependency list. As each variable is defined, referenced, or modified, a notation is made on the list.

The verification code reading uncovers the use of a variable prior to its definition. This error is documented on an error list by the producer. In addition, each of the problems detected earlier during the code reading (as performed by each individual) is discussed and documented.

At the end of the review, the error list is summarized to the group by the producer. Since none of the problems are major, the participants agree to accept the code with the agreed to minor modifications. The producer then uses the error/problem list for reference when making modifications to the component.

20.7. EFFECTIVENESS

Studies have been conducted that identify the following qualitative benefits of peer reviews.

- Higher status visibility
- Decreased debugging time

- Early detection of design and analysis errors (much more costly to correct in later development phases)
- Identification of design or code inefficiencies
- Ensuring adherence to standards
- Increased program readability
- Increased user satisfaction
- Communication of new ideas or technology
- Increased maintainability

Little data is available that identifies the quantitative benefits attributable to the use of a particular form of peer review. However, one source estimates that the number of errors in production programs was reduced by a factor of 10 by utilizing walkthroughs. Another source estimates that a project employing inspections achieved 23 percent higher programer productivity than with walkthroughs. No data was available indicating the amount of increased programmer productivity attributable to the inspections alone.

20.8. APPLICABILITY

Peer reviews are applicable to large or small projects during all development phases and are not limited by project type or complexity.

20.9. LEARNING

None of the peer reviews discussed require extensive training to implement. They do require familiarity with the concept and methodology involved. Experience has shown that peer reviews are most successful when the individual with responsibility for directing the review is knowledgeable about the process and its intended results.

20.10. COSTS

The reviews require no special tools or equipment. The main cost involved is that of human resources. If the reviews are conducted in accordance with the resource guidelines expressed in most references, the cost depends upon the number of reviews required. Most references suggest that peer reviews should be no longer than two hours, preferably one half to one hour. Preparation time can amount to as little as one half hour and should not require longer than one half day per review.

21.1. NAME. PHYSICAL UNITS CHECKING

21.2. BASIC FEATURES

Many (scientific, engineering, and control) programs perform computations whose results are interpreted in terms of physical units, such as feet, meters, watts, and joules. Physical units checking enables specification and checking of units in program computations, in a manner similar to dimensional analysis. Operations between variables that are not commensurate, such as adding gallons and feet, are detected.

21.3. INFORMATION INPUT

Units checking requires three things to be specified within a program: 1) the set of elementary units used (such as feet, inches, acres), 2) relationships between the elementary units (such as feet equals 12 inches, acre equals 43,560 square feet), and 3) the association of units with program variables. The programming language used must support such specifications, or the program must be preprocessed by a units checker.

21.4. INFORMATION OUTPUT

The information output depends upon the specific capabilities of the language processor or preprocessor. At a minimum, all operations involving variables that are not commensurate are detected and reported. If variables are commensurate but not identical (i.e., they are the same type of quantity, such as units of length, but one requires application of a scalar multiplier to place it in the same units as the other), the system may insert the required multiplication into the code, or may only report what factor must be applied by the programmer.

21.5. OUTLINE OF METHOD

The specification of the input items is the extent of the actions required by the user. Some systems may allow the association of a units expression with an expression within the actual program. Thus, one may write LOTSIZE (LENGTH * WIDTH * square feet) as a boolean expression, where the product of LENGTH and WIDTH must be in units of square feet. The process of ensuring that LENGTH * WIDTH is in square feet is the responsibility of the processing system.

21.6. EXAMPLE

A short program in Pascal-like notation is shown for computing the volume and total surface area of a right circular cylinder. The program requires as input the radius of the circular base and the height of the cylinder. Because of peculiarities in the usage environment of the program, the radius is specified in inches, the height in feet; volume is required in cubic feet, and the surface area in acres. Several errors are present in the program, all of which will be detected by the units checker.

In the following, comments are made explaining the program, the errors it contains, and how they are detected. The comments are keyed by line number to the program.

Line Number	*Comment*
2	All variables in the program that are quantities will be expressed in terms of these basic units.
3	These are the relationships between the units known to the units checker.
5–10	Variable radius is in units of inches, height is in units of feet, and so forth.
12	Input values are read into variables radius and height.
13	Lateral surface must be expressed in square feet. (RADIUS/12) is in feet, and can be so verified by the checker.
15	Lateral-surface and top-surface are both expressed in square feet; thus, their sum is in square feet also. Area is expressed in acres, however, and the checker will issue a message to the effect that though the two sides are commensurate, the conversion factor of 43,560 was omitted from the right side of the assignment.
16	The checker will detect that the two sides of the assignment are not commensurate. The right side is in units of feet quadrupled; the left is in feet cubed.

(1)   program cylinder (input, output);
(2)   elementary units inches, feet, acre;

(3)　　units relationships feet = 12 inches; acre=43,560 feet**2;

(4)　　constant pi = 3.1415927

(5)　　var radius (inches),

(6)　　　　height (feet),

(7)　　　　volume (feet**3),

(8)　　　　area (acre),

(9)　　　　lateral-surface (feet**2),

(10)　　　　top-surface (feet**2): real;

(11)　　begin

(12)　　　　read (radius, height);

(13)　　　　lateral-surface := 2*PI*(radius/12)*height;

(14)　　　　top-surface := PI* (radius/12)**2

(15)　　　　area := lateral-surface + 2* top-surface;

(16)　　　　volume := PI *((radius**3)*height);

(17)　　　　write (area, volume);

(18)　　end;

21.7.　EFFECTIVENESS

The effectiveness of units checking is limited only by the capabilities of the units processor.

Simple units checkers may only be able to verify that two variables are commensurate, but not determine if proper conversion factors have been applied. That is, a relationship such as 12 inches equal feet may not be fully used in checking the computations in a statement, such as line 13 of the example. There we asserted that (radius/12) would be interpreted as converting inches to feet. The checker may not support this kind of analysis, however, to avoid ambiguities with expressions such as "one-twelfth of the radius."

21.8.　APPLICABILITY

Certain application areas, such as engineering and scientific, often deal with physical units. In others, however, it may be difficult to find analogies to physical units. In particular, if a program deals only in one type of quantity, such as dollars, the technique will not be useful.

Units checking can be performed during all stages of software development, beginning with requirements specifications.

21.9. LEARNING

Dimensional analysis is commonly taught in first-year college physics on statics; conversion from English to metric units is common throughout society. Direct application of these principles in programming, using a units checker, should require no additional training beyond understanding the capabilities of the specific units checker and the means for specifying units-related information.

21.10. COST

If the units checking capabilities are incorporated directly in a compiler, its usage cost should be negligible. If a preprocessor is used, such systems are typically much slower than a compiler (perhaps operating at one-tenth of compilation speed), but only a single analysis of the program is required. The analysis is only repeated when the program is changed.

22.1. NAME. REGRESSION TESTING

22.2. BASIC FEATURES

Regression testing is a technique whereby spurious errors caused by system modifications or corrections may be detected.

22.3. INFORMATION INPUT

Regression testing requires that a set of system test cases be maintained and available throughout the entire life of the system. The test cases should be complete enough so that all of the system's functional capabilities are thoroughly tested. If available, acceptance tests should be used to form the base set of tests.

In addition to the individual test cases themselves, detailed descriptions or samples of the actual expected output produced by each test case must also be supplied and maintained.

22.4. INFORMATION OUTPUT

The output from regression testing is simply the output produced by the system from the execution of each of the individual test cases. When the output from previous acceptance tests has been kept, additional output from regression testing should be a comparison of the before and after executions.

22.5.   OUTLINE OF METHOD

Regression testing is the process of retesting the system in order to detect errors that may have been caused by program changes. The technique requires the utilization of a set of test cases that have been developed (ideally, using functional testing) to test all of the system's functional capabilities. If an absolute determination can be made of which portions of the system can be potentially affected by a given change, then only those portions need to be tested. Associated with each test case is a description or sample of the correct output for that test case. When the tests have been executed, the actual output is compared with the expected output for correctness. As errors are detected during the actual operation of the system that were not detected by regression testing, a test case that could have uncovered the error should be constructed and included with the existing test cases.

Although not required, tools can be used to aid in performing regression testing. Automatic test harnesses can be used to assist the managing of test cases and in controlling the test execution. File comparators can often be useful in verifying actual output with expected output. Assertion processors are also useful in verifying the correctness of the output for a given test.

22.6.   EXAMPLE

a.   Application.   A transaction processing system contains a dynamic data field editor that provides a variety of input/output field editing capabilities. Each transaction comprises data fields as specified by a data element dictionary entry. The input and output edit routine used by each data field is specified by a fixed identifier contained in a data field descriptor in the dictionary entry. When a transaction is input, each field is edited by the appropriate input editor routine as specified in the dictionary entry. Output editing consists of utilizing output editor routines to format the output.

b.   Error.   An input edit routine to edit numeric data fields was modified to perform a fairly restrictive range check needed by a particular transaction program. Current system documentation indicated that this particular edit routine was only being used by that single transaction program. However, the documentation was not up-to-date in that another, highly critical transaction program also used the routine, often with data falling outside of the range check needed by the other program.

c. Error discovery. Regression testing would uncover the error given that a sufficient set of functional tests was used for performing the testing. Had only the transaction program for which the modification was made been tested, the error would not have been discovered until actual operation.

22.7. EFFECTIVENESS

The effectiveness of the technique depends upon the quality of the data used for performing the regression testing. If functional testing, i.e., tests based on the functional requirements, is used to create the test data, the effectiveness is high. The burden and expense associated with the technique, particularly for small changes, can appear to be prohibitive. It is, however, often quite straightforward to determine which functions can be potentially affected by a given change. In such cases, the extent of the testing can be reduced to a more tractable size.

22.8. APPLICABILITY

This method is generally applicable.

22.9. LEARNING

No special training is required in order to apply the technique. If tools are used in support of regression testing, however, knowledge of their use will be required. Moreover, successful application of the technique will require establishment of procedures and the management control necessary to ensure adherence to those procedures.

22.10. COSTS

Since testing is required as a result of system modifications anyway, no additional burden need result because of the method (assuming that only the necessary functional capabilities are retested). The use of tools to support it, however, could increase the cost, but it would also increase its effectiveness.

23.1. NAME. REQUIREMENTS ANALYZER

23.2. BASIC FEATURES

The requirements for a system will normally be specified using some formal language that may be graphical and/or textual in nature. A requirements analyzer can check for syntactical errors in the requirements specifications and then produce a useful analysis of the relationships between system inputs, outputs, processes, and data. Logical inconsistencies or ambiguities in the specifications can also be identified by the requirements analyzer.

23.3. INFORMATION INPUT

The form and content of the input will vary greatly for different requirements languages. Generally, there will be requirements regarding what the system must produce (outputs) and what types of inputs it must accept. There will usually be specifications describing the types of processes or functions the system must apply to the inputs in order to produce the outputs. Additional requirements may concern timing and volume of inputs, outputs, and processes as well as performance measures regarding such things as response time and reliability of operations. The form of the inputs to the requirements analyzer is specified by the requirements specification language and varies considerably for different languages. In some cases all inputs are textual, whereas some languages utilize all graphical inputs from a display terminal (e.g., boxes might represent processes, and arrows between boxes might represent information flow).

23.4. INFORMATION OUTPUT

Nearly all analyzers produce error reports showing syntactical errors or inconsistencies in the specifications. For example, the syntax may require that the outputs from a process at one level of system decomposition must include all outputs from a decomposition of that process at a more detailed level. Similarly, for each system output, there should be a process that produces that output. Any deviations from these rules would result in error diagnostics.

Each requirements analyzer produces a representation of the system that indicates static relationships among system inputs, outputs, processes, and data. Some analyzers also represent dynamic relationships and provide an analysis of them. This may be a precedence relationship, e.g., process A must execute before process B. It may also include information regarding how often a given process must execute in order to produce the volume of output required. Some analyzers produce a detailed representation of relationships between different data items. This output can sometimes be used for developing a database for the system. A few requirements analyzers go even further and provide a mechanism for simulating the requirements using the generated system representation including the performance and timing requirements.

23.5. OUTLINE OF METHOD

The user must provide the requirements specifications as input for the analyzer. The analyzer carries out the analysis in an automated manner and provides it to the user who must then interpret the results. Often the user can request selected types of outputs, e.g., an alphabetical list of all the processes or a list of all the data items of a given type. Some analyzers can be used either interactively or in a batch mode. Once the requirements specifications are considered acceptable, a few analyzers provide the capability for simulating the requirements. It is necessary that the data structure and data values generated from the requirements specifications be used as input to the simulation, otherwise the simulation may not truly represent the requirements.

23.6. EXAMPLE

Suppose that a process called PROCESS B produces two files named H2 and H3 from an input file named M2. (The purposes of the files are irrelevant to the discussion.) Suppose also that PROCESS D accepts Files H2 and H3 as input and produces Files J3 and J6 output. In addition, PROCESS G is a subprocess of PROCESS D, and it accepts File H3 as input and produces File J6. Then the pseudo-specification statements, Figure 23.6-1, might be used to describe the requirements. (Note that these requirements are close to design, but this is often the case.)

PROCESS B
-
-
-

USES FILE M2
PRODUCES FILES H2, H3

PROCESS D
-
-
-

USES FILES H2, H3
PRODUCES FILES J3, J6

PROCESS G
-
-
-

SUBPROCESS OF PROCESS D
USES FILE H3
PRODUCES FILE J6

Figure 23.6-1. Requirements specification statements.

The requirements specifications imply a certain precedence of operations, e.g., PROCESS D cannot execute until PROCESS B has produced files H2 and H3. Detailed descriptions of what each process does would normally be included, but are emitted for brevity. The requirements analyzer will probably generate a diagnostic, since the statement for PROCESS D fails to indicate that it includes the subprocess G. A diagnostic will also be generated unless there are other statements that specify that file M2, needed by PROCESS B, is available as an existing file or else is produced by some other process. Similarly, other processes must be specified that use files J3 and J6 as input unless they are specified as files to be output from the system. Otherwise, additional diagnostics will be generated. It can be seen that some of the checks are similar to data flow analysis for a computer program.

However, for large systems the analysis of requirements becomes very complex if requirements for timing and performance are included, and if timing and volume analysis are to be carried out. (Volume analysis is concerned with such things as how often various processes must execute if the system is to accept and/or produce a specified volume of data in a single given period of time.)

23.7. EFFECTIVENESS

Some requirements analyzers are very effective for maintaining accurate requirements specifications. For large systems with a large number of requirements, they are essential. On the other hand, most existing requirements analyzers are rather expensive to obtain and use, and they may not be cost-effective for development of small systems.

23.8. APPLICABILITY

Requirements analyzers are applicable for use in developing most systems. They are particularly useful for analysis of requirements for large and complex systems.

23.9. LEARNING

Most requirements analyzers require a considerable amount of personnel training.

23.10. COST

Most requirements analyzers are expensive to obtain and use. They generally require a large amount of storage within a computer and so can only be used on large computers.

24.1. NAME. REQUIREMENTS TRACING

24.2. BASIC FEATURES

Requirements tracing provides a means of verifying that the software of a system addresses each requirement of that system and that the testing of the software produces adequate and appropriate response to those requirements.

24.3. INFORMATION INPUT

The information needed to perform requirements tracing consists of a set of system requirements and the software that embodies the capability to satisfy the requirements.

24.4. INFORMATION OUTPUT

The information output by requirements tracers is the correspondence found between the requirements of a system and the software that is intended to realize these requirements.

24.5. OUTLINE OF METHOD

Requirements tracing generally serves two major purposes. The first is to ensure that each specified requirement of a system is addressed by an identifiable element of the system software. The second is to ensure that the testing of that software produces results that are adequate responses in satisfying each of these requirements.

A common technique used to assist in making these assurances is the use of test evaluation matrices. These matrices represent a visual scheme of identifying which requirements of a system have been adequately and appropriately addressed and which have not. There are two basic forms of test evaluation matrices. The first form identifies a mapping that exists between the requirements specifications of a system and the modules of that system. This matrix determines whether each requirement is realized by some module in the system and, conversely, whether each module is directly associated with a specific system requirement. If the matrix reveals that a requirement is not addressed by any module, then that requirement has probably been overlooked in the software design activity. If a module does not correspond to any requirement of the system, then that module is superfluous to the system. In either case, the design of the software must be further scrutinized, and the system must be modified accordingly to effect an acceptable requirements-design mapping.

The second form of a test evaluation matrix provides a similar mapping, except the mapping exists between the modules of a system and the set of test cases performed on the system. This matrix determines which modules are invoked by each test case. Used with the previous matrix, it also determines which requirements will be demonstrated to be satisfied by the execution of a particular test case in the test plan. During actual code development, it can be used to determine which requirements specifications will relate to a particular module. In this way, it is possible to have each module print out a message during execution of a test indicating which requirement is referenced by the execution of this module. The code module itself may also contain comments about the applicable requirements.

If these matrices are to be used most effectively in a requirements tracing activity, the two matrices should be used together. The second matrix is built prior to software development. After the software has been developed and the test cases have been designed (based upon this matrix), it is necessary to determine whether the execution of the test plan will actually demonstrate satisfaction of the requirements of the software system. By analyzing the results of each test case, the first matrix can be constructed to determine the relationship that exists between the requirements and software reality.

The first matrix is mainly useful for analyzing the functional requirements of a system. However, the second matrix is also useful in analyzing the performance, interface, and design requirements of the system, in addition to the functional requirements. Both are often used in support of a more general requirements tracing activity, that of preliminary and critical design reviews. This is a procedure used to ensure verification of the traceability of all the above-mentioned requirements to the design of the system. In addition to the use of test evaluation matrices, these design reviews may include the tracing of individual subdivisions in the software design document back to applicable specifications made in the requirements document. This is a constructive technique used to ensure verification of requirements traceability.

24.6. EXAMPLE

a. Application. A new payroll system is to be tested. Among the requirements of this system is the specification that all employees of age 65 or older:

1. Receive semi-retirement benefits

2. Have their social security tax rate readjusted

To ensure that these particular requirements are appropriately addressed in the system software, test evaluation matrices have been constructed and filled out for the system.

b. Error. An omission in the software causes the social security tax rate of individuals of age 65 or older to remain unchanged.

c. Error discovery. The test evaluation matrices reveal that the requirement that employees of age 65 or older have their social security tax rate adjusted has not been addressed by the payroll program. No module in the system had been designed to respond to this specification. The software is revised accordingly to accommodate this requirement, and a test evaluation matrix is used to ensure that the added module is tested in the set of test cases for the system.

24.7. EFFECTIVENESS

Requirements tracing is a highly effective technique in discovering errors during the design and coding phases of software development. This technique has proven to be a valuable aid in verifying the completeness, consistency, and testability of software. If a system requirement is modified, it also provides much assistance in retesting software by clearly indicating which modules must be rewritten and retested. Requirements tracing can be a very effective technique in detecting errors early in the software development cycle that could otherwise prove to be very expensive if discovered later.

24.8. APPLICABILITY

This technique is generally applicable in large or small system testing and for all types of computing applications. However, if the system requirements themselves are not clearly specified and documented, proper requirements tracing can be very difficult to accomplish in any application.

24.9. LEARNING

Knowledge and a clear understanding of the requirements of the system are essential. More complex systems will result in a corresponding increase in required learning.

24.10. COSTS

No special tools or equipment are needed to carry out this technique if done manually. The major cost in requirements tracing is that associated with human labor expended. Requirements tracing is often a feature of requirements analyzers, which are expensive to obtain and use.

25.1. NAME. SOFTWARE MONITORS

25.2. BASIC FEATURES

These tools monitor the execution of a program in order to locate and identify possible areas of inefficiency in the program. Execution data is obtained while the program executes in its normal environment. At the end of execution, reports are generated by the monitor summarizing the resource usage of the program.

25.3. INFORMATION INPUT

Software monitors require as input the program source code to be executed and any data necessary for the program to run. Certain commands must also be provided by the user in specifying the information to be extracted by the monitor and in specifying the format of the generated output reports. These commands may specify:

- What is to be measured (e.g., execution times, I/O usage, core usage, paging activity, program waits)
- The specific modules to be monitored
- The frequency with which data is to be extracted during program execution (sampling interval)
- The titles, headings, content of each output report
- The units used to construct graphs
- Whether the graphs are to be displayed as plots or histograms

25.4. INFORMATION OUTPUT

The output of a software monitor is a set of one or more reports describing the execution characteristics of the program. Information that may be contained in these reports is given below.

- A summary of all the sample counts made during data extraction, e.g., the number of samples taken where the program was executing instructions, waiting for the completion of an I/O event, or otherwise blocked from execution.
- A summary of the activity of each load module.
- An instruction location graph that gives the percentage of time spent for each group of instructions partitioned in memory.

- A program timeline that traces the path of control through time.
- A control passing summary that gives the number of times control is passed from one module to another.
- A wait profile showing the number of waits encountered for each group of instructions.
- A paging activity profile that displays pages-in and pages-out for each group of instructions.

This information is often represented in histograms and/or plotted graphs.

25.5.   OUTLINE OF METHOD

Software monitors typically consist of two processing units. The first unit runs the program being monitored and collects data concerning the execution characteristics of the program. The second unit reads the collected data and generates reports from it.

A software monitor monitors a program by determining its status at periodic intervals. The period between samples is usually controlled through an elapsed interval timing facility of the operating system. Samples are taken from the entire address range addressable by the executing task. Each sample may contain an indication of the status of the program, the load module in which the activity was detected, and the absolute location of the instruction being executed. Small sample intervals increase sampling accuracy, but result in a corresponding increase in the overhead required by the CPU.

The statistics gathered by the data extraction unit are collected and summarized in reports generated by the data analysis unit. References to program locations in these reports will be in terms of absolute addresses. However, in order to relate the absolute locations to source statements in the program, the reports also provide a means to locate in a compiler listing the source statement that corresponds to that instruction. In this way, sources of waits and program locations that use significant amounts of CPU time can be identified directly in the source code; any performance improvements to the program will occur at these identified statements.

Software monitors are similar to another tool used to monitor program execution, test coverage analyzers. Test coverage analyzers keep track of and report on the number of times that certain elementary program constructs in a program have been traversed during a sequence of tests. During the monitoring of a program, both tools count the frequency of certain events. After program execution, both generate reports summarizing the data collected. However, because these tools serve different functions, they are different in their techniques of gathering information and in the type of information each collects. Test coverage analyzers are used to measure the completeness of a set of program tests, while software monitors measure the resource usage of a program as a means of evaluating program efficiency. As an evaluation of program efficiency requires consideration of execution time expenditure, software monitors utilize a strict timing mechanism during the collection of data. This is absent in monitors such as test coverage analyzers, which are not used to evaluate program performance.

25.6. EXAMPLE

a.   Application.   A program that solves a set of simultaneous equations is constructed. The program first generates a set of coefficients and a right-hand side for the system being solved. It then proceeds to solve the system and output the solution.

b.   Error.   In the set of calculations required to solve the system, a row of coefficients is divided by a constant and then subtracted from another row of coefficients. The divisions are performed within a nested DO-loop, but should be moved outside the innermost loop, as the dividend and divisors within the loop do not change.

c.   Error discovery.   The performance of the program is evaluated through the use of a software monitor. Examination of the output reveals that the program spends almost 85 percent of its time in a particular address range. Further analysis shows that 16.65 percent of all CPU time is used by a single instruction. A compiler listing of the program is used to locate the source statement that generated this instruction, which is found to be the statement containing the division instruction. Once the location of the inefficiency is discovered, it is left to the programmer to determine whether and how the code can be optimized.

25.7. EFFECTIVENESS

Software monitors are valuable tools in identifying performance problems in a program. Their overall effectiveness, however, is dependent upon the quality of their use.

25.8. APPLICABILITY

Software monitors can be applied to any kind of program in any programming language.

25.9. LEARNING

There are no special learning requirements for the use of software monitors. In order for the tools to be used effectively, however, the input parameters to the monitor must be carefully selected in determining the most relevant reports to be generated. Once the areas of a program that are most inefficient have been identified, it requires skill to modify the program to improve its performance.

25.10. COSTS

The largest cost in using a software monitor is that incurred by the CPU to extract the data during execution. In one implementation, extraction of data resulted in an increase of user program CPU time by 1 percent to 50 percent. Storage requirements also increase in order to provide memory for diagnostic tables and the necessary program modules of the tool.

26.1. NAME. SPECIFICATION-BASED FUNCTIONAL TESTING

26.2. BASIC FEATURES

Functional testing can be used to generate system test data from the information in requirements and design specifications. It is used to test both the overall functional capabilities of a system and functions that originate during system design.

26.3. INFORMATION INPUT

a. Data information. The technique requires the availability of detailed requirements and design specifications and, in particular, detailed descriptions of input data, files, and databases. Both the concrete and algebraic abstract properties of all data must be described. Concrete properties include type, value ranges and bounds, record structures, and bounds on file data structure and database dimensions. Abstract properties include subclasses of data that correspond to different functional capabilities in the system and subcomponents of compound data items that correspond to separate subfunctional activities in the system.

b. Function information. The requirements and design specifications must also describe the different functions implemented in the system.

Requirements functions correspond to the overall functional capabilities of a system or to subfunctions that are visible at the requirements stage and are necessary to implement overall capabilities. Different overall functional capabilities correspond to conceptually distinct classes of operations that can be carried out using the system. Different kinds of subfunctions can also be identified. Process descriptions in structured specifications, for example, describe data transformations that are visible at requirements time and that correspond to requirements subfunctions. Requirements subfunctions also occur implicitly in database schemata. Database functions are used to reference, update, and create databases and files.

The designer of a system will have to invent both general and detailed functional constructs in order to implement the functions in requirements specifications. Structured design techniques are particularly useful for identifying and documenting design functions. Designs are represented as an abstract hierarchy of functions. The functions at the top of the hierarchy denote the overall functional capabilities of a program or system and may correspond to requirements functions. Functions at lower levels correspond to the functional capabilities required to implement the higher-level functions. General design functions often correspond to modules or parts of programs that are identified as separate functions by comments. Detailed design functions may be invented during the programming stage of system development and may correspond to single lines of code.

26.4. INFORMATION OUTPUT

The output to be examined depends on the nature of the tested function. if it is a straight input/output function, then output values are examined. The testing of other classes of functions may involve the examination of the state of a database or file.

26.5. OUTLINE OF METHOD

The basic idea in functional testing is to identify "functionally important" classes of data. The two most important classes of data are *extremal values* and *special values*. Different kinds of sets of data have different kinds of extremal values, and different classes of special values must be used to test different kinds of functions.

   a.   Extremal values. The simplest kinds of extremal values are associated with elementary data items. If a variable is constrained to take on values that lie in the range (a,b), then the extremal values are a and b. If a variable is constrained to take on values from a small set of discrete values, then each of those values can be thought of as an extremal case.

   The construction of extremal cases for data structures (e.g., group data items) can be more complicated. It is necessary to construct extremal values of both the component elementary parts of the data structure as well as its dimensions. The data structure can be treated as a single quantity. In this case, when it takes on an extremal value, all of its elements take on that value. It is also possible to consider its components as a set of values in which one, more, or all of the components have extremal values. The construction of extremal values for files and databases is similar to that for data structures. Files with extremal dimensions contain the smallest possible and largest possible number of records. If the records are variable-sized, they contain records of the smallest and largest dimensions.

   b.   Special values. There appear to be two kinds of special values that are important for data processing programs. The first is useful for testing functional capabilities in which data is moved around from one location to another, as in a transaction-update program. Functions of this type should be tested over distinct sets of data (i.e., values in different files, records, variables, or data structure elements should be different) in order to detect the transfer of the incorrect data from the wrong source or into the wrong destination. The second kind of special data is useful for testing logical functional capabilities that carry out different operations on the basis of relationships between different data items. It is important to test functional capabilities of this type over special values such as those in which sets of data that enter into the comparison are all the same.

   Additional kinds of special values are important for scientific programs or programs that do arithmetic calculations. They include zero, positive and negative values "close" to zero, and large negative and positive values.

Functional testing requires that tests be constructed in which the input data is extremal, non-extremal, and special, as well as tests that result in program output that is extremal, non-extremal, or special.

26.6. EXAMPLES

Example 1: Testing of Requirements Functions.

a. Application. A computerized dating system was built in which a sequential file of potential dates was maintained. Each client for the service offered would submit a completed questionnaire, which was used to find the five most compatible dates. Certain criteria had to be satisfied before any potential date was selected, and it is possible that no date could be found for a client or fewer than five dates were found

b. Error. An error in the file processing logic causes the program to select the last potential date in the sequential file whenever there is no potential date for a client.

c. Error discovery. The number of dates that are found for each client is a dimension of the output data and has extremal values 0 and 5. If the "find-a-date" functional capability of the system is tested over data for a client for which no date should exist, then the presence of the error will be revealed.

Example 2: Testing of Detailed Design Functions.

a. Application. The designer of the computerized dating system in Example 1 decided to process the file of potential dates for a client by reading in the records in sets of 50 records each. A simple function was designed to compute the number of record subsets.

b. Error. The number of subsets function returns the value 2 when there are less than 50 records in the file.

c. Error discovery. The error will be discovered if the design function is tested using the extremal case, which should generate the minimal output value of 1. Note that this error is not revealed (except by chance) when the program is tested at the requirements specifications level. It will also not necessarily be revealed unless the code implementing the design function is tested independently and not in combination with the rest of the system.

26.7. EFFECTIVENESS

Studies have been carried out that indicate functional testing to be highly effective. Its use depends on specific descriptions of system input and output data and a complete list of all functional capabilities. The method is essentially manual and somewhat informal. If a formal language could be designed for describing all input and output datasets, then a tool could be used to check the completeness of these descriptions. Automated generation of extremal, nonextremal, and special cases might be difficult, since no rigorous procedure has been developed for this purpose.

For many errors it is necessary to consider combinations of extremal, nonextremal, and special values for "functionally related" input data variables. In order to avoid combinatorial explosions, combinations must be restricted to a small number of variables. Attempts have been made to identify important combinations, but there are no absolute rules, only suggestions and guidelines.

26.8. APPLICABILITY

This method is generally applicable.

26.9. LEARNING

It is necessary to develop some expertise with the identification of extremal and special cases and to avoid the combinatorial explosions that may occur when combinations of extremal and special values for different data items are considered. It is also necessary to become skilled in the identification of specifications functions, although this process is simplified if a systematic approach is followed for the representation of requirements and design.

26.10. COSTS

The method requires no special tools or equipment and contains no hidden excessive tests.

27.1. NAME. SYMBOLIC EXECUTION

27.2. BASIC FEATURES

Symbolic execution is applied to paths through programs. It can be used to generate expressions that describe the cumulative effect of the computations occurring in a program path. It can also be used to generate a system of predicates describing the subset of the input domain that causes a specified path to be traversed. The user is expected to verify the correctness of the output that is generated by symbolic execution in the same way that output is verified that has been generated by executing a program over actual values. It is used as a basis for data flow analysis and proof of correctness.

27.3. INFORMATION INPUT

a. Source code. The method requires the availability of the program source code.

b. Program paths. The path or paths through the program that are to be symbolically evaluated must be specified. The paths may be specified directly by the user or, in some symbolic evaluation systems, selected automatically.

c. Input values. Symbolic values must be assigned to each of the "input" variables for the path or paths that are to be symbolically evaluated. The user may be responsible for selecting these values, or the symbolic evaluation system used may select them automatically.

27.4. INFORMATION OUTPUT

a. Values of variables. The variables whose final symbolic values are of interest must be specified. Symbolic execution will result in the generation of expressions that describe the values of these variables in terms of the dummy symbolic values assigned to input variables.

b. System of predicates. Each of the branch-predicates that occur along a program path constrains the input that causes that path to be followed. The symbolically evaluated system of predicates for a path describes the subset of the input domain that causes that path to be followed.

27.5. OUTLINE OF METHOD

a. Symbolic execution. Symbolic values are symbols standing for sets of values rather than actual values. The symbolic execution of a path is carried out by symbolically executing the sequence of assignment statements occurring in the path. Assignment statements are symbolically executed by symbolically evaluating the expressions on the right-hand side of the assignment. The resulting symbolic value becomes the new symbolic value of the variable on the left-hand side. An arithmetic or logical expression is symbolically executed by substituting the symbolic values of the variables in the expression for the variables.

The branch conditions or branch predicates that occur in conditional branching statements can be symbolically executed to form symbolic predicates. The symbolic system of predicates for a path can be constructed by symbolically executing both assignment statements and branch predicates during the symbolic execution of the path. The symbolic system of predicates consists of the sequences of symbolic predicates that are generated by the execution of the branch predicates.

b. Symbolic execution systems. All symbolic execution systems must contain facilities for: selecting program paths to be symbolically executed, symbolically executing paths, and generating the required symbolic output.

Three types of path selection techniques have been used: interactive, static, and automatic. In the interactive approach, the symbolic execution system is constructed so that control returns to the user each time it is necessary to make a decision as to which branch to take during the symbolic execution of a program. In the static approach, the user specifies the paths he wants executed in advance. In the automatic approach, the symbolic execution system attempts to execute all those program paths having a consistent symbolic system of predicates. A system of predicates is consistent if it has a solution.

The details of symbolic execution algorithms in different systems are largely technical. Symbolic execution systems may differ in other than technical details in the types of symbolic output they generate. Some systems contain, for example, facilities for solving systems of branch predicates. Such systems are capable of automatically generating test data for selected program paths (i.e., program input data that will cause the path to be followed when the program is executed over that data).

27.6. EXAMPLE

a. Application. A FORTRAN program called SIN was written to compute the sine function using the McLaurin series.

PREDICATES:

(X**3/6).GE.E
(X**5/120).GE.E
(X**7/5040).LT.E

OUTPUT

SIN = ?SUM − (X**3/6) − (X**5/120)

Symbolic output for SIN

Figure 27.6-1. Symbolic execution example.

b. Errors. The program contained three errors, including an uninitialized variable, the use of the expression $-1**(I/2)$ instead of $(-1)**(I/2)$, and the failure to add the last term computed in the series onto the final computed sum.

Different paths through SIN correspond to different numbers of iterations of iterations of the loop in the program that is used to compute terms in the series. The symbolic output in Figure 27.6-1 was generated by symbolically evaluating the path that involves exactly three iterations of the loop.

c. Error discovery. The errors in the program are discovered by comparing the symbolic output with the standard formula for the McLaurin series. The symbolic evaluator that was used to generate the output represents the values of variables that have been uninitialized with a question mark and the name of the variable. The error involving the expression $(-1)**(I/2)$ results in the generation of the same rather than alternating signs in the series sum. The failure to use the last computed term can be detected by comparing the predicates for the symbolically evaluated path with the symbolic output value for SIN.

27.7. EFFECTIVENESS

Studies have been carried out that indicate that symbolic evaluation is useful for discovering a variety of errors, but that, except in a small number of cases, it is not more effective than the combined use of other methods such as dynamic and static analysis.

One of the primary uses of symbolic evaluation is in raising the confidence level of a user in a program. Correct symbolic output expressions confirm to the user that the code carries out the desired computations. It is especially useful for nonprogrammer users.

27.8. APPLICABILITY

The method is primarily useful for programs written in languages that involve operations that can be represented In a concise, formal way. Most of the symbolic evaluation systems that have been built are for use with algebraic programming languages such as FORTRAN and PL-1. Algebraic programs involve computations that can be easily represented using arithmetic expressions. It is difficult to generate symbolic output from programs that involve complex operations with "wordy" representations such as the REPLACE and MOVE CORRESPONDING operations in COBOL.

27.9. LEARNING

It takes a certain amount of practice to choose paths and parts of paths for symbolic evaluation. The user must avoid the selection of long paths or parts of paths that result in the generation of expressions that are so large that they are unreadable. If the symbolic evaluation system being used gives the user control over the types of expression simplification that are carried out, then he must learn to use this in a way that results in the generation of the most revealing expressions.

27.10. COSTS

Storage and execution time costs for symbolic evaluation have been calculated in terms of program size, path length, number of program variables, and the cost of interpreting (rather than compiling and executing) a program path.

The storage required for symbolically evaluating a path of length P in a program with S statements containing N variables is estimated to be on the order of $10(P + S + V)$. Let Cl be the cost of preprocessing a program for interpretation, C2 the cost of interpreting a program path, Cons the cost of checking the consistency (i.e., solvability) of a system of symbolic predicates, and Cond the cost of evaluating a condition in a conditional statement. Cons and Cond are expressed in units of the cost of interpreting a statement in a program. The cost (in execution time) of symbolically executing a program path is estimated to be on the order of $C1 + C2 (1 + E + Cons/10 + Cond/100)$.

28.1. NAME. TEST COVERAGE ANALYZERS

28.2. BASIC FEATURES

Test coverage analyzers monitor the execution of a program during program testing in order to measure the completeness of a set of program tests Completeness is measured in terms of the branches, statements, or other elementary program constructs that are used during the execution of the program over the tests.

28.3. INFORMATION INPUT

Test coverage analyzers use the program source code and a set of program tests to generate test coverage reports. Sophisticated coverage analyzers may also involve input parameters that describe which of several alternative coverage measures are to be used.

28.4. INFORMATION OUTPUT

Typical output consists of a report that describes the relevant feature of the program that has been "exercised" over a sequence of tests. Branch coverage analyzers keep track of and report on the number of times that each branch in a program has been traversed during a sequence of tests. A program branch is any transfer of control from one program statement to another, either through execution of a control transfer instruction or through normal sequential flow of control from one statement to the next.

Different kinds of coverage analyzers will report different kinds of information. Analyzers that measure coverage in terms of pairs of branches, loop iteration patterns, or elementary program functions have been proposed, but branch coverage analyzers are the most widely used. In addition to coverage information, analyzers may also record and print variable range and subroutine call information. The minimum and maximum values assumed by each variable in a program, the minimum and maximum number of times that loops are iterated during the executions of a loop, and a record of each subroutine call may be reported.

28.5.   OUTLINE OF METHOD

a.   Branch analyzers.   Branch coverage analyzers typically consist of two parts, a preprocessor and a postprocessor. The preprocessor inserts "probes" into the program for which test coverage analysis is required.

The probes call subroutines or update matrices that record the execution of the part of the program containing the probe. Theoretical studies have been carried out to determine the minimum number of probes required to determine which branches are executed during a program execution. The probes may also record information for determining minimal and maximal variable values, loop iteration counts, and subroutine calls.

The information generated by program probes has to be processed before test coverage reports can be generated. If a sequence of tests has been carried out, the information from the different tests has to be merged. The operation of the information generated by probes during program testing is processed and reports are generated by the coverage analyzer postprocessor.

b.   Function analyzers.   Function analyzers are based on the idea that each program construct implements one or more elementary functions. Loop constructs, for example, involve functions that determine if a loop is to be entered, when it is to be exited, how many times it is to be iterated, the initial value of the loop index variable (if present), and subsequent values of the loop index. It is possible to define complete sets of tests for these functions that will cause the function to act incorrectly on at least one test if the function contains one of a predefined set of possible functional errors. Test coverage analyzers can be built that keep track of the data over which constructs are executed and that report on the functional completeness of the data used in the execution of the constructs. Function coverage analyzers can be constructed using the preprocessor probe insertion and postprocessor report generation approach used for branch coverage analyzers.

28.6.   EXAMPLE

a.   Application.   A quicksort program was constructed that contains a branch to a separate part of the program code that carries out an insertion sort. The quicksort part of the code branches to the insertion sort whenever the size of the original list to be sorted or a section of the original list is below some threshold value. Insertion sorts are more effective than quicksorts for small lists and sections of lists because of the smaller constants in their execution time formulae.

  b. Error. The correct threshold value is 11. Due to a typographical error, the branch to the insertion sort is made whenever the length of the original list, or the section of the list currently being processed, is less than or equal to 1.

  c. Error discovery. Parts of the insertion sort code are not executed unless the list or list section being sorted is of length greater than 1. Examination of the output from a branch coverage analyzer will reveal that parts of the program are never executed, regardless of the program tests used. This will alert and draw the attention of the programmer to the presence of the error.

  It is interesting to note that this error is not discoverable by the examination of test output data alone, since the program will still correctly sort lists.

28.7. EFFECTIVENESS

Research results confirm that test coverage analyzers are a necessary and important tool for software validation. Previously assumed "complete" test sets for production software have been found to test less than 50 percent of the branches in a program. The use of test coverage analyzers reveals the inadequacy of such test sets.

  Studies indicate that although test coverage of all parts of a program is important, it is not enough to simply test all branches, or even all program paths. A large percentage of errors are only detectable when a program is tested over extremal cases or special values that are closely related to the functions performed in the program. There appear to be three situations in which branch coverage is effective in finding errors. The first is that in which an error in part of a program is so destructive that any test that causes that part of the program to be executed will result in incorrect output. The second is that in which parts of a program are never used during any program execution, and the third, that in which unexpected parts of a program are used during some test. Other kinds of errors require additional test selection techniques, such as functional testing.

28.8. APPLICABILITY

Test coverage analysis can be applied to any kind of program in any programming language.

28.9. LEARNING

There are no special learning requirements for the use of test coverage analyzers. Once a set of tests has been found to be inadequate, it requires skill to generate data that will cause the unexercised features of the program to be used during program execution.

28.10. COSTS

Test coverage analyzers can be inexpensive to use. The major expense is the capital cost for the tool. It is estimated that the construction of a test coverage tool requires a level of effort that is more than that required for a parser but less than twice that effort. The major part of the test coverage analyzer consists of the parser that is used to determine probe insertion points for a program.

29.1. NAME. TEST DATA GENERATOR

29.2. BASIC FEATURES

Test data generators are tools that generate test data to exercise a target program. They may generate data through analysis of the program itself or through analysis of the expected input to the program in its normal operating environment. Test data generators may use numerical integrators and random number generators to create the data.

29.3. INFORMATION INPUT

Test data generators require as input:
a. The program for which data is to be generated, or
b. A quantifiable description of the domain of possible inputs to the program from which the test data generator is to produce representative values.

29.4. INFORMATION OUTPUT

The output produced by test data generators is a set of data that can be used effectively to detect execution-time errors in a program. It is generally intended that such test data causes the program to be thoroughly exercised when executed. It is also desirable to have this input data be representative of the actual data used in real program operation in order to properly evaluate results obtained from program execution.

29.5. OUTLINE OF METHOD

Test data generators generate test data for a program in a systematic, deterministic manner. There are two major methods currently used to generate test data. Both methods can be implemented as fully automated tools.

One method of test data generation analyzes the structure of a program and, based upon this analysis, generates a set of test data that will drive execution along a comprehensive set of program paths. This method attempts to maximize the structural coverage achieved during execution with the derived data. Though this approach requires a detailed, rigorous structural analysis of a program (which is often quite difficult, if not impossible), tools have been developed that aid in the automation of this analysis. There are tools that can analyze a program and identify certain structural elements in that program. Data is then automatically generated that will drive execution through each of these program elements.

If it is desirable to increase the coverage achieved by the test data, there also exist tools that use automated program analysis to aid in accomplishing this. After monitoring program execution with the generated data, it may be possible to increase the current structural coverage achieved by using automated tools that assist in determining how to alter the current set of test data as necessary to cause different branching conditions to occur. Test data generators that create test data based upon the amount of structural coverage that the data will achieve are generally very sophisticated tools. Much research and development work is currently being done in this area.

A second approach to generating test data is based upon analysis of the possible inputs to a program under real, operational usage. This technique requires more knowledge of the software for which input data is to be generated than the previous technique. However, in this approach the output generated from program execution provides more meaningful results to the user during testing. One such tool that utilizes this technique examines the domain of all possible input values to a program under normal program operation and partitions this domain into mutually exclusive subdomains. For each subdomain there is an associated probability that a sequence of actual input values will belong to that partition. Data is then generated by sampling from each subdomain, with the distribution of sampling determined by the subdomain's associated probability. Automated tools have been built to assist in computing these probabilities and in sampling from the appropriate partitions.

This technique attempts to mirror the intended operation of a program by generating test data that is representative of its operational input. This mode of program testing can be very useful during a preliminary period of software operational use. With this technique, reasonably accurate predictions can be made on the software's performance in real operation.

Other test data generators exist that use less sophisticated techniques than those described above. Many of them generate databased upon commands given by the user and/or from data descriptions in a program, such as in a COBOL program's data definition section. This is mainly a COBOL-oriented technique in which the test data is intended to simulate transaction inputs in a database management situation. This technique, however, can be adapted to other environments.

29.6. EXAMPLE

Test data is required for a new payroll program. A test data generator is used to generate data normally contained in the payroll records of each employee on the payroll. The data fields in these records consist of:

- Employee identification number
- Employee name
- Indication of hourly or salaried employee
- Salary rate (if salaried)
- Hourly rate (if hourly)
- Number of hours worked during last pay period
- Number of tax exemptions declared
- Federal withholding tax rate
- Social security tax rate
- Marital status

A file of records containing this information is created by the test data generator. For each field in a record, a value with the appropriate data type is randomly generated (e.g., alphanumeric for Employee Name, integer for Employee Identification Number, real for Federal Withholding Tax Rate). The file is then reformatted in an organization that is acceptable to the payroll system as input. The generated test data will then be fed to the payroll program to be tested.

29.7. EFFECTIVENESS

The overall effectiveness of automated test data generators in use today is generally poor. Though these tools permit the generation of more test data than any human tester could create (thereby devising more test cases), a burden is placed on the human tester to evaluate all the test results obtained from program execution with the generated data. Unfortunately, test data generators themselves do not have a facility by which to verify these test results. In addition, most of the test data generators in use today create data in a manner totally insensitive to the functional peculiarities of a program. The data may often be meaningless in content. It may focus testing upon an unimportant portion of the program and totally ignore critical portions. A human tester, however, often has a certain intuition about which program areas need to be more thoroughly tested than others and so creates his test data accordingly. The overall ignorance of test data generators in determining which data items offer the most potential in discovering errors is the major factor behind their current ineffectiveness in program testing.

29.8. APPLICABILITY

Test data generators are generally applicable for any system requiring input data for operation.

29.9. LEARNING

For those test data generators that only require as input the source program for which test data is desired, very little learning is required to use these tools. The user interface with the tool will always be the same, and the user manual for the tool should provide sufficient information for its operation. For those data generators that create databased upon the domain of expected inputs to the program, much more learning is required. It is necessary to acquire some knowledge about the application environment and operational usage of the software so that representative input data can be generated.

29.10. COSTS

Automated test data generators are generally quite expensive. This is primarily due to the relatively infrequent use of these tools in actual testing environments. The initial costs in building test data generators have very rarely been offset by benefits obtained in using them. As yet, the derived utilization of the more sophisticated tools that exist have not justified their cost. Accordingly, test data generators are among the most costly testing tools that exist today.

30.1. NAME. TEST SUPPORT FACILITIES

30.2. BASIC FEATURES

An environment simulation, or test bed, is a test site used to test a component of software. This test site simulates the environment under which the software will normally operate. A test bed permits full control of inputs and computer characteristics, allows processing of intermediate outputs without destroying simulated execution time, and allows full test repeatability and diagnostics. To be effective, the controlled circumstances of the test bed must truly represent the behavior of the system of which the software is a part.

30.3. INFORMATION INPUT

The information input to a test bed is the software for which a testing environment is to be simulated and which will later be installed in a real system.

30.4. INFORMATION OUTPUT

The information output by a test bed is the results observed through execution of the software installed in the test bed. This information is used as a preliminary means of determining whether the software will operate as intended in its real environment

30.5. OUTLINE OF METHOD

Test beds provide an environment in which to monitor the operation of software prior to installation in a real system. To be of value, this environment must realistically reflect those properties of the system that will affect or be affected by the operation of the software. However, the test bed should simulate only those components in the system that the software requires as a minimum interface with the system. This will permit testing to focus only on the software component for which the test bed is built.

Test beds are built through the consideration of, and proper balance between, three major factors:

- The amount of realism required by the test bed to properly reflect the operation of system properties

- Resources available to build the test bed

- The ability of the test bed to focus only on the software being tested

Test beds come in many forms, depending on the level of testing desired. For single-module testing, a test bed may consist merely of test data and a test driver. A test driver is a program that feeds input data to the program module being tested, causes the module to be executed, and collects the output generated during the program execution. If a completed, but non-final, version of software is to be tested, the test bed may also include stubs. A stub is a dummy routine that simulates the operation of a module that is invoked within a test. Stubs can be as simple as routines that automatically return on a call, or they can be more complicated and return simulated results. The final version of the software may be linked with other software subsystems in a larger total system. The test bed for one component in the system may consist of those system components that directly interface with the component being tested.

As illustrated in the above examples, test beds permit the testing of a component of a system without requiring the availability of the full, complete system. They merely supply the inputs required by the software component to be executed and provide a repository in which to place outputs for analysis. In addition, test beds may contain monitoring devices that collect and display intermediate outputs during program execution. In this way, test beds provide the means of observing the operation of software as a component of a system without requiring the availability of other system components, which may be unreliable.

30.6. EXAMPLE

The federal government has just distributed to all American corporations new tax rates to be imposed on the earnings of all employees beginning at the start of next year. Due to these new tax rates, Company XYZ has had to revise its current payroll program so that it will accommodate the new federal regulations by January 1.

In order to test this new program, a test bed is being constructed to simulate the operation of the payroll system. To simulate the inputs to this system, a test file of data containing all the information necessary for the system to operate is created. The file consists of a record of information for each employee in the company. Each record contains the following data:

- Employee identification number
- Employee name
- Indication of hourly or salaried employee
- Salary rate (if salaried)
- Hourly rate (if hourly)
- Number of hours worked during last pay period
- Number of tax exemptions declared
- Federal withholding tax rate
- Social security tax rate
- Marital status

A test driver controls the execution of the payroll program. It feeds the above data to the program in the proper format. At the end of program execution, the driver simulates the check-writing facility of the payroll system in the following manner. It directs the output of the payroll program to an output file. The output consists of a record of data for each company employee. Each record contains the following information:

- Employee name
- Employee social security number
- Check date
- Total employee earnings less deductions

The test driver then dumps this information from the output file onto a hardcopy device so that the output can be analyzed and verified for correctness.

30.7. EFFECTIVENESS

The use of test beds has proven to be a highly effective and widely used technique to test the operation of software. The use of test drivers, in particular, is one of the most widely used testing techniques.

30.8. APPLICABILITY

This method is generally applicable, from single-module to large-system testing and for all types of computing applications.

30.9. LEARNING

In order to build an effective test bed, it is necessary to develop a solid understanding of the software and its dynamic operation in a system. This understanding should aid in determining what parts of the test bed deserve the most attention during its construction. In addition, knowledge of the dynamic nature of a program in a system is required in gathering useful intermediate outputs during program execution and in properly examining these results.

30.10. COST

The amount of realism desired in a test bed will be the largest factor affecting cost. Building a realistic test bed may require the purchasing of new hardware and the development of additional software in order to properly simulate an entire system. In addition, these added resources may be so specialized that they may seldom, if ever, be used again in other applications. In this way, very sophisticated test beds may not prove to be highly cost-effective.

31.1. NAME. WALKTHROUGHS

31.2. BASIC FEATURES

Walkthroughs (WT) constitute a structured series of peer reviews of a system component used to enforce standards, detect errors, and improve development visibility and system quality. They may be conducted during any of the life cycle phases and may also be applied to documentation. An identifying feature of a WT is that it is generally presented by the creator or producer of the material being reviewed rather than by an independent or third party. In addition, because of the presenter's advance preparation and his familiarity with the material, less preparation by other members is required.

31.3. INFORMATION INPUT

a.   Walkthrough package. This set of materials includes all necessary backup documentation for the WT. Examples of materials made available include (but are not limited to) module flowcharts, system flowcharts, HIPO charts (or other high-level representation schemes), and module listings. Other important materials may include sections of the Functional Specification, System/Subsystem Specification and Database Specification (as applicable) that pertain to the component under review. Often, copies of applicable standards are also part of the WT input.

b.   Questions list. Some organizations that practice a more formal version of a WT require reviewers to submit the component to the presenter prior to the WT. This enables the presenter to be better prepared to respond to the questions at the WT.

31.4. INFORMATION OUTPUT

a.   Action list. During the WT, a list of problems and questions is recorded. This action list is distributed to all participants and is used by the producer (reviewee) as the basis for subsequent changes to the component.

b.   Walkthroughs form. During the course of the WT, this form is completed by an individual with recording responsibilities. The form identifies participants and their responsibilities, the agenda for the WT, the decision of the WT (accept as-is, revise, revise and schedule another WT), and is signed by all participants at the end of the WT.

31.5. OUTLINE OF METHOD

a.   Roles and responsibilities. The group of individuals participating in a WT are usually referred to as reviewers. The leader of the

WT is called the coordinator. The coordinator is responsible for WT planning, organization, and distribution of materials. The WT is called to order, moderated, and summarized by the coordinator.

The producer (or reviewee) is that individual whose module or component is to be reviewed during the WT. In most cases, the producer is generally responsible for selecting the coordinator and review team (in most situations; sometimes management may perform this function) and providing the WT package materials to the coordinator. During the WT, the producer initially provides a general description of the module, then leads the reviewers through a detailed, step-by-step description of the module. After the WT, the producer should objectively consider every item on the action list and make changes to his product as he deems appropriate.

The reviewers are composed of individuals from varying backgrounds and fulfill responsibilities based upon their area of specialization. Some roles fulfilled are those of recorder and representatives of the user, standards, and maintenance groups. In general, these participants are responsible for being familiar with the material being presented, submitting comments prior to the review, and listening and contributing during the WT. At the end of the review, each must cast a vote indicating whether the module is acceptable, needs revision, or is rejected.

Because of the organization that each is representing, some specific responsibilities are associated with each reviewer. In addition to contributing to the WT, the recorder must make written note of the participants assembled and the action items that result from the review.

The user representative is often involved during early WTs of a module (i.e., during requirements analysis and design). His responsibility is to ensure that the proposed solution is usable and does, in fact, meet the needs of his organization.

The standards representative, referred to by some sources as a "standards bearer," is responsible for checking that the product being reviewed adheres to organization standards. In some cases, he may be asked to provide input to a request to deviate from a standard.

The maintenance representative, referred to by some sources as the "maintenance oracle," must view the product from the standpoint of the group who will be required to maintain the product. Items that may be of prime concern to this individual are documentation and program comments, program functionality or modularity, naming conventions, and data decomposition.

b. The process. Many organizations practice walkthroughs that differ radically in formality. The process described in the following paragraphs falls at the midpoint between these extremes. There are four basic steps in the process.

1. *Scheduling.* When the work item module is very near completion (including documentation), the producer notifies management and selects the WT participants. The WT date is agreed upon and facilities are scheduled. The WT should not exceed two hours and is best kept to less than one hour. This implies that the work item is of manageable size. Sources suggest the following guidelines for work package size:

   - 5–10 pages of specifications for a requirements WT
   - 1–5 structure charts (or HIPO diagrams) for a preliminary or detailed design WT
   - 50–100 lines of code for a code or test WT

2. *Preparation.* The producer collects appropriate information for use at the WT and gives it to the coordinator for distribution. Each reviewer studies the materials, making a note of questions or comments. Most sources estimate that a maximum of one hour of preparation by reviewers is necessary.

3. *Walkthrough meeting.* After the coordinator opens the review, the producer uses test data to simulate the operation of the component. Each specification, design phrase, or line of code is reviewed. The recorder documents comments or questions using the action list. Each reviewer signs the Walkthrough, documenting the decision of the meeting (accept product as-is, accept with modification, or reject). The recorder provides a copy of the action list to all participants and supplies a copy of the Walkthrough form to management.

4. *Rework.* The producer reviews each action item, making product changes as he feels necessary. He may decide to implement all, part, or none of the suggested changes. No follow-up is held to ensure that suggestions are incorporated; it is assumed that the

producer is in the best position to make implementation decisions. Major items on the action list may be summarized at the next WT for the module.

31.6. EXAMPLE

One week prior to completion of the coding of a module of 75–100 lines, the producer notifies his line manager of the need for a WT. Upon management approval, the producer selects a coordinator (one of the lead analysts from the development shop), a standards representative (from the Quality Assurance group), a maintenance representative (from the Production Program organization), and a user representative (from the group requesting the system). Three days prior to the inspection, he notifies the coordinator of the planned WT and suggested participants. At this time, he gives the coordinator copies of the program listing (including comments), a systems-level flowchart depicting how it interfaces with other modules, a data dictionary, a set of test data items, and a section from the Functional Specification detailing the user requirement associated with the module.

The coordinator notifies the selected participants, receives their commitment to attend, and distributes to each a copy of the materials furnished by the producer.

Each participant reviews the materials. The standards representative finds two instances of deviations from published standards and notifies the coordinator (who in turn notifies the producer). The user representative verifies that the code addresses each designed aspect by reviewing the proceedings of the previous design WT. He is satisfied that each requirement has been addressed and notifies the coordinator that he finds no errors and feels that his presence is not required for the code walkthrough. The maintenance representative finds no immediate concerns with the code, but makes a note to inquire about the structure of the data files.

The WT begins with a brief introduction by the coordinator, who then turns the review over to the producer. He uses the system flowchart to give a summary of the functions of the module and proceeds to go line by line through the code using the selected test data. When the lines of concern to the standards representative are reached, a brief discussion occurs to explain the reasons for the deviations from standard. In this instance, the reviewers are satisfied that the deviations are justified. The recorder so notes on the action list and the meeting proceeds. The maintenance representative points out one line of highly complex code and suggests that it be broken up into two less complex steps. Agreement cannot be immediately reached, so the suggestion is added to the action list.

At the end of the module review, the coordinator seeks a decision from the reviewers about the module. They agree to give their approval, providing that the suggested changes are made and that the producer will further investigate the effect of breaking up the complex line of code. Each signs the Walkthrough form and the meeting is adjourned.

The recorder distributes a copy of the action to all participants. The producer makes the changes he feels are necessary. He runs a benchmark of the module with the complex code and again with the code broken down. Since no significant loss of efficiency results, he modifies the code. The module is now ready for a unit test, which may be followed by another WT.

31.7. EFFECTIVENESS

Studies have been conducted that identify the following qualitative benefits of Walkthroughs:
- Higher status visibility
- Decreased debugging time
- Early detection of design and analysis errors (much more costly to correct in later development phases)
- Identification of design or code inefficiencies
- Ensuring adherence to standards
- Increased program readability
- Increased user satisfaction
- Communication of new ideas or technology
- Increased maintainability

Little data is available to identify the quantitative benefits attributable to the use of Walkthroughs. However, one source estimates that the number of errors in production programs was reduced by a factor of 10.

31.8. APPLICABILITY

The Walkthrough is applicable to large or small projects during all development phases and is not limited by project type or complexity.

31.9. LEARNING

The Walkthrough does not require special training to implement. However, experience has shown that the effectiveness of the Walkthrough increases as the WT experience of the reviewers increases.

31.10. COSTS

The WT requires no special tools or equipment to implement. The direct costs are equal to the expense associated with the human resources involved.

Index

Acceptable level of risk, 210
Acceptance metrics, 542
Access control, 460, 228
Accounting logs, 570
Adaptive maintenance, 366
Administrative planning, 156
Air contaminants, 462
American Institute of Certified
  Public Accountants, 208
Analyze, 22
Anomaly-detecting metrics, 542
Application
    control objectives, 209
    control review, 242
    history, 89
    review questionnaire, 244
Attributes of quality software, 312
Audit
    ability, 482
    requirement, 14
    trails, 482
Auditor and control, 608
Auditors on the Quality Assurance
  review team, 616
Authorization rules, 465
Autoexec, 466
Automatic test systems, 354
Automating scheduling, 160
Automating the Quality
  Assurance function, 290
Availability, 585

Backup, 587
    and contingency planning, 477
    considerations, 480
    media, 479
Base case, 263
    QA technique, 279
Batch process, 242
Boundary value analysis, 334

Cause-effect graphing, 335
Causes of goal failures, 120
Certification, 314
Changes, 126
    and debug facilities, 403
    control, 397
    request, 398
Checklist, 262
    QA review technique, 274
Code, 378
    and review techniques, 393, 395
    audit, 398
    conventions, 388
Commented code, 391
Common
    data definitions, 372
    system vulnerabilities, 218
Commonality index, 422
Communications
    environments, 484
    system failure, 226

Comparators, 401
Compiler extensions, 392
Complex program structure, 379
Complexity, 15, 99
    based testing, 339
    of application, 89
Compliance, 28
Computer
    center, 268
    hardware, 268
    operation controls, 227
    software, 268
    systems design, 268
Conducting a Quality Assurance
    review, 171
Conducting the review, 173
Confirmation, 263
Console operator logs, 572
Construction, 318
Consultant, 14, 263
    (advice) QA technique, 284
    services, 445
Control
    adaptive maintenance, 385
    changes, 398
    corrective maintenance, 386
    in an MIS environment, 606
    measures, 493
    perfective maintenance, 382
    software changes, 382
    standards, 24, 442
Conversion, 123, 139
    checklist, 201
    phase, 29, 155, 197
Corrective maintenance, 367
Cost
    of quality assurance, 44
    overruns, 126
    versus benefit trade-off, 552
Cost-effective, 139
    curve of control, 211
Coverage-based testing, 337
Critical software attributes, 550
Criteria, 544
Cross-referencer, 401
Cross-training, 617
Cryptographic systems, 504
Cryptography, 470

Damage protection, 460

Data, 237
    center operations, 447
    encryption standard, 472
    error, 242
    input, 242
    integrity controls, 476
    integrity, 475
    labels, 467
    output, 243
Databases, 90
Definition of software maintenance, 364
Design, 317
    phase, 28, 152
Design-based functional testing, 336
Desk checking, 326
Developing the Quality Assurance
    function, 63
Diagnostic routines, 402, 572
Disaster recovery controls, 228
Discretionary controls, 216
Documentation, 137, 373, 381, 477
    guidelines, 392
    libraries, 403
    standards, 24
Dynamic analysis techniques, 350
Dynamic assertions, 351
Dynamic testing, 321

Effort to develop, 90
Electrical power quality, 461
Emergency procedures, 478
Emulation mode, 380
Enforce documentation, 410
Enhancements, 106
Entrance conference, 162
Environment control objectives, 208
Environmental controls, 461
    hazards, 462
    review questionnaire, 229
Equipment, 459
    cover locks, 460
    enclosures, 460
    lockdown devices, 460
Erroneous or falsified data input, 218
Errors, 22
    guessing, 335
    seeding, 341
Evaluate all requests for changes, 409
Evaluating reliability, 569
Evaluation objectives, 27

Exchange of reports, 617
Exposure to loss, 89

Factor, 544
Factors that affect source
  code maintainability, 387
Failure, 118, 119
Fault
  avoidance, 589
  tolerance, 590
Feasibility
  of software reuse, 427
  phase, 28
  study, 151
File
  access control, 503
  backup, 478
  controls, 228
Financial
  applications, 88
  considerations, 596
Fire and water damage, 462
Fixed disk devices, 463
Flexible diskettes, 463
Flow analysis, 345
Foreign corrupt practices act, 208
Framework for measuring
  quality, 544
Functional definition, 364
Functional testing techniques, 333

GAAP, 210
Gantt Chart, 159
General business experience, 268
General systems design, 267
Goals, 5
  evaluation matrix, 133
  of software maintenance, 407
Government
  reports, 148
  standards, 136
Guidelines, 10

Hard-coded parameters, 381
Hardware
  and software monitors, 576
  measurements, 579
  selection analysis, 443
Heat and humidity, 461
Human measurements, 582

Identification, 465
Impact of a failure, 587
Importance levels, 586
Improving software maintenance, 387
Inadequate design, 122
Independence, 605
Industry reports, 148
Ineffective security practices, 220
Information security policy, 492
Initiating systems review, 145
Inspections, 327
Internal audit, 92, 148, 603
  responsibilities, 604
Internal control defined, 207
Interviews, 262
  QA techniques, 271
Inventory of applications, 492

Job description, 74, 77
Judgment, 263, 539
  QA technique, 282

Large modules, 380
Laws and regulations, 210
Life cycle verification activities, 317
Logic flow, 379
Logical access controls, 468

Magnetic media protection, 462, 503
Maintainer, 375, 381
Maintenance, 319
  personnel, 411
Management 123
Management's role, 491
Managing software maintenance, 404
Manual versus automated testing, 324
McCabe metrics, 340
Memory protection features, 458
Methods, 5
  evaluation matrix, 138
  for selecting applications, 86
Metrics, 539, 541
Missing or incomplete design
  specifications, 382
Mission impact, 97, 98
Misuse by authorized end users, 219
Morale, 405
MTBF, 581
MTTR, 581
Mutation analysis, 343

NASA, 416
Nondiscretionary controls, 216

Objectivity, 80
Observation, 262
  (examination) QA technique, 272
Operating system flaws, 225
Operational controls, 476
Optimize
  hardware, 139
  people, 139
Organizational
  controls, 227
  structure, 64, 65, 71

PC security problem, 456
Peer review, 326, 395
People, 91
Perfective maintenance, 365
Performance, 6
  acceptance criteria, 584
Personal computer, 455, 483
  self-assessment questionnaire, 495
Personnel, 375
  screening, 490
Physical accessibility, 457
Planning, 156, 296
Policies, 10
  and procedures, 210
  for controlling software changes, 383
Poor software design, 370
Poorly coded software, 371
Portability, 434
Postreview conference, 304
Predictive metrics, 542
Prioritization process, 94
Privileged instructions, 458
Problems, 7
Procedural errors, 221
Procedures, 10, 59
Productivity, 423
Program
  debugging, 315
  errors, 223
  phase, 154
Programming, 268
  language, 372
  phase, 28, 188

Project
  control, 160
  documentation review
technique, 269
  documentation, 262
  management, 267
  selection procedures, 57
  tickler card, 158
Proof of correctness, 315
  correctness techniques, 329
Protection strategies, 487
Prototyping, 432

QA staff, 70
Quality, 4, 423
  areas, 117
  assurance , 5, 19
  candidates, 69
  charter, 33, 45
  control, 19
  costs, 36
  documentation, 164
  factors, 545
  functions, 21
  group, 146
  measurement, 542
  objectives, 9
  requirements, 543
  results, 306
  review and assessment
    procedures, 58
  review points, 149, 172
  review techniques, 261
  staffing alternatives, 67
  support staff, 76
  tasks, 19
  work plan, 49
Quantifiable goals, 552
Quantitative analysis, 263, 509

RADC, 541
Ratings, 509
  individual applications, 93
Reauthentication, 467
Recovery
  levels, 594
  procedures, 593
  strategy, 593

Recurring review procedure, 60
Redesign, 377
Reducing losses, 212
Reducing risks, 213
Relationships, 78
    with internal auditors, 614
Reliability, 101, 565
    distinctions, 567
    metrics, 578
    program, 595
    requirements, 567
Reporting Quality Assurance results, 293
Requirements, 316, 373
Residue control, 473
Resource requirements, 380
Restrict code changes, 410
Retention of test data, 404
Reusability, 415
Reusable software classification, 420
Reusable software information, 417
Reuse of software, 413
Reuse process, 417
Review, 327
    applications, 26
    controls, 217
    environmental controls, 227
    of an application system, 115
    of goals, 128
    of methods, 134
    of performance, 137
    point evaluation forms, 514
    points, 54
    the adequacy of application
        controls, 207
RFP, 433
Risk
    analysis, 488, 569
    assessment, 493
    evaluation, 96
    scoring, 102

Schedule maintenance, 410
Scoring the QA review, 514
Security, 123
    concerns 455
    management, 487, 489
    mechanisms, 457
    objectives, 456
    problem, 486

Selecting applications for review, 85
Selection criteria, 92
Simulation, 331
Simulation/modeling, 263
    QA technique, 282
Skill, 92, 264
Software
    acquisition, 433
    commonality, 421
    crisis, 414
    designed for outdated hardware, 371
    development, 475
    factory approach, 431
    maintenance policy, 407
    maintenance process, 368
    maintenance tools, 400
    maintenance, 361
    measurements, 580
    quality requirements survey form, 547
    quality, 370
    reuse, 422
    selection analysis, 443
Source code guidelines, 388
Sources of information, 147
Special requests, 107
Special value analysis, 335
Staffing, 72
    alternatives, 66
    the quality assurance review, 155
Standards, 10
    data definitions, 391
Static analysis techniques, 345
Static testing, 323
Statistical analyses, 341
Status report, 160
Statutory requirements, 89
Storage, 480
Storage media, 222
Structural testing techniques, 337
Structural versus functional testing, 322
Structured modular software, 390
Subroutines, 380
Symbolic execution, 347
System
    design phase, 179
    development standards, 15
    documentation Quality Assurance
        technique, 270
    documentation, 262
    environment, 100

error messages, 572
failures — methods, 121
failures — performance, 123
failures, 378
incident reports, 572
interruptions, 586
justification phase, 174
performance meetings, 578
programming practices, 444
review priorities, 85
size, 99

Task force, 66
Technical advice, 25
Technical problems, 446
Technology, 12, 90
   integration, 101
Telecommunications, 243
Test
   analysis, 341
   data, 263
   documentation, 353
   drivers, 353
   generation, 332
   languages, 354
   phase, 154
   plan, 194
   QA technique, 277
   results, 196
   support tools, 352
Testing, 123, 263, 311, 315, 320
   (verification) QA technique, 277
   phase, 28, 193
   standards, 399
   techniques and tools, 357
Threshold value assessment, 584
Time span, 90
Top-down review, 126
Top-down/bottom-up approach, 395
Training MIS personnel, 444

Uncontrolled system access, 220
Usage monitoring, 483
Users, 374
   identification, 466
   involvement, 91
   level of satisfaction, 578
   responsibilities, 458
Utility libraries, 402

Validation, 311, 314
Verification, 311, 314
   techniques, 325

Walkthroughs, 327, 396
Workload scheduling, 587
Workpaper retention, 167
Workpapers, 165